BUSINESS
AND SOCIETY

Other Books by George A. Steiner

Top Management Planning
Strategic Factors in Business Success
Industrial Project Management (with William G. Ryan)
Multinational Corporate Planning (with Warren M. Cannon)
Managerial Long-range Planning
National Defense and Southern California, 1961–1970
Government's Role in Economic Life
Wartime Industrial Statistics (with David Novick)
Economic Problems of War
Economic Problems of National Defense

BUSINESS
AND SOCIETY

Second Edition

George A. Steiner

University of California
Los Angeles

CONSULTING EDITOR: Barry M. Richman
University of California at Los Angeles

Random House New York

Second Edition

987654321

Copyright © 1971, 1975 by Random House, Inc.

All rights reserved under International and Pan-American Copyright Conventions. No part of this book may be reproduced in any form or by any means, electronic or mechanical, including photocopying, without permission in writing from the publisher. All inquiries should be addressed to Random House, Inc., 201 East 50th Street, New York, N.Y. 10022. Published in the United States by Random House, Inc., and simultaneously in Canada by Random House of Canada Limited, Toronto.

Library of Congress Cataloging in Publication Data

Steiner, George Albert, 1912–
  Business and society.

  Bibliography: p.
  1. Industry—Social aspects—United States.
2. Industry and state—United States.   I.   Title.
HD60.5.U5S8 1975   658.4'08   74-18279
ISBN 0-394-31902-8

Manufactured in the United States of America. Composed by Colonial Press, Clinton, Mass. Printed and bound by Kingsport Press, Kingsport, Tenn.

To my students
past, present, and future

Preface

There have been few, if any, times in our history when the interrelationships between business and society have been more complex, more dynamic, and more significant to the future of both business and society. For the first time in our history questions are being raised about the fundamental functions society expects its business institutions to perform. At no time in our history has there been more widespread criticism of business. It seems, as Eric Hoffer has observed, "that the social landscape has begun to tilt away from business." Yet, at no time in our history has business been a greater beneficial force in so many major areas of society. At no time in the past have business managers thought so much or so deeply about the impact of their companies on their environment and the present and future potential influence of the environment on their companies.

Today, there are few topics more exciting and important to both business and society than the interrelationships which exist between the two, the subject with which this book is concerned.

My major objective is to paint on a wide canvas as many of the significant interrelationships, issues, philosophies, and points of view as possible within the confines of a book of this size. To do this I have reviewed and condensed a mountain of literature to which I have copiously referred for those wishing to dig deeper into particular subjects.

This book is designed for college students, business managers, and the general reader interested in business-society interrelationships. In recent years there has been a rapid growth of courses in universities and colleges in business and society, business and its environment, social responsibility of business, business policy and organizational environment, and comparable subjects. It is my hope that instructors of such courses and their students will find in this book all of the basic issues which they find interesting and important. It is also my hope that they will find the analyses to be of sufficient depth to provide the basis for provocative classroom discussion on those subjects they choose to emphasize.

I have found in my classes that students like to discuss freely cases in the business-society relationship. To satisfy this urge, which I think should be encouraged, I have prepared *Cases in Business and Society*, which Random House is publishing simultaneously with this book. Also, for additional readings, an instructor may wish to use my *Issues in Business and Society*, published by Random House in 1972. With these books it is possible to structure classroom discussions in many different and provocative ways.

This book is also for the businessman who wishes to discover the underlying forces that are changing the relationship of his company with society. Richard Gerstenberg, when chairman of the board of the General Motors Corporation, commented: "The most successful business in the years ahead will be the one that not only offers quality products at competitive prices, but also succeeds in matching its resources to society's changing demands, the business that is best able to give creative response to the social aspirations of the people it serves. Conversely, the business that fails in the years ahead will be the one that fails to understand how it is related to the society around it and will therefore overlook opportunities for service, for growth, and for profit" (1973). I hope businessmen find help in this book in determining what their relationships with society are and ought to be, and I will be disappointed if the business reader does not see in these pages concrete suggestions to help his company meet society's new demands.

I have tried to encompass a broad range of the more important current interrelationships and issues between business and society. I have tried to emphasize the importance of identifying the major underlying trends and issues and of getting the pertinent facts before coming to conclusions about business or social policy. The historical perspective is not neglected. Also I have emphasized processes in business and government which affect the relationship between the two. Finally, I have employed the systems approach to analysis by looking at the many interrelationships among different types of business activities and social elements in a multiple rather than a unilateral approach and by analyzing issues on the basis of the most relevant areas of knowledge.

Following an introductory chapter dealing with the nature and scope of the business-society relationship and the approaches of the book, there are three short chapters on the historical developments leading to today's complex business-society interrelationships. Part Two of the book presents an overview of today's business environment, the demands made on business, and its new role in society. Part Three covers a broad range of changing values affecting society and business. Part Four deals with major community problems in which business is deeply involved. Part Five is concerned with business-government interrelationships. In Part Six the relationships between business and its employees are examined; and, in Part Seven, future potential business-society connections are discussed.

Many people made helpful comments and suggestions in the preparation of this second edition, too many to name them all here. I do want to express my appreciation, however, to the following professors for their substantive suggestions: John C. Athanassiades, Georgia State University; Robert L. Clewett, Pennsylvania State University; John W. Collins, Syracuse University; Frederick G. Crane, Drake University; Neil H. Jacoby, UCLA; Rosemary Pledger, Northeast Louisiana University; Paul Prasow, UCLA; Don Sandlin, East Los Angeles College and California State University—Los Angeles; Hans Schollhammer, UCLA; Edward V. Sedgwick, UCLA; Richard Stead, Colorado State University; John F. Steiner, California State University —Los Angeles; Alfred W. Stoess, University of Nevada; and J. Fred Weston, UCLA. Special thanks are due my wife, Jean E. Steiner, who carefully edited the manuscript and to Miss Sharon Outzen who carried the burden of typing the manuscript. I hope there will be a third edition of this book and that those reading it will feel free to give me their comments so that it will be an improvement over this edition.

George A. Steiner

January 1974

Contents

Preface   vii

1. The Structure of Business Ecology   3

Part One   The Road to Today's Complex Interrelationships

2. Antecedents to Capitalism   17
3. The Theory of Classical Capitalism   35
4. The American Experience   46

Part Two   Today's Business Setting: An Overview

5. The Changing Business Environment   69
6. The New Demands on Business and the Changing
Business Role   85
7. Corporate Powers: Myth and Reality   106

Part Three   Business and Changing Values

8. Changing Values in Society   121
9. Business Ideologies   137
10. The Social Responsibilities of Business   153
11. Making Social Responsibilities Operational in Business   185

12. The Social Audit   196
13. Business Ethics   210

Part Four Business and Major Community Problems

14. Business and Our Polluted Environment   231
15. Business and Consumers   253
16. Business, Community Problems, and Disadvantaged
Minorities   281
17. Business and Education   307
18. Business and the Arts   315
19. Business and Technology   320
20. Affluence, Growth, and the Post-Industrial Society   338

Part Five Business and Government

21. Government-Business Interrelationships: An Overview   355
22. The Political Role of Business in Public Affairs   370
23. The Convergence of Business and Government
Planning   393
24. Economic Concentration and Public Policy   415
25. Business and International Policy   444
26. Other Issues in Government Regulation of Business   464

Part Six Business and Its Employees

27. The Changing Role of People in Organizations   499
28. Labor Unions and Managerial Authority   523

Part Seven The Future

29. Future Forces and Patterns in the Business-Society
Relationship   543

Bibliography   569

Index   599

BUSINESS
AND SOCIETY

CHAPTER ONE The Structure of Business Ecology

INTRODUCTION

Ecology is concerned with the mutual relations between organisms and their environments. Business ecology, therefore, deals with the relationships of business with elements of society. The ecology of business is obviously an important and broad area of inquiry. It is the purpose of this chapter to describe some major dimensions of its significance, to define its scope, and to examine approaches to its study.

IMPORTANCE OF BUSINESS-SOCIETY RELATIONSHIPS

It is not easy to underscore in a few words the enormous significance of the interrelationships between business and society. The following comments, however, may be useful in introducing the subject.

Business Is a Major Institution in Society A casual review of any major newspaper will reveal many headlines concerned with the business-society nexus. This is so, of course, because business is such a dominant institution in society. It has a strong impact on the institutions and actions in society, and what goes on in society has a powerful influence on it.

Throughout history there have been many eras when the business-society connection has taken on a special significance; for instance, during the Industrial Revolution, in the days of the swashbuckling industrial buccaneer in the latter part of the nineteenth century, in the depression of the 1930s, and in World War II. None of these periods, however, transcends in importance the interrelationships of today.

American society currently is in the process of reshuffling in a fundamental way its institutions and priorities. Business is not only a catalyst, but is itself deeply influenced by this process.

Some Paradoxes Business finds itself in a number of paradoxical situations. On the one hand, American business institutions have created the most productive machine for turning out goods and services that the world has ever seen. Yet, at the very same time, and in no small measure because of the great capability of this machine to produce goods and services, business values are being attacked and condemned.

Today's business community is far more concerned with its social responsibilities than ever before in history; yet it is attacked because it is not doing enough. There are those who assert that sooner than many people think, the largest companies of this nation will be judged not on productive prowess alone, but on what they do about air and water pollution, product safety, community well-being, social goals, and the quality of the lives of those who work in and are affected by the company. On the other hand, there are those who assert that if business becomes too concerned with social and political activities, it will erode its economic capability to be efficient in producing goods and services. Not at all surprising is the claim of some people that business is the one great hope for solving many of the serious social problems that exist today.

Managerial Attention to Environment More and more, managers, especially in the large companies, are becoming aware of the fact that the success of their enterprises depends upon the way in which they adjust to their environment. Their attention is therefore shifting dramatically from methods of improving the internal allocation of resources to developing strategies that will best adapt their companies to changes in society. And the subject of the interrelationships between business and society has moved from a very low place on managerial priority lists to the highest position for many top managements.

To my knowledge, no studies have been made that seek to determine the number and frequency of decisions made by managers which relate in whole or in part to environmental forces. Empirical observations of businessmen, however, leave no doubt in my mind that the higher a manager moves up the hierarchical chain and the larger the business enterprise, the more of his decisions and the more of his time concern his company's environment. At the top levels of the larger companies, I would judge that the great majority of decisions are influenced by environmental considerations and that managers spend far more time thinking about the environment and their interaction with it than about any other force affecting their business.

The Nature of the Issues The issues involved in the business-society interrelationship cover a vast range from the most profoundly significant to the trivial, and from the highest levels of abstraction to the grubby details. At higher levels of abstraction are such questions as: To what extent should government regulate individual businesses in the public interest? Should an effort be made to slow down economic growth and technological advance in order to solve our pollution problems and to conserve limited natural resources? To what extent are changing social values altering the organization and operation of business? How will this, in turn, change the nature of our society? Does business have social responsibilities? If so, how should business discharge them?

At lower levels of abstraction, one finds other challenging issues, such as how much support the government should give to business research and development. At the practical level of daily activity, one finds important issues such as those concerning hanky-panky in business campaign contributions to get favorable contracts from local politicians. Businessmen, large and small, are continuously seeking favors from government, and many issues arise in connection with their ability to influence legislators or other public officials. Is changing local zoning ordinance X justified in the public interest, or is it being modified to favor a particular business? On the other hand, throughout government there exists a myriad of detailed regulations, many of which are trivial and irritating to business. For example, are *all* the local building codes really necessary, or even desirable?

These are but a few illustrations of the many difficult and significant issues which permeate the business-society relationship. How they are resolved will have a very important bearing on the way the American people will live tomorrow.

BUSINESS, BUSINESSMEN, AND SOCIETY DEFINED

Business is a broad term encompassing a range of action from simple personal pursuits to the work of giant corporations. In this book, business covers manufacturing, commercial, trade, and other economic activities of both individuals and business institutions; for the most part, however, the discussion relates to business organizations and principally to corporations. A business institution is not wholly an economic organization, for it has social as well as political characteristics. In relating business to society, and in understanding the impact of social changes on business, the discussion therefore considers all three of these aspects of business activity.

In historical discussions the words "business" and "businessmen" will be used although these words did not come into general usage until the latter part of the nineteenth and the early twentieth centuries. In the early history of the United States, the words most commonly used to describe business and businessmen were "commerce" and "merchant." During this period people spoke of "going into business" and "going into merchandising," and the word "businessman" was rarely heard (East, 1946: 16).

"Society," as the term is used in this book, means essentially that which is conceived when one speaks of this nation, or the American civilization. It means the entire scope of the functional and structural parts of our society, the entire mode of life of our people. Inherent in this concept one finds three fundamental interrelated parts which comprise the abstraction of society. They are: (1) ideas or beliefs, (2) institutions, and (3) material things.

Ideas include such things as attitudes, ideologies, and beliefs. They are arranged in scales of values, or preference systems, which help individuals and society to set and seek common ends. They establish the broad goals of life expressed in terms of what is considered to be good, true, right, beautiful, and acceptable. The common cord of a cohesive society is that unifying thread which runs through ideas and beliefs and ties them together into a scale of values. These ideas and beliefs underlie and dominate the systems of institutional arrangements in society, of which business is one.

Institutions are those more or less formalized ways by which society tries to do something. They are forms, conditions, procedures, and methods of group activities. They are systems of control. The business institution, for instance, is accepted by society as a means to use scarce resources to produce in an efficient manner those goods and services that society wants and is willing to pay for. Other institutional systems are, for example, the political system, labor unions, the educational system, the language system, and the legal system.

The third element in society encompasses tangible material things such as stocks of resources, land, and all manufactured goods. These things help to shape, and are partly products of, man's institutions, his ideas, and his beliefs. His economic institutions, together with his stock of resources, determine in large part the type and quantity of his material things. As his types and quantities of material things change, so do his ideas and beliefs.

Figure 1–1. Business and Its Major Societal Areas of Interrelationship

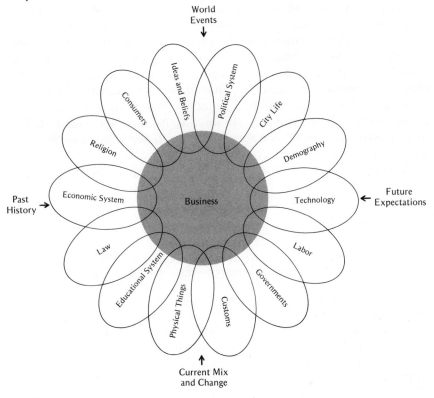

THE SPECTRUM OF BUSINESS-SOCIETY INTERRELATIONSHIPS

Figure 1–1 conceptualizes one set of interrelationships between business and society. The outer ring of circles includes only those areas of primary interest in this book. Additional areas of importance to business would include weather, natural resources, military events, language, medicine, geography, and agriculture. The illustration shows that past history has an impact on the current mix of relationships in society. The mix and its direction of change are also influenced by current world events and by what is going on in this society at the present time. The changes are influenced as well by future expectations.

In examining the many interrelationships between business and society, one must distinguish among businesses. The business system is not a unified structure. There are giant firms which are larger, at least in terms of cash flows, than most governments of the world.

There are also millions of small enterprises. (Most of the economic activity of the nation is conducted through several thousand of the largest companies, and for this reason a large part of this book is concerned with these companies.) Some companies do business only in the United States, while others operate in many foreign countries. Some companies are in service trades, and others only mine or manufacture. Some managers have committed their enterprises to improving the quality of life of their employees and people generally, while others feel their objective is only to optimize stockholder wealth. Every company is unique. No two are exactly alike. As a consequence, what is a sensible thing to say about the relationship of one business to society may be complete nonsense if applied to another. When discussing the social responsibilities of business, for instance, that which may be true for a huge highly profitable corporation may not apply at all to a very small company striving to avoid bankruptcy.

FUNDAMENTAL INTERRELATIONSHIPS BETWEEN BUSINESS AND SOCIETY

It is obvious, yet quite important, to note that the business system is only one system in a larger system we call society. Society is composed of many institutions or systems which interrelate and work together—sometimes in harmony and often in conflict—to achieve the goals which society sets for itself. All institutions influence one another. All are interdependent.

Institutions, or systems, in society are not created and accepted as the result of some mystical conception. They are created and accepted by society in order to perform important societal functions. At any one point in time there is a working relationship between society and its institutions which sets the interconnections between the institution and society as a whole and among institutions. This is called the social contract. This contract is partly written in legislation but also is found in customs, precedent, and articulated societal approval or disapproval. Whether explicit or implicit, the social contract is the basis for institutional actions.

This fundamental interrelationship between business and society leads to a number of important conclusions. One is that the business institution operates, basically, to serve society's interests as society sees them. Another is that generalizations about the interrelationship between business and society in the past may not be valid today or tomorrow. The social contract changes continuously. In periods of great change, such as today, there is more pervasive and fundamental rewriting of the contract than in tranquil times. Indeed, today there are many people who feel that the social contract is being rewritten in a fundamental way.

The business system operates on the legacy of the past and in light of the current and perceived future environment. The past has resulted in a body of laws, customs, and habits of thought that govern current business actions. The current and future environments open up opportunities for business and also pose threats. Some businesses react solely to current environmental changes on a day-to-day basis. More and more businesses, however, survey future environmental horizons for opportunities and threats so that they may make current decisions to exploit the opportunities and to avoid the threats. Hence, business today reacts not only to today's environment but also to that which is perceived in the future.

Society has goals that may or may not coincide with those of business enterprises. For example, society's desire to prosper matches in general the goal of a company; as each prospers the goals of each are met. But society's goal of growth with stable prices may result in governmental actions that restrain growth goals of a business. As Chamberlain observes: "Each seeks a stable relationship in which its own advantage is secured, and each is continually upsetting and reconstituting it in a way that it hopes will be advantageous to itself" (1968: 143). He concludes: "To society, the firm is an instrument to be used. To the firm, society is a field to be exploited" (144).

While the business firm finds itself constrained by government and other systems in society, it still possesses many options for action. Government, too, is constrained in its relationships with business and yet has power to restrain business. The paradox is explained in terms of specific relationships and in matters of degree. The privacy or autonomy of the corporation is protected as a basic social value against government interference. But when government considers it necessary to constrain business in order to achieve a societal purpose, it does so.

CHARACTERISTICS OF THE ANALYSIS

I have sought to accomplish a number of purposes in this book and in so doing have used many different analytical approaches. These are presented not to be argumentative or defensive, but merely to provide a clearer picture of the nature of the contents of this volume.

Comprehensive Scope I have sought to make this book comprehensive in scope, yet reasonably succinct. I have tried to cover the large canvas, sketching out all of the most important interrelationships between business and society. This approach is in contrast to that of selecting and concentrating intensively and exclusively on a few major areas, such as business social responsibility, pollution, and consumerism. I think it is far better for the student in a basic course in the business-society interrelationship to be exposed to the major interrelationships, even if the exposure is often "light," than for him to dig deeply into only a few major areas. It seems to me that the last approach short-changes the student. The student can concentrate later, and with a better chance for enrichment, if he starts from a broad base.

Identifying Issues, Getting the Facts, and Reaching Conclusions
This book emphasizes issues in the business-society nexus. One goal is to help students to identify the "correct" issues. This means asking the "right" questions and framing the "right" problems. What is "right" often depends upon who is asking the question. Nevertheless, students of this subject must try to get at the basic and strategic questions. For instance, there is no question about the fact that technological advance has had serious and unwanted side effects. Is the question how to slow down technology advance to reduce these side effects, as some people advocate, or is it, as others suggest, how to inject into decision-making processes incentives to avoid the unwanted side impacts? Or is it something else? Students of this subject should understand that framing the "right" question is often very difficult in this area. They also should remember that proposed solutions follow the question once it is asked.

Many times in this book questions will be asked and no answers given. This is because there are no answers. Even if there are no answers, we still are progressing if the right questions are posed.

Once the issues have been identified, what are the facts? Getting the facts may be extremely difficult. For example, what are the facts about the safety of nuclear power plants? What are the facts about the human and economic damage caused by various types of pollution? What are the facts about the expectations of society on the social responsibilities of business? We do not have enough facts about these and many other crucial questions.

Once the facts are gathered it is essential to use them in a proper context. For example, some critics charge that business has not really solved major social problems and its failure to do so indicates more concern with profits than the social welfare. The first part of the statement is correct but not the second. The facts are correct—business has not solved major social problems—but the perspective of the critics is wrong. It is not business's responsibility to solve major social problems, with a few exceptions to be noted later.

Even with the right issue at hand and all the facts that are available, reasonable men may come to radically different conclusions about preferred policy on major issues. The reason, of course, is that men come to the issues and facts with differing ideologies, scales of values, and interests. The attorney-general of the United States looks at the antitrust laws somewhat differently than the chief executive of General Motors. At the very least, however, reason is more likely to prevail in society when men can communicate with one another about commonly identified issues and the real facts. In some instances, but not all, I have explained my position on the issue being examined. This has not been done to intrude my views on the reader, but rather to help in the analysis, for this book is not designed to "sell" or "explain" one particular point of view. Its purpose is to identify major issues and to stimulate full, informed, and thoughtful debate about them.

Because judgment is often the final determinant of one's position on a particular issue, this is not an excuse to ignore the facts of a case. A charming story about Michelangelo will illustrate this situation. When Michelangelo had completed his carving of David, the governor of Florence came to look at the finished piece. He was pleased with what he saw, but as he looked at it he mused, "The nose . . . the nose is too large, is it not?" Michelangelo looked carefully at David's nose and quietly answered, "Yes, I think it is a little too large." He picked up his chisel and mallet, and also a handful of marble dust, and mounted the scaffolding. Carefully he hammered, permitting small amounts of dust to fall to the ground with each blow. He finally stopped and asked: "Now, look at the nose. Is it not correct?" "Ah," responded the governor, "I like it . . . I like it even better. You have given it life." Michelangelo descended, according to an old chronicle, "with great compassion for those who desire to appear to be good judges of matters whereof they know nothing" (Lerman, 1942: 168–69).

To deplore "shooting-from-the-hip," so to speak, does not suggest as an objective to "know all there is about business and society." I find myself in complete accord with J. Robert Oppenheimer when he observed: "No man should escape our universities without . . . some sense of the fact that not through his fault, but in the nature of things, he is going to be an ignorant man, and so is everyone else." It is an appropriate posture to approach the subject of this book with humility.

Emphasis on Current and Significant Issues   I have tried to emphasize the more current and socially significant issues. Thus, there is emphasis upon business's relationships with major current social problems, rather than upon older government regulation of business; upon today's changing social values and their potential impact on business, rather than on social attitudes toward business in the past; upon emerging new issues such as "consumerism," rather than on the evolution of laws to protect consumers. While I realize there are no uninteresting subjects, I have tried to emphasize what I think are generally the more interesting and exciting issues between business and society.

The Business-Society Focus On the business side, the main focus is on the impact of society on the business institution—business's role in society, the philosophy of managers, managerial practices, and business structure. On the societal side the focus is on how business brings change—to values, institutions, institutional relationships, and decision-making processes. Also emphasized are total societal welfare, preferred balances between business and societal roles, and interrelated decision-making between the two.

A Fundamental Analytical Structure While emphasis is on issues in this book, issues come and go. What is hot today will be cold tomorrow. What will be front and center tomorrow may not now be discernible. A main purpose of this book is to provide a basic tool kit for examining not only today's issues but also those of tomorrow. I, therefore, have emphasized the fundamental processes for decision-making and change in both business and other institutions in society, particularly the government. I have tried to employ the most pertinent analytical methods in dealing with selected issues. I have also tried to develop a theory underlying the subject matter of business and society. Following are a few comments about selected analytical methods used in the book.

The Interdisciplinary Approach In this book, I have applied managerial, behavioral, historical, technical, religious, and political knowledge and methodology where appropriate. It seems to me that it is wrong to think one discipline alone can explain or provide the required understanding throughout the business-society interface. Of course, in certain areas and certain subjects, particular disciplines have more to say than others. In employing the interdisciplinary approach, I have tried to use the pertinent tools and methods in the different disciplines.

Historical Perspective It is a fundamental thesis of this book that one cannot fully understand the present—or the future—without a comprehension and appreciation of the past. One cannot understand the conflicts among businessmen about social responsibilities, for instance, without a knowledge of the way in which capitalist theory has developed and the impact that environment has had on it. Historical perspective has other advantages. With history as a base, it is easier for one to avoid being deceived by cliches, "red herrings," and irrelevant observations. As Justice Holmes once suggested, history is the first step toward an enlightened skepticism. Furthermore, it is important to know that there are historical causes for current events and that the pattern of future events is being shaped today. The inevitability of change not only provides a key to an understanding of shifting relationships between business and its environment, but it should warn against clinging tenaciously to any rigidly fixed set of abstractions, generalizations, or institutions as being the best inter-relationship between business and society for all time.

Perhaps the most valuable lesson of history is the knowledge of the very short period of time men have lived in freedom, and how easy it is to lose this precious jewel in the crown of civilization. Political and economic freedom are the great prizes men seek. History teaches the significance of this goal to men. It also teaches the grave difficulties in determining for any age the proper balance among freedom, the requirements for order, and the rights of men. On the other hand, one must guard against the human tendency to deprecate the present in favor of the past. It is easy, for instance, to praise the indomitable spirit of old New England, but not so easy to see it as often being frost cold and granite hard. There is a proclivity in men to remember the pleasant and forget the unpleasant. Then, too, the precise lessons of the past may not always be clear or applicable in today's setting.

It is often said today that history is irrelevant. In times of great change history is, in fact, often rejected. Chateaubriand, in 1832, remarked that "When a people, changed by time, does not want to remain what it has been, the first symptom of its malaise is disrespect for its past, and for the virtues of its ancestors." The pace of change in recent years has been so swift that events often seem to be discontinuous with the past. This may be so for some things, but for the massive underlying forces in society, there is continuity with the past and there will be continuity between the present and the future.

History is not useful in the sense that a knowledge of chemistry is. But it can be at least as valuable in providing insights into who we are, how we got here, options which may be open, solutions which may be best for society, and where we may be heading. "A moment's insight," wrote Justice Holmes, "is worth a lifetime of experience." And, says Lynn T. White, this is very important, especially today, "when insight is much scarcer than information" (Davidson, 1971).

The Systems Approach I have used this approach throughout the book. The systems approach looks at the way in which parts and subsystems of a system interrelate. Generally, the objective is to examine the parts to see how they can contribute to the optimization of the entire system. In connection with the pollution problem, for instance, the systems approach asks whether the costs of taking an action in one area will be greater or less than the benefits to society as a whole. Whether or not one can answer such questions with precision, the value of the systems approach rests in improving understanding. Churchman observes on this point: "We seem forced to conclude that anyone who actually believes in the possibility of improving systems is faced with the problem of understanding the properties of the whole system, and that he cannot concentrate his attention merely on one sector. The problem of system improvement is the problem of the 'ethics of the whole system' " (1968: 4).

In the systems approach, the impact of business on society and the impact of changes in society on business are examined directly. For example, there is in the book a discussion of the way in which business has been responsible for technological change, how technological change has affected social values and expectations, and how these in turn have influenced business.

Underlying Forces, Trends, and Processes I have tried to identify and explain the underlying forces that affect business-society interconnections and the main trends which appear today and may be reasonably projected into the future. Understanding forces and trends is indispensable to insight and the illumination of issues and possibilities for the future.

Finally, I have tried to explain the basic processes in business and other institutions in society which have a major impact on business (e.g., government, unions). It is difficult to understand the interrelationships between business and society without comprehension of the way in which the managerial and economic processes in business operate. I have, therefore, tried to be specific about these processes.

PART ONE

The Road to Today's Complex Interrelationships

what-program
how-much
when-schedule
who- responsibility

Tuesday

Discussion for class

CHAPTER TWO

Antecedents to Capitalism

INTRODUCTION

The American economy has been and is a capitalist system, although its characteristics have changed significantly over time. So, too, have the interrelationships between business and society altered throughout recorded history. In this chapter I shall try to capture the main trends in the broad sweep of recorded history leading to the rise of American capitalism. Even though little more can be done here than to express broad generalities, such background material provides a firm basis for understanding today's business-society relationships. (In this and the next chapter I have borrowed liberally from my book *Government's Role in Economic Life* (1953).

THE ANCIENT WORLD

The emergence of business in society is lost in the past. We know, however, that various forms of business flourished in the Mediterranean area some 3,000 years ago. The Mesopotamian merchant roamed over far-distant seas to ply his trade and had at his disposal a number of techniques which we know today to be fundamental in the conduct of business. Miriam Beard writes that the businessman formed trading companies; wrote contracts; operated on the basis of laws governing trading, including regulations over market pricing; and was subject to government control. We know that these merchants had access to mass-production techniques, for there was dis-

17

covered in Brittany a deposit of 4,000 hatchets, neatly tied together with wire, which were traced to Mesopotamian producers of the period 1800–1200 B.C. One further bit of evidence of the importance of trade in these early days is the Code of Hammurabi, issued around 2000 B.C. It contained more than 300 laws, many of which concerned business activities.

Business life in the Mediterranean Basin was surprisingly advanced and reached a golden age between 800 and 450 B.C. During this period, the businessman had freed himself from the control of the Near Eastern despots and had not yet fallen under the heel of the Roman legions. But the position of the businessman varied in different parts of this world.

In Athens and Sparta, for example, traders were not well regarded. Here, agrarian and military interests were dominant. Indeed, throughout early Greek history and extending into and through the period of the Roman Empire, warriors were at odds with businessmen. In Greece, business as an occupation was stamped with disapproval. A merchant could not hold public office, could not own property, and in time of war was impressed into the army and given the lowest rank. Plato downgraded the importance of private property and the accumulation of wealth in the ideal society he described in *The Republic.* Citizens in this ideal society were to be prevented from accumulating profits in commercial activities lest this nourish the growth of avarice and lead to a process of social decay. Plato's pupil, Aristotle, was similarly dismayed by the practice of accumulating excessive wealth through the accumulation of profits made in commercial enterprise. These views are still held by people in different parts of the world.

On the other hand, there were great trading cities such as Carthage, Tyre, Rhodes, and Corinth, where the businessmen were rich and dominated government offices. In these cities the concepts of property, profit, division of labor, banking, and commercial law were well advanced, and the businessman was highly respected.

THE ROMAN WORLD

The Punic Wars (236–146 B.C.) completely changed the Mediterranean world of business. The great trading cities fell one by one, and all the seats of power of the businessman were in ruins or reduced to ashes. His wealth and prestige were lost, and the means for his revival were gone. Beard points out that Roman historians vilified the businessman by emphasizing his bad traits and glorifying the agrarian and the warrior. This stamp of social inferiority clung to the businessman for centuries (1962).

In the Roman Empire there existed a marriage between the aristocracy and the businessman unmatched in history for its convenience, cleavage, and ultimate catastrophe. Despite the inferior position of the businessman in Roman life and thought, his assumption of a more and more important role was predetermined by a number of forces. Rome was unable to feed its people and needed imports of food. Roman generals found it necessary to borrow money to wage war, and hoped that booty could repay the debt. And as Rome prospered, the demand for luxury goods grew. Finally, the Roman government had essential services performed by contractual arrangements with businessmen; coinage, the building of roads and aqueducts, and even the collecting of taxes (in the early period) was done not by civil servants, but by an entrepreneur who obtained the contract.   *FART*

The cleavage between the aristocracy and the businessman grew *louder and louder.* from many sources. Noblemen who fought the wars were made painfully aware of the greed of merchants who charged exorbitant rates of interest on their loans. As businessmen grew richer, their duel with the aristocracy for political power intensified, for never in Rome was the businessman able to hold government office. This cleavage reached a peak of sorts when Cassius (113–53 B.C.), who was an extremely wealthy businessman, sought to become ruler of Rome. He came close, as a co-ruler with Julius Caesar (100–44 B.C.), but eventually lost and committed suicide. The hatred between rich Alexandrian traders and Roman officials was of such proportions that it eventually led to war, and the conflict between businessmen and the aristocracy led to the ruin of both.

Throughout the history of the empire, the Greek view of the businessman persisted. In the earliest days of the empire, for example, brick-making was the only enterprise considered to be respectable, because it was based on the earth. Late in the empire, however, wealth became more and more an esteemed goal. But the businessman was never allowed to hold political power despite his wealth or the help of his gold in conquest. He was accepted for his aid but scorned for his trade.

At the height of the empire, business flourished. Technology was esteemed, there was an advanced money and banking system, trade was widespread, the profit motive was strong, business was organized, an advanced legal system existed (after which our system is patterned), and in many other ways the empire was an advanced commercial world. But a new influence, Christianity, brought still more social censure to business. Church doctrine was not at all sympathetic to business, but throughout the life of the later empire, it did not adversely affect business. The collapse of the Roman Empire grew out of many complex forces upon which we shall not dwell except to say that the immediate cause was the conquest of Rome by the barbarians, culminating in the "official" end of the empire in A.D. 476.

THE MEDIEVAL WORLD

The medieval world is generally considered to have extended from the break-up of the Roman Empire to the fifteenth century. These are arbitrary dates, for at both ends change was neither sudden nor abrupt. The period is generally broken into parts: the Dark Ages, which extended from the end of the empire to about A.D. 1000; the High Middle Ages, which extended through the thirteenth century; and the Later Middle Ages.

In contrast with the centralized and highly developed world of the Roman Empire, the world of the Dark Ages was one of extreme and primitive localism. As the central authority of Rome decayed, large chunks of real estate were administered and controlled by local manorial lords. The masses of the people were serfs who tilled land owned by a manorial lord and used his grain mills, his wine presses, and his agricultural implements. They were shackled as tightly to their lord as were the slaves of the Roman world to their masters. A third class in society was the freeman who, as the name implies, was able to move about as he chose. Traders were found in this group, but they were few because of the constant danger to person in an age of violence. A fourth group was the clergy, whose influence constantly increased. Society was linked together in local groups by a cordon of privilege, obligation, custom, and religion. People lived simply to feed, clothe, and shelter themselves; to work in the interests of the lord in payment for his protection; and to seek salvation in the hereafter. This was a world of rules which governed everything, spiritual and earthly. Trade dwindled to practically nothing.

The dominant institution was the Catholic Church, whose supreme function was the salvation of man. Man was considered to be a citizen not only of this earth, but also of a more important kingdom in the hereafter. Church doctrine held that entrance into this other world was not easy because man had sinned by disobeying God. It was only through the Church that the vast redeeming store of grace given man through God's Son could be utilized to absolve sin and gain entrance into the Kingdom of Heaven. And it was to this end that the entire population directed its efforts.

This other-worldly attitude was hostile to business. Trade was considered to be founded on greed, which was sinful, and trade also turned the minds of men to the material aspects of this life rather than to the spiritual glory of the next. Businessmen were held in low esteem, the accumulation of capital for production was discouraged, lending money at interest was opposed, prices had to be "just," and actions had to be in conformity with a moral code established by the Church.

Toward the end of the Middle Ages, the Church became the largest landowner in Christendom, largely because the belief was widely held that expiation for sin could be found in making gifts (including land) to the Church. In the eighth century bishops, whose cathedrals were located in towns, were given complete authority over the people on the lands the Church controlled. Churchmen thus became manorial lords controlling thousands of serfs. The wealth of the Church thus gave it an enormous temporal power to complement its unrivaled spiritual power.

Minute controls were exercised by local craft and merchant guilds to ensure the monopoly of their position and to preserve an orderly life. Town governments passed ordinances and regulations controlling the trade of the town and the administration of its property. Over all lay the heavy hand of custom, privilege, and theology, whose economic restraints few men chose to disregard.

There were, however, a few offsetting forces stimulating trade. In most towns there were markets where local merchandise was traded on a more or less regular basis. There were also larger fairs, held at irregular intervals, which attracted wares and traders from distant cities and lands. Then, in the eighth century, the invasions of Islam changed the Mediterranean from a Roman to a Muslim lake. The Crusades (the first of which began in 1095) were organized to expel the invaders, restore Christianity, and regain control of the Holy Land. A major side effect was the stimulation of trade.

As economic activity increased, the Church found itself faced with a growing gap between its own practices and philosophy and actual life. Priests made loans to parishioners and borrowed money to build churches; and the Church itself had become an important economic revenue-producing institution as a landlord. St. Thomas Aquinas (1225–1274) is regarded as the greatest of the Scholastics for his systematic attempt to reconcile theological dogma with actual conditions in his *Summa Theologica*. He felt that trade, although not good or natural, was permissible if used to maintain the household or to benefit the country. Profit and interest charges were accepted with a few modifications. In general he, like his contemporary churchmen, did not like what was going on in the commercial world but could not stop it. He therefore set out to reconcile commercial practices with theology as much as possible.

The stability of medieval localism was long in the process of transformation before the scope and direction of change became apparent. Under the hammer blows of extensive economic, political, religious, and social change, the medieval world in the fifteenth century merged into a world dominated by powerful nationalistic states and strong business-oriented cities.

The End of the Medieval World   The decline of the medieval world was hastened by four important events: the Black Death, the Renaissance, expanding trade, and a change in theology. First, the Black Death (1348–1349) was a terrible scourge that took the lives of about one-third of the population of Europe. No society can stand such a catastrophe without major changes. From an economic view, for example, losses in revenues by manorial lords weakened their control, and peasants left their lands to form bodies of free workers for hire. Widespread social unrest developed throughout the century. Second, there was an intellectual awakening beginning in Italy around 1350 which spread throughout Europe for another hundred years. The people of medieval Europe probably knew less than did men at the time of the birth of Christ. Reclaiming the vast lost knowledge and discovering more blew a fresh invigorating wind through medieval society. Universities were established, the rebirth of intellectual freedom stimulated new ideals of individual freedom, and more enlightened ideas about business were accepted. Through such forces as these there developed a society which discovered new ways to do things. Indeed, says Lynn White, "The chief glory of the later Middle Ages was not its cathedrals or its epics or its scholasticism: it was the building for the first time in history of a complex civilization which rested not on the backs of sweating slaves or coolies but primarily on non-human power" (White, 1940: 156). Third, the Crusades (extending from the eleventh to the thirteenth centuries) brought economic revival. Fleets of ships were built, the Mediterranean was opened to navigation, agriculture was stimulated by the demands for food, and commerce flourished. This burst of economic activity at first was confined to the port cities, but a rapid inland penetration soon took place. These developments were further expanded by the search for new trade routes to the East in the late fifteenth century.

Finally, there was the change from an other-worldly to a this-worldly theology brought on by the Protestant Reformation in the early sixteenth century. The beginning of this revolution is usually attributed to Martin Luther (1483–1546), but there were dissidents before him in Florence. At any rate, he did not set out to free business, although that was the net result. He, like other churchmen of the day, disapproved of much of commercial activity. Luther's starting point was a rejection of the Catholic ideals of the ascetic and monastic life as a way to salvation, and of the view that the required morality could not be found in secular life. Luther said that one could find salvation in any walk of life. What counted was a man's faith, not his works. As time went on there were subtle changes in Luther's views which favored economic activity. He felt, for example, that daily events were the manifestation of the Providence of God, that it was a Christian's duty to accept involvement in daily affairs and to be happy about them since they were determined by God. Luther did not open up the economic possibilities in these views; that remained for others to do. While Luther's theology was contemplative and passive, Calvin's was aggressively active. To Calvin, the center of everything was God, and it was man's chief end to glorify God. Salvation could be assured by the demonstrated ability of a man to perform good works consistently with the consciousness that this was made possible by the power of God working through man. As a result, there existed a tremendous pressure for hard work. Hard work was not in itself the means of winning salvation, but a sign of man's willingness to fulfill God's will. Here is the idea that one serves God through his occupation.

The Puritans added another dimension and welded the spirit of entrepreneurship tightly to the spirit of God. There were two principal objectives of work to the Puritans. One was a sort of discipline, a means to keep a person busy and thereby avoid evil thoughts and actions. The other was to enhance the glory of God. The Puritans laid great stress on the need to work hard, and to live to work, not work to live. Hard work inevitably would lead to riches, but this accumulation of wealth was for God, not for the pleasures of the flesh. On this point the Puritans were on the horns of a dilemma. To work hard would bring riches, but both the pursuit and the possession of riches were dangerous because they diverted man from his main task of achieving the glory of God. John Wesley, the great preacher, avoided the dilemma this way: "After you have gained all you can and saved all you can, spend not one pound, one shilling, one penny, to gratify either the desire of the flesh, the desire of the eyes, or the pride of life, or for any other end than to please and glorify God" (Fullerton, 1928: 163–91). The certainty of salvation lay in hard, constant, and continuous work in one's calling. The wealth accumulated was a mark of faithfulness in the discharge of one's work. Benjamin Franklin translated this theology into pragmatic axioms that caught the very heart of the spirit of capitalism and individual entrepreneurship. Franklin quoted with approval Proverbs 22, 29: "Seest thou a man diligent in business? He shall stand before kings." To him, time was money. Man should not love money, he said, but he had an obligation to make money. Making money was a duty. It was an end in itself.

Here is the Protestant Ethic, which has had such a powerful impact on American economic activity. It emphasized the virtue of work, the evil of idleness, the sacred nature of private property, the dignity and worth of the individual, personal independence, the emphasis on thrift, and the justification for the accumulation of wealth.

The Jewish religion stressed the virtues of hard work, sobriety, thrift, and the accumulation of riches. But the Jews also felt that riches were the blessings of the Lord and should be enjoyed for God's sake.

Max Weber, the great sociologist, believed that the very "spirit of capitalism" came as a byproduct of the religious ethic of Calvinism, but this view has been challenged (Green, 1959). The chain of cause and effect in the economic implications of changing theology after Luther is not at all clear, but it is abundantly obvious that the new theology fostered and nurtured the very spirit of capitalism in a fashion impossible with preceding religious beliefs. It is probably better to say that religion and the rise of capitalism were intimately intertwined.

MERCANTILISM

The break-up of the medieval world brought a variety of changes in the major countries of Europe. In most countries, power tended to concentrate in the hands of kings, as for example in France and England, and these rulers set about to control the economic life of their countries. The body of thought associated with that effort has been called mercantilism, and the states have been called mercantilist states.

Mercantilist practices differed among the European states. The mercantilist states generally sought to maintain centralized political power at home and a military power which could be exercised in the foreign interests of the sovereign. A strong national state, the mercantilists reasoned, was one which was wealthy, and precious metals were the most desirable forms of national wealth. These states therefore determined to control their economic systems at home and to expand their empires abroad in order to acquire as much of the world's precious metals as possible. Controls centered on foreign trade because it was through a favorable balance of trade that precious metals could most readily be acquired. Exports were stimulated and imports restricted. Efforts to produce a favorable trade balance did not stop at the point of foreign exchange; they extended back through the manufacturing chain to individual procedures. New industries were encouraged by government, output was controlled, and distribution regulated. To stimulate wool manufacture, for example, an English law of 1571 required that every person over six years of age had to wear, on Sundays and holidays, a wool cap made in England (Cheyney, 1912: 175). Colonies were considered to be useful in achieving the major purpose of accumulating precious metals not only as sources of the metal through mining, but, more importantly, through trade. Colonies could provide raw materials to the mother country and be a source of sales of finished goods.

Colonies were therefore sought and when acquired were sharply regulated in the mother countries' interests. No form of economic life (at home or in colonies) escaped the regulatory eye of central government; detailed rules were prescribed for labor, finance, agriculture, manufacturing, and consumption.

While most European businessmen were suffering under restrictive central government controls, there were cases in which they were comparatively free and powerful. In mercantilist states like France and England, for instance, grants of monopoly were rather freely given by the king. Royalties were paid to the crown, of course, but the system favored a few at the expense of the many. In Florence, Italy, there was great fluid wealth which was used to stimulate the arts and nourish the religious, political, and military ambitions of businessmen such as the Medici, who were dominant in the fifteenth, sixteenth, and seventeenth centuries. Jacob Fugger (1449–1525) of Augsburg, Germany, was a man of enormous wealth who controlled the destinies of governments. In Holland there were many wealthy merchants and bankers who assumed high political office.

Like their predecessor states, the nationalist states underwent gradual change and were replaced by a system of capitalism, the principal features of which exist to this day. But American capitalism today is a far different system from that which immediately followed mercantilism. To really understand business-social relationships in the United States over the course of its history, as well as to comprehend a number of major issues which are current today, it is necessary to have more than a snapshot view of what happened in the past. For this reason, the remainder of the chapter will be devoted to the events leading to the rise of capitalism.

THE RISE OF CAPITALISM

Demands for Freedom from Legal Restraints Mercantilism sowed the seeds of its own destruction. The material philosophy of mercantilism rescued individuals from the business restraints of medieval life, and in so doing, provided society with a new way of thinking about advancing its material well-being through trade opportunities. Although mercantilism directed individual economic activity in conformity with the interests of a centralized authority, the objectives and methods of state control became less acceptable to men who sought more and more to pursue self-interest and to exploit for themselves the opportunities offered in the expanding trade fostered by mercantilism.

One important result of this situation was that the pattern of mercantilistic controls tended to be modified in favor of individuals. In England, for example, there was a quite noticeable drift in the early seventeenth century for government, in order to stimulate new manufactures, to relieve new industries from the minute regulations that applied to older industries. This, together with other events, led to pressure to relieve from regulations those businesses which were still controlled. Also, although the statutes in England included a vast body of regulations, they were less and less strictly enforced as counterpressures mounted. The demands of a growing entrepreneurial class for more economic freedom provided first by growing trade, then by relaxation of controls, and finally by the spectacular mechanical inventions in England were stronger than mercantilistic restraints could withstand.

The Great Inventions Beginning in the textile industry in England, a series of inventions laid the basis for revolutionary changes in manufacturing methods. John Kay invented the flying shuttle in 1733; Hargreaves patented his spinning jenny in 1770; Arkwright's power-operated spinning machines were patented in 1769; and Compton's inventions in 1779 permitted machines to produce fine, delicate muslins.

At first, the machines were operated by water power, but toward the end of the century (1781) came the invention of Watt's steam engine. Meanwhile, new techniques were being developed to replace charcoal with coal in the extraction of metals. Early in the century Darby succeeded in smelting iron from coal, a strategic invention for England, which was running out of wood for charcoal. In the middle of the century the process was improved, and mills could produce a purer iron and run it through rolling mills. At about the same time steel manufacture was greatly improved. So it went in other areas—chemicals, machinery, agricultural equipment, and pumps.

The immediate impact of such inventions was to introduce the factory system. The older system was a domestic system in which individuals worked in their own homes and owned their own simple tools. Except in a few institutions such as the joint-stock companies, capital and capital equipment for manufacture were widely scattered. But with these inventions it became desirable to aggregate capital to buy machinery and collect scattered workers together in a factory to run the machinery. Factories in the modern sense were introduced for the first time in history. The result was an explosive growth of production and a lasting impact on all sorts of social institutions.

The Agricultural Revolution In the meantime a double-pronged revolution took place in agriculture. A long series of Enclosure Acts permitted farmers in one locality to throw together their scattered pieces of land and then to redivide the land thus aggregated in such a way that each received his proportionate share. This share was in one block and subject to the owner's control. A farmer with many scattered pieces of land could, in a sense, trade in the separate plots on a single new tract without sacrificing acreage. Although it had originated around the middle of the fifteenth century, the process was suspended during the seventeenth century, and not reactivated until the eighteenth. This movement was accompanied by the introduction of new methods of farming: crop rotation, fertilization, drainage, better stock, and accumulation of capital equipment. These changes opened up new opportunities for those with capital, knowledge, and initiative. The result was a revolution in agriculture paralleling, but by no means equaling, the revolution in industry.

THE INSTITUTIONS OF CAPITALISM

On the economic side, history had also provided the people of the seventeenth and eighteenth centuries with other basic institutions by means of which individual enterprise could be expressed advantageously once it was freed from restraints. By the eighteenth century some of the institutions were perfected, while others were yet in infancy.

It is worthwhile to list a few of these institutions, which are essential to the operation of the individual enterprise system. From the time of the Romans to eighteenth-century England, legal rights to hold and use property were gradually strengthened in favor of individuals. So also were laws relating to the sanctity of contracts. Over a long period of time a body of free workers had accumulated in society. The existence of this group, in combination with accumulations of capital and an entrepreneurial class (capitalist proprietors), established one base for the introduction of the factory system. This group also provided a foundation for the division of labor and the wage system so important in the development of the modern economy. The great trading companies set a pattern for the evolution of the modern corporation as a business form. Accounting systems for business enterprise, although not in very polished form, existed and were recognized as important. A system of money had long existed, but it was not until the seventeenth and eighteenth centuries that money transactions increased rapidly. A credit system, although long in existence, paralleled the expansion in the use of money. The Bank of England, founded in 1691, facilitated extension of the use of credit. Medieval town fairs, continued in the mercantilistic world, helped set a pattern of competitive price behavior. The worth of the businessman in society, and a recognition of his inherent right to trade for profit, was becoming more and more accepted. Fire and life insurance companies developed in the latter part of the seventeenth century and stimulated risk taking. In sum, the basic institutions and behavior patterns of a free economy existed. But if government restraints and the heavy hand of custom were lifted, would the result be chaos, or order?

New Business Organizations Great economic progress in England during the seventeenth and eighteenth centuries was due in large part to the efficiency of its business organizations in exploiting trade opportunities and new technology. Of more significance for us, however, is the fact that the joint-stock companies of this period were the prototypes of the modern business corporation, which is undeniably one of the world's greatest inventions.

The first English joint-stock company was chartered by Mary Tudor, Queen of England, in 1553 to expand trade with Russia. Additional companies were chartered in this century, but the greater growth was in the next century. These companies had many features of the modern corporation, but they differed much in scope and purpose. The East India Company (1600–1874), for instance, engaged in trade, but it was primarily a political power and was supposed to promote the welfare of the English people and increase the revenues of the crown. It had the right, for example, to make and enforce laws and to coin money. Indeed, its charter empowered it to "seize all ships, vessels, goods and wares going to or coming from the East Indies." One-half the booty went to the company and the rest to the crown (Davis, 1961: II, 126). While many joint-stock companies had economic and political, and some military powers, they were formed for many different purposes, such as trade, colonization, manufacturing, fishing, mining, and banking. By 1700 there were about 140 of these companies in England (Johnson and Krooss, 1953: 144).

There were other forms of business organizations in England at this time but none with the potential significance of the joint-stock company. The joint-stock company did, however, draw some of its features from these other organizational forms (Davis, 1961: II, 66–156).

At the beginning of the eighteenth century a speculative fever in England was accompanied by fraud in some companies, particularly the South Sea Company (chartered in 1711). The Bubble Act was passed in 1720 to regulate new promotions, but its wording was so murky that it led to the abandonment of the joint-stock form for almost a century, except for companies like the East India Company, which were exempt from the provisions of the act, and for unchartered joint-stock companies. The unchartered companies did not have a limited liability for common stock owners, nor could they sue and be sued in a common name. These two characteristics were finally granted at the time of the repeal of the Bubble Act in 1825 and the passage of the Companies Act in 1862, which provided for a general system of incorporation by registration. In the meantime, the corporate form flourished in America.

THE RISE OF NEW IDEAS

Revolutionary economic events preceding and accompanying the Industrial Revolution were paralleled by scarcely less significant changes in the realm of ideas, particularly ideas concerned with the position of individuals in economic and social life.

Natural Laws Newton's discovery of the laws of gravity and the publication of his *Philosophiae Naturalis Principia Mathematica* in 1687 stimulated a rapid development of the natural sciences. The discovery and formulation of immutable physical laws governing these sciences stirred men to seek the laws of nature that guided the actions of individuals. Men no longer blindly accepted the view that it was natural and desirable for government to regulate economic and social life. Rather, the idea flowered that it was natural and desirable for government not to interfere in social and economic life. There must be, it was reasoned, a "natural order" which governed men's lives.

This philosophical fermentation led in the latter part of the seventeenth and early eighteenth centuries to a reformulation of a theory of natural law, or natural order, which directed the affairs of men. The new revelation of natural law bridged a gap which spanned time back to imperial Rome, when lawyers had tried to discover the fundamental "laws of nature" which they thought underlay and integrated all legal codes. They were led to develop the law of property and contract which to this day is fundamental in economic life, but they did not discover the universal laws they sought.

Typical of the newer doctrines of natural order was that of John Locke, who, in his second *Treatise on Civil Government* published in 1691, advanced the idea that men in the original state of nature were free and equal and were not subject to subordination or subjection. In this state of nature there were natural laws which governed relationships among men. It is true, he argued, that in the state of nature a lack of "executive power" created the necessity for government, but society subjected itself to government only by consent. Since men in a state of nature had "natural" and "inalienable" rights of "life, liberty, and estate," government created by men should not abridge them. If it did so, it was guilty of interfering with natural law and subject to overthrow by its victims.

This philosophy was more comforting than convincing. Subsequent elaboration by such philosophers as Hume, Hutchison, the Physiocrats in France, and even Adam Smith in his *Theory of Moral Sentiments* failed to find the key to its underlying scientific logic. To these men, the natural order was that which God ordained for the happiness of mankind. It was a benevolent order in which all was in harmony. Such laws, however, were not set forth concretely. They were, rather, "obvious." Obvious to whom? Not to every person, but "to intelligent, thoughtful, and trained men who sought the inner laws of society." The natural order was not revealed by observation of external facts, but rather by "discovering the principle within." This concept was in the tradition of the scholastic idiom of the medieval world, which described a fixed order of rights, duties, and obligations.

The theory of natural laws was too naive and nebulous to fit the requirements of economic life, but it contained three ideas that were to flower and engulf the philosophy and practice of the regulated state. They were ideas about individualism, laissez faire, and an orderly economic system operating on the basis of individual self-interest rather than government control.

Individualism The operation of the individual enterprise system and political democracy is predicated on the theory of individualism. "Individualism" is a comparatively new word used to express a philosophy as old as antiquity. It is the idea of the supreme importance of the individual in society, the idea of the inherent decency of man, and a belief in his rationality. These concepts, of course, led to the conclusion that authority over men should be held to a minimum. The idea of the infinite worth of the individual in society is threaded in the entire intellectual history of mankind. It extends back to the Stoics, who incorporated it in their search for natural order. Undoubtedly they found the idea in others before them. The Greeks, at about the time of the Peloponnesian Wars, founded a society extolling the individual rather than the group. The Judeo-Christian theology rests on the doctrine of human equality and the worth of the individual. So the idea, as well as its practice, is not so modern as the word used today to describe it.

If individualism has had a long and venerable heritage, why speak of its great significance in the eighteenth century? The reason is simple. Although the idea found application in practice in a few scattered previous periods of history, its comparatively widespread acceptance in the eighteenth century altered the economic and political history of the world in the most profound sense—and for the better.

An idea so old and so fundamental in the thoughts of mankind quite obviously has had different meanings to peoples at various times in history. Individualism to the Romans, for example, meant the importance of individuals of only certain classes. Sources of authority for extolling the virtues of individual rights have ranged from pure reason, righteousness, and history to nature and God. The individualism of Herbert Spencer approached anarchy, as did that of Tocqueville. On the other hand, the individualism of Saint Simon led him to theocracy. In all these shades of meaning, however, the idea of the supremacy of the individual persisted.

Individualism to the early founders of the American Constitution and to the economists and philosophers who propounded the advantages of individual initiative was not vague. It meant something very specific. It meant relief from the shackles of mercantilism. Politically, it meant the right of people to legislate in their own behalf, to be taxed only by their representatives, to be free to choose their government representatives, to be free to overthrow the government if they so chose, and to have economic liberty and freedom. It meant that individual liberty was a fundamental objective of the political system. It was not a means to an end: it was the foremost political end. The American Declaration of Independence eloquently expressed these ideas. Economically, individualism meant freedom of individual activity and association. Again, the idea was concrete. It meant that each individual should be free to choose his own occupation, to choose his own economic ends and the means for realizing them, to choose to use resources at his disposal as he saw fit, to be freed from mercantilistic-type pressures on his economic valuations, to exchange freely with others, and to be free to organize a business with others. In short, it was a freedom to improve his economic position as he saw fit, to enjoy freely the results of his labors, and to manage his own affairs with a minimum of government regulation.

Laissez Faire The phrase *laissez faire,* first used by the French, meant that government should literally "let us alone." Specifically, it meant government should not undertake to dictate to individuals the terms of trade, how much should be produced, in what quantity, with what quality, and so on. It meant that the economic freedom embodied in the theory of individualism should not be restricted by government regulations. Laissez faire was more than a negative reflection of individualism. It was, to writers in the eighteenth and nineteenth centuries, a positive necessity for the preservation of individualism. They did not mean that government should exercise no control over economic activity, but rather that its controls should be held to a minimum. To these men, laissez faire naturally grew from the idea that the individual and not the state was the primary object of concern. The welfare of the individual and society, it was argued, could best be served by individual initiative rather than state dictation. Theirs was the idea that state interference on the whole was inimical to the best interests of individuals and society.

A Free Economic System If government restraints were lifted, through a policy of laissez faire, would the result be chaos or order?

It remained for an English professor of moral philosophy named Adam Smith in his *Wealth of Nations* (1776), and his followers, to show clearly and persuasively how the wealth of a nation and the best interests of individuals in it could be maximized if individuals were allowed to pursue their self-interests without government interference. The explanation is that of the classical exposition of the operation of the free enterprise system. This is presented in the next chapter.

The basis for laissez faire was not solely economic. It was political as well. The close relationship between politics and economics was framed in the expression "political economy." On the economic side, Adam Smith and his followers, with a clarity born of genius, persuasively showed that interference by government in economic life would jeopardize the natural tendency for men, in pursuit of their individual interests, to obtain the greatest want satisfactions from limited resources. Interference in the free market mechanism, they argued, would prevent the most efficient utilization of resources in improving the well-being of both individuals and society.

Application of the Ideas of Individualism and Laissez Faire The world was receptive to the philosophy of individualism and laissez faire. With the creation of workable systems to guide political and economic life, they became reality. The reception of Smith's *Wealth of Nations* and the circumstances surrounding the American Revolution and the drafting of the Constitution illustrate the power of ideas when the world is receptive to them.

Smith's political economy had a wide and profound effect on the world of affairs. Businessmen were delighted to have a scholar's eulogies of their dominant position in society, a position which they knew in fact existed although it was not generally recognized. They were also glad to see an explanation of the beneficent results to be achieved for society by relieving them of government restraints. They welcomed a comforting rationale for the pursuit of their own selfish interests and a justification for regarding their pursuit of profits as being unselfish. Of course, business wholeheartedly accepted Smith's teachings, but politicians and the people also accepted them.

What of the United States, or more precisely, the American colonies? The American Revolution was fought in 1776, the very year in which Smith's book appeared. The two events were not unconnected, for each found its affinity in the economic and philosophical stirrings in which the world pressed for individual and political freedom against arbitrary control by a central government. The Americans, like Smith, found a superb target in British mercantilism.

In the New World, the seeds of individualism and the idea of representative government were planted in fertile soil. Confidence in individual initiative took on new meaning in a rich continent awaiting development by the enterprising. Many of the institutions of a free economy were in unrestricted operation in the colonies as a result of illicit trade and the relaxation of mercantilistic regulations because of the distance from the mother government as well as the slackening of enforcement at home and abroad. Yet the American colonists felt themselves restrained by the mercantilistic controls that still remained. Probably even worse than the controls themselves in the eyes of the colonists was the arbitrary way in which regulations were enforced by a government in which the colonists were denied representation. Then too, the mother government rarely hesitated to impose controls ex post facto whenever the occasion seemed to warrant it.

The grievances of the colonists were specific. They objected to such controls as tax levies on sugar, molasses, tea; laws pertaining to quitrents and land tenure; subjection of home rule to anachronistic central imperial policies evidenced, for example, in British vetoes of bankruptcy laws; and laws requiring colonial billeting of English soldiers. The flames of discontent were fanned by economic depression following the Seven Years' War. Explosive elements in the colonies could no longer be contained and the Revolution was fought.

SOME CONCLUDING OBSERVATIONS

Although more will be said in later chapters about the history of the businessman and his relationships with society, it may be useful to pause here to draw a few conclusions about the historical perspective given thus far. It may seem to an observer of today that changes are coming so swiftly in society that history has no meaning. This is a dangerous notion, for history has many lessons of importance for us, a few of which follow from the discussion of these chapters.

First, there has been much variation in the relationship between business and society over a long period of time. Social change over the past 4,000 years has brought enormous differences in the role of business and businessmen in society. Second, business and businessmen have been of great importance in bringing about social change. The break-up of the medieval world as well as the decline of mercantilism illustrates the point. Third, changes taking place in society also have had great impact on business and the businessman. The influence on business of the Protestant Reformation and the Punic War illustrates the point. Fourth, institutions of society have changed when the need for change to meet social objectives has become evident. Mercantilism, for example, declined as the demand for and advantage of personal freedom became clearer. Fifth, capitalism has roots extending back over 2,000 years. Sixth, fundamental ideas have a long life and reside deeply in the attitudes of individuals. Despite the very rapid changes of today, many of the fundamental ideas that drive people are the same as those of centuries ago. For example, such ideas as the worth of the individual, a deep resistance to government regulation (laissez faire), an antipathy to business monopoly, and the Protestant Ethic. Seventh, the short-run dynamics of social life do not usually create forces which abruptly break the evolutionary process of changing social organization. The breakdown and disintegration of civilizations takes place over a relatively long period of time (often centuries). The undercurrents seem to be more important in directing the flow of the river than its surface eddies. While the characteristics of human beings during different periods of time have not been treated in these two chapters, it is sobering to contemplate the Durants' conclusion that "known history shows little alteration in the conduct of mankind. . . . Evolution in man during recorded time has been social rather than biological . . ." (Durant and Durant, 1968: 34). Eighth, although businessmen have changed many types of social ideas and activities, and vice versa, the most important relationships in the past have been with government, religion, wars, and technology. Ninth, the businessman has never ruled over a unified society, although he has often had a powerful influence. He has, however, ruled as a patrician, a political office-holder, or a city "father" over both small and large metropolitan areas. This sort of thing flourished in some pre-Roman cities. It was not until A.D. 1000 that a second wave of merchant-managed cities developed and it reached its peak in 1500. Finally, and of the greatest significance, is the fact that the type of political and economic freedom enjoyed in the United States has existed for a relatively short period of time, less than 200 years. The great bulk of recorded history is one of dictatorial control over individuals and economic repression.

CHAPTER THREE

The
Theory
of Classical
Capitalism

INTRODUCTION

Adam Smith was the founder of the capitalist ideology. For a century and a half after his *Wealth of Nations* appeared, the mainstream of economic thought was concerned with perfecting the fundamental ideas articulated in his book. This chapter presents a composite view of how the economic system was supposed to bring wealth to individuals and nations when the restraints by governments, such as those practiced under mercantilism, were eliminated.

One might well ask: Why discuss capitalist theories of men who wrote more than a century ago? There are many answers to this question, but several stand out. The application of the basic ideas of these early writers explains much in the history of business-society relationships in the United States. Over a long period of time these ideas have clashed with others, but many of them still are held strongly by many people in and out of business. The result, of course, is a conflict which explains some important verbal battles that rage around business-society relationships. These conflicting views sometimes exist in the same managers, which creates problems for them in their decision-making.

What is described in this chapter is the theory of the operation of the individual enterprise system. This name, in wide use today, was unknown in early America. The economic order which Adam Smith, and those who immediately followed him, wrote about was called capitalism. What is described in this chapter technically is the classical theory of capitalism. Fundamentally, capitalism is an economic order founded on the profit motive. Emphasis on different parts of capitalism has led to distinguishing types of capitalism. For instance, mercantile capitalism recognized private property and profit, but was restrained in a framework of laws promulgated by the state. Industrial capitalism emphasizes freedom of individual initiative to profit from industrial activities. Finance capitalism describes control of private property by financial interests rather than by owner-managers. State or national capitalism exists when there is major state control over business in the national as well as business interests. This is a modern version of mercantile capitalism (Hacker, 1947). What is described here can also be called the classical exposition of the individual enterprise system, to distinguish it from some modern theories which seek to explain how the individual enterprise system works today as compared with classical theory.

THE ECONOMIC DISCIPLINE OF ADAM SMITH

Adam Smith, in his *Wealth of Nations,* was the first person to offer an analysis of the whole range of economic processes which explained the order of the capitalistic system which underlay its surface chaos. Smith was a firm believer in the natural order of things, and he had inherent faith in the value of unrestrained individual pursuit of self-interest and natural liberty. His genius lay in his ability to show how an economic system founded on these principles could be relied upon to reach the economic goals of mercantilism more surely than the regulated mercantilistic system itself.

Individual Freedom Smith's main thesis can be summarized syllogistically. He recognized the age-old urge of individuals to increase their wealth. Each individual in his own local situation, he said, is better able to judge the most profitable utilization of the resources at his disposal than a distant government. The wealth of a nation is the aggregate wealth of the individual members of the population. Thus, the wealth of a nation will increase most rapidly if each individual is left free to pursue his own interests as he sees fit. In a famous passage, Smith elaborates this conclusion further by saying:

> As every individual, therefore, endeavours as much as he can both to employ his capital in the support of domestic industry, and so to direct that industry that its produce may be of the greatest value; every individual necessarily labours to render the annual revenue of the society as great as he can. He generally, indeed neither intends to promote the public interest, nor knows how much he is promoting it. By preferring the support of domestic to that of foreign industry, he intends only his own security; and by directing that industry in such a manner as its produce may be of the greatest value, he intends only his own gain, and he

is in this, as in many other cases, led by an invisible hand to promote an end which was no part of his intention. Nor is it always the worse for the society that it was no part of it. By pursuing his own interest he frequently promotes that of the society more effectually than when he really intends to promote it. (1776: 423)

Role of Government Adam Smith did not accept a rigorous laissez-faire policy. Adam Smith the believer in natural harmony was constantly checked by another Adam Smith—a shrewd, somewhat cynical, and realistic Scot. At some points Smith took solace in the beneficence of an "invisible hand," but at other points he was unwilling to shake it. Advocating a quite limited sphere of government interference in economic affairs at one point, Smith throughout his *Wealth of Nations* presents one exception after another to minimal government interference. He presented the duties of government as follows:

> According to the system of natural liberty, the sovereign has only three duties to attend to; three duties of great importance, indeed, but plain and intelligible to common understanding: first, the duty of protecting the society from the violence and invasion of other independent societies; secondly, the duty of protecting as far as possible, every member of the society from the injustice or oppression of every other member of it, or the duty of establishing an exact administration of justice; and thirdly, the duty of erecting and maintaining certain public works and certain public institutions, which it can never be for the interest of any individual, or small number of individuals, to erect and maintain; because the profit could never repay the expense to any individual or small number of individuals, though it may frequently do much more than repay it to a great society. (1776: 651)

Smith did not consider these limitations so restrictive as to reduce government's role in economic activity to virtually zero, as some people think. For example, he advocated extending some mercantilistic regulations over business, curbing monopoly, freeing slaves from masters, public ownership and management of highways and toll bridges, and levying heavier taxes over toll bridges for carriages of the rich than of the poor (Viner, 1927). Smith's was, in the words of Hobson (1926: 69), a "baggy" system. It is possible to pick it up at various points, drop it, and find that it falls into rather different shapes. It so happens that the mainstream of economists in the nineteenth century shook it and found it expounded a rather limited laissez-faire doctrine. But Smith's views of the relationships between government and economic activity could be used to support a thesis of major government interference in economic activity. The fundamental view in American thought until very recent times, however, was that government intervention in economic life should be severely limited. Some people still think so.

THE STRATEGIC REGULATOR OF ECONOMIC ACTIVITY
IS THE FREE MARKET MECHANISM

Adam Smith and his followers developed a powerful and widely accepted theory of how efficiency and order are assured in economic life when individuals pursue their self-interests unrestrained by government. The central regulator, they argued, was the free market mechanism. The following is an oversimplified, composite explanation by classical economists of how capitalism (or the individual enterprise system) operated.

Under a free market mechanism, equilibrium among economic factors will provide the best utilization of scarce resources in satisfying human material wants. The mechanism constantly pushes toward and seeks to reach equilibrium. As it does so, society achieves the maximum want satisfaction from every unit of scarce resources. To put it in another way, the free market mechanism, it was argued, will ensure that every productive resource is in that position in the economic organization in which it will make the greatest possible addition to the total social dividend, as measured in price terms.

Competition is the touchstone, the regulator, the mechanism, by means of which this result is achieved. Competition literally means "seeking together," with an implication of rivalry and mutual exclusivity of goal by those who seek. Competition is the attempt of two or more persons to get the same thing, each guided by his own valuations and unrestrained by outside forces. Valuation and freedom to compete are two essential conditions for an acceptable competitive effort.

Individual valuations are expressed in the market in terms of price. Prices in a free market mechanism reflect simply and quantitatively a matrix of influences determining individual economic valuations. Buyers and sellers alike express their choice through price. Consumers continually express their choice in the market for one product in favor of another. On the other side of the market, producers express a willingness to accept a proposed price. In so doing, they exercise a choice as to whether to continue production at the price buyers are willing to pay.

In the classical view, freedom to compete meant essentially the absence of control by either buyers or sellers in the market. Sellers, on the one hand, individually should not materially influence supply on the market. Buyers, on the other hand, should not materially influence demand. No buyer and seller should be important enough or able to influence market price by exerting pressure, other than that involved in registering his own vote, on demand or supply or price. This is the "atomistic" view of market competition which has been called "pure" competition. Under such conditions of competition, both buyers and sellers have acceptable alternative courses of action. Buyers can choose to purchase a given commodity from among a larger number of sellers. They also, of course, have recourse to acceptable substitute commodities. Sellers are faced with a large number of individual buyers and can combine their resources to produce a commodity in demand in place of one not in demand, if they so choose.

Sellers in striving to increase their profits benefit both consumers and society. No individual buyer can be guaranteed the best possible bargain at all times, but neither is he ever obliged to accept an unjustly poor bargain. Sellers must so apply their resources that they will yield a profit after costs are met. If resources are incapable of returning a profit to producers at market prices for the commodity produced, they are free to rearrange and apply resources in producing a product that will yield a profit. Producers will constantly rearrange resources so as to get the highest possible profit out of their use. In this way a constant adjustment of resources is made in producing commodities in the public favor, as expressed by market demand. As public demand for a commodity falls, the resources used in producing it will be devoted to other uses more in demand. All agents of production, in conformity with these principles, will continuously tend to be used in that combination which will yield the greatest volume of want satisfactions to society out of the limited resources at its disposal.

In reaching this end, free competition produces many advantages to society, including the assurance that goods and services will be produced at the lowest possible cost; that profits will be held to the minimum; that resources will be used to produce what society wants; that constant efforts will be made to widen the choice of goods available to consumers; that prices will be kept low; and that there will be a continuous improvement in the scale of living.

UNDERLYING ENABLING INSTITUTIONAL ARRANGEMENTS AND ASSUMPTIONS

The efficient operation of the free market mechanism is, in the classical view, predicated upon the existence of a number of fundamental institutional arrangements and upon the validity of certain underlying assumptions about the way people act. These are the *sine qua non* of the system.

Perspective in Examining Assumptions   Four considerations should be kept in mind in reviewing the following discussion. First, the individual enterprise system cannot be said to operate on the basis of any one principle. The system is one broad integrated process. In this process all fundamental elements operate simultaneously and are constantly being influenced by all other elements. Second, some elements are predominantly of an economic character, such as division of labor. Some are essentially noneconomic, such as popular government and law. Others are a mixture of economic as well as noneconomic, such as the profit motive. But all elements are inextricably interwoven. Third, to the extent that fundamental elements do not in reality exist, or theoretical assumptions are contrary to fact, the idealized operation of the system cannot be expected to take place. On the other hand, it should be observed that the operation of the system has always been considered sufficiently flexible to be efficient in the face of all but extremely serious deviations from theoretical assumptions. Fourth, the reader should be aware that much of the expansion of government regulation of economic life has grown out of the fact that over a long period of time the underlying assumptions have become less and less valid in practice. Government has been forced by the community to step into economic life, in part, to bridge this dichotomy.

Now, what are the major underlying assumptions and institutional arrangements, in classical theory, for the efficient operation of the individual enterprise system?

Property First, the ability of individuals to own and use property is of strategic importance. This institution has a great many ramifications, of which the following are a few: (1) The ability of individuals to own property is a powerful incentive for them to pursue their own economic interests and in so doing to benefit society. Property ownership does not provide the only incentive to economic action, but the incentive to produce is strongest under conditions where individuals can own property and use it to their own benefit with comparatively little restriction. (2) The ability of individuals to save, or to accumulate past rewards, results in the aggregation of privately owned capital. Capital accumulation is a fundamental means for increasing the productivity of the economic system. (3) The ability of individuals to exert control over property provides a needed flexibility in the use of resources. Without such flexibility, it would be difficult to solve effectively the basic problem of maximizing the satisfaction of human wants out of limited resources. (4) As the natural law philosophers observed, there is a psychological fulfillment in the ownership of property which indirectly manifests itself in economic institutions. The ownership of property provides a sense of security, a pride of ownership, a satisfaction of participation in society, and a respect for the property rights of others.

The Profit Motive Second, profit-making is closely associated with the institution of property. In some respects, it is another way of looking at the same thing; in other aspects, it is something more.

The possibility of making a profit, of course, is a powerful economic incentive to better one's economic position, and has often been spoken of as the mainspring of the individual enterprise system. A fundamental reason for so describing it is that profit is a reward for three fundamental functions without which economic progress can hardly take place. These three functions are awareness of consumer demand, risk-taking, and management of resources. Awareness of consumer demand is a function of conceiving a good or service which can be produced and sold. This is not a matter of invention, although it can be that. It is a question of detecting a market desire for a product and determining the possibility of producing it at a price consumers will pay which will leave a margin above costs for the producer. Risk-taking, of course, involves committing factors of production to making a good or service which an uncertain future market may or may not accept. Each enterpriser, therefore, accepts the possibility of risk of loss of his capital. Finally, management of the resources at the disposal of producers must be efficient for society to obtain the maximum benefits from their use in terms of price, quality, and quantity. Those performing these functions receive profits if they are efficient, and incur losses if they are inefficient.

Division of Labor Division of labor is a third essential element in the operation of the individual enterprise system. Division of labor is of two kinds. One is the specialization of enterprises in the production of individual types of commodities and the other is individual occupational specialization. The growth of economic productivity is based upon both kinds of division of labor.

Individual Freedom A fourth fundamental assumption is that individuals are "free" to pursue their own self-interest and that they will do so. Each individual, it is reasoned, is interested in bettering himself. If he has economic freedom he will, by pursuing his individual self-interest, ensure economic progress. Thus, for example, competition cannot exist where individuals are not free to change jobs, to employ their capital and land as they see fit, to consume as they choose, and to enter into contracts with others as they wish. If an individual has economic freedom, he will strive on the one hand to increase his wealth, and on the other hand to avoid losing it. This hedonistic principle—the hope of gain and the fear of loss—is central in stimulating economic activity. Individuals thus motivated will maximize their own want satisfactions and in so doing will ensure economic progress and a growing social dividend. Self-interest is assumed to be a universal principle with universal motivation and advantage.

The Economic Man Closely associated with this assumption is a fifth, that man is rational. Man is assumed to be an "economic man." An economic man will know when his interests will be served by a given course of action and will take that course of action. This broad assumption is based upon a number of subsidiary assumptions.

It is assumed that a consumer has full knowledge of the various alternatives open to him on the market. He will know variations in price of different producers of the same product, will know variations in quality, and will buy the cheapest good of best quality. This further assumes, of course, that consumers who need the good will have the ability to buy. It means, too, that consumers are free to buy or not to buy, according to the choice their self-interest dictates. And it means, of course, that consumers will make the "right" choice, that is, they will in fact buy the cheapest good with best quality which ideally satisfies their need.

Producers also are considered to be "economic men." It is assumed that they have full knowledge of consumer wants and alternative courses of action open to them in combining resources. They, too, will know which goods to produce in order to make the greatest profit. In addition, once they know of such alternatives, they will direct their resources correspondingly. This assumes, of course, mobility of capital and labor.

Workers, likewise, are considered to be "economic men." Their interest will be to strive to raise wages, shorten hours of work, and improve working conditions. It is assumed that they can act in conformance with such self-interests and will do so. For this to happen, workers are assumed to have complete market information about job opportunities. They are assumed to have an ability and a willingness to use this information by shifting jobs if need be. This, of course, also assumes great mobility of labor. It assumes workers can and will discriminate between "good" and "bad" employers so as to eliminate substandard employers. It assumes an equality of bargaining power between workers and employees, and it assumes virtually complete and continuous full employment of resources.

Consumer Supremacy A sixth fundamental assumption is that the interests of enterprisers and consumers are closely correlated. Consumption is the end purpose of production, and business could not exist if it did not strive to satisfy and serve the consumer.

Limited Role of Government A seventh assumption is that government interference in economic life will be held to a minimum. It is this idea, compared with the older mercantilistic view of full government domination over economic life, that is most responsible for the label "liberalism" being attached to classical capitalistic theory. The most influential early economic theorists spoke eloquently against government intervention on two counts. One was economic, the other political; and both were interrelated.

On the economic side, the laissez-faire doctrine held that government intervention in the market mechanism was not only inappropriate, but also unnecessary. Government intervention in the market mechanism was inappropriate because it tended to lessen the efficiency of the market in fulfilling the objective set for it. This objective, of course, was providing the greatest want satisfactions from the limited resources available to society. As we have observed, the functioning of the economic system was predicated on the assumptions of virtually complete individual economic freedom. When individuals were free to act in conformity with their self-interests, they would ensure that a balance was struck between consumer wants and the most effective utilization of resources in satisfying them. Thus, producers had to be free to use their resources as profit opportunities dictated. Consumers had to be free to exercise unrestrained choice in the market. Workers had to be free to move from one occupation to the next as their self-interests dictated. Any interference in this freedom, of course, placed artificial roadblocks in the process by which resources and human wants were equated. Central in the operation of this system was a flexible pricing on the market. Above all else, government should not interfere in market pricing, for such action would strike a mortal blow at the very heart of the system.

Government intervention in economic activity was thought to be unnecessary. Was it supposed that in the operation of this system all men were angels and none would try to take advantage of others? Of course not. But the government need not interfere where economic interests were concerned, because the regulative force of competition would establish effective control over diverse interests. Because of competition, each individual would be given a powerful incentive to observe the interests of others. If producers attempted to cheat consumers by adulterating goods, reducing quality, or raising prices unnecessarily, they would soon find that consumers would go elsewhere to buy. If producers failed to protect workers from industrial accidents, or failed to provide reasonable working conditions, or hammered down their wages, workers would go to an employer who treated them better.

Parenthetically, it might be observed that herein lies an important inconsistency in the logic of classical capitalistic economics. If it is unnecessary to protect consumers and workers from unscrupulous employers, why is it necessary to protect one unscrupulous employer from another? Classical theory accepted government regulation which would protect individuals against fraud, breach of contract, and the rights attached to property. Could not one reason on a comparable basis that if one person found he could not trust another in contractual dealings, he could be expected to have no further dealings with that person?

Does all this mean that government had no functions? It does not. Government had some clearly defined roles and others not so concretely limited. Government certainly was obliged to provide national security from aggression. Government had a recognized function in preserving internal law and order. It should also establish a framework within which individuals could more efficiently engage in economic activity, such as assuring a uniform system of coinage, measures, bankruptcy laws, and so on. Certain activities which individuals could not effectively provide, such as lighthouses, were permitted. In general, however, government's function was to maintain law and order and comparatively little else; individuals were to ensure economic progress.

It should be noticed that none of these permissible functions included direct interference in the market mechanism. Interference in the market mechanism was quite generally forbidden to government. Justifiable public action stopped at the point at which the equilibrium of demand-supply conditions was tampered with. But where was this point? How about tariff measures? Most classical thinkers considered tariffs as evils, but the tradition in England was much more free-trade than in the United States. In this country, under the leadership of Alexander Hamilton, Matthew Carey, and later Friedrich List, tariffs were accepted as not only desirable but necessary functions of government (Hamilton, 1791; Carey, 1822; List, 1841). How about antimonopoly laws? These were within the laissez-faire tradition because they restored rather than restricted competitive conditions. But direct price controls touching anything else were wrong.

Early capitalist theorists evidenced a strong bias against government encroachment in the economic sphere for political reasons. John Stuart Mill, for example, argued brilliantly in favor of restricting government economic regulation in order to avoid political evils (Mill, 1870). He said: "Every increase of the functions devolving on the government is an increase of its power, both in the form of authority, and still more, in the direct form of influence." In democracies, as in oligarchies, Mill observed a strong tendency for governmental usurpation of power. "Experience . . . proves," he thought, "that the depositaries of power who are mere delegates of the people, that is of a majority, are quite as ready . . . as any organs of oligarchy, to assume arbitrary power, and encroach unduly on the liberty of private life." Perhaps it is more important in a democracy than in any other form of political society to exercise restraint on the use of state power, "because, where public opinion is sovereign, an individual who is oppressed by the sovereign does not, as in most other states of things, find a rival power to which he can appeal for relief, or, at all events, for sympathy." But whatever the form of power, the individual should be surrounded "with the most powerful defences" against it, "in order to maintain that originality of mind and individuality of character, which are the only sources of any real progress, and of most of the qualities which make the human race much superior to any herd of animals." Mill's strongest reason against the extension of government power is the social debilitation he feels government regulation tends to bring. He argued that whenever a people looks continuously to government to resolve problems of their joint concern, whenever people expect to have everything done for them except matters of mere routine, their faculties are only half developed.

These views were definitely intended to restrict government economic intervention. But Mill, like Smith, was driven by his own insight into the realities of the world to accept more government regulation than he would have tolerated in his more abstract philosophical concepts.

This does not exhaust the list of assumptions and institutional arrangements required for the best operation of capitalism. It does, however, present the main economic and political ones. The principal Anglo-American thinkers in the liberal tradition in the nineteenth century did not say or expect that all these assumptions were absolutely true or that even if they were, the system would always operate perfectly. They would agree with Pope that:

Whoever thinks a faultless piece to see,
Thinks what ne'er was, nor is, nor e'er shall be.

Two Basic Dogmas But there were two underlying observations to which contemplation of this system and its assumptions led. They can be considered dogmas of liberal nineteenth-century thought. They were, first, that under a system of individual enterprise a higher level of well-being is attainable than under any other form of economic organization; and second, that such an economic system with its individual economic freedom is the only one compatible with the maintenance of political democracy. One dogma is economic; one is political.

In this light, the so-called classical or liberal tradition was perhaps more of a way of thinking than a fixed discipline in which individual principles always fitted with orderly and perfect precision. Liberalism was the central thought. It was literally *liber* (free) + *al* (pertaining to) + *ism* (an idea or practice) = freedom from state interference in economic and political life. This was the liberal society. An underlying pattern of principles, however, provided a framework for the ordering of the liberal economic society.

CHAPTER FOUR

The American Experience

INTRODUCTION

Throughout its history, the dominant business of the United States has been business. Other nations have sought as a first goal empire, glory, conquest, peace, and independence. The United States has sought freedom and prosperity. Business has been the primary instrument in the constant pursuit of these objectives, but business has not been independent of other elements in American society. The relationship of business with forces in its environment has been close, constantly changing, and increasingly complex over time.

This chapter presents a thumbnail sketch of the major linkages between business and society throughout the history of the United States. Rather than a chronological sketch of evolving relationships, the focus is on selected aspects of the ties that cut across time. This technique loses something of the thrust of concurrent historical developments, but I feel it is a more effective method for catching important relationships, for gaining perspective, and for discovering the insights that are so important in understanding what has happened, what is happening today, and what is likely to happen tomorrow.

DOMINANT ROLE OF BUSINESS AND BUSINESSMEN

From the very beginnings of this society with the exception of a few periods, business has been of predominant concern and businessmen have been held in high esteem. This is in great contrast to preceding

Western history, for with the few exceptions of city-states dominated by businessmen, both business and businessmen have been scorned.

The earliest colonies were formed by English trading companies operated by private individuals who hoped to make a profit. It is true that in some instances the motive for colonization was to avoid religious persecution, but the backers of the Pilgrims, for instance, hoped to make a profit. The commercial spirit manifested itself in different ways in colonial America, but it was dominant in most walks of life. The farmer was not a peasant bound to the soil with a pattern of life dictated by custom. While his way of life was different from that of the retail merchant in the town, they both engaged in buying and selling to make a profit. As the farmer accumulated wealth, he built and ran grain mills and in other ways employed his capital exactly as a merchant. Even lawyers reflected commercial interests in their work, and many became businessmen in their dealings with trading ventures, land acquisitions, and other commercial actions for a profit (Letwin, 1969: 5). Businessmen were at the top of colonial society not so much because of their wealth, but because they were not rejected for such positions. There was no aristocracy or ruling elite to suppress them. In addition, everyone in the society, with few exceptions, not only aspired to these positions, but felt it their duty to do so.

Criticisms of businessmen, however, are to be found in all eras of American history. In the early colonial world farmers were criticized for being boorish, grain millers for charging too much, merchants for being greedy, and so on. These attacks for the most part were directed at specific abuses. Greed was often associated with business efforts, but there was no attack on the pursuit of wealth itself. Nor was the high status of businessmen attacked as such.

After the Civil War, farmers assailed railroads and grain elevator operators for charging excessive prices and discriminating among customers. This led to the so-called Granger Laws in many states to prevent unjust practices. Toward the end of the nineteenth century, however, assaults on businessmen and business became bitter and powerful. The businessman was accused of being a greedy, avaricious rascal who robbed investors with worthless stocks, exploited employees in company-owned stores, charged consumers monopoly prices, ran roughshod over weaker competitors, bludgeoned government to act in his behalf, shot striking employees, maintained horrible working conditions, and in other ways evidenced a crude, predatory, and thoroughly unlikable character. The abuses of business during this period were widely publicized by the so-called muckrakers, who were principally journalists employed by new, rapidgrowing magazines and newspapers. They were later joined by novelists, such as Upton Sinclair.

There is no doubt that much of the attack was justified. The label "robber baron" was applied to the captains of industry in this period. Although some historians think this phrase a bit overdrawn, the appellation has stuck. There are still defenders of this view, but the current trend of historiography is away from it (Bridges, 1958). Such a trend does not deny the validity of the bases for the attacks, but only asserts that the cultural setting in which the businessman operated permitted and accepted these abuses. What was done was in a social and moral context which accepted a certain amount of ruthlessness in competition. Furthermore, despite the excesses, there were offsetting gains made by these men in moving American business into a highly advanced stage of capitalism (Destler, 1946).

In the 1930s business in general was under attack for the first time in our history. During the 1920s the idea was advanced, partly by businessmen, that business knew how to achieve a continuing economic prosperity, and it was widely accepted. The deep depression of the 1930s proved this view to be wrong, and in addition brought to light serious instances of extremely poor judgment, outright criminal negligence, and blatant fraud and theft on the part of prominent and heretofore highly respected businessmen. There was a popular feeling that the economic collapse would not have occurred if business managers had been more capable. This view was accentuated by conservative ideas expressed by a majority of businessmen about the limited role of government in helping to relieve human distress after the collapse of the economic system.

As a result of the high level of performance of American industry during World War II, business and businessmen regained a good measure of respect. This respect, centered largely in recognition of businesses' ability to solve problems and advance the economic well-being of the nation, continued with only moderate erosion to the late 1960s. Thereafter, as will be noted particularly in Chapter 5, respect for business dropped precipitously.

THE RISE OF THE MODERN CORPORATION
IN THE UNITED STATES

Throughout the business history of the United States, the fundamental forms of business organization have been the individual proprietorship, the partnership, and the corporation. While the first two have always been much greater in numbers than the corporation, the corporate form has shown a spectacular growth in its control over business assets. So impressive has this been that some people speak of today's culture as the "corporate society."

In England, the corporate form was associated with speculative excesses as well as the exercise of economic and political monopoly power. As a result, there were very few corporations in the American colonies prior to the Revolution, and strenuous efforts were made to control them after the new national government was formed.

At the Constitutional Convention a proposal to give the federal government power to incorporate businesses was rejected. It was felt that the corporation had privileges which eventually would lead to dominant monopoly power. As a result, the delegates specifically denied the federal government the power to incorporate, leaving the matter to the states on the assumption that they would know how to and could better control this potential monster. Restraint on federal incorporation survived until 1791, when it became expedient for the federal government to create a bank. The constitutionality of this act was tested in 1819 in *McCulloch v. Maryland,* in which Justice Marshall declared that the federal government had implied powers which included the power to charter a corporation if that was apposite and highly pertinent to a particular function the government legally could and wanted to perform. Since the government had the power to coin money, reasoned the Court, it also had the power to charter a corporation to do it.

In the meantime, the states sought to control the formation of corporations. At first, the state legislatures dealt with charters one at a time and conceived of each corporation chartered as being principally an agency of government endowed with public attributes and political power. Charters were therefore given mostly for functions conceived to be responsibilities of the state, such as promoting turnpikes and operating banks. People were fearful of corporations, and efforts were made to limit their lives. New York, for example, passed a law limiting the life of a manufacturing company to twenty-five years, but this idea did not prevail.

At the turn of the nineteenth century the groundwork was laid for the subsequent rapid development of the modern business corporation. A first step came in the passing of incorporation laws. In 1799 Massachusetts approved the first general incorporation laws for companies to build aqueducts. If the corporation laws were satisfied, it was no longer necessary to get a charter directly from the legislature. In 1811 New York passed the first general incorporation law applying to manufacturing companies. Finally, in 1837, Connecticut passed the first general incorporation law allowing any lawful business to be incorporated when the provisions of the law were satisfied.

In the Dartmouth College case of 1819, a solid legal shield was forged for corporations. In 1816 the legislature of New Hampshire amended the charter of Dartmouth College to make it a public institution. The trustees objected and sued to regain the original charter. The Supreme Court said that state legislatures could not pass any law impairing the obligation of a contract. The Court said the charter "is a contract, the obligation of which cannot be impaired without violating the constitution of the U.S." The corporate form was thus cleansed from the legal status of a monopoly and given freedom from arbitrary legislative interference.

This protective armor was further strengthened in the Santa Clara case in 1886. The Supreme Court cloaked the corporation with the mantle of the Fourteenth Amendment to the Constitution. This amendment was passed in 1868 to protect blacks, and it forbade states to abridge the privileges and immunities of citizens; to deprive any person of life, liberty, or property without due process of law; or to deny to any person within its jurisdiction the equal protection of the laws. The Court said a corporation is a person and the benefits of the amendment therefore extended to it. Corporations were thus protected from abusive statutes. States could and did regulate corporations, but the regulations had to be developed through accepted legal procedures, be nondiscriminatory as compared with individual citizens, and be in conformity with all laws protecting persons.

The corporate form, protected by law and blessed by immaculate state conception, had characteristics which fitted the environment of early America. Business's tasks were large and growing in size; money was scarce and the corporation could collect large pools of capital by tapping small amounts from individuals; individuals were optimistic and willing to bear risks; marketability of shares was favored by a mobile population; group activity was characteristic of early America; and it was easy to get charters. By 1800 there were about 300 corporations, and their growth thereafter was rapid (Cochran, 1959: 40).

GROWTH OF THE AMERICAN ECONOMY

From the point of view of such measures as personal income and total output of goods and services, the United States economy has been spectacularly successful. From a tiny society in 1800, the United States has developed into a society that produces more goods and services than the remainder of the world combined. A few of the statistics along this route follow.

Data for the period around 1800 are scarce and unreliable, but their relative magnitudes are acceptable and impressive in light of what happened afterward. Total private production income in 1800 was about $668 million. The total population numbered 5.3 million, and per capita income was therefore around $141. Revenue of the federal government was $11 million. There was a handful of small factories, but many items, such as nails, were made at home.

During the first half of the nineteenth century population expanded rapidly. Production income was $1.3 billion in 1839, and jumped to $7 billion in 1869. The factory system got a footing follow-ing the Embargo Act of 1807 and grew rapidly. It was not until 1853, however, that the first manufacturing company boasted assets of $1 million. Railroad construction leaped from 23 miles in 1830 to 30,000 miles in 1860. This network strengthened the sinews of trade, and a territorial division of occupations, as well as a national market for trade, was perfected to become the base for an unprecedented in-dustrial expansion in the second half of the century (Bureau of the Census, 1949).

Total national output (in 1944 prices) increased from $8 billion in 1860 to $25 billion in 1900 (Dewhurst, 1950). This growth was ac-complished in the face of a decline in the work week from 69 hours in 1860 to 61 hours in 1900. This was an age, too, of ex-traordinary inventions, the rise of mass-production manufacturing, intense exploitation of natural resources, huge capital accumulation, new monetary and financial institutions, and corporate consolidation and combination.

The record of the economic growth of the United States during the twentieth century reveals an industrial revolution on top of an industrial revolution despite monumental economic, political, and military disturbances. The tiny population of 1800 had expanded to a giant nation of 210 million by 1973. Between 1909 and 1973 the total output of goods and services rose over ten times (in constant prices).

This aggregate economic growth resulted in an expanding real purchasing power of individuals, particularly in recent years. As late as the 1930s it was estimated that one-third of the nation lived in poverty but, as will be examined in Chapter 19, the incidence of poverty in recent years has declined impressively. Data about in-come distribution in the past are not very good but enough is known to conclude that there has always been great inequality in the dis-tribution of income. This has created tensions but not serious prob-lems because the total pie to be distributed has grown rapidly with but few exceptions noted later in this chapter.

ECONOMIC AND SOCIAL PROBLEMS PARALLELING GROWTH

Enormous growth such as this was not without its social costs and problems. This part of American history is important, and covers a wide spectrum of problems which can be illustrated here in only a few areas.

During the first half of the nineteenth century, many people believed in a theory called the "Iron Law of Wages." This theory, read into David Ricardo's work by a German Socialist named Fer-dinand Lassalle, was comforting to the businessman who wanted to pay low wages. It was reasoned that laborers should get low wages for their own good. If workers got high wages, they would raise large families. When the children grew up, they would swell the ranks of labor and, in conformity with the inexorable laws of supply and demand, competition for jobs would drive wages down to bare subsistence levels. Why start this painful process when low wages in the first place will maintain the proper supply of workers? This theory was buttressed by economic attitudes which condoned poor working conditions, exploitation of children and women, long hours of work at low pay, and shortened life expectancy. Labor unions were prohibited by law, so there could be no redress by collective bargaining, and courts of law prevented government from taking vigorous action. Conditions such as these existed into the twentieth century.

Throughout our history, the social costs of business development have been significant. By social costs we mean the unpaid costs of industry. They affect interests which the legal system does not cover and those which can be invaded without consent or compensation. An illustration is damage to property values in an area adjacent to a chemical plant belching foul smoke into the air. The costs of an increasingly complex society are not, of course, created by business alone. They are inherent in the progress of this society to which many institutions have contributed. Among these costs is increasing urbanization, which has brought frightening problems of unemployment, poverty, crime, complex interdependencies of people, and personal insecurity.

There is little question about the fact that the social costs of progress have increased throughout our history to the point where many of them are now intolerable. On the other hand, the net gains to society up to the present day are far beyond the costs.

THE ROLE OF BUSINESS IN ECONOMIC GROWTH

Prospects for great economic growth were dim when the Constitution was ratified in 1789. Most of the population was engaged in subsistence agriculture, European demand for American products was down, and the merchant marine was restricted by the mercantile policies of European nations. The colonists faced an economic depression, but they were optimistic about the future.

To what extent was business responsible for our great economic growth? One approach to this question is to try to measure the contribution of business to the expansion of Gross National Product (GNP). This is difficult, but it was attempted by Denison (1962) for the first half of the twentieth century. He concluded that about 58 percent of GNP growth was due to improvements in technology and organization of production, and the remainder to improvements in the quality of the labor force due to education and to expansion in the quantity of capital available. Business organization, of course, was instrumental in developing structures to improve the productivity of workers, and business raised the capital needed to improve worker productivity. But government was instrumental in educating workers, did help to develop the financial institutions through which capital could be provided, and promoted economic conditions that helped to expand markets, which in turn increased the demand for business products.

There were also many other important environmental factors. One must include mores and values which accepted the sanctity of a contract, the importance of private property, and the significance of personal liberty. There was also the willingness of labor to treat its relationships with management on a contractual basis, subject to bargaining. We should mention basic ideas and values in society which stimulated aggressive entrepreneurship.

The best answer to what was responsible for the great economic growth of the United States probably lies in this view: There was a set of social, political, and economic conditions that provided a framework for business activity which stimulated a spirited response to the profit incentive and created a willingness of business to reinvest capital. No one can fully describe the relative importance of the forces operating in this moving and constantly changing setting. Government clearly has been of great importance, but so also were the value systems of most people in this society. But, given the proper setting, the businessman was Hamlet in this industrial drama.

GOVERNMENT AND BUSINESS

The Myth of Laissez Faire Operational laissez faire has increasingly diverged from conceptual laissez faire in the United States. From the very beginning of our history, government has exerted more power over economic activity than is considered acceptable in classical capitalistic theory. The framers of the Constitution were determined to give the federal government more, not less, power. From that day to this the businessmen, the farmers, and other interest groups have exerted pressures on government to act in their behalf. Government has responded, and there has therefore been an increasing divergence of practice from theory. To paraphrase Wesley Mitchell, we look with pride on the rugged individualists in our early history who cleared the soil and carried on the business of that small society. But when the record is examined in detail, it becomes clear that they were not at all content with their world and pressured the government for help.

The political process has always been used by individuals and organizations to redress grievances which could not be achieved through the market mechanism or courts of law. Naturally, as this society grew and became more complex, problems of individuals and institutions also mounted. The result, of course, was that government was increasingly asked to interfere in the economic processes to help individuals. It can be said that until the depression of the 1930s governmental regulation of business was within the tolerable limits of a classical laissez-faire philosophy. Controls over business have experienced their greatest growth since then.

Changing Scope and Types of Government Controls on Business
Several broad patterns are apparent in the evolution of government actions which have an important bearing on business. From 1790 to 1837 government activities were predominantly promotional. The second law passed by the newly formed Congress, for example, gave a 10 percent discount on tariffs to goods brought here in American ships. The recognition of a need for better transportation, growing out of difficulties during the Revolutionary War and the War of 1812; an inherent understanding of the values of a better transportation system to society; and pressures from agrarian interests led government to promote transportation. Substantial loans were made to turnpikes and later to railroads and huge grants of land were given to them which were to be sold to finance construction.

The second major period of government activity toward business took place during the last part of the nineteenth century. As a result of overproduction, farm prices fell sharply during and after 1865, and the farmers turned on the railroads in their disappointment. A number of states enacted Granger Laws to control railroad abuses (for example, charging more for a short than a long haul) and instituted reforms (for example, state prescription of maximum rates). Sometime later, in 1887, the federal government created the Interstate Commerce Commission to regulate interstate railroads. The great wave of industrial consolidations in the 1880s led to the Sherman Antitrust Act in 1890 to control them. While there were some promotional enactments, the period was more one of expanding government regulation to curb the abuses of an ebullient, aggressive, and often irresponsible business world. On the other hand, efforts to introduce social reforms, such as permitting workers to strike and improving working conditions, met with repeated rebuffs by the Supreme Court.

The third major change took place in World War I with the introduction of detailed nationwide controls over production, prices, the movement of commodities, and the allocation of commodities to users. The war ended before these controls began to "bite," but their introduction constituted the prototype of the comprehensive and minute nationwide regulations over business which were adopted during World War II and again during the Korean War.

The depression of the 1930s brought a new pattern in the scope and extent of federal actions. This depression was one of the severest human and economic catastrophes ever to strike the American people. In combating this crisis the federal government assumed an entirely new role in economic life and in its relationship with business.

The statistics of this depression starkly reveal the extraordinary tragedy. For instance, GNP dropped (in current dollars) from $103.1 billion in 1929 to $58 billion in 1932. Industrial production was almost halved between these two dates. Durable goods production in 1932 was one-third the 1929 level. Steel production in 1932 was at 20 percent of capacity. The unemployment rate rose in 1933 to 25 percent of the labor force. Thousands of businessmen and farmers went bankrupt, and millions of investors lost their life savings. The calamity itself and the subsequent actions of government introduced into this society new social values and institutional arrangements that affected subsequent events and will continue to do so for a long time to come.

The New Deal of Franklin D. Roosevelt broke new ground in three major ways. The federal government for the first time assumed responsibility for stimulating business activity out of an economic depression. The federal government assumed responsibility for correcting abuses in the economic machinery of the nation, particularly in business, and amassed more laws to this end in a shorter period of time than ever before or since. The federal government for the first time assumed responsibility on a large scale for relieving the distress of businessmen, farmers, workers, homeowners, consumers, investors, and other groups because of adverse economic events. This truly was a social revolution, and fortunately a peaceful one.

Today's body of government controls over business activity is a blend of these types. The totality of government actions that are related to business has, of course, grown immensely. Whether it has increased very much, if at all, in relation to the totality of business actions is a debatable point.

In 1971 a fifth major change in government controls took place when the federal government introduced an overall wage-price freeze on the American economy. This action established a precedent for comprehensive controls in peacetime. It is true that the United States was engaged in a major war, the Vietnam War, and that during wartime in the past the government had instituted such controls. But there was something different about the 1971 experience. The Vietnam War was winding down, but inflation was not under control. Also, the controls were continued after the end of the war.

Finally, in more recent times a new trend of expanding government-industry partnership in resolving major problems was begun. COMSAT, formed as a joint government-industry project to exploit satellite communications technology, is a case in point.

The Omnipresence of Government The agenda of permissible government action in economic life has become so expanded that practically no aspect of business and general economic activity is closed to it if an important reason for intervention can justify action. The limits to the exercise of federal economic power today rest on political and social tests, not on economic doctrine.

A Mixed, Free Economy Despite a comparative open door to intervention and the growth of the government, the remarkable fact about the American mixed economy is not how much of economic life the governments, particularly the federal government, control but how much they do not. Although the federal government directly controls or indirectly influences economic activity to a significant degree, the economy cannot at all be said to be centrally administered or controlled, except in time of major war. Indeed, even in World War II and the Korean War, while the economy ostensibly was centrally controlled, there was a surprising amount of activity where unfettered individual decision was possible.

The great bulk of goods and services are produced by individual business firms whose resources are not owned or managed by government. Millions of individual proprietors, consumers, and workers are relatively free to choose among alternative courses of action. Corporations, labor unions, and farm cooperatives have considerable freedom in choosing among courses of action. These groups and individuals determine in large degree how scarce resources are used. It is true that some of these decisions are made within a framework of rules laid down by government and law, but within these rules, which are often very loose and flexible, men are rather free to pursue their economic interests as they see fit.

The great bulk of the national income is spent by individuals and businesses with comparatively little restriction. The mere fact that the American economy is highly competitive indicates by definition a great deal of comparatively free economic decision-making. It indicates that government influence is not so dominant as one who looks only to certain types of controls or measures might suppose. When the total realm of economic decision is studied in detail, it is not at all difficult to see that the economy operates primarily on the basis of decentralized decision-making of individuals singly and in groups. Actions of the millions of business enterprises, and millions of workers and consumers are only in part, and often in small part, patterned by government regulations.

In the past, when government regulation of economic life was at a minimum, the automatic working of the free market mechanism was relied upon to achieve comparative equilibrium in the social and economic system. Today, social and economic equilibrium must be achieved through the interworkings of conscious collective public and individual action in the marketplace. This complex, intricate, and productive economy cannot operate in any other way.

IMPACT OF CHANGING SOCIAL AND RELIGIOUS VALUES ON BUSINESS

Social values have had great influence on business, and business has influenced them. The following are a few selected values of significance to business.

The Protestant Ethic The Protestant Ethic, discussed previously, has been predominant throughout our history. Also significant in our history has been another set of religious values following the Judeo-Christian religious views. Parts of these two ethics collided in the depression of the 1930s and the collision was accompanied by a major change in the actions of government toward economic distress. The Protestant Ethic postulated that a man was poor because of his own shortcomings and not because of any particular economic or social structure. Hard work, thrift, and piety were ways to end poverty. Those that were poor because they did not take this route were improvident and undeserving of help. Benjamin Franklin voiced such views in these adages: "God helps those who help themselves." "Laxness travels so slowly that Poverty soon overtakes him." "Diligence is the mother of good luck, and God gives all things to industry."

Another dominant theme in the Judeo-Christian tradition is the idea that "Greater love hath no man than to lay down his life for his friends." In this view men did have an obligation to one another, and a man could become poor and a businessman could fail through no fault of his own. Up to the 1930s the former view, plus other philosophies like that of Social Darwinism, inhibited help to those in need, whether individuals or businessmen. The second view became more dominant in the 1930s. It better fits a complex, interdependent, and affluent society. But both views still exist, and sometimes both exist in the same person. There are thus raised moral conflicts to which we will return in a later chapter.

Individualism and Laissez Faire These major philosophies extending through our history were discussed in Chapter 2. The additional comment that seems appropriate here is that individualism holds in high esteem not only a person, but an orderly and progressive society in which there is free association in organizations. For business this has meant freedom of individuals to form groups, emphasis on participation in groups, and the right to leave groups. An individual's freedom is, of course, basic in the philosophy of individualism. Throughout our history the dilemma has arisen as to how much of a man's freedom should be denied in order to increase the freedoms of someone else. It is recognized, of course, that each man's rights must be conditioned by the rights of others. There is no final answer to where the balance lies in this equation. We have solved it in the United States reasonably well, with a comparatively few exceptions in our history, such as the Civil War. Enough has been said heretofore about laissez faire.

Materialism Ours unquestionably has been a materialistic society from the very beginning, although early in our history materialism was modified considerably by austere religious views about spending money. Materialism means a way of life directed toward satisfying material wants. Following capitalist ideology, materialism emphasizes individual profitability through satisfying the material wants of others. The materialistic attitudes found in the United States do not mean that these are the only motivating forces in society. This clearly was not the case in colonial America, and it is not the case today. Rather, it means that justification for seeking money is an overpowering philosophy in this materialistic society. Tocqueville, when visiting the United States around 1800, said, "The Americans carry their business-like qualities and their trading passions" into all their activities. Several decades later when Dickens visited America, he said he found a hard materialistic spirit everywhere. These statements should not be translated into an indictment of the materialistic spirit as one of greed, or one that condones any means to achieve a materialistic end. To Veblen, businessmen were motivated by greed. To Schumpeter, materialism meant that businessmen were making a "creative response" to opportunities confronting them.

For most of our history materialism meant production to meet consumer needs with the hope of the producer that a profit would be made. More recently, materialism seems to be directed toward assuring for the possessor of money the "good life," the "quality life." Most businessmen I know seek money not for money's sake, but because of the "good life" it will give them and their families.

Optimism Americans have generally had great faith in the future of their country; in democracy, equality, liberty, business; and in other people. This spirit, of course, is the reverse of a philosophy of despair, and has provided Americans with a buoyant attitude throughout most of their history. Some people think this spirit of optimism is being eroded today.

Antipathy to Monopoly A deep-seated feeling against monopoly extends back through the ages, certainly into the medieval world, and has been constant in our own history. It fostered pre-Constitutional government price controls of local monopolists, such as grain millers and beer distillers. It was extended during the nineteenth century to public utilities and giant manufacturing concerns. This spirit is significant today in current attacks on the large corporations.

Fundamental Law Early in our history there was a blending of the doctrine of natural rights with the acceptance of the external will of a just and loving God. It was the idea, mentioned before, that there are fundamental laws that govern the life of man. This view gave great security and stability to society, although it condoned what we conceive today to be social abuses. It is not a dominant tenet today.

Social Darwinism When Charles Darwin's *Origin of Species* appeared in 1859, Herbert Spencer, an English philosopher, applied Darwin's findings to social organizations and coined the phrase, "the survival of the fittest." Spencer believed that the struggle of man in the marketplace was socially benign in eliminating the weak and unsuccessful. "The poverty of the incapable," he wrote, "the distresses that come upon the imprudent, the starvation of the idle, and those shoulderings aside of the weak by the strong, which leave so many in shallows and in miseries, are the decrees of a large, far-seeing benevolence" (Spencer, 1868: 353–54). Those that were left were best fitted to survive. These were the best, and the resulting organization was the best. This was called Social Darwinism by some; Justice Holmes called it the law of the jungle. Spencer was an uncompromising proponent of individualism who believed that any interference in the natural evolution of events would prevent the betterment of mankind and lead to social destruction.

Spencer's views were highly popular among leading intellectuals and businessmen in the United States from about 1870 to 1890. His theory coincided with the great industrial expansion and the amassing of huge business fortunes during this period. Spencer not only explained why rich men were rich, but asserted that it was all for the good of mankind. Andrew Carnegie identified the work of Herbert Spencer as of great influence and comfort to his thinking (Hofstadter, 1955: 44–45). Spencer's popularity was short-lived because the excesses of businessmen and widespread economic distress led to business reforms and social legislation. There are still today, however, a few people who do not completely reject his philosophy.

Pragmatism Spencer's philosophy was replaced at the turn of the twentieth century by a philosophy of pragmatism enunciated by William James and John Dewey. This philosophy rejected absolutes, fixed formulas, and the formalism of social organizations. It took the view that society could be controlled by man for the betterment of man. Pragmatism opposed theoretical abstractions and asked whether an idea or an institution worked, whether it was practical, and whether it made sense. This was in tune with a vigorous, changing society because it stimulated experimentation and innovation for the benefit of society as well as for the gain of the individual.

Attitudes Toward Government The typical American, including businessmen, has viewed government through bifocal lenses. On the one hand, this democracy was so established that voters could exert pressures on the government to help in solving their problems. On the other hand, there has been a deep antipathy to government's exercise of power. Undoubtedly this attitude finds its roots in the dictatorial excesses of most governments preceding our own, but I suspect it also is in response to a deep conviction that governmental power must be held in check to prevent its misuse, even in a political democracy. On the one hand, therefore, increasing government intervention in business has been accepted, but on the other hand, social attitudes have exerted a general restraint.

Efficiency Efficiency, especially in business, has been a driving force throughout our history and has diminished little if at all as a goal of high value. An overriding goal set by society for business has been the use of a minimum amount of resources to achieve a maximum output of goods and services. Until very recently our society has subordinated other goals, such as clean air and shorter working hours, to the task of getting more economic output through efficient use of resources. In recent years, as this society has become more affluent, other goals have risen in priority. But business is still expected to be efficient while achieving other goals, such as cleaning up the environment.

Science and Technology From the earliest colonial period, typified by the technical achievements of Benjamin Franklin, our society has been scientifically oriented. The search for the new way to do things better through intervention not only has been encouraged but well rewarded. This orientation has resulted in concentrated efforts in major institutions—government, business, universities, nonprofit "think tanks," and foundations—to advance technology and science. Reliance upon, and efforts to advance, science and technology have grown in intensity rather than diminished.

Other Values There are, of course, many other values which have existed throughout our history which have had an important impact on business, and which have been much influenced by business. For example the meaning of work, the role of the family in society, fairness in contractual dealings, social responsibilities, patriotism, equality of opportunity, and democratic decision-making in the political arena.

Certain dominant values have been characteristic of our society and have been largely responsible for the ways in which our society in general, and business in particular, has advanced. One cannot understand the evolution of the business-society interrelationship throughout our history without a knowledge of these values and the way they have influenced the relationship.

CHANGES IN TYPES OF INDUSTRIAL ORGANIZATIONS AND DOMINANT BUSINESSMEN

The most dominant businessmen in society have differed over time. In colonial times the overwhelming majority of businesses were small. The dominant businessmen in the north in terms of wealth were the merchants who financed the building of ships, engaged in foreign commerce, and supplied the colonies with their needs from abroad; and the wealthy landowners. In the south it was the planter aristocracy, built on slave labor and cotton, that was predominant until the Civil War. In the period from 1800 to 1850 a class of large and wealthy wholesalers developed who took advantage of the new geographical specialization of commerce. Wholesalers engaged in foreign commerce and operated across the total American market. Many specialized in single commodities, financed trade, stimulated new innovations, and altogether played a major role in business activity. In the period from 1850 to 1900 the manufacturing owner-manager rose to a dominant position. After the depression of 1873, he replaced the wholesaler as the most prominent businessman in society. During the twentieth century the professional manager of large corporations, who controlled but did not own his company, became the dominant business figure.

Shifts have taken place in major industries. To about 1850, American industry was based upon the technologies of the Industrial Revolution—coal, steam, machine tools, and textiles. In the later nineteenth and early twentieth centuries new technologies and industries were developed on the basis of such inventions as steel, the incandescent lamp, organic chemicals, the internal combustion engine, and the telephone. In the 1960s completely new industries developed from new technologies in petrochemicals, synthetic fibers, computers, atomic energy, and electronics. In effect, there have been three industrial revolutions in the United States.

Both the individual enterprise and the corporate form of organization have existed throughout our history. Small business has been clearly predominant in terms of numbers. During the period 1870 to 1890 an impressive concentration of economic power in large corporations appeared as industrialists sought to control entire industries. Big business became our most preeminent economic institution. From that time to this there has been a high concentration of business assets and income in the largest companies.

A very important changing pattern of employment in major sectors of the economy should also be noted. The accompanying table shows clearly the changes taking place in employment in agriculture, industry, and services. Up to the 1920s the movement was principally from agriculture to industry. Thereafter, the shift has been much greater to services. A revolution in agricultural productivity has provided the manpower for expanding goods and services in the non-agricultural sectors of the economy.

Table 4–1.   Distribution of Employment, by Sector, 1870–1972

SECTOR	1870	1900	1920	1947	1965	1972
Agriculture	50.8%	38.1%	27.6%	12.1%	5.7%	4.2%
Industry	30.0	37.8	44.8	42.1	39.6	30.4
Service	19.2	24.1	27.6	45.8	54.8	65.3

SOURCE: Data for 1870–1965 from Victor R. Fuchs (1968, pp. 19, 24). Data for 1972 from U.S. Department of Labor (1973).

ORGANIZATIONAL PROLIFERATION

There has been a rapidly increasing proliferation of organizations in the United States over our history. Today, the number of organizations which have a direct or indirect impact on business is exceedingly large. They range from religious, fraternal, educational, military, and political, to economic. The communications media exert a special type of continuous influence on business. One hundred years ago there were no labor unions, no giant manufacturing companies, no trade associations, and no employers' associations. There were very few professional associations. Government played a very small part in economic life (the percentage of federal taxes from national income from 1851 to 1860 was 1.8). There were comparatively few organizations, and those few were quite small.

Contrast this with today's society, in which business organizations alone number in the millions. There are about 10 million sole proprietors and active partnerships in industry. In addition, there are around 1.6 million corporations. Since most farms are businesses, we should add another 3.2 million organizations. Within the business sector there are thousands of trade associations and business-oriented groups. Add to this the millions of workers in organized groups and additional millions of organizations in the nonprofit sector.

Paralleling the proliferation of organizations in society is their growing size and concentration of power. Drucker observes that historians in several hundred years are likely to see as a central feature of today's society the emergence of large organizations which are entrusted with social tasks of importance (1969 (A): 171).

IMPACT OF ECONOMIC DEPRESSIONS ON BUSINESS

The occurrence of economic depressions has always had an associated impact on business, aside from the inevitable loss of earnings. We have already noted the impact of the depression of the 1930s. A few other illustrations may be useful. A number of circumstances growing out of the depression immediately following the Declaration of Independence led the Constitutional Convention to draft a new Constitution. The depression of 1837 resulted in prohibitions in state constitutions to prevent states from lending money to business. Financial reforms followed the depressions of 1857 and 1907. Fortunately there have been no economic depressions in the United States since that of the 1930s.

IMPACT OF SUPREME COURT DECISIONS ON BUSINESS

Businesses operate within a legal framework. This is an important observation, but it does not begin to catch the drama of the many changing impacts of law on business enterprise in the United States. Only a few illustrations will be given here.

One should begin with the fact that the Constitution is the supreme law of the land, and that the Constitution is what the Supreme Court says it is. This is not meant to be a flippant statement, but merely to record the fact that there can be different meanings for words, phrases, and sentences in the Constitution. Only the Supreme Court can decide what they mean. Indeed, the Supreme Court has the power to declare acts of Congress, orders of the executive branch of the federal government, and acts of state and local governments to be invalid when it thinks there is a conflict with the Constitution.

Law fundamentally codifies the values society seeks to preserve. In this sense, law and the interpretation of law do not change swiftly. There is a reverence in law for accepting the authority of past decisions as applicable to similar future cases. On the other hand, the Supreme Court has reflected in the long run the dominant currents of public sentiment.

In a broad sweeping observation it can be said that throughout the nineteenth century, and well into the present century, the Supreme Court's decisions were highly favorable to business. The Court erected a tough legal shield that protected business from federal and state controls as well as from the collective bargaining power of labor unions. At the same time, however, by broad interpretations of the Constitution, the precedent was laid for far-ranging controls initiated by the federal government.

The commerce clause (Art. 1, Sec. 8) of the Constitution, for example, gives Congress the power "to regulate Commerce with foreign nations, and among the several states, and with the Indian tribes." The framers of the Constitution wanted to give the national government power to prevent the states from placing barriers around the free flow of commerce among the states and with foreign countries. They probably would blink with disbelief if they could see the extent to which this simple sentence has, through Supreme Court interpretations, supported all sorts of regulations on business. It is not an exaggeration to say that this clause is one of the most fruitful sources in the Constitution, as interpreted by the Court, for the regulatory powers of the federal government. This power today supports federal controls over such diverse activities as railroads, air transport, stockyards, boards of trade, communications, warehouses, security exchanges, the quality of foods and drugs, standards and classifications of commodities, monopolistic practices, and unfair trade practices. The list is endless.

IMPACT OF WARS ON BUSINESS

Wars have always had an impact on business, both stimulating and depressing. The Seven Years' War led England to impose controls on the American colonies which resulted in the American Revolution and freedom for colonial businessmen. The War of 1812 stimulated the nation's first major land transportation construction, which, in turn, laid the base for a vigorous industrial expansion. The Civil War ruined many businessmen throughout the nation. World War I left in its wake serious world problems which eventually resulted in the greatest depression ever to hit the United States and very hard times for business and the rest of the population. World War II, the Korean War, and the so-called Cold War brought great stimulation to technological developments. The Vietnam War brought great changes in the values held by society. As will be shown later the impact on business has been significant.

THE PACE OF CHANGE

It is commonplace today to say that the pace of change has never been quicker. This is not as accurate a statement as to say that the pace of change has always been rapid in the United States. This has not been a stagnant society. But the pace of change has been set by different elements at different stages in our development. While our GNP today is at superlative heights, the percentage rates of real growth in recent years do not compare with some periods in the nineteenth century when the nation was expanding rapidly. The long-range average annual rates of growth, however, are higher today. This is because throughout the nineteenth century and during the first half of the twentieth, the business cycle showed extraordinary instability. Fortunately, GNP has been rising at a stable rate since World War II. Railroad building set a feverish pace between 1830 and 1860. The industrial track was fast in the 1870–1890 period. But it is also true that throughout the nineteenth century, and well into the twentieth, most basic social values were remarkably stable.

During the past quarter century the United States has undergone its most rapid acceleration of certain types of social, technical, economic, and military changes. No period in our history matches the huge changes taking place in today's society with respect to threats of annihilation, the increase in real income of the average family, the rise of education, telescoped product life cycles, migration of farm workers to cities, urbanization, exacerbation of social problems, popular consciousness of social problems, decline in new births, and numbers and potentiality of new discoveries and technological innovations. Considering all these together, it is correct to say that total social change and ferment in the United States probably has never been greater than during the past twenty-five years.

PART TWO

Today's Business Setting: An Overview

CHAPTER FIVE **The Changing Business Environment**

INTRODUCTION

It was said previously that the business environment is extremely complex and is changing in deep and fundamental ways. As a point of perspective for the remainder of this book I think it useful now to sketch some of the major changes taking place. The business environment is, of course, a vast territory, the full range of which certainly cannot be captured here. This discussion, therefore, will be limited to a brief description of significant changes taking place in selected areas of the environment. The discussion will begin with a short examination of the implications for business of changes taking place in major areas of its environment. This is followed by a note on business's impact on its environment. There is then examined those fundamental underlying forces operating in the environment from which all other change is derivative.

CRITICISMS OF BUSINESS

One of the outstanding environmental changes is the growing criticism of business. This is a fact to which business, especially the larger companies, is becoming painfully aware. Business has always had sharp, vocal, and powerful critics (Walton, 1966; Saloutos in Steiner, 1972; and Michelman, 1969). There has been nothing in the past, however, except possibly in the 1930s, equaling today's criticisms of business and demands for changes.

There is today a paradox in the business-society relationship. On the one hand there is great hostility to business. As David Rockefeller put it: "It is scarcely an exaggeration to say that right now American business is facing its most severe public disfavor since the 1930's. We are assailed for demeaning the worker, deceiving the consumer, destroying the environment and disillusioning the younger generation" (1971). Yet at no time in our history has business been a greater beneficial force in society. At no time in our history have businessmen thought more about the consequences of their action on the environment and the people in it.

A recent opinion poll revealed that 60 percent of the American people said they had "little approval" of business (Benham, 1972). This figure had risen from 46 percent in 1967. In 1971 11 percent of the sample said they had "high approval" of business compared with 20 percent in 1967. These numbers reveal widespread dissatisfaction.

The list of criticisms of business is virtually endless and growing. Jacoby examined the current criticisms of business and found that they centered on five allegations, as follows: (1) corporations exercise concentrated economic power contrary to the public interest; (2) corporations use their political power contrary to the public interest; (3) corporations are controlled by self-perpetuating, irresponsible power elites; (4) business exploits and dehumanizes workers and consumers; and (5) business degrades the environment and lowers the quality of life (1973). Epstein surveyed the critical literature and adds a few other major allegations, such as: business reinforces inequality in the distribution of wealth and power; business is imperialistic in bringing an expansion of military, political, economic, and cultural domination to both underdeveloped and mature nations; and business contributes to cultural philistinism by promoting commercial rather than humanistic or artistic criteria in its functioning and communications (in Steiner, 1974). The multinational corporation is subject to these criticisms plus many others, such as exploitation of host underdeveloped countries, siphoning off profits and depleting capital in host countries, exporting jobs from the United States, and behaving badly with respect to local customs and national plans.

A different dimension of attack lumps together alleged shortcomings of the economic system and, in strident tone, demands the abolition of capitalism and, of course, the business institution. An example:

> Capitalism stinks! It is a highly destructive, wasteful, exploitative and irrational way to organize the resources of a society like ours. As a system, it stands in irreconcilable opposition to the fulfillment of the needs of the great majority of the people who live under its rule and to the creation of the Good Society. We can only solve our social problems and create that Good Society by doing away with capitalism and the institutions that support it (Christoffel et al., 1970).

This list by no means exhausts the major themes in the attacks on business. Each, of course, accommodates more detailed verses. To present these criticisms here without analysis of their validity is not, of course, to accept them. The more important criticisms will be examined throughout the book.

The sharpness of attacks on business and the prescription for eliminating the perceived ills differ among critics. To oversimplify, there are three major groups of business critics (Bronfenbrenner in Steiner, 1972). First are the reformist critics. This group accepts the basic institutional framework of contemporary society but insists upon reforms in the way in which business and other institutions operate and the interrelationships among institutions. Most contemporary critics of American business, including this author, fall into this category.

A striking feature of today's business environment is the growth in numbers and diversity of self-appointed so-called public-interest or activist groups to exert pressure on corporations to meet their demands. Most can be classified as reformists. They range widely in shape, size, expertise, and power. But never before have there been so many. Their targets spread from environmental pollution to employment practices of American companies in South Africa and Angola. Their tactics range from lobbying in legislatures to confrontations with managers at annual meetings of stockholders. There are only a few, however, that have influenced importantly legislative and corporate voluntary action (*Business and Society*, 1973).

Second, are so-called leftist critics. They reject current institutional structures and demand some sort of socialist state. While there are different schools of thought among this class—Marxism, Leninism, Maoism—the fundamental idea is central control of prices, production, resource allocation, and other economic activities. This is, of course, the antithesis of capitalism. In the United States this group of critics has been very small and ineffective relative to the others.

The third group is the utopian critics. Here one finds the hippies, who seek to achieve their objectives through nonviolence, and in contrast, the Yippies, who want to tear down everything, violently if necessary, and start all over. Reich and his following would also be included here. Each sect, however, has one thing in common: They all reject today's political, social, and economic institutions and values and wish to see, instead, some sort of cooperative utopia in which wealth is equally distributed, work is shared, and the human spirit is free to achieve its fullest potential. The members of this broad group grew rapidly in the late 1960s, but recently have leveled off if not declined. In numbers and influence this group is small relative to the reformists.

Despite the adverse statistics of opinion polls I believe that there is a vast reservoir of respect in society for the capabilities of business in problem-solving and in meeting the needs of society. This is reflected in the fact that people generally are looking to business rather than to government to meet many of their demands. This is a fact of high significance.

Popular antipathy to business stems, I think, from a number of fundamental causes. First, as will be discussed at length later in the chapter, society expects business to help society improve the quality of life, and expectations are running ahead of reality. Business is criticized for not bridging the gap. There is a cynicism among the people that business will not budge from its traditional narrow self-interest to meet new demands. Second, there is a general misunderstanding of how business operates and what its role in society is and should be. In speaking to this point Estes says that business is like sex:

> . . . it is the subject of fantasies, mythology, frustrations, wounded psyches, and unrealistic anticipations. Unlike sex, there is little or no curiosity about the facts; few seem highly motivated to pursue the facts when the myths are so much more exciting (Steiner, 1972).

Businessmen have been accused of not communicating very well with the public concerning what business is all about. There is truth to this criticism but it takes two to communicate. For instance, newspapers and magazines carry the facts of business profits but opinion polls periodically show that the public thinks business earns 28 percent on sales after taxes! Actually profit margins have declined from 1965 to late 1973, when this is being written, and today the average annual after-tax-profit return on sales is around 4.5 percent.

Third, there is general dissatisfaction today with major institutions in society. Causes of disaffection among them are often applied to business whether appropriate or not. Fourth, there is a deep innate antipathy and distrust of institutions which exercise power over society. Business does have power and therefore is viewed with suspicion. Finally, there is the continuous and mounting dissemination of information about wrongdoings, actual and imagined, of businessmen and companies. Widespread exposure of criminal activities of companies like Equity Funding Corporation tend to stain the image of all business. Criticisms, whether true or not, which are leveled at business by various consumer and environmental activist groups also tend to tarnish the image of business.

CHANGING VALUES

The ferment in the business-society relationship reflects changes in the values people hold. In Part Three of this book this subject will be explored in depth. Here it is sufficient to note that some rather important value changes are taking place and are having a major impact on business. For instance, we have always had a conflict between materialistic and humane values, but the balance today is much more in favor of the latter than in the past. This has resulted, among other things, in looking at present goods and services in a much different light than in the past.

There is no doubt about the fact that the goods and services available to the American people today are the best the world has ever seen. Yet there is criticism of business and its products. One reason is that people no longer look primarily to the physical characteristics and functions of economic goods and services. They now inquire more and more into their contributions to the quality of life. They no longer look at goods and services in terms of simple possession and utility but to the drain their production makes on the world's resources, the working conditions in factories where they are made, the pollution that their production entails, their reliability and safety, and the way the fruits of production are distributed. This new way of looking at goods and services constitutes a fundamental difference from the past.

A noticeable value change in the young is timing of self-gratification. Today, contrasted with the immediate past, young people want their satisfactions now rather than later. They want the good things of life immediately. This value shift is, of course, a product of an affluent society. It brings with it new and high expectations of business capability in meeting it.

We have many conflicts in values. For instance, we want price stability as well as economic growth. This conflict today is bringing new problems to both government and business in restraining price inflation at full employment levels.

Broadly, there are changes taking place in society's values which influence the way business will operate. There are also ample signs that many basic values are not changing that concern the fundamental institutional relationships in society, as well as the structure and operation of the business institution. How these two rates of change will finally influence business remains to be seen.

MAJOR SOCIAL PROBLEMS

There seems little doubt but that people are dissatisfied with all major institutions, including business, because they are frustrated in resolving today's big social problems. The crust of American society is split with social San Andreas faults. These are the great social problems which have been evolving for a long time and which are now of such colossal proportions as to create for us potential social earthquakes. Of top priority are the festering sores in our central cities; pockets of deep and abject poverty; malnutrition among the poor; racial strife; unemployment among minority groups; widespread water, air, and noise pollution; traffic congestion; general social unrest; and a shortage of energy.

Another problem is how to assure that society is self-renewing, innovative, and capable of exerting the required consensus in achieving its objectives and solving its major problems. This is far from easy or sure. Diffused loyalties of individuals in many groups provide the opportunity for minority groups to exert excessive power on issues that arouse their members. Minorities can and do dominate majorities. As society becomes more complex and power more diffused, it becomes increasingly difficult for diverse groups to organize to offset the power of specific groups. For instance, public opinion polls show that Americans are overwhelmingly in favor of free trade, yet in every session of Congress there are laws proposed or passed which violate this principle.

Perhaps of greater significance is the problem of getting the necessary consensus from many groups to deal more forthrightly with some of our social problems. Attacking with more hope of success the problems of New York City, for instance, requires a coordination among groups that has not yet been achieved. It is and will continue to be a major problem to ensure the emergence of new alignments of power to master social change. This must be facilitated by the development of new methods and techniques. Mastering problems such as these involves business directly, indirectly, and massively.

THE ECONOMIC ENVIRONMENT

The economic environment covers a vast territory and is, of course, of arresting significance to business. It is a source of opportunity as well as threat. The managerial task today is far more complex than in the past in large part because of the rapid changes taking place in the business economic environment to which a firm must adapt for survival and profitable growth. The following is presented only to illustrate some of the dimensions of today's economic environment in which business finds itself.

In a very broad sense there has been a constant encroachment on business freedom of decision-making in the marketplace because of growing government regulations. This has not been solely a matter of changing the rules of the game in which business operates, it also involves more direct controls over managerial decision-making. Governmental direction to automobile manufacturers to produce a reliable automobile airbag is a case in point. Less direct, but highly important to the automobile industry, have been results of a combination of forces springing from federal clean air standards, federal automobile safety standards, and increasing concern about gasoline shortages. Small car sales have risen from 37.8 percent of the total in

1967 to 61 percent of the market in mid-1973. This shift, if it continues, will reduce profits of automobile manufacturers because the margin is less on smaller automobiles than on larger ones.

At this writing in mid–1974, the economic environment is filled with serious problems. Economic danger flags are flying. We have double-digit price inflation and double-digit prime interest rates. The economic machine is operating at capacity but unemployment is rising. Shortages of raw materials and components are disrupting production lines and add to both inflation and unemployment. The collapse of the stock market has dried up equity financing sources for business. Business profits are rising in current dollars but falling in constant dollars. International money markets are more stable than at any time since the end of World War II. Not since World War II has the economic outlook been so uncertain.

At a different level, to illustrate the complexities of business economic environment, risks of production are rising. The life cycle of a typical product (e.g., from introduction on a market until it is either taken off the market or is substantially remodeled) is becoming shorter. At the same time the research and development time and costs to produce a typical product are increasing (Steiner, 1969: 555–560). Competition generally is increasing, both at home and abroad. In a number of recent years wage rates have risen faster than worker productivity. Costs of borrowing money have risen substantially in recent years. Such pressures are reflected in declining profits per dollar of sales, as noted previously.

On the other hand there are elements in the economic environment which provide great profit opportunities. The size of the American market is itself a source of opportunity. Despite undulations above and below gross-national-product trend lines, business activity in the past three decades has shown remarkably stable growth when compared with the past. New technologies are opening up opportunities for business. Despite costs of capital compared with the past, financial means are available for business expansion and investment at home and abroad. If we are successful during the next few years in stabilizing international financial and trade relationships, world markets will present great new opportunities for American companies.

There are so many other forces operating on the economic environment that clamor for mention. But this discussion must suffice for the present.

THE LEGAL ENVIRONMENT

An executive of a large company remarked recently that ten years ago his chief legal worries centered on antitrust matters and everything else was lumped together as a poor second. Not today, he commented. Now, there are many areas of great urgency, the priorities of which change from month to month, and the number of problems have exploded.

Fortune magazine recently conducted an analysis of a cross-section of American industry to determine changes taking place in their legal environment. It found eight major areas of concern, as follows: antitrust, securities and stockholder matters, consumerism, environment, fair employment practices, safety, government contracts, and wage-price controls. Companies were asked to designate those areas of most concern to them. For individual companies, certain areas easily dominated their concern but for industry as a whole there were no clear standouts.

While examination of the daily newspaper might lead to the conclusion that consumer suits were dominating corporate legal history, the facts are otherwise. The major source of new corporate legal miseries is the federal government, said forty-four of the sixty-five companies in *Fortune*'s survey. Second place went to state and local governments, but ten companies ranked the private sector first and twenty-five placed it second.

Not only have legal actions in all areas increased rapidly but exposure and potential liability for business also have risen explosively. One reason, clearly, is the extraordinary number of laws which have been passed recently to govern business activity. One executive correctly lamented "the volume of laws and regulations is such that no one can comply faithfully with all rules. No large organization can effectively police all its employees" (Carruth, 1973: 157). So governmental legal hounds can easily find bones to pick in the most law-abiding companies. People are concerned also about business practices that affect them and the general ethos in society encourages them to take legal action to redress grievances they perceive.

A major cause of corporate legal headaches is the class action suit. Some call it "judicial populism"; some say it is "legalized blackmail." All see it as a major instrument of social activism. The ability of plaintiffs to join into a class in a single lawsuit to resolve many claims at one time is of long standing. In 1966, however, the Supreme Court changed the rules of the game to permit something that was not possible before—a single individual could act on behalf of all similarly injured persons and if he won they all won damages. As more class action suits were brought before the courts the definition of what constituted a common cause for banding together was broadened. Courts have reaffirmed the rights of individuals not only to sue companies in their own private pecuniary interests but also in the public interest. This means that individuals have the right to sue a company on behalf of the public for violating a pollution law. In May 1974, however, the Supreme Court ruled that anyone bringing a class action suit must notify each person affected by the litigation, no matter how much the cost. This decision raised a formidable barrier to anyone bringing a class action suit.

There is no doubt at all about the fact that the legal environment of business is opening up new areas of litigation. The volume of legal actions is growing rapidly but, more seriously, liability is being attached to actions for which manufacturers were heretofore immune and for all companies potential liability is unlimited.

THE GOVERNMENTAL ENVIRONMENT

There is today practically no aspect of business that the federal government cannot regulate if the occasion arises to do so and popular or legislative support exists. There have been those who have advocated more government policy-making over business and less detailed regulation but so far government controls over business have been plentiful in both areas (Drucker, 1969). Never before in our history (except in wartime) has government been involved in so many details of business.

As noted earlier in this chapter, the criticisms of business are mounting. These are not general criticisms but concern specific business activities such as product safety, product labeling, advertising honesty, pollution, and worker safety. The government has responded to these criticisms with specific legislation constraining business. The trend is up and not down.

Government, however, has been supportive of business. Trade negotiations between our government and foreign countries seek to benefit our export businesses. The government is beginning to support business nondefense research and development. This is likely to grow rather than taper off. A new set of opportunities and dangers for business exist in the formation of more government-business partnerships to do things society wants.

In considering the government environment one should note that the power of business in the political process is eroding. When such a large part of society feels as strongly against business as is apparent from the data presented earlier, it is much easier for critical voices to be heard in the political process. Legislators still listen carefully to the voters and pressure groups. This point is sharpened because of the growth, power, constituency, technical know-how, and persistence, of groups which have arisen to protect something—the consumer, the environment, morality, and so on. The net conclusion is that the power of government over business is being used more frequently to achieve the purposes of groups critical of business.

THE INTERNAL BUSINESS ENVIRONMENT

Individuals within organizations are demanding that their interests be considered in the managerial decision-making process. In the past, and within the law, business could make decisions wholly on the basis of economic factors. This is no longer possible. Individuals want more creative jobs, they want to participate in the decision-making process, they want to avoid routine mind-numbing jobs, they want more pleasant surroundings, they want higher wages and more generous pensions, and they want shorter hours and more vacations. At the same time, competitive pressures constrain passing off increased costs in higher prices and force productivity and cost-reduction programs. Such forces face business with contradictory pressures and painful choices.

CHANGING CONSTITUENT ROLES

In the distant past a businessman could be successful if, working within the rules of the game laid down by government, he tried to satisfy only his customers and stockholders. In most companies the stockholders owned and ran the business. Today, corporations of any size are run by professional managers who own little stock. The typical stockholder does not act or think like the traditional owner but as an investor.

An increasing part of the stock of larger corporations is owned by institutional investors. In the past these investors exerted very little pressure or none at all on corporate managers. If they did not like what was going on, they sold their stock. Now they are beginning to exercise their power by putting pressure on managers to assume social responsibilities.

Individuals and groups interested in the decision-making process of a larger company today include, aside from the owners and investors, the managers and employees of the company, customers, suppliers, labor, professional staff groups, the community, government, business associations, self-appointed activist groups, and the public at large. Not only is it becoming more essential for larger companies to consider these various interests and to take them into account in decision-making, but the roles and interests of these groups are changing. For instance, customers are not only becoming more sophisticated but are being led by activist groups to exert power over companies directly or through government. Ours is a pluralistic society and it is becoming more so, a fact of great importance to business.

PLURALISM — *diffused power*

A pluralistic society is one which has many semi-autonomous and autonomous groups through which power is diffused. No one group has overwhelming power over all others, and each has direct or indirect impact on all the others. The existence of power in so many decentralized groups makes less possible the tyranny of a majority over a minority.

The pluralistic society has two dimensions, both of which are important in the diffusion of power. First, various social functions have different structures. For instance, one set of institutions is concerned with business activity. Second, within each major functional area there are organizations having dissimilar degrees of independence and interdependence. In business, for example, there is a multiplicity of organizations having disparate goals, values, methods of operation, autonomy, power, and interrelationships.

Implicit in American pluralism is the freedom of individuals to join associations and thereby to express their desires and to seek fulfillment through many different avenues. This freedom is essential to Americans for we are, as Tocqueville first observed, the "joiningest" society in the world. This right also encourages the growth of new forms of association to meet new needs of society and of individuals.

For business, a pluralistic society means, first, that many groups can exert power over business. Second, there is a continuous question of the use and exercise of business power as compared with the power of other groups in society. Third, business can express itself through many different organizational combinations. Fourth, there is the implication that business is in no small degree a joint venture among a number of other responsible groups in society. Fifth, pluralism may lead to consensus or it may lead to conflict among groups. In either event, business may join other groups or it may be the target. Finally, there is great awareness in groups of what is happening elsewhere. Businesses are sensitive to their profit position, share of market, general economic conditions, and so on. Labor unions are sensitive to general economic conditions, dissatisfactions among members, business pressures on Congress, wage rates, and fringe benefits. This awareness of one organization of another's actions is characteristic of the present American economy. It explains the dynamism of this society as change—technological, ideological, social, political—tends to affect every part of society.

It should be noted that pluralism is not a natural state of affairs. It was an alien concept in Rome, throughout the medieval world, and under early mercantilism. It was in the medieval world that widespread attacks on authority gave rise to the concept, but it was not until the end of the eighteenth century that the idea was made workable in practice. Pluralism and political democracy are handmaidens. If democracy is to survive, diffusion of power among groups must exist and be guarded.

The existence of pluralism in a political democracy fosters self-preservation, since individual groups are given strong voices and bargaining power. Furthermore, overlapping membership in many groups diversifies loyalties and minimizes the danger that a strong leader in any one group can command the power of all members. The fact that people belong to many groups also increases their tolerance of other views.

INTERDEPENDENCE AMONG MAJOR GROUPS

The social and economic system today is one in which interdependence among major groups in society is an outstanding characteristic. The economic model now contains three major sectors: the profit-seeking, or private; the nonprofit; and the government. Organizations in each are inextricably interrelated with those in other sectors. All influence one another both as stimulants and as restrictions on the exercise of power. None can exist without the others—or at least, none could be as strong as it now is without the others.

Business depends upon governments to purchase approximately 30 percent of the total GNP. It looks to the nonprofit educational system for skilled managers and workers. Business relies on labor organizations to negotiate in good faith, and vice versa, rather than to seek goals through a sort of industrial guerrilla warfare. Business seeks government help in preventing unfair competition at home and abroad, in maintaining conditions under which resources are fully employed, and in absorbing various types of economic risks. Government, of course, depends upon business for revenues, for meeting the demands of society for goods and services, and for advice.

So interdependent are business and government that Adolph Berle, a long and astute student of the modern corporation, has observed:

> I here suggest that there is no way of knowing whether any enterprise in the United States, taken by itself, makes or loses money, and that the utility or non-utility of goods or services it produces or provides is not necessarily the factor determining the profit. I believe that the profit-and-loss statements made up at the end of the year really reflect whether the enterprise holds a favored or an unfortunate niche in the whole (political, social and economic) aggregate (1963: 32–33).

OTHER ENVIRONMENTS

There are other systems in the general business environment that are changing and of importance to business. For instance, our proliferating technology provides growing opportunities as well as threats to any particular business. The growth and influence of universities not only is a source of challenge to business values but also a portent of new values which might challenge the old in the work environment as students enter business. Changing rates of population fertility will have a continuing impact on business. The growing concentration of people in urban centers is complicating city governance and, in turn, raises demands for business aid. It also erodes the environment in which business is done. The consequences to business of changes in these and many other areas are almost infinite as they fan out in impact and time.

The future environment of business, as noted in Figure 1-1, has an impact on today's business. Toffler has popularized the words "future shock" to describe the psychological impacts of current and accelerating future changes on people (1970). He has explored with ample detail how these changes affect today's thinking, decision-making, and other aspects of life. The perceived future must always be considered in today's business environment.

BUSINESS'S IMPACT ON ITS ENVIRONMENTS

The business institution is not a passive agent which reflects all demands made upon it. Nor is it an impassive one that rejects all demands. Business managers, particularly of the larger corporations, are very sensitive to changing public demands and criticisms.

The reaction of a business to societal demands will depend upon a number of factors. Among them are the size of a company, its profitability, the timing of pressures, the type of pressure, the degree of public consensus, and the value systems of its top managers.

What business does directly or indirectly influences every facet of this society. Its introduction of technology into society brings in its wake changes in values which in turn affects what society believes and does. Because of its dominant role in society there is a tendency for business values to be accepted. Being on time for work, for instance, is a value which is applied in nonwork situations.

Business also has power over its economic and political environments. When a company decides to move from one community to another its influence in these areas can be decisive. On other occasions business power is negligible. For instance, the automobile companies exerted all the power at their command to change the automobile emissions standards for 1975 and 1976 incorporated in the Air Quality Control Act of 1971 because, they said at the time, they could not technically meet the standards. They were correct but at the time their power did not prevail and the act was passed.

UNDERLYING FORCES IN TODAY'S CHANGING
BUSINESS ENVIRONMENT

The business environment has never been static but today it is changing in scope and depth to a degree not encountered for several hundred years. So significant is the change that one observer speaks of "the second American Revolution" (Rockfeller, 1973). I think it is impressive enough to warrant saying that we are redefining capitalism

(Steiner, 1972). To justify such expressions there must be powerful forces in our society which will continue to operate for some time. Among the most important I mention the following.

Changing National Priorities There are two major trends which underlie the changing business environment and which have great impact on business management. The first is the belief that this American society has now virtually solved the age-old "economic problem." This means that for the first time in the history of civilization it is perceived that a large society is capable of providing an acceptable minimum of goods and services for the great bulk of its population. Notice that this statement does not say that today everyone can get from our economic system all that he needs or wants. We still have pockets of poverty, there are people who do not have enough to eat, there are ghettos and barrios, and we do have extremely difficult economic and social problems. While we are a few years away from assuring that everyone can have a minimum level of goods and services, the achievement is clearly in sight. This is a phenomenon of extraordinary importance.

Dow Votaw commented recently that: "In a land of scarcity, economics is king; in a land of plenty, economics is just another member of the royal court" (1972: 30). From the beginning of our history the central concern of society has been to satisfy minimum economic needs. The success of our industrial system in meeting this challenge provides the occasion for today's society to consider other priorities.

This economic success story has coincided with the sudden rise of unprecedented social problems. While there is diversity of judgment about the criticalness of many of these problems, and the priorities of resources to be allocated to them, there is a national consensus that they must receive higher priority. In an important degree, our social problems are an outgrowth of the spectacular success of our industrial system in meeting yesterday's priorities for producing more and more goods and services. In the past, society accepted heavy social costs of business in order to get production. Now it is asking business to bear more of the cost.

The shift is vividly illustrated in this way. Only a few years ago a belching smokestack was hailed by a community with rejoicing. Why? Because it meant jobs, and jobs meant access to the goods of the economic system. Today, a smoking chimney is viewed with disdain because it pollutes the environment.

Business is not being asked to replace its past emphasis on productivity. Society still wants higher production, but its demands on business have broadened to include business's help in improving the quality of life.

Progression Up the Hierarchy of Man's Needs Another outgrowth of growing affluence in this society is ascension of more and more people to higher need levels. Maslow (1943) said that a person's needs are rank ordered in five levels—from the lowest level of basic physiological demand for food, clothing, shelter, and rest; through security needs; to social needs for affection and belonging; to ego needs for prestige, identity, and self respect; and on to the highest levels of self-fulfillment (See Chapter 27). As most people find lower-level demands being met satisfactorily their needs become more intense at higher levels. These levels focus more on individual psychological satisfactions. To meet these needs business is being asked to pay more attention to human requirements both inside and outside individual businesses.

Rising Expectations When human beings perceive the possibility of achieving important gains for themselves from their environment, their expectations escalate faster than reality bears the fruit they seek. Tocqueville wrote with remarkable insight on this point in the eighteenth century: "The evil which was suffered patiently as inevitable, seems unendurable as soon as the idea of escaping from it crosses men's minds. All the abuses then removed call attention to those that remain, and they now appear the more galling. The evil, it is true, has become less, but sensibility to it has become more acute." We are witnessing today in the United States a great upsurge of expectations in conformance with this phenomenon. They associate with rising real income, cleaning up the environment, immediate rather than delayed gratifications, city rebuilding, an end to all poverty, and so on.

Jacoby has pointed out that the conceived importance of our social problems is determined by public expectations as much as by real conditions (1971). He defines a "social problem" as a gap between society's expectations of a social condition and present realities. Furthermore, he says, the major cause of expanding social "problems" in the United States has been rising expectations and not a failure of reality to improve.

Our society, accustomed to steady progress, generates high expectations. Not only have accelerating expectations put increasing pressure on all institutions to perform better, but failure to achieve expectations has resulted in violence, dissension, and growing criticism of all institutions in our society.

Future expectations have an impact on business and can take highly exaggerated forms. For instance, fears of future high concentration of business assets in the largest corporations are giving rise to demands to limit the size of large companies now. Some recent studies have looked at population growth (Ehrlich, 1968), and some have related population growth with other trends (such as pollution and food production) and have derived visions of the Apocalypse (Meadows, 1972). We shall return to these studies later but at this point it is relevant to note that a future doom that they see is generating demands to slow down economic growth.

PERSPECTIVES IN VIEWING THE AMERICAN ENVIRONMENT

There are two extreme positions from which American culture is viewed. One, assumed by observers such as Charles Reich (1970A) and Ronald Segal (1968), sees all the blemishes, problems, and weaknesses but none of the strengths, accomplishments, and successes. The other extreme, exemplified by a current popular automobile bumper sticker "America: Love it Or Leave it," sees nothing that needs change. It takes the position that all is right with America and those who want to change it are wrong, at best, and enemy subversives, at worst.

Those in the first group see the United States on the verge of revolution, or eventual catastrophic collapse, or continuous turmoil and conflict which will eventually rend the social fabric to tatters. The others see a vigorous and strong society continuing to thrive on the basic principles and institutions of political, social, and economic life hammered out in the past. The first, at the very least, wants to see revolutionary changes made; the latter insists on the status quo. There are, of course, stances in between.

Both extremes are very wrong. This society is too complex for its essence to be captured in simple observations, no matter how discerning. Like a kaleidoscope its image changes from time to time, issue to issue, event to event, observer to observer.

The New Demands on Business and the Changing Business Role

CHAPTER SIX

INTRODUCTION

In the previous chapter there were a number of comments concerning the new demands being made today on business by society. In this chapter the nature of these demands will be discussed in some detail. First is the demand that business help society to achieve its goals. Next is the demand that business help people to achieve a quality of life. This is followed by specific demands made upon a large company. The wide gap between public expectations on business and reality is then noted. Finally, the chapter concludes with an examination of how these demands are changing managerial philosophies and business practice.

TO HELP SOCIETY ACHIEVE ITS GOALS

Institutions in society, as noted previously, exist to help society achieve one or more of its goals. Business is no exception. Unfortunately, for that manager who wishes to help society achieve its goals, there is no official list of national goals that he can consult nor, if he finds a goal he wants to help achieve, is there any guidance to tell him precisely how far he is obliged to help.

The first effort to develop national goals was made by a Presidential Commission in 1960 (President's Commission on National Goals, 1960). Thereafter, there have been other attempts to describe national goals (Edwards, 1964; Lecht, 1966). In July 1969 President Nixon established a National Goals Research Staff in the White House with a responsibility to forecast future developments, calculate ranges of social choice, and develop social indicators to reflect the present and future quality of life. It was hoped that the work of this group would provoke national discussion which would lead to the establishment of specific goals in 1976, the 200th anniversary of the founding of this Republic. The staff followed this philosophy and its report "does not presume to say *what* our choices should be. Rather, it defines the questions, analyzes the debates and examines the alternative sets of consequences" (23). We can hope that by 1976 we shall have a set of goals developed from informed debate, but the probabilities of getting it are low.

Although there have been no polls of public opinion on, or other efforts to help formulate, those ends which society seems to want today for its economic and social system, I think it is useful to come to some conclusions, no matter how tentative. In the absence of any convincing consensus of what people want, the objectives in Table 6–1 seem to me to reflect today's mood.

Table 6–1.   Major Goals of the American Society

1. An end to engagement in war, a foreign policy to ensure lasting peace, and in the meantime an adequate national defense establishment.
2. Full employment of persons and resources with reasonable price stability.
3. Economic progress, in the sense of high and expanding production, national income, and standards of living.
4. A favorable balance of international trade, international financial stability, and growing foreign trade.
5. Resolution of great social problems such as air and water pollution, city deterioration, transportation congestion, poverty, unemployment, racial tensions, and drug abuse.
6. More security for individuals against economic risks, such as loss of pensions.
7. More law and order and less crime.
8. Less inequality in the distribution of income.
9. More equity in taxation.
10. Preservation of political and economic freedom.
11. Political stability to ensure orderly rather than revolutionary change.
12. More efficiency and higher morality in government.
13. Responsibility of government to act in the common good in a degree commensurate with its size and authority.
14. Conservation of natural resources.
15. An independent energy supply and basic material resources equal to demand.
16. Preservation of the basic institutions and character of the "free enterprise system," while at the same time expecting business to meet new social demands.
17. A society in which the human dignity, creativity, self-satisfaction, and potential of all men can be fulfilled. People want to live "quality lives."

There are many other objectives which might be added, but these serve the purposes at hand. They establish the broad goals toward which our social and economic system is supposed to move. Precisely what these goals mean is not at all clear and would take another volume to analyze. For example, what does more security for individuals really mean? Then, too, priorities among these goals change over time and bring about a much different total profile. For instance, in recent years there has been a growing increase in the importance of goals 5 and 16 to more and more people. So strong is the desire for these goals, and so likely is it to continue, that some people are beginning to wonder whether in the 1970s economic growth goals may have to be less aggressive in order to satisfy demands for a better quality of life.

In sum, these goals are very difficult to define; there are great differences in society about the priorities of each one; the swings in emphasis during the past few years have been impressive; there are conflicts among them; and the list is not complete. Despite these shortcomings, the list does lay some basis for more detailed specification of the objectives to which business may contribute and the expectations of society about what business ought to contribute.

TO IMPROVE THE QUALITY OF LIFE

The demand on business today is to produce goods and services efficiently and in quantity, as in the past, and at the same time to improve the quality of life. This is not a peripheral or modest addition to the businesses agenda. It is, Drucker says, ". . . a demand that business and businessmen make concern for society central to the conduct of business itself. It is a demand that the quality of life become the business of business" (1969(B): 77).

At a high level of abstraction I would guess that most people combine these ideas and would say that quality of life refers to: (1) a high and rising level of personal minimum income, (2) an up-to-date concept of human equality, (3) an opportunity for individual self-fulfillment, (4) a pollution-free environment, and (5) resolution of major social and economic problems (Corson, 1971). Can we get more specific about the meaning of quality of life?

Much is written and said about the quality of life. Despite the attention given to it, however, this remains an elusive phrase. Frequently the words refer to environment and the external factors important to an individual's quality of life, such as air, housing, transportation, law and order, racial equality, and employment. Factors such as these do, indeed, determine in important degree how satisfactory an individual's life is. But, as Dalkey reminds us, these include only a limited part of the sum of satisfactions that make life worthwhile (1972: 9). So he and others define the quality of life in terms of a person's sense of well-being, happiness or unhappiness, as determined by psychological and emotional factors such as love, affection, and self-respect. Combining these two points of view suggests, of course, that quality of life can be determined by identifying and measuring both types of factors.

One reason, among others, why there is no consensus about the meaning of a quality of life is that the subject can be approached from points of view other than those noted above. For instance, definition may be in terms of these perspectives: economic, social, psychological, or environmental. Also, the quality of life definition will depend upon life styles, age, interests, economic levels, education, and a combination of all.

The development of quality of life factors has paralleled the search for social indicators. Social indicators were first proposed in a report of a task force by John Gardner when he was Secretary of the Department of Health Education and Welfare (HEW) (Bell Report, 1969). The task force defined a social indicator "to be a statistic of direct normative interest which facilitates concise, comprehensive, and balanced judgments about the condition of major aspects to a society" (97). It was hoped that eventually there would be identified factors of major social concern in raising or lowering quality of life together with quantitative measures of how well we were doing in improving the quality of life. So far, progress has been very slow in identifying a list of factors of high social concern which is generally accepted. Much less progress has been made to date in developing suitable measures (Environmental Protection Agency, 1973).

The Organization for Economic Co-Operation and Development (OECD) sought to identify major social consensus common to its membership countries for which a set of acceptable indicators and systematic assessments are needed (1973). The list of indicators that OECD prepared is shown in Table 6–2. Eight major areas are covered, and, in a number of these areas, detailed concerns are identified.

Dalkey has been developing lists of factors which appear to be most important to an individual's sense of well-being, personal satisfactions, and happiness (1972). He accumulated about 250 factors which eventually he classified into 48 categories. In a survey among upper division and graduate students at UCLA he ranked his factors in descending order of importance. The most important ones are shown in Table 6–3.

Dalkey says that the basic components of the quality of life are common to practically all individuals and are only weakly dependent upon ethnic or socioeconomic status. He also says that differences between individuals in relative emphasis or relative priorities "are due in large part to the fact that trade-offs among the components

TABLE 6–2. Social Indicators

FUNDAMENTAL SOCIAL CONCERNS	SUB-CONCERNS
HEALTH	
A-1. The probability of a healthy life through all stages of the life cycle	
A-2. The impact of health impairments on individuals	**A-2-a.** The quality of health care in terms of reducing pain and restoring functional capabilities
	A-2-b. The extent of universal distribution in the delivery of health care
	A-2-c. The ability of the chronically impaired and permanently handicapped to participate more effectively in society
INDIVIDUAL DEVELOPMENT THROUGH LEARNING	
B-1. The acquisition by children of the basic knowledge, skills and values necessary for their individual development and their successful functioning as citizens in their society	**B-1-a.** The extent to which children from economically and socially disadvantaged families reach the basic standards of achievement
	B-1-b. The extent to which the physically and mentally handicapped receive educational services for their individual development through learning and for their more effective participation in social life
	B-1-c. The proportion of other children reaching the basic standards of achievement
B-2. The availability of opportunities for continuing self-development and the propensity of individuals to use them	
B-3. The maintenance and development by individuals of the knowledge, skills, and flexibility required to fulfil their economic potential and to enable them to integrate themselves in the economic process if they wish to do so	

FUNDAMENTAL SOCIAL CONCERNS	SUB-CONCERNS
B-4. The individual's satisfaction with the process of individual development through learning, while he is in the process	
B-5. The maintenance and development of the cultural heritage relative to its positive contribution to the well-being of the members of various social groups	
EMPLOYMENT AND QUALITY OF WORKING LIFE	
C-1. The availability of gainful employment for those who desire it	
C-2. The quality of working life	**C-2-a.** Working conditions
	C-2-b. Earnings and fringe benefits
	C-2-c. Employment-time, employment-related time and paid holidays
	C-2-d. Employment security
	C-2-e. Career prospects
	C-2-f. Industrial conflict
C-3. Individual satisfaction with the experience of working life	**C-3-a.** Working conditions
	C-3-b. Earnings and fringe benefits
	C-3-c. Employment-time, employment-related time and paid holidays
	C-3-d. Employment security
	C-3-e. Career prospects
	C-3-f. Relations among and participation by employees
	C-3-g. Supervision, autonomy, and job-challenge
TIME AND LEISURE	
D-1. The availability of effective choices for the use of time	**D-1-a.** The flexibility of patterns of working time
	D-1-b. The accessibility and quality of leisure-time opportunities
	D-1-c. The time available for personal development, family and social obligations, and social participation

FUNDAMENTAL SOCIAL CONCERNS	SUB-CONCERNS
COMMAND OVER GOODS AND SERVICES	
E-1. The personal command over goods and services	
E-2. The number of individuals experiencing material deprivation	
E-3. The extent of equity in the distribution of command over goods and services	**E-3-a.** The extent of relative impoverishment **E-3-b.** The dispersion in the structure of income and wealth
E-4. The quality, range of choice, and accessibility of private and public goods and services	**E-4-a.** Whether individuals have the information needed to make effective choices **E-4-b.** Individuals' satisfaction with the quality, range of choice, and accessibility of the private and public goods and services they consume
E-5. The protection of individuals and families against economic hazards	**E-5-a.** The extent to which individuals and families obtain insurance or other compensation for predictable and unpredictable income losses **E-5-b.** The extent to which individuals and families obtain assistance for significant expansions of obligatory expenditures particular to them **E-5-c.** The extent to which individuals and families perceive themselves as secure against adverse change in their economic status
PHYSICAL ENVIRONMENT	
F-1. Housing conditions	**F-1-a.** Cost and availability of suitable dwellings **F-1-b.** Living space and utilities of dwellings **F-1-c.** Accessibility to neighborhood shops and services, and work places **F-1-d.** Neighborhood and environmental amenities

FUNDAMENTAL SOCIAL CONCERNS	SUB-CONCERNS
F-2. Population exposure to harmful and/or unpleasant pollutants	**F-2-a.** Air
	F-2-b. Noise
	F-2-c. Pervasive and persistent pollutants
	F-2-d. Water
	F-2-e. Land
F-3. The benefit derived by the population from the use and management of the environment	**F-3-a.** Land management
	F-3-b. Water management
	F-3-c. Management of the urban and rural landscape
	F-3-d. Housing conditions
	F-3-e. Control of pollution
	F-3-f. Reduction of congestion
	F-3-g. Accessibility among social services and functions
	F-3-h. Environmental contribution to recreation and amenity
	F-3-i. Other aspects of urban and rural life
PERSONAL SAFETY AND THE ADMINISTRATION OF JUSTICE	
G-1. Violence, victimization, and harassment suffered by individuals	**G-1-a.** Involving persons
	G-1-b. Involving property
	G-1-c. Involving perceptions of danger to safety and security
G-2. Fairness and humanity of the administration of justice	**G-2-a.** In the administration of criminal law
	G-2-b. In the administration of civil law
	G-2-c. In the administrative practice
G-3. The extent of confidence in the administration of justice	
SOCIAL OPPORTUNITY AND PARTICIPATION	
H-1. The degree of social inequality	**H-1-a.** The degree of inequality among social strata
	H-1-b. The extent of opportunity for social mobility
	H-1-c. The position of disadvantaged groups
H-2. The extent of opportunity for participation in community life, institutions, and decision-making	

SOURCE: OECD, 1973: 14–17.

TABLE 6–3. Major Elements in an Individual's Quality of Life Ranked in Order of Importance

RANK FACTOR	RELATIVE IMPORTANCE
1. Love, caring, affection, communication, interpersonal understanding; friendship, companionship; honesty, sincerity, truthfulness; tolerance, acceptance of others; faith, religious awareness.	15.0
2. Self-respect, self-acceptance, self-satisfaction; self-confidence, egoism; security; stability, familiarity, sense of permanence; self-knowledge, self-awareness, growth.	11.5
3. Peace of mind, emotional stability, lack of conflict; fear, anxiety; suffering, pain; humiliation, belittlement; escape, fantasy.	10.0
4. Sex, sexual satisfaction, sexual pleasure.	9.5
5. Challenge, stimulation; competition, competitiveness; ambition; opportunity, social mobility, luck; educational, intellectual stimulation.	8.0
6. Social acceptance, popularity; needed, feeling of being wanted; loneliness, impersonality; flattering, positive feedback, reinforcement.	8.0
7. Achievement, accomplishment, job satisfaction; success; failure, defeat, losing; money, acquisitiveness, material greed; status, reputation, recognition, prestige.	7.0
8. Individuality; conformity; spontaneity, impulsive, uninhibited; freedom.	6.0
9. Involvement, participation; concern, altruism, consideration.	6.0
10. Comfort, economic well-being, relaxation, leisure; good health.	6.0
11. Novelty, change, newness, variety, surprise; boredom; humorous, amusing, witty.	5.0
12. Dominance, superiority; dependence, impotence, helplessness; aggression, violence, hostility; power, control, independence.	3.5
13. Privacy.	2.0

SOURCE: Dalkey, 1972: 71.

depend upon how much the individual is receiving of each. These variations in trade offs are also part of the underlying value structures common to most people. The wealthy may rate material comfort lower than sense of achievement, whereas the poor man may reverse this rating." This, he says, is not a difference in basic values. "The same poor man, if he manages to become wealthy, will switch priorities, not because of any fundamental change in his value system, but simply because the relative value of comfort declines as more is obtained" (1972: 9–10).

Different approaches have been suggested for measuring desired levels of and progress being made toward specific social indicators (EPA, 1973). We have developed some measures; for example, levels of income for different areas below which families and persons are considered to be living in poverty. We have reasonably good, although far from perfect, data on the number of poor. Information on life expectancy is acceptable. For too many indicators of the quality of life, however, measurement criteria are not acceptable or nonexistent (Terleckyj, 1970; Hoffenberg, 1970; EPA, 1973).

In sum, there is not available for the businessman a set of factors of the quality of life which has a consensus. Even more serious is the fact that the state-of-the-art of measurement is today not helpful to the businessman. (We shall return to the problem of measuring the social performance of business in some detail in Chapter 11.)

SPECIFIC DEMANDS ON A LARGE COMPANY

The General Electric Company is, to my knowledge, the first large corporation to attempt to identify a complete range of demands and complaints that it faces. Table 6–4 gives the results of GE's analysis. It lists ninety-seven specific demands and hazards that seem to be arising out of the new social pressures on business.

Even a cursory glance at the list makes a number of points obvious. First, a large corporation is, indeed, subject to a wide range of demands. Second, not even the largest and most profitable company can satisfy all the demands made upon it. Third, there are obvious conflicts among the demands. C. B. McCoy, when president of Du-Pont, complained:

> What we are getting is a lot of different demands and requests, some of them contradictory.
>
> We are expected to create more jobs, but to do this we must remain competitive in world markets, and that calls for more productivity, investment and technology. At the same time, we are asked (often by the same people) to slow down technology, put more money into pollution control, and increase our commitments to education and urban improvement.
>
> Something has to give. It just isn't possible to optimize for all these goals at the same time (1971).

GE is now measuring these demands and setting priorities to identify those which appear to be the most urgent and which must be met to the extent that company resources, interests, and other pressures permit. More and more large companies will undoubtedly follow this precedent.

Table 6–4.   Social Demands on and Threats to a Large Company

A. MARKETING/FINANCIAL POWER

Federal chartering of corporations, with provision for periodic rechartering

Attacks on "shared monopolies" (re cereal case): restructuring and reorganization of major companies and industries

Limitations on (a) number of businesses one company may engage in, and (b) share of market one company may possess

Dismemberment of large, diversified companies

Nationalization of some industries (e.g., R.R.)

Prenotification of mergers: all mergers barred to top 200 corporations

Higher corporate taxes; perhaps, excess profits tax or progressive corporate income tax

Prenotification of price increases; permanent wage/price/profit controls on major corporations

Divestiture of finance affiliates

Public control of large corporations because they are either immune from, or (for the public good) they must be shielded from normal economic and political/legal constraints

B. PRODUCTION OPERATIONS

Stringent effluents/emissions standards; fines for violations—and possible plant closings

Internalization of all negative "social costs"

National/regional/state land use planning re plant siting, etc.

Environmental impact statements required for new plants, new processes, etc.

Equal pay (and benefits) for equal work

Provision (or support) of day care centers

Tighter enforcement of occupational health and safety standards

Due process for employees (ombudsman)

Human assets accounting, to reveal managerial performance re human resources

Special groups—e.g. minorities, women—demand separate collective bargaining rights

Strikes, sit-ins, class action suits to enforce demands

White collar unionization, including middle-management, professionals

Restrictions on "management rights" (to limit exercise of arbitrary authority)

"Co-ordinated (coalition) bargaining" with major companies/industries

Escalation of labor's bargaining power

Union political power overshadows that of business

C. GOVERNANCE

Broader representation of other constituencies, viewpoints on boards; "co-determination" demands by unions

Table 6–4. (Continued)

Appointment of public members to boards

Management should not have right or power to nominate directors

Greater personalization of accountability and responsibility, among board members and top managers; public financial statements to permit identification of any conflicts of interest

Broader, more explicit accounting of corporate performance (economic and social)

Picketing, disruptions at shareowner meetings

Large, institutional owners use proxies bloc voting of stock and other influences for pressure-group purposes

D. COMMUNICATIONS

Greater disclosure, breakdown of information (e.g. product line; EEO; pollution control)

Stronger FTC controls on advertising standards; provision for "counter-advertising"

More technical information re products (e.g. contents, performance, life, safety) should be made available

Divestiture of all press and broadcasting outlets (to free press from corporate control)

Stronger SEC backing for shareowner resolutions

FCC pressures to dismember communications monopolies

E. COMMUNITY & GOVERNMENT RELATIONS

More government intervention as a third party in almost every significant area of corporate decision making

A "populist" dominated government

Organization of political power blocs (minorities, consumers, environmentalists, elderly, poor, etc.)

More disclosure, control of businessmen's political contributions

Corporations should work more positively and closely with government in, e.g. establishing national priorities; planning, goal-setting, establishing performance criteria, controlling government expenditures, taxation, policies (VAT, etc.) revenue sharing

More vocal and positive support for social reform programs

Entry into "social needs" markets (products, systems, services), even at some curtailment of profit; participate in "Marshall Plan for the Cities"

Privatizing of some government services; quasi-public corporations (e.g. COMSAT)

Contribute know-how to improve governmental efficiency, productivity

More generous leaves for employees to engage in community and government service

More government control directly (or by tax and subsidy) over amount, location and type of business capital investment

Table 6–4.   (Continued)

Loyalties among members of the business community could be severely strained by competition for government aid, by customer suits, etc.

Bureaucratic procedures become more burdensome to cope with government regulations

F. DEFENSE PRODUCTION

Get out of defense work

Shift from defense domination of national budget

More subcontracting to small business

Tougher agency, GAO controls on costs

Control of profit margins

No title (or no exclusive right) to patents developed under government contracts

Picketing of defense facilities

G. INTERNATIONAL OPERATIONS

Establishment of a "U.S.A., Inc." arrangement with more government help, more government controls

Controls on overseas investment, licensing arrangements, use of technology

Shift toward protectionism

End tax deferrals for offshore profits

Restraints on imports from offshore subsidiaries

Report wage scales paid on offshore manufacturing subsidiaries

Labeling to show country of origin

Federal standards for accounting in multinational operations

Multinational government agreements on control of MNC's; create autonomous international body to supervise multinational companies

"Coalition bargaining" by multinational unions (e.g. *re* transfer of operations)

Get out of Angola, South Africa, etc., or reform programs, practices there

World-wide minimum wage standards

Redistribution of corp. profit in low-wage countries

Repeal tariff incentives for creating foreign manufacturing subsidiaries

Repeal tax incentives for overseas operations

SOURCE: Estes in Steiner, 1973: 34–41.

The list of threats and demands shown in Table 6–4 permits organized speculation about the major challenges which large corporations will feel in the next decade. The results of one projection are presented in Table 6–5.

Table 6–5.   Major Areas of Challenge in the Future Business
Environment

1. Constraints on corporate growth—a spectrum of issues ranging from national growth policy through economic controls and environmental protection to questions of antitrust policy and industrial structure.
2. Corporate governance—including matters of accountability, personal liability of managers and directors, board representation, and disclosure of
   information.
3. Managing the "new work force"—dealing with the growing demands for
   job enlargement, more flexible scheduling, more equality of opportunity,
   greater participation and individualization.
4. External constraints on employee relations—the new pressures from government (EEO, health and safety, "federalization" of benefits), unions
   (coalition bargaining) and other groups (class action suits, "whistle-
   blowing").
5. Problems and opportunities of business-government partnership—including a redefinition of the role of the private sector in public problem-
   solving.
6. "Politicizing" of economic decision-making—the growing government
   involvement in corporate decisions through consumerism, environmen-
   talism, industrial reorganization, inflation control., etc.

SOURCE: Estes, in Steiner 1973, p. 30.

CRITICAL PUBLIC ISSUES IN THE SEVENTIES

A review of Table 6–4 permits one to speculate about what may be
the more important public issues in the 1970s concerning the corporation. Estes did this and derived Table 6–6. The reader can compare
his conclusions with those of the table.

EXPECTATIONS VERSUS REALITY

In the last chapter the idea that expectations were outracing reality
was presented. This is a difficult phenomenon to measure. A recent
cross-section poll of the population, however, does provide a basis
for believing there is a wide gap between what reasonably can be
expected of corporations, in light of the way in which the socioeconomic system operates, and what the public thinks business should
do.

   The public was asked whether business should provide special
leadership in dealing with any of sixteen specific societal problems.
The results for the years 1966 and 1973 are shown in Table 6–7. Three
surprising conclusions can be reached with a quick glance at the
numbers. First, there has been a rapid increase between 1966 and
1973 in the expectations of what business ought to do. Second, the

Table 6–6. Some Critical Public Issues of the 'Seventies*

1. Role of corporation in society	Mission; legitimacy; social needs role; governance; accountability and measurement
2. Reordering of national priorities	Social needs v. defense/space; public and private sector roles; goal setting and "social accounting"
3. Consumerism	Product quality, safety; warranties; advertising; consumer rights
4. Environmentalism	Pollution control; plant siting; waste management; recycling; internalizing costs; technology assessment
5. Equality	Equal employment opportunity; taxation; educational opportunity; political power; participation and control
6. Individualism	Self-development, self-actualization; privacy; due process; diversity of life styles
7. National growth policy	Population (size and distribution); energy; full employment; resource depletion; R & D policy
8. Multinational corporation	U. S. competitiveness: balance of payments and trade policy; nationalism; international controls; governance; multinational unions; international economic policy
9. Urban renewal	Finances (revenue sharing); "new cities," metropolitan/regional government; housing, transportation
10. Inflation and controls	Structural reforms; wage/price policies; labor-management policies
11. Unemployment	Manpower policies; vocational education; government as "employer of last resort"
12. Education	Financing; curriculum; educational technology; career-long education; day care/child development
13. Productivity	Motivation; "management rights;" investment policies; behavioral research
14. Law and order	crime control; drugs; prison and court reform
15. Welfare	Guaranteed income; "workfare" proposal; built-in COL adjustments
16. Health care	National health insurance; delivery systems; HMO's; "biomedical revolution"
17. Occupational health safety	Mechanical/systems safety; air pollution; noise; toxic substances protection; rest periods

SOURCE: Estes in Steiner, 1973: pp. 32–33.
* *Not* in order of priority.

percentage of the population which expects leadership from business in most areas is very high. Third, business is expected to take leadership in areas in which it traditionally has had no responsibility (e.g., controlling population growth). Leadership in many of the areas shown in Table 6–7 has been generally assumed by the government.

The population was asked: "As far as you know, has business helped solve this problem, or not?" The responses and their comparisons with the data in Table 6–7 are shown in Table 6–8.

Table 6–7. Popular Views About Whether Business Should Provide Special Leadership to Specific Societal Problems

	SHOULD TAKE LEADERSHIP		
	1973	1966	CHANGE FROM 1966
Controlling air and water pollution	92%	69%	+23%
Eliminating economic depressions	88	73	+15
Rebuilding our cities	85	74	+11
Enabling people to use their talents creatively	85	73	+12
Eliminating racial discrimination	84	69	+15
Wiping out poverty	83	69	+14
Raising living standards around the world	80	43	+37
Finding cures for disease	76	63	+13
Giving a college education to all qualified	75	71	+4
Controlling crime	73	42	+31
Cutting down accidents on highways	72	50	+22
Raising moral standards	70	48	+22
Reducing the threat of war	68	55	+13
Eliminating religious prejudice	63	37	+26
Cutting out government red tape	57	34	+23
Controlling too rapid population growth	44	17	+27

SOURCE: Harris, 1973: 36.

Two conclusions are obvious. First, there is a very wide gap between what people think business should be doing and what they say it is doing. Second, the gap has widened significantly between 1966 and 1973.

Numbers such as those shown in the accompanying tables are not, of course, highly accurate because polls from which they are derived are subject to many shortcomings. Nevertheless, the magnitudes shown obviously reflect popular attitudes in a general way and are, therefore, views which should be taken seriously. Broadly they reflect paradoxical trends. One shows rising public expectations from business; one shows that the public thinks business's performance is de-

Table 6–8. Popular Views About Whether Business Has Been and Should Be Taking Special Leadership in Specific Areas

	1973				CHANGE IN GAP
	HAS BEEN	SHOULD BE	GAP	1966 GAP	FROM 1966
Rebuilding our cities	60%	92%	−32%	+7%	−39%
Raising living standards around the world	52	80	−28	+18	−46
Eliminating racial discrimination	50	84	−34	−11	−23
Finding cures for disease	47	76	−29	+8	−37
Enabling people to use their talents creatively	41	85	−44	−8	−36
Eliminating economic depressions	41	88	−47	+2	−49
Giving a college education to all qualified	40	75	−35	−6	−29
Controlling air and water pollution	36	92	−56	−34	−22
Wiping out poverty	35	83	−48	−6	−42
Cutting down accidents on highways	29	72	−43	−21	−22
Eliminating religious prejudice	28	63	−35	−3	−32
Controlling crime	23	73	−50	12	−38
Raising moral standards	21	70	−49	−10	−39
Controlling too rapid population growth	21	44	−23	−6	−29
Reducing the threat of war	18	68	−50	32	−18
Cutting out government red tape	11	57	−46	15	−31

SOURCE: Harris, 1973: 37.

clining. It is like asking a man to fly like a bird and criticizing him because he is not doing it.

SHIFTING MANAGERIAL PHILOSOPHIES

Managers of businesses, especially the larger ones, are aware of the new demands being made upon them. There are, of course, great variations among them about the extent to which they and their companies should respond. It is not too much to say, however, that the net result is an important change from past philosophy about how and for whom businesses should be managed. This is a subject which will be addressed in a number of later chapters. At this point, as evi-

Table 6–9.   Bank of America's Standards for Top Executives

1. Receptivity to change

"We cannot afford senior management personnel who . . . chart the corporation's course in terms of yesterday's realities. . . . To succeed at BankAmerica, a person must understand that it is not enough to react to change. It is not even enough to anticipate change. It is necessary to capitalize on change. . . ."

2. Awareness of people

". . . the senior manager today and tomorrow must understand in both mind and heart that new philosophical forces are changing the value systems of today's work force. The manager must see the reality behind the rising cry for job enrichment. There must be increased awareness of the growing demand, particularly from younger members of the work force, for greater freedom of action, for greater responsibility, or both."

3. Global outlook

". . . an international bank cannot develop its policies in anything but a global context. The management of this corporation must . . . possess the ability to see things in a worldwide context."

4. Sociopolitical sensitivity

". . . it is imperative that the senior corporate manager understand . . . socio-political forces. . . . While there are many of these forces, if I were asked today to rank them in terms of their importance . . . I would suggest this order: (1) consumerism; (2) demands of minorities; (3) demands of women, and (4) the crisis of the environment.

". . . we do not feel that anyone can aspire to a senior management position in BankAmerica . . . without an acute awareness of the impact these forces may have on our operations."

5. Market orientation

"Any individual who hopes to be a senior manager in BankAmerica must be attuned to the change in values evolving in the marketplace . . . nothing is taken for granted anymore, neither reliability, nor quality, nor service, nor value for the money. The consumer is demanding honest and factual information and what he perceives is a fair shake. . . . Almost every corporation dealing in the consumer market will have to take into consideration this new milieu."

6. Congeneric perception

"Four or five years ago, it was possible for a person who was simply . . . an astute and knowledgeable commercial banker to become a policy-maker. At this corporation and at most other large banks, this is no longer true. . . . Our management now . . . must be acutely aware of the opportunities presented by the one-bank holding company concept. Today's manager must understand the interrelationships of financial services, the opportunities in financial services other than commercial banking . . ."

7. Profit consciousness

"I have deliberately placed the most important dimension last. . . . I have left it until last because each of the other characteristics we seek in a

Table 6–9.   (Continued)

senior manager is necessary to preserve, protect, and enhance our ability to generate a profit. . . . It is our considered judgment . . . that without the other six dimensions, a management may run grave risks of having some good profit years and then some bad ones. . . .

"A manager at BankAmerica Corp. must know that profit is an obligation we owe to the 175,000 shareholders. . . . A manager must know in the fiber of his being that profit is the measure of the efficiency and effectiveness with which a corporation serves the needs of the public. . . . Our would-be manager must realize that for every hundred reasons given to cut a profit margin, probably no more than five or six are valid. . . .

"Finally, a potential senior manager must know that, while profitability is not the only yardstick for measuring performance, it is now and will be in the future the most important yardstick."

dence of this changing view of managerial responsibilities, I present in Table 6–9 seven criteria to be used in the selection of senior management which A. W. Clausen, president and chief executive officer of the BankAmerica Corporation, recently set forth for his company. These are not, of course, the sole criteria upon which advancement at the Bank of America is made. Personality, intellectual capability, and physical characteristics obviously would be considered. It is the general thrust of the criteria that highlights managerial concern and adaptability to the new environment which is of high interest here. Notice also that profit consciousness is mentioned last, not because it is unimportant but because the bank feels that without the first six qualities there is risk of lower profit.

CHANGING MANAGERIAL PRACTICES

Accompanying changes in the way in which managers think about their responsibilities are new managerial practices. There is no doubt that the ways in which things are done in business today, especially in the larger companies, are different from the past because of the changing environment in which business finds itself. Many of the current trends will accelerate. In my presidential speech before the Academy of Management I expressed my position in this regard as follows: ". . . future managerial practices and theory will have changed drastically in response to society's new demands that business improve the quality of life. However, the changes will be evolutionary—rapidly evolutionary—but not revolutionary. We today would recognize the changes in management practices and theories which will take place over the next few decades. The total picture, a decade or two in the future, however, will be substantially different from that of today" (1972:2).

Table 6–10. Recent Past Versus Future Managerial Practices

RECENT PAST	TOWARD FUTURE
Assumption that a business manager's sole responsibility is to optimize stockholder wealth	Profit still dominant but modified by the assumption that a business manager has other social responsibilities
Business performance measured only by economic standards	Application of both an economic and social measure of performance
Emphasis on quantity of production	Emphasis on quantity *and* quality
Authoritarian management	Permissive/democratic management
Short-term intuitive planning	Long-range comprehensive structured planning
Entrepreneur	Renaissance manager
Control	Creativity
People subordinate	People dominant
Financial accounting	Financial and human resources accounting
Caveat emptor	Ombudsman
Centralized decision-making	Decentralized and small group decision-making
Concentration in internal functioning	Concentration on external ingredients to company success
Dominance of solely economic forecasts in decision-making	Major use of social, technical, and political forecasts as well as economic forecasts
Business viewed as a single system	Business viewed as a system of systems within a larger social system
Business ideology calls for aloofness from government	Business-government cooperation and convergence of planning
Business has little concern for social costs of production	Increasing concern for internalizing social costs of production

SOURCE: Steiner, 1972(B): 4.

In Table 6–10 I have tried to picture briefly a few of the major business practices which are undergoing change and the direction in which they point. Other research has developed much more detail about possible changes [NICB, 1973 (A)] which will be considered in later chapters.

CONCLUDING OBSERVATIONS

It is abundantly clear from what has been said in this and the previous chapter that new and significant demands are being placed on corporations, particularly the larger ones. Business is an important change agent and is responding to societal pressures. To some people the pace of change is too slow. To some others it is too rapid. The better managers, I believe, feel that the better a corporation is able to reflect societal demands and adapt to them the more successful it is likely to be.

CHAPTER SEVEN Corporate
Powers:
Myth
and Reality

INTRODUCTION

Adolph Berle caught the paradox of the modern corporation nicely in these words:

> . . . the modern corporation as an institution is entitled to much more respect than it has frequently received. The dangers inherent in its use are also great enough to require serious attention. The possibilities of its continued development are, so far as one can see, unlimited. It is, in fact, an institution at a crossroad in history, capable of becoming one of the master tools of society—capable also of surprising abuse; worthy of the attention of the community as well as of scholars (Berle, 1954: 22).

Debate today swirls about whether the modern corporation is a basic institution whose fundamental attributes must be preserved in the national interest, or whether it is subject to such abusive exercise of powers that drastic reform is obligatory in the public interest. It is the purpose of this chapter to provide an overview of the powers of the modern large corporation and the many issues they raise. Subsequent chapters will take a deeper look at political, economic, and social powers of the corporation.

THE NATURE OF CORPORATE POWER

What is Power? Power is one of those value-laden words about which there is general agreement on definition but wide disagreement on meaning in an operational setting. Fundamentally, power is the ability of an individual, group, or organization to influence or determine the behavior of other individuals, groups, or organizations to conform to one's own wishes. There is some argument among scholars about whether power refers to actual influence, or a potential that can be used if the occasion arises, or both.

The mechanics of power, or the way in which it is exercised, are often confused with power. Authority may be viewed as the right to exercise power. Coercion can be either a form or a component of power. Dominance or domination is a form of power. Influence is a persuasive form of power. Force is a form or tool of power. Prestige is a consequence of power (Votaw, 1966).

The Concepts of Power In our society there are some strongly held views about the existence and the exercise of power. Traditionally, for instance, people in this country distrust those who hold or exercise power. As a result, few Americans profess to seek or admit having any power. Corporate presidents, for instance, speak of themselves as being "employees" or "agents" of someone or a group having power over them (Votaw, 1966: 76). There is also in the United States the concept that power is necessarily evil. A limited power supply concept asserts that if one person acquires power another will lose some. Another view is that power corrupts. This is expressed in Lord Acton's celebrated dictum that "power tends to corrupt and absolute power corrupts absolutely."

In analyzing these and other traditional concepts of power Votaw found that: "With no little trepidation, we have concluded that many of these beliefs are misleading, dangerous, useless, or do not conform to reality" (1966: 86). The modern concepts of power look more towards the functions performed by the posessor of power than did earlier concepts, cross a wider range of social experience than traditional power concepts, and see power as a force to resolve societal problems. The older power concepts were formed principally by political theorists; the modern ones are developed by sociologists, economists, lawyers, and social psychologists, as well as political scientists.

Votaw identifies three primary assumptions of modern concepts of power as follows:

1. That power is a resource of society which can be used to solve some of society's problems; that power is itself a source of order; though subject to abuse and corruption, power has a positive as well as a negative side.
2. That power is essentially a relationship between individual and individual, between individual and group, between group and group; that the relationship is reciprocal in nature, requiring "empowering responses" for its existence; that power is based, in large measure, "on interpersonal expectations and attitudes."
3. That power, like wealth, is not static in quantity but is constantly being produced and destroyed (1966: 81).

Modern power theory is breaking away from the old concept that institutions exercise power, to the reality that it is men in institutions who use power. It may be convenient to say "the company" did this or did that but it is not nearly as accurate as saying that the chairman of the board made the decision that led to this or to that. Modern power theory is developing a much sharper understanding of the way power in large business organizations is actually exercised. Adolph Berle was a pioneer and longtime scholar in this field (1932, 1954, 1959, 1963), but there were many others such as Selekman and Selekman (1956), Hamilton (1957), Mason (1960), Eells (1962), Moore (1962), and Cook and Peterffy (1966).

Spheres of Business Power There are six major spheres of business power as follows:

Economic power is the ability of the holder to influence events, activities, and people by virtue of control over economic resources, particularly property. It is an ability to influence or determine price, quality, production, and distribution of goods and resources.

Social and cultural power is the ability to influence social activities, values, and systems. It is the ability to influence social institutions, such as the family; and cultural values, mores, customs, life styles, and habits.

Power over the individual concerns the impact on individuals having direct relationships with a corporation (such as employees, stockholders, suppliers, and community members); and on the general characteristics of individuals as well as concepts of individualism in society.

Technological power is the influence over the thrust, rate, characteristics, and consequences of technology.

Environmental power relates to the impact of a company's actions on the physical environment such as air and water pollution, use of resources, and general community development.

Political power is the ability to influence public policies and laws.

These areas of power obviously are related. For instance, technological developments of corporations will influence their own economic power as well as social and cultural values. An affirmative use of political power can, of course, increase a corporation's economic power. A coherent view of corporate power of necessity looks at all six areas of power.

Levels of Analysis In each of these spheres it is possible to examine business power at different levels of application. For instance, the economic power of the business system as a whole may be examined. Power may be exercised in coalitions of business interests, or business and other interests. Then, of course, the power exercised by an individual firm or its components (departments or plants) may be studied. Finally, business power may be examined from the point of view of an individual business leader.

HOW MUCH POWER DOES BUSINESS HAVE?

There is no answer to this question either for the totality of business or for any particular company. In none of the spheres noted above, nor at any level, are there measures of power which are accurate and generally accepted. There are some quantitative measures in the economic sphere which some people use as indicators of power, such as share of the market or volume of assets relative to others, but there is no consensus. The state of the art of measurement of business power is not very advanced, hence there can be no conclusive answer to the question of how much power business really has.

Despite inability to measure accurately the power of business, or a firm, there is no doubt about the fact that great power rests in and is exercised by this institution. For instance, a large multinational company can, by its investments, radically alter the social and economic structure of a small country. It can, also, by its investments and treatment of cash flows, upset the United States balance of payments accounts and accentuate currency price fluctuations. A company that divests itself of a plant in a community in which it is a major employer is exercising a power of great importance to that community. When a company decides to allocate funds to support or prevent passage of legislation, it is exerting social and political power. The powers of a company over the physical conditions in which its employees work are obvious.

The use or restraint of power very often is a complex question. For example, some firms are faced with the question of whether they may remain neutral in a major public controversy in an area in which they have power. In September 1963, for example, racial turmoil developed in Birmingham, Alabama, where a plant of the U.S. Steel Corporation was the largest employer. Pressure was placed on Roger Blough, then chairman of the board of the company, to exert the power of his company to ease, if not resolve, the problems. The company sought to be neutral, and in the face of mounting criticisms Mr. Blough commented on his position at length. At a news conference, he said:

> Economic influence, which I presume to mean some kind of economic force to bring about some kind of change, is I think an improper matter upon which to criticize . . . United States Steel. . . . I do not either believe that it would be a wise thing for United States Steel to be other than a good citizen in a community, or to attempt to have its ideas of what is right for the community enforced upon that com-

munity by some sort of economic means. This is repugnant to me personally and I am sure it is repugnant to my fellow officers in United States Steel (*Congressional Record*, Nov. 4, 1963: A6864–65).

A *New York Times* editorial commented critically as follows:

> . . . he . . . has put some severe limits on the exercise of corporate responsibility, for he rejects the suggestion that U.S. Steel, the biggest employer in Birmingham, Alabama, should use its economic influence to erase racial tension. . . . This hands-off strategy surely underestimates the potential influence of a corporation as big as U.S. Steel, particularly at the local level. It could, without affecting its profit margins adversely or getting itself directly involved in politics, actively work with these groups in Birmingham trying to better race relations (October 30, 1963).

A large corporation influences community affairs whether it acts or does not act. There is frequently no position it can take that is really neutral. This is especially true when a company has had a history of using its powers in issues of its own choosing. One of the ironies of power is that he who wields it does not see his position as one of power so much as one of restraint. Presidents of large companies are not so much concerned with what powers they have, as with the powers of other groups which serve to restrain them. In addition, they are often painfully aware of strong and aggressive pressures on them to use the powers they do possess in ways in which they may be reluctant to move. Such was the position of Mr. Blough.

THE CONCENTRATION OF ECONOMIC POWER

We have always distrusted large size and concentrated power whether in public or private institutions. In much economic theory there is a yearning for a return to the simple economies of the past when businesses were small and free and unfettered competition existed. This is matched with a nostalgia for simpler times which, presumably, a diminution of concentrated economic power could return. The visible large business firms are, therefore, the targets of our traditional thinking stimulated by strong attacks against them, as will be noted shortly.

The most frequently used measure of the degree and extent of corporate economic power is concentration of assets. The first creditable compilation of concentration data was made by Berle and Means in 1932. They concluded, after an exhaustive study, that the 200 largest nonfinancial corporations in the United States in 1929 (less than seven-hundredths of 1 percent of all nonfinancial corporations) controlled nearly 50 percent of all corporate wealth and 22 percent of the national wealth (Berle and Means, 1932). Chapter 23 will show that this concentration has remained relatively stable or has risen sharply, depending upon the numbers used.

A comparison of the U.S. Steel Corporation in 1901, when it was the largest company in this country, with the giants of today gives some perspective on the extent of the growth of huge corporations. In 1901 the assets of U.S. Steel were placed at $1.4 billion (although the actual market value of outstanding stock was around $793 million) (Hacker, 1968: 436). General Motors is the largest manufacturing company in the nation today, so far as sales and profits are concerned. Its sales in 1972 were $28.3 billion, profits were $1.9 billion, and assets were $18.2 billion. (Among all manufacturing firms, its assets were exceeded only by Standard Oil of New Jersey, with a total of $20.3 billion.) The level of sales of General Motors is exceeded by the GNPs of only about 16 nations in the world, including the United States, and only a few states in this country. Three banks and two insurance companies have assets greater than Standard Oil (N.J.). In terms of assets, the largest company in the United States is American Telephone & Telegraph, with total assets in 1972 of $60.6 billion. U.S. Steel's assets were $4.9 billion in 1972 the eighth largest industrial company in the United States on the basis of that measure.

Large size is not solely a business phenomenon. The size and power of the federal government have increased significantly. Universities which twenty-five years ago were small or not even in existence now must cope with 30,000 to 50,000 students at one time.

To many people such sheer size is a perfectly acceptable index of monopoly power which not only should be feared but broken up. As indicated in Chapter 23, there was for some time statistical evidence to support the view that concentrated economic power was used to administer prices, raise prices, and reap excessive profits. There were those, however, who challeged this simple conclusion and said that it was not mere size nor how concentrated were sales in an industry in a handful of firms that was important. What was important was how they performed and behaved. More recently, as will be shown in Chapter 24, statistical evidence is accumulating that confirms the view that concentrated economic power has not been abused.

The facts are, however, that we do have concentrations of economic power which sometimes is used contrary to the public interest. It is generally being used in a way beneficial to society, however, because of the many pressures and constraints which exist. Enlightened public policy, of course, should assure that there is continuous vigilance in the exercise of this power in the public interest.

THE LITERATURE OF BUSINESS POWER

The literature dealing with business power has grown rapidly in recent years. A list of the older classics and some of the more recent writings include Barber, 1970; Berle and Means, 1932; Burnham, 1941; Dahl,

1962; Domhoff, 1967; Finn, 1969; Galbraith, 1956, 1967, 1973; Green and Moore, 1972; Jacoby, 1973; Josephson, 1934; Heilbroner, 1972; Hunter, 1963; Kolko, 1962; Lundberg, 1968; McConnell, 1966; Melman, 1970; Miliband, 1969; Mills, 1959; Mintz and Cohen, 1971; Nader and Green, 1973; Nossiter, 1964; Phelan and Pozen, 1972; Reich, 1970(A); Rose, 1967; and Weinstein, 1968. Some of this literature is conservative in tone and a frank defense of the classical powers of business. Other studies are written by confirmed critics of business and the biases show. Some studies are results of solid scholarship while others masquerade as scholarship or are frankly polemical. The purpose of some studies is to show business in a poor light while the intent of others is to present a reasonably balanced view of the nature of business power. Some studies deal only with abuses of power.

Any analysis of the literature on corporate power must deal with extremely difficult obstacles. For example, it is virtually impossible to find "representative" materials in the huge polyglot writings on the subject. There exists a methodological quagmire in which are found conflicting theoretical assumptions and tools for viewing power. Often the subject matter is not examined in a rigorous fashion. So, concludes Epstein: ". . . despite the volume of writing on the subject, our knowledge is fragmentary and often contradictory because our analytical tools are both rudimentary and dull and our access to the relevant materials is limited. As scholars we should, therefore, view pronouncements regarding business power with a skeptical eye, keeping in mind the existing state of the art in this field of analysis" (in Steiner, 1974).

All this leads to this conclusion: Beware of the premises, methodology, facts, and conclusions of writings dealing with business power.

Quite obviously this is no place to attempt any extended analysis of the literature. I do want to comment a little, however, on one basic concept of corporate power which has been widely accepted and which is of dubious validity.

DOES THE LARGE FIRM HAVE MONOLITHIC POWER?

"American society has been amalgamated into a single monolith of power—the corporate state—which includes both the private and public structures. This monolith is not responsible to democratic or even executive control. The Corporate State is mindless and irrational. It rolls along with a momentum of its own, producing a society that is evermore at war with its own inhabitants" (Reich, 1970(B)). This statement, elaborated at length in The Greening of America by Reich (1970(A)), was quoted to well over 3,000 businessmen who were asked: "In general, do you agree or disagree with Professor Reich's statement?" Following was the response:

Of all respondents (3,453 subscribers to the *Harvard Business Review* of which 94 percent were in business) 28 percent said they were in general agreement with the indictment.

Public relations managers were more in agreement with the quotation than the average respondent since 42 percent of them accepted it.

More than one third of the managers under thirty agreed with it.

At Harvard University, 46 percent of the business school students accepted the quotation. At a midwestern university the total was 51 percent (Ewing, 1971).

The significance of this response depends much upon whether the respondents accepted the quotation as a literal description of reality or an emotional reaction. The word "monolithic" means one massive undifferentiated whole, exhibiting solid uniformity and one harmonious pattern throughout. Even the most unskilled and unperceptive effort to find the truth can easily discover the distortion in Reich's statement if this definition is in mind. Why then do so many persons in business accept it? It is my guess, shared by Ewing in correspondence on the subject, that the high response represented an emotional reaction against the power of big business and big government. It was a reaction based more upon literature about power than from personal experience. It was a reaction predicated upon a "feel" of power in terms of its presence as contrasted with an actual observation of how power is used and felt.

Reich's views about the monolithic "corporate state," explained in detail in his book, is based heavily on Galbraith's *The New Industrial State*, a fact Reich acknowledges. Galbraith's views have been accepted not only by Reich but by others concerned with business power. Central in Galbraith's thesis is that group decision-making in large organizations has replaced the old entrepreneurs. This he calls the "technostructure" and it, "not the management, is the guiding intelligence—the brain—of the enterprise" (1967: 71). The technostructure, says Galbraith, is more interested in its own survival and sustained growth of the firm. Profits are secondary. To achieve its goals the technostructure engages in planning. It "reaches forward to control its markets and on beyond to manage the market behavior and shape the social attitudes of those, ostensibly, that it serves" (1967: 212). This he calls the "revised sequence."

There is in Galbraith's book much that is true about American industry but this particular description is a gross distortion of reality. The top management of most companies makes the major decisions, not some amorphous group. Styles of management differ among companies and so does the decision making process (Mintzberg, 1973; Silk, in Graubard, 1969).

I have been creating, reviewing, and writing about comprehensive corporate planning systems of business firms, large and small, for twenty years and do not recognize the so-called revised sequence of Galbraith or the "corporate state" of Reich (1970(B). Nor do other competent observers of the business scene (Scott, 1973; Bower, 1970).

In reality, Galbraith's description of corporate power and its use is much overstated. If his and comparable descriptions are taken as dangers to be avoided the results can be healthy; if they are accepted as literal truth the results can be unhealthy.

HAS CORPORATE POWER BEEN USED RESPONSIBLY?

There is no conclusive answer to this question. Some people answer it with a resounding yes and others with a cold no. If one looks at the economic accomplishments of the modern corporation and the ways in which individuals are treated it is easy to find plenty of support for an affirmative view (Jacoby, 1973). On the other hand, if one looks only at abuses, the warts on the anatomy of the corporation, the view is just the opposite (Heilbroner, 1972).

During the latter part of the nineteenth and early twentieth centuries, the practice was to use power in the self-interest, narrowly defined, of the possessor. There were, as a result, outrageous abuses of corporate power which over time led to laws designed to prevent future abuses. These laws today provide a major restraint on the use of corporate power in ways contrary to the public interest. There has been for a long time, and there is today, an obviously growing trend, particularly among the larger companies, to use corporate powers in the social interest. An assessment of how and why this trend has come about will be given in detail in later chapters.

WILL POWER BE CONTROLLED IN THE FUTURE?

It is, of course, comforting that in recent years economic power in large companies has generally been used responsibly. Will it be in the future? There are a number of potent reasons for believing that corporate powers will continue to be used responsibly, even more responsibly than now. Berle sets forth the power of public consensus in preventing unsuitable exercises of corporate power (1959: 110–16). I think this force will be strong and effective in ensuring the responsible exercise of power by those who hold it. Berle says that the public consensus follows the force of "the conclusion of careful university professors, the reasoned opinions of specialists, the statements of responsible journalists, and at times the solid pronouncements of respected politicians. . . . These, and men like them, are thus the real tribunal to which the American system is finally accountable" (1959: 113). They are numerous and they are at times strong. Collectively, they help the public to develop consensuses and establish standards of performance, the violation of which can lead to serious consequences for unscrupulous business managers.

So long as the general values of the managerial group are tuned to the achievement of priority social objectives, the concentration of power in the large companies is likely to be used responsibly toward such ends. Should American society become controlled by a small elite with objectives different from those we now hold, the great concentrations of economic power could be used toward other ends. Such authoritarianism, of course, is contrary to political democracy, and it is to be hoped will always be rejected by the American people.

Business leaders themselves have been taught certain general philosophical and ethical premises in schools, universities, and churches which tend to lead to the responsible exercise of power. It is also true that chief executives of large companies, despite their assertions to the contrary, are often conformists. They are conformists to the general values of their group, and in the immediate past this has been for responsible use of their power as compared with a "public be damned" attitude. Some writers think, and I agree with them, that an increased professionalization of management will push managers toward a more responsible exercise of power. There are those, too, with whom I disagree, who think that a viable self-accountability of management plus professionalization is sufficient to bring the needed degree of responsible exercise of power (Gaddis, 1964). While this may be true today, there can be no guarantee that this alone is enough.

These forces are and will be reinforced by the diffusion of power in our pluralistic society; by the existence of other major power centers such as universities, labor unions, agricultural cooperatives, and many governments; by continuous surveillance of self-interest groups; and by expanding perspectives of top business leaders about the social responsibilities of their companies.

Three major checks on power are thus discernible. The general atmosphere in society is resistant to the excessive power and its use. Displays of power are apt to result in legislative restraint. Power will remain insecure and insecure power is restrained power.

THE ISSUE OF LEGITIMACY

Legitimacy refers to the rightful possession of power. Fundamentally, the source of power conferred upon corporations is the authority granted by society over the ownership of property. Society has accepted laws, beliefs, and customs associated with the exercise of powers over possessed property. So far as the corporation is concerned, the stockholders as owners are conferred powers over the use of their property to conduct a business by buying and selling commodities, hiring workers, and attending to other matters concerned with production for profit. In the simplest terms, the stockholders elect the board of directors, who in turn choose the managers, who in turn operate the business under the policy direction of the board in the interests of the stockholders. In an even simpler case, the stockholders may be the directors and managers of a corporation. In both instances it is clear that legally and actually the managers of the enterprise are accountable to the stockholders who are the owners.

In the large corporations of today this simple chain of relationships does not exist. By virtue of the diffusion of stock ownership and the comparatively small proportion of the total stock owned by one individual or group, managements in effect control property they do not own. Futhermore, although the stockholders theoretically choose management, the fact is that they are completely unable to do so and do not, except in rare instances, even try. The general procedure is for managers to solicit, and get, proxy statements from shareholders which are then used to elect directors. Directors generally are chosen by management and elected legally by these proxies. As a result, the managements of many large companies are, in the words of Berle (1959), "automatic self-perpetuating oligarchies."

This situation raises important questions of legitimacy: Who chooses these men to exercise the powers over the property they control? The answer is simple: they choose themselves. To whom, then, are they responsible? The answer to this question is far from clear.

With these developments has come a change in the nature of the property owned by stockholders. In the simple case of a small corporation, the stockholders' property is possessory when the owner manages the property. In the large corporation controlled by managers, possessory property is broken into two parts. One is "passive receptive," which is held by stockholders. They receive benefits from the use of the property, but do not control it. The other is that over which management has control. The manager is the real possessor of the property. He has possession without title; the stockholder has title without possession (Berle, 1969). It is true, of course, that in thousands of corporations where there is little diffusion of stock ownership the older model of corporate authority still exists, but in more and more of the largest corporations, the newer model is the more realistic. Power exists without mandate, a situation which, says Berle, exists because no one has come up with a better plan.

In the past, the accountability of managers was to the source of power, but this channel is not at all clear in the management-controlled companies. Today there is only a weak linkage between mandate of power and the exercise of it. So, to whom are they accountable? If, as Berle contends, this situation is accepted by a public consensus, then it is to the public that these managers are accountable. This opens up an entirely different set of questions.

It is perfectly clear that in the largest corporations we are in need of better guidelines to the uses of power. But, as Berle points out, the worst that can be said for this situation is that it is not very satisfactory. The best that can be said is that it has worked very well, much better in fact than in many instances where there has been concentrated stockholder control. Directors of corporations whose control is held by hundreds of thousands or millions of stockholders which are widely scattered "probably pay greater attention to . . . the public consensus than do the holders of undisputed control" (Berle, 1959: 109).

PART THREE

Business and Changing Values

CHAPTER EIGHT

Changing Values in Society

INTRODUCTION

The fundamental determinants of the relationships between business and society are the values held in society. Some major value linkages between business and society were treated in previous chapters, but the subject is so important that this chapter will delve more deeply into it.

Values are not fixed and immutable; they change, and as they undergo change, society and its institutions change. It is not too much to say that the destiny of a society is determined by and is reflected in its values.

While the connections between business and social values have never been simple, even in primitive societies, there have been few if any times when the interrelationships have been more complex than they are today. Seldom, if ever, in our history have so many values changed more rapidly than in the past few years. Business has been a major catalyst in stimulating this change, and it will in turn feel the effects of the new value patterns. It is the purpose of this chapter to describe the meaning of values, the ways in which value change is brought about, the role of business in this change, the impact of value changes on business, and the resulting issues in business-society relationships.

WHAT IS MEANT BY VALUES?

There is no generally accepted definition or classification of values. The definitions given here are therefore by no means universally accepted, but are rather a reflection of recent advances in value theory.

Values establish the standards by which the importance of everything in society is judged. All men seek some ends, ends that represent those things they want above all else. Their value systems establish not only those ends, but the means to achieve them. Values are settled habits of regarding, and attitudes toward, events or phenomena. They include that which an individual, a group, or a nation may prize and desire in or for himself, his society, his nation, his culture, his fellowmen, or his environment. Values are based on a belief that, when applied, they will benefit or penalize some individual, group, or institution. They are held for a reason—a benefit—and hence are different from a personal whim, taste, or liking. In this light, values are *conceptions of desirable states of affairs* that are utilized in selective conduct as *criteria* for preference or choice or as *justifications* for proposed or actual behavior" (Williams, 1967: 23). Values change in individuals and in groups when evidence shows that they do not yield expected benefits. (Baier and Rescher, 1969).

At any time the values of a society are those "so generally acknowledged and widely diffused throughout the society that explicit, overt appeal to them can well be expected from publicly recognized spokesmen for values: newspaper editorialists, graduation exercise speakers, religio-moral sermonizers, political orators, and the like" (Baier and Rescher, 1969: 73). A register of such American values is given in Exhibit 8–1. These are values for the entire society and not those espoused by one group, such as businessmen, lawyers, Methodists, or Southerners, although these groups may cherish some of them. Nor are the values in Exhibit 8–1 held only by people as personal attitudes. They are espoused by and for people in general. We can say this while recognizing that there is and can be strong dissent among certain individuals and groups about some of these values.

There are value-belief clusters. For instance, associated with freedom are law and order, individualism, and government controls. Williams says there are fifteen major clusterings in the American culture, as follows: (1) activity and work, (2) achievement and success, (3) moral orientation, (4) humanitarianism, (5) efficiency and practicality, (6) science and secular rationality, (7) material comfort, (8) progress, (9) equality, (10) freedom, (11) democracy, (12) external conformity, (13) nationalism and patriotism, (14) individual personality, (15) racism and related group superiority (1967: 33).

Exhibit 8–1.   A Tentative Register of American Values

I. *Self-oriented values*
   A. Personal "material" welfare (the right to life and the pursuit of happiness)
      1. Health (physical and mental well-being)
      2. Economic security and well-being ("materialism" and the American way of life)
      3. Personal security (stability of the conditions of life)
   B. Self-respect (the right to be treated *as a person* and *as a member in good standing of the community*; honor, honorableness)
   C. Self-reliance (self-sufficiency, rugged individualism and the pioneer tradition)
   D. Personal liberty (the right to endeavor to "shape one's own life," to work out major facets of one's own life," to work out major facets of one's own destiny and to go one's own way)
      1. Freedom (from interference)
      2. Privacy
      3. Property rights
   E. Self-advancement ("success," ambition, diligence)
   F. Self-fulfillment (and "the pursuit of happiness")
   G. Skill and prowess
      1. The intellectual virtues (intelligence, education, know-how, realism, practicality, versatility)
      2. The physical virtues (strength, dexterity, endurance, good appearance, cleanliness)
      3. The virtues of the will (strengths of character)
         a. Readiness for hard work (industriousness)
         b. Toughness (fortitude, endurance, bravery, courage)
         c. Initiative and activism (the "go getter" approach)
         d. Self-control (temperateness, sobriety)
         e. Perseverance and steadfastness
      4. Competence (pride of workmanship)
      5. Inventiveness and innovativeness
      6. Initiative (the "self-starter")
      7. Well-informedness (access to information, being "in the know")
      8. Faith ("believing in something" including "having a sense of values")
      9. Appreciation and appreciativeness (of "the good things of life")
II. *Group-oriented values*
   A. Respectability (group acceptance, avoidance of reproach, good repute, conformity, the "done thing" and the "herd instinct")
   B. Rectitude and personal morality (honesty, fairness,

Exhibit 8–1. (Continued)

probity, reliability, truthfulness, trustworthiness—the "man of honor")

C. Reasonableness and rationality (objectivity)

D. The domestic virtues (love, pride in family role, providence, simplicity, thrift, prudence)

E. The civic virtues (involvement, good citizenship, law-abidance, civic pride—the "greatest little town" syndrome)

F. Conscientiousness
   1. Devotion to family, duty
   2. Personal responsibility and accountability
   3. Devotion to principle (especially of one's religion—"the godfearing man")

G. Friendship and friendliness
   1. Friendship proper
   2. Loyalty (to friends, associates)
   3. Friendliness, kindliness, helpfulness, cooperativeness, and courteousness (the good scout; "getting along with people")
   4. Fellow-feeling (compassion, sympathy, and "love of one's fellows")
   5. Gregariousness
   6. Receptivity (openness, patience, "the good listener")
   7. Personal tolerance ("live and let live," "getting along with people")
   8. Patience

H. Service (devotion to the well-being of others)

I. Generosity (charity, openhandedness)

J. Idealism (belief in human solutions to human problems)

K. Recognition (getting due public credit for the good points scored in the game of life; success and status)

L. Forthrightness (frankness, openness, sincerity, genuineness; keeping things "above board," the fair deal)

M. Fair play (the "good sport")

III. *Society-oriented values*

A. Social welfare (indeed, "social consciousness" as such)

B. Equality
   1. Tolerance
   2. "Fair play," fairness
   3. Civil rights

C. Justice (including legality, proper procedure, recourse)

D. Liberty (the "open society"; the various "freedoms")

E. Order (public order, "law and order")

Exhibit 8–1.   (Continued)

F. Opportunity ("land of opportunity" concept; the square deal for all)
G. Charity (help for the "underdog")
H. Progressivism, optimism (faith in the society's ability to solve its problems)
I. Pride in "our culture" and "our way of life"

IV. *National-oriented values*

A. The patriotic virtues (love of country, devotion to country, national pride)
1. National freedom and independence
2. National prosperity and national achievement
3. Patriotism and national pride
4. Concern for the national welfare
5. Loyalty (to country)
6. Chauvinism (nationalism, pride in national power and preeminence)

B. Democracy and "the American way"
C. "Public service" in the sense of service of country (the nation)

V. *Mankind-oriented values*

A. The "welfare of mankind"
1. Peace
2. Material achievement and progress
3. Cultural and intellectual achievement and progress

B. Humanitarianism and the "brotherhood of man"
C. Internationalism
D. Pride in the achievements of "the human community"
E. Reverence for life
F. Human dignity and the "worth of the individual"

VI. *Environment-oriented values*

A. Esthetic values (environmental beauty)
B. Novelty

SOURCE: Reprinted with permission of The Macmillan Company from *Values and the Future* by Kurt Baier and Nicholas Rescher (eds.). Copyright © 1969 by The Free Press, a Division of The Macmillan Company, pp. 92–95.

Values can and do conflict. The value of full employment of resources conflicts with the value of price stability. Values associated with environmental pollution clean up are today conflicting with technology, individual rights, job security values, and monetary values. Efficiency as a value is often in conflict with individualism.

Throughout this chapter our concern is with values that seem to be held rather generally in society. These values are necessarily abstract and stated at a high level of generalization. They are a composite of individual values—and yet they are more than that. Individuals in society influence one another; they cooperate and work toward common ends. Their values, therefore, reflect their subjective preferences, but the common values held by society collectively are also reflected in their attitudes and actions.

A MODEL OF VALUE CHANGE

Numerous illustrations of important interrelationships between business and the values of society were given in previous chapters. It is time now to explain further how each can and does affect the other. Figure 8–1 presents a simple conceptual model of what in reality is a very complex process of mutual influence. It focuses attention on new technology because this is a major way in which business affects social values, as will be explained shortly. This is not the whole story by any means. Business affects many other things in society which in turn influence value change. Also, many other things going on in and outside society influence values in society. These interrelationships Figure 8–1 reveals.

Beginning at the left, the chart shows that a variety of forces and institutions influence research and development, from which springs technology. For instance, the competitive environment of a large technically-oriented company such as Union Carbide or du Pont de Nemours will stimulate their research and development activity. This is not the only driving force within a company. There are the value systems of top managers, directors of research, and individual scientists and engineers. Because of political, military, intellectual, economic, and other pressures, government is a major stimulator of research and development. Its influence is felt predominantly through financial support to business institutions to undertake research and development, although government itself also produces new technology independently of business. Furthermore, government supports educational institutions, which are major contributors to new knowledge leading to new technology. Figure 8–1 also shows private individual effort which is not connected with any of the other three institutions.

It is easy to see that business, stimulated by economic pressures and government support, strengthened by knowledge developed in the academic world and by private individual efforts, is a major producer of research and development leading to new technology. The model shows also that economic, social, political, military, religious, and intellectual forces directly influence and are affected by the development and use of new technology. These forces feed back into the process and influence both the volume and direction of research and development. Russia's Sputnik, for instance, brought about a major change in the United States space program. Historically, economic

Figure 8–1.   A Conceptual Model of Major Forces Causing and Influenced by Changing Values

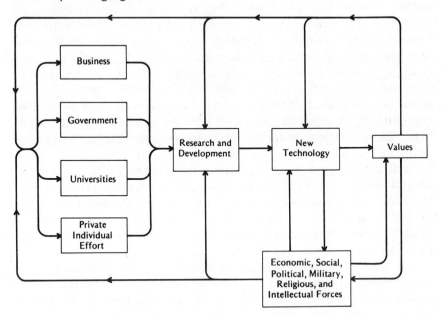

forces have been more prominent than others in directing the scope of new research and development into new technology. More recently, however, military and political forces have become of greater significance. Figure 8–1 also shows that the new technology, as well as other changes in society, affects the values of society. The ways in which this phenomenon takes place will be elaborated upon below. Once values are changed, the impact is felt throughout the model in research and development scope and direction; new technology and its uses; and social, religious, and other forces in society.

CONCEPTUAL TYPES OF VALUE CHANGE

A first approach to understanding how changes in the values of society may take place is to look at the many ways, conceptually, that this phenomenon can occur. This and the next section follow the work of Nicholas Rescher (Baier and Rescher, 1969: 68–81).

Sometimes a small group or minority of people may subscribe to a value and, as a result of their efforts and changing events, the value may be redistributed throughout society and become accepted generally. Today's rising consumer expectations (Chapter 15), for example, began with a small group of outraged citizens and spread rapidly as a result of their efforts. At any one time events can occur which

will serve to emphasize or deemphasize values. Some values are so
solidly held that only catastrophic events will change them. Others
are less strongly held and readily alter as events change. Values about
the personal dignity of individuals, for example, are very deeply entrenched in our society and change only slowly. Values associated
with the roles of individuals in organizations, however, are now
changing rapidly. Individuals hold some sets of values in a scale of
importance representing the degree of commitment to them. The position on the scale is determined by many factors, such as cost of
commitment, changes in conceived benefits derived from a commitment, and alterations in technology which create alternative ways of
doing things. As changes take place in society, rescaling of values by
individuals and groups occurs. Values generally hold within a given
area of application, but may be extended in coverage. The value of
legal and political equality, for example, has recently been much extended to include the rights of black Americans and other minority
groups. This is value redeployment, or the redefinition of area of application of old values.

A type of value shift which is sensitive to social, economic, or
technological change concerns the standards of implementation of a
value. Existing standards for application can be altered or new standards introduced. For instance, people still hold in high priority values
of safety, speed, reliability, and comfort in transportation. But they
expect these to be realized in higher degree in an airplane than they
did in the Model T Ford of the 1930s. The minimum they accept has
risen greatly with the jet airplane. Values associated with a man's
standard of living, especially the minimum, have been continuously
reevaluated in this country in recent years as per capita income has
grown and been more equitably distributed. Value implementation
retargeting takes place when a person or group changes the target or
objective to achieve an underlying value. For instance, the value of
maintaining competition can be implemented through a number of
means, such as preventing price discrimination, stopping collusive
price actions, and preventing monopoly.

Modes of upgrading and corresponding modes of downgrading
can be discerned for each of these varieties of change. For instance,
value acquisition would be upgrading and value abandonment would
be downgrading; increased redistribution would be upgrading and
decreased redistribution would be downgrading; rescaling upward
would be upgrading and rescaling downward would be downgrading, and so on.

CAUSAL ORIGINS OF VALUE CHANGE

As noted in the accompanying model a major cause of societal value
change is technology. A fundamental reason is that technology pro-

vides new options to people and as a result brings shifts in their values (Mesthene, 1970, 1968). For example, the automobile was instrumental in changing the way of life in this country because of new options it gave people (Jones, 1972). The automobile has upgraded values concerned with pleasure, time, self-reliance, power, privacy, novelty, convenience, and human dignity. It has downgraded love and affection, reasonableness and rationality, devotion to family, law and order, freedom from interference, natural beauty, reverence for life, and courtesy (Hazard, in Baier and Rescher, 1969: 325). As everyone knows there are today great changes being made in values concerning the automobile. As someone has said the past love affair of Americans with the automobile is over.

Technology has made possible high urbanization in modern society which, in turn, has brought a chain of forces to alter older values. For instance, downgraded are such values as natural beauty, tranquility, independence, closeness to nature, privacy, and love of mankind. Upgraded are pleasure, materialism, interdependence, convenience, power, and novelty. New medical discoveries have lengthened the life span and thereby changed significantly ways of life and values around the world. New technologies also bring new organizational arrangements which in turn start a chain of value change. The shift from the household to the factory system during the Industrial Revolution is one illustration. There are, however, significant changes being made in today's business structures because of technology change (Jacoby, 1962).

Value change can take place indirectly or derivatively, as a result of changes in other values. For instance, an upward rescaling in the value of the role of a corporation in society will indirectly affect the subsidiary value of the obligation of management toward the interests of the stockholder.

New information brings changes in values. For instance, evidence that automation was not going to result in widespread unemployment altered national values with respect to the protection of workers from this type of innovation. Values are changed by ideological and political events. The rise of the Nazi party in Germany in the mid-1930s brought widespread value changes in that society and eventually in many others. Early political ideologies in the United States concerned with the benefits of mass education eventually broke down resistance to public educational institutions. Value erosion can result from boredom, disillusionment, or reaction. When a value is achieved fully, and possibly with surfeit, it may be downgraded—for example, economic security in a welfare state. Or, it may lose its savor in a hopeless situation—for instance, national independence in an emerging nation that finds itself in chaos. In the past, in the United States most basic values changed slowly and in conformity with an overriding value that held slow value change in high esteem. Today, change is being more and more accepted as desirable in itself. One result is an erosion of values which have been unchanged for centuries.

The mere increase in population affects values concerned with privacy and association. Shifts in population from agricultural to urban areas bring with them a chain of consequences altering values. Fundamentally, although not completely, many demographic changes are facilitated or permitted by technological developments. The substantial increase of young people as a proportion of total population has had a major impact on values about them and their role in society. This growth was not due to technological forces. On the other hand, the affluence of this society fostered values in the younger generation which, when coupled with values associated with their role in society, have been of importance in stimulating changes in values throughout society.

TODAY'S CHANGING VALUES

There is controversy about the depth and thrust of today's changing values. There are some who feel strongly that values in society are changing so deeply that the inevitable result will be a revolution (Reich, 1970). Others feel that "there are a few inches of topsoil that blow around, but then you hit rock" (Roche, 1969). There are, of course, many views standing between these two poles.

Various opinion polls can be used to support a variety of views. For instance, one Gallup poll found that 52 percent of the American public thought they were conservative, 34 percent said they were liberal, and 14 percent had no opinion (1970). The conservatism of the average American was confirmed in another poll reported under the title "It's a Wyeth, not a Warhol, World" (Wells, 1970).

On the other hand, various polls reveal significant value changes among certain elements of the population, especially certain youths. For instance, Yankelovich polled so-called practical-minded and forerunner students. Among the latter group there were reported some rather significant value changes (*Fortune*, 1969). But, among youths who do not go to college there is a much lower degree of deviation from traditional values (*Life*, 1971).

One perspective on changing values is offered by Mitchell (1971). He says Americans can be divided broadly into three kinds of people. Each type has a markedly different set of needs, values, and beliefs. The first is the "man-against-society model." The central need of this group revolves around survival and security. People in it highly value economic and physical well-being, solidarity, law and order. Their world revolves around struggle, conflict, fear, and anxiety. In this group one finds the disfranchised, the minorities, the poor and un-successful.

The second group seeks homeostasis, or stability with the envi-ronment. People in this group try to achieve stability with environ-ment. They see for themselves a good chance for a satisfactory life. Their values are materialistic, comforming, competitive, hard work-ing, possession-conscious, and achieving. In this group are the suc-cessful middle and upper classes who have sufficient means to lead a "good" life.

The third group are the unfolders. These people are seeking self-fulfillment or self-actualization to use Maslow's phrase. They are hu-manistic, democratic, self-reliant, and have a reverence for life and beauty. Here one finds rebelling students as well as leaders in busi-ness, government, and the professions.

Mitchell "guestimates" that today about 25 percent of the popu-lation is in the first group, 65 to 70 percent in the second group, and 2 or 3 percent, but not over 5 percent, in the third group. So, if he is at all close to the mark, and I think he is, one's views of today's chang-ing general value system are different depending upon where he is looking.

With respect to business, however, as noted previously, values are changing significantly. Among all these groups there is disaffec-tion with business. There is some comfort to business, however, I think in the above surveys since they indicate no great upheaval in the basic societal value system. But this is not static. As Ewing has observed: "The social, cultural, and political environment of industry is changing. The change is not sharp or tangible but subtle and ubiq-uitous—more like the profound alternation of water and sky that sailors call a 'sea change' than like a line storm. It is taking place not only in the United States but also in many other nations. . . ." (1971: 149).

WHAT OF THE FUTURE?

In recent years there has been an explosion of interest in and specu-lation about the future. "Futurism" is the word applied to it. The magazine *Futurist* is devoted to this subject and all the relevant refer-ences to the literature can be found in it.

Forecasting Methods Among the more frequently used analytical methods to forecast future changing values are the following. The first is extrapolation, or the extension of present trends with appropriate modification for future anticipations. Second are analytical forecast-ing models which survey future causal factors and calculate their impact on values, or take given values and determine the impact of future causal factors on them. Third are questionnaire techniques which are designed to get from informed persons their considered judgments about future developments. The most popular of these techniques for forecasting values is the Delphi (Gordon and Helmer, 1964; and Dalkey and Helmer, 1963).

Cost-Benefit Analysis A key concept in all value forecasts is cost-benefit analysis. If one holds a value, he expects that its realization will benefit someone (himself or others). But actions reflecting the commitment will also cost something. Analysis of this cost-benefit relationship can yield conclusions about possible changes on each side and consequent revisions in values as one side or the other alters.

Costs may be considered in terms of money, time, effort, or discomfort. Benefits are of many more types—convenience, comfort, pleasure, quality of life, leisure, and so on—and are generally much harder to calculate than are costs. At best, the cost-benefit equation of forces operating on values can be only roughly approximated (Baier and Rescher, 1969: 76–88). Cost will have an influence on the maintenance of a value. To illustrate, privacy becomes increasingly expensive as urbanization advances. When the cost gets too high, the value is downgraded relative to others, or lower standards may be accepted.

In 1970–1972 there was a rapid escalation in the value attached to clean air and water. In 1973 there was some decline in that value as the costs of achieving it began to become better known. If costs fall to very low levels, there is a tendency to depreciate the value. This happened to lighting from electric power before the emergencies of 1973.

Correspondingly, changes in benefits alter both the intensity with which values are held as well as their position on a scale. Benefit reflects a need for a value, and as need changes, so will values. For instance, the demand for scientific and intellectual skills has increased greatly in recent years and, as a result, the associated values have risen in importance. In an affluent society, the benefits of wealth decline and change attitudes about riches. In sum, changes in environment from whatever cause alter the cost-benefit elements of values and bring about an upgrading or a downgrading.

Evaluations of change can begin with a value and proceed with an analysis of changes of environment likely to alter the cost-benefit equation of the value. Costs and benefits of value can also be analyzed in relation to other values. For example, a higher value placed on leisure may lead to a search for self-fulfillment that increased education can help to satisfy. For certain types of education, such as home study, educational TV, and university extension courses, costs are quite low and much below benefits for millions of people. If this type of education helps individuals to get desirable jobs, it tends to bring an upgrading in educational values.

Evaluations of change can begin with a causal force, such as technology, and proceed to examine its impact on values. Consider a possible system with the following characteristics: a computerized, small-car, very low-cost mass transportation system by means of which individuals have easy access to cars, push a button for destination, experience no delays over two minutes, and ride in noiseless comfort at great speed. Such a system would upgrade values associated with personal dignity, convenience, comfort, rationality, and peace. Perhaps values associated with beauty might be enhanced if the system were esthetically pleasing. If the rider were able to read in comfort, values associated with intellectual virtues would also be upgraded. On the other hand, certain values might be downgraded, such as self-reliance, individualism, and privacy.

SOME PROJECTIONS

The Delphi technique has been used to develop a consensus about changing values in the United States from today to the year 2000, and several of the major conclusions are of interest here (Baier and Rescher, 1969: 134–47). First, there is likely to be a continuing commitment to present-day values, except for a greater emphasis upon social and a lesser emphasis upon religious values. Second, some substantial changes are expected in specific values. For instance, increased emphasis is anticipated in each of the following value groupings (in descending order of increased emphasis):

> Material (personal comfort, economic security)
> Social (social justice, service to others)
> International (the brotherhood of man, peace)
> Intellect (intelligence, wit)
> Esthetic (attractiveness in design of furniture, etc.)
> Other-regarding values (service to others, tolerance)
> Humanitarian ("idealism," human dignity)
> Personal (self-reliance, intelligence)
> Self-oriented (success, prestige)
> Self-regarding values (prudence, self-advancement)
> Character (conscientiousness, reasonableness)
> Prowess (fitness, physical skill)

Those value groupings where decreased emphasis is expected are (in order of decreased emphasis):

Religious (piety, self-sacrifice)

Parochial (family pride, fraternity loyalties)

National (patriotism, national pride)

Local (civic pride)

Spiritual (reverence for life)

Third, the results are optimistic in the sense that in the great majority of cases anticipated changes are considered to be "a good thing" by the respondents. Exceptions are the decline in self-reliance and devotion to family. Finally, important variations in values are anticipated from developments in technology, political-economic-sociological developments, education and psychotechnics, biotechnics, and economic-technological developments. So far as the first group is concerned, the respondents seemed to think that value schemes have already discounted the potential effects of these developments.

Wilson has identified a few major value changes which he feels will alter public and private values. They are:

An emphasis on the "quality of life," from the quality of products to the quality of environment.

A growing belief that leisure is acceptable in its own right.

A rejection of authoritarianism.

A growing belief in pluralism, decentralization, participation, and involvement.

An increased public impatience, or lower frustration tolerance, with economic hardship, such as poverty and unemployment and with social injustice.

A move from the concept of independence to interdependence.

From the satisfaction of private material needs, to meeting public needs.

From primary emphasis on technical efficiency, to more social justice and equity.

From the preservation of a systems status quo to the development and acceptance of change (1971).

Finally, Mitchell projects that within the coming generation Americans falling within his "unfolding" group will rise to 15 or 20 percent. If this takes place, he says, ". . . this nation will be launched upon a societal phase-change of momentous proportions" (1971: 219). I think the thrust of his forecast is correct but with lower percentages.

In the succeeding parts of this book further changes in social values in different aspects of the business-society interrelationship will be examined. Before going on, however, a few comments about evolving issues are in order.

EMERGING ISSUES FOR BUSINESS-SOCIETY RELATIONSHIPS

The preceding analysis makes clear that business affects and is affected by society's values. Cursory examination of the results of forecasts of value changes brings to light modifications which will have a bearing upon business and the way it relates to society. The implications of a more educated society, for instance, will ramify through many business activities. Altering expectations of individuals entering business, as well as a more literate society, will necessitate different managerial and organizational arrangements. Downgrading of self-reliance, conscientiousness, and motivation to work, if actually experienced, will be matters of concern to business. Increased emphasis on economic security, social justice, and service to others will undoubtedly move government to take actions having a bearing on business, such as increasing the production of public goods relative to private goods. All these issues, and many more, will be treated at some length in the remainder of this book.

Traditionally, businesses have been regarded as economic institutions. Now they are, particularly the larger ones, also being seen by some observers as social and political systems. This opens up the door for the entrance of a whole new set of value systems about them (Bell, 1973; Elbing and Elbing, 1967; Galbraith, 1964). Under the hammer blows of rapidly developing technology, and influenced by such attributes of this society as affluence, poverty in the midst of plenty, growing humanism, and rising demands for social justice, it is easy to see how impressive changes in the values of large segments of society will occur. These values will reflect the rising needs of the new supersociety into which this nation is evolving. On the other hand, the traditional society made possible the supersociety as a result of the fundamental values to which the society adhered. For large segments of society, these values will continue to hold their traditional importance and relationships one with another.

The outcome of the struggle between these two monolithic value systems will determine the fate of the supersociety. If the supersociety destroys the values of traditional society upon which it rests, it will destroy itself. On the other hand, if the traditional society does not adjust to the needs of the supersociety, it will collapse. And the relationships between business and society will become embroiled in this struggle. I am optimistic about the outcome. We see increasing signs that our traditional values are changing to accommodate to the new world we have created. They are not, perhaps, changing rapidly enough to satisfy some groups, but they are changing. There is no major block of society implacably opposed to the values of other major blocks. There are only minorities at the extremes in polarized opposition. Society as a whole seems to be mixing a new blend of old and new values in new scales. There will doubtless be a period of struggle, but we must strive to assure that this nation will retain in the latter part of this century its unique capability to change for the better.

CHAPTER NINE

Business Ideologies

INTRODUCTION

Because business has always been a dominant force in this society, its ideologies have had a strong influence on public policy, the ways in which businessmen conducted their businesses and themselves, and the methods they used to control their environment. One cannot understand the evolving relationships between business and society—past, present, or future—without some comprehension of changing business ideologies.

Business ideology is anchored in the basic value system of society; however, it is not the same thing. An ideology, as will be explained shortly, is a rather different set of views held for a different purpose than the basic value system generally found throughout society. This chapter will summarize current business ideologies, explain their basic nature and purposes, show how they are rooted in the basic values held by society, comment on their inconsistencies and the gaps which can be found in them, describe some competing ideologies, and explain why business ideologies have been rather stable over a long period of time. It is not my purpose to argue with or evaluate any particular part of the ideologies, although some comments will be made about their applicability in today's and tomorrow's societies.

WHAT IS A BUSINESS IDEOLOGY?

A business ideology is the content of the patterns of thought characteristic of the business classes. It is their system of beliefs, values, and objectives as related to business. In this respect, ideology is synonymous with business creed and philosophy. An ideology has several important characteristics. It is selective in subject matter, in that it does not seek to cover every facet of business interest. Public expressions of the ideology generally are only of those elements of it having some popular acceptance. It is based on intuitive views, education, logical argument, and subjective values. More often than not, it is a reflection of self-interest. Business ideology, like other ideologies, is often expressed in language designed to appeal to the emotions of the listeners. Usually the language is simple, if not oversimplified. Ideology in business, as elsewhere, often tolerates no competing ideology or appeal to facts. An ideology is designed to serve the purposes of its advocates. It also satisfies the human desire for explanation and interpretation of experience.

Generally speaking, ideologies may be designed to fill a number of purposes of the groups espousing them. So far as the business ideology is concerned, it might be said to fill such needs of the business group as these: to justify and rationalize the existence and the actions of business; to describe ideals to be sought; to establish standards for judging or appraising business organizations, their policies, and their leaders; and to provide an explanation of causal factors in the event of failure (Monsen, 1963: 9–10).

Sutton, Harris, Kaysen, and Tobin, in a masterful study of the business ideology, advanced the "strain" theory in these words:

> Briefly, our thesis is that the content of the business ideology can best be explained in terms of the *strains* to which men in the business role are almost inevitably subject. Businessmen adhere to their particular kind of ideology because of the emotional conflicts, the anxieties, and the doubts engendered by the actions which their roles as businessmen compel them to take, and by the conflicting demands of other social roles which they must play in family and community. Within the resources of the cultural tradition and within the limits of what is publicly acceptable, the content of the ideology is shaped so as to resolve these conflicts, alleviate these anxieties, overcome these doubts. For the individual businessman, the function of the ideology is to help him maintain his psychological ability to meet the demands of his occupation. It follows that the ideology has functional importance also for those on whom the actions of businessmen impinge and for the whole society (Sutton et al., 1956: 11).

In taking this position, these scholars reject the "interest" theory that ideologies simply reflect narrow self-interest as conceived by their adherents. More specifically, they reject the idea that the business ideology is designed to persuade others to take action which will result in a profit advantage to businessmen. There is truth, but not the whole truth, in this theory. One cannot explain the determined resistance of many businessmen to an unbalanced federal budget, for instance, as one that has a direct beneficial influence on their profits. If this view governed public policy it would sooner or later reduce profits.

The businessman plays many roles and often finds conflicts among the values associated with different roles. He is a manager, an owner, a voter, a member of society, a friend, a competitor, a husband, a father, a church member, and so on. Modes of behavior are culturally determined in these different roles. His problems in deciding what to do as he assumes these roles can become difficult and create major strains and stresses. For example, economic life demands that a manager be competitive, but this may conflict with his role as a good neighbor to the competitor his action forces out of business. The businessman is faced with uncertainties of environment; he is responsible for outcomes of decisions over which he has limited control. Some of his roles place on him a responsibility—for community welfare, for instance—which he may feel conflicts with other roles—protector of stockholder interests, for instance.

Another theory is that the creed may serve to slow down, rather than prevent, institutional changes and reforms. The established business order is thus given time to find ways of adapting to these modifications (Berg, 1968: 147). In this view, the businessman who is himself an architect of change turns conservative and seeks more stability in his environment.

Finally, the typical businessman thinks of himself, and of business in general, as being important to the progress of society. He feels that threats to the business system are threats to society in general and to his role in particular. His ideology, therefore, is a shield against the erosion of his and his group's role. He knows the origin of the classical capitalist ideology rested in an effort to rescue the businessman from a suppression which was contrary to his and society's interests, and he does not want this to happen again.

CHANGING BUSINESS IDEOLOGIES

For the better part of our history when people spoke of the business ideology there was a general understanding of what was meant, even though not everyone subscribed to all of its principles. This was the classical, or traditional, ideology which found its taproot in the classical exposition of the individual enterprise system described in Chapter 3.

In the 1920s the first major break with that tradition took place when managers of larger corporations said their responsibility was not to serve solely the common stockholder as in the classical ideology, but was to coordinate the many interests focused on the company. They used words like "trusteeship" and "stewardship" to symbolize their obligations to different interests. The word "service" came into usage to express these new responsibilities of managers.

The meaning of "service" remained a puzzle until it was replaced by the words "social responsibility" which first were used in the 1930s. At that time they were merely substitutes for "service" which had become overused and still quite unclear. Over time, the idea that business had social responsibilities continued to be discussed but it was not until the late 1960s and the early 1970s that it became of dominant concern to business. In the meantime, businesses grew in size, professional managers replaced more and more entrepreneurs, environment became much more complex, and other changes suggested new ideas about the business role.

As a result, there has evolved over the past several decades a new business ideology which, while incorporating much of the old classical ideology, is so different as to present, for the first time, a challenge to some of the basic tenets of the old ideology. There is no name for this new ideology. I shall call it the "modern managerial social responsibility ideology," or the "modern managerial ideology" for short.

There never was a consensus about the classical ideology, nor is there one today. There probably is less of a consensus about the modern ideology. Different classes of businessmen embrace different aspects of these ideologies in different degrees and with different emphasis. Ideologies of top managers of the largest companies may differ from those of managers of smaller companies. Ideologies may also vary among managers in the same companies. For instance, the top management of a large company may have a liberal set of views about public responsibilities shared by newly-hired MBAs but not by older middle-level managers. Ideologies about such matters as competition, government power, and free trade may differ from industry to industry. For instance, the steel industry would much like to have the government raise tariffs on imported steel. Aircraft manufacturers, however, push for free trade. Older managers may have more conservative views than younger managers. Managers with diverse educational backgrounds may, of course, not think alike about many things. Finally, a company that is brilliantly successful in making money may have a creed unlike one that is desperately trying to survive.

It must not be thought that either of these major creeds is a monolithic body of American capitalistic thought which is reasonably complete, well-structured, and stable. Each is incomplete, has gaping holes in it, is continuously under attack, and is constantly changing.

THE CLASSICAL TRADITION

Government The classical view of government, as noted in Chapter 3, is one of hostility and distrust. Government is considered to be inherently evil, powerless to create, and negative in its relations to industry. There are many reasonable explanations of why businessmen hold this view. Government may be a scapegoat for those obscure forces which cause the outcomes of business decisions to differ from expectations. Business denigrates government because its administrators are not held to the same types of accountability imposed on businessmen. Government is a regulator of business and is naturally resented. Government is a suitable target for resentments built up by a businessman. The hostile attitudes reflected in the American revolt against tyranny of a central government have probably carried over to this day.

Government Finance Taxes are always too high, and ideology demands their reduction. The rationale is that taxes divert resources from business and consumers to be used by government in making unnecessary expenditures. Taxes, furthermore, stifle individual initiative and risk-taking, reduce the capital available to a firm, and inhibit business investment.

Government debt is regarded in the same way as the debt of an individual or a company; the mounting federal debt, to the classical creed, is a clear sign of impending bankruptcy if the trend continues. Correct budgetary practice is quite obvious—budgets must be balanced at all times, and when surpluses are generated the debt should be paid off. The general business view is that expenditures just about always are higher than they should be.

Profit Prominent in the traditional philosophy, of course, is the importance of profit. Managers should seek to maximize profits for the benefit of the common stockholders. High profit levels indicate that managers are doing a good job and performing their proper role in society.

Competition Competition is the touchstone of the economic system which, when allowed to operate freely without interference by government or by monopoly, will produce an overall harmony with many benefits to society. The ideology is filled with warnings of the evils attendant upon government and labor interference in the competitive processes. The businessman holding the classical ideology still talks as though he is always faced with a cold, impersonal market mechanism over which he has no control.

Consumers and Service Consumers and service to them hold a supreme position in classical ideology. The consumer is pictured as having great and ultimate power over the fate of businessmen. If businessmen meet consumer demands, they will succeed; if not, they will fail. Consumers are considered to be independent and fickle. Aggressive advertising is necessary and in the community interest because it stimulates consumers and business activity. Service likewise is emphasized as being in the interests both of consumers and society by "bringing a better life to all."

Labor Many businessmen insist that bargaining between employee and employer should be on an individual basis, free of compulsion, or coercion by government or unions. This idea is captured in the slogan "right to work," which stands in opposition to the closed shop and other union security rules, including effective strikes. Large numbers of businessmen, however, today accept the right of employees to join unions, to bargain collectively, and to maintain job security irrespective of union membership. On the other hand, the creed insists that a worker should be free to join a union or not, and not be subject to union coercion. The right to strike is accepted, but the creed insists that other rights must also be protected. This means, for instance, that violence, boycotts, organized picketing, and other such kinds of union activity should be prohibited. Furthermore, unions are considered to be monopolies and should therefore be subject to the antitrust laws. The traditionalist sees industry-wide bargaining as a monopoly power, and he resists it.

Management, according to the creed, has a right to administer its property as it sees fit without union interference. Encroachment on what are considered to be managerial prerogatives by contract work rules is resisted. The ideology says that wage-rate increases should be correlated with rises in productivity. Union restrictions of output are deplored. Indeed, the ideology asserts that the true road to prosperity for all is increased productivity.

International Trade Not unexpectedly, one finds a schism in attitudes toward trade. The classical theory, of course, is foursquare for free trade; but when free trade conflicts with self-interest, as it often does, protectionism is advocated. Today, therefore, industries threatened by cheaper foreign imports want to be protected. Others not so threatened and benefiting from foreign trade want continual reductions in trade barriers throughout the world.

Economic Growth The creed places faith in the natural operation of the competitive system to recover from cyclical downswings and to ensure higher levels of economic output over time. Given freedom from interferences by government and labor unions, the system is held to be self-correcting.

Importance of the Businessman One of the dominant themes in the classical ideology is praise for the achievements of the business system—rising output, higher standards of living, and "the conversion

of the luxuries of yesterday's rich to the necessities of today's masses"
(Sutton et al., 1956: 19). Nonmaterial benefits are also praised, such
as the creation in and by business of a spirit of service, the ability of
those with talent to find personal achievement in the business world,
and the great possibilities to find a type of freedom which this system alone makes possible. The importance of businessmen and the
justification for their relatively high salaries are not neglected.

Underlying Values The values underlying traditional business
ideology are well known. Central is individualism, which stresses
responsibility and freedom. One aspect of this value enjoins each
person to work hard and accept the consequences of his own actions;
another is that individuals must be able to make choices freely in
pursuit of their own self-interests. To the traditionalist, these values
lead to just distribution of income.

High praise for the material benefits resulting from the economic
system is based upon materialistic value. The unabashed faith in the
future finds support in a value of optimism. The dominance of the
religious values of the Puritan Ethic has been covered in previous
chapters. A certain universalism also underlies the creed, one expression of which is that "what is good for business is good for all."
Finally, it should be mentioned that the tone of the traditional ideology is practical, assured, austere, and unbending in its assumption
of rightness.

Reality v. Ideology It is fair and important to say that no matter
how far removed from reality some of these views may seem to be,
most of them are still held by a majority of businessmen. Reality and
ideology generally are not the same. The significance of the ideology
is lost if it is not understood that, fundamentally, it is not meant to be
a description of what is going on today but rather it is a prescription
of what ought to be. For many businessmen, especially in the larger
companies, such events as the jolt of the depression of the 1930s, the
Keynesian economic revolution, and the more recent concern about
major social problems have resulted in significant disagreement with
important parts of the classical ideology.

THE SMALL BUSINESS IDEOLOGY

The ideology of the small businessman, say Monsen and Cannon
(1965: 43), is but a minor variation of the classical creed. The traditional creed expounds the view that business generally is small, and
larger companies maintain this tradition by decentralizing operations.
Large corporations are accepted, however, and their social benefits
extolled, but small businessmen often find themselves in opposition
to big business. Small businessmen also unashamedly seek and ac-

cept government aid for their class. Other businesses seek government aid for themselves or their industry, but generally not for their class. The small businessman is not as well organized as other business groups in expounding his beliefs.

THE MODERN IDEOLOGY

Rather than develop the history of this creed, which has been done well by others (Krooss, 1970; Mason, 1960), I shall describe the ideology today by summarizing some of the policy recommendations made by the Committee for Economic Development (CED), the views of top executives of large companies as expressed in the McKinsey Lectures given at Columbia University between 1956 and 1967, and statements of other business leaders.

The CED is a group of some 300 business executives and educators who conduct research on topics of their own choosing and prepare policy recommendations. Millions of copies of these documents have been distributed and discussed by CED-sponsored business groups throughout the nation. The CED does not presume to promote the special interests of business, nor does it assume it speaks for any other group (Schriftgiesser, 1960: 26). It is a body of men, most of whom are from large companies who speak principally from a business point of view and only for themselves. Since its creation in 1942, the CED has published almost 200 carefully prepared research monographs covering nearly 100 major subjects. In light of this huge compilation and scope of inquiry, the resume presented here can no more than touch lightly upon a few highlights of the disseminated ideology.

The McKinsey Lecture Series The McKinsey Lectures, sponsored first in 1956 by the Graduate School of Business, Columbia University, were given by executives of the largest business organizations in the United States. Each lecture was on a topic chosen by the speaker and later published in book form (Cordiner, 1956; Houser, 1957; Blough, 1959; Greenewalt, 1959; Kappel, 1960; Folsom, 1962; Watson, 1963; Rockefeller, 1964; Donner, 1967; and Wright, 1967). Neither individually nor collectively was there an effort to present a complete ideology. Compared with the flamboyant confidence and arrogance of the business speeches of the late nineteenth and early twentieth centuries, the tone of the McKinsey Lectures was calm, thoughtful, cautious, and perhaps at times a bit apologetic.

Business Seen in a New Setting The CED was formed because its originators felt the old ideology was deficient in dealing with the anticipated economic problems following the end of World War II, particularly the need to reduce the disastrous effects of an expected economic depression. This group felt that business in cooperation with government and other institutions in society had to pool resources to combat this prospect. As its fields of inquiry have expanded, its questioning of older ideology has become more widespread. In assessing the first fourteen years of CED, Zellerbach commented: "Through CED, businessmen have proved themselves able to renounce what is hardest for all men to forsake—their preconceptions" (1956: 10).

In the first McKinsey lecture, Cordiner commented on the new world and the need for describing it, as follows:

> Many thoughtful persons have observed that the United States has evolved a wholly new form of capitalism, variously called democratic capitalism, mass capitalism, or—more aptly—people's capitalism. As the first nation in the world to break through the ancient barriers of scarcity into an economy of abundance, we have a unique experience that we ourselves need fully to understand and to communicate to the rest of the world. But somehow we have not yet been able to do it well—to describe this new people's capitalism, and all that it means to the spiritual and cultural life of the people, as well as to their material well-being (1956: 1).

The holder of the traditional view sees little change in the economic system in the last fifty years, or ignores it. The managerial ideology sees change and seeks to reflect it. The CED and McKinsey lecturers see a new economic system structurally different from the old and interrelated in new ways with society.

Professional Managerial Responsibilities Cordiner's first lecture set the theme of a new managerial role, which was defined by Rockefeller in the following passage:

> The old concept that the owner of a business had a right to use his property as he pleased to maximize profits has evolved into the belief that ownership carries certain binding social obligations. Today's manager serves as trustee not only for the owners but for the workers and indeed for our entire society. . . . Corporations have developed a sensitive awareness of their responsibility for maintaining an equitable balance among the claims of stockholders, employees, customers, and the public at large (1964: 22–23).

The professional manager is obliged to plan ahead to ensure the survival and prosperity of his enterprise (p. 49); he has deep responsibilities for the people of his organization, and he has broad social responsibilities. This theme can be seen throughout the lectures and the many publications of the CED.

Cooperation and Acceptance of the Power of Government Quite contrary to the classical philosophy, the modern ideology accepts a certain partnership with government in society. James Roche expressed it this way:

> Business and government can ill afford to be adversaries. So mutual are our interests, so formidable are our challenges, that our times demand our strengthened alliance. The success of each largely depends upon the other. Today, business and government are each becoming more involved in the affairs of the other (1969: 6).

While this view is generally accepted in many CED publications and among most McKinsey lecturers, there is not complete agreement. Cordiner and Blough, for instance, expressed fear of rapidly growing federal power. Comparable fears have been found in some dissents in CED policy recommendations. There is no doubt, however, that the way the managerial ideology sees government is a clear break with the traditional business antipathy to government.

A paper prepared by the CED strongly supported the principles of the Employment Act of 1946 and was influential in getting this legislation passed (CED, 1946). (The act was vigorously opposed by most businessmen.) This meant, of course, that the CED accepted a strong government hand in economic life in fulfilling the purposes of the act. It meant, too, that the CED accepted the Keynesian idea that balancing the federal budget annually was less important than economic stability (CED, 1947, 1958, 1966). While accepting budgetary deficits to promote economic activity, the prevailing managerial creed advocates that surpluses in prosperous years offset deficits in poor years so that the budget is in balance over the entire business cycle. There is not the same fear of debt as in the traditional view, but its size is bothersome, and managers would be happier to see it reduced in prosperous years. The CED was an advocate of rebuilding Europe (CED, 1948) and accelerating United States economic development programs in underdeveloped countries (CED, 1956, 1957).

Business leaders advocate much more participation of their peers in governmental affairs, from advice to full-time jobs (Folsom, 1962: 134–37). One of the reasons for the sympathetic view of the CED toward government lies in the fact that the CED is dominated by executives from large firms who understand the importance of government action in providing an environment in which business can prosper. Another is that many of these executives have held important positions in the federal government and understand its problems, its motivations, and the requirements placed upon it.

Need for Big Organizations Justification of large organizations is not well articulated in traditional ideology, a shortcoming which the managerial ideology seeks to fill. In the McKinsey lectures, as one might expect, the emphasis is on large, not small, businesses, and the writers point with pride to the accomplishments of and the need for large organizations. Cordiner, for example, said, "Without . . . large-scale economic enterprises, a nation is today a second-rate power and its people suffer both lower standards of living and greater vulnerability to attack by aggressive nations" (1956: 3). The McKinsey lecturers also took pains (for instance, Blough, 1959: 10–11) to point out that competition among large companies was much different from that among small companies, but equally rigorous and demanding. Kappel dwelt at length on a theme which would not be denied by others of this group—that large organizations can be imaginative, innovative, and satisfying places in which to work. A number of the lecturers pointed out that through decentralization the great advantages accruing to size can be achieved.

Stress on Human Values Every one of the McKinsey lecturers dwelt at some length on the treatment of men in organizations. Indeed, it is the most dominant of all the themes in this series. The views of the managerial ideology are in stark contrast to the one-sided doctrine of self-interest in the classical creed.

Houser feels the most important tasks of managers concern people. He says:

> It can no longer be taken for granted that ability will find its own level. In this age of the corporation, management must take specific steps to make sure that people have an opportunity to grow and develop; otherwise too many of them are likely to be lost in the labyrinthine processes of the organization. This is one of the major responsibilities of management today, a responsibility not only to its own people but to our free society (1957: 4).

Kappel asks the question: "What makes a vital business?" and answers it: "Vital people make it" (1960: 5). He then elaborates at length on why and how. Watson says he believes IBM's most important philosophy is "our respect for the individual" (1963: 13, italics omitted).

There are many aspects of this increasing concern for individuals. For instance, several writers (Kappel, Blough, and Greenewalt) point out that some conformity is necessary, but that a large organization can stimulate innovation and creativity in people, can provide satisfying jobs, and can facilitate individual growth.

Closely associated with this topic is general education, a subject which has concerned the CED. In 1960 the CED published its first statement about the importance of and requirements for educating businessmen. This was followed by another report in 1964. More recently it has become interested in general education (1965, 1968a, 1968b).

Labor Issues concerning labor are exceedingly complex and a matter of concern to management. Despite the great importance of labor power, which businessmen see as a formidable competitor, very few CED reports have been published on the subject; and, except for a discussion by Blough, the matter was almost completely ignored by the McKinsey lecturers. Managers of the largest companies now accept the necessity of organized labor, as explained in Chapter 28. For many businessmen, the classical ideology regarding labor is still fundamental. For more and more of them, however, the legitimacy of labor unions is accepted with relative equanimity.

International Trade The CED takes a more liberal view of free trade than the classical ideology, which although equivocal, leans to protectionism. In one statement (1959) the CED saw advantages in some protection from free world markets, but in later statements it has put itself in the ranks of those seeking to reduce tariff barriers. For example, in 1964 the CED said, "Our principal recommendation is that the United States should seek in free world trade negotiations to obtain tariff reductions from its trade partners in return for reciprocal United States concessions, coming as close as possible to cutting free world tariffs by fifty percent, across the board" (CED, 1964: 8).

Agriculture The CED is in agreement with the traditional creed, as well as with many academic economists, in advocating for agriculture a return to a free market which will set price levels, rather than having the government do it (CED, 1956, 1957).

GAPS IN IDEOLOGIES

There are, of course, many other issues included in the ideologies, but rather than examine them, it seems more useful to consider some of the major blanks or inadequately covered issues. Business ideology, particularly the traditional branch, covers only part of the landscape and generally ignores things not easily explained, not agreeable, or not pleasant to consider. For instance, the old ideology is rather silent on business bearing any of the social costs of progress, such as unemployment, water pollution, or urbanization problems. In their evaluation of the creed, Sutton and his colleagues point out that it "rarely makes any claim on the esthetic quality of modern life, the superiority of the moral standards of our present society over those of earlier societies or of other countries, or the piety of life under the System. . . . Nowhere in the creed is there any suggestion that conflict exists between religion and capitalism, humanitarianism and money seeking. . . ." (Sutton et al., 1956: 49). Strangely enough, little space is given to the great improvements in such noneconomic values as health, span of life, or equal opportunity. The creed fails to point out that there are many reasons for the success of this society in improving the well-being of its people aside from business, as important as business is.

INCONSISTENCIES IN THE IDEOLOGY

A number of major conflicts have been noted between the classical and managerial ideologies. In both creeds there are inconsistencies; for instance, in attitudes toward competition. The classical ideology strongly favors competition, but when businessmen are dealing with their own situation, there is considerable deviation from the generality. The same sort of inconsistency may arise when a particular businessman is concerned with details of immediate concern to himself as distinct from the generalities of the creed.

Imprecations about violation of the ideology have often been ignored by both society and businessmen in dealing with specific issues. We are a pragmatic people, but we also are responsive to value systems held by important segments of society. The business ideology, as a prescription for human behavior in the economic world, and as a moral doctrine, influences thinking and action, but does not always determine it. On occasion, I have listened with amusement to managerial friends repeat the liturgy of the function of managers to maximize profits, because I have seen these same men in their decision-making assume socially responsible positions contrary to the narrow interests of stockholders, at least in the short run. There often is, therefore, inconsistency between the doctrine and action.

COMPETING IDEOLOGIES

The business ideology has never gone unchallenged, but the strength of opposing views is greater today than ever before. A major competitor is, of course, the federal government, whose exercise of power is based upon its own ideological rationalizations of its actions. The ideology of government is a strong challenger because it is a determinant of ultimate aims to which the business system moves as well as of the means employed to get there. Much of government's activity is based upon pressures from various groups in the community, including business, which often find their own ideologies in contradiction to the business creed. But the civil bureaucracy itself follows its own ideology. So does the military bureaucracy within the executive branch, and political parties in the legislative branch. Other groups with competing ideologies of importance to business are labor, agriculture, public school teachers, and intellectuals (Monsen and Cannon, 1965). Major parts of these other ideologies are in direct conflict with critical parts of business ideology, but some common ground with business doctrine can be found in most of them. Their collective strength, however, is a major neutralizing force for business ideology (Brayman, 1967).

WHITHER THE BUSINESS IDEOLOGY?

The business creed today is composed of an underlying traditional ideology upon which has been superimposed the new managerial ideology. The latter has both added important dimensions to the traditional ideology and significantly modified some older doctrine. As such, the total ideology is a mix of the anachronistic debris of the past and enlightened adaptations to fit the needs of contemporary society. It is altogether likely that the newer activities of faith will gradually find greater acceptance and replace or downgrade some of the more obsolete classical formulations. We do not know how much of the CED or McKinsey Lecture Series philosophy is accepted by medium-sized and small businessmen. There are signs, however, that dissemination and acceptance are taking place.

Before taking too extreme a position against parts of the classical tradition, it is important to note that it contains some fundamental ideas and considerations of major significance to the workings of this society. Rigorous competition, the pursuit of self-interest, the importance of the individual, strong questioning of government use of power, the operation of laws of supply and demand in the marketplace, efficient utilization of economic resources, and so on, are still relevant to the type of society we have and wish to keep. It is not so much the ideas and values that need modification as the often irrelevant way in which the business ideology formulates and uses them to resist change in specific cases. Reformulation of some old doctrines, together with greater attention to filling blanks and resolving inconsistencies, would strengthen the ideology.

Does the ideology fulfill its purpose and will it continue to do so? Naturally, the answer to this question must be based on the purpose businessmen conceive for it. If it is designed principally, as Sutton and his colleagues say, to ease the strains of their calling, it has done this and probably will continue to do so. If it is designed to slow down changes in environment so as to permit the businessman to adjust, that too has been achieved. However, the businessman now accepts a wide range of social legislation which he initially resisted with all the power at his command. If the ideology is intended to help the businessman wrestle with future uncertainties and to bolster his sense of importance, it also does that.

It is fair to ask whether the ideology is flexible, perceptive, and inspiring enough to help the nation through today's social and vexatious economic problems to that promising post-industrial world so many people see in the last part of this century. The answer to the question is not clear, but in recent years the ideology has shown remarkable ability to adapt to events. It is somewhat perceptive in dealing with the fundamental issues of relevance to this society. How inspiring it will be as it undergoes change remains to be seen. If the beliefs and recommendations of the CED publications and the McKinsey lecturers are taken at face value and not as public relations statements (which, except in minor detail, they are not), there is promise that the business ideology will meet the challenge.

Heilbroner raises doubts about the business ideology being sufficiently inspirational in the trying days ahead. This is in part, he says, because

> . . . it is the more or less transparent defense of privilege masquerading as philosophy, the search for sanction clothed as a search for truth, the little evasions and whitewashings that cheapen what purports to be a fearless confrontation of great issues. And yet, these are only surface flaws. At its core, the business ideology as a spiritual creed or as an historic beacon is vitiated by something that is missing—I cannot but think fatally missing—from its deepest conception. What it lacks is a grandiose image of society, a projection of human possibilities cast in a larger mold than is offered by today's institutions (in Chiet, 1964: 25).

I am not sure, however, that the ideology will fail to rise to the need. There has been a great deal of thought given to the present and future needs of society by leading businessmen. As one reads the views of these men, a number of major themes seem to be loud and clear, such as the following:

A better world is possible, especially if we plan for it rather than only react to events.

Businessmen are in a position to influence the quality of our lives, for better or worse.

The modern business leader has far broader interests than short-range profit. He is socially and politically (civically) concerned and active. He takes professional pride in his role and is continuously in the process of learning.

The modern business leader accepts a responsibility to use the resources at his command to balance the many interests focused on his company. It is important to discover new and better ways to improve public decision-making.

The better businessmen are informed about factors that affect business and the full range of our social, economic and political problems, the better they will be able to formulate positive programs for the protection and improvement of our society, and the more likely they will be to want to do so.

As society becomes more affluent and enlightened, the greater is the responsibility of managers to consider more carefully human values both within and outside the firm.

Businessmen do have social responsibilities and must face up to discharging them.

How rapidly such ideas will spread through the business community in thought and action cannot be foretold. If these views become more generally accepted by businessmen and replace elements of the traditional views with which they conflict, the business ideology will be more in tune with the changing expectations of society and more likely, therefore, to be a significant positive force in the achievement of the great society which is the dream of tomorrow.

INDIVIDUAL COMPANY VALUE SYSTEMS

There are fundamental beliefs, convictions, attitudes, and ideas, explicit or implicit, for every individual business firm. These are not so much ideologies, although they can draw from ideologies and complement them, as value systems. Because individuals differ in every company, these value systems are unique to each company. These values constitute the fundamental driving force in each business and may be more important in its success than its material assets. Thomas Watson emphasized this point as follows:

> This then is my thesis: I firmly believe that any organization, in order to survive and achieve success, must have a sound set of beliefs on which it premises all its policies and actions. Next, I believe that the most important single factor in corporate success is faithful adherence to those beliefs. . . . In other words, the basic philosophy, spirit, and drive of an organization have far more to do with its relative achievements than do technological or economic resources, organizational structure, innovation and timing. All these things weigh heavily on success. But they are, I think, transcended by how strongly the people in the organization believe in its basic precepts and how faithfully they carry them out (Watson, 1963: 3).

CHAPTER TEN

The Social
Responsibilities
of Business

INTRODUCTION

Within the past few years there have been pronounced changes in the views of many business managers about their social responsibilities which have paralleled and partly reflected the changing priorities and expectations of society about business's social functions. As a result, there are today few subjects of more concern to business than this one. This chapter explores various aspects of this issue. There is no one who "has the answers" about what should be done, when, how, or by whom. In this chapter, therefore, the reader will find an exploratory examination of the issues and a few guidelines to action, rather than a neat framework of definitive theoretical or operational conclusions.

FROM PROFIT MAXIMIZATION TO BROADER SOCIAL RESPONSIBILITIES

At the outset some perspective about the shift in objectives of business is useful. The idea that a business has one and only one objective—to maximize profits—has been the majority view of business for the better part of our history. This is the view that business managers exist only to serve the best interests of the stockholders. The first break from this came in the 1930s. The view was advanced and accepted that managers of large companies must make decisions which maintain an equitable balance among the claims of stockholders, employers, customers, suppliers, and the general public. Managers were considered trustees for these interests. Although decisions might be made which resulted in short-range profits at less than a maximum, many of those who held this view argued that if the balancing was done correctly, the long-range profit interests of the company would be maximized. There were some who felt that some actions not directly related to profits might be taken, but their acceptable range was negligible.

Another major break from the older concept is now taking place. It is the view that business must get deeply involved in dealing with major social problems. Although this involvement is partly justified by its proponents because it may be done profitably, there is a growing body of opinion, in and out of business, that significant business actions can and should be taken even though there is no direct relationship with profit. There are some people who talk as though business alone can handle the social problems the government has failed to resolve. Most observers see the lack of reality in this view, but many assert that business must reexamine the profit concept. It is evident that things must be done which are not permitted within the traditional boundaries of business decision-making. Paralleling this thought is a deep concern about the human values of the employees of corporations. Here, too, actions may be accepted which do not directly increase and may actually reduce profits, at least in the short run. While there is no consensus about these current ideas, it does seem clear that the underlying thought is distinctly different from the past views of balancing interests and of profit maximization (Adizes and Weston, 1973). These three views are not, of course, sequential. Among managers, the public, government officials, and students of business, each idea can be found today as a basis for action and thought (Richman, 1973).

WHAT IS MEANT BY THE SOCIAL RESPONSIBILITY OF BUSINESS?

In the classical view, a business was acting in a socially responsible fashion if it strived to utilize as efficiently as possible the resources at its disposal in meeting the goods and services that society wanted at prices consumers were willing to pay. If this were done well, said classical economic theory, businessmen would maximize profits. The concept of socially responsible action has been broadened today far beyond this boundary, but there is no consensus on either a definition or the limits of action.

For our purposes business's social responsibilities may be defined from three points of view: The conceptual, the impact of the responsibilities on profits, and specific social programs. All are closely interrelated, not mutually exclusive, and, as will be shown later, by no means capable of covering all meanings of social responsibility in use today.

Conceptual Social responsibilities refer to "the businessman's decisions and actions taken for reasons at least partially beyond the firm's direct economic or technical interest" (Davis, 1960: 70). A somewhat broader view says they are obligations to "pursue those policies, to make those decisions, or to follow those lines of action which are desirable in terms of the objectives and values of our society" (Bowen, 1953: 6). Perhaps an even wider dimension is the following:

> By "social responsibility" we mean the intelligent and objective concern for the welfare of society that restrains individual and corporate behavior from ultimately destructive activities, no matter how immediately profitable, and leads in the direction of positive contributions to human betterment, variously as the latter may be defined (Andrews, 1971: 120).

Fundamentally, these definitions say that actions taken by a business which in some degree helps society to achieve one or more of its objectives are socially responsible actions.

Specific Corporate Social Programs In an evaluation of corporate social responsibilities it is useful to drop down from high levels of abstraction to concrete specific programs. The first comprehensive list of program areas was prepared by the Committee for Economic Development (CED) and is shown in Exhibit 10–1. (For a more recent

Exhibit 10–1. Spectrum of Current Corporate Activities

Economic Growth and Efficiency
    Increasing productivity in the private sector of the economy
    Improving the innovativeness and performance of business management
    Enhancing competition
    Cooperating with the government in developing more effective measures to control inflation and achieve high levels of employment
    Supporting fiscal and monetary policies for steady economic growth
    Helping with the post-Vietnam conversion of the economy
Education
    Direct financial aid to schools, including scholarships, grants, and tuition refunds
    Support for increases in school budgets
    Donation of equipment and skilled personnel

Exhibit 10–1. (Continued)

Assistance in curriculum development
Aid in counseling and remedial education
Establishment of new schools, running schools and school systems
Assistance in the management and financing of colleges

Employment and Training
Active recruitment of the disadvantaged
Special functional training, remedial education, and counseling
Provision of day-care centers for children of working mothers
Improvement of work/career opportunities
Retraining of workers affected by automation or other causes of joblessness
Establishment of company programs to remove the hazards of old age and sickness
Supporting where needed and appropriate the extension of government accident, unemployment, health and retirement systems

Civil Rights and Equal Opportunity
Ensuring employment and advancement opportunities for minorities
Facilitating equality of results by continued training and other special programs
Supporting and aiding the improvement of black educational facilities, and special programs for blacks and other minorities in integrated institutions
Encouraging adoption of open-housing ordinances
Building plants and sales offices in the ghettos
Providing financing and managerial assistance to minority enterprises and participating with minorities in joint ventures

Urban Renewal and Development
Leadership and financial support for city and regional planning and development
Building or improving low-income housing
Building shopping centers, new communities, new cities
Improving transportation systems

Pollution Abatement
Installation of modern equipment
Engineering new facilities for minimum environmental effects
Research and technological development
Cooperating with municipalities in joint treatment facilities
Cooperating with local, state, regional, and federal agencies in developing improved systems of environmental management

Exhibit 10–1.   (Continued)

Developing more effective programs for recycling and reusing disposable materials

Conservation and Recreation

Augmenting the supply of replenishable resources, such as trees, with more productive species

Preserving animal life and the ecology of forests and comparable areas

Providing recreational and aesthetic facilities for public use

Restoring esthetically depleted properties such as strip mines

Improving the yield of scarce materials and recycling to conserve the supply

Culture and the Arts

Direct financial support to art institutions and the performing arts

Development of indirect support as a business expense through gifts in kind, sponsoring artistic talent, and advertising

Participation on boards to give advice on legal, labor, and financial management problems

Helping secure government financial support for local or state arts councils and the National Endowment for the Arts

Medical Care

Helping plan community health activities

Designing and operating low-cost medical-care programs

Designing and running new hospitals, clinics, and extended-care facilities

Improving the administration and effectiveness of medical care

Developing better systems for medical education, nurses' training

Developing and supporting a better national system of health care

Government

Helping improve management performance at all levels of government

Supporting adequate compensation and development programs for government executives and employees

Working for the modernization of the nation's governmental structure

Facilitating the reorganization of government to improve its responsiveness and performance

Advocating and supporting reforms in the election system and the legislative process

Designing programs to enhance the effectiveness of the civil services

Exhibit 10–1.   (Continued)

Promoting reforms in the public welfare system, law
enforcement, and other major governmental
operations

SOURCE: CED, 1971: 31–40.

and larger list see McAdam, 1973). In a survey on the social audit,
which will be discussed later, respondents were asked to add to this
"laundry list" and responded by suggesting as major new categories:
product safety, advertising, consumer services, general community
services, and improving employee self-satisfaction. Thousands of
more detailed programs can, of course, be imagined under these
main programs.

In thinking about social programs it is useful to distinguish between those which may be classified as internal in or external to a
business. Internal social responsibilities, for instance, can be concerned with assuring due process, justice, equity, and morality in
employee selection, training, promotion, and firing. Or, they may
relate to such things as increasing employee productivity, or improving worker physical environment. External social responsibilities refer
to such actions as stimulating minority entrepreneurship, improving
the balance of payments, or training and hiring hard-core unemployed.

Impact on Profits A company may take socially responsible actions which serve to improve short-range profits. For instance, a company may install a machine to replace one which is hazardous to
workers. In doing so it may also set forth new rules concerning
worker bonuses and promotion which result in higher productivity
while at the same time erasing injustices.

The impact on profits may be diffused and unclear. For instance,
giving or increasing scholarships to children of employees may reduce short-range profits. The program may be justified, however, on
the grounds that employee loyalty will strengthen and bring higher
long-range profits. Also, hiring educated children of employees will
bring new talents to the company which may be profitable. Such
programs may be justified also on the grounds that the company believes society needs better educated people and that somehow the
net result will be to the advantage of the company. This latter justification can be selfish or altruistic.

Finally, of course, actions can be taken which clearly reduce
profits. Installing expensive antipollution devices, the costs of which
cannot be passed on to consumers, will do so.

Businessmen will not take actions which will reduce both short- and long-range profits. They may be willing to take an action that reduces short-range profits if they believe that it will somehow increase long-range profits. It may not always be easy, however, to draw a creditable relationship between a current action and its impact on long-range profits. Hence, rationalization of specific actions which cut short-range profits on the grounds that long-range profits will be expanded may lack conviction. Cleaning up a ghetto may improve the climate for business generally but if one company does it the long-range impact on the profits of that company may not be seen with much clarity.

Other Definitions of Social Responsibilities Almost every author writing in this field has his or her own definition. The following are a few perspectives other than those mentioned from which social responsibilities have been defined: theological (Baumhart, 1971; Purcell, 1967); sociological (Bell, 1971); esthetics (Eells, 1968); social problems (Rockefeller, 1973); internalizing costs (Barkley and Seckler, 1972); and how future society judges today's performance (Farmer and Hogue, 1973). Social responsibility may also refer to an obligation, a liability, social consciousness, corporate legitimacy, charitable contributions, "do goodism," managerial enlightenment, and so on (Votaw, 1972: 1–2; 1973: 25). Social responsibility means something different, depending upon how one looks at the concept and the corporate role in society.

Most businessmen prefer words other than social responsibility because these words to them connote a fixed obligation with unclear commitments. They prefer such synonyms as social concern, social programs, social challenge, social commitment, or concern with public problems.

Some Conclusions Aside from the lack of consensus about definition several conclusions are clear. The assumption of social responsibility, in my definition, does not necessarily mean a reduction of either short- or long-range profits. Also, many of the requirements for socially responsible action are identical with what used to be called business integrity or acting ethically or being good corporate citizens. Today's demands for socially responsible actions by business, however, go well beyond the traditional social expectations.

These concepts of social responsibility are broad and general. They do not explain very precisely what social responsibilities are for all businesses, nor what those of a single business are at a particular point in time. Unfortunately, there is no formula for either case, and both are the subject of substantial disagreement and the cause of frustrating dilemmas for business managers. One objective of this chapter and other discussions in this book is to help to clarify these questions.

THE CASE AGAINST BUSINESS'S ASSUMPTION OF SOCIAL RESPONSIBILITIES

The core of the strongest arguments against business's assumption of any responsibilities other than to produce goods and services efficiently and to make as much money as possible for stockholders is that business is an economic institution and economic values should be the sole determinant of performance. The manager of a business is the employee of the stockholder and responsible only to the stockholder. Legal opposition to social responsibilities rest also on this central concept. This is called the classical view.

Contrary to the Basic Functions of Business Milton Friedman, a widely respected economist, is on the side of the classicists in this clear statement:

> . . . there is one and only one social responsibility of business—to use its resources and engage in activities designed to increase its profits so long as it stays within the rules of the game, which is to say, engages in open and free competition, without deception or fraud. . . . Few trends could so thoroughly undermine the very foundations of our free society as the acceptance by corporate officials of a social responsibility other than to make as much money for their stockholders as possible. This is a fundamentally subversive doctrine (1962: 133).

Friedman argues that in a free enterprise, private property system, a manager is an employee of the owners of the business and is directly responsible to them as his employers. Since stockholders want to make as much profit as possible the manager's sole objective should be to try to do this. If a manager spends stockholder money in the public interest he is spending stockholder money without stockholder approval and perhaps in ways stockholders would oppose. Similarly, if the cost of social action is passed on to consumers in higher prices the manager is spending their money also. This is "taxation without representation," says Friedman, and should be rejected (1970).

Furthermore, if price on the market for a product does not truly reflect the relative costs of producing it, but includes costs for social action, the allocative mechanism of the marketplace is distorted. "Either the customer pays a price greater than that necessary to call the good into the market or the firm's product-mix provides less consumer satisfaction" (Browne and Haas, 1971: 9).

Friedman argues that the doctrine of social responsibility means acceptance of the socialist view that political mechanisms rather than market mechanisms are the appropriate ways to allocate scarce resources to alternative uses (1971). A manager undertaking activities in the public realm is performing social and political functions and becomes a civil servant. The result is that the businessman will ". . . sooner or later, be chosen by the public techniques of election and appointment" (1962: 132). As this process evolves, there will be an erosion of the drive to use resources efficiently and a loss of the great productivity of the present economic mechanism.

As a manager moves further away from the simple rule of profit maximization that guides his actions into the social and political realm he has no guides to help him know what social responsibilities he should take in the public interest. Furthermore, the businessman should not try to determine what is the public interest because "The economic system is not a playground on which businessmen may exercise their peculiar preferences" (Heyne, 1971: 26).

Closely associated with this argument is the view that businessmen have no special skills to deal with social matters. As explained by one observer: "The spectacle of otherwise sophisticated people going on bended knee to companies and pleading with them to have the kind of conscience and moral sensibilities only rarely found in individuals is nothing less than laughable" (Henderson, 1968: 81). There are many others who believe that businessmen have a primeval greed and a single-minded grasp for money which makes them obviously philosophically and emotionally unfit to deal with social problems.

We Do Not Want Business Values to Dominate Us Theodore Levitt supports the classical view because he fears domination of business values. He says:

> But at the rate we are going, there is more than a contingent probability that, with all its resounding good intentions, business statesmanship may create the corporate equivalent of the unitary state. Its proliferating employee welfare programs, its serpentine involvement in community, government, charitable, and educational affairs, its prodigious currying of political and public favor through hundreds of peripheral preoccupations, all these well-intended but insidious contrivances are greasing the rails for our collective descent into a social order that would be as repugnant to the corporations themselves as to their critics. The danger is that all these things will turn the corporation into a twentieth-century equivalent of the medieval Church. The corporation would eventually invest itself with all-embracing duties, obligations, and finally powers—ministering to the whole man and molding him and society in the image of the corporation's narrow ambitions and its essentially unsocial needs (1958: 44).

His fear, of course, is that the values of the more prominent business managers will dominate the values of society. He does not want social values determined in this way, and I do not blame him. In the past the results were not good for the society whose values were determined by one major institution, whether it was the church, the military, business, or something else.

Other Opposing Arguments The following may be mentioned among the additional more important arguments on this side. There is no substitute for the power of self-interest to get people to act. Any replacement of altruism for self-interest will therefore be fatal to the efficiency of the system. The rigors of the market mechanism will place in jeopardy the competitive position of that firm which adds to its costs by assuming social responsibilities. Pressure for business assumption of social responsibilities grows out of defects in the economy, and the way to solve the problem is not to push business into the assumption of social responsibilities, but to improve the workings of competition (Friedman, 1962: 120; Lewis, in Mansfield, 1964). There is a close connection between personal political and economic freedom in the ability of a person to use his property in his own interests, as permitted by the social system. The use of stockholders' property by managers for purposes other than the direct benefit of the stockholders is dangerous, for the loss of economic freedom will in the end bring a loss of political freedom (Hayek, 1944). Therefore, managers should manage only in the interests of shareholders, and shareholders should be put in a position to decide how their property will be used. The opposition also asserts, "Taken seriously, the doctrine of social responsibility fosters megalomania in its adherents. It places upon the businessman's conscience intolerable burdens that tempt him continually to arrogance and pharisaism" (Heyne, 1968: 104). Finally, there is serious question about whether or not any but trivial diversion of stockholder equity is legal (Manne, 1972).

James Russell Lowell caught the essence of this side of the argument in the following rhyme:

> Not a deed would he do
>   Not a word would he utter
> Till he weighed its relation
>   To plain bread and butter.

THE CASE FOR BUSINESS ASSUMPTION OF SOCIAL RESPONSIBILITIES

There is no one core idea in the argument that business has social responsibilities. Fundamentally, there seem to be three major core ideas, not mutually exclusive: corporations are creatures of society and should respond to societal demands, the long-run self-interests of business are best served when business assumes social responsibilities, and it is the moral and right thing to do.

Society Expects Business to Assume Social Responsibilities The argument is that corporations are creatures sanctioned by society and when society's expectations about their functioning change so should the corporation's actions. Many business leaders accept this argument and express it in different ways. John W. Hill, chairman of Hill and Knowlton, puts it this way: "Corporate enterprise operates under franchise from public opinion, and that franchise can be modified or withdrawn by the people's representatives in government at any time they so wish" (Clapp, 1968: 7). Gerhard Bleichen, chairman of the board of the John Hancock Mutual Life Insurance Company, says: ". . . it never occurred to me that there was a time when American business was at liberty to operate in conflict with the interests of society" (1972).

A businessman operates within a set of cultural norms and restraints. These are certainly economic but also legal, political, social, and technical. They are powerful and the businessman knows instinctively that as they change, as for instance with respect to social actions today, they must be incorporated in his decision-making processes. Johnson expresses this in terms of utility theory as follows: "A growing number of executives today are socialized to have utility functions of the more altruistic . . . type; along with profits and income, they genuinely seek the well-being of others" (1971: 61).

The managers of the biggest companies know that as a business gets larger, the public takes more of an interest in it because it has a greater impact on the community. The antennas of these managers are tuned to public opinion and they react to it. They seek to maintain a "proper" image of their company in the public mind. This leads to the assumption of greater social responsibilities.

It can be said in truth that many businessmen accept the argument expressed above that because society expects them to assume social responsibilities they must try to do so. If not, the argument runs, society will either force them to do so through laws or society may no longer permit them to survive. In either case it is in the enlightened self-interest of a company to react to society's wishes. History confirms that an institution with power that is not used in conformance with society's desires will lose that power.

Long-run Self-interest of Business In a milestone policy statement of the CED a group of prominent businessmen concluded: ". . . it is in the enlightened self interest of corporations to promote the public welfare in a positive way" (1971: 25). The statement continued: "Indeed, the corporate interest broadly defined by management can support involvement in helping to solve virtually any social problem, because people who have a good environment, education, and opportunity make better employees, customers, and neighbors for business than those who are poor, ignorant, and oppressed" (1971: 26).

Arjay Miller adds a different dimension to self-interest in these words:

Under current conditions, management cannot effectively discharge its long-run responsibilities to shareholders unless it also behaves responsibly toward employees, customers, government, education and the public at large. The ability of a corporation to protect and enhance the stockholder's equity depends crucially upon the prosperity, goodwill and confidence of the larger community. Acceptance of a large measure of responsibility toward the community is therefore good business as well as good citizenship (1966: 2–3).

The same point holds with respect to other aspects of social responsibility. For example, more managers are learning that it is possible to ensure greater harmony between corporate and personal goals and that when this occurs the productivity of people in organizations can be enhanced. It is simply in the best interests of the company to understand and respond to the needs of people in the organization. Although this attitude is akin to the self-interest of classical theory, it has different dimensions. The older was an often irresponsible self-interest; the newer is enlightened in that it reaches out to benefit society while at the same time favoring the company. The new self-interested businessman sees that justice, due process, and concern for employees can harmonize with the company's best interests. There is a social as well as an economic character to this attitude.

Avoidance of Government Regulations   Businessmen recognize that if they do not step up to social action programs the government will. They reason correctly that the more business responds to societal pressures the less pressure will be placed on government to step in. B. X. Yarrington, president of American Oil Company, comments: "Somewhere down the road, corporations that ignore this need for the parallel development of social and traditional investments will feel the wrath of society—expressed, I'm sure, through the agencies of government" (1972).

If a businessman avoids government regulation by keeping up with social demands, he will reduce his costs, since regulation in general is expensive for him. He will also retain his flexibility and freedom in making decisions and meeting competition; restrain concentration of power in government; and thereby advance his own and the public's interests.

Furthermore, says Melvin Anshen, if business steps up to its social responsibilities, it will retain a needed creditability with the public and will be invited to, not restrained from, participating in the political decision-making process when new rules of the game are being written for business. "There can be no greater danger," he writes, "than to permit the new rules to be formulated by either the small group of critics armed only with malevolence toward the existing system or the much larger group sincerely motivated by concern for ameliorating social ills but grossly handicapped by their ignorance of the techniques and dynamics of private enterprise" (1970: 12). Business will be denied participation in hammering out these new rules if it volunteers its services only after its stubborn resistance to change has been overcome by public pressure.

Businessmen Are Concerned Citizens Like everyone else, businessmen wear a number of hats. As citizens they see the need for social action. As executives they may have the power to do something and accept the challenge. Most of what executives do in the social area may be reactive to societal pressures and justified in their minds on the grounds of self-interest, in one or more facets of these multidimensional terms. Yet, as concerned citizens they may welcome the opportunity, however they justify it, to participate in the development of a better world.

Other Arguments Following are a few more views about why business should assume social responsibilities. It is possible that some managers will accept the argument that to assume social responsibilities will assure a legitimacy that often becomes tenuous and fuzzy. If managers find themselves in control of a company in which they possess a small stock ownership, to whom are they responsible? Stockholders who do not control? The public? It is sometimes argued that businessmen have great social power and should step up to assuming an equal amount of social responsibility. Another argument is that government has tried to solve an assortment of social problems and has not done very well. Thus, why not let business try its hand? Business is innovative and creative, another argument says, so why not take advantage of this capability in the social as well as the economic area? Also, if business undertakes social responsibilities, it will find ways to make its actions profitable. If business cannot profit by existing market forces and legal constraints, the government should provide the proper incentives for business. In either event business will profit as well as the general public. Since neither the law nor custom obligates managers to pursue maximum profit, why not endorse pursuit of social activities (Hetherington, 1969)? Finally, as Andrews points out: ". . . corporate executives of the caliber, integrity, intelligence, and humanity required to run substantial companies cannot be expected to confine themselves to their narrow economic activity and to ignore its social consequences" (1971: 133).

AN ASSESSMENT OF THE ARGUMENTS

The arguments of those who oppose a corporation's doing nothing but optimizing stockholder wealth are weak on two grounds. First, they overstate the trend and ultimate magnitude of businesses voluntary assumption of social responsibilities. Second, they want corporations to do something they cannot do and that is to ignore societal demands on them. This is not to say that these arguments have no substance. They do contain warning signals that caution against excessive thrusts away from economic motivations and measures of performance.

Some of the opponents of corporate social responsibilities rest their case on a description of how business operated under the comparatively simple conditions of one hundred years ago. In dismissing this point of view Adolf Berle said the author was "endeavoring to describe late 20th-Century processes . . . in terms of 19th-Century economic folklore" (*Business Week*, 1971(B)). The stockholders of the larger corporations do not control the managers nor do the managers feel they are responsible solely to the stockholders. Wallich and McGowan argue that:

> Once it is recognized that corporations are not usually owned by a group of investors who own shares in only one corporation, but by individuals who as a group typically own shares in a very large number of corporations, the whole concept of stockholder interest becomes extremely fuzzy (in Baumol, et al., 1970: 55).

If stockholders feel their interests are not being served by the social policies of a company whose stock they own they will sell the stock. If there is much investor disaffection with a company's policies the message will be read through a drop in its stock price and a rise in the costs of its equity capital.

Opponents of social responsibility often assert that there is a sharp conflict between economic and social goals of business. It seems worthwhile to quote at some length how the General Electric Company views this matter:

> As a statement of *purpose*, "maximizing of profits" is not only unsatisfying: it is not even accurate. . . . A more realistic statement has to be more complicated . . . in General Electric: "The corporation is a creation of society whose purpose is the production and distribution of needed goods and services, to the profit of society and itself." *Each* element of that statement is needed, if the whole is to be accurate; you cannot drop one element without doing violence to the facts.

> The corporation *is* a creation of society. It is created by a charter which can be revoked either literally by legal action, or figuratively by the action of the marketplace.

Its principal activity lies in satisfying the *economic* needs of society through the supply of goods and—more and more, in our changing society—of services.

And these goods and services must be *needed:* if they do not meet some individual or communal need, they will not be purchased and the would-be supplying company will have failed to justify its existence.

Finally, if this cycle of events is completed successfully—and success, after all, is the aim—*both* the corporation *and* society will profit. This mutuality of interest is important and inescapable. If society sees no benefit to itself from a corporation's activities, then in the long run (and the long run is what a corporation plans for) that business will not be profitable. Or, if society benefits but the business does not make money, then the company will go out of business—in the short run.

I would like to return to this question of profit, but for the moment I want to expand this statement of purpose even further. As a microcosm of society, a corporation must reflect *all* of that society's shared values— social, moral, political and legal, as well as economic. It must change as society changes; but, as a dynamic institution, it can also seek to influence the ultimate form and expression of those changes (Day, 1969).

This is a view shared by many businessmen and academic scholars (Henry Ford II, 1972; Harold Johnson, 1971).

The proponents of social responsibilities are saying that society is not substituting one set of expectations for another. Rather it is broadening the standards by means of which corporate performance is to be judged. But obviously, what is meant by this differs from person to person. On the one hand, there are those who seem to believe that a business enterprise really has responsibilities which may require actions that "have no direct bearing on profits" (Rockefeller, 1964: 23). Others feel that business has a responsibility to find profit opportunities in solving social problems, but no obligation to do more than that.

The issue is entangled in semantics. There are some people who assert that the new views about social responsibilities represent nothing more than a modification of the old profit-maximizing goal of business. In the past the emphasis of business was on maximizing short-run profit, but now a shift has taken place to put a greater emphasis on maximizing long-range profit. The basis for the shift is that businessmen see that many things are happening in the environment today which will affect future profits, and they feel they must take action, even though it reduces short-term profits, to optimize long-range profits. The businessman, therefore, is still strictly an economic man.

In considering this position, it is important to understand the meaning of profit maximization. To the economist, this is a precise concept that can be measured quantitatively. It means that a firm will attempt to increase its output so long as the marginal revenue from the last item produced is greater than the marginal cost of that item. At that point where marginal cost equals marginal revenue, the firm will receive its maximum profit. This concept is found in all elementary economics textbooks; it means literally that a firm which seeks to maximize profits in this sense will not make any decision which will prevent it from getting the highest possible profit for its stockholders. As I have argued elsewhere, the economist's strict concept of profit maximization is not an acceptable operational goal for today's larger corporations—assuming they could achieve such a goal, which they rarely can (Steiner, 1969: 168–73). Much more appropriate is a concept of "required and rising profits," "or those needed to satisfy the many claims made on the enterprise, including the level necessary to meet the self-satisfactions of managers from participating in the resolution of social problems, improving the quality of life of employees and making this a better society." The level of required and rising profits may be achieved despite the assumption of expenditures for social responsibilities which may have little direct bearing on long-range profits. A company that can reach the level of profits required to balance properly the interests focused on its operations is in a position to take social actions. A company not in so favored a position may be unable to assume them.

Business decision-making today is a mixture of altruism, self-interest, and good citizenship. Managers do take actions which are in the social interest even though there is a cost involved and the connection with long-range profits is quite remote. These actions traditionally were considered to be in the category of "good deeds." The issue today is that some people expect, and some managers wonder whether they should respond to, business's assuming a central role in resolving major social problems of the day in the name of social responsibility. This is the view that business is responsible for achieving the quality of life which is considered to be possible in this evolving society. It would be disastrous for business and society if the latter view prevailed. Business cannot do this, nor should it try. Larger corporations, however, clearly feel that the old-fashioned single-minded lust for profits tempered with a few boy-scout good deeds must be modified in favor of a new social concern. Society also expects its business leaders to be concerned. The issue is not whether business has social responsibilities. It has them. The fundamental issue is to identify them for business in general and for the individual company.

THE CONCEPT OF VOLUNTARISM

In Exhibit 10–2 I have tried to capture in a simple picture some important concepts. It will be noted in the left drawing that a major pressure on business is economic, that is, to be efficient in dealing with its economic function of production, employing people, grow-

Exhibit 10–2.   Voluntary Business Social Responsibilities
Compared with Total Business Social Responsibilities
and Decisions

TOTAL BUSINESS SOCIAL RESPONSIBILITIES	TOTAL BUSINESS DECISIONS
100%	100%
	Voluntary area
Expectations beyond reality	Government-dictated. Demands made by outside groups and met by business under pressure
Voluntary area	
Government-dictated. Demands made by outside groups and met by business under pressure	
	Response to traditional "free" market forces
Traditional efficient production	
0%	0%

ing in a balanced fashion, and so on. In doing this, as noted previously, a company is being socially responsible. Beyond this are social responsibilities established by government and expressed in legal requirements. Included here, also, are responsibilities demanded by outside groups and accepted under pressure by business (e.g., union contracts). Next is an area marked "voluntary action," undertaken in response to an awareness of changing social values and priorities. Beyond this is a much larger area which encompasses emerging and amorphous responsibilities that society may expect business to assume. To the right of the chart are areas making up the totality of business decisions. Most decisions are made in response to traditional economic forces. Fewer are dictated by government and even fewer are voluntary social actions.

The magnitudes and relationships among these areas in the chart are not, of course, presumed to be accurate. Yet, I do think they serve in a somewhat elementary fashion to reveal several significant points. First, a comparable drawing of one hundred or even twenty-five years ago would show substantially different magnitudes. Second, the area of voluntarism is not really great in terms of the totality of business social responsibilities or the totality of total corporate actions. Yet, it is of very great significance to business as well as to society.

Within the voluntary area are zones of action. First, there are programs which might be called "legal plus." These are actions which go beyond present legislation and are considered to be socially responsible, such as employee safety, antipollution measures, or minority hiring and promotion programs. Second are programs about which there is a national consensus, such as contributing to local charities or to education. Third is an area about which there is no consensus. For instance, the United Church of Christ insists that Gulf Oil Corporation should get out of Angola as a socially responsible action. Others do not agree with this position.

Another way to look at this area of voluntarism is in terms of correlation with social expectations. The U.S. Chamber of Commerce sees four levels of business social responsibilities, as follows: first, conforming to existing legal requirements in fulfilling the economic function; second, meeting recognized public expectations and social demands; third, anticipating new social demands and preparing in advance to meet them; and fourth, serving as leaders in setting new standards of business social performance (1973). John D. Rockefeller, 3rd, takes a similar position in his book on *The Second American Revolution*. He concludes:

> The challenge is to be successful in business *and* in serving the needs of society. Is it unreasonable to assume that the same abilities and qualities apply in both cases? I think not (1973: 95).

Today there is no broad-based social pressure for every business, large and small, to assume all the programs that various well-meaning groups, as well as extreme activists, demand. The greater part of whatever pressure *does* exist is brought to bear on the large businesses, rather than on the small. However, even the larger ones are not expected to try to do everything. Individual companies can pick and choose those actions they wish to take in response to society's demands.

VOLUNTARISM VERSUS SOCIAL REFORMISM

The voluntary approach is rejected not only by many people who have a very conservative view of corporate responsibility, but also by the more radical activists. The voluntaristic view accepts the present political-economic system and seeks to make incremental reforms in it. Some social reformists, on the other hand, say that such an approach is superficial and inadequate for getting at the deep-rooted problems of this society. They believe that there can be no effective resolution of today's social ills, as they see them, short of major changes in national policy and in our basic institutions (including business). There is, of course, a spectrum of positions within each of these two opposed camps. Students of business's social responsibility should recognize the very different conclusions reached at these extreme points of departure (Bronfenbrenner, in Steiner, ed., 1972(A); Wish, Johnson, in Steiner, ed., 1973(A)).

IS THE DOCTRINE OF VOLUNTARY SOCIAL RESPONSIBILITY NEW?

The answer to the above question is no. Throughout history philosophers and theologians charged the businessman with responsibilities extending beyond merely operating efficiently and making money. In modern times prominent economists such as J. M. Clark (1934) and respected critics of business such as Adolph Berle (1932, 1954) supported this view. Despite these dissenters from Adam Smith's theory of strict self-interest (1776), the main thrust of economic theory has been in the classical tradition (Bell, 1967). So, too, with the practices of corporations. Throughout this country's history, individual corporations have taken on a rather surprising variety of programs that would receive top marks today in any register of high-minded social programs (Heald, 1970). However, in business history, as in economic theory, despite these activities (and they became more numerous with the passage of time), the main thrust of endeavor has been the pursuit of strictly economic goals.

HOW TOP MANAGERS VIEW THEIR SOCIAL RESPONSIBILITIES

Empirical observation, research studies, and polls leave no doubt that top managers of companies—particularly in the larger corporations—not only are highly concerned about social programs, but also are increasingly leading their companies into them. A recent survey of the annual reports of sixty companies (including the forty largest companies in the United States) shows a sharp rise in expression of social responsibilities. The number of socially responsible actions and statements steadily increased from 167 in the 1965 annual reports of these companies, to 576 in 1971 (Coppock, et al., 1972). Altogether, for the years 1965, 1967, 1969, 1970, and 1971, the survey found a total of 1,963 issues reported. The mix had changed considerably. Philanthropic activities and social and community involvement accounted for 48 percent of all items reported in 1965; this declined to 22 percent in 1971. Environmental issues, which accounted for 16 percent of all items in 1965, reached 42 percent in 1971. Consumer issues rose from 7 percent in 1965 to 11 percent in 1971. Of course, many reports were merely verbal statements of concern. However, examination of annual reports over this period clearly shows a very rapid increase in specific action programs in the social area.

These findings corroborate and amplify a poll of 350 executives taken in 1969 by *Fortune* magazine (Louis, 1969). The *Fortune* poll revealed varying opinions on the interrelationships between the amassing of profits and the assumption of social programs. At one end of the spectrum 10 percent of the survey sample said that the sole business of business was to make a profit. At the other extreme 17 percent said that business should assume social responsibilities even at the cost of reduced profits. Another 20 percent said that business should concentrate on profits, but pay more taxes and provide more human resources to help solve social problems. Another 8 percent said that business should improve its skills in solving social problems and make its knowledge available to government. The largest group—42 percent—said that business "first must make an *adequate* profit, then must assume public responsibilities that may not be profitable" (Louis, 1969: 94). Despite these variations, 94 percent of the executives said their companies were involved in social programs, such as training and employing the hard-core unemployed. Among the 10 percent who said business's sole responsibility was to make a profit, 60 percent said they had programs in full operation rather than merely in the thinking or pilot stage.

A survey made by the *Harvard Business Review* of 3,453 subscribers asked how valid they thought were the following four statements: (1) "A corporation's duty is to its owners and only to its owners." (2) "A corporation's duty is primarily to its owners and secondarily to employees, customers, and the public." (3) "A corporation's duty is to serve as fairly and equitably as it can the interests of four sometimes competing groups—owners, employees, customers, and the public." (4) "The primary duty of the enterprise is to itself—to ensure its future growth and continued functioning as a profit-making supplier of goods and services." Seventy-four percent responded that the first statement was the least valid of the four. Only 2 percent said it was the most valid. Sixty-one percent said that the third statement was the most valid of the four. Only 2 percent said that the second statement was the most valid (Ewing, 1971: 147). A study of 209 managers in a large Midwestern area were asked the same question and responded in essentially the same way (Krishnan, 1973).

What can one conclude from such surveys? Managers are undoubtedly more involved in dealing with social problems today than they were a decade or even a few years ago. (For two recent massive compilations of business social programs, see Moss, 1972; and Nowlan and Sharon, 1972.) They probably are not involved as much as some managers, and many people in general, would like them to be. In reviewing this situation one prominent businessman (Goldston, 1971: 76) asks critics of business to be patient and remember a prayer that the late Martin Luther King was fond of quoting from a black Southern minister:

> Lord, we ain't what we ought to be.
> We ain't what we want to be.
> We ain't what we're going to be.
> But, thank the Lord, we ain't what we was.

SHAREHOLDER PROPOSALS

Public interest groups literally have been swarming over the larger corporations in an effort to get them to act in conformance with the views of the activist groups. Every conceivable legitimate and potentially effective method has been employed in this drive. The use of the shareholder proposal by activist groups is of recent origin, at least in terms of scope of activity, and is discussed here briefly to illustrate one important type of pressure put upon companies to act in a socially responsible way.

One of the earliest uses of the stockholder proposal took place in 1967 at the Eastman Kodak Company. A civil rights organization using the acronym FIGHT sought to get Kodak to increase its hiring of minority workers. One of FIGHT's strategies was to buy a few shares of Kodak stock, so as to gain admission to the annual meeting of the shareholders, and be in a position to exert pressure directly on the management. FIGHT also solicited proxies from several church groups who held Kodak stock. While the votes in favor of FIGHT's proposals were insignificant in comparison to the total votes cast, the company eventually did increase its employment of black workers.

Two years later the Project on Corporate Responsibility was formed in Ralph Nader's organization. The proposal for the organization expressed the hypothesis that many of the most important political decisions made in the United States are made not by government but by major corporations. Corporate executives, it said, could do much more to solve major social problems. Unfortunately, however, they are heavily insulated from the kinds of pressures which other policy makers must respond to. Also, their chief concern is profit maximization rather than public weal (Center for Law and Social Policy, 1969).

"The Project on Corporate Responsibility," therefore said the proposal, "will attempt to make corporate decision-makers more responsive to legitimate social demands. . . . By harnessing the hitherto untapped power of shareholders to express political preferences, the Project will try to increase executive awareness of the social (rather than financial) consequences of their decisions."

The proposal went on to say that the project would solicit proxies from various institutions holding stock in the corporations at which its shareholder proposals would be made. It added, "the Project is not structured to take control of corporations. Instead, the project's strategies will be designed to take advantage of a corporation's need for a good public image and the desire of corporation executives to be part of a socially responsible (and acceptable) institution. In addition, occasionally litigation will be utilized to compel corporations to obey the law. . . ." The proposal then went on to describe in great detail the strategies to be used at stockholder meetings.

The first attack of the project was Campaign GM. In 1970 the project bought a few shares of General Motors' stock and introduced a shareholder proposal with two major demands at the annual stockholders' meeting. One was to put three "public interest" directors on the board. The other was to set up a committee on corporate responsibility to examine GM's performance in dealing with social and environmental issues and recommend actions "to make GM responsible." In subsequent years the project introduced other resolutions at stockholder meetings of GM and many other companies. While votes in all instances have been heavily against the project, its pressures have undoubtedly moved companies to take actions in the directions the project has aimed.

This movement has grown until in 1973 one listing showed thirty-one major organized protest actions at annual meetings of corporations. Another listing showed that one group alone (Church Project on U.S. Investments in Southern Africa (CPASA)) planned to present shareholder proposals at twenty-one corporations (*Economic Priorities Report*, 1973).

This movement has been paralleled by the growing concern of large institutional investors about the use of their investments to advance socially responsible actions of corporations. Pressures and interests have come from within and outside of these institutions. Top executives of large institutional investors, for example, have expressed concern about social aspects of their investment policy (Greenough, 1971). Pressures have been placed upon university investment officers by students. This has resulted in a number of reports to help guide university investment portfolio selection and proxies (Longstreth and Rosenbloom, 1973). These reports, by and large, have made suggestions for exercising stockholder powers to make corporations act in a more socially responsible fashion, although they generally have recommended that this be done with caution in light of conventional goals to maximize safety and yield. Several mutual funds were formed in 1971 to invest in companies having acceptable social programs. The most publicized was the Dreyfus Third Century Fund.

To find out how responsive institutional investors have been to the social point of view the Ford Foundation conducted a study of 115 institutions (religious, universities, foundations, insurance companies, banks, and mutual funds). The significant findings were as follows: 57.4 percent said "they take social considerations into account in the selection and retention of investments"; 40.0 percent said they consider "on the merits" all proxies relating to social and political matters; and 23.5 percent said they had special procedural mechanisms to take social considerations into account in their investment process or have policy statements on the matter (Longstreth and Rosenbloom, 1973: 42–43).

The mutual funds formed to invest in stocks of companies having good social action programs to the date of this writing (mid-1973) did not do well (Shapiro, 1973). One reason has been that many companies who received high marks as being socially responsible did not chalk up the same good score in profit margins during the 1971–1973 period.

Arguments for and against this kind of pressure by institutional investors on corporations range across a spectrum with opposite positions at the extremes. Manne, for example, opposes strongly the pressures of groups such as the Project on Corporate Responsibility (1971, 1972). At the other extreme are such activist groups as the United Church of Christ (1970).

In an analysis of the issues Malkiel and Quandt raise some significant questions (1971). They ask, first, how can a person decide which companies should be favored and which avoided? Xerox, for example, is condemned by some activist groups for being in South Africa and yet Xerox is high on many lists of the most socially responsible companies. Malkiel and Quandt say that so interrelated is business activity that once a precedent is established for buying or selling stocks for social reasons, a case can be made for avoiding investment in virtually any company. Second, they ask, is sale of securities in companies less socially minded the best course of action? They believe that direct pressure on management through the proxy vote and contacts is likely to yield better results than the sale of stock. Third, they ask whether an investment manager's trusteeship would be violated if, because of the application of noneconomic criteria, returns on his portfolio were lower. They seem to think so. Fourth, so far as university funds are concerned, they raise a question about whether the use of social and moral criteria might endanger the basic purpose of the university. They reason that "if the university were to take a formal position in moral, social, or political matters, as a corporate entity, the freedom of its members to hold and teach contrary positions would be seriously compromised in principle and eventually eroded in practice" (44). This issue does not apply, of course, to other institutional investors.

In the final analysis there is no reason why managers of investment portfolios ought not exert pressures on companies in whom they invest. However, it would seem that the pressures ought to be in the interests of the constituents of the investment manager as they see their interests and not as the manager thinks he sees them.

BUSINESS AND MAJOR SOCIAL PROBLEMS

Business Is Not Solely Responsible for Solving Social Problems Business is a predominant instrumentality in society for dealing with major social problems, but it is not the institution of sole or last responsibility. It is government that has the central role in dealing with such problems. Business has major incentives for working on these problems, as noted previously. It has great talents which it can exert, ranging from the development of new equipment to reduce pollutions of various types to contributing managerial knowledge free to government agencies. A central issue in dealing with social problems concerns the extent to which government should provide incentives for business to become involved in solving social problems when it does not appear to business to be profitable to do so. It also must be pointed out that other institutions in society such as universities, labor unions, and religious institutions and people themselves, individually and in groups, can make valuable contributions to overcoming major social problems.

Social Responsibility and the Costs of Doing Business Will not the socially responsible company be put at a competitive disadvantage? If it goes too far, the answer is yes. However, a great many social responsibilities can be pursued without substantial costs to an enterprise—for example, improving due process within the company, encouraging managers to lend their knowledge in resolving local community as well as national problems, and locating plants in underprivileged areas. Many social responsibilities can be pursued, as noted before, while making profits. Some may be costly, such as not closing a marginal plant in a community dependent upon it, making large capital equipment expenditures to reduce the pollution of the company's environment, and giving substantial funds to the community for beautification.

Business must develop a new concept of costs. Costs of doing business are not solely those concerned with purchasing, producing, and distributing goods and services in the traditional accounting sense. Most managers say that their most precious assets are people. If so, the preservation and use of those assets entail a cost beyond the money wage. All thinking managers know that much of the cost borne by society for many activities (education, for instance) is of enormous benefit to business. Business does pay taxes, but it is questionable that it bears a cost equal to the benefits derived. Finally, there are many costs borne by society as a result of business activity which business does not fully defray. For the first two groups of costs, a business may ask itself whether it is doing enough to carry its share, and if not, whether it wishes to assume further responsibilities to do so. In the last case there are two questions. One concerns the social responsibility a firm may feel for bearing some of these costs, and the other deals with legal liabilities. The boundaries overlap.

How Much Social Cost Should Business Bear? Social costs are the total costs of business activity, including immediate costs of production plus all other costs. For instance, a factory dumping pollutants into a clear stream incurs two kinds of costs. One is the cost of its operation; the other is the costs that result from changes in the stream's ecology—perhaps human and animal disease, perhaps the destruction of natural beauty. To the extent that business does not bear these external costs, they must be borne by others.

These "other costs" include a spectrum of elements. They may involve direct and indirect losses of third persons, such as reduced real estate values from nearby factory noise. They include human damage in the form of disease, accident, loss of jobs, disturbance of social relationships, and changes in the life style of groups. They may include defaced landscapes, ugly buildings, or traffic congestion. Some costs are incurred immediately; others may take a long time to be felt. Some costs can be measured in dollar terms, such as the price for cleaning up a polluted stream. Others, such as the impairment of health resulting from air pollution, cannot be gauged in quantitative terms. Indeed, the determination of many social costs depends upon the value society attaches to a particular impact and its relationships to the benefits of social change.

Capitalism has been called "an economy of unpaid costs" (Kapp, 1950: 231). By this is meant that a large part of actual costs of production are not counted as business expenses, but are shifted to and borne by third persons or by the community as a whole. As society has become more complex, there has been a rise in the unpaid costs

of business. In our earlier history these costs generally were considered to be implicit byproducts of economic life and regarded
as the short-run price to be paid for the higher economic efficiency
and long-run social advantage resulting from the operation of the
economic system. Eventually, laws were passed to force business
to meet unpaid costs where injury to third parties could be reasonably determined. The political history of the United States increasingly
reflected the unwillingness of the masses of the people to bear the
social costs of economic development without help from government.
Throughout this history business pressure groups sought to avoid
the assumption of social costs that had been transferred to others.

In considering business responsibility for social costs, it should
be remembered that business creates social values. Important benefits accrue to society through business's activities. A business, for
instance, may introduce an innovation that will cut the costs of
making a particular product. Assuming no other significant cost than
that of production, the result is a net gain in social value. A company may erect a beautiful building, tastefully landscaped. Or a
company may contribute to advancing knowledge. Theoretically, a
business firm should in the long run cover all costs of production and
should profit from the social benefits it creates. This attitude suggests that in the long run, social costs should be borne by those
responsible for creating them or those who bear them should be
compensated. It also suggests that a firm should receive compensation in accordance with its contribution to social benefit. Unfortunately, in only a comparatively few instances can such cause and
effect relationships be isolated and measured. More often, the determinants cannot be identified or quantified.

What then is the operating liability of a company? From an
ethical point of view, a company "should consider carefully both
the social costs involved in its operations and the social values it
creates, and do what it can in the light of its competitive situation to
compensate for the net social costs for which it is responsible"
(Bowen, 1953: 214). This, of course, leaves much room for interpretation.

The Legality of Corporate Philanthropy During the nineteenth
century, courts of law held that a corporation existed only to provide
profits for distribution to stockholders. Corporate giving was identified as an *ultra vires* act. In 1919, in *Dodge v. Ford Motor Company*,
a Michigan court said that business was to be operated primarily for
the profit of stockholders and forced the company to declare a dividend, which it had not done for many years. The older restraints to
corporate giving were removed by the A.P. Smith case in 1953, in
which the Supreme Court refused to review a decision of the highest
court in New Jersey. The board of directors of the A.P. Smith

Company, manufacturers of machinery and equipment for water and gas industries, gave Princeton University $1,500 as a contribution toward its general maintenance. Questioned by the stockholders, the corporation sought a declaratory judgment asking that its action be sustained. The New Jersey Supreme Court, in affirming a lower court decision, said:

> It seems to us that just as the conditions prevailing when corporations were originally created required that they serve public as well as private interests, modern conditions require that corporations acknowledge and discharge social as well as private responsibilities as members of the communities within which they operate. Within this broad concept there is no difficulty in sustaining, as incidental to their proper objects and in aid of the public welfare, the power of corporations to contribute corporate funds within reasonable limits in support of academic institutions. But even if we confine ourselves to the terms of the common law rule in its application to current conditions, such expenditures may likewise readily be justified as being for the benefit of the corporation; indeed, if need be the matter may be viewed strictly in terms of actual survival of the corporation in a free enterprise system . . . [*A. P. Smith Manufacturing Company v. Barlow et al.,* 26 N.J. Super. 106 (1953); affirmed, 98 Atl. (2d) 581; appeal to U.S. Supreme Court dismissed, 346 U.S. 861 (1953)].

In the Revenue Act of 1935, Congress made it possible for corporations to deduct from taxable earnings their charitable contributions up to 5 percent of net profits. Most states also have such legislation. The legal requirements which require directors to exercise sound business judgment and to act in a fiduciary capacity to corporate interests are not relaxed, however.

Is Business in Danger of Going Overboard? Assertions by some business leaders give the impression that they are ready to assume significant social responsibilities. Is business in danger of going overboard and trying to do too much?

Since 1935, when the Revenue Act permitted deductions for charitable donations, the annual average charitable contributions of corporations have been much less than 1 percent of gross profits. This is, however, an impressive aggregate sum, for it is today well over $1 billion annually. In comparison with the total contributions of Americans to charitable purposes of around $20 billion, however, it is not large. Nor is it outstanding in comparison with corporate before tax profits in 1973 of around $125 billion. At the present time, David Finn, a public relations expert and inside observer of corporate top managements, concludes that the typical top manager is still rooted to making profits and "has shown little inclination to make community betterment his goal" (1969: 248). Until there is a great change in top management's point of view, it is doubtful that corporate contributions will rise to the 5 percent credit allowed by the Revenue Act.

It is not fair to judge corporate managements solely on the basis of tax deductions. Managers spend many hours of work on community problems and other issues associated with social responsibilities. Actions are taken, such as a delay in moving an unprofitable plant, which they know will reduce profits. They do keep on the payroll employees who are not as productive as new ones who could replace them. They do take costly measures to reduce air and water pollution. They do spend huge sums of money in undertaking product research to improve product quality and safety. All this gets mixed into self-interest, "good business," better "image," and other such motivations. If it were possible to put a dollar cost on such actions, the figure, I am sure, would be in excess of charitable contributions.

All this does not add up to a major deviation from past philosophy. Eli Goldston, when president of Eastern Gas and Fuel Associates, said that "net profit per share is more important to professional managers than many current theorists assume. . . ." (Goldston, in *Daedalus*, 1969: 80). Given these dimensions of corporate assumption of social responsibilities, we are so far from going to excess that the theses of Friedman and Levitt explained early in the chapter are equivalent to fearing that a leaky faucet will bring on the Johnstown flood.

CRITERIA FOR DETERMINING THE SOCIAL RESPONSIBILITIES OF BUSINESS

I am not so much concerned about business going overboard in assuming social responsibilities as I am that social expectations of what business can and should do may get out of hand. For both business and society generally, clearer boundaries than now exist for the assumption of social responsibilities must be set. In the light of today's economic realities, of the intensity of social problems in and out of an individual business, and of society's expectations and goals, what might be acceptable overall guides to business's assumption of social responsibilities? I suggest the following:

First, there is no formula for all businesses or any one business. Each firm must decide for itself. Business can take action, but it is not compelled to do so except when law and custom determine otherwise. I suppose that the first social responsibility of each business is to think carefully before acting about what it thinks its social responsibilities really are. In doing this, each company must not underestimate the magnitude of the tasks involved in dealing with major social problems. A proper estimate is important, for studies show that in the recent past companies have tended to move with more energy than discretion in dealing with some social problems.

They have confessed that they underestimated the tasks they accepted and that more money, time, and thought were required than they originally had calculated (Cohn, 1970: 68–82).

In deciding what to do, the values and interests of top managers are, of course, guiding considerations. Companies are run by men at the top, and in more and more companies there are oligarchies, or groups of men, who set major guides for company actions. These men have systems of values and interests which are important to them. Since part of the fun of managing a company is in advancing one's own self-satisfaction and self-fulfillment, the power of the company can and should be used to satisfy the socially responsible values and interests of top management. The generous contributions of many companies to the performing arts is one reflection of the values of their top managements. The levels and directions of public expectations which top management thinks are focused on the company are also guiding considerations. Companies are expected to be philanthropic in the communities in which they do business. A public utility is naturally expected to take special pains in training and hiring underprivileged local unemployed workers. The public expects an aircraft manufacturer to be especially careful about the safety of his products as compared with the expectation, for instance, of a manufacturer of lawn mowers. Some sort of crude cost-benefit analysis ought to be helpful to a company in its consideration of social responsibilities.

Second, business must be considered to be predominantly an economic institution with a strong profit motive. Business should not be used to meet noneconomic objectives of society in a major way without financial incentives. Whatever we do, and whatever we expect business to do, it is of paramount importance that no action be taken to erode the profit motive. The fundamental justification for this view is supported by Will and Ariel Durant, who looked over the broad sweep of history they so assiduously chronicled and concluded that "the experience of the past leaves little doubt that every economic system must sooner or later rely upon some form of the profit motive to stir individuals and groups to productivity. Substitutes like slavery, police supervision, or ideological enthusiasm prove too unproductive, too expensive, or too transient" (Durant, 1968: 54). We must continue to judge business performance primarily on the basis of economic criteria. Business should be expected to make its greatest contribution to the resolution of social problems through making a profit by discovering new opportunities itself, or by being given incentives by other institutions to profit by its actions. Conscience and profit may pull in the same direction. Business's search for profitable opportunities in the past has reduced or eliminated many hard social problems and can do so in the future.

Third, business should be expected to take the long view and perform socially responsible actions that might temporarily lessen net profits but that are in the profit interests of the company in the long run. It is quite clear that the long-range self-interest of business lies in correcting such problems as unemployment, civil disorders, environmental pollution, and crime.

Fourth, an individual business has social responsibilities, says Keith Davis, commensurate with its social powers (1960: 71). This seems simple enough, but putting the principle into practice can be complicated. That power and responsibility go hand in hand is an idea as old as civilization itself. This can be only a rough guide to action, but it can be a useful one. For instance, company A is the major employer in a town, and company B is an employer of only 5 percent of the people in the town. Both companies are planning to move. It would seem that, other things being equal, company A should give more thought to its social responsibilities in moving than should company B. Having said this, however, we still do not know to what extent the formula of co-equal power and responsibility should alter the decision of company A. This sort of problem is what Davis calls a "socio-economic responsibility."

There are also, he says, "socio-human responsibilities" of companies. Considering a business as only an economic institution may lead to the conclusion that it has some responsibilities concerned with the economic costs of unemployment, but not with the erosion of human dignity or social disorganization following loss of a job. Or a business may be concerned with increasing creative capability in individuals to improve productivity, but not with attempting to help workers get more self-fulfillment from their jobs. Davis says this is wrong because business deals with the whole man in a whole social structure. Furthermore, businessmen have socio-human power, that is, power over the quality of a man's life. As such, they have socio-human responsibilities commensurate with that power. Again, this equation yields no sure answers in any situation, but it should help.

Fifth, and closely associated with the preceding point, is the matter of company size and type. As a firm grows larger, it has an actual and potential influence on more and more people: society then takes a greater interest in what it does, and the company in turn thinks more carefully about its responsibilities. It tends to become affected with a public interest. Everyone knows there is always a potential for the abusive use of power. As corporations acquire more power over people, therefore, there is pressure for them to install protective policies, rules, and actions so that individuals are less likely to be injured unjustly or without due process. The social responsibilities of the smallest entrepreneur-owner business are not many, but there are some. For example, a very small business in a ghetto area has a social responsibility not to raise prices arbitrarily nor to sell defective goods as first quality. As an institution, however, society does not expect many social responsibilities of small business other than to provide goods and services within the law and codes of honesty and integrity.

Social responsibilities differ with respect to types of company. The special position of public utilities was noted above. A company involved in the mass production of a very competitively priced product is in a much different position with respect to the feelings and personal interests of employees in leading the good life at work than, say, a technically oriented and highly profitable laboratory manned by Ph.Ds. A mining company is in a different position with respect to employee safety than, say, a small real estate office.

Sixth, no one should expect a business voluntarily to jeopardize its ability to attract stockholder investment. If a corporation diverts substantial sums of money to social purposes, it will significantly reduce its average return on capital which in turn will bring reduced growth rates, a lower market evaluation of its securities, or both. This sort of thing cannot, of course, long continue. A company guilty of serious air and water pollution may be forced to clean up its waste even though the impact may have great profit consequences. On the other hand, a company which has profit levels well above the industry average may find leverage in assuming social responsibilities of greater magnitude than a company much below the industry average.

Seventh, an effort should be made to determine which agencies in society are best able to undertake tasks in dealing with social problems, and proper responsibilities should be assigned to them. In some areas the government is clearly the best agent (for example, national security). In other areas business is the best (for example, in producing goods). An individual business should choose only those social responsibilities it can best manage. Traditionally, business does a better job when the task entails a minimum of political involvement, does not get directly into the democratic political processes, deals with a physical problem that can be quantified and measured, and is one in which it has experience. These conflict a bit. For instance, training the hard-core unemployed is not a physical but a people activity, although it is one with which business has had much experience and recent success. A business that can pass on costs to consumers (for example, a public utility may use less efficient workers and get higher rates because of higher costs) may do more than one faced with a highly elastic and declining demand for its product.

Eighth, business should be obliged to internalize more of its external costs. In the past, businesses were excused from bearing such costs of production as air and water pollution, scarring hillsides in the search of coal and defacing natural beauty. Society then held the economic output of business to be of higher priority. Today, priorities are shifting and business is expected to bear more social costs. This is, however, a complex problem to which we will return later.

As both guides and boundaries, these criteria can justify the assumption of almost no social responsibilities or rather substantial ones. There are, however, a few overriding generalizations that may sharpen the focus.

It seems to me that when a company can assume social responsibilities with almost no cost or very small ones, it has an obligation to do so (for example, social justice inside the company). One area of potential high payoff for little or no cost is informing the public about the operation and social value of the business system. Indeed, I think this is an important social responsibility which business has not fulfilled. If people do not know, or misunderstand, they are much more likely to be swayed by irresponsible criticism and to expect far more from the business institution than they should in their own long-range self-interests. This is a responsibility which should also be borne by the academic world and government.

The shift in the thinking of more and more businessmen is away from short-run to long-run profits. There is also an important philosophical drift from unbridled self-interest to an enlightened social interest. It is a new way of looking at business power, interest, and operation. It can accommodate a good bit of what we now speak of as social responsibility without eroding the economic incentive. Indeed, a great deal of the socially responsible action that can be accepted by business will strengthen the profit incentive.

CHAPTER ELEVEN

Making Social Responsibilities Operational in Business

INTRODUCTION

The question of whether or not business has social responsibilities is settled in the minds of most observers and managers of larger companies. Today managers are wrestling with the problem of how to identify which social programs their company should pursue on a voluntary basis, how much to do, and how to inject the social view into the company's decision-making processes. These questions are examined in this chapter.

INSTITUTIONALIZING SOCIAL ACTION IN THE DECISION-MAKING PROCESS

From a societal view, as well as from the view of top managers who accept the idea of social responsibilities for their firms, it is desirable to have the social point of view institutionalized. This means that once a top social policy has been formulated, its implementation becomes a part of the day-to-day routine decision-making processes throughout the company. Managers consider it in their decision-making without continuous surveillance by higher-level managers.

It is important to distinguish among three types of social action programs in this connection. First are the programs pursued because of legislation, such as equal opportunity or safety. In this category also are programs undertaken because of contractual arrangements with labor unions, such as those concerning equitable hiring, promoting, and firing of employees. The second category includes company social programs which top management decides voluntarily to undertake. The third are social programs undertaken by managers throughout an organization on a voluntary basis and not dictated by higher-level managers. These managers have a social point of view which leads them to act as individuals, or for their particular organizations, in ways fitting into but not determined by top management attitudes and policies.

If a company is to avoid legal penalties for noncompliance it must, in the case of the first class of actions, establish policies, plans, procedures, control mechanisms, and incentives to assure that goals are achieved in conformance with law and contract. In this way the social program is entwined in the decision-making processes of the company, from top to bottom. If this is not done and if top management does not continuously survey activities, lower-level managers may sabotage the program if they find themselves in opposition to it on value, economic, or other grounds.

Similarly, actions of the second type may not be undertaken in organizations even when top policy has been announced, in the absence of implementation procedures, rewards, and penalties. The problem here is somewhat different, however, because now the motivating force results from greater top management interest and not from any legal compulsion. Lower-level managers not in complete sympathy with the program may be more difficult to persuade than when legal sanctions are involved. This is especially true, as noted below, if social goals and manager-financial goals are in conflict.

Finally, it is even more difficult for top managers to get lower-level managers to act in the third category if they are not disposed to do so. There is a world of difference between lofty top management rhetoric at high levels of abstraction—olympian megathoughts, as one manager put it—and specific actions on the front lines of lower-level managers.

Because of such considerations most companies begin the pursuit of voluntary social programs gradually and only slowly develop full-scale programs by means of which they become institutionalized in the decision-making process. Before examining this transition it is worthwhile to comment further as to why there is resistance to institutionalizing social programs (both government-dictated and voluntarily undertaken) in many companies.

REALITIES OF INJECTING VOLUNTARY SOCIAL ACTION IN THE DECISION-MAKING PROCESS

Chief executives of companies are thought to have extraordinary power to get things done in their enterprises. When asked about their power, however, they begin talking about how little power they have. President John Kennedy used to comment frequently to a visitor as follows: "I agree with you, but I cannot speak for the State Department." What he meant was that even with all the power at his command he found it difficult to move the State Department to act as he wanted it to act. Much the same problem exists with the chief executive of a large company.

At a particular time a company operates on the basis of a set of established policies and procedures, customs, precedents, human values, and managerial styles. Chief executives have an important hand in the design of the system over which they preside, but they also must operate within the system. The system itself restrains the use of power except as prescribed by the system. Power of chief executives is also restrained because they know that if they force a significant change in the system, the results may not be entirely what they want. There are risks in injecting change in corporate systems. This does not mean chief executives do not have power. They do. It means that wise managers exercise their power very carefully and, if possible, gradually and with the concurrence of other managers.

To illustrate, consider the incentive and control systems of most businesses today. The focus in most firms is on net profit in the short run. Objectives are directed toward its improvement, plans are laid to achieve profit objectives, controls are exerted to assure that plans are implemented, and managerial rewards are based upon accomplishment of profit goals. The rules and controls are well-established and expressed in quantitative terms. Actions can be assessed readily in terms of impact on profits.

To inject into this well-established and well-understood system new objectives and new values concerned with social programs which cannot be easily evaluated in terms of desirability or performance, is a very complex, difficult, and risky operation. In a centralized functional type of organization where the managerial lines of control are comparatively short and tight, the problems in injecting important social values are challenging, to say the least. They are more challenging in a company with decentralized profit centers.

Typically, in an organization such as the latter, the top management of the company headquarters lays down company policies, strategies, objectives, and standards of performance. Within this framework the top managers of the divisions develop their own policies, strategies, objectives, and detailed plans. The top management of divisions have wide authority to act as they see fit. Their performance is measured by headquarters and, as noted above, evaluation is made in terms of profit. In this system the top management of the company does not interfere in the detailed operations of the divisions. A division manager, in this system, is not likely to undertake social programs which may significantly increase his costs and reduce his net profit.

This is an oversimplified picture but is closer to reality than the assumption that a chief executive can do anything he wants to do in his company. It is important to note in this connection that most corporate business is done in decentralized companies. Ackerman examined the 500 largest companies in the U.S. and found that in 1949 less than 20 percent had product divisions, compared with over 75 percent in 1969. (Presumably, most if not all had some degree of decentralized authority.) In 1949, about 63 percent of the companies had functional organizations, compared with 11 percent in 1969 (1973).

Wide gaps exist among different levels of managers concerning the wisdom of social programs. To test this hypothesis a study was made of 1,135 managers at different levels in one company. Each manager was questioned about his attitude toward the following propositions:

(1) Many contemporary social problems will not be solved unless corporate managers commit their companies to helping to find solutions; (2) corporations have a definite obligation to clean up air and water pollution; (3) corporations have a definite responsibility to provide greater job opportunities for minority groups; and (4) corporations have a definite obligation to provide greater job opportunities for women. In each instance top level managers held their beliefs more strongly than those at lower levels. The gap became progressively wider at each level (Collins, 1973). Quite obviously in this company the gap should be narrowed if the "privates" are to follow the policy rhetoric of the "generals."

FROM TOP MANAGEMENT CONCERN
TO INSTITUTIONALIZATION OF SOCIAL PROGRAMS

An interest in having a company undertake social programs can arise anywhere in the company. Top management must accept the idea, however, if the company is to become seriously concerned about social programs on a company-wide basis. Once top management is convinced, however, the implementation of the social point of view is by no means simple or automatic. For most companies the transition from top management social concern to institutionalization of social programs takes place step by step and on the basis of a number of different methods.

Following are a few organizational methods used today to implement voluntary social policies. They are not sequential. In actual practice, some are more likely to succeed than others.

Moral Suasion The top management of a company by its example or through persuasion and encouragement may seek to stimulate managers and employees to pursue social actions. The assumption is that managers by this method will be willing and anxious to comply with the basic policies of top management without being subject to detailed procedures and controls. The process usually involves distribution of memoranda, speeches, and other documents which explain top management's social views. Sometimes staff offices at company headquarters continue the moral persuasion through follow-up memoranda and discussion.

This technique will surely fail to produce satisfactory results in the business setting described above. Managers who are measured on a short-term ROI will not easily be moved to undertake programs which will lower their financial performance. Antagonisms can develop between managers and staff groups and become intensified, perhaps by guilt pangs of managers who would like to be more socially conscious, but feel they cannot be, in their own self-interest.

Compulsion Top management can, of course, decide what social programs a company will pursue and then can make implementation of these programs compulsory for its managers. This technique will not work unless it is accompanied with appropriate detailed policies, procedures, controls, and rewards or penalties for performance against a standard. Such a system can work, but as noted previously, it will create serious tensions in a company if it forces managers to do things which they feel are not in their self-interests. Skillful managers may find ways to erase conflicts between their financial goals and the company social goals. If they cannot, however, the basis for serious conflicts in the company will exist.

Using the Board of Directors A company that is seriously concerned with social affairs may add to the board one or more directors with a broad social point of view. This is not a suggestion that such directors "represent" society but that they bring the societal view to the top decision-making level of the company.

A number of companies have created board committees to give social policy direction. In 1970 General Motors Corporation created the Public Policy Committee composed of five members of the GM board. All members of the committee are outside members of the board. The committee meets once a month and has made a number of recommendations to the GM management covering a wide range of subject matter. It has no direct power but the committee has been highly influential in getting social programs under way at GM. Other companies having comparable board committees are Ford Motor Company, IBM, Kimberly Clark, and Philip Morris.

Top-Level Officers, Staffs, and Committees In a significant number of larger companies responsibility for social programs has been given to top level officers, staffs, and committees. In the fall of 1973 under the auspices of the Committee for Economic Development I conducted a survey of the state of the art of the social audit in American companies. A survey was mailed to 750 companies and 284 usable responses were received. Most of the companies were large, only 5 percent had annual sales under $100 million (Steiner, 1973; Corson and Steiner, 1974). The question was asked: "Has your company given any person, organizational unit or group responsibility for surveying more or less continuously the evolving demands on your company for social action programs?" A total of 70 percent answered yes. Among these, 42 percent said the responsibility was lodged in the public and community affairs department; another 14 percent said it was placed in a senior vice president; 11 percent said it was in an environmental and urban affairs staff; 6 percent said in corporate relations; 6 percent in a vice president of personnel; 4 percent in a board committee on corporate responsibility; 3 percent in the board of directors; and lesser percentages in the senior vice president—human resources; ad hoc executive task force; and director of planning and budgeting.

Many, but not all of the departments concerned with public and community affairs trace their roots to corporate staffs which were created in the 1950s to deal with governmental relations. Since then the functions of these staffs have expanded rapidly. While functions vary from company to company these staffs are now involved in five major areas: government relations, encouragement of employee participation in political and civic affairs, political and economic education programs for employees, corporate contributions and community service programs, and socioeconomic programs. (For more details see Chapter 22.)

A large part of the work of officers of these departments is concerned with communications with company constituencies, both outside and inside. Increasingly, however, these officers are becoming involved in policy-making and program implementation in their companies in the broad area of social responsibility. One survey showed, for example, that 90 percent of public affairs officers in forty-one companies said their companies had made organizational changes recently in response to public expectations of increased social responsibility (Bradt, 1972). While Bradt's study does not make clear that it was the public affairs officer that stimulated the organizational change, it is implied, probably correctly, that he did so and/or had an important role in making the decision. The changes made include the establishment of corporate committees to conduct studies of company environmental practices, the determination of company objectives, and the formulation of social policies for the company.

A number of companies have formed ad hoc top-level committees of senior officers to frame social policy. The Bank of America, for instance, formed such a committee in 1971. It recommended that the bank concentrate on the following four major social problem areas: housing in minority areas; jobs, job training, business opportunities, and education among minorities; environment, including loans which will improve or protect the environment, area development services, including bank research publications; and social unrest, including student relations programs, student awards and loans, foundation support, and so on.

The Security Pacific Bank has developed a program which, to oversimplify, establishes weights for determining whether a specific social program should be undertaken and with what emphasis. Criteria are established for factors relating to how the program fits into company strategy and how it relates to various managerial considerations. Many managers participate in the selection process and those programs which get the highest number of points are the ones from which top management makes the final selection.

Management by Objective Once program areas of interest are identified, action programs can be carried out by several methods. The Southern California Edison Company, for instance, identified four major areas of concern, as follows: education, urban and regional planning, environmental preservation, and governmental effectiveness. A management-by-objective program was developed in which general policy in each of the four problem areas was formulated. Specific actions to be taken within each of the policies in each area were identified, and responsibility for carrying out the policies and programs was assigned to a specific department, officer or manager, or other individual. The system was then assessed and reports of performance routinely made.

THE REWARD AND PERFORMANCE MEASUREMENT SYSTEM

Managers respond best when specific goals are set for their performance and when their rewards are determined by how well they perform in meeting those goals. If lower-level managers are to be made responsible for social programs to meet new societal expectations, and are expected to inject the social point of view in their planning and decision-making, it would be self-defeating if their efforts were measured solely by old narrow economic criteria. What can be done? Obviously the answer is to inject new standards for evaluating managerial performance. This is not easy, as will be discussed later, because acceptable quantitative measures of performance in the social area have not been invented. In the meantime, a number of companies measure managerial performance for bonuses and promotion on the basis of a point system. If measurement is on a scale where, say, 100 is perfect, most of the points will be determined by economic performance. This can be measured quantitatively. For socially responsible activities, and other actions not measurable quantitatively, subjective evaluations will add additional points. The values of perfect performance on the point scale can, of course, be set forth for different activities so that a manager will know how many points a perfect performance in a given area will gain for him.

COST NEGOTIATION

If a manager is to be held accountable solely or primarily for the net profit performance of his organization he will, as noted previously, be very reluctant to undertake programs in the name of social responsibility if they threaten reduction of his profits. One way to avoid conflict between the financial goals of such a manager and the social goals of top management is to negotiate costs. If top management wishes to increase the proportion of minorities in managerial positions in the divisions it may be necessary to increase the costs of training. If the divisional manager can be assured that the company will not burden his budget with the increased training costs, he will be much more amenable to implementing top management's policies in this regard.

COMPREHENSIVE SOCIAL POLICIES FOR A COMPANY

Another step which some companies are now taking is that of developing over-all policies to serve as guides for specific actions relating to social programs. The following policies are suggested for a comprehensive approach to institutionalizing the social point of view in a company (Steiner, 1972). Each item should be prefaced by: "It is the policy of this company . . ."

1. to think carefully about its social responsibilities. This policy does not commit a company to any particular social program, but it does say that the company feels its first social responsibility is to think carefully about its social responsibilities.
2. to make full use of tax deductibility laws through contributions, when profit margins permit. This policy simply takes advantage of the tax laws but does not commit the company beyond its current minimum philanthropy unless it feels that profit margins are high enough to warrant further giving.
3. to bear the social costs attendant upon its operations when it is

possible to do so without jeopardizing its competitive or financial position. This policy says the company wishes to avoid the adverse side effects on society of its operations to the extent that it can do so.

4. to concentrate action programs on limited objectives. No company can take significant action in every area of social responsibility. It can achieve more if it selects areas in which to concentrate its efforts. This policy, therefore, sets limits on social programs.

5. to concentrate action programs on areas strategically related to the present and prospective functions of the business, to begin action programs close to home before acting in far distant regions, and to deal first with what appears to be the most urgent areas of concern to the company. This policy has many facets to it. For example, it does not say that a company should take only that action which is closest to its self-interest. It does say that it should concentrate its efforts in areas that will be importantly related to its survival and healthy growth. To implement this policy it will be necessary for a company to assess carefully the various expectations of its many constituencies, especially those close to it, lay out priorities for action, and then see to implementation. It says, for example, that it is much more important for a public utility to pay attention to what people in and out of the company expect by way of social action than to make contributions to charities far removed geographically from the company.

6. to facilitate employee actions which can be taken as individuals rather than as representatives of the company. This is an encouragement to try to free people who want to be released. A company should not force employees to go out in the community to do good deeds but there is a great opportunity for companies to encourage and provide means for their employees to pursue their community interests.

7. to search for product and service opportunities to permit our company and others to make profits while at the same time advancing the social interests; but not all social actions should be taken solely for profit. This policy recognizes that there are many things a company can do that are socially responsible and profitable. The combination should be encouraged.

8. to take actions in the name of social responsibilities but not at the expense of that required level of rising profits needed to maintain the economic strength and dynamism desired by top management. Actions taken in the name of social responsibility should enhance the economic strength of the company and/or the business community. The over-all mission of the company is two-pronged, as follows:

> To set forth and achieve corporate objectives which meet specified social challenges ranging from product quality to the "quality of life" requirements, both internally and externally.

> To increase the company's earnings per share at a rate required to meet share-owner/profit expectations *and* these new requirements.

This policy does not replace traditional profit policy but expands it. Some companies, the Chase Manhattan Corporation, for example (1971), have embraced this policy.

9. to take socially responsive actions on a continuous basis, rather than *ad hoc,* one at a time, or for a short duration. This policy is based upon the conviction that a company will be able to make a much greater impact, at less cost, with continuous as compared with on-again-off-again actions.

10. to examine carefully before proceeding the socially responsive needs which the company wishes to address, the contributions which the company can make, the risks involved for the company, and the potential benefits to both the company and society. This is a warning to "look before you leap." Many companies in the past got into trouble because they acted more on impulse than reason. This policy commits the company to take action which is organized, sensible, systematic, and extended over a period of time. It is the opposite of putting out fires or answering alarm bells in response to outside pressures and, after the pressures disappear, going back to practices existing before the stimulus. This policy says: "Let's make a careful cost/benefit analysis before making important commitments."

POLICIES IN FUNCTIONAL AREAS

These company-wide policies can be used to develop subpolicies in selected functional areas. To illustrate, in the marketing area subpolicies might be set forth as follows (Schwartz, 1971):

1. Advertising will avoid statements which take advantage of unsophisticated buyers (such as children and the less educated), shall avoid exploiting emotions, and shall be honest.
2. Products in the company's product line will not be injurious to users and will achieve the highest possible quality and service for the price.
3. Research and development will be oriented, to the greatest extent possible, to produce products which are nonpollutants.

SPECIFIC COMPANY ACTIONS

Policies lead to action. A few specific actions which a company might consider taking are:

1. Establish responsibility within the company for defining the company's social responsibilities.
2. Define specific corporate objectives in specific areas of social responsibilities, and set forth concrete strategies and plans to achieve them. (In this process, carefully examine costs and problems for each major action and company capabilities.)
3. Establish policies and procedures for the contributions of a philanthropic nature made by the company.

4. Lay out policies and plans to stimulate socially responsible actions by individuals in the company.
5. Revise the measurement and reward system to make sure that managers set goals in terms of both social and economic ends, and develop rewards to reflect accomplishment in both.
6. Develop cost/benefit analyses which are appropriate for different levels of decision-making and which will serve to improve decision-making in the area of social responsibilities.
7. Prepare a social audit.

CONCLUDING COMMENT

A surprisingly large number of companies today are preparing reports for internal as well as external consumption on the social programs which they are undertaking. These are called social audits. They are a major managerial tool not only for making social programs operational but for reporting on what is being done. So important is this new development that the next chapter will be devoted to it.

CHAPTER TWELVE

The
Social
Audit

INTRODUCTION

The notion that a business should make a social audit of its activities was first proposed twenty years ago by Bowen (1953: 155–156). The idea lay dormant for almost as long. It has been only during the past two to three years that American corporations have thought seriously about social audits. It is a concept, however, which is evolving rapidly and the basic thrust today is for a requirement in the future that all corporations, especially the larger ones, prepare a social audit for public distribution.

WHAT IS A SOCIAL AUDIT?

There is probably agreement, at a high level of abstraction, that the business social audit is a report of social performance in contrast to the financial report which is concerned with economic performance. There consensus ends.

There are fundamentally two different types of social audits. One is an audit required by the government. A large corporation must account to the government for many different programs. For example, the FDA and the FTC require companies to report on the characteristics of products (e.g. tests of flammable textiles and drugs). The EPA has set air pollution standards against which corporations must report their experience. The Equal Employment Opportunity Commission requires submission of data on employment of members of minority groups. The Department of Labor, the Securities and Exchange Commission, and many other federal, state, and local agencies require reports. Many concern economic programs and many relate to social programs. The reporting is piecemeal, that is, one report is made at a time, covering only one subject.

The second type of social audit is that for programs voluntarily undertaken by a company. This is the type of audit which will be discussed here.

There are at least five different concepts of and approaches to making a business social audit (Corson and Steiner, 1974). First is that which identifies expenditures which have been made for social programs and/or describes in qualitative terms what has been done. This approach is concerned only with cost inputs and not benefits or accomplishments. A second concept is the valuation of human assets. This audit is concerned with valuations of the productive capability of the company's human organization, the valuation of shareholder loyalty and banker or community good will, customer loyalty, and so on (Likert, in Baumol, et al., 1970). The Barry Corporation of Columbus, Ohio, is one of the very few companies that combines such valuations with traditional financial reports in its annual report to stockholders. A third concept is a "program management approach." Used by the Bank of America, this concept seeks to measure costs and effectiveness of those activities the company is engaged in voluntarily for social reasons (Butcher, 1972). A fourth concept, which might be called "the inventory approach," involves the cataloguing of what the company is doing in each major social program or not doing in social areas where there is a social expectation that it should be active. For each identified area this approach calls for data and/or a narrative description of what is or is not being done. A final concept may be called the "balance sheet approach." This approach, which will be discussed later, tries to quantify values contributed to society (assets) and detriments to society for actions taken or not taken (liabilities) (Abt, 1972(A); Linowes, 1972).

The great majority of social audits which have been made and distributed currently are of the first or fourth types. A good illustration is the pamphlet published by General Motors Corporation in 1972 and 1973 called Report on Progress in Areas of Public Concern. A few cost/benefit type audits have been made but not widely publicized. The second and fifth types are more proposals than practice, although Abt Associates, Inc., made a fifth type audit (Abt, 1972(B)).

It is worth adding that while the name "social audit" is likely to stick, many businessmen prefer other terms, such as "social statement" or "social report" or "business response to social priorities" or "report on corporate societal policies and actions." The social audit carries with it a connotation of quantification which, as will be shown later, is not achievable today. The other terms imply a more descriptive or qualitative definition, which is more in line with today's state of the art.

WHY COMPANIES HAVE MADE SOCIAL AUDITS

In the social audit survey noted earlier (Steiner, 1973) the question was asked: "Has your company attempted within the period since January 1, 1972, to inventory or to assess what has been done in any of a series of 'activity fields'?" A surprising 76 percent of the respondents answered yes to the question. Of the companies responding affirmatively, 89 percent said they had examined more than one activity field. It should be noted that the words "social audit" were not used, although respondents knew that was what was meant.

Table 12–1. Purposes Which Led Companies to Make a Social Audit

	NUMBER	PERCENTAGE	RANK
1. To identify those social pressures which the company feels pressured to undertake	55	5	9
2. To identify those social programs which the company feels it ought to be pursuing	157	14	3
3. To examine what the company is actually doing in selected areas	194	17	1
4. To appraise or evaluate performance in selected areas	162	14	2
5. To determine areas where our company may be vulnerable to attack	101	9	5
6. To inject into the general thinking of managers a social point of view	122	11	4
7. To ensure that specific decision-making processes incorporate a social point of view	95	8	6
8. To inform the public of what the company is doing	70	6	8
9. To offset irresponsible audits made by outside self-appointed groups	41	4	10
10. To meet public demands for corporate accountability in the social area	78	7	7
11. To increase profits	37	3	11
12. Other	17	2	12

Note: 196 companies checked one or more purposes.

Also, the questionnaire contained the CED list of possible areas of business social action (see Exhibit 10–1) to which respondents could refer.

Each corporation was also asked why it had undertaken to assess and in some cases to report on its social performance. A list of possible purposes was provided and respondents were asked to check the purposes which best explained their making a social audit. The answers are shown in Table 12–1. It is noteworthy that the most significant reasons were to examine what the company was doing and to appraise performance. It is also noteworthy that the social audits were not undertaken to offset audits of self-appointed outside groups or to increase profits. Respondents were asked what other motives prompted their making a social audit, and a wide variety of answers were received, including: "as a guide to internal management," "part of marketing strategy," "part of long-range planning," "to balance commitment to social activity against job activity," and "to make sure the company is fulfilling its promises and commitments."

THE SPECTRUM OF SOCIAL ACTIVITIES REPORTED

The survey showed that some companies were involved in every one of the CED social programs listed in Exhibit 10–1. In addition, respondents listed 46 additional programs which they said they were pursuing. Some of these were subsets of CED programs but there were also many new ones (Corson and Steiner, 1974).

Respondents were asked to identify those programs which involved significant commitments of money and/or personnel time. Those which ranked highest are shown in Table 12–2.

THRUST TOWARD THE ACCOUNTABILITY SOCIAL AUDIT

As noted in Table 12-2, a social audit can be designed to achieve a wide variety of purposes. Space does not permit an examination of what audits might include for different purposes or how they should be made. From a social point of view the most significant social audit is an accounting of social performance made to the constituents of the company. While most social audits up to the present time have not been directed at giving a comprehensive accounting to a wide audience, the pressures are in that direction. It is quite likely, if such pressures grow, that the major purpose of social audits in the future will be to make an accounting to various legitimate interests concerned with corporate social activities (Corson and Steiner, 1974).

By accountability is meant reporting on or explantation of the discharge of responsibilities. In the case of the social audit the accountability, of course, concerns social responsibilities.

Table 12–2.   Rank Order Listing of Activities Which Were Noted Most Frequently to Involve Significant Commitments of Money and/or Personnel Time

RANK *		NUMBER OF RESPONSES
1.	Ensuring employment and advancement opportunities for minorities	244
2.	Direct financial aid to schools, including scholarships, grants, and tuition refunds	238
3.	Active recruitment of the disadvantaged	199
4.	Improvement of work/career opportunities	191
5.	Installation of modern pollution abatement equipment	189
6.	Increasing productivity in the private sector of the economy	180
7.	Direct financial support to art institutions and the performing arts	177
8.	Facilitating equality of results by continued training and other special programs (civil rights and equal opportunity)	176
9.	Improving the innovative and performance of business management	174
10.	Engineering new facilities for minimum environmental effects	169

* RANK: (1) indicates highest commitment.

There is little question that there is an escalation of demand that all institutions, especially the larger and more important ones, be accountable to society for the discharge of their responsibilities. This fundamental idea is not new. Financial reports of corporations, for instance, represent long-established statements of accountability. Reporting by corporations, however, is not keeping pace with responsibilities they have accepted let alone those which various groups think they may have. As a result demands for an accounting are outracing practice.

There is a thrust today to get corporations to report activities in the social area on a systematic and audited basis comparable to the annual financial report. I do not think this is likely to happen soon. This does not mean, however, that corporations cannot make an accounting to the public which will be generally accepted as fulfilling reporting requirements. Take philanthropy, for instance. I think the public will accept a simple statement by a company that it gave away so many dollars for different categories of activity. Acceptability of such an accounting will not depend upon sophisticated cost/benefit analyses.

My guess is that we shall have a great deal of experimentation with various reporting methods before corporations settle on any general patterns of response. The mere fact that corporations are making social audits, however, reflects an acceptance of the idea of social responsibilities. The fact that many corporations are making social audits public is a reflection of the acceptance of the idea of accountability. Neither one of these ideas has a crystal-clear consensus about meaning. The ideas and standard practice will evolve. In the meantime, there are a great many different ways a corporation can discharge its conceived obligations (Bauer and Fenn, 1973).

WHAT SHOULD THE ACCOUNTABILITY SOCIAL AUDIT ENCOMPASS?

It has been demonstrated sufficiently in preceding chapters, and it will be further documented in later chapters, that society's expectations have grown to include a wide range of amenities, products, services, and information for the government, employees, consumers, investors, and the community. If a social audit is to include all such activities, it embraces everything a corporation is doing or not doing. If the social audit is to verify the various costs entailed and the benefits produced, it becomes an impossible task and the information which might be produced, were a large company to try to make it available, would most likely be indigestible.

On the other hand, if a social audit includes only a cataloging of activities which top managers are interested in pursuing and/or those activities which might improve the public image of the company if publicized, the principal function of the social audit will not be performed. The corporation really would not be making an accounting of the extent to which its social performance met expectations of its constituencies.

The social audit should, like the financial audit, satisfy the informational needs of those it is designed to serve—employees, consumers, shareholders, the general public, opinion makers, reformers, and others. The needs, of course, will change from time to time. Basically they will include: (a) activities required by legislation (e.g., equal opportunities for minority group members), (b) activities performed to meet contractual arrangements with labor unions (e.g., employee rights in layoffs), (c) activities voluntarily undertaken by the company (e.g., philanthropic undertakings), and (d) socially useful programs designed to make a profit (e.g., contracts to train hard-core unemployed for useful jobs).

Of strategic importance in defining the scope of the audit is the identification of those activities of such concern to the constituencies of the company at a particular time as to merit inclusion in the social audit. This is a difficult task but must be performed if the accountability social audit is to become reality.

IDENTIFYING AND RESPONDING
TO CONSTITUENT EXPECTATIONS

Today the scope of few if any social audits are accountings of acceptable expectations of constituents. There are many reasons for this but three seem to stand out: (a) the whole idea of public accountable reporting is new; (b) the methodology for identifying social expectations and determining appropriate corporate response is in its infancy; (c) very little has been done to develop creditable measures of social performance. Enough has been said about (a) but more needs to be said about the other two.

Society has a number of ways to send messages to business about its expectations. One of the clearest, of course, is to put pressures upon the legislative process to enact laws. But there are other ways. Among them are crusading reformers; opinion makers in all walks of life, including business; various organized groups, such as unions, environmentalists, and trade associations; stockholders; government agencies; and public opinion polls.

As pointed out in Chapter 6, larger companies are now surveying these sources to identify expectations. The process is done by staff analysis of various message channels. There is no accurate and unchallenged method, however, to identify those constituent expectations of importance to a company nor the degree of obligation of the company to respond. The evolution of the accountability social audit will be restrained until an acceptable methodology to do this is perfected. Table 12–3 is a matrix, developed by General Electric, which could be used to spell out systematically constituent expectations. Notice that the list of activities is somewhat different from the CED list.

Once constituent expectations are identified, a major problem for a company arises in appraising the strength and direction of the expectations. There are really no accurate and tested ways to do this. Assuming that some conclusions can be reached about thrusts of expectations, the problem then becomes one of determining to what extent, if any, a company should respond. If it chooses not to respond, is it obliged to mention it in the social audit? We do not have satisfactory answers to these questions.

THE MEASUREMENT PROBLEM IN EVALUATING
BUSINESS SOCIAL PROGRAMS

The art and science of the social audit will not get very far without acceptable measures of business social performance. Such measures do not now exist and the problems involved in getting them are severe.

Table 12–3. Matrix Table for Recording Expectations of Major Company Constituents by Selected Social Program

	SOCIAL AUDIT MATRIX								
	Customers	Investors	Employees	Dealers Distributors	Suppliers	Competitors	Communities	Public	Government
Product and technical performance									
Economic performance									
Employment performance									
Environment and natural resources									
Community welfare and development									
Government-Business relations									
International trade and development									

The nature of social performance measures depends upon who is looking at the programs and why. This suggests at least four different types of measures, as follows:

Contributions to Constituents This approach focuses attention on "consumers" of social activities—society as a whole, a community, or groups and individuals, etc.—with respect to either their broad needs or specific demands. Measurement may be in terms of values received or benefits related to costs incurred.

If the evaluation is in terms of the extent to which a business social program helps society achieve the goals it sets for itself there is a deep problem of measurement. To begin with, this society has no well-formulated goals, let alone measures for determining how well we are achieving them, as explained in detail in Chapter 6.

Attempts have been made to develop cost/benefit evaluations of a company's social programs and to arrive at a sort of aggregate measure of net contribution to society. Probably the most ambitious one is that of Clark Abt (1972(A)). He lists, in financial terms, in a sort of modified and combined balance sheet and income statement, social assets of a company; social commitments, obligations and equity; and social benefits and costs to staff, to the community, and to the general public, and comes to a net social income to clients. This method would be prohibitively expensive for a company of even moderate size. Linowes proposes a "Socio-Economic Operating Statement" which calculates, in dollars, for specific major programs, the "social improvements" and "detriments" that are involved. He winds up, like Abt, with an aggregate plus or minus for society (1972). While simpler than Abt's Linowes' Method is still too complex for practical application.

Subjective polls of opinion can also be used in evaluation. Some activist groups periodically poll their readers and publish the results in the form of ranked standings of companies with respect to how socially responsible they are deemed to be. Opinions of individuals about how they perceive the impact of social programs on themselves can be useful measures. An example is Blum's poll made to determine the extent to which a company was satisfying the basic human needs of its employees (1958).

Traditional Business Measures A company may wish to evaluate its social programs in terms of benefits to itself. The standard may be in the form of the traditional return on investment. This is, of course, a cost/benefit equation from the company's point of view. In every instance brought to my attention the cost/benefit analyses have been extremely rough and far from complete in the sense of considering all the major costs and benefits. The reason for this will be clear shortly.

In response to criticism about its activities in South Africa the Mobil Oil Corporation published an "audit" of its employment policies in South Africa. It was a comparison of nonwhite and white employees in various jobs in terms of percentage of total employees, wages, and benefits. These are, of course, traditional business measures of performance.

Efficient Conduct of Programs One might ask: How efficiently has the company conducted its programs? For most programs this evaluation must be subjective. In some instances, however, evaluation can be quantitative. For instance, we have had for some time mathematical models to improve company efficiency and these are now being directed to social programs. To illustrate, one input-output matrix has been developed to show how a firm can minimize wasteful use of resources (Elliott-Jones, 1972).

Survey Research This approach uses whatever disciplines and measures are available and can be employed appropriately in evaluation. The Council on Economic Priorities, for instance, has been making rather detailed examinations of programs of different industries (Council on Economic Priorities, 1973; American Institute of Certified Public Accountants, 1972: 39–40, 72–74).

THE MEASUREMENT PROBLEM IS CRITICAL

The above illustrates the range of approaches to measurement that exists today. The literature on the subject is rather bleak at the present time. It is a fact that there are today no creditable generally accepted standards for measuring businesses social performance in general or with respect to most if not all of the social programs undertaken by business. There are understandable reasons why this is so.

For a standard to be generally accepted it must be understood; it must be measurable, preferably quantitatively; it should be comparatively simple; and two independent researchers should be able to derive the same or very close answers. This set of criteria is hard to satisfy in the social area in making a cost/benefit analysis which is central in the preparation of a sophisticated social audit.

For example, on the benefit side, trouble arises immediately. There will be for most programs no consensus about which benefits ought to be evaluated nor how much weight should be given to each one. Of great concern is the fact that benefits stretch over a long period of time which will make any quantification extremely difficult. Benefits will also depend upon things that a company cannot control.

Equally difficult questions arise on the cost side. Direct costs are easy to measure, but measuring indirect costs becomes more difficult. Opportunity costs, or opportunities foregone, become even more difficult to measure. Then there is the difficult economic question of joint costs.

Each social program must be considered individually and standards must be developed for it. The approach will range from essentially a quantitative measure, such as percentage of minority employees to total employees, modified as appropriate by qualitative considerations such as subtle racial or other injustices. For some programs, such as antipollution programs, cost/benefit analyses may be the best approach. But here, as noted above, it is a long way from deciding upon a cost/benefit analysis to developing acceptable cost and benefit measures.

For many programs there is no way to go but to prepare description scenarios of what constitutes acceptable performance. For instance, suppose a utility says that one of its major social programs is to help local governments (where it is doing business) to improve their regional physical plans. One approach to evaluating performance will be to ask what constitutes reasonable, acceptable action.

To answer this question further questions such as the following will have to be answered: Has the utility assigned a man full-time to the work? What does the local government think about the help it is getting? Are there tangible benefits which are discernible? By building a scenario such as this, one can begin to determine whether performance has been acceptable. Acceptable to whom? To reasonable people like you and me! If this approach is pursued with care I do think a model can be built for many important social programs, with both qualitative and quantitative elements, which will make it possible to decide upon magnitudes of performance along a spectrum from "extremely poor" to "exceptionally satisfactory."

It will be a long time, however, before such measures are developed and receive wide acceptance in and out of business.

In developing measures it must be widely understood that a measure suitable for evaluating one purpose of a company's social program may be completely inadequate to measure a different objective. Furthermore, it will be impossible to satisfy all dimensions of the problem of measurement and evaluation. There are certain dimensions that defy quantification and sometimes they may be the most important ones to evaluate.

It is in point to observe that at the present time efficient economic operation of a company is a major social responsibility and we do have rather clear and generally acceptable measures to evaluate such performance. They are not perfect but better than those in existence for social programs. This is fortunate because in terms of total social contribution that the typical corporation can make today the greatest benefit will come from its economic function.

Until better measures of social performance are available much of what passes for social audits will be in descriptive terms.

SHOULD MAKING A SOCIAL AUDIT BE MANDATORY?

There is logic in making a social audit mandatory. The present-day annual financial reporting of corporations is mandatory. It reflects an accounting of performance which society in decades past has expected from corporations. Today, as amply described in preceeding chapters, society is expecting much more from its corporations. Why should corporate performance in meeting these new demands not be the subject of mandatory reporting? Actually, as noted previously, reporting is mandatory for many of the government's dictated social programs. It is not for voluntarily undertaken programs or for societal expectations not registered in law or contract. Once the problem of identifying expectations which corporations properly should meet has been reasonably well resolved, and once the measurement issue is reasonably resolved, the logic of mandatory reporting seems apparent.

Respondents of the CED social audit survey were asked: "In general, do you think that business firms will be required to make a social audit in the future?" A surprising 46 percent of the respondents answered this question affirmatively. The larger the corporation the higher the proportion of "yes" responses. Respondents were asked whether they felt this prospect was acceptable to business. The great bulk of those who said they thought reporting would be required also said they thought the requirement would be acceptable to business. A large number took the time to explain their positions (Corson and Steiner, 1974, Appendix B). Some typical responses are as follows:

"Yes. It's a matter of being responsive to a changing climate of public attitudes and demands. . . ."

"Yes, it places a healthy discipline on management to perform."

"The prospect is not only acceptable but I deem it to be necessary."

Respondents were asked what major obstacles they felt stood in the way of developing the social audit. The results are shown in Table 12–4.

Table 12–4. Important Obstacles to the Development of the Social Audit

	ORDER OF IMPORTANCE *					
	1	2	3	4	5	RANK
1. Inability to develop consensus on ways to organize information	15	29	43	41	22	4
2. Inability to develop consensus as to what activities shall be covered	38	35	50	34	8	3
3. Danger to the company in publishing the results of social audits	8	18	15	14	66	5
4. Inability to develop measures of performance which everyone will accept	98	57	29	8	4	1
5. General decline in pressures on business to undertake social programs	9	7	5	7	73	6
6. Inability to make creditable cost/benefit analysis to guide company actions	58	63	25	32	8	2

* Companies identified 1, 2, 3, 4, 5, in order of importance.

Given a resolution of the scope and measurement issues executives obviously do not see a major problem in preparing a comprehensive social audit. This probably is due to the fact that companies now make many reports to the public and government agencies and it is considered not a monumental leap to add other items and prepare a comprehensive report.

A MODEL FOR SOCIAL ACCOUNTABILITY AUDITING/REPORTING

If the respondents to the CED survey are correct and reporting is mandatory how will corporations be likely to meet the requirement? Until some format is developed by consensus or legislated by government, corporations will continue on a trial-and-error basis to develop ways to assess and report on the performance of social programs. To provoke thought about a uniform format the following model is suggested:

Table 12–5.   A Model for Social Auditing/Reporting

1. An enumeration of social expectations and the corporation's response	A summary and candid enumeration, by program areas (e.g., consumer affairs, employee relations, physical environment, local community development), of what is expected and the corporation's reasoning as to why it has undertaken certain activities and not others.
2. A statement of the corporate social objectives and the priorities attached to specific activities	For each program area the corporation would report what it will strive to accomplish and what priority it places on various activities.
3. A description of the corporation's goals in each program area and of the activities it will carry on	For each priority activity, the corporation will state a specific goal (in quantitative terms when possible) and describe how it is striving to reach that goal (e.g., to better educational facilities in the community, it will make available qualified teachers from among members of its staff).
4. Statement indicating the resources committed to achieve objectives and goals	A summary report, in quantitative terms, by program area and activity of the costs, direct and indirect, assumed by the corporation.
5. A statement of the accomplishments and/or progress made in achieving each objective and each goal	A summary, describing in quantitative measures when feasible and through objective, narrative statement when quantification is impracticable, the extent of achievement of each objective and each goal.

SOURCE: Corson and Steiner, 1974.

The report, of course, should provide enough information to permit the reader—internal managers as well as the public—to compare the company's activities with those of other companies acting in the same social area.

So long as corporations can choose on a voluntary basis which social programs to pursue, the creditability of the social report may rest on the comprehensiveness and candor with which it is prepared. Creditability also can be increased if an "independent" analyst examines the corporate report and certifies to its accuracy. The social report might also be more readily accepted if the board of directors of the company reviews and approves it.

CONCLUDING OBSERVATION

"Business functions by public consent," the CED statement on *Social Responsibilities of Business Corporations* said ". . . its basic purpose is to serve constructively the needs of society—to the satisfaction of society" (p. 11). Demands are growing and are not likely to diminish that corporations, especially the larger ones, continue to expand their efforts to appraise and inform about how well they are serving the needs of society. The social audit is a tool to do this. It is my judgment that it is not a current fad which will soon disappear. It is a new managerial requirement. How it will evolve, however, is not as clear.

CHAPTER THIRTEEN

Business
Ethics

INTRODUCTION

The world of business ethics is quite broad and its outer edges spread into a number of areas in the larger sphere of business-society relationships. The social responsibilities of businessmen, for instance, clearly involve ethics and morality. Other areas concerned with ethics discussed in previous chapters are religion, the value systems of society, and business ideologies.

I think it useful, however, despite these other analyses, to focus directly in this chapter on some major issues of morality in business decision-making. There are four reasons why I do this. First, various systems of values and views in society about what is right and wrong are reflected in the value systems of individual businessmen and affect business practice. Second, business is a major activity in society and influences morals both in terms of what it does and through the products it produces. Third, there are a number of ethical systems in society bearing different injunctions to the businessman. As a result, doubts are often raised in the mind of the businessman about what is and what is not ethical. The frustrations this conflict causes seem to be getting worse rather than better. Finally, one cannot understand business, or business-society relationships, without knowledge of the ethics and ethical problems of businessmen and of what society thinks is the state of business ethics compared with what society expects from business.

Business ethics are filled with abstractions and precepts very difficult to apply with certainty to many specific business problems.

This vagueness tends to make many businessmen uncomfortable. They cannot, however, brush this subject aside as did a student who finally gave up on an examination question in a course on ethics by writing: "This is one of those issues I am happy to leave with my elders until I am old enough to leave it to my children."

In this chapter I want to define business ethics, examine the state of ethics in business today, analyze the applicability of different ethical systems and guidelines to business decision-making, and inquire into what may be done to clarify ethical standards for businessmen. Mark Twain once said: "To be good is noble. To tell people how to be good is even nobler, and much less trouble." This chapter is not designed to tell people how to be good, but rather to explain why businessmen do not always have clear-cut ethical guides in making decisions, and to suggest a few useful approaches to improving ethical behavior.

WHAT IS BUSINESS ETHICS?

There is a mountainous literature on the subject, but no universally accepted definition of the word "ethics." A number of writers draw a distinction between morals (what people do) and ethics (what they think they ought to do), but I shall use the two words synonymously. It is a mass of moral principles or sets of values about what conduct *ought* to be. Ethics may be specified by a written or unwritten set of codes or principles governing a profession. Major attributes of ethics may be summarized as follows (Bachman, in Bartels, 1963: 116):

Concept: The field of ethics may be conceived as a discipline, science, study, or evaluation.

Content: The subject matter of ethics is concerned with what is good or bad, right or wrong. Words frequently encountered in discussions of ethics are true, fair, just, right, proper, and their antonyms.

Judgment: Judgment is required to determine whether human action is ethical or not. The judgment concerns the overt act, not the motivations behind it. Behavior and not its cause is that which is judged.

Standards: Judgment is based upon standards which are, of course, values.

Values: The final element of ethics, therefore, is the sets of values and criteria used as standards for judging human conduct.

Business ethics, of course, relate to the behavior of a businessman in a business situation. They are concerned primarily with the impacts of decisions on people, within and without the firm, individually and collectively in communities or other groups. They are concerned with actions measured by ethical rules, as contrasted with, say, strictly economic or financial rules. Business ethical behavior is conduct that is fair and just over and above obedience to constitutional laws and valid government regulations. It is always ethical for a businessman to obey the laws even though he may personally believe them to be unjust or immoral. If he feels that the laws are unfair, the proper remedy is to seek change by argument and persuasion rather than by civil disobedience. The distinction between legality and ethical behavior is important, because the boundaries of each do not coincide.

WHAT IS THE ETHICAL PROBLEM IN BUSINESS?

Today's ethical problem in business is far more difficult than in the past. In the medieval world, the Church set the standards of morality. They were fixed, simple, and not to be disobeyed. Throughout a long period of our history, the question of ethics was either neglected by businessmen or was not an object of doubt for most of them. Dan Drew, builder of churches and founder of Drew Theological Seminary, typified the compartmentalization of businessmen's decision-making in the nineteenth century in these words:

> Sentiment is all right up in the part of the city where your home is. But downtown, no. Down there the dog that snaps the quickest gets the bone. Friendship is very nice for a Sunday afternoon when you're sitting around the dinner table with your relations, talking about the sermon that morning. But nine o'clock Monday morning, notions should be brushed aside like cobwebs from a machine. I never took any stock in a man who mixed up business with anything else. He can go into other things outside of business hours, but when he's in the office, he ought not to have a relation in the world—and least of all a poor relation (Stone, in Bartels, 1963: 35).

The ethical quandary in business today stems partly from the fact that a company is in a sense a social system, and as such reflects social values. Furthermore, the expectations of society, for instance with respect to the social responsibilities discussed at length in Chapter 10, are placing a heavier responsibility on businessmen to meet ethical standards. Finally, businessmen are human beings with ethical values that cannot be separated from their business lives. As a result, more and more business decisions involve ethical and moral issues.

As the ethical content of business decisions is increasing, the consensus of ethical standards and norms is being eroded. The fact of the matter is quite plain that there is no single clear standard of approved ethical action available to a businessman to use in making specific operational decisions. The diversity of cultural patterns has brought moral diversity. While there is a consensus in society on underlying values, as discussed in Chapter 8, when detailed specification of approved actions is promulgated, the consensus tends to disintegrate, and different actions, often contrary, can find sources of approval in society. The broad ethical norms are fuzzy, as are many laws, and detailed rules of conduct are often contradictory. The body of ethical standards influencing a businessman is a composite of strands of values woven together from many repositories, each having different degrees of acceptance, each containing inconsistencies within its own area and often in conflict with other ethical systems, and each having deep-rooted values which are generally accepted in society.

It seems paradoxical to say that there are ethical standards which have a social consensus and yet the businessman is left without a clear navigational system to steer him through ethical waters. The explanation, of course, is that there is a social consensus on many values when they are expressed at a high level of abstraction that disappears when specific decisions are required. In commenting on general ethical principles applicable to marketing, one businessman said: "We found them almost everywhere applicable, and almost nowhere sufficient in themselves to resolve the kinds of ethical problems we faced" (Clasen, 1967: 79). For instance, I think society would generally assert that business advertising should be truthful, and there are laws which attempt to make businessmen meet specific standards of truth. Nevertheless, in many specific cases a businessman is not sure what is right or wrong. To illustrate: Is it moral to use pretty, scantily-clad young women to help sell automobiles? Is it truthful to advertise, "Max's hamburgers are the best buy in town"? Neither is illegal. It is obvious that there is a generally accepted truth system peculiar to advertising, but it is often not clear to an advertiser at just what point that system is violated, socially or legally.

One other point needs mention, namely, that very frequently a businessman's choice is not between obvious right or wrong, good or bad. For instance, is a businessman right or wrong in discharging an older worker (for whom he has no other job) because he has become a danger not only to his own life, but to the lives of others in a machine shop? Is it ethical for one businessman to take over a company, against the will of the management, by borrowing money and using acquired stock as collateral, and then firing the old management so that the buyer's brother-in-law can be given a company to run? Is it ethical to get information about a competitor from an employee of the competitor, if no money is exchanged?

Granted that executives are faced with different sets of ethical systems, Walton asserts that "A morally responsible executive is one who knows the various kinds of value systems that may be employed in a particular situation and has a rather clear idea of what values hold ascendancy over others in a conflict" (Walton, 1969: 64). The problem of an executive frequently is not that of finding an ethical norm or principle to use, but of applying an accepted rule in a particular situation. In many important business decision areas the ethical course of action is not clear even to those most determined to act ethically.

A different problem arises for a businessman when he thinks he is acting ethically, but his behavior is not considered ethical by observers. For instance, a businessman may extol the importance of competition to society and then by merger reduce or eliminate it. The businessman may see no conflict; his observer may not know the true facts, may distort them, or may come to a different conclusion with the same facts.

HOW ETHICAL IS BUSINESS TODAY?

Most observers of the business scene think that the ethical standards of American businessmen are at an all-time high, but most also think there is plenty of room for improvement (Leys, 1968; Hess, 1968;). There have been few systematic attempts to measure the state of ethics of American business. Such a project is handicapped because of differing and conflicting standards of measurement and the equally difficult problem of determining what a man actually believes as compared with what he says he believes. Baumhart, a Jesuit priest, made a thorough survey several years ago of business ethics. Highlights of his basic finds are as follows (N = number of respondents answering a particular question):

> When several thousand managers were asked this question, 83 percent agreed: "For corporation executives to act in the interest of shareholders alone, and not also in the interest of employees and consumers, is unethical."
>
> Most businessmen think they are more ethical than other businessmen. They rate their company higher than the average in their industry.
>
> The general level of ethics in business is not considered particularly high by the general public and by students.
>
> When asked whether they had ever had a conflict between their role as a profit-oriented businessman and an ethical person (N = 610), 32 percent said they had not. Those that had experienced a conflict said the most important ones (24 percent) were personnel problems (firing and layoffs). Dishonesty (advertising, contracts, and promises) was noted by 18 percent.
>
> When asked what influences businessmen to make ethical decisions (N = 807), the greatest influence was said to be a man's personal code of ethics; next was formal company policy; then the behavior of a man's superiors in the company, the ethical climate of the industry; last, the behavior of a man's peers in the company.
>
> When asked what influences a businessman to make an unethical decision (N = 705), the most important force was the behavior of a man's superiors in the company, the next was ethical climate in the industry, and the last was personal financial needs.
>
> The chief executive is very important in the ethical conduct of people in his company. Men tend to accept the values of their superiors.

Men in staff and line positions tend to have the same replies to ethical questions put to them. Also, men at different levels of management tend to have similar responses.

Businessmen think that good ethics is good business in the long run because it leads to repeat sales, lower employee turnover, good reputation, and consistent behavior.

When asked the most important personal influences on ethical actions (N = 100), 26 percent ranked father as first, 18 percent ranked both parents as first, 11 percent ranked the boss as first, 8 percent placed the clergy first, and 8 percent put teachers first.

The older a businessman becomes, the more ethical seem to be his attitudes (N = 1512). Three out of four businessmen were not surprised when shown this conclusion.

Many businessmen would rather go bankrupt than act unethically. When asked (N = 100) whether it was ethical to make decisions contrary to the dictates of conscience when business insolvency was at stake, 87 percent said no, and only 11 percent said yes.

Businessmen think it is easier to be ethical in certain occupations, such as accounting and engineering. It is harder in purchasing and selling.

Nineteen percent of businessmen (N = 100) said they had quit a company for ethical reasons.

Size of company makes a difference in responses of managers. Testing of 1,200 managers showed that those in companies with less than 50 employees answered less ethically than those from companies with over 10,000 employees. But, those in the smallest companies responded as ethically as those in companies with 1,000 to 9,999 employees. The differences, however, were not great. For instance, when asked whether it was ethical for executives to act solely in the interests of stockholders, 80 percent in the companies with less than 50 employees said no, and 85 percent in the largest companies said no.

The most important influence on industry ethical levels is the state of competition. Unethical practices mount with too much as well as too little competition.

Most managers think that government regulations help to improve ethical behavior in business.

Most businessmen favor an industry code of ethics (N = 1,471). Half, 50 percent, strongly favor a code, and 21 percent favor one somewhat. Most (87 percent) felt a code would be welcome when a manager wanted to refuse an unethical request, 71 percent felt a code would raise the ethical standards of an industry, and 57 percent said that people would violate the code when they could avoid detection. Only 4 percent of the executives would like to see a government agency enforce codes. Most wanted industry self-enforcement.

A college education and courses in ethics apparently do not influence a manager to act more or less ethically. He does, however, improve his sensitivity to ethical problems and thinks and speaks about them with more ability.

Businessmen affiliated with a church apparently have no better ethical attitudes than those who are not church members. Ethics is probably neither more nor less important to the average businessman than to the average American (1968).

A number of interesting conclusions can be drawn from this summary. To note just a few, the toughness of competition is important in the use of ethical standards; what top management does is influential in the conduct of others in a company; a surprising 32 percent in one survey said they had never been faced with a conflict of ethics; and an astonishing 87 percent said they would rather go bankrupt than make a decision contrary to their conscience. This latter finding seems a bit inconsistent with some of the others.

A commonly held attitude about businessmen is that, unlike people in other professions, they seek money primarily and have an excessively materialistic set of values. Other professions are popularly pictured as exemplary in holding human values and public service over financial gains. This, of course, is a phony stereotype. Like all groups in society, some businessmen may neglect ethical norms for monetary gain. As a group, they are probably faced by and succumb more frequently than the average person to temptation. On the other hand, faced with the exigencies of making a profit in a rigorously competitive situation, it is remarkable that so many businessmen have commendable ethical standards.

WHY TRY TO BE ETHICAL?

Oliver Sheldon, one of the first business moralists of this century, said that administration of a business was primarily a matter of both scientific and ethical principles (1923). This is the view that a manager does not make a technical decision and then superimpose the ethical consideration; decision-making intermixes both. An executive can try to be amoral if he chooses and obey only the letter of the law and his own self-interests. Most businessmen, however, would agree with Sheldon. Why do they try to be ethical in their decision-making? Perhaps some businessmen feel intuitively that no one has ever learned how to hold a society together without ethical standards and that business, as a part of society, cannot operate without some ethical standards. Even the austere capitalistic system, which glorified the pursuit of self-interest above all other values, operated on the basis of an ethical system that was not for many businessmen the equivalent of what was legal (standards concerned with paying debts, putting in an honest day's work, and meeting contractual obligations). It is understood that business cannot operate unless businessmen can depend upon the actions of others.

Some businessmen feel that it is good business to be ethical. Observers think this is supported by the fact that if one businessman behaves ethically, it will stimulate others to do likewise, that ethical behavior is a sort of insurance against retaliatory acts, and that a man who tries to be ethical will eventually overtake his unethical adversary (Learned, Dooley, and Katz, 1959: 115–16). This explanation was corroborated by Baumhart's surveys (1968: 60).

Businessmen think that practicing good ethics will help their business because customers repeat sales; employees like to work for an ethical manager; a good reputation will attract business; a reputation for sharp business practice is not an asset; and consistent behavior is valued by customers (Baumhart, 1968: 53). On the other hand, Baumhart found that rarely did he meet a manager who used the assertion that "good ethics is good business in the long run" as a major reason or guide for his decisions (1968: 50).

In a famous article on religion in business practice, Ohmann asserted that the good managers "have the mental equipment to understand the business and set sound long-term objectives, but the best ones have in addition the philosophical and character values which help them to relate the over-all goals of the enterprise to eternal values. This is precisely the point at which deep-seated religious convictions can serve an integrative function since they represent the most long-range of all possible goals" (Ohmann, 1955: 38).

A final answer to the question, and implicit in some of the above, is that if a businessman does not abide by some ethical norms, he will suffer unpleasant consequences. If the norm is codified into law, he will be hauled into court. Or, he may be penalized by social condemnation, disappearing customers, pangs of conscience, and the disdain of superiors and peers. These generalizations must, of course, be tempered by the principle of the degree to which particular ethical standards are used. In holding views such as these, managers would not, for example, accept the "turn the other cheek" biblical injunction when dealing with competitors. Nor would they honestly respond with complete candor to a competitor's query about a new product they were developing which might replace that of the competitor. This would not be considered unethical. At the same time, most businessmen would consider it ethical to meet commitments with competitors, to avoid hiring competitors' employees to learn trade secrets, and to resist circulating dishonest rumors about competitors' products. To act ethically does not mean to try to abide by all ethical standards in the businessman's ethos. This will become clear in the next section.

SOURCES OF THE BUSINESSMAN'S ETHOS

Every executive is the center of a web of values which connect into various value systems that, while different from one another, have interconnections. There are five principal repositories of values influencing businessmen: religious, philosophical, cultural, legal, and professional. Some of the strands in these systems reach back into pre-Christian antiquity; others are of more modern origin. These systems assume varying degrees of authority over individuals, and in the same individual over time. Common bonds threaded through these systems, however, such as the Ten Commandments, bind together the great majority of individuals in this society.

Religion The fundamental conception of what is right and wrong in many areas of life is rooted in biblical morality. There are differences, however, such as the morality of birth control, capital punishment, and detailed matters of daily living, but deep in society's values is the idea that moral values are of divine origin and rest on a theistic foundation. The major religions agree on emphasis on the dignity and worth of the individual, which in turn is the basis of the need to recognize the rights and obligations of others. From Catholicism comes the view that a well-ordered social system is necessary to achieve human dignity. Both Catholicism and Judaism emphasize in their tenets the social responsibility of men to act in such a way as to contribute to the welfare of the social system or, at least, not to act to harm it in any way. Built upon such verities are many other rules of conduct.

Philosophical Systems A major stream of thought, antedating the Judeo-Christian ethic, is that of the philosophical views of great thinkers. From Plato to contemporary philosophers, the idea has prevailed that reasoning can produce ethical norms. Ancient Greeks, like Socrates, Aristotle, and Plato, had a great deal to say about ethics, although they did not produce fully articulated philosophical systems. It was Aristotle, for instance, who laid down the Golden Rule: "We should behave to friends as we would wish them to behave to us." The Epicureans held the view that pleasure is sufficient grounds for saying that an act is good. On the other hand, the Stoics preached the spartan, sober, industrious life, which the Puritans espoused and which is practiced by some businessmen today. In a great leap in time, Immanuel Kant (1724–1804) tried to find universal laws of morality to guide men's conduct. Jeremy Bentham (1748–1832) developed a utilitarian system as a guide to ethics, a concept perfected by John Stuart Mill, David Hume, and John Locke in the nineteenth century. Bentham observed that mankind was governed by two masters: pain and pleasure, and the moral worth of an act was the extent to which it produced the greatest excess of pleasure over pain. A practical ramification of this philosophy was the idea of majority rule which underlies political democracy. There is no such thing as a unified system of values flowing from the thinking of the great philosophers, but they did develop many standards of ethics, and their beliefs are measures of ethical standards in contemporary society (Leys, 1952; Olafson, 1961).

Cultural Experience The life and development of a society are both based upon and produce values. Drawn from religion, for instance, is the dominant ethic of preserving the social system. Relationships among groups, the ethical responsibilities of large corporations, and ethics of labor unions are examples of systems arising from cultural experience.

The Legal System The law is a codification of customs, ideas, beliefs, and ethical standards which society wishes to preserve and enforce. As social views about what is right and wrong change and crystallize, they are reflected in new laws or the abandonment or neglect of old laws. A major cause of higher ethical standards in business is the addition of laws to prevent the violations of what society considers proper ethical practice.

It is a mistake, of course, to consider the law as establishing the standards of ethics for society. The law simply cannot cover all ethical conduct. The law usually seeks to prevent only the grossest violations of what society considers to be ethical standards. Furthermore, there are many instances where the law is not clear, and the businessman is faced with a gray area of interpretation. The law, for instance, sets standards for labeling products, price discrimination, and management's dealings with unions, but there are thousands of court cases in these areas attesting to different interpretations of the law.

Professional Codes Professional codes are an increasing source of ethical norms for businessmen. There are three types which deserve mention here. First are so-called company creeds or philosophies, which are usually short, widely distributed, and cover those basic philosophies that presumably govern the business (Thompson, 1958; Steiner, 1969: 144–50; Towle, 1964: 267–74; Heermance, 1924). There is no standard format for creeds. Some of them are fundamentally economic statements, but many are basically codes of ethics. Most creeds are written at high levels of abstraction and contain the injunctions of the systems of ethical standards discussed above. The Golden Rule, for instance, is found in many of them.

Are company creeds merely public relations documents? Are all these codes that seek to guide a businessman merely window dressing to make people think they seek to act ethically? For some companies, the creeds are indeed public relations documents, and for many managers the codes which presume to guide them are matters to be ignored. There is ample evidence, however, to show that company creeds really do guide action in many companies and are bases of company plans. There also is no doubt about the fact that many managers who want to act ethically do respond favorably to industry, technical, and other codes.

A second type of code is found in company/operational policies which set up guides to action that have an ethical content. For instance, specific policy statements concerning such matters as procedures for hiring, promoting, and firing employees; making decisions about dealers; or handling customer complaints. These policy statements are often rather detailed.

Third, businessmen are members of clubs and other groups and are encouraged to follow codes laid down by these organizations. Many industry associations have codes of ethics. Professional societies, such as those of accountants and engineers, have codes of ethics which serve as standards of ethical conduct for members whether they are in a business firm or not. The accounting code, for instance, is strict about honest reporting of information, and the engineering code is firm on such matters as adherence to high standards of performance and quality.

POPULAR GUIDES TO ETHICAL CONDUCT

There are scores of fundamental ethical guides in a manager's ethos. Those he holds in highest esteem depend upon his beliefs. In this section I want to discuss two of the more widely held standards of ethical conduct and also present a few other guides that seem to have high applicability in business decision-making.

The Golden Rule Though stated in varying forms, the Golden Rule is found among many religions. The Book of Matthew states it: "All things whatsoever ye would that men should do to you, do ye so unto them: for this is the Law of the Prophets." "Do unto others as you would have them do unto you," is the popular version. It is a generally accepted fairness ethic standard in and out of business. Developed in the biblical world of agriculture, nomads, and small population, how suitable is it today for business? It may have applicability in the simplest of ethical dilemmas, but generally it is inadequate. It has multiple meanings, ranging from "an eye for an eye" to "every girl has a father" (Lundberg, 1968: 36). A number of assumptions underlying the Golden Rule are unrealistic in the world of business. One assumption is that "others" are capable of reciprocating behavior. Even if they were able to reciprocate, there is no guarantee that they would want to. Also, would the first party want to receive the reciprocal action? This brings to mind Bernard Shaw's version: "Don't do unto other as you would have them do unto you because their tastes may be different."

Greatest Good for the Greatest Number This is a basic foundation of democracy, as noted before. Is it applicable to business affairs? Again, in simple dilemmas it may be helpful, but in specific cases it is inadequate. In a company whose stock is held by a few wealthy men and whose payroll is in the hundreds of thousands of dollars, a large wage increase far beyond productivity or industry-wage levels which is justified on this precept would not square with other more generally held ethical norms in business. On the other hand, failing to spend money to protect workers cannot be justified on the grounds that there are more stockholders than workers and that this, therefore, would result in the greatest good for the greatest number.

The Principle of Proportionality In an effort to provide more direct guidance to businessmen in determining ethical action in specific cases, Garrett has distilled the views of writers on ethics into the principle of proportionality, or limited responsibility. The principle states: "I am responsible for whatever I will as a means or an end. If both the means and the end I am willing are good in and of themselves, I may ethically permit or risk the foreseen but unwilled side effects if, and only if, I have a proportionate reason for doing so" (Garrett, 1966: 8). Conversely, "I am not responsible for unwilled side effects if I have a sufficient reason for risking or permitting them, granted always that what I do will as a means or an end is good" (Garrett, 1966: 8, italics omitted).

What is meant by "proportionality" in this principle? Garrett lists five types. One is the type of good or evil involved: "a necessary good will outweigh a merely useful good." An action needed to keep a business from going into bankruptcy will have precedent over a stockholder dividend, although the loss of a dividend may have serious consequences to a stockholder. A second is the probability of effect: a serious harm that is no more than slightly probable is outweighed by a certain good. Firing an employee who can get another job is outweighed by the saving of his wage if there is no work for him or his efficiency is low. A third is the urgency of the situation. While research is important to a business, it is outweighed, if it can be postponed, by the need to meet the payroll. A fourth is the intensity of one's influence over effects. If a worker is often drunk, firing him will work a hardship on his family; but if the employer is not responsible for the drunkenness, his obligation disappears. Finally, is the availability of alternate means. If good effects can be achieved by other goods, with lesser evils or no evil side effects, it would be unethical not to choose them, other things being equal. If an inefficient worker can be made more efficient without cost, this is the ethical thing to do rather than to fire him (Garrett, 1966: 9–11).

Critical Questions The above guides are prescriptive. They seek to tell an executive how to act. Another approach is to help the executive guide himself by his asking a series of questions, the answers to which will lead to more ethical conduct. Leys has surveyed the systems of the great philosophers and has derived 36 critical questions for the decision-maker (1952: 189–91). The following are a few examples: What are the authoritative rules and precedents, the agreements, and accepted practices? If there is a conflict of principles, can you find a more abstract statement, a "third principle," which will reconcile the conflicting principles? What is not within our power? What are the undesirable extremes in human dispositions? Has sufficient consideration been given to the disguised selfish interests? What is my station and its duties? To what can we all be loyal? Does the language that you use prejudge the issues?

In 1961 the Secretary of Commerce appointed a Business Ethics Advisory Council of twenty-six leading businessmen, educators, clergymen, and journalists who, after an exhaustive study, issued a document suggesting several dozen pragmatic questions which businessmen should ask themselves. The council said no single list could possibly encompass all the needs of business, but these were the types of questions each business enterprise should answer if it is to achieve the highest levels of ethical action: do we know whether our officers and employees apply in their daily activities the ethical standards we have promulgated? Do we reward those who do so and penalize those who do not? Do we have adequate internal checks on our compliance with law? Do we have a current, well-considered statement of policy regarding potential conflict of interest problems of our directors, officers, and employees? Have we reviewed our company policies in the light of our responsibilities to society? Do we have a clearly understood concept of our obligation to assess our responsibilities to stockholders, employees, customers, suppliers, our community, and the public (Sporn, Hickman, and Hodges, 1963: 48–50)?

Even though the approach is for the businessman to ask these questions, his problems in deciding what to do will be much like those discussed in connection with the Golden Rule. The one advantage is that the questions posed should stimulate more thinking about what is or is not ethical.

Response of Peers When I became involved in the allocation of all steel, copper, and aluminum throughout the country during the Korean War, I was faced with many perplexing issues which could not be resolved by quantitative logic. One fundamental rule I used in approaching these problems was to so conduct my basic analysis and make my final decisions that any serious inquiry by experts in Congress, agencies of government, or other areas would lead to the conclusion that no decision was incompetently derived or unethical. The maxim is: "So behave that you can justify your action before a technically competent and impartial board of inquiry" (Towle, 1964: 46). This does not mean, of course, that simply because an action can be explained technically, it is necessarily ethical. Rather, it means to me that a decision was reached on the basis of technical competence, that the major elements of the decision can be explained, and that an impartial jury would accept the approach to and the ethics of the conclusions.

Commitment Some writers on ethics think that if a businessman begins to think seriously about what is wrong and what is right, he has made the first and most important commitment to ethical conduct. There is much truth to this, because honest men do disagree about specific human actions; there is no universal formula. This commitment leads a businessman to find in the business ethos those strands which for him will result in ethical action.

Structural Change Patterson (1969) points out that structural approaches to controlling power and preventing unethical actions are much more satisfactory than exhortations of the "Thou shalt not" variety. The power of A over B is a function of the dependency of B on A. There is no reason, necessarily, why the powers of A and B should be equal; but if the inequality is to be reduced in order to prevent unethical acts by A over B, there are two approaches. The first is to define specifically the obligations of A to B, and their relationships. The second is to eliminate the power balance so that reciprocal duties can be determined by bargaining between A and B. Collective bargaining, the Sherman Antitrust Act, and the Truth in Lending Act are examples of structural devices for developing a better workable power balance among groups in society. Much of the federal legislation that affects business is of the structural change variety. This is, of course, an important force for assuring more equitable dealings in business, but it does not cover all cases needing correction, and it opens up areas of gray where the legality of action is uncertain.

Game Ethics Some experienced observers of today's scene conclude that business ethics is like the ethics of playing poker. The ethics of business, says Carr, are game ethics and not at all the same as the ethics of religion. As in poker, the game "calls for distrust of the other fellow"; "it is right and proper to bluff a friend," it is acceptable "to put the other players at an unfair disadvantage," and "the major tests of every move in business, as in all games of strategy, are legality and profit." Carr says: "A wise businessman will not seek advantage to the point where he generates dangerous hostility among employees, competitors, customers, government, or the public at large. But decisions in this area are, in the final test, decisions of strategy, not of ethics" (Carr, 1968: 149).

As might be expected, there was strong reaction pro and con to Carr's article. There were twice as many against him as for him (Blodgett, 1968). In responding to his critics, Carr concluded that "sound long-range business strategy and ethical considerations are usually served by the same policy" (Blodgett, 1968: 170).

TYPES OF BUSINESS MORALITIES

One of the problems in applying universal standards of ethics is that, as Chester Barnard (1958) reminds us, there are different types of moralities in a company. One is personal responsibility. This refers to the personal beliefs of an individual about such matters as honesty, avoiding criminal acts, and being willing to perform accepted duties. A second is representative or official responsibility. This refers to the fact that a manager's actions are often representative rather than personal. He may be an agent of constituents, and as such must act in their interests. Thus, a bank trustee represents a client and may do things, or be prevented from doing things, that he as an individual would—or would not—do. His behavior is determined by deeds of trusts, wills, mortgages, and other legal documents. He may, however, have choices, and when he does the decision should be in the client's interests and not the result of his own personal predisposition. Throughout business there are men who represent a business, and their ethics of personal behavior do not necessarily coincide with their representative behavior. How many times in business and government does one hear an executive say: "I would very much like to do what you ask. It is the right thing to do. But my hands are tied. Regulations simply forbid my doing it."

There are the personal loyalties which one individual has to another—such as the loyalties of a subordinate to his supervisor—when they are acting in their official capacities. Frequently, these loyalties are in conflict with the ethical standards an individual applies when acting as an individual. For instance, the general manager of a division of a large company withheld information from central headquarters about impending disastrous financial troubles. Several of his subordinates, who were men of high moral character and who had close connections with headquarters managers, did not inform headquarters of the problems principally because of strong personal loyalty to their superior officer.

There are corporate responsibilities. Corporations, as entities, have moral responsibilities which are not necessarily matters of law and which are not necessarily identical with the personal moral codes of the executives who run them. These may be internal—for instance, deciding matters connected with stockholders, customers, employees, creditors, and officers—or they may be external, such as matters affecting the interests of communities, competitors, governments, and society.

There are organizational loyalties. Many people, as Barnard points out, have a deep sense of loyalty to an organization as an entity that far transcends their self-interest. I have seen many men jeopardize their health and work excessively long hours without pay, contrary to their selfish interests, because of their loyalty to their task and/or company.

There are economic responsibilities. This type of morality guides individual action of an economic nature. For example, "Waste not, want not," or "Willful waste makes woeful want," are standards of ethical conduct which are deep in some individuals. Some businessmen think it is immoral to go into debt.

There is technical morality. As noted previously, professional people have moral codes that guide their actions. Many of these ethical standards are deep-seated. For instance, I am convinced that the high standards of most engineers in the aerospace industry would prevent them from making a cheap lawn mower. They are so used to working with exceedingly close tolerances and high quality that they could not bring themselves to the task. The acceptance of lower standards would be morally repugnant to them.

Finally, there is legal responsibility. Barnard had in mind in this category more than an intention to conform to laws, court decisions, administrative orders, and so on. He had in mind following those rules that are necessary to the operation of formal organizations. It is a morality that transcends conformity to law. It is a deep belief in the importance of and need for effective cooperation, the proper distribution of responsibilities, and the necessity of equity and justice in organized life.

These different moralities carry subsystems of ethics unique to each. Yet they exist side by side in an individual along with other ethical systems. As noted, there can be and often is conflict with these subsystems and other systems; sometimes there is harmony.

FORCES DOWNGRADING AND UPGRADING ETHICAL CONDUCT

It seems to me that ethical standards in business will continue to improve because the forces that tend to lower ethical standards tend to be offset by forces that raise standards. Among forces downgrading ethics in business are the following: The philosophy of materialism is still predominant in the United States and drives some businessmen to be oriented exclusively to monetary rewards. Higher income taxes induce many companies to engage in dubious practices in the compensation of their executives, which does not foster higher ethical standards in other managers. Loopholes in tax laws and efforts to take advantage of them tend to lower ethical standards. Despite assertions to the contrary, competition is still rigorous and, as Baumhart discovered, men under such circumstances tend to neglect ethical standards.

On the other hand, federal government surveillance of business activities is increasing and the number of laws prescribing ethical conduct is growing. Legal standards of ethical conduct are rising. Popular expectations for higher ethical standards in business are rising and are accepted by businessmen. Materialism, while strong, is declining in acceptance relative to business and other interests in the quality of life. Management is rapidly becoming professionalized and, for that reason alone, more ethical. This last point is particularly important in light of the fact, as discovered by Baumhart (1968) and Clark (1966), that the conduct of a manager is significantly influenced by top management and his peers. As corporations become larger, their standards of ethical conduct tend to rise. This is because of their greater public exposure.

The exposure of Watergate in 1973 and 1974 undoubtedly will result in legislation to raise ethical standards in and out of business. While the exposures may tempt some people to lower their ethical standards (e.g., on income tax returns "because others have been getting away with not reporting honestly"), the net impact, I think, will be to raise standards generally because people will think more about improving ethical standards.

CASE APPLICATIONS

A great deal of the foregoing has been general, prescriptive, and procedural. Little has applied directly to a particular case. The problems businessmen have in applying ethical systems to their decision-making can only be appreciated by examining particular cases. The reader is referred to Garrett, Baumhart, Purcell, and Roets (1968); Smith and Matthews (1967); Leys (1952); and Steiner (1975).

IMPROVING A COMPANY'S ETHICAL BEHAVIOR

The following approaches may be attractive to those managers who want to improve or maintain high standards of ethical conduct in their companies. First, top management must make a commitment to think about and improve the ethical conduct of managers and other employees in the company. Part of this commitment is an intent to be ahead of the average company in equitable and just treatment of interests of persons and groups affected by company actions. Second, codes of ethics, policies, questions to be asked in decision-making, and procedures to secure more ethical actions are helpful. Codes of ethics and policies should express simply and at a high level of abstraction the standards set by top management. Statements of application of these standards can be more specific in terms of concrete problems and how they should be approached and handled. For instance, in dealing with hiring and firing policy, or employee promotion, the most likely problem situations may be defined and the proper courses of action delineated for employees having to make decisions in these cases. Finally, in light of the fact that a man's boss greatly influences his behavior, top management must set a good example of high ethical conduct. This will flow downward in the administrative structure and be felt at the lowest levels.

PART FOUR

Business and Major Community Problems

CHAPTER FOURTEEN

Business and Our Polluted Environment

INTRODUCTION

Ill fares the land, to hastening ills a prey,
Where wealth accumulates and men decay.

So wrote Oliver Goldsmith in 1770. Environmental pollution has for centuries been a problem to man. Today, however, for the first time there is fear that man may not be able to survive on this planet if massive corrective measures are not taken to control pollution. For the first time widespread attention is being given to the extent of business responsibility for pollution. The types of environmental pollution treated in this chapter are those of air, water, solid waste, noise, and chemical pesticides. Our concern is principally with the American urban physical environment and the business-society interface. The central questions addressed are: Why be concerned? Who is to blame? What are the merits of the many diverse prescriptions for solving the problem? What are the major problems in determining the facts to set acceptable standards? What are the types of conflicts that arise between pollution standards and goals in other societal systems? Can cost/benefit analysis help in decision-making? Who should pay the pollution costs? What are government and business doing about meeting the problems? Major themes in this chapter are the seriousness of pollution problems, their intricate interrelationship with other areas of society, and the low level of our knowledge about the problems and their solution.

Why Be Concerned? In a classic understatement President Nixon in a special message to Congress concerned with pollution (February 10, 1970) said: "Like those in the last century who tilled a plot of land to exhaustion and then moved on to another, we in this century have too casually and too long abused our natural environment. The time has come when we can wait no longer to repair the damage already done, and to establish new criteria to guide us in the future. . . ." As we have sought to control nature to meet society's needs for goods and services we have also destroyed many of the amenities of our surroundings. Economic growth has been achieved at the cost of reduced natural amenities.

Up to a decade or so ago the amount of pollution in most parts of this nation did not exceed levels which could be tolerated by the seemingly limitless cleansing capacities of our air and water systems. This is no longer the case. Within the past decade the public suddenly has become aware that in many areas certain natural amenities are below thresholds of tolerability.

Air Air pollution is no new problem. London's air in the seventeenth century was described as "an impure and thick mist accompanied by a fuliginous [dusky, smoky, sooty] and filthy vapor." In 1948 the town of Donora, Pennsylvania, became enveloped in a thick layer of poisonous air from local industrial plants, and about half its population became ill as a result.

The Council on Environmental Quality (CEQ) has found that there has been improvement in air quality in the U.S. between 1968 and 1970 but that most of the population still lives in areas where the quality of air is below standards set by the Environmental Protection Agency (EPA) (1970). The worst air conditions are in the larger cities, which surprises no one. What is surprising, says the CEQ, is that communities with population under 100,000 are suffering problems almost as severe as in the large cities. The EPA sampled the population to determine the number of people exposed to air pollution that exceeded the EPA primary (health protection) standards. It found that: "While 43 percent of the sample population lived in areas where the monitoring data indicated that the sulfur dioxide primary standards were exceeded, the level of photochemical oxidants exceeded the standard in all the areas sampled" (CEQ, 1972).

Such dangers to health are, of course, very serious. There are other costs, however, of sobering magnitude. Economic losses from damage to property (rot, discoloration, rust, erosion), agricultural losses, and timber deterioration run into many billions of dollars each year. Aside from this sort of damage, air pollution increases risks of accidents in travel, has an adverse physiological and psychological impact on people, and reduces the esthetic enjoyment of life.

Water Water pollution has existed for centuries and from time to time has resulted in massive deaths because of water-borne diseases such as typhoid. The pollution problem today has ramifications far beyond a potential outbreak of typhoid. The EPA sampled the nation's waters and found in 1970 that 27 percent of the country's stream and shoreline miles were polluted. In 1971 the prevalence of pollution rose to 29 percent. These are average and very rough numbers.

Throughout the land, swimmers find waters off limits, fishermen cannot eat their catch, and drinking the water without purifying it is unthinkable. Water pollution is a continuous and increasing source of danger to public health. Economic losses from the destruction of fishing grounds, industrial requirements for equipment to purify water, and the break-up of watershed ecology easily range in the billions of dollars annually. It is also, of course, a clear erosion of the quality of life when formerly clear and beautiful streams become sinkholes of filth.

Solid Wastes We are becoming inundated in a sea of solid wastes—metal cans, glass and plastic bottles, garbage, old automobiles, and many other items that do not easily disintegrate even after the lapse of much time. The Bureau of Solid Waste Management in the Department of Health, Education and Welfare, estimates that for each person in the nation over five pounds of refuse is collected each day by public and private collection agencies. By 1980 the figure is expected to be eight pounds. Automobile disposal is becoming such a problem that President Nixon in his message to Congress on pollution in 1970 suggested that the cost of disposing junked automobiles ought to be included in the car's purchase price. City after city is running out of land space on which to dump solid wastes. The problem is not only one of disposal but of esthetics as well, as more and more waste, like abandoned automobiles, erodes the natural beauty of the countryside and clogs city streets.

Noise Scientists have been warning the public for years about the health dangers inherent in the rising crescendo of environmental noise. Except for extreme noises, such as jet aircraft on takeoff, however, the American public has not yet become aroused about this problem. If there is not noise abatement, however, widespread human illness can result from rising noise levels. Tolerance thresholds for noise vary among individuals, but the annoyance threshold ranges from 50 to 90 decibels. For many people, nervous systems begin to react adversely at 70 decibels, the equivalent to the sound of average city traffic. Even at 55 decibels, sleep may be disturbed though the sleeper does not awaken. These standards may be measured against a noisy sports car or heavy truck (90 db at 20 feet), a chipping hammer (110 db at 3 feet), a pneumatic jackhammer (120 db at 5 feet), or a jet on takeoff (140 db at 80 feet). We are also beginning to understand how intense vibration, even with little or no sound, may create physical illness. Awareness of noise and its impact on the human body is comparatively new, but evidence supports the need for concern.

Pesticides Excess amounts of pesticides can contaminate air, water, soil, or food. Rachael Carson in her best-selling book *Silent Spring* (1962) first alerted the world to the dangers of widely used chemical pesticides, particularly the organo-chlorine types of DDT and its related DDE and dieldrin. These agents have been found to interfere with life processes. It was not Carson's position that these agents should never be used, but that their widespread use without prudent concern for the harmful effects gave promise of grave danger in the future for soil, water, wildlife, and man himself.

There are more than 200 basic chemicals used in modern pest control, and they are combined in more than 60,000 separate compounds. Each of these reacts differently on organisms (Graham, 1970: 107). It has been demonstrated clearly that birdlife is endangered by pesticides such as DDT because they cause birds to lay eggs with thin shells that lessen the chances of hatching, and they interfere with the normal breeding cycle. A great danger of such chemicals is that they remain remarkably stable over periods of years, and as they move up the food chain from plants through herbivores to larger carnivores, the poisons become more concentrated in living tissues. The immediate danger is not to man directly, but to the food chain (Graham, 1970: 111).

Concluding Comment All this adds up to something approaching a nightmare that is in the forefront of public thinking. Senator Muskie, a long-time but only recently-heard protagonist for pollution control, underscores the seriousness of the situation in these words: "From this time forward we must devote as much energy and ingenuity to the elimination of man-made hazards to man as we have to the expansion of his ability to harness energy and materials to his desires." This is a broad statement, but he just may be right. We have made much progress during the past few years in coming to grips with the pollution problem, but we have a long way to go to achieve our objectives of environmental quality.

WHO IS TO BLAME?

The issue of blame is not particularly controversial nor of high priority in today's setting, but a word or two about it is useful. Business, government, and people generally are all guilty of polluting the environment in one way or another. Industry, of course, is a major contributor to all forms of pollution. But government is far from blameless. In February 1970, to illustrate, President Nixon ordered all federal government installations to stop contributing to air and water pollution, promised them a $359 million fund to use in obeying his directive, and commented that the federal government is "one of the nation's worst polluters." Local communities across the land are guilty of dumping raw sewage into lakes and streams. Nature is a heavy contributor to pollution. A few volcanoes like Krakatoa in the East Indies and Katmai in Alaska, for instance, have put more sulfuric contaminants into the air than all the products of combusion since the beginning of recorded civilization.

The deep-rooted causes of our environmental problems are different from these. One is a growing population and greater concentration of people. Between 1910 and 1970 the proportion of the population living in urban areas of 2,500 or more jumped from 45.7 to 73.5 percent and the number of people in these centers leaped from 42 to 150 million. Sewage systems, collection agencies, and traffic controls have not kept pace with the resulting concentrated increase in pollutions. This factor has been exacerbated by rising per capita incomes which permit people to buy more things—automobiles, electrical devices, paper products, and so on. Both these forces have accelerated the rise of pollution because of new technological, economic, and managerial developments that have expanded the variety of products available for consumption. All this has increased per capita consumption of energy which, in turn, has further added to air, water, and solid waste pollution. Between 1960 and 1970 a 10 percent increase in population (181 to 205 million) resulted in a 14 percent rise in metropolitan population, a 33 percent increase in vehicles, a 65 percent growth in industrial production, and a 100 percent leap in electric power generation.

To this should be added other deep-rooted causes of our environmental problems. The CEQ identifies them as follows: "our past tendency to emphasize quantitative growth at the expense of qualitative growth; the failure of our economy to provide full accounting for the social costs of environmental pollution; the failure to take environmental factors into account as a normal and necessary part of our planning and decision-making; the inadequacy of our institutions for dealing with problems that cut across traditional political boundaries; our dependence on conveniences, without regard for their impact on the environment; and more fundamentally, our failure to perceive the environment as a totality and to understand and to recognize the fundamental interdependence of all its parts, including man himself" (1970: vii).

It is worth noting that our pollution problems are also the result of success in raising per capita income, in reducing infant mortality which in turn resulted in a population explosion, in raising farm out-put which has fed a growing population and which also has caused growing insecticide and animal pollution, and in increasing produc-tivity which has made it possible for people to buy more goods with the same income.

SCHOOLS OF THOUGHT ABOUT
THE POLLUTION PROBLEM

For a subject as recent as the pollution crisis, which can be viewed from many different disciplines (economic, medical, social political, scientific), and which can arouse high emotions, it is not surprising that there are different schools of thought about it. Each has a unique diagnosis of the problem and a prescription for its solution.

Doomsday Those in this school of thought take the position that we are doomed; we are on the verge of catastrophe; we are strangling ourselves with overpopulation; and it is too late to do anything about it (Ehrlich, 1968). There is much too much evidence today that if we have the will we can achieve a desired environmental quality. In this light these apocalyptic views of the problem should be rejected.

Arrest Growth This school asserts that not only the growing population but rising production, growing use of raw materials, and increasing consumption are bringing environmental degradation. Eventually, resource depletion will bring worldwide starvation (Mead-ows, et. al., 1972; Mishan, 1971). This subject will be dealt with at length in Chapter 20. At this point it may be asserted that not only may faster economic growth and improving environment coincide, but that the former is essential for the latter.

Capitalist Mismanagement This school sees the pollution prob-lem as the inevitable result of capitalistic exploitation. The only answer is to replace private property and the profit motive with state ownership of resources and centralized planning. The invalidity of this prescription has been revealed by Marshall Goldman in a study which shows that in many areas the pollution problem is worse in the Soviet Union than here (1972).

Systems Balance This school views the pollution problem as soluble. It asserts that much can be done to achieve environmental quality but that the problems are immense. Adequate resources must therefore be devoted to their solution. The solutions must not be piecemeal but must be found by a systems approach. Taking action to reduce pollution will affect other systems in society and, as a result, the proper action is one which will achieve an optimization of the goal of the entire societal system. This is, of course, a conceptual and not an operational approach. But it is the one most suitable for this society.

THE "ISSUE-ATTENTION CYCLE"

"Public perception of most 'crises' in American domestic life," says Downs, "does not reflect changes in real conditions as much as it reflects the operation of a systematic cycle of heightening public interest and then increasing boredom with major issues" (1972: 39). The cycle has five stages.

In the first, preproblem stage, a highly undesirable condition exists which has not yet captured public attention. This is followed by a second stage of alarmed discovery which is coupled with euphoric enthusiasm and confidence about society's ability to solve the problem within a relatively short time. The third stage begins when there is a realization of the "costs" involved in overcoming the problem. In time, this stage phases into a fourth one in which a decline in public interest is brought about by a combination of boredom, discouragement, partial solution of the problem, and the rise of other problems in the public mind. Finally, a fifth stage is reached when the problem receives low public attention.

Generally the "issue-attention cycle" for a problem does not cover a long span of years. The pollution problem is moving today from stage two into stage three but it is doubtful whether it will move very quickly into the later stages. There are many reasons for this. The problem is visible and is threatening to almost everyone. There are only a few visible targets, or scapegoats, and business is a favorite one. Public interest groups, therefore, can stir public interest against "powerful" polluters. Finally, politicians can easily gain support for the ambiguous and all-encompassing goal of "improving the quality of environment." While one should never underestimate the public's capacity to become bored it is altogether likely that the pollution issue, for reasons such as these will probably be of high public concern for many years (Downs, 1972).

WHAT IS AN ACCEPTABLE ENVIRONMENT?

During the past few years standards have been established for major pollutions. Under the authority of the Clean Air Act of 1970 the EPA established in 1971 primary and secondary national ambient air quality standards for six of the most widespread air pollutants—particulate matter, sulfur oxides, carbon monoxide, hydrocarbons, oxides of nitrogen and photochemical oxidants. The act called upon states to develop plans to achieve, within three years after approval by EPA, primary standards to protect public health. Secondary standards—to safeguard aesthetics, vegetation, and materials—are to be achieved "within a reasonable period of time." EPA has approved or partially approved most plans from the states. The Clean Air Act also set some tough standards for automobile emissions. Standards for other pollutions have also been set, such as lead and phosphorous in gasoline, aircraft smoke, water, use of insecticides, toxic substances, lead in paint, and many others (CEQ, 1972).

Setting such standards is a simplistic answer to the question of what constitutes an acceptable quality of environment. For example, if a state has an area where the air is cleaner than the EPA standard, can it allow industry to pollute the air up to the limits of the EPA standard? This question was brought to the Supreme Court by the Sierra Club and in 1973 the Court ruled that states with relatively clean air must bar any new industry that causes "significant" air pollution even though EPA standards are not violated. This decision, of course, raises a question about how clean should air be in any particular area.

But the problem of defining air quality goes far beyond this issue. It is obvious that acceptable standards of water purity, air cleanliness, solid waste disposal, and noise will and should vary depending upon geography, population, user, time, and other factors. Is it as necessary to have pure water at the mouth of the Mississippi as at its head? Should air purity be maintained at identical levels for Los Angeles and Aspen, Colorado? If the air is too clean, there will be no rain and plants will not grow. If water is too pure, fish will not live in it. Honest men will differ radically about answers to questions of how pure is pure?

Not too much question has been raised in the past about standards of purity established by the government but as costs are considered the controversy will rise. A major pollution policy issue is, of course: How much is society willing to pay to achieve a given standard? This turns out, as will be demonstrated shortly, to be an extraordinarily difficult question to answer. In many instances it is impossible to answer it with conviction. We do know, for instance, about how much it will cost a steel mill to reduce specific levels of sulfur oxides in its smoke. We do not know how much it will cost to purify Lake Erie.

Pollution control involves a series of standards for different levels of pollution, different types of polluters, and varying levels of expenditures. Pollution control must take place in a dynamic environment; as environment changes, so will the standards. In light of such factors as these, it is no wonder that we do not have a clear answer to the question of what is an acceptable environment. Nor is it likely that we will soon have an answer on which most people will agree.

The National Science Board of the National Science Foundation reviewed the state of the art of environmental science and concluded:

> Environmental science, today, is unable to match the needs of society for definitive information, predictive capability, and the analysis of environmental systems as systems. Because existing data and current theoretical models are inadequate, environmental science remains unable in virtually all areas of application to offer more than qualitative interpretations or suggestions of environmental change that may occur in response to specific actions (1971: viii).

The board said this "constitutes a crisis for the Nation. . . . The current mismatch between capability and need is at least comparable to any other challenge to science and technology that was encountered during this century" (ix).

CONFLICTS WITH OTHER SOCIAL SYSTEMS

Pollution controls will affect other major areas of society. Past failures to examine the impacts of pollution standards on other social systems has resulted in some severe problems, a point deserving illustration.

The Energy Crisis There is in the United States today an energy "crisis" which concern about the environment has helped to create. The crisis illustrates the necessity for a systems approach to dealing with pollution problems. For example, local power utilities have faced severe problems and delays in locating power plants in populated areas because they contribute to air and water pollution. The traditional fuel for power plants has been the fossil fuels—coal, oil and gas. We have sufficient coal for all of our power needs but getting it out of the ground and using it produces major environmental degradation. Strip mining, of course, defaces the earth. Coal also contains a large number of air pollutants, such as the sulfur compounds. In order to reduce pollution the power companies have turned to gas, which is a lower polluter, and in the process have helped to create a gas shortage. To offset these problems the power companies have increased their usage of oil. Environmental restrictions on drilling for oil on the continental shelf because of leakage damage to marine environment and concern with the ecological impact of oil pipelines (such as that in Prudhoe Bay in Alaska) have slowed down exploration of oil reserves in the United States. There is a shortage of gasoline and heating oil brought on by many causes. However, the shortage has been deepened because fuel consumption of new automobiles has been substantially increased because of the catalytic converter added to engines to reduce polluting emissions, and the added vehicle weight in complying with federal safety standards. (More will be said about the energy crisis in Chapter 26.)

Building nuclear energy plants would go a long way toward erasing the energy crisis but environmentalists have blocked their construction. They are supported by some scientists who say that such plants constitute a health and safety hazard. Other equally prestigious scientists say radiation hazards are very low and the plants should be built (*Time*, November 1, 1971). At the moment, however, the "doomsday cloud" that hangs over the industry is delaying the construction of a majority of proposed nuclear power plants.

Life Styles in Cities The standards of the Clean Air Act, if applied meticulously, would necessitate drastic changes in living and working habits in many cities. Ruckelshaus, when Administrator of the EPA, said: "In Los Angeles, for example, it [the act] could bring commercial activity to a near halt; for we can see no alternative under the law but to impose gas rationing sufficient to cut traffic to 20 percent of its current level" (1973: 7). Since the city has virtually no public transportation, this would radically alter city social and economic life. Los Angeles is not alone. Boston, New York City, Minneapolis, Pittsburgh, and other big cities would also be obliged to curtail automobile traffic to an extent which would seriously change life styles and cause incalculable economic damage if present EPA standards are enforced.

The Emissions Battle The Clean Air Act requires that by 1975 new car emissions of carbon monoxide, and hydrocarbons must be 90 percent below the 1970 standards. Also, the 1976 standards for oxides of nitrogen must be under 90 percent of the 1970 emission levels, which were of course uncontrolled. The 1973 cars had reduced these pollutants to about 32 percent of the 1970 emissions. To get to under 10 percent of the 1970 levels, however, would create extraordinary technical problems and excessive costs in the opinion of the automobile manufacturers. The environmentalists were stubbornly opposed to extending the deadlines beyond 1975 and 1976. The Clean Air Act provided, however, that the Administrator of EPA could extend the deadline for one year if the public interest, health and welfare demanded it. He did extend the deadline one year in light of the automobile industry pleas, but he also established strict interim standards which raised howls in the industry. The controversy leading to the EPA decision generated its own smog of conflicting figures, technical testimony, and emotion (Burck, 1973).

Aside from the technical problems the automobile industry says that getting the last few degrees of emission reduction up to the 90 percent will be extremely costly compared with the small amount of reduction. The numbers are controversial but to reduce emissions from 80 to 90 percent of the 1970 levels could be three to five times the cost to the motorist to get from 1973 standards to 80 percent.

The cost to the motorist is a matter of controversy. The EPA calculated that the catalytic converter needed to meet the 1975 standards for emissions would cost about $185 per car. The automobile companies claim that the lowest estimate for the converter and accompanying components would be about $275. The fuel cost penalty could be as high as 30 percent, they say, and that would add another $100 per car per year. In addition, the converters would require repairs and eventual replacement. If these numbers are correct they result in high total costs. What such costs will do to the elasticity of automobile demand, thence to automobile production, is not clear but the impact could be significant. Since the automobile industry is such a large part of total GNP the impacts would spread throughout the nation.

Other Impacts Without elaboration it may be noted that adding antipollution costs to exporting industries will, of course, make them less competitive with foreign producers not forced to reduce pollution. Banning pesticides may reduce agricultural productivity with consequent impacts not only on agricultural income but on human lives.

All this is not said to restrain or reduce antipollution laws and standards. Rather it is to demonstrate the intricate interrelationships between pollution actions and other segments of society. There are important cost/benefit interrelationships and trade offs which simply must be considered. Up to the present time standards have been set with too little regard for the trade-offs.

The Arab Oil Embargo At the time of this writing, January 1974, the partial Arab embargo of crude oil and increased prices has seriously exascerbated what before was a manageable demand-supply deficiency for oil. In order to manage the deficiency of oil many environmental standards have been temporarily lifted. Oil drilling on our shorelines, is now proceeding; under prescribed conditions electric utilities may use high-sulfur oil and in some cases coal; and construction of nuclear power plants is being speeded. The greater becomes the demand-supply deficiency for energy the more environmental standards are likely to be loosened. As the oil crisis eases it is predictable that efforts will again be exerted to enforce the environmental standards.

COSTS AND BENEFITS: AN OVERVIEW

The CEQ calculated total pollution control expenditures for the decade of the 1970s and came to a grand total of $287.1 billions. The council began with costs already incurred and added costs of meeting new standards, the costs of providing control for increasing population and new productive capacity. Total ten-year costs for air pollution control came to $106.5 billion; for water pollution control, $87.3 billion; for noise (commercial jet aircraft) control, $.9 to $2.7 billion; for nuclear power plant radiation control, $2.1 billion; for solid waste control, $86.1 billion; and for surface mining and reclamation, $5.1 billion. Annual incremental costs rise from $10.4 billion in 1970 to $33.3 billion in 1980. This, says CEQ, represents an increase from $51 per person in 1970 to around $145 per person in 1980 (1972: 277–278). Actual business investment in pollution control, for comparative purposes, was estimated at $4.9 billion in 1972.

To get a grasp of the economic impact of pollution standards on certain industries the CEQ commissioned technical consulting firms to make microeconomic studies of those industries. Included were industries such as automobiles, cement, iron foundries, pulp and paper mills, and steelmaking. Following were major conclusions (CEQ 1972: 285–301):

1. Depending upon the industry, annual price increases up to 1976, the period studied, will range from 0 to 2 percent. Companies that cannot pass along increased costs in higher prices will suffer a profit squeeze.
2. Among the 12,000 plants in the 11 industries studied, from 200 to 300 will be closed by 1976 because of pollution-control requirements. Most of these plants are or will be marginal and probably would close for other reasons.
3. From 50,000 to 125,000 jobs will be lost by 1976. This is about 1 to 4 percent of the workforce in the 11 industries and .05 percent of the total national current workforce.
4. About 150 communities will be affected but the data did not reveal what the impact on any one would be.

The CEQ also asked what the macroeconomic impact would be of annual antipollution expenditures of $26 billion (in 1971 dollars) over the 1972–1980 period of time. The conclusion was that there would be adverse impacts on prices, balance of payments, and employment, but that the magnitudes would be rather small (CEQ 1972: 301–304).

Substantial benefits could offset these costs. It has been calculated that a 50 percent reduction in the amount of particulates and sulfur oxide in the air over urban areas would reduce illness and premature death from bronchitis by 25 percent and maybe by 50 percent; morbidity and mortality from heart disease would shrink by perhaps 20 percent and from respiratory diseases by 25 percent. The death rate from lung cancer would fall by 25 percent or more. Such a reduction in air pollution would add from three to five years to the life expectancy of the average adult in urban centers. This translates into 5,000 fewer deaths each year from lung cancer and 16,000 fewer deaths from heart disease (Lave and Seskin, 1970). A very conservative calculation of savings in medical bills and personal earnings that would not be lost through illness would amount to around $2 billion per year (Butler, 1972: 22). No one knows what a reduction in air pollution would save in property and crop damages but $15 billion per year might not be far off the real mark. To these numbers must be added benefits from esthetic, psychological, and human relations points of views. Numbers cannot be ascribed to these benefits but they could be very large.

The same sorts of guestimates can be made for other pollution controls. Even these rough estimates seem to indicate that despite the size of the antipollution bill the benefits seem to be greater.

POLLUTION CONTROL DECISION ANALYSIS

From what was said above it is obvious that setting pollution standards is an extremely difficult task if an effort is made to do it in such a way that maximum benefits to society are received for minimum costs. In recent years a number of tools have been developed to make more rational decisions with respect to such questions, although they are not yet as sharp as needed.

Cost/Benefit Analysis This technique is designed to show whether it is worthwhile to incur a particular cost. The basic approach is to take a project, such as a proposed air pollution standard, and find all the direct and indirect costs that would be incurred. Then all relevant benefits are identified and translated into dollar terms. The difference is identified in one dollar number.

This method immediately encounters obvious problems. It is extremely difficult to get good cost estimates. It is even more difficult to determine creditable dollar estimates for benefits. For instance, clean air reduces morbidity and mortality of heart disease. How much is that worth in dollars? Clean water reduces foul odors. How much is that worth?

It is sometimes thought that cost/benefit analyses must be made only in dollar terms. That is not necessary. Qualitative conclusions can be reached about such matters as better visibility, odors, general psychic conditions, and health improvement. When such qualitative considerations are made some speak of this as cost/effectiveness analysis.

Whether the analysis sticks to dollars or not it is possible that two analysts may agree on the basic benefits and costs to be measured. It is quite unlikely, however, that there will be agreement on either the dollar translations or qualitative conclusions. This is so because the estimates involve judgments in the absence of hard facts.

Trade-off Analysis This is an analysis to determine whether one proposed system is better than another. It starts with cost/effectiveness analysis for each system being considered. Other issues which must be considered in a final decision may be, for instance, moral. One pollution control method may require a slowdown of automobile speed as against another method which reduces total mileage driven over a period of time. Preventing a power plant from burning coal may help the ambient air in Montana but bring a power shortage to Minneapolis. There are scores of trade-offs involved in choosing among pollution controls which may or may not be amenable to quantitative conclusions. Frequently they involve individual scales of values, remote impacts, and heavy impacts on a few to serve the many.

To underscore the complexity of the pollution problem consider a number of possible ways to "solve" the air pollution problem in the Los Angeles basin. Among possible ways for dealing with the problem are the setting of standards for automobile emissions, as is now being done; setting of limits for other types of emissions, such as sulfur oxides from smokestacks; moving residents out of the basin; rationing gasoline; increasing the price of gasoline until enough travel is discouraged to control pollution; sending workers home when smog levels get to certain points; taxing automobiles with no emission controls; building a rapid transit system and prohibiting automobiles in certain areas; subsidizing automobile drivers who reduce mileage; forcing car pooling; and persuading people to use various means to voluntarily reduce pollution. Which method and/or mix is most desirable? No one really knows the answer, but looking at the alternatives reveals many trade-offs.

Systems Analysis A classic example of the need for systems analysis is the present energy crisis. Meadows' study of the limits of growth referred to previously (1972) is a systems analysis. In a systems analysis an effort is made to simulate reality by relating the most significant parts of the system to determine how the system will react when one or more parts of it are changed. To illustrate, Egypt's Aswan Dam is a marvelous engineering accomplishment but an ecological disaster. Floods have been controlled by the construction of the dam but arable land along the Nile is declining. One result is that Egyptians have electricity and television sets, because of the dam, but are running the risk of not having enough food and of food costs rising.

Furthermore, some of the silt which previously was flushed into the Mediterranean provided food for fish. That has declined and so has the crop of fish.

Concluding Observation Conceptually these tools sound attractive. They are powerful when data are available. But the most pertinent data are not readily available. Nor will the required information be soon available. As a consequence, the sort of unilaterally established standards used in the Clean Air Act must be considered an acceptable approach (de Nevers, 1973). But an effort should be made to get information so the tools described here can be used (Edmunds and Letey, 1973).

WHO SHOULD BEAR THE COST OF POLLUTION CONTROL?

From an economic point of view a strong case can be made for each business assuming all of the social costs it creates. For a theoretical optimal allocation of resources the full costs of each good or service should be taken into account in its price. The cost, therefore, is either absorbed by the polluter or is borne by the consumer of the product or service. For other types of pollution, e.g., city sewage, costs can be allocated to polluters through higher utility rates and/or taxes. In both instances government action is required. In the first case the market mechanism is incapable of internalizing the costs of pollution. In the latter case collective action is needed to reduce pollution.

Any company that incurred heavy antipollution-control expenses would find itself in competitive difficulties if other companies in the industry did not do the same. For individuals, pollution is often cheaper than nonpolluting. General Motors found this out when, beginning on May 15, 1971, it launched a two-month advertising campaign in the Phoenix, Arizona, area to induce motorists to buy a kit to reduce automobile emissions. The campaign was intensive and was conducted through the radio, television, newspapers, billboards, and among automobile dealers. The kits were capable of reducing emissions up to 50 percent from older cars and cost $9.95. They were easy to install, but if a mechanic was hired to do the job the cost should have been less than $20. Out of 334,000 pre-1968 cars in the area only 528 owners bought and installed a kit.

Government can take one of a number of approaches, or a mix of them to determine how the pollution bill is paid. First, is to depend upon private negotiation through courts of law. Up until recently victims of pollution had no redress but to seek damages in a court of law. Second, is direct public regulation and control. This can take the form of establishing an ambient standard of quality and emission limitations designed to meet the standard. Or a substance may be prohibited from use, such as some pesticides like DDT. Third, is public investment, subsidy, and incentives. This has been a time-honored approach in this country. Fourth, government may encourage users of polluting products and polluters to reduce consumption voluntarily or undertake recycling or other programs to reduce pollution. The pricing mechanism may be employed by taxing polluters. Each approach has its own strengths and problems.

The first approach is, of course, completely inadequate to deal with today's pollution problems. It never was used extensively simply because it was so difficult for the victim to prove in a court of law that he suffered damages.

The regulatory approach is the one most favored at the present time. It has the merit of fitting the political decision-making process. Various interests can be heard and then uniform standards set. Control machinery which can be managed by government can then be erected to assure compliance. This approach can cause problems, such as the following.

If national standards were applied across-the-board two competitors might find themselves in very different positions. One might discover that his costs for nonpollution of water might be nil, since he had access to high-quality water, whereas another might be forced to incur heavy costs since his water source was of low quality. If industry were forced to comply with nationally prescribed standards, other changes in the industrial structure would follow. Companies have located plants up to now for reasons having nothing to do with pollution. Antipollution standards which industry now had to meet out of its own pocket would force some plants to relocate. All companies would take these standards into consideration in locating new plants in the future. This conceivably could be at a heavy social cost. For instance, a company might be willing, pollution control aside, to locate in a low-income area in order to use the labor supply and to help achieve society's goals in bringing such people in the mainstream of economic life. It could be, however, that a company could not justify such a location because of stringent antipollution standards.

Government investment, subsidy, and economic incentives are used widely in pollution control. For instance, the federal government has contributed close to $20 billion to municipal governments for construction of sewage-treatment plants. When the question is raised about how to get business to do something, the invariable answer is "let's have a tax incentive." The claimed advantage is that it would make profitable a socially desirable objective not otherwise economical for a business. It would also achieve a social objective without direct government intervention and administrative overhead. Most people have in mind something like the 7 percent tax credit for industrial new machinery and equipment purchases. This is very attractive. Tax incentives are, of course, indirect government expenditures, and as such have inherent disadvantages. By their very nature they do not involve scrutiny by government, and the privilege may be abused. Their costs are buried in tax returns and are difficult to disentangle from other business expenditures. As a result, it is virtually impossible to make a cost-benefit calculation of such expenditures. It might well be, depending upon circumstances, that a tax incentive would have a better cost-benefit payoff than other incentives, but this should not automatically be assumed. As a general rule, it probably would be better from the social point of view to use tax incentives only when the cost-benefit equation is clearly more favorable than other incentives and its benefits outweigh its disadvantages.

There are other incentives which government may offer. For instance, government can make contracts with companies to do certain things, such as invent new equipment to reduce pollution, or find new ways to meet particular standards at designated costs. Great opportunities exist for industry alone or through government contracts to find new ways to dispose of the solid wastes that are covering the landscape—garbage, trash, cans, and so on. Not only is there profit in disposing of this waste, but there is profit in turning it into salable products such as fertilizers, fuel, or usable metals.

The government has not done much to try to persuade people to reduce pollutions voluntarily. One example is a very exhaustive list of things consumers can do to reduce the demand for energy (Office of Emergency Preparedness, 1973). Voluntary action has never proven to be very effective.

The economist's favorite approach is the last suggested—the pricing mechanism. One suggestion is for some government agency to measure pollution from each industrial plant and announce a set of prices, with different prices for differences in damage caused. Prices would vary according to geographic location, time of year, maybe even day of week, wind direction, and so on. "But every producer of a given type of pollution at the same time and place must pay the same price" (Ruff, 1969). Under this scheme, firms would be free to adjust to the price any way they liked. If the pollution price were high and business raised the price to consumers—which it would have to do or go out of business—consumers then would naturally switch from businesses which were high polluters to those which were low polluters. Plants would be encouraged to change their products; they might relocate to places where their pollution would do less harm; or they might produce less during a smoggy season (in the case of air).

This sounds logical and fair. To implement such a plan on a comprehensive scale, however, would raise serious problems. Setting these prices on a comprehensive scale just once, not to mention changing them as conditions alter, would be an operational nightmare. Aside from the complexities of the administrative task, there would be widespread inducements to fraud which probably would not be completely resisted. Furthermore, much pollution is the result of joint activities of industry and others, which raises questions of joint costs and their allocation.

These arguments do not lead to the conclusion that the basic idea of a tax on pollution is without merit. Quite the contrary. A system of taxation on polluters has merit when it is possible to identify gross violations of acceptable pollution standards; when the violator is clearly guilty; when no greater social costs are thereby created; and when there is no effort to introduce a comprehensive and detailed system covering all plants, all forms of pollution, in all geographical areas of the country.

A field study of water pollution in the Delaware River Basin showed that costs of achieving a given level of pollution control under a fee or tax system would be only half that of a fixed uniform regulatory system (Chase Manhattan, 1972). When certain criteria are met the tax on pollution has impressive advantages. But it is not without serious problems under certain circumstances and under certain circumstances other approaches to paying the pollution bill may have greater merit.

In the end, society is going to have to pay the bill. The question becomes one of how the bill shall be paid, what the mix will be among those who will bear the initial cost, and what the trade-offs will be among different costs incurred as a result of the first anti-pollution cost.

MAIN LEGISLATIVE ENACTMENTS

The first federal law concerning air pollution was the Air Pollution Control Act of 1955, which authorized funds for research. The Clean Air Act of 1963, replacing the 1955 law, made available more financial assistance to state and local governments. The amendments to this act in 1970 provided the basis for the high standards which are in effect today.

Congress passed a law in 1899, the Refuse Act, which prohibited dumping impediments into navigable waters. This act is still in use and has been invoked recently. The first major modern legislation was the First Water Pollution Control Act of 1948, which was extended in 1952 and again in 1956. The most important feature of this law was its provision for substantial aid to local governments in constructing sewage-treatment plants. The Water Quality Act of 1965 permitted the federal government to establish water quality standards for interstate waters. The Clean Water Restoration Act of 1966 provided more money for building treatment facilities. The Water Quality Improvement Act of 1970 provided tighter controls over oil pollution, vessel pollution, and pollution from federal activities. The Federal Water Pollution Control Act Amendments of 1972, however, was the first comprehensive legislation to control water pollution. Vetoed by the President, but passed by the Congress over his veto, the act seeks nothing less than to eliminate all pollution in navigable waters by 1985. An interim goal, by July 1, 1983, is to make as many bodies of water as possible clean enough for swimming. To attain these goals, new standards and enforcement machinery are created and federal expenditures totaling $25 billion are authorized. Most of this is to aid local governments in building sewage treatment plants. Industrial plants can be ordered to stop all pollution of waters by mid-1983 but there are loopholes to avoid this tough standard. Because actual dollar allocations to municipal governments are low and because of these loopholes this legislation may be a case of clean rhetoric and dirty water (Freeman and Haveman, 1972).

The Noise Control Act of 1972 gives the EPA broad authority to establish noise levels for new motors and engines and for transportation, construction, and electrical equipment. All new products which are noisy and may adversely affect public health and welfare will require labels to say so.

It was not until 1965 when the Solid Waste Disposal Act was passed that the federal government assumed a major role in this area. This act made the federal government responsible for research, training, demonstrations of new technology, grants, etc., for solid-waste planning programs. Stiffer legislation is now before the Congress in proposed amendments to this act.

As a result of concern over pesticides, the Federal Pest Control Review Board was created in 1961 to review and coordinate federal programs of pesticide use. A more effective program was created in the Federal Committee on Pest Control of 1964. In the same year the Secretary of Interior banned the use of DDT on Department of the Interior lands. In 1967 and 1970 a number of states prohibited the use of DDT and its derivatives.

There have been, of course, literally hundreds of other pieces of legislation—federal, state, and local—concerning pollution. All we can do is note that fact here. There is one final enactment of great importance, however, that deserves mention. It is the National Environmental Policy Act of 1969. It established the Council on Environmental Quality. The CEQ is charged with assisting the President in preparing an annual environmental quality report and making recommendations to him on national policies for improving environmental quality.

The council also has responsibility for evaluating environmental impact studies which the act requires every U.S. government agency to make before undertaking a project affecting the environment. Along with this new legislation the President, by executive order, reorganized federal agencies dealing with pollution into the Environmental Protection Agency.

ENVIRONMENTAL IMPACT STUDIES

Section 102 of the National Environmental Policy Act of 1969 provides that each agency of the U.S. government must ". . . include in every recommendation or report on proposals for legislation and other major federal actions significantly affecting the quality of the human environment, a detailed statement by the responsible official on: (i) the environmental impact of the proposed action, (ii) any adverse environmental effects which cannot be avoided should the proposal be implemented, (iii) alternatives to the proposed action, (iv) the relationship between local short-term use of man's environment and the maintenance and enhancement of long-term productivity, and (v) any irreversible and irretrievable commitments of resources which would be involved if the proposed action should be implemented." This legislation has encouraged some states to require similar impact studies by both business and state agencies.

In explaining the type of analysis required, the CEQ said, among other things, that the study should include "the probable impact of the proposed action on the environment, including impact on ecological systems such as wildlife, fish, and marine life. Both primary and secondary significant consequences for the environment should be included in the analysis. For example, the implications, if any, of the action for population distribution or concentration should be estimated and an assessment made of the effect of any possible change in population patterns upon the resources base, including land use, water, and public services, of the area in question" (*Federal Register*, April 23, 1971: 7ff).

Without elaboration of other specifications it can be said that the requirement is for a deep and thorough research analysis. To illustrate, the U.S. Geological Survey has proposed a procedure for evaluating environmental impact of proposed projects to comply with the requirements of the act. The framework for analysis is a matrix with a list of 88 items concerned with "existing characteristics and conditions of the environment" on the vertical column, and another check-off list of 100 items concerned with "proposed actions which may cause environmental impact" on the horizontal part of the matrix. There are thus 8,800 possible interactions to be examined.

Assessment of environmental impact, if done thoroughly, is a difficult undertaking involving many different approaches, methods, and techniques (Edmunds and Letey, 1973). It has started a new discipline of analysis. As it matures, it will provide the nation with invaluable information and evaluating techniques concerning the improvement of the environment.

THE BUSINESS RESPONSE

A fair assessment of the business response to pollution controls is that business generally has accepted and approved. Indeed, in some cases business has stimulated government to establish standards of performance. Business is taking action and is expanding its efforts.

Henry (1972) conducted a survey of the impact of environmental protection on major companies and found that thirty-eight out of forty-nine had a formal written policy on environmental protection. Illustrative of such policies is the following:

> It is the policy of the General Electric Company to contribute to environmental protection by eliminating or limiting to lowest practicable levels, and in any event limiting to statutorily defined levels, all adverse environmental effects from its products, facilities and activities, and by offering products and processes which will help solve environmental problems.

Capital expenditures of business for pollution control have increased in aggregate dollars as well as a percentage of total business capital expenditures. Actual business investment in pollution control for air and water in 1971 was $3.2 billion. Planned investment in 1972 was $4.9 billion (CEQ, 1972). This was about 5.3 percent of total planned capital investment for that year.

In the "polluting" industries there have been important increases in investment. For instance, in the paper and allied products industry expenditures in 1970 were $26.7 million and $66.3 million in 1972. In stone, clay, and glass products the rise in the same period was from $8.2 to $24.2 million. In the primary metals industry the increase was from $100.2 to $132.1 million, and in petroleum and coal products from $289.2 to $474.2 million. As percentages of total industry capital expenditures, the rise was from 2.3 percent in 1970 to 15 percent in 1972 in the stone, clay, and glass products industry. In the paper and allied products industry the rise, in the same period, was from 7.3 to 22.8 percent. In primary metals it was from 8.2 to 16.4 percent, and in petroleum and coal products it was from 6 to 10.1 percent (Lund, 1973).

Not all businessmen have accepted pollution controls. Those whose profits have been eroded as a result, and those whose competitive position has been weakened at home or abroad, have complained. In the case of the automobile companies the complaint has been centered on technological problems of compliance. More and more businessmen are now turning to the question of how to comply and make a profit from compliance. Gerstacker of Dow Chemical Company, for instance, commented as follows: "I cringe everytime I hear a company say how much it's costing to clean up pollution. The opposite is true. We expect to make a profit at it" (*Business*

Week, January 1, 1972: 32). One way to do this, of course, is to recycle waste materials for use or sale which in the past were discarded or dumped into the air or water systems. Another avenue to profit is, of course, to produce equipment which reduces pollution at very low cost.

CHAPTER FIFTEEN

Business
and
Consumers

INTRODUCTION

From the very beginning of our history governments have enacted legislation to protect consumers from unscrupulous businessmen. Until recent years efforts to protect consumer interests were intermittent. They were usually stimulated by a shocking exposé or a visible disaster. Today, there is a different kind of concern for the consumer. Consumers and their spokesmen are continuously aggressive in demanding and getting better treatment from business, both through legislation and voluntarily. The movement, called "consumerism," is widespread, organized, and powerful.

It is the purpose of this chapter to examine the nature of "consumerism" and the underlying reasons for its growth, to review briefly the past history of consumer protection, and then to discuss some major issues such as the independence of the consumer, regulation of advertising on behalf of consumers, the morality of product obsolescence, automobile safety, manufacturer liability for defective products, and the response businessmen should make to consumerism.

CONSUMERISM

President Nixon began his special message to Congress on consumer rights (October 30, 1969) with these words: "Consumerism—Upton Sinclair and Rachel Carson would be glad to know—is a healthy development that is here to stay." He was referring to a broad and increasingly aggressive movement, supported by government and the population in general, to protect consumers from a wide range of dangers connected with the products and services they buy and use. The protection sought is not only against outright fraud and physical harm, but against more subtle injuries from such practices as deceptive advertising and fine print in warranties which void seller guarantees.

The beginning of what today we call consumerism is not clear, but may be marked by President Kennedy's special message to Congress on March 15, 1962. Momentum picked up a little with a few new pieces of legislation in 1964 and 1965 and an important boost was given to the movement by the publicity associated with the publication in 1965 of Ralph Nader's book *Unsafe at Any Speed*. The American public which for so long had been patient about product and service abuses began to express itself in strident ways. There was no rallying motto but had there been it well could have been one recommended by Denenberg: "Populus iamdudum defatatus est" (the consumer has been screwed long enough) (*Newsweek*, March 5, 1973: 60). Politicians heard: a flood of bills inundated Congress, and many were passed.

One characteristic of today's consumer revolt—and that probably is not too harsh a term for what is happening—is rising expectation for better product performance, more product safety, and better information to permit consumers to make more informed choices. The threshold of acceptable performance is rising. Consumers are demanding and legislation is reflecting a new consumers' bill of rights. President Kennedy spoke of certain rights which all consumers had. President Nixon in his message picked up these rights and said:

> Consumerism in the America of the 70's means that we have adopted the concept of "buyer's rights."
>
> I believe that the buyer in America today has the right to make an intelligent choice among products and services.
>
> The buyer has the right to accurate information on which to make his free choice.
>
> The buyer has the right to register his dissatisfaction, and have his complaint heard and weighed, when his interests are badly served.
>
> This "Buyer's Bill of Rights" will help provide greater personal freedom for individuals as well as better business for everyone engaged in trade.

Consumerism does not mean that *caveat emptor*—let the buyer beware—is replaced by *caveat venditor*—let the seller beware. It does mean, however, that protecting the consumer is politically acceptable and that the government will survey consumer demands for better treatment and respond to them with new guidelines for and regulations over business.

WHAT IS BEHIND CONSUMERISM?

It seems paradoxical that the American consumer is at one and the same time the envy of the world for the quality and abundance of the products and services he consumes, and himself dissatisfied with those products and services. Why the paradox?

General Discontent This is an age of discontent, of skepticism, and challenge to established authority. Begun by the young, these attitudes have extended into other areas of American life, including consumer reactions. Today's consumers are much better educated than those of the past and now challenge older practices which they heretofore bore in silence. They question the authority of the uncontrolled marketplace. This is an age, too, of vocal expression of discontent; and consumers, fed up with bad treatment at the hands of manufacturers, advertisers, merchants, and repairmen, are voicing their complaints.

Are the complaints justified? Every consumer would say yes, because every consumer has been frustrated with a variety of consumption problems. Furthermore, consumers are bombarded almost daily in the press with illustrations of product and services deficiencies, recalls, and deceptions. Businessmen claim that dissatisfied consumers represent only a small fraction of the total. This may be so, but the rising tide of consumer complaints is based upon solid and often painful cases, as the following paragraphs will show.

Unsafe, Impure, and Defective Products The National Commission on Product Safety concluded in a thorough study that "the exposure of consumers to unreasonable consumer product hazards is excessive by any standard of measurement" (1970: 1). There are 20 million Americans, the commission said, who are injured each year in the home as a result of incidents connected with consumer products and the annual cost to the nation of these product-related injuries may exceed $5.5 billion. This and many other reports, including daily newspapers, are filled with notices of products with highly lethal defects, such as imported eyeglass frames made of a highly flammable cellulose nitrate; an infant's rattle that easily comes apart to expose three-inch spikes; toys with electrical, mechanical, or excessive heat hazards; and TV sets with radiation danger.

Deceptive Promotion The consumer is beset with advertising claims that are distorted, untrue, and deceptive. For instance, the National Academy of Science's National Research Council reviewed almost 4,000 drug preparations for the FDA in 1969 and concluded that most were effective for the claims made for their use. However, 7 percent—or close to 300—were not. Included in this list were mouthwashes, the sales of which totaled over $200 million each year, which when used as a part of a daily hygiene regimen were found to have no therapeutic advantage as a germ-killer over salt water or even plain water. The consumer has so often found products having less utility than advertised that the experience is considered normal (Cox, et al. 1969: 13–33).

Following hearings on games before the Subcommittee on Investigation of Sweepstakes Promotion, House Small Business Committee Chairman Dingell concluded:

> . . . our accumulated data show that an average of only about 10% of the prizes advertised and ostensibly "offered" are ever, in fact, actually awarded—and, even worse, that 90% of the few prizes that are awarded are of the least expensive variety, more being mere trifles worth perhaps a dime or a quarter. Seldom, indeed, are the first, second or third prizes—the large ones that enticed millions of people to enter the "contests"—prizes such as automobiles, vacations in Europe, yachts, color television consoles, $10,000 in cash, $100 a week for life—ever awarded (U.S. Congress, Select Committee on Small Business, 1969).

Illusive Guarantees In an examination of warranties and guarantees on major house appliances, the FTC concluded that ". . . it is fair to state that in some instances the exclusions, disclaimers, and exceptions so diminished the obligations of the manufacturer that it was deceptive to designate the document as a warranty, because the remaining obligations were lacking in substance" (Presidential Task Force on Appliance Warranties and Service, 1969: 47). Out of 200 warranties examined, 34 had some exceptions, disclaimers, and exclusions. Several warranties contained all of these, and in some of them the same exceptions were stated more than once.

Failure to Fulfill Guarantees Equally serious are the complaints of consumers that manufacturers and retailers fail to meet their warranties.

In commenting on the unhappy lot of the consumer who gets no satisfaction from his local dealer and goes to the manufacturer, the FTC said:

> It is not uncommon for the manufacturer to ignore the appeal altogether and make no response. Some do respond and advise the consumer to contact the dealer about whose conduct she complained. Others recommend contact with a distributor or area service representative. This often leads to what is described as the "run around" with a considerable exchange of correspondence, broken appointments, and nothing being done, with the manufacturer, distributor, and retailer all disclaiming any blame or ability to solve the problem (Presidential Task Force on Appliance Warranties, 1969: 61).

Sloppy and Excessively Priced Repair Service A survey was made of TV repair service in New York City. In twenty homes a tube was made inoperable by opening the filament, which is equivalent to a tube burning out. Of the twenty servicemen called to repair the sets, seventeen were reported to be dishonest or incompetent. Repair costs ranged from $4 to $30 on what should have been a total cost of $8.93, including the charge for service and labor (Weiss, 1968: 14). Independent repair services have deteriorated to such an extent that manufacturers are developing their own training programs for mechanics.

No Forum for Complaint A major problem for consumers is that when they are dissatisfied, they literally have no place to complain. If the problem is one of clear fraud, redress might be made through Better Business Bureaus or the courts. For obvious reasons, however, the purchaser of an inoperable or defective home appliance is not likely to seek redress in a court of law for the failure of the retailer, distributor, or manufacturer to conform to the terms of a warranty.

Journalistic Exposés The flames of consumer discontent have been both lit and fanned by a number of writers whose books have become best sellers. Among the leaders are, in order of the appearance, Vance Packard's *The Hidden Persuaders* (1957) and *The Waste Makers* (1960). In the first volume Packard attacked the use of motivation research and what he called "manipulation" of consumers by advertising. In the second volume he attacked planned obsolescence. In 1962 Rachel Carson published her *Silent Spring*, a devastating account of how our products are polluting our environment. Jessica Mitford's best-selling criticism of the undertaking industry was published in 1963 under the title *The American Way of Death*. Ralph Nader's *Unsafe at Any Speed* came in 1965, and John Galbraith's *The New Industrial State*, which among other things popularized the large company as a monster that held the consumer completely in its grip, appeared in 1967. This same theme was emphasized in 1973 in his *Economics and the Public Purpose*. Heilbroner's *In the Name of Profit*, published in 1972, revealed some dramatic stories of some irresponsible business decisions. There were many more (Vogel, 1973; Nader, ed., 1973), but these books all were highly critical of business, all were best sellers, and all gave consumers information which they had never before had about products and business practices.

Rising Expectations As mentioned previously, expectations are rising in this society. Consumers have much higher standards concerning the products and services consumed than ever before. Expectations frequently outrace reality. They not only are a reflection of rising sophistication but also a yearning for the ideal (Anderson and Jolson, 1973). They are a root cause of rising consumer dissatisfaction.

Other Problems This does not exhaust the list of problem areas for consumers. There is the area of hidden charges in the form of service costs. The complexity of new products is so great that manufacturers find it difficult to communicate to consumers adequate information about how to use a product. As President Kennedy observed in his special message to Congress noted above, "The housewife is called up to be an amateur electrician, mechanic, chemist, toxicologist, dietitian, and mathematician—but she is rarely furnished the information she needs to perform these tasks proficiently." Manuals purporting to describe how products can be put together and used efficiently are sometimes models of incomprehensible English. Despite the Truth-in-Lending Act of 1968, many consumers still do not know just how much they pay for credit. These problems are only illustrations; the full list is far longer.

THE CONSUMER ADVOCATE

One of the phenomena of today's consumerism, in contrast to that of the past, is the rise of consumer advocates. They are self-appointed vigilantes of the consumer and are very numerous. The most outstanding are Ralph Nader and his "raiders." His role is partly that of the muckraker of the past, but it goes further to embrace active representation of the consumer in the courts, in government agencies, in legislatures, and in corporations. Consumerism is not a mass movement of our 210 million consumers speaking as a unit in their own interests. It is rather an amorphous mass of disgruntled consumers partly led and partly pushed by activists who champion what appear to them to be issues beneficial to consumers (Brunk, 1971).

Consumer advocates demand a wide range of remedies to protect the consumer. High on the list, of course, are safe products whose quality meets prescribed standards. They demand an end to false and distorted advertising. Not only do they want better caliber people in regulatory agencies, but they want the regulatory agencies divorced from those who are regulated. They demand that disgruntled consumers find ready and satisfactory redress of grievances. They seek to institutionalize in governmental machinery their fervor by urging the Congress to establish an agency empowered to intervene in the proceedings of all other federal agencies concerned with consumers. Consumer groups seek to protect the environment from damage and to purify the environment that has been degraded.

While consumer advocates have incurred the bitter enmity of many businessmen, there are many who consider Nader's crusade to be beneficial to both business and the community. Edward Rust, when president of the U.S. Chamber of Commerce, said that he was in full agreement with Nader when he concerned himself with producing better products and services. "Nader's focus," he said, "is usually on the first business of business—its products and services. His primary insistence is on products that perform as they are supposed to, on warranties that protect the buyer at least as much as the seller, on services that genuinely serve. . . . I think we are forced to the conclusion that his commitment is to make the system work" (1973). He went on to point out, also, that while Nader was sometimes shrill, and often overdramatized his points, this type of performance is necessary to gain attention in the marketplace of ideas.

There are those who challenge the quality of scholarship of some of Nader's publications (Burck, 1973). Others accuse him of employing the same sort of distorted advertising to promote his books and ideas that he deplores in business (Leff, 1972). There are also some who ask whether his demands really always advance the interests of consumers (Winter, 1972; Brunk, 1971).

Fundamentally, consumer advocates are reformists. On net balance they have served the best interests of consumers, business, and the community. As will be discussed later, however, they are for the most part polemicists and their "factual" assertions, arguments, and policy recommendations must be examined critically.

THE BUSINESS RESPONSE: AN OVERVIEW

The response of businessmen to the rising crescendo of consumer complaints has been mixed. There is plenty of evidence that many companies are seeking to meet consumer complaints honestly and with high commitment to consumer interests. For instance, larger companies particularly are increasingly establishing offices of consumer affairs, frequently at the vice-presidential level, to coordinate all corporate activities which are concerned with consumer satisfactions. They interpret the consumer point of view to the company and provide meaningful communications between the company and the consumer (Blum, Steward and Wheatley, 1972).

The public apparently is not convinced, however, that these efforts are enough, and the justification of their feelings is confirmed. In a 1960 poll 70 percent of consumers said business was striking a fair balance between making a profit and providing a service. Currently, only 29 percent think so (Yankelovich, 1972). In a study of 157 companies, Webster concluded: "Only a small number of companies . . . appear to have a well thought-out, planned, and integrated program working toward a common objective of improved service to the consumer" (1973: 91).

On the legislative front, particular business interests have fought against just about every new piece of legislation designed to protect consumers. When they have lost that battle, they have sought to de-fang the regulations by weakening the bite of regulatory agencies either by pressuring Congress to pass less rigorous laws or to deny funds to enforce them. The business attitude generally is that "present laws are adequate," or "what is all the fuss about, the number of complaints is very few."

On the other hand there have been many instances where busi-nessmen have organized to ask government to set standards which their industry should be meeting in order to serve consumer interests better. For example, in 1971 the National Canners Association pre-pared some forty-eight pages of regulations which it asked the FDA to adopt so as to assure proper sealing and sterilization of canned foods.

Although not as many companies are stepping up to consumer-ism pressures as might be desired by consumer advocates there is plenty of evidence to conclude that more and more companies are responding responsibly. Among leaders are Eastman Kodak, Whirl-pool, Quaker Oats, Motorola, General Electric, Westinghouse, and RCA, to mention but a few (Webster, 1973: 93; and Aaker and Day, 1972). The thrust of the larger corporation that deals directly with the consumer is to follow these leaders and, as a consequence, one should be wary of using generalizations about business's response to consumerism to apply to a specific company.

A BRIEF RESUMÉ OF CONSUMER LEGISLATION

The history of consumer protection by governments follows the grow-ing complexity of products, multiplying opportunities for abuse; new methods to bilk the consumer; and consumer disasters and com-plaints. Legislation on the statute books is a result of efforts to protect businessmen, of outrage at some business practices, or of a genuine effort to protect consumers before disaster strikes.

From the beginning of our history governments have passed laws to protect consumers. In the earliest days, however, redress for most grievances was worked out through the courts, case by case, or by consumers expressing dissatisfaction in the marketplace. Gradually, governments built legislative protections in an expanding number of areas, including weights and measures, public health and safety, trans-portation, communications, finance, licensing of workers and profes-sionals, zoning, and other essential services.

In the latter part of the nineteenth century, state and local gov-ernments created commissions to prevent railroads and other public utilities from exploiting the public. This idea was picked up by the federal government with the passage, for example, of the Interstate

Commerce Commission Act of 1890, which created a federal commission to regulate railroads in the public interest. A milestone in the entrance of the federal government into consumer protective legislation was made in 1872 with the passage of a law prohibiting the use of the mails to defraud. The National Bureau of Standards was created in 1901 to fix measures for use by business and state and local governments. A major precedent was set in 1906 with the passage of the Pure Food and Drug Law, which forbade the misbranding of drugs. One year later sanitation in the meat-packing industry came under congressional scrutiny, and the Meat Inspection Act of 1907 was passed to authorize the Department of Agriculture to inspect slaughtering, packing, and canning plants. The passage of this act followed a period of agitation arising from Upton Sinclair's The Jungle, which described in lurid detail the lack of sanitation in meat-packing plants.

Around the time of World War I there was a surge of legislation to protect consumers. For example, the Clayton Act of 1914 and its creation of the Federal Trade Commission protected consumers from unfair trade practices. The Water Power Act of 1920 established the Federal Power Commission to protect the public from public utility monopolistic practices. The next major surge of legislation came in the 1930s under the Roosevelt New Deal Administration. Many pieces of legislation during this period tightened past laws and added new ones. One noteworthy one was the Sea Food Act of 1934, which permitted the FDA to inspect processing plants. There were a number of important actions protecting the financial interests of consumers, such as the creation of the Securities and Exchange Commission in 1933. The Wool Labeling Act of 1939 was the first law dealing with a particular type of product. This law benefited consumers because it required fabric labeling, but it was passed because wool growers wanted to limit competition from processors of reused wool and from artificial fibers.

In the minor wave of new legislation in the 1950s the Flammable Fabrics Act of 1953 was passed because of indignation resulting from burns suffered by children dressed in flammable materials. The act prohibits making apparel from flammable fabrics. Other acts were passed concerning fur products and textile fiber products. The Kefauver-Harris Drug Amendments of 1962 to the Food and Drug Act required pre-market testing of drugs for efficacy as well as safety and prescribed that the labels show the common or generic name for the drug.

This brief resumé of consumer protective legislation reveals several characteristics. First, the range of such legislation covered all industries, but was largely aimed at abuses in specific industries such as railroads, foods, drugs, and electric utilities. Second, consumer legislation generally was passed only after some shocking revelations stirred public opinion enough to overcome special business interest pressures on legislators. Third, consumer legislation often was passed during periods of rising prices when consumer complaints increased. Finally, journalistic exposés were important in stimulating interest in protecting consumers.

In the past few years an unprecedented concern for consumers has resulted in the passage of over several dozen major pieces of legislation. To illustrate but a few, the Fair Packaging and Labeling Act of 1966 was finally passed after five years of hearings. The Consumer Protection Credit Act of 1968 required full disclosure of interest rates charged to borrowers. The Securities Markets Review Act of 1968 required full information about over-the-counter stocks. Legislation was passed to establish standards and/or regulations for automobile safety, cigarette advertising, meat inspection, poultry inspection, fire research and safety, consumer counseling, sizes for children's clothing, toxic insecticides, electrical equipment, and gas pipeline safety. In 1968 the Congress passed the Child Protection and Toy Safety Act which has permitted the FDA to crack down on hazardous playthings. In response to the *Report of the National Commission on Product Safety* (1970), the Congress in 1972 created the Commission on Consumer Product Safety and gave it broad authority over a wide range of products.

President Johnson created a new White House post of Special Assistant for Consumer Affairs. In his message to Congress in 1969 President Nixon asked for and got a new Office of Consumer Affairs in the Executive Office of the President with greater responsibilities than held by the Special Assistant for Consumer Affairs. By executive order President Nixon created the National Business Council for Consumer Affairs in 1971 to advise him and government agencies, through the Secretary of Commerce, on programs of business relating to consumer affairs. In the meantime a proposal was before the Congress to establish a Department of Consumer Affairs (U.S. Congress, Hearings on S.1177 and H.R. 10835, 1971; and Hearings on S. 860 and S. 2045, 1969).

Recent legislation on behalf of the consumer has been massive. It is estimated that there are some 50 federal agencies and bureaus now performing some 200 to 300 functions affecting consumers (U.S. Congress, Hearings on S. 1177 and H.R. 10835, 1971: 19). These numbers are easily exceeded by state and local protective legislation. The consumer can hardly be said to be the prey today of malevolent businessmen with such protective armor on the statute books. Yet new abuses appear daily which demand new protections.

There are radically opposing views about the efficiency of agencies administering consumer protective legislation. Nader complains (1973) as does Galbraith (1973) that regulatory agencies are, at best, not protecting consumers as the law requires, and, at worst, are acting in the interests of business rather than consumers. At the other extreme is the thesis that most regulations should be abolished for the sovereignty of the consumer is being undermined in the name of protection (Peterson, 1971).

The vast flood of legislation and government programs of the past eight years on behalf of consumers represents a strong move to protect consumers before rather than after disaster strikes. It is more comprehensive in scope and represents a stronger affirmation by government of its intention to protect the rights of consumers than any previous flurry of consumer legislation (Gaedeke, 1970). On the whole it seems to me that it does protect consumers without unjust or inappropriate restraints on business. This fact is not offset by distortions of impact and faulty administration which is important but not great in relation to the totality of regulatory need.

IS THE CONSUMER SOVEREIGN OR CAPTIVE?

Traditional economic theory presumed "consumer sovereignty" in the marketplace. In this view, the initiative for and choice of what is produced lie with the consumer. Goods and services are produced in response to his wants. It is the vote of the consumer in the marketplace that spells financial success or loss for producers. In this theory, the consumer is considered to be well informed about costs, quality, and other characteristics of products and services and in a position to make a choice in conformity with his own self-interests. Here is the "economic man" who, when duped by one producer or retailer, will take his business elsewhere and will by such actions force producers and distributors to accede to the interests of consumers. Under such circumstances, complaints are few, and those producers who understand consumers and satisfy consumer wishes will be the most successful in making profits.

This is completely the reverse of the facts, says Galbraith. To Galbraith, the consumer is the pawn of business. The mature corporation is in a position to manage what the consumer buys at the prices the corporation controls: ". . . the producing firm reaches forward to control its markets and on beyond to manage the market behavior and shape the social attitudes of those, ostensibly, that it serves" (1967: 212). This is the view that managements lay plans to trap the consumer into doing what the company wants through sophisticated advertising, packaging, product design, and other marketing and merchandising techniques. The consumer has so many choices that he has trouble in making a decision, and the right sort of appeal will determine his choice. That which survives on the market may not necessarily be the best product, but the one that is most effectively "sold." Far from being a sovereign, the consumer is a puppet, a captive of business.

Which of these views is correct? Neither is, but both have a certain degree of validity. There is no question at all that advertising does have an important influence on the consumer, but there is reason to believe that it is not as great as asserted by Galbraith (Trivoli, 1970). In a thorough study of the subject, Bauer and Greyser conclude that the consumer is no helpless passive target of communication (1968). No amount of company planning was able to save the Corvair automobile following adverse publicity about its safety. Much depends upon the consumer, the product, the time of purchase, information and other circumstances about his purchase to determine whether he is in control or is being controlled. It is probably fair to say, however, that the growing complexity of products, the paucity of information about them, and uncertainties in the minds of consumers about many characteristics of products make consumers more amenable to the blandishments and hoopla of advertising.

FALSE AND DECEPTIVE ADVERTISING

Mark Twain once said: "When in doubt, tell the truth. It will amaze most people, delight your friends and confuse your enemies." American advertising, which costs around $25 billion a year, has not paid enough attention to Twain's recommendation.

Advertising has the legitimate function of providing factual information for consumers at reasonable cost. But when does simple information become irresistible persuasion? When is an advertiser telling the truth? What is the difference between puffery and prevarication? At what point in advertising should government intervene? What should government's penalties be? When is cost excessive? These are tough questions the answers to which are very often quite unclear.

The FTC long has regulated advertising but in recent years it has stepped up its activity, especially in a number of controversial areas. The original legislation creating the FTC in 1914 gave the agency power to regulate unfair methods of competition. In 1916 the FTC decided this meant false advertising and moved to stop it. In 1931 the FTC for the first time extended its jurisdiction to deceptive advertising and had its knuckles rapped by the Supreme Court for doing so. As a result, the Wheeler-Lea Amendment to the original legislation was passed in 1938 to prohibit unfair and deceptive trade practices, including false and misleading product advertising. Since then there have been many pieces of legislation extending and expanding the power of the FTC over advertising.

For the most part false advertising was not too difficult to detect and correct. Thus, the FTC had little trouble early in its life in stopping advertising claims that coffee could cure malaria. The traditional remedy applied by the FTC when it caught wrongdoing was to issue a cease-and-desist order. If advertisers did not comply with the order they were subject to a fine of $5,000 each day for each violation. One difficulty with this remedy was that the wrongdoer was often left in possession of a market unlawfully earned. As a result the FTC began "corrective advertising" in 1971.

In a well-publicized case concerning Profile Bread the FTC said its advertising was misleading. The Continental Company, a subsidiary of International Telephone and Telegraph, the maker of the bread, was accused of deceptively advertising that its bread was a weight-control product. Actually, the only difference from other breads was that the slices of the advertised product were half the size of other brands. The FTC ordered "corrective advertising" which meant the company had to spend 25 percent of its annual advertising budget to disclaim Profile's weight-control capabilities (*Fortune*, 1972).

The FTC effort, of course, was to restore the market to the condition before the deceptive advertising. This remedy raised such controversial issues as: how much do consumers really remember? What is the real impact on consumers of advertising? What should corrective advertising be to remedy past "bad" memories? Might not clever corrective advertising provide an opportunity to capitalize on past wrongdoing as seen by the FTC?

In 1971 the FTC moved to force advertisers to make available written evidence of advertising claims. The automobile companies were asked to substantiate their claims. The FTC wanted written proof, for example, that Ford's LTD is "quieter than some of the world's most expensive cars." In 1972 the FTC asked for substantiation of dog-food advertising. The FTC gave Campbell Soup sixty days, for instance, to explain how its Champion Valley Farms dog food is "completely balanced." In 1973 the FTC wanted proof of claims from shampoo firms.

Pitofsky, a former FTC official, speculates that in the future the FTC attacks on advertising are likely to move in three directions. First, to limit advertising that is persuasive rather than informative. Persuasive advertising he defined as "those efforts to impart information which substantially all consumers already have" (1973: 9). Such advertising, he says, is socially wasteful. He did not advocate across-the-board limitations but only in specific cases such as where all products are essentially identical so that little information is added from successive advertisement of the product.

Second is anticompetitive advertising, such as advertising used to barricade entry to firms; or when by merger or joint venture national advertising is begun in a market where there was none; or where there is a joint monopoly with high advertising, high prices, and high profits. The cereal industry at this writing is being prose-

cuted as falling in the last category. Six manufacturers control 90 percent of the market with few, if any, low-priced competition.

The third area, according to Pitofsky, is false and deceptive advertising. FTC's aggressive action in this area will not likely be seen
as an effort just to crack down on false and misleading claims, but as
a larger governmental effort to improve consumer protections.

Over-all, it appears that FTC's efforts are moving more and more
to assuring that advertising provides to the consumer clearer, more
accurate, and sufficient information about products. This does not
portend, of course, less attention to false and deceptive advertising.
On the contrary, the two are intimately interrelated.

All this raises many issues. I shall confine comment to one,
namely, puffery versus prevarication. Levitt, in a brilliant article,
pointed out that people buy things for many purposes and advertisers may be accused of prevarication when they are only engaged
in puffery to satisfy the wants of consumers. Consumers, he says, want
"truth," but also they need "the alleviating imagery and tantalizing
promises of the advertiser and designer" (1970: 92). Business, he says,
is caught in the middle. Most companies would go bankrupt if they
did not provide "fluff" because no one buys pure functionality. On
the other hand, if too much fluff is used the advertiser invites further
government legislation. The middle ground may not always be clear,
but Levitt thinks it can be clearer if business thinks more purposively
in trying to find it (1973: 92).

HOW MUCH FREEDOM OF CHOICE?

There have been occasions when the government has strongly restricted consumer choice. Perhaps the most famous case was Prohibition in 1919 when the government decided it was in the public
interest to prohibit the manufacture, sale, and consumption of alco-
holic beverages. From time to time the government steps into the
marketplace to prohibit the use of a particular product, such as DDT,
or to restrain its usage in some fashion, such as the use of cigarettes.
In some instances where products are obviously dangerous, such as
flammable children's clothing, restrictions are easily justified. In other
cases, such as cyclamates, valid arguments pro and con can be made.

There are some broad principles which can be advanced to justify government's restraint of consumer choice. For instance, government clearly is justified in imposing safety regulations, especially
when someone other than the buyer or seller is subject to injury.
Hazardous toys are a case in point. Consumers also clearly should be
protected from false advertising. Consumers clearly must be protected from dangerous, addictive, and poisonous foods and drugs.
Government also has the clear responsibility to make sure that consumers have enough information to make rational choices.

The criteria for deciding why, when, and how much consumer freedom shall be limited, however, are not always clear within these broad guidelines. Each case is subject to controversy and must be decided upon the circumstances surrounding it. Restrictive legislation with respect to cigarette advertising is a case in point.

Beginning with the Surgeon-General's report on cigarette smoking made public on January 11, 1964, and in subsequent studies, overwhelming evidence that cigarette smoking is injurious to health and shortens life expectancy has been made public. In quick response to the Surgeon-General's report the FTC on June 22, 1964, issued a trade regulation rule providing that all cigarette labeling and advertising must carry a health warning statement. The Congress in 1964, by passing the Federal Cigarette Labeling and Advertising Act, reaffirmed the regulation of the FTC. The warning requirement was changed in subsequent legislation and is now: "Warning: The Surgeon-General has determined that cigarette smoking is dangerous to your health." This statement is not and never has been as strongly worded as desired by the FTC.

The FTC also has restricted cigarette advertising to protect the public health. One basis for the FTC's action is the 1938 Wheeler-Lea Amendment to the 1914 Federal Trade Commission Act. The FTC contends that cigarette advertising is particularly misleading since it implies that smoking is not harmful. Indeed, as one commissioner put it, "The industry spends hundreds of millions of dollars each year on such advertising—and the rate of expenditure is increasing—to obscure the fact that cigarette smoking is a dangerous and harmful habit which each year shortens the lives of hundreds of thousands of people" (Elman, in *FTC Report to Congress,* 1968: Appendix).

Professor Milton Friedman, a nonsmoker, objects to the FTC anti-cigarette-advertising approach because he believes that it is "hostile to the maintenance of a free society." Whenever we ride in an automobile, he says, we risk our lives. We do it, however, because the advantage is worth the risk. Similarly, a smoker may view the pleasure of smoking as justifying the cost to him in reduced length of life. Why not ban Marx's *Das Kapital* or Hitler's *Mein Kampf*? They have caused far more deaths than cigarettes. Or, why not require them to carry a label: "Reading Is Dangerous to Mental Health and May Cause Death from Revolution and Other Disturbances"? "In a free society," he says, "government has no business to propagandize for some views and to prevent the transmission of others. Freedom of speech includes the freedom to preach for or against Communism, for or against Fascism—and also for or against smoking" (*Newsweek,* June 16, 1969: 53).

This is a ringing call to freedom of speech with which no one can disagree, but it is not the whole of the issue. Does not the government have some responsibility to protect the public health? Constitutional guarantees of freedom of speech are paralleled by rights of all the people, including protection of public health and welfare. Freedom of speech is not without some limits of responsibility. The government does have a right, authorized by the Wheeler-Lee Amendment, and the people have a right, to be protected from false and misleading advertising. Despite industry claims to the contrary, is not cigarette advertising grossly misleading? Does not the government have a duty to assure that advertising is more truthful than untruthful?

There is a real question whether freedom of speech is abridged when powerful industries can saturate the communications media with strong messages favoring their interests when contrary views which favor the consumer cannot be expressed as forcefully. May this circumstance not be more harmful to freedom of speech than government regulation of advertising? Beyond this point, however, there seems to me to be a basic implied obligation of government to act in such circumstances, because there seems to be a growing feeling among consumers that if the government does not react adversely to a product on the market, it must be all right. As we have seen previously, this is far from the case. Finally, the implication in Friedman's statement that only the smoker is injured is contrary to the facts. In this day of publicly supported medical care, the better the health of the nation, the lower the cost to all taxpayers. Higher medical costs associated with diseases caused by cigarette smoking are charges everyone must bear. Does not the public generally therefore have a right to take action which will in its judgment reduce the total medical costs all society bears?

This particular case raises other issues aside from advertising. For instance, why attack advertising and not production? Since the production of cigarettes is legal, it cannot now be forbidden, and it is not likely that Congress will pass legislation authorizing its stoppage. Not only are powerful business and agricultural interests against ceasing production, but large numbers of consumers also would oppose such a move. Furthermore, with the disastrous results of Prohibition still within memory, Congress is not likely to repeat that type of blunder. In light of the legality of production, it does not make much sense to place a complete ban on broadcast advertising. The government's attack on advertising, however, is based on the assumption that limiting or eliminating broadcast advertising will have a positive effect on reducing smoking and keeping people from starting to smoke. Whether this will, in fact, occur remains to be seen. In the meantime, restricting the marketing of a legal product is a new precedent in regulation and opens up a Pandora's Box of potential problems. For example, does this precedent mean that advertising of guns, of dairy products (a source of cholesterol), or of alcohol faces similar restrictions?

On the assumption that the basic objective of the government to protect the public health is a sound one, how best can this objective be achieved? Aside from current programs to restrain advertising and mass education about the hazards of cigarette smoking, taxes on cigarettes may be increased to discourage consumption, taxes on cigarettes may be increased to finance research that seeks to make cigarettes with fewer or no health hazards, standards for tar and nicotine content may be required on all packages of cigarettes and in advertisements, existing purchase laws for minors can be enforced, and the current educational program may be so intensified as to constitute a new program.

In sum, even though there may be a general consensus that governmental restrictive legislation is required there frequently is controversy about just how much restraint will be exercised and by what methods. The limits are not usually clear.

PRODUCT OBSOLESCENCE

Critics claim that manufacturers' self-interests lead them to engage in what is called "product obsolescence." This can mean a deliberate underengineering of a product to produce a shorter life-span to force consumers to make premature replacement purchases. It can also mean styling changes or advertising that persuade consumers to replace products before their usefulness is ended. Automobiles, household appliances, light bulbs, and toys are often cited as products with built in obsolescence. Is a producer acting responsibly when he makes a product that lasts for five years when it could be made to serve much longer? Critics see built-in obsolescence as a waste. They say that expenditures for replacements could be used for other products, and purposely shortening the life of a product is a loss to consumers and society. On the other hand, the defenders of underengineering point out that the fickle consumer will turn away from the higher-priced product which lasts longer in favor of the lower-priced product with a shorter life. The consumer will also react favorably to styling because he wants change and newness. Critics assert that such consumer reactions are induced by manufacturers, but the defenders of product obsolescence say this is the way consumers are and manufacturers are doing no more than meeting consumer interests.

Product obsolescence results partly from the effort of manufacturers to induce mass consumption in order that they and society may reap the benefits of mass production. With mass production, producers can cut costs per unit, which in turn will increase demand for products having elastic demands. Under such circumstances, there are opportunities for profits. All this is quite legitimate and morally responsible in our society. Product obsolescence involves a question of trade-off. Electric light bulbs, for instance, can be made to last longer, and long-life bulbs are on the market and cost only a little more than ordinary bulbs. The informed purchaser knows, however, that the long-life bulbs have thicker filaments and use more power. Light bills are therefore higher for the same illumination. A watch made to last almost indefinitely would cost far more than the cheap watch that lasts but a few years. For most products, there is a trade-off between length of life and such factors as cost, quality, safety, and performance. Who is to make such decisions? In modern business they are made by managers and engineers who must, in turn, base their conclusions on many forces, not the least of which is the response of customers.

It should be pointed out in this connection that consumer attitudes in the United States run more toward newness, innovation, and style than toward sameness and utilitarianism. There are those who assert that advertising is the cause of this consumer philosophy. There is some truth to this, but I think there are deeper values in society which lead generally to the preference for the new over the old product.

The social responsibilities of a manager are discharged if the consumer understands the facts about his product in sufficient degree to appraise the value of purchasing an alternative product that promises a longer life. It is a breach of morality, says Walton, with whom I agree, when "(a) obsolescence is deliberately engineered into a product that may be legitimately presumed by the ordinary reasonable man to have a longer period of service, and (b) this presupposition is deliberately exploited by the vendor" (1969: 200).

MANUFACTURER LIABILITY FOR DEFECTIVE PRODUCTS

Consumers are sometimes injured in the use of products. The question of liability has long been a matter of concern for the courts, businessmen in the chain of manufacturer and distribution, and of course, consumers. Until recent years consumers had difficulties in collecting damages from anyone, especially the original manufacturer. More recently, however, laws and judicial rulings have expanded importantly the liabilities of manufacturers and have permitted consumers to collect greater damages from them. Some of the milestones in this evolution follow.

Until a few years ago manufacturers were well-protected from consumer liability suits. An injured plaintiff proceeded to collect damages through either contract or tort law. Under contract law the disgruntled consumer had to plea that the manufacturer was bound by a warranty (implied or expressed) that his product was reasonably fit to do what it was supposed to do without injury to the user. In the absence of a direct contract between the manufacturer and the consumer, called "privity," the courts would argue that the plaintiff had no case against the producer but had to go to the retailer. If the retailer lost a suit, he would sue the wholesaler, and he in turn the manufacturer. This chain seldom resulted in redress to consumers.

If the injured consumer used tort law he had to argue that a manufacturer was negligent in producing a product. This was very difficult to prove because courts of law found manufacturers guiltless if they exercised reasonable care in producing a product, whether or not it caused injury.

The first major change occurred in 1916 in the case of *Mac-Pherson v. Buick Motor Company*. In this case General Motors was held liable, irrespective of privity, for injuries resulting from the use of its product. In this case a wheel was found defective when it fell off while the car was going fifteen miles per hour. In *Randy Knitwear v. American Cyanamid* the court held that: "It is highly unrealistic to limit a purchaser's protection to warranties made directly to him by his immediate seller. The protection he really needs is against the manufacturer whose published representations caused him to make the purchase" (1962). As a result of decisions like these it is now possible for injured consumers to sue and have a good chance of collecting damages from manufacturers when they are injured by a product that is defective.

There have also been important changes in tort law. Now it is held that a manufacturer is liable for unfit products that unreasonably threaten a consumer's personal safety. This is called strict liability under tort and means that liability exists when a wrong is done. The crucial case in this regard was *Henningsen v. Bloomfield Motors, Inc.,* in 1960. In 1962 in *Greenman v. Yuba Power Products, Inc.,* the doctrine held, and the court said: "A manufacturer is strictly liable in tort when an article he places on the market, knowing that it will be used without inspection, proves to have a defect that causes injury to a human being." Today, it is not necessary to prove fault on the part of the manufacturer. It is only necessary to show that the product was defective when sold and caused injury.

These decisions were further expanded by *Larson v. General Motors Corporation* in 1968 when the court granted damages to a plaintiff who said the design of a steering-column assembly constituted an increased hazard to the driver when the automobile was involved in an accident. The court held that it is the duty of the manufacturer to design a product that is reasonably fit for its intended use and free of hidden defects that could make it unsafe. The court held that: "While all risks cannot be eliminated nor can a crash-proof vehicle be designed under the present state of the art, there are many common sense factors in design which are or should be well-known to the manufacturer that will minimize or lessen the injurious effects of a collision."

In sum, the burden of proving blame has been lifted from complaining consumers. It is now far easier than ever before to collect damages from a manufacturer. Courts clearly have decided that injuries resulting from defective products should be paid for by producers, not by the injured persons. Paralleling these legal changes is an increase in liability suits. One estimate is that such actions rose from 50,000 per year in 1960 to 800,000 per year in 1970 (McGuire, 1973: 61).

This trend means, obviously, that manufacturers must pay close attention to possible defects in and injuries from the use of their products. The entire production and marketing chain must be reexamined to assure as much as possible that the design, manufacture, sales, and service of products will not injure users nor bring catastrophic damage suits. Failure of companies to do this invites bankruptcy.

PRODUCT SAFETY: THE CASE OF AUTOMOBILES

Consumers have recently become much more conscious about product safety and they, together with their advocates, are pressing legislatures for higher standards to be met by producers. Legislatures, especially the Congress, have responded and the number of laws regulating product design and functioning has been mounting. This trend undoubtedly will continue into the future. Many issues arise when government prescribes safety standards for a product. To illustrate some important ones, and these vary from case to case, the following discussion deals primarily with automobiles.

Importance of Automobile Safety Automobile safety is a particularly dramatic issue because of the huge numbers of casualties involved, because most everyone rides in automobiles, and because the federal government is expanding continuously its prescription for safety devices on vehicles. Last year some 56,000 Americans died as a result of motor-vehicle accidents. Of this number about 28,000 were riding bicycles, motorcycles and vehicles other than automobiles or were on foot. About 2,000,000 people were disabled beyond the day of an accident. Permanently disabling injuries are estimated to outnumber fatalities three to one. Total "societal costs" associated with these accidents (including property) are estimated to run between $40 to $45 billion a year (Bowen, 1972). These are large enough numbers to merit the concern of everyone.

Attacks on Automobile Manufacturers, 1965–1966 In 1965 and 1966 the automobile industry was jolted by a series of events relating to automobile safety features. For some time the federal government had been moving to upgrade automobile safety standards by raising requirements for government-purchased automobiles. In 1965 Senator Ribicoff introduced a bill in Congress to expand federal research into traffic safety, and invited representatives of the four major automobile companies to testify before his committee. In the meantime Ralph Nader's *Unsafe at Any Speed* (1965) appeared. All this coincided with increasing public concern over mounting highway deaths and injuries and consumer complaints about the quality of automobiles. The net result was widespread publicity for and action associated with improving automobile safety features.

Accusations against the automotive industry ranged from the hysterical to the sophisticated and technical. On the more extreme side, the industry was accused of being more concerned about profits than human lives (O'Connell and Myers, 1966). The industry was charged with being more concerned with styling than safety. It was charged, with proof, that automobile manufacturers did produce automobiles with known, but correctable, defects. For instance, Nader and others argued that General Motors knew of hazards in the rear-end suspension system of the popular Corvair automobile which tended to make it unstable and unsafe in turns even at moderate speeds. The industry also was charged with ignoring information developed from research which would minimize injury in an accident. In 1952, for instance, research at Cornell University showed clearly the value of the safety belt. Other research showed the value of eliminating knobs and other projections inside the automobile, improving door latches, and adding interior padding as means to reduce hazards to individuals when an accident occurred. The industry, however, missed the opportunity to apply such findings.

The Industry Response Some aspects of the response of the industry to these new charges were not constructive. The industry fought to defeat some legislation before Congress dealing with automobile safety features. In a more enlightened approach, industry spokesmen pointed out that their critics seemed to give the impression that cars were carelessly put together in some styling studio and unveiled suddenly to an innocent world. This is far from the case, they correctly asserted, since years of development and experimentation preceded the beginning of each new assembly line. Over the years the automobile has become increasingly safe through research and experience. While manufacturers are concerned with design, they have clearly not ignored safety. Indeed, they point out that the industry for years has allocated about half a billion dollars annually for safety improvements *(Nation's Business,* May 1966: 39). Many safety features have been introduced in automobiles without government threats.

Industry spokesmen also pointed out that the public has not reacted favorably either to certain safety features or to the costs for them. For example, when the American Motors Corporation in 1950 adopted seat belts as a standard item, some dealers and customers felt this was a negative factor and cut them off. Nevertheless, over the years automobiles have incorporated more and more safety features. The industry claims that for many years it has been interested in and has taken action to avoid accidents by eliminating the causes of accidents. For instance, it has sought to get states to pass motor vehicle inspection laws to weed out and correct deficiencies in unsafe automobiles and drivers.

An Appraisal of the Debate There was, of course, truth on both sides. No one can read the minutes of the hearings before Senator Ribicoff's Senate Subcommittee on Executive Reorganization investigating traffic safety without a feeling that the automobile manufacturers had not been as concerned about the safety of drivers as they should have been. On the other hand, they certainly had not been indifferent to consumer safety.

In issues of this type it is always difficult to tell when industry resistance to government pressure and sharp criticism is a cover-up for shortcomings, an effort to avoid regulations, a defense to avoid legal liabilities, or all three. In the latter case, for instance, automobile manufacturers naturally can be expected to seek to avoid any situation where liability for product defects can be easily placed on them. With 100 million cars in operation, the potential of legal liabilities is frightening to manufacturers. On the other hand, of course, loss of life or injury to a motorist is of the highest importance.

I think that an appraisal of the events associated with this debate leads to the conclusion that the industry response was not effective in combating the criticism, that the general threshold of sensitivity of people to automobile safety was considerably reduced, and that confidence in industry leaders was not enhanced. There seems little doubt that in this as in other consumer areas there was a shift in priorities and expectations. Whereas consumers in the past concentrated on style, power, and gadgetry, there was an increasing concern among them for safety even at an increased cost and at the expense of styling. Furthermore, consumers wanted better performance from their automobiles. Even though automobiles had been improving in performance and safety, in 1966 they were far from meeting the expectations of opinion leaders. The gap continues to this day. It is very true, as Nader pointed out in his book, that because of lack of information in the past, consumer expectations about new automobile innovations were maintained at a low level and geared more to annual style change and engine performance than to safety. With specific information about what safety might be like, the expectations of consumers took a sudden jump in this direction. On the legislative front, the result was a new type of regulation over the industry that has brought greater and stricter control.

New Legislation and Federal Programs Two major pieces of legislation resulted from the debates on automobile safety. The first was the Motor Vehicle Safety Standards Act of 1966. The National Highway Traffic Safety Administration (NHTSA) now administers this legislation. The second was the Highway Safety Act of the same year.

The Motor Vehicle Safety Standards Act introduced federal standards for automobile safety. Provision was made in the bill for the government to undertake research, development, and testing to improve automobile safety. Once standards are established, producers have a limited time within which to introduce devices or design in new models, and the U.S. District Courts have authority to restrain the sale of automobiles not so equipped or designed. Foreign automobiles also must comply with the new standards. There are several other noteworthy features of this law, such as the government may establish uniform federal motor vehicle safety standards for all used vehicles; government inspectors may enter factories and warehouses to inspect cars; manufacturers are required to reimburse the dealer for cars requiring work after shipment from the factory; and manufacturers must notify automobile purchasers of any established defects.

The Highway Safety Act deals with safety programs. Each state is required to prepare a safety program to be approved by the federal government. Standards are to include driver performance, recording of accidents, vehicle registration, driver licensing, and so on. Enforcement is encouraged by the threat of withholding certain federal funds in cases of noncompliance.

A great many safety standards have been enacted under or stimulated by the new legislation. Among them are seat and shoulder belts, windshield washers, head restraints, defrosting and defogging systems, nonpopout windshields, energy-absorbing steering columns, safer fuel tanks, better tire rims, safer bumpers, safer tires, and passive restraint systems such as air bags.

Today, the automobile makers say they have no basic quarrel with the idea of federally mandated safety standards. Controversy is concerned only with technicalities of new requirements for future application and the speed with which they are supposed to be introduced (Bowen, 1972).

On the basis of past experience and a continuing consumerism, it is likely that the government will tighten existing standards and introduce new ones. For 1974 models the front bumpers must provide 5-mph barrier impact protection. In the 1975 models this standard will apply to rear bumpers. One can be sure that this standard will rise in future models. Safety standards for the 1974–1975 models require that belt restraints be coupled with ignition so that automobiles will not start until belts are secured. More effective passive restraint systems will be required for later models. (These are systems, like air bags, that are effective without anyone in the car taking action.) The present director of NHTSA wants to achieve in the future a set of safety standards which will make crashes "absolutely survivable." This will, of course, require that many stiff standards be met. Beyond such regulations the government may introduce new rules to reduce repair costs through altering car design. Government may decide to set standards concerning the potential life of parts—for instance, by requiring the use of certain types of materials that will increase life expectancy. There is no doubt that the automobile industry will have an important partner in government in the future.

Major Issues in Legislating Product Safety For any one product a series of issues arise in dealing with safety. How safe is safe? Aspirin is safe and therapeutic when properly used. When used improperly it can kill. "Too safe" may involve costs so high that consumers cannot buy the product; "too unsafe" causes needless injuries and loss of lives. Acceptable risks must be tolerated. But what are such risks? What is a minimum risk? Can a $20 power tool be expected to be as safe as a $500 one? Are products supposed to be safe even when used by boobs and idiots?

Since some residual lack of safety will always remain, anyone who can effectively dramatize these elements can develop a large following. But a careful evaluation requires balancing achievements, costs, remaining hazards, and what consumers really will buy and use.

Should the government legislate safety standards which consumers would not pay for (e.g., safety belts) if they had a choice? If a consumer is required by law to buy a safety feature but does not use it, should he be required by law to use it?

There are many trade-offs between styling and safety features, production costs and safety features, and repair costs and safety features. Who shall make these decisions and what criteria will be used?

Each safety device raises its own issues. The principal argument for air bags, for instance, is that people who won't use seat belts will be automatically protected with air bags. The manufacturers say, however, that they will be expensive, will not do anything that seat and shoulder belts will not do if used properly, and that there are serious problems of reliability. Manufacturers assert it would be better to devise means to make sure seat and shoulder belts are used.

Questions of costs must also be addressed. As more safety features are introduced the cost of the automobile will rise. Where do costs and safety equate in general and for each safety item? The manufacturers complain that seat belts and shoulder harness cost consumers around $200 million per year and only about 35 percent of the drivers use them. This raises the question as to whether this is the best way to spend this money. Many assert that proper driver licensing and vehicle inspection would reduce accidents by 75 percent [*Business Week,* February 27, 1971(a): 79]. Iacocca, the president of Ford Motor Company says that the price of the Pinto will rise from $2,000 to around $3,000 in five years because of safety features and engine pollution controls [*Business Week,* 1971(C)]. What will this do to consumption of cars? If rising costs adversely affect production there will be other costs introduced into the economy in the form of unemployment.

Who Is Responsible for Automobile Accidents? Manufacturers do not, of course, carry the blame for automobile accidents. Reducing accidents and deaths requires a widespread attack on the many factors which are responsible. The more appropriate analysis of responsible factors would include the driver, pedestrians, other drivers, roads and highways, and other factors. The driver himself, of course, is a major cause of accidents. When speed limits were reduced in late 1973 because of the energy crisis, fatal accidents dropped dramatically.

Drinking is involved in probably half of all automobile accidents; and one study concluded that if 20 percent of driver licenses (those held by the accident-prone) were withdrawn, total accidents would drop by 80 percent (Sypher, 1968: 30). The psychology of drivers is, of course, highly important. As cars become safer, drivers feel they can drive more safely at higher speeds. Most vehicles on the highways are old and have the defects of age. It is, of course, impossible to produce automobiles that will be completely safe throughout their entire lifetimes. Among the other factors might be mentioned weather, time of day, road signs, lighting conditions, and so on.

A nationwide effort to reduce automobile accidents must deal with all these factors, any one of which can be the sole cause for any particular accident. It is important to distinguish here, however, between the initial accident and what has been called the second accident, or that which takes place inside an automobile once there is a collision. It is to the latter situation that much of the criticism of the automobile companies has been directed. It is here that automobile design and safety features are of great significance in reducing injury.

This by no means exhausts the list of issues concerned with automobile, or other product, safety. It should, however, serve to illustrate that the problem is massive, the issues are many and controversial, and there are few absolutes.

Have New Safety Features Reduced Fatalities? There is no evidence that the new safety rules have cut the toll of highway deaths.

There is evidence, however, to show that the chances of surviving an accident are improving. For example, deaths caused by drivers striking the steering wheel have been practically eliminated at speeds up to 50 miles per hour (*Business Week*, September 20, 1969). The director of North Carolina's Highway Safety Research Center completed a study of accidents throughout his state and concluded: "The circumstances that would have produced 115 accident injuries in 1961 would produce only 66 injuries in 1970" (General Motors Corporation, 1972: 17).

THE CONSUMER PRODUCT SAFETY COMMISSION

Before leaving the subject of product safety note should be made of the newly appointed Consumer Product Safety Commission. In 1972 the Congress passed the Consumer Product Safety Act which adopted most of the recommendations of the thorough study of the National Commission on Product Safety, referred to previously. The new commission has sweeping powers to regulate virtually all consumer products not now regulated. In the later category are automotive products, most foods, tobacco, and drugs. Industrial products are exempted but if there is only token usage by consumers they, too, fall under the powers of the commission. The commission can force design change in products or ban them if they are considered to be unduly hazardous. One of the first acts of the commission was to publicize a list of 400 product categories it considered to be hazardous. The implication was that if manufacturers did not make the products less hazardous the commission would force them to produce safer products. As a result of this legislation there should be a continuing improvement in product safety.

PERSPECTIVES ON CONSUMERISM

In considering the many issues concerned with consumerism it is important to understand that powerful and articulate writers and organizations assume extreme contradictory positions. For instance, there are those who take a strong position against much if not all government regulation of business on behalf of consumers (Peterson, 1971). Others take strong stands against particular pieces of legislation. At the other extreme are consumer advocates who seek ideal or extremely high protective standards for consumers. Galbraith, for instance, would socialize large companies to prevent exploitation of consumers (1973). Nader and his associates press for ideal standards of protection in consumer interests (Turner, 1970; Cox, 1969; Nader, 1973).

Both sides are unafraid to use exaggerated and unsupported fact to support their position. One side sees a complete breakdown of government regulation and asserts unblushingly that no regulation is better than regulation. Galbraith says flatly that the large corporation is nothing short of a monolithic giant which forces consumers to do its bidding. Nader also sees the consumer in the grip of corporations "able to divert scarce resources to uses that have little human benefit or are positively harmful" (1973: 14). Senator Hart places a number on the outrage by saying that in 1969 out of $780 billion of purchases by consumers $200 billion were spent on products having no value (Winter, 1972: 3).

Remedies sought by either extreme position should be considered with caution. I do not mean to say that proposals of either should be dismissed out of hand. They should, however, be examined very carefully. Business performance should not be measured against unrealistic standards or distorted views of reality. The systems approach and cost/benefit analysis, as noted previously, is a better way to appraise public policy than accepting without reservation "facts" presented at either extreme.

Even what appear at face value to be reasonable demands for consumer protection can turn out, on analysis, not to be in the best interests of consumers. For example, it would appear to reasonable people that drugs ought to be tested thoroughly to prevent another thalidomide disaster. But how much testing? Peltzman examined very carefully the results of the 1962 Kefauver-Harris Amendments to the Food, Drug and Cosmetic Act which prevents a manufacturer from marketing a new drug until it has proven the effects claimed for it to the satisfaction of the FDA. He concludes that the losses to consumers because of new drugs which have not been put on the market, and the delay in getting new drugs to the market, far outweigh savings. The deaths caused by lack of drugs, in other words, are each year far beyond those saved through thorough investigation before marketing (in Steiner, 1974).

HOW SHOULD BUSINESS RESPOND TO CONSUMERISM?

As noted previously business is responding but perhaps not as rapidly and in as socially responsible a way as some people wish. There are two broad approaches to stepping up the business response to consumerism on the assumption that pressures will continue. One is by industry self-regulation and the other is for each company to take appropriate action.

Beyond these actions a company may establish a high-level contact point for meeting consumer complaints, such as an Office of Consumer Affairs. Much can be done to create advertising messages that are fair, honest, and meet consumer needs and expectations. Dialogue with consumers individually and in groups could be profitable. Policies to reduce after-sale consumer frustrations also can pay off (Berry, 1972; Nickels and Zabriskie, 1973). Also, an individual manager can be responsive to consumerism by pressing legislatures for enlightened consumer protections (Levitt, 1970). A company can take steps to institutionalize the social point of view in the decision-making process throughout the company, as was discussed in Chapter 11.

CHAPTER SIXTEEN

Business, Community Problems, and Disadvantaged Minorities

INTRODUCTION

One night in July 1967 James Roche, then the president of General Motors Corporation, was working late on the fourteenth floor of the GM Building in Detroit. As he was pondering his company's problems, he gradually became conscious of an eerie flickering light. He looked out the window to see the city in flames, the result of massive rioting. "I never thought I would see anything like that," he is reported to have said. This event galvanized him into action and "the city" became his most urgent business. In a similar fashion, businessmen in many other cities either faced or were threatened with the same kinds of widespread disorders. They, too, became vitally and instantly involved in the urban crisis.

While businessmen have always been involved in urban problems, the crises brought on by city riots in the 1960s launched them into an acceleration of old programs and the development of new ones. These riots riveted attention on programs that not only promised to reduce tensions but, hopefully, would speed the disadvantaged into the affluent society.

Among the more prominent and widespread programs were those concerned with equal opportunity, training, and employment of the disadvantaged, stimulating minority business enterprises, and eliminating substandard housing. These will be the principal subjects of this chapter. Business found itself involved in many other programs but space does not permit much more than a brief mention of some of them. The chapter begins with a few comments about critical urban problem areas and the role of business in their resolution. Following an examination of major programs, some guidelines for both business and government, based on experience with these programs, conclude the chapter.

DIFFERENT URBAN SETTINGS

To say that there are really two distinct areas in most large cities is an oversimplification, yet an illuminating one. There is the suburban area and the ghetto or barrio. The problems of each and the relationships of business to them vary radically. Again, in highly oversimplified terms, in the first are most frequently found the affluent and in the latter the disadvantaged.

These and other oversimplifications about urban phenomenon, however, are dangerous. For instance, the census of 1970 showed that in the central cities there were 1.8 million families, or 33.6 percent of all poor families. Suburban areas, however, had 1.2 million, or 22.4 percent of the total. The remainder of 2.3 million or 44 percent were outside metropolitan areas.

Population concentration in metropolitan areas has continued in the United States for decades. The 1970 census counted 73.5 percent of us living in urban areas. It is generally conceded that rising concentration is directly associated with many of our urban ills. Yet the Bureau of the Census includes as an "urban place" any settlement having a population over 2,500. Now, clearly the problems of Palm Springs, California, are radically different from those of Boston, Massachusetts.

There have grown up in our larger cities, however, concentrations of disadvantaged minorities. It was the plight of this group that heightened business concern for them in the past decade. They are still a major concern of business, but expanding federal programs have drawn attention to the disadvantaged wherever they are found.

Statistics about these people and the areas in which they live are not very good and those which are available can be interpreted in different ways (see Chapter 19). There is no doubt about the fact, however, that in the ghetto areas of major cities one finds the highest incidence of poverty, unemployment, air pollution, substandard housing, deficient or nonexistent transportation, crime, uncollected garbage, poverty, and eroding human spirits. In most cities the majority of the population in these areas is black. In some, the proportion of Mexican-Americans and American Indians is high. There is in these areas a culture of poverty to which many forces contribute. Lack of income leads to ill health and lack of medical attention. Inadequate housing, poor education, little or no transportation, discrimination, societal neglect, degrading welfare practices, inadequate birth control, and a nonreligious spiritual malaise interact with one another to form a bondage which is difficult for society to break and even more difficult for individuals to escape. Harvey Perloff explains it this way:

> The ghetto is not just a place with many unemployed and subemployed persons; it is a place that saps motivation, erodes the capacity to learn, pulls young persons out of national mainstream activities by overwhelming them with human temptation and risk. It is also a place where it is difficult, inconvenient, costly, and risky to carry out economic activities (Committee on Science and Astronautics, 1969: 93).

In the ghetto areas of our major cities the plight of disadvantaged minorities is visible and of deep concern to all responsible citizens. But there are disadvantaged minorities throughout the nation, although in smaller concentrations and having less visibility. The requirements among the disadvantaged, and programs to meet them, vary enormously. The elderly indigent, for instance, need income and medical care. Poor unwanted children need foster homes. But as noted earlier, all these programs cannot be covered in this chapter and we shall, therefore, concentrate on a few major ones that are indispensable to any significant rehabilitation of the disadvantaged and of major concern to business.

WHAT IS THE BUSINESS ROLE IN DEALING WITH PROBLEMS OF THE DISADVANTAGED?

The answer to this question will depend upon who is looking. At one extreme are those who feel that since governments have failed so badly in resolving such problems, it is now the responsibility of business to do the job. At the other extreme are those who feel business has no responsibility whatever other than to be efficient and gradually raise employment and per capita income. In between are those who see that the business role is very complex and interrelated with other institutions.

A Historical Note It should be remembered that businessmen throughout history have been intimately involved in community affairs. This has been done in their roles as managers of businesses but also as citizens, as holders of political office, and as volunteer members of all types of community institutions. Their motivations have not always been centered on their pocketbooks. In a sweeping historical examination of business in its relations to the community Heald concludes:

> American businessmen fully shared the social concerns and preoccupations of their fellow citizens. Although they have often been depicted— indeed caricatured—as single-minded pursuers of profit, the facts are quite otherwise. The nature of their activities often brought them into

close contact with the harsher aspects of the life of a rapidly industrializing society. Like others, they were frequently troubled by the conditions they saw; and, also like others, they numbered in their ranks men who contributed both their ideas and their resources to redress social imbalance and disorganization (1970: 1).

To say that businessmen in their dealings with the community were not guided solely by profits is not to say they were paragons of civic virtue. Throughout our history prominent businessmen have served our communities in highly unselfish ways. Others have exploited the environment for their own gain. In general, I think the following observation of Heald has become more true as time has moved on. He said: "From the outset, self-interest combined with idealism to foster sensitivity to social conditions on the part of the business community" (1970: 2).

There is not today nor has there been in the past any single pattern to the interrelationship of business to community life. Sometimes a single business has dominated a community. In others, political leaders have dominated business. If any pattern is general it is that businessmen have always been scattered throughout community organizations (such as hospitals, recreation groups, arts groups, etc.) to help in planning, financing, and managing. The motivations naturally range from pure self-interest to unquestioned idealism.

One should distinguish between individual activities in the community and corporate programs, although the two are not always easy to separate. Most of the remaining discussion concerns corporate actions, but it must always be in mind that corporations are run by people and their motivations become intermixed with business purposes.

Business Actions During the past half dozen years business firms, especially the larger corporations, have impressively stepped up their activities in dealing with general community problems. In reviewing what has been done it is useful to think of several categories of action. First are those which are dictated by government, such as equal opportunity programs. Second are those performed by business under government incentives, such as contracts for training hard-core unemployed. Third are those undertaken strictly for profit, such as collecting garbage under a city contract. Fourth are those undertaken in conformance with a pure social interest, such as philanthropic giving. And finally are those undertaken for a variety of reasons such as supporting a minority enterprise to increase employment to advance the idea of private enterprise, or to help stimulate economic activity in decaying neighborhoods.

With a recent great burst of federal programs, corporate activities in the first two categories have risen sharply. Activities in the third area are also growing. Business has come to see that there are opportunities for profit in dealing with urban problems. This is not to be criticized, as some people do, but to be applauded where profit and social benefit parallel one another. Recycling waste, providing transportation, or renovating housing are illustrations. The fourth area has been given new attention. To illustrate, in one study of 247 corporations there were 175 who said they had revised their annual donations since 1967 to provide funds to groups identified specifically with urban problems (Cohn, 1971: 11). Activities in this and the last group have expanded over a very wide spectrum—drugs, play centers, aid to youth, help for the elderly, minority business assistance, hospitals, etc. (Dennis, 1973; MacEachen, 1972; Cohn, 1971; McGuire and Parrish, 1971).

Aside from antipollution programs those which have received the greatest amount of business money and personnel attention are, in the order ranked by the respondents of one survey (total n = 284), as follows: ensuring employment and advancement opportunities for minorities (244), direct financial aid to schools (238), and active recruitment of the disadvantaged (199). High on the list also were support and aid to improvement of black educational facilities and special programs for them and other minorities (159), providing assistance to minority enterprises (134), leadership and financial support for city and regional planning (135), and help in planning community health activities (Corson and Steiner, 1974).

Overall, there is no doubt that business social programs to help mitigate major urban problems have increased. However, while the statistical evidence is not at hand, it appears that many companies have become discouraged with their programs, and activities which they alone support may have declined in the past few years (Case, in Steiner, 1974).

The Business Commitment The fact that business is undertaking these programs clearly indicates its commitment to doing something about the problems to which they are addressed. This statement is supported by one study in which nine of ten respondents (N = 247) said the step-up in corporate urban social programs was permanent. Most thought the involvement would broaden and intensify with time (McGuire and Parrish, 1971). Commitment is also indicated by the increase in the number of companies that have appointed senior persons or created new staff groups at the top levels of companies to deal with urban affairs. Most large companies now have made such assignments and in most of them the officer in charge has been given more responsibilities. The business commitment is founded upon and justified by the many forces underlying business assumption of social responsibilities, set forth in detail in Chapter 10.

EQUAL OPPORTUNITY AND AFFIRMATIVE ACTION

There has long been widespread discrimination against minorities, especially the blacks, in American business. It has only been in the past decade that there has been any concerted attempt to remedy this situation. The responsibility was assumed by the federal government in a series of enactments, executive orders, and guidelines, and implemented by business, as well as government, in revised employment practices.

Basic Legislation The cornerstone of the structure of laws and regulations enforcing equal opportunity is the Civil Rights Act of 1964. Title VII clearly prohibits discrimination in compensation, terms, or conditions of employment because of an individual's race, color, religion, sex, or national origin. This law is administered by the Equal Employment Opportunity Commission (EEOC), an independent agency whose five members are appointed by the President with the approval of the Senate. Originally, the EEOC was given no enforcement powers. It could only investigate and seek voluntary correction of allegedly unlawful employment practices. That has been corrected and the EEOC today has power to issue guidelines, basic procedures, and to take employers and unions to court to stop discriminatory practices. Also the budget of the agency has been expanded. The budget request for Fiscal Year 1974 is $47 million to cover 2,388 positions.

Executive order 11246, effective in September 1965, provided that all government contracts include provisions that contractors take "affirmative action" to assure implementation of the provisions of the Civil Rights Act. In the Allen-Bradley Company case in 1968 Secretary of Labor Shultz said that affirmative action meant a company should not wait for minorities to appear but should seek them out. It also meant a company should avoid carrying forward unnecessary adverse impacts resulting from past discriminations. The Office of Federal Contract Compliance (OFCC) now requires that each organization holding a federal contract must make a written affirmative action program acceptable to the OFCC in each of its plants. If the goals of such programs are not met and the organization cannot show "good faith" in trying to meet them it may lose its federal contracts as well as the right to bid on future federal contracts. Various federal orders have extended this program to nonmanufacturing organizations associated with the federal government, such as banks and educational institutions.

The Equal Pay Act of 1963 prohibited discrimination in employment on the basis of sex and was, of course, reinforced by the Civil Rights Act of the next year. The OFCC in 1971 ordered that affirmative action goals and timetables, required under acts and orders noted above, also be applied to women in job categories in which they were currently underrepresented.

Griggs v. Duke Power Company The courts reinforced the hand of the EEOC in this milestone case in 1971. Black employees challenged the company's requirements for a high school education and passing of a number of tests which were not related to the job before employment was possible. "The Civil Rights Act," said the court, "proscribes not only overt discrimination but also practices that are fair in form, but discriminatory in operation. The touchstone is business necessity. If an employment practice which operates to exclude Negroes cannot be shown to be related to job performance, the practice is prohibited." This case probably marked a turning point in the attitudes of businessmen. Heretofore, many regulations were somewhat fuzzy and the attitude of the courts was not clear. Those companies that had taken a "wait and see" position saw that with judicial blessing the federal government meant business (Shaeffer, 1973).

The ultimate goal is parity in the workforce for minorities, to be achieved on a timetable. As time goes by there will develop a body of case law to reinforce the rights of minorities in reaching this goal. For instance, in a recent court decision it was held that once hired black people must be given the job training necessary to enable them to perform their jobs.

The General Electric Program In most companies, policies and procedures are clear and reach throughout the organization. At General Electric, to illustrate, "the overall corporate goal . . . is, as it must be, the creation of a self-sustaining system that results in true equality of opportunity at all levels of the organization" (General Electric, 1970). The basic statement of policy of the company issued in 1969 is as follows:

> It is the policy of the General Electric Company to provide employment, training, compensation, promotion and other conditions of employment without regard to race, color, religion, national origin, sex or age, except where age or sex are essential, bona fide occupational requirements.
>
> In addition, while it is the policy to apply appropriate job related standards to the conditions of employment and to maintain such standards at a level consistent with the healthy growth of the Company's business in a highly competitive economy, it is also the policy to take affirmative action to seek out individuals whose potential has not been developed, with the objective of assisting them to meet these standards. Affirmative action will include finding additional sources of applicants who can become qualified, utilizing appropriate training which will assist these individuals towards full qualification, and developing programs to assure upward mobility for qualified individuals.

A major goal of the Company is also to become a civic leader in programs and activities which enhance equal employment opportunities within the various communities in which the Company operates and throughout the Nation.

The application of the policy is prescribed as follows:

Each manager is responsible for the application of this Policy within his component. This includes initiating or supporting programs and practices designed to develop understanding, acceptance, commitment and compliance within the framework of this Policy. All employees and specifically each manager will be responsible for complying with all the requirements and laws of the government, and in applying this Policy to achieve Company objectives.

Specifically, each Manager will be responsible for:

Making certain that individuals in his components who make or recommend employment and other personnel decisions are fully aware and comply with this Company Policy

Notifying both applicants and sources of applicants that the Company is an "Equal Opportunity Employer"

Taking affirmative steps to encourage the application and qualification of individuals for available job openings

Assuring that promotion and development opportunities at all levels within his component are made without regard to race, religion, color, national origin, sex or age, except where sex or age are essential bona fide occupational requirements

Cooperating with compliance reviews by appropriate government agencies

Demonstrating leadership among other responsible business and civic leaders in observing the spirit and intent of federal, state and local laws concerning nondiscrimination.

Each Division General Manager, Department General Manager and Corporate Staff Officer will assure that this Policy on Equal Employment Opportunity and Affirmative Action is appropriately communicated and uniformly applied by all levels of management.

At least once each year progress and performance in the area of Equal Opportunity and Affirmative Action will be measured for each Department, Division, Group, Corporate Staff, as well as the Company as a whole.

This policy and procedure is carried out through a lacework of committees and reporting forms (General Electric, 1970). As a result of its programs this company in mid-1973 could observe that one out of every ten of its employees is of a minority group; of 40,000 new people hired in 1972, 20.5 percent were minorities, or more than one in every five joining the company; and that employment of minority college graduates represented 13 percent of the total hired in 1972. The company adds that it is not complacent about these results for there still is progress to be made in filling openings at higher managerial levels with minorities (General Electric, 1973).

An Evaluation The survey noted above showed clearly that corporate efforts in this area were given more emphasis than in any other social program. While no over-all results have been measurable it does seem that equality of opportunity for minorities has advanced significantly during the past two to three years. The current commitment of business to meet the objectives of equal opportunity legislation results from a meeting of clear federal guidelines, energetic surveillance, court decisions reaffirming the laws, and a readiness on the part of industry to meet the requirements.

In more and more corporations one finds the creation of mechanisms to assure conformance with federal equal opportunity policy. In many companies appraisal of how managers are meeting these programs is important in determining their rewards. At Xerox, for instance, the chairman of the board said, in emphasizing the importance of progress in placing minorities and women in upper managerial positions, ". . . a key element in each manager's over-all performance appraisal will be his progress in this important area. No manager should expect a satisfactory appraisal if he meets other objectives, but fails here" (quoted in *Fortune,* September 1972: 146). Still obsolete seniority systems and procedures, many embedded deeply in contractual arrangements with unions and/or past prejudices in the minds of men, remain to be changed before the fullest achievement of the objective of equal opportunity policies is met.

TRAINING AND EMPLOYMENT OF THE DISADVANTAGED

Paralleling the rise of laws concerning economic opportunity were programs to train and get into the workforce people having various disadvantages which were barriers to their gainful employment. Federal manpower programs are based on the assumption that persons with severe employment handicaps are not very likely to improve their employment experience without assistance.

Federal Manpower Programs There have been and are today a bewildering number of programs to train and assist the disadvantaged to get employment. The fiscal year 1974 budget request for these programs is almost $5 billion, a small decline from fiscal year 1973. The budget anticipates enrollment at all levels of 3.3 million people. Most of the people helped are enrolled in school-work support programs, training programs for veterans and unemployed aerospace engineers, training programs for welfare recipients, remedial education and skill training, and the rehabilitation of physically and mentally disabled persons, to mention but a few categories.

Of particular interest for business is the Job Opportunities in the Business Sector (JOBS) program, which is operated in conjunction with the National Alliance of Businessmen (NAB). This program contracts with individual firms to hire and train disadvantaged workers. Budget outlays for fiscal year 1974 are requested at $566 million, a sum higher than in 1973, to take care of 371 thousand enrollees.

JOBS and NAB The NAB was formed by Henry Ford II and a group of businessmen in response to President Johnson's manpower message to Congress on January 23, 1968. The President recognized that previous methods to relate government job-training programs to actual jobs had not been successful because employers were not directly involved. The NAB sought their involvement. A goal of putting 100,000 hard-core unemployed to work was set for the summer of 1969 and 500,000 by 1971. It was thought at the time that the continued unemployment of these people was the fundamental cause of urban unrest. It was estimated at the time, also, that there were from 500,000 to 750,000 of these disadvantaged individuals. The word "hard-core," applied to this group, meant that they had specific characteristics such as: on the average they had been unemployed for eighteen months; they had never received intensive skill training; they needed medical care; they lived with other families; they were married and had three children; their diet was inadequate; and they had been in jail.

When a company joins NAB, it agrees to hire a certain number of unemployed in its plants and offices. The employer can get information from NAB headquarters about available unemployed, but the employer hires whomever he chooses. Most of the candidates, however, have never bothered to look for a job. The NAB has information about past experience in hiring, training, and employing the hard-core unemployed which an employer can use if he chooses. The program is financed by both government and business. The government will cover the extraordinary costs of training the hard-core unemployed, meaning costs over and above what a company would normally spend to prepare any newly recruited worker for a job. The average cost of training a hard-core individual is about $3,500. This includes training, needed medical attention, transportation, and maybe day care for dependent children.

A majority of companies acting under the NAB program has taken no federal funds (Janger, 1972). This is not a matter of altruism. In many cases, costs of training the hard-core are little or no different from typical training. In some cases, the companies do not want to be bound by the screening and certification procedures of the government. Others do not want the government examining payroll records, personnel folders, and training practices, all of which is required if the companies accept federal funds. Some companies feel that the burdens of government inspection are more costly than the additional training costs incurred.

At least several dozen companies, mostly larger firms, have established subsidiaries in ghetto areas specifically to recruit, train, and hire hard-core unemployed and other disadvantaged people. One of the first was Aerojet General Corporation's creation of the Watts Manufacturing Company in 1965 to make tents for the Army. In most large cities, jobs are in the suburban areas, and the unemployed are in central city areas. Typically, the poor have no or inadequate transportation to get to jobs with any reliability and at low cost. Despite the great need and advantage of ghetto subsidiaries, it is unlikely that this method will make a major dent in the employment problem without large government subsidies. Land in the central city is scarce and expensive, insurance and tax rates are high, buildings are scarce and often in poor shape, and production efficiency is not likely to be equal to that of a comparable operating plant in a suburban area. For such reasons, ghetto plants generally operate at a competitive disadvantage (Garrity, 1968).

The enthusiasm with which the program was first received waned with declining business activity and other economic problems in 1971 and after. To date there have been about 30,000 companies involved in the program in all major urban areas in the United States. Companies have loaned about 8,000 executives to the program. In recent years company pledges have dropped off and there has been less assurance that pledges once made will be met (Janger, 1972).

Of significance is the fact that over time the problem of getting the poor into jobs was no longer seen as getting 500,000 hard-core unemployed to work. Rather it was viewed as a more universal problem. The task is now seen as one of getting perhaps 11 million people to work who are members of minority groups and who would not be hired by business without changes in the recruiting and selection procedures of firms. This group includes 4.5 million from the disadvantaged minorities, 4 million under twenty-one years of age, and 3 million who live in the urban slums (Nixon, 1969: 141). Traditionally, private employers developed elaborate recruiting, screening, and training programs which were specifically designed to reject such persons. In their search for efficient operations, they tried to identify and reject the inefficient, the illiterate, the inept, the inexperienced, the miscast, the juvenile delinquents, and those having other undesirable characteristics from the conventional business point of view. If any of these types did slip through the screening mechanisms, personnel systems and front-line supervisors were trained to spot them and to replace them with more efficient performers.

These are the very persons recruiting systems are now designed to find, and these are the very persons industry is seeking to train and employ permanently. Why? What happened? One significant stimulant to change was the widespread city rioting in 1967. Businessmen were concerned and were quite receptive to President Johnson's appeal to them early in 1968 to organize a nationwide effort to hire the hard-core unemployed with government help. This coincided with a general increase in the social responsiveness of businessmen, as discussed in Chapter 10. Deep in the cause of the about-face change in recruitment policy was also the feeling that rejection of the chronically unemployed from the labor market would inevitably lead to government action which businessmen might find distasteful and that, if this type of unemployment were not reduced sharply, the problems of cities would become virtually insoluble.

An Evaluation of the Program   The program has achieved significant results but the expectations for it have not been reached. Statistics about NAB are not solid and quantitative conclusions are, therefore, only approximate. It is probable that between 250,000 and 300,000 NAB trainees are still at work. The retention rate on the average is around 50 percent. This is somewhat lower, as might be expected, than the national retention averages for all workers.

The program has been conducted principally through the largest companies. Over 90 percent of the hiring companies had over 10,000 employees. Most of the companies involved, such as the regulated utilities, had relationships with the government that "induced" their participation.

Perhaps one of the most significant accomplishments, as reported by Janger is the:

> Provision of special programing to meet the special employment problems of the disadvantaged—generally dismissed as preferential treatment before 1968—has become a way of life for the vast majority of the companies surveyed (1972: Highlights).

On the other hand, the degree of participation of companies has been disappointing. Furthermore, even among the larger companies, NAB has had little success in persuading companies that had not already been involved in hiring the disadvantaged. Most executives feel that the 50 to 60 percent turnover rate of the program is economically unsatisfactory and must be lowered if employment of the disadvantaged is to become more than a species of philanthropy.

In sum, however, most executives in a survey of 2,500 companies said their experience with NAB programs was generally favorable.

The conclusion is that "NAB/JOBS evidently does represent definite progress toward the goal of regularized employment, training and retention of the disadvantaged" (Janger, 1972: 58).

Business's Learning Experience From this experience, industry has learned that it has a great deal to learn about recruiting, training, and employing the disadvantaged. This is not the place to go into detail about this but simply to register the fact. But, to illustrate, business found it had to go into the ghettos and recruit the hard-core unemployed for their training programs. It found that the problems of these disadvantaged required very different training and employment approaches than for the ordinary worker. Many managers found to their pleasant surprise that many of the disadvantaged were not lazy, dull, indifferent, and immoral, but honest, hardworking, and intelligent. Business learned that the most effective training was that for a specific job the trainee could see waiting for him or her after the training period ended (Burack, Staszak and Pati, 1972; Janger and Shaeffer, 1970; Cohn, 1970; Janger, 1969).

BUSINESS AND MINORITY ENTERPRISES

During the past half dozen years efforts have been made by individual business firms on their own initiative, as well as with government incentives, and by the federal government acting directly, to foster and nourish minority enterprises. Some of the highlights of the major programs are presented here.

Why Such Programs? The first census of minority enterprises made in 1969 revealed a great disparity which common observation heretofore identified but could not substantiate statistically. Only 4 percent of the businesses in the United States, or 322,000, were minority-owned. The total receipts of these businesses were $10.6 billion or .7 percent of receipts of all businesses in the United States. At the time, the proportion of minorities to the total population was 17 percent. Negroes ran 163,000 of the businesses, Spanish-speaking Americans ran 100,000, and other minorities operated 59,000. The great majority of these businesses were small service enterprises. A total of 232,000 had no paid employees (Bureau of the Census, 1971).

Aside from the inequity shown in these numbers there are other reasons why help to minority enterprises is deemed to be of great importance. A survey of executives whose companies were helping ghetto enterprises said that a dominant explanation of involvement was "to extend the benefits of the U.S. enterprise system to ghetto residents . . ." (Brown and Lusterman, 1971: 6). Traditionally in the United States the ownership and operation of a small business has been an important avenue to prosperity not only for the owner, but through him, for the community as well. As Cross put it: "Unless we are content with future generations of minorities in which nobody is poor but few are affluent, we must also build equities, foster the ownership of capital, and create wealth in the ghetto" (1969: 14).

Businessmen also have other motivations which lead them to take the initiative and/or respond when government incentives are offered. They are: to ensure a healthy and vital economic and social environment which business needs to survive; to protect company facilities in or near ghetto areas; to reduce the need for taxes to pay for welfare, housing, crime control, and other services in ghettos; and to increase the purchasing power of the millions of residents of ghettos with all the benefits to business and people in ghettos that can bring (Brown and Lusterman, 1971). These justifications show a logical self-interest but also a recognition of a wider social concern.

Major Barriers to Minority Entrepreneurship The chances of success when any individual starts a business are slim. When he is a member of a minority group, and especially when living in a ghetto area, the chances for success are even narrower. A prospective entrepreneur in a ghetto area faces formidable obstacles. To begin with, his motivation and ability to save to acquire venture capital are almost nil. If he seeks credit, he finds it almost impossible to get. He is a poor risk, and lenders either will deny him credit or charge such a high price for it that it is unobtainable. Except in rare cases, he is completely without management skills so that even if he does get equity capital, his ability to use it at a profit is questionable. He is also faced with cost problems, mentioned earlier, which put him in a poor competitive position. In addition, basic attitudes in the ghetto culture hold business in low esteem (McKersie, 1968: 90). There seems to be a resistance to the profit incentive and an opposition to investment or technical assistance from the world outside the ghetto (Cross, 1969: 204). There is, in short, to use the words of Cross, a formidable list of "disincentives," or wealth-forbidding conditions.

Government Programs The greatest support to minority enterprises is given by the federal government. The catalog of federal programs assisting minority enterprises is very long [Office of Minority Business Enterprise (OMBE), 1971]. The most significant ones are administered by the OMBE, although many other government agencies have programs for small and minority-owned enterprises.

The OMBE was established by Executive Order 11458 in 1969. It is a center for coordinating federal government activities; promoting programs of all governments and businesses in helping minority enterprises; and acting as a center of information. The initiatives of the OMBE have taken many forms, such as a program to stimulate bank deposits in minority-owned banks, the establishment of National Minority Purchasing Councils designed to stimulate purchasing agents of corporations to buy from minorities, educational programs to train minority enterprisers to manage better their business, leadership in making loans to minority businesses, and getting federal contracts for them.

The Small Business Administration (SBA) is a major source of funds for small minority enterprises. In 1972 the federal government, mainly through the SBA, had made loans, guarantees, and other forms of credit support to minority firms in the amount of $353 million. This was a threefold increase over 1969. Another major source of financial support, and potentially much greater, are the Minority Enterprise Small Business Investment Companies (MESBICs). These are licensed, regulated, and partly financed by SBA. Each MESBIC initially is capitalized with at least $150,000 of a private corporate sponsor's money and $300,000 from SBA. There are now fifty-one MESBICs with a total private capitalization of $17.5 million. This original capital can be expanded fifteen times and thus make available substantial funding.

OMBE has been successful in significantly increasing government purchases from minority firms. In fiscal year 1972 federal procurement amounted to almost $400 million. Of this total about 70 percent was bought on a noncompetitive basis (OMBE, 1972).

Business Minority Enterprise Programs A number of companies have independently initiated, supported, and watched over operations of new minority-owned and managed enterprises. Mattel, Inc., support of Shindana Toys is a good illustration of a company that initiated and supported another company that was in competition with it. Mattel initially extended financing but Chase Manhattan Capital Corporation later refinanced the loan. The General Electric Company probably started the first black-owned aerospace company when it awarded a subcontract to Progress Aerospace Enterprises. Many companies systematically attempt to coordinate their purchasing so as to assure that minority enterprises are fully recognized.

A different type of program is that of the nonprofit Rochester Business Opportunities Corporation (RBOC). The impetus for this organization came from the Eastman Kodak Company in 1967. RBOC's board includes representatives from major companies in the Rochester area plus a few black businessmen. Its funds come from private enterprise and are loaned to minority enterprises. The SBA also participates in its lending. RBOC seeks out individuals who might start enterprises. Some of the large company supporters of this organization, such as Xerox, stimulate the development of a company, guarantee to buy its products, help to train the management, and stand ready to aid in resolving various problems in getting started and operating profitably. Since its inception in 1968 it has assisted more than seventy-five companies with an investment of $2.5 million.

Some companies have limited their activities in the under-privileged areas to establishing their own branches and employing ghetto residents. Others lean over backward to buy from minority enterprises. Some agree to buy minority-owned products if the firms can get started with aid from the government or others. Many banks have special minority enterprise loan departments. There is no over-all survey of such activities but two studies contain many other illustrations like these (MacEachen, 1972; Brown and Lusterman, 1971).

An Evaluation Instances of successful new minority-owned enterprises which hire more than a handful of people are rare. Larger companies are still creating plants in depressed areas but less energetically than after the city riots in the sixties. Companies that aided minority enterprises in the past still help, although there have been a few instances where heavy losses have forced sponsor withdrawal. Financial and other unforeseen problems are partly responsible for the reluctance of business to initiate more minority-owned subsidiaries or independent companies. The federal government's more aggressive aid to minority-owned enterprises is mostly responsible for the growth of these organizations in numbers and sales during the past half dozen years. However, it is doubtful that the ratio of minority-owned enterprises to all enterprises has changed much since 1969. There have been more failures than successes, by far. One study in Chicago showed that 80 percent of the black-owned firms that were founded in 1972 folded by the end of the year (*Time*, July 9, 1973). Since government regulations limit the amount of money that MESBICs can put into one enterprise they have tended to finance only small "mom and pop" type businesses and have avoided minority interests in larger risks.

Minority entrepreneurship should be encouraged because of its obvious advantage to minority groups and to society generally. Much has been learned about how to make such firms more successful, but the assurance of success without subsidy cannot be given. It is not easy to run a successful small business, and it is even more difficult to expand a one-man shop into a firm hiring many people. While expansion of minority enterprises on the basis of the programs discussed above is not likely to be the salvation of problems of disadvantaged minorities, a modest yet successful program can have many payoffs (Farmer, 1970). In the long run the more significant programs for increasing the number of minority managers in the business world unquestionably are those which train and employ them at higher managerial levels in established corporations.

SUBSTANDARD HOUSING

The National Housing Act of 1934 committed this nation to providing "a decent home" for every American family. This has not happened. The federal government has failed to meet the need despite countless programs. Private industry has failed to meet the need despite pressures on it to do so, pressures sweetened with government incentives. Fundamentally, the government programs have been underfunded, and incentives to industry have been inadequate.

Dimensions of the Problem The Housing and Urban Development Act of 1968 established as a goal the construction or rehabilitation of 26 million housing units, 6 million of which should be for low- and moderate-income families, within the following decade. For the past ten years total new housing starts for all income levels have been around 1.5 million per year, although in recent years the annual starts have been over 2 million.

Hard data concerning housing needs of the disadvantaged are not available. The CED estimated in 1973 that 8.8 million households existed in "housing poverty" or one out of seven households in the nation (1973: 47). The CED concluded that black families account for about 2.3 million within this total, or roughly 2½ times what their numbers in the total population would predict. Case says there is evidence that the underhoused families are most likely to be living in rental quarters in the inner city; are likely to be nonwhite, sixty-five or older, and have an annual income of under $3,000 (1972: 31). To provide new "adequate housing" for the inner-city's underhoused families could require, he calculated ". . . three to seven percent of the Gross National Product, a diversion of the major thrust of the private housing industry from its attention to the upper one-half of the residential housing market, and significant changes in the public sector investment in public facilities for inner-city neighborhoods" (Case, 1971: 427). He also concluded that such efforts were not likely to be made. He was right.

These cold numbers do not catch the full dimensions of the problem. Inadequate housing has far-reaching impacts on the underhoused as Charles Abrams has pointed out:

> The housing problem is more than the slum and more than the predicament of the low-income family. It spurs migration from cities and deters movements into them. It is the source of many discontents among the millions of mishoused and dishoused families yearning to be rehoused. It affects family budgets, security, happiness, and stability. It is tied to the issues of segregation and neighborhood decay. . . . Few other problems have more serious impacts on the economic well-being of cities and the social well-being of their citizens (Abrams, 1965: 40).

What Has the Government Done? The interests of the federal government in housing extend back to 1890 when Congress held hearings on slums and urban blight. Major pieces of legislation in recent years have been the Housing Act of 1959 which provided federal aid for low-income groups through subsidies for publicly developed and owned projects; The Housing Act of 1961 which authorized rent supplements for the poor; the Demonstration Cities and Metropolitan Development Act of 1966 which committed the government to planning model neighborhoods; and the Housing Act of 1968 which authorized a variety of programs to rebuild cities and provide suitable homes for rural dwellers.

In reviewing the history of housing President Nixon in his State of the Union Message in March 1973 reached several significant conclusions. On the one hand, he said, much progress has been made. He claimed that in 1940 there were 46 percent of our people living in substandard housing. This dropped to 37 percent in 1950, he said, to 18 percent in 1960, and to 8 percent in 1970. On the other hand, he said, despite the expenditure of between $63 and $95 billion to provide decent homes over the past forty years, federal efforts to provide adequate housing for the poor have failed.

He said that the federal government was the biggest slumlord in history. He complained that there was high disillusionment over shoddy construction, profiteering by real estate interests, inequitable programs, and waste. In the place of the old subsidy programs he proposed that direct housing allowance be given to the underhoused so that they could seek better housing in the private market. Authorized subsidies for approximately 300,000 units for 1973 would be continued, he said, but after January 1973 further subsidy would be suspended.

To make better progress, the President asked the Congress to establish a Department of Community Development to deal with major problems such as housing, transportation, and disasters. Also, he proposed that the federal government reduce its spending for many programs and give the money to local governments to spend as they saw fit. The Congress has not yet approved the new department but the revenue-sharing program with state and local governments has been accepted.

Why Has Not the Need Been Met? The Douglas Commission answered this question succinctly in these words:

> Despite the magnitude of needs and the interest in urgent action on housing and other aspects of the urban crisis, a complex of factors has inhibited the full implementation of the program:
>
> 1. Fiscal limitations,
> 2. Congressional limitations,

3. Administrative restrictions,
4. Inhibitions at the community level, and
5. Limitations on private participation (1968: 13–20).

Space does not permit analysis of these problems but the role of business should be noted. The building industry in the United States has a capacity far beyond current and past production rates. Today's 60 to 70 million housing units are testimony to its capabilities. But the simple and sad fact is that today, and for some time in the past, it has not been profitable for business to build low-cost housing for the poor. While the need is there, the effective demand is not. Millions of people simply cannot afford to pay for what today is considered a socially acceptable minimum standard of housing.

Although the building industry is one of the largest in the country, it is composed of small entrepreneurs working in localized markets on rather thin margins. As a result, it is economically not possible for these producers to invest in the management overhead needed to participate extensively in federal programs or to risk short-term profits with the likelihood of lifting long-term profits. They have little bargaining power to hold down construction worker wage-rate increases and insufficient resources to undertake research and development programs with a view toward holding down construction costs.

And there is more to the inability of low-income groups to find adequate housing. Rising costs of housing as a result of increases in land values, material, and labor prices, and inefficiencies resulting from building codes and ordinances play an important part. The incentive to invest in areas where low-income groups live is weakened by the high risks and the need for higher-than-average interest rates on mortgage financing, assuming that such financing can even be found.

From an economic point of view, the market has not supplied and cannot supply housing that people cannot afford. The government has offered subsidy programs to offset the difference between ability to pay and market price, but they have been unable to fill the need.

The Industry Response To the extent that low-income housing has been profitable, the profit-making sector has responded in the traditional way. In recent years, however, industry has sporadically taken the initiative to undertake new programs, even though the risks appeared to be higher than normal and the potential profits less than alternative investment opportunities. These programs have been stimulated by a combination of social-mindedness and profit potential, the mixture varying from case to case. For example, the Allegheny Conference on Community Development (ACCD), formed in 1943 and privately financed, was designed to organize business participation in a major community development program in Pittsburgh to erase blight in that city. ACCD has been responsible for twenty redevelopment projects involving a private investment of $500 million in new buildings. Smith Kline & French undertook a community revitalization project in Philadelphia a few years ago which involved not only housing, but job training, education, and general information services. A number of companies have programs to buy and renovate dilapidated houses. Some seek a profit and others do not. Many banks have special loan programs to stimulate the construction of low-income housing.

These are but a few illustrations of the ways in which larger companies have entered the low-income housing market. The number of new structures built or renovated has not been impressive in light of the total need. Perhaps the most impressive thing about the efforts is that corporations are responding to the social need for low-income housing and are taking risks which would have been rejected even a few years ago. The leaders of the American life insurance industry in 1968 agreed to divert $1 billion of their investment funds to underwrite investment in slum areas for construction and to create jobs for slum dwellers. One of the leaders commented that this investment "will be far less profitable than alternative investments. The difference in the returns may very plausibly be considered as a self-imposed 'tax,' designed to speed social progress— and it may be a big tax" (McQuade, 1968: 162). Many companies see in the huge demand for low-income housing an opportunity for profit and are therefore underwriting the risks of research and development programs to improve construction technology with the hope that new innovations will find a profitable market in the future. This is true of many building suppliers, such as U.S. Gypsum and Armstrong Cork Company.

Toward a Decent Home for Everyone Unfortunately, ensuring a decent home for everyone is no simple task. It is something that neither industry nor government can do alone. How the two can best work together with those who are involved is something that has not yet been determined. A good bit of attention has been given to the demand dimension of inadequate housing, but comparatively little has been devoted to the market mechanisms by means of which demand and supply can be equated.

Fred Case (1972) persuasively points out that the first step to a solution is the identification of the special characteristics of underhoused families, such as income, age, family size, location, and so on. The next step is to develop a model showing the system through which housing is supplied. This, of course, is a complex flow chart showing how government, financial institutions, material suppliers, labor, industry, family income, and the stock of housing units are related. The special needs of the underhoused then must be related to market processes to determine where the market mechanism can be improved and subsidization used with greatest payoff.

This will involve a complex system of actions. Something will have to be done to help the underhoused solve their problems so that they can pay for adequate housing. New technical developments should be identified to make house construction more efficient and lower priced per unit of labor input. Government programs must be revised to provide greater incentives for private investment in low-cost housing. Federal incentives ought also to motivate industry to develop new research programs to reduce housing costs, and local governments should see that obsolete building codes do not prevent the introduction of acceptable cost-reducing building materials and methods. Finally, government must find adequate funding for its incentives and subsidies. Quite obviously, such a systems approach is neither simple nor easy. When one digs into the low-cost housing problem, not only does everything seem to influence everything else, but its resolution does not lie in a simple scheme.

OTHER PROGRAMS INVOLVING BUSINESSMEN

From a financial point of view, the programs discussed above are those receiving the most attention from business. There are others, however, whose financial dimensions are increasing. Cash donations are on the rise. Business is becoming more active in educating the underprivileged, a subject which will be examined in Chapter 16. Businessmen are working more frequently with local, state, and national governments in developing systems analyses and feasibility studies concerning community transportation problems. Some companies help to recruit and train police cadets. Some are involved in programs to improve community-police relationships. Many companies conduct youth programs ranging from recreation and summer camps to education.

Businessmen are becoming much more active than they used to be in serving on committees to help governments formulate policies, in making special studies for government, and in other ways contributing their talents without compensation in helping the community to resolve its problems. The creation and operation of the Urban Coalition illustrates the way in which business leaders have rallied to help society attack pressing urban problems. This organization was formed in 1967 by businessmen, and they have played a dominant part in its activities since then. It functions to deal with urgent social problems by promoting legislation, stimulating the development of local coalitions, and providing local groups with the information needed for them to come to grips with local social problems. There are many cities where the mayors have established advisory councils to help them deal with city problems. Businessmen are often prominent on such committees.

AN OVERALL EVALUATION

One of the potentially significant achievements during the past few years has been the growing accessibility to local governments of the special talents resting in individual businesses, especially the larger companies. For example, managerial, analytical, research, and technical skills have high transferability to community problems. This is not an injection of business values as much as of business techniques into community problem-solving. If such knowledge, together with that of the universities, can be continuously tapped—and most of it is without cost to government—it may turn out to be the most significant of current business not-for-profit community activities. Overall, however, there seems to be a general feeling among people in and out of business that business is not doing enough. NICB in 1968 surveyed city officials in 114 cities with populations over 50,000, and they rated business efforts in helping to solve urban problems as only "fair." Looking at business's performance from their own point of view, these city officials tended to emphasize these faults:

> Business is a latecomer to the field, but a very welcome one, nonetheless.
> When called upon to help, business is usually cooperative, yet it is hesitant to advance remedies for urban ills or to offer unsolicited aid to government.
> Businessmen need to become much more aware of the problems and workings of city government if their help is to be effective.
> Business too often becomes involved only when urban problems are closely related to its own interests rather than being genuinely concerned with those having broader social and economic implications for the community (Finley, 1968: 2).

Among a number of large companies, however, I am sure that the top managements would say they are pulling their weight. On the other hand, Cohn found in his study (1971) that many businessmen were not happy with what they have been able to do and with what they consider to be a waning interest on the part of the federal government. Other observers conclude that while business may have gotten involved in dealing with urban problems the net impact has not been very great (Bartimole, 1973).

The fact of the matter is quite clear, however, that even with a doubling of the efforts of business the major community problems cannot even be brought under control, not to mention solved. Governments at all levels, especially the federal government, must do more and also must provide more incentives to encourage the business sector to apply fully its capabilities.

TOWARD CLOSER GOVERNMENT-BUSINESS
COOPERATION

Simon Ramo forecasts that "in the future we will see the formation of new organizational teamings of government and private elements of our society, business, the professions, the universities. A new 'Social-Industrial Complex' will grow up to attack the problems of the period in response to insistent citizen demand" (in NICB, 1972: 22). He points specifically, although not exclusively, to city problems such as housing and transportation.

We need to accommodate in the next twenty-five to thirty years an additional 75 to 100 million people. Most of them will live in expanded cities. To accommodate large numbers of people in present city areas will necessitate major changes in housing, transportation, and other areas. The costs will be in the billions of dollars. Suppose new cities are built? Ramo says that to build a city of 100,000 will require an investment of about a billion dollars. No individual company can step up to such expenditures.

Beyond the issue of cost, however, is the necessity for looking at all the interrelationships involved in such developments. This is the systems approach. To get the many different interests involved in city planning to coordinate their efforts is an extremely difficult problem. It can only be done by major groups working closely together.

Involved is not only the power of government to secure needed coordination but incentives to business to unlock its decision-making capabilities. This is not to say that business is the dominant partner in this arrangement. Government should be. More importantly, the two, and others, must find a working mechanism which will permit each to contribute that for which it is more capable than the others. We are not very good at doing this sort of thing (Branch, 1970), but we must learn to do it well and quickly.

Experience teaches a few lessons which can be used in improving the relationships of business with community problems, and between business and government in dealing with such problems. This chapter concludes with a few of them.

GUIDELINES FOR BUSINESS SUCCESS IN UNDERTAKING
URBAN AFFAIRS PROGRAMS

The following guidelines are suggested for guidance in areas of particular concern to the disadvantaged (Cohn, 1970: 81–82):

1. As in every other serious long-range program, there should be a careful effort to establish the objectives top management wishes to achieve. The company may seek many objectives—reputation, experience with a potential future payoff, stability of environment, aid

to the unskilled, and so on—but whatever it seeks ought to be established in realistic and, if possible, concrete terms.

2. Alternative strategies ought to be explored and choices made. If a company wishes to improve housing conditions in a city in which it does business, for instance, there are many options open to it, ranging from contributions of cash for studies to research in new ways to build low-cost housing at prices the potential inhabitants can afford to pay.

3. Management should try to foresee the various impact on the company of the actions that are planned. For instance, it should ask itself what the effect on other employees and on production may be of a program to train and hire a given number of hard-core unemployed. It should inquire into the value of lending top managers to a community task force for X days a month.

4. Attention should be paid to the likely total costs to the company of a given course of not-for-profit action, and the volume of its resources which may legitimately be allocated to urban affairs. It is not to the advantage of the company or the community to have the company suddenly discover that a given program is costing much too much and then abruptly stop all community service.

5. If a company creates an urban affairs department, care in staffing and organizing it will pay off for the company and society. Like any other top-level staff job, it should not be the resting place for problem executives who are not performing well in other functions. If the urban affairs activity is more than extension of the typical personnel, public relations, or government affairs departments, it may pay to set up a new organization reporting to the chief executive or to a second in command.

6. Many businessmen have found that certain types of involvement in urban affairs require knowledge and understanding that go beyond the usual managerial and technical business talents. Political skills, deep understanding of community problems, and an ability to settle problems in a far different cultural setting are requisites for some activities.

GUIDELINES FOR GOVERNMENT

The following guidelines are suggested for government in its dealings with business as a partner in meeting social problems in urban areas of a type discussed in this chapter:

1. Government must take the lead. Resolving major social problems is predominantly a government responsibility. Business does have some responsibility, but its best efforts can be obtained by proper incentives—either through the normal operation of the market system or through government incentives.

2. It is more efficient if government sets policy and lets business do the work (e.g., training hard-core unemployed or constructing houses).

3. Tax incentives should be used sparingly, as contrasted with contracts. A special panel on private enterprise of the Kerner Commission recommended tax incentives to industry to get the hard-core disadvantaged to work. Briefly, the panel suggested that each hard-core unemployed be given a green card. An employer hiring a green-card holder would be eligible for a tax credit equal to a share of the wages and fringe benefits paid to the holder. The share would be 75 percent for the first six months, 50 percent for the next half year, and 25 percent for the second year. No credit would be paid if the person employed did not stay on the job at least six months.

This is a direct approach to the problem and offers incentives of value to employers. A major defect is that this system would cost more than the current contract system for any given level of employment. Under the contract system the government could set standards which industry would have to meet and could make sure that government support would cover only the true costs of employing a certified worker. The tax incentive approach would be self-enforcing. It could not distinguish among jobs that would be dead-end, routine, or that would require no training, as compared with those that would require training and would lead to better jobs. The result is that the government would inevitably pay for much that otherwise would be done without government support, and would find itself paying for training that would not be given. To close these loopholes would require an administrative hierarchy which in itself would be costly and resisted by business.

4. Government can come to grips with pressing urban problems in a more powerful way if it replaces much of the rhetoric of social legislation with cash. Social legislation has been inadequately funded in many areas, particularly in low-income housing. Funding has been more adequate, however, for manpower training.

5. Government should stimulate a massive research program to clarify the dimensions and nature of major social problems and to determine how best to mix the efforts of government, the people directly involved, and industry.

BUSINESS AND THE NONCRISIS CITY AREAS

The point should be made, although I shall not dwell on it, that business has been instrumental in the improvement of city life in certain areas. All city life is not like that discussed in this chapter (Banfield, 1970). Many cities have beautiful suburban and downtown areas. Much more attention is paid today than ever before in our history to the esthetics of office and factory construction and the amenities of life of the people who work in them. Businessmen in many cities, such as New York, Pittsburgh, Atlanta, and Los Angeles, have stimulated and contributed heavily to the development of art centers and theaters for the performing arts. Rising incomes provided by business have, of course, contributed to the quality of life of people, most of whom live in cities. In surveying what business has not done about city problems, in general, and those of disadvantaged minority groups in particular, it is well to remember what its fundamental role should be.

CHAPTER SEVENTEEN

Business
and
Education

INTRODUCTION

A vast and growing domain of education is often spoken of today as the "knowledge industry," a phrase first coined by Fritz Machlup in 1962. One fundamental facet of this world is research, which creates knowledge; another is education, which disseminates knowledge. Both work in tandem to produce knowledge in people, which is the central resource of this society (Drucker, 1968: 263). Knowledge is a foundation upon which business activity takes place. It also has a major relevance to business, because it is a means to greater productivity to enable people to lead more satisfying lives, to master and change their institutions, and to control an increasingly unstable and unlivable environment.

Today, the interrelationship between business and education is deep and intimate. This chapter explores the reasons why business increasingly supports education and the major interrelationships between the two.

HISTORICAL RELATIONSHIPS

It was not until the middle of this century that the corporation developed a comprehensive, overt, and managed interest in education. Before then, business and businessmen did take a position on various questions about education, but their attitudes were generally aloof and distant. In the early colonial period businessmen, like everyone else, believed that education was the responsibility of the churches, individual families, or private philanthropists. Only in the case of the extremely poor was it thought valid for the state to intervene to provide free education. This "pauper view" of public education endured well into the nineteenth century. Around the turn of the nineteenth century businessmen supported the creation of private schools to teach "practical" subjects like arithmetic, navigation, and surveying. Some of the businessmen leaders of the American Revolution supported free general education, but they were in the minority.

During the first half of the nineteenth century more businesses made philanthropic contributions to education, but education was low on the list of business charitable programs. The relative position of education in business priorities rose after midcentury because of the obvious need by business for new knowledge, educated manpower, and an improved environment. Nevertheless, the relationships between business and general education were not close. Indeed, there was a strange lack of communication and understanding between industry and education (Patrick and Eells, 1969: 1).

Beginning around 1950, the connections between the interests of business and education increased in number and intensity. The result was a whole new relationship between them which differed in kind and scope from that of the past.

THE RATIONALE FOR BUSINESS SUPPORT OF EDUCATION

One major branch of the new relationship between business and education is the extensive support business provides. The reasons given to justify corporate help to education range from the purely pragmatic to the altruistic, from short-term advantage to long-range potential benefits, and from company to personal motivations. Surveys show clearly that business support of education is becoming increasingly associated with social responsibilities that go beyond the quest for profits. When 300 chief executives of the largest companies in the country were shown a list of social problems and causes in which business might get involved and asked to list their highest priorities for activities, "supporting education" topped the list (Louis, 1969: 94).

Many companies justify their help because they get direct benefits from the educational system. The more skilled the educated human product of the educational system, the greater the benefits to business. More and more companies are observing that the knowledge of their people is their most important asset, and they are right. While companies pay taxes to support education and make cash contributions, the net cost to them of these talented people is far less than the actual cost to society. Many companies justify their contributions because they are direct beneficiaries of the research results of educational institutions. Not only do companies find value in the technical research of universities (for example, physics, chemistry, engineering), but they gain from research in nontechnical areas (for example, new techniques to manage a business, and research in human behavior in organizations).

A less tangible but nonetheless a powerful motivation is that a better-educated people will more likely assure a congenial economic, political, and social environment for business. Business and education are interlocked in developing a better society. As Harlow Curtice (then chairman of the board of General Motors) said, "In the further evolution of . . . society, intellectual and cultural development and market advances must necessarily go hand in hand. The first is primarily the responsibility of higher education, the second that of business and industry. Both are indivisible aspects of our growth as a nation" (1955: 357). In addition, there is still in the minds of many businessmen the thought that if they do not contribute, the government will increase its activities and its control over educaion. While the business contribution to education is vitally important, it is not large enough, in relation to the total cost of education paid mostly by society through government, to have much of an impact. Anyway, traditional fears of government control of education as its support expands have never been justified in practice, especially at the university level.

Businessmen do have pragmatic reasons for giving, aside from those mentioned above. For instance, they give to enhance their image in the educational world as well as generally. Scholarships bearing the name of the company, for instance, may help recruit better employees. Donating equipment to a school will get the company name before students who may later buy its product. Relationships with consumers can be improved through general gifts and research grants. Some agree with Lawrence Cremin's observation: "Education is good economics, sensible politics, and sound defense; it trains character, helps people get ahead; and incidentally keeps them off the labor market for protracted periods of time" (1966: 31).

There are, of course, many personal reasons for business aid. Feelings of deep gratitude on the part of managers for their education, nostalgia for alma mater, and self-satisfaction growing from association with universities and the youth of the nation—all are important motivators. One cannot read the policy statements of businesses or listen to the speeches of businessmen without getting the strong feeling that a good bit of altruism is involved in corporate aid to education. The attitudes of many companies are generous, unselfish, and public-spirited (Patrick and Eells, 1969: 121–38; Watson, 1965: 7–8). The following reasons for giving are typical: "it is socially responsible to do so"; "the company is a good citizen"; "it is necessary to preserve the individual enterprise system"; "society needs better educated people"; "Jefferson was right when he said a democracy could not survive without an educated electorate"; and "the better educated people are the more they will understand business." Homer Turner, long-time director of the U.S. Steel Foundation, which has given millions of dollars to education, declared that "motivation for corporate contributions is closely linked to the general character of life in these United States, including the historic concern for the preservation of freedom and justice for the individual and for all autonomous groups comprising the spectrum of voluntary associations in a free society" (Patrick and Eells, 1969: 129).

In recent years a new reason for corporate involvement with the universities grows out of the rising antipathy of students to business. A surprising number of students know very little about business and categorically condemn it for being immoral; as being responsible for all sorts of social ills from pollution to social unrest; for supporting the wrong values; and for fostering discrimination, deception, and conflict (Wierzynski, 1969). Many businessmen are concerned about such attitudes and are frustrated about what to do. Nonetheless, such attitudes are driving them into more involvement with education. On the other hand, there seems little doubt that student unrest has caused businessmen to withdraw their support.

While there are no statistics on the subject there is no question that businessmen and people in the academic world are talking more and more with one another. This is an extremely healthy development, in my judgment, because I believe this is by far the best way for each to understand the thinking, problems, and practices of the other.

THE NATURE OF BUSINESS PROGRAMS TO AID EDUCATION

Business aids to education cover a wide spectrum of programs, which may be classified into five categories: cash contributions, equipment and material, teaching aids, employee time and company facilities, and direct attacks on social educational problems. A surprising number of companies contribute to education, and few of them limit their support to one program. Many large companies have multiple approaches and a large staff to administer educational programs.

Cash Contributions Direct corporate aid to all of education in 1972 was approximately $365 million, according to the Council for Financial Aid to Education (1972). Of this total $275 million went to universities and colleges. This compares with $2.02 billion given from all private sources to colleges and universities in the year 1971–1972. The total corporate aid to education has been comparatively level since about 1966. In 1950 the total was $43 million (Patrick and Eells, 1969: 7). Aid to education has risen from 10 percent of total corporate giving for all purposes in 1950 to 43 percent of the total in 1972.

Cash contributions take many forms, such as unrestricted grants, scholarships, faculty chairs, research support, and grants for equipment and buildings. Many companies have foundations which administer such programs. A number of companies follow a policy of setting aside a fixed percentage of corporate income after taxes to be devoted to their giving program, a good part of which often is for education. Some companies will match contributions of employees, up to a given amount, to educational institutions, a practice begun by General Electric.

Equipment and Material Companies give equipment and material to schools to influence future purchases, to encourage research about the product, or to put it to good use at a minimum cost to the company. One study of business contributions showed that 34 percent of the companies surveyed gave samples of their raw materials or finished products to schools (Watson, 1965). Many companies, like American Cyanamid, have policies which require that equipment to be disposed of be first routinely referred to the education cooperation representative to see whether it might best be transferred to a school.

Teaching Aids A survey of 248 companies in 1964 showed that 64 percent had prepared and distributed informational booklets on many subjects (for example, science, history, economics) for distribution to schools as teaching aids. Almost as many had provided paper, filmstrips, film recordings, and tapes. Much of this, of course, is self-serving, but not all. Babcock and Wilcox, for instance, each year distributes to schools textbooks it has prepared on the generation of steam and the burning of fuels (Watson, 1965: 44). The Standard Oil Company of California publishes a booklet that it mails to schools at all levels describing the materials which it has prepared as teaching aids and which are available for the asking.

Time and Facilities Many companies make available to schools their special knowledge, their time, and their facilities. Illustrative of these programs are: student field trips to offices and factories; company representatives addressing classes and meeting with students, teachers, and educational administrators on all sorts of topics; the company providing information for student and faculty research projects and giving school administrators advice on business, scientific, political—and, occasionally—curricular matters. Giving advice on curriculum is a touchy subject, especially when it may involve an injection of business values into the educational system. It can be healthy and valuable when, for instance, businessmen look ahead to their needs for different types of talent and help schools to design their curriculum so that students can take advantage of the new demands and avoid becoming part of surplus talent in an obsolete discipline. Many businessmen serve on school boards, advisory committees, and boards of regents or trustees.

Direct Action on Educational Problems In recent years a number of companies have hired staff to make a direct attack on social problems, including educational problems. For instance, the Xerox Corporation created an educational department with a large staff of professional educators, part of whose responsibility was to develop a model educational park. Most direct educational programs, however, concern projects to help the disadvantaged, particularly in ghetto areas, or to educate company employees. This subject was treated at some length in Chapter 16.

The key words to define the role of business in education are supportive and cooperative. There is a sort of partnership between the two (Finley, 1973).

BUSINESS EDUCATIONAL PROGRAMS

Twenty years ago I visited the headquarters of a large company in Chicago and, being an educator, noticed the absence of books and other reference documents in the offices of the managers. I inquired about this and was told that the top management felt the display of books and magazines indicated time was spent on reading which could much better be devoted to company business. This attitude was typical. Today the company encourages managers to improve their knowledge, and books and other reference materials are found in most offices of the company.

The day when a business manager could be complacent with the education he received years before has passed. In the past ten years there has been a remarkable addition of knowledge about how better to manage a business. Furthermore, doing a better management job is becoming increasingly difficult for managers at all levels. As a consequence, business today is highly education-minded for its own personnel. Educational programs for company personnel both inside and outside companies are increasing rapidly.

Programs naturally are numerous and vary from company to company. On-the-job educational programs include such methods as job rotation, planned progression, psychological guidance, special research projects, special assignments, committee meetings, multiple management, and staff meetings. Off-the-job methods are: class work and special courses, seminars and conferences, attending the company institute, special lectures and conferences, membership in professional organizations, planned reading courses, and executive programs in universities. Some companies have, in effect, their own universities (for example, General Motors, General Electric, and AT&T), where managers receive advanced management education. A large number of companies send their managers to scheduled university executive programs, encourage them to get advanced degrees, or motivate them to take special courses.

These programs generally are for managers, but companies also have in-house and off-site training programs for other employees. They are designed principally to permit them to upgrade their skills and further their personal and career development.

THE EDUCATIONAL MARKET

Education is big business and an increasingly important customer of business. In 1973, total costs for all elementary and secondary schools, universities, and colleges amounted to over $90 billion. Enrolled in the system were 60 million students, and around 4 million men and women were employed to educate and take care of them. Outside of government itself, this is the largest industry in the country.

Traditionally, the school system has been a good market for many businesses, from construction to books and teaching aids. Two important changes, however, have taken place. First, the market has shown rapid growth in the past decade and will continue to expand in the future. Second, new opportunities are opening for the sale of different types of goods and services. New demands are growing rapidly for equipment connected with computer-managed instruction, audiovisual aids, and reproduction machines. Some companies are now attempting to improve the abilities of students (for example, reading) on a contractual basis. This is an important new development.

FUTURE RELATIONSHIPS

There seems little doubt that education will become even more a central element of life in the future than it is today. The world of tomorrow will be a learning society; most professional men will engage in continuous, life-long education, and education will increase in importance relative to industry. Business in this world will become even more interrelated with education.

It seems safe to forecast that business will increase its contribution to education, in cash as well as in materials and services. It is likely that the contribution will grow as a percentage of total corporate giving and total corporate income. A current trend for business to expand its aid to secondary and elementary schools is likely to continue. Many companies today contribute only to private institutions on the grounds that they already support public institutions through taxes. In reality, private institutions receive public support either directly in governmental cash contributions or indirectly in tax exemptions, so that the difference between the public and private educational institution is blurring. Several companies who made gifts only to private institutions examined their policy and discovered that they were giving much less proportionately to public institutions in their taxes than to private institutions in direct gifts (Watson, 1965: 16–17). The increasing financial difficulties of private institutions will result in greater public support for them. Since many large companies have scores of Ph.Ds and conduct scheduled classroom work, it will not be surprising to see a cooperative effort between large companies and local educational institutions in granting joint degrees. DuPont, for example, has more Ph.Ds on its payroll than many colleges. The growth of educational programs in business will elevate the position of the educational coordinator.

Of the many issues which will arise concerning this relationship, two deserve comment here. The first is whether or not this growing intimacy will lead to the injection of business values into the educational process. Should business try to advance its values in the educational process? My answer is no, because this should be left to the marketplace of ideas working through professional educators. No one group, however dominant in society, should try to foist its value systems on the student population as a charge for its aid. Business has not tried to do this. Business has tried to get the educational world to understand its purpose and functioning and to get its values accepted. It has not tried, to my knowledge, to do this as a part of its educational aid program, and I do not think it will try to do so in the future.

A second issue is whether business will in the future, as in the past, find job opportunities for an ever-better-educated work force. This is a vitally important question, because any substantial unemployment, underemployment, or employment at jobs demanding only low skills of a highly educated group of people will produce a dangerous social force. Such people will not long accept these conditions and will take radical measures, if necessary, to correct them. My own view is that business will continue to absorb an educated work force and will continue to demand a better-educated work force.

CHAPTER EIGHTEEN

Business
and
the Arts

INTRODUCTION

It has been only within the last decade that business support of the arts has matured. Prior to this time business support of the arts was virtually nonexistent.

After defining the area of the arts, this chapter briefly traces business support of the arts and their interrelationship. Support to the arts is not a leading business concern, but it is most important to the arts and to society.

WHAT ARE THE ARTS?

There is no consensus about what is covered by the "arts." Barnett advances one classification as follows: *fine arts,* including music, literature, and the visual arts; *the combined arts,* which include the dance, the theater, and the opera; and *the applied arts,* which embrace such specialties as ceramics, textile design, architecture, and miniature painting (Barnett in Merton, et. al., 1959). If the area of the arts is conceived in this way it is clear that it includes a vast activity interlaced throughout society. It covers activity which is of direct relevance to corporate functions.

If the arts are defined in terms of purpose the definitions are different. For instance, Susanne K. Langer says art is "the practice of creating perceptible forms expressive of human feeling" (1964: 21). Other definitions view art as a creative process which expresses a mood, a feeling, and spirit. It is a "messenger of discontent," a mode of understanding, an essential to the human spirit, a window to reality, a path to knowledge (Eells, 1967). These definitions underscore the pervasiveness as well as the deep significance of the arts in society. Defined in this way the arts perform functions of high interest to business.

SUPPORT FOR THE ARTS

Before World War II the typical businessman regarded the arts as an unsuitable area for his corporate contributions. Indeed, there was some antipathy to certain of the arts and some artists, a view which was shared by many artists. As Eells put it: "Almost everything about business and the corporation is likely to appear prosaic, utilitarian, perhaps even repugnant, to the artist. To the corporate executive, the necessity for profit making may seem far removed from esthetics" (1965: 37). This view gradually underwent change in the 1960s. Businessmen increased their contributions to the arts but did so as philanthropy. Gradually many businessmen came to perceive a mutually rewarding relationship with the arts. For example, some local businessmen discovered that by supporting local artistic endeavors it was possible to attract tourists, and tourist dollars to their communities. At the same time the artist saw the need of business support to assure a healthy development for the arts. For example, many areas of the performing arts saw the need of community support, including business's, if they were to survive and prosper.

In the mid-1960s a report sponsored by the Rockefeller Brothers Fund dramatized the economic plight of the arts and elevated their priority for business support (Baumol and Bowen, 1965). Corporate contributions rose, but more importantly the Business Committee for the Arts was established to lead business to the same generous support of the arts that it had given to higher education. This organization, composed of over a hundred business leaders, stimulated a variety of imaginative programs to aid the arts.

In 1965, the first year that corporate contributions for supporting the arts were tabulated separately, 2.8 percent of corporate donations were made to this area. The proportion rose to over 5 percent in 1970. If this percentage holds (and it is likely to be higher today) the current cash outlays of business to the arts are over $50 million. Other business aids, however, are equally if not of greater significance to the development of the arts. A few types of such programs are lending company personnel, giving office space, donating equipment or selling it at a discount, stimulating the development of local organizations to support and develop arts projects, educating arts groups to be better managers, buying works of art for office improvement, employing artists in residence, and subsidizing employees to attend performances (Chagy, 1970, 1971; Reiss, 1972).

A milestone in the relationship of business with the arts was passed in 1972 when a large corporation, Dayton Hudson of Minneapolis, created a position of corporate director of cultural affairs. To my knowledge this was the first full-time appointment of this type. The position went to a former director of the Art Institute of Akron, Ohio. He was made responsible for coordinating the corporate arts program, evaluating criteria for arts support, establishing a program of continuing education and communication in the arts for company employees, and developing (with the help of cultural groups and community leaders) new projects in a wide range of areas (*Arts Management,* 1972).

Private foundations have also been heavy contributors in recent years to the arts. The Ford Foundation, for instance, began in 1966 a ten-year $80 million program of assistance to sixty-one orchestras in thirty-three states, the District of Columbia, and Puerto Rico. It recognized the significance of supporting the orchestras in light of their economic problems. The foundation pointed out that: "Unlike business or industry, the arts cannot raise productivity beyond a certain minimal level—only so many concerts, for example, can be given in a day or week and it takes just as long to rehearse a Mozart symphony now as it did in Mozart's day. Only a small percentage of rising costs can be passed on to the consumer in the form of higher ticket prices without driving away all but the wealthy or unusually devoted" (1973). This type of economic problem exists in other areas of the arts and provides one convincing reason for need. More fundamentally, however, as will be discussed later, the corporation needs the arts.

The federal government has also in recent years become a supporter of the arts. President Kennedy set up the President's Advisory Council on the Arts in 1963 to survey needs and recommend action. The Congress has had before it recommended legislation to support the arts since 1877, but it was President Johnson that got the first legislation to support the arts in the form of the National Council on Arts, established in 1964. To provide funds for the council the Congress passed in 1965 an act establishing the National Foundation on the Arts and Humanities. In 1973 its budget was approximately $80 million.

We seem to be entering a period of general public recognition of the importance of supporting the arts. In the business world we seem to be passing from the old donative system to one which fits better the modern views of corporate social responsibilities as well as a deeper understanding of mutual advantage. In the older view corporate support was more or less made in a philanthropic context. This, says Eells, ". . . is denigrative of the artists and of the arts, as though they had little or nothing to contribute and had always to be on the receiving end of a passive relationship" (1967: 214).

The more modern view is that a corporation may see in supporting the arts an opportunity to fulfill the growing social demands for the improvement of a quality of life. Furthermore, there is a recognition that the artist and the arts have much to contribute to the corporation. They do have common goals to which each can contribute to the advantage of the other. There are mutual responsibilities and, as Eells says ". . . there is the need for bilateral action grounded in mutual respect for unique contributions on both sides" (1967: 214).

COMMON GOALS

The modern corporation thrives in a society which is open, pluralistic, creative, flexible, free, and sensitive to societal values. The arts and the artist also seek and prosper in such an environment. Each seeks these goals in a different way, but each benefits when they are achieved. The late Armand Erpf, an investment banker and patron of the arts, said that a healthy artistic community is a vital environmental influence which encourages private enterprise to be innovate and experimental. He also said that: "The creative instinct of a businessman may well be comparable to the creative force of an artist: it is just that the two are working with quite different materials and in different media" (1967: 85). Freedom to create and to innovate is a necessary condition for a flourishing art and a dynamic and prosperous business community.

Individualism, as pointed out repeatedly in this book, is a major value in our society. In this connection, Frank Stanton's words are important: ". . . the first place to worry about American life losing its vital qualities of individualism is in the arts. If this happens, no liberal education will save our kind of society, and *no business enterprise will long prosper* in what is left of it" (1967: 13).

The productivity of modern industry depends heavily upon a large variety of human resources which are characterized by technical specialities, imagination, sensitivity, and the need for intellectual stimulation. These people just happen to need music, museums, the theatre, and other arts. To attract them corporations as a matter of personnel policy attempt to stimulate a more congenial arts environment in the community.

As corporations become more involved in improving the quality of life, it is likely that their relationships with the arts will become more attractive. As Erpf says ". . . as we become more affluent and leisured, all of us need beautiful things and beautiful talk to avoid becoming bored, and corporations should be interested in helping satisfy this need. Moreover, since people are becoming more educated, the old folk culture, which sufficed in the 19th century, will no longer be enough" (1967: 88). Today, the arts provide a source of increasing satisfaction and become ever more necessary to that elevation of the human sense of fulfillment to which people aspire.

The last chapter emphasized a direct and important relationship between education and business. Eells notes, "Society is a comprehensive educational adventure, and all institutions play their respective parts. Business and cultural institutions have integral roles in the educational process thus broadly conceived. The arts and the corporation meet on this common ground" (1967: 226). There are so many interrelationships between art and education. Both are concerned with knowing, with the search for the truth, with assimilation of knowledge, and with transmission of knowledge. Of significance also is the stimulation which the arts provide. Alfred North Whitehead once remarked that religion was a powerful influence in the nineteenth century; then it was science early in this century; and in the 1930s it was education. He added that "in another generation or so, the germinating power in American civilization may be the artist—using that term in its broadest sense—the creator's" (1956: 141). One does not have to stretch one's imagination to see the point that the arts do inject a significant stimulus into life wherever they thrive. This is true in the educational world as everywhere else.

In a substantive fashion the corporation and the arts interrelate at many points and areas. To mention but a few: product design, architectural design, human relations, work environment and the human need for beauty. These interrelationships, of course, make for close bonds.

Finally, the businessman and the artist find common ground in the area of communications. Business operates on the basis of communications systems. The better and more imaginative they are the better business functions and relates itself to the community. The arts and the artist are communicators but in a much different dimension, for the most part. The artist is constantly seeking to improve his communications with his patron, audience, and society generally. The artist participates directly, of course, in many communications programs of business. The deeper mutual reliance, however, is the stimulation to and improvement in communications each contributes to the other, especially the arts to business.

CHAPTER NINETEEN

Business
and
Technology

INTRODUCTION

In very recent years there has been a unique and momentous interlinking of business and technology which has produced what some have referred to as the "technological revolution," "the age of science," "the age of technology," or "the age of acceleration." Whatever the name given to this period in man's history, the facts are clear that technology is the primary force stimulating great change in society and that it is business which has been the principal instrument for translating this knowledge into goods and services.

Previous chapters touched upon a number of issues associated with technology, such as the way technology brings social change, the impact of technology on social values, and the question of who should bear the costs of technological progress. In this chapter, following a definition of technology and the recent rapid changes in it, the question of whether technology is a destroyer or savior of society will be examined. This will be followed by an analysis of whether or not technology can be better planned. The question of how far government should support research and development will then be addressed. This is followed by an analysis of the impact of technology on economic growth, on employment profiles, and on business structures.

WHAT IS TECHNOLOGY?

Fundamentally, technology refers to the knowledge of how to do things. Generally, the word technology is associated with the industrial arts, applied science, engineering, and with physical things. The dictionary explains that technology also is "the sum of the ways in which a social group provides itself with the material objects of its civilization." It includes fundamental knowledge about physical and social phenomena, such as the laws of aerodynamics and properties of materials; knowledge about how these principles are applied to production, such as the application of lift/drag ratios to airplane production; and knowledge about the day-to-day production process, such as rules-of-thumb of workers (Mansfield, 1968: 10). Technology is concerned with the use of new knowledge, whereas science is devoted to understanding phenomena and is thought of as producing new basic principles and laws of phenomena. New knowledge can also be produced through simple observation and not involve any new discoveries of basic principles. Such, for example, was the idea of making a clothespin. Technological change takes place when new ideas from whatever source are introduced into the productive system to make a new product or service. Involved are both the idea and its development into a useful product or service. Some businessmen have learned that the latter is frequently more difficult than the former.

SCIENTISTS, ENGINEERS, AND RESEARCH AND DEVELOPMENT (R&D) OUTLAYS

There are many causes of the great change taking place in today's world, but none is as pervasive and dynamic as the advances in science and the many technologies founded on them. Muller reminds us that the rise of science was one of the quietest and at the same time one of the profoundest revolutions in history (Muller 1957: 277). It is still going on.

Underneath the enormous changes taking place is a rapid acceleration in both the number of scientists and engineers and in the resources placed at their disposal. The technical labor force in the United States (including scientists and engineers) has been growing rapidly. Numbering very few in 1800, scientists and engineers totaled 30,000 in 1890. They numbered well over 300,000 in 1930, more than 700,000 in 1950 and about 1.2 million in 1969. In the 1960s it was estimated by competent observers that 80 to 90 percent of all scientists that had ever lived were then alive (Walker, 1968). This suggests an accelerating technology on a scale never before experienced.

The explosive rate of growth of technology is also illustrated by estimates of research and development (R&D) expenditures in recent years. In 1928 American industry spent less than $100 million on R&D and the federal government spent considerably less than that (Silk, 1960: 159). By 1943 the total national R&D expenditure was around $5 billion. A rapid increase took place thereafter so that by 1965 the total was over $20 billion, and the estimated 1972 outlay was $28 billion. Industry historically spends about 70 percent of this total, a good bit of which is supported by the government. In 1972, to illustrate, total industry R&D was estimated to be $19.2 billion, of which the federal government contributed $8.7 billion, or 42 percent. The government proportion is declining; in 1965, for example, its contribution was 55 percent of the total (National Science Foundation, 1969: 9). For fiscal 1974 total federal R&D is projected to be about $17.4 billion ($9.4 for defense, $2.5 for space, and $5.5 for civilian programs). The result is a technology base which, given sufficient time, capital, wise choice of priorities for expenditure, and motivation, probably can meet the great bulk of known and prospective human demands. If this statement is true, and I think it is, it is of the profoundest significance for business and for society.

Yet another dimension illustrating the growth of technology is speed of change. In the past it took, literally, centuries for a new idea to be translated into practical use. Today the time span is in years and sometimes months. For instance, it was centuries between the time Paracelsus discovered that ether could be used as an anaesthetic and its general use for that purpose. The first patent for a typewriter was issued in England in 1714 but it was a century and a half before typewriters were commercially available. Charles Babbage invented the computer in the early 1800s but it was not until 1946 that the first modern electronic digital computer was built. Within a few years this invention revolutionized information processing. Today for some new food products the time span from conception to production is measured in months. So rapid are today's technological changes, and so numerous are they, that Toffler says we have a major disease of change. He calls it "future shock" in a book by that name (1970).

TECHNOLOGY: DESTROYER OR SAVIOR?

For well over 200 years there have been two extreme views about science and technology. One sees it as a savior of mankind and the other sees it as a destroyer of society and the people in it.

One view sees technology as an unqualified blessing that should be encouraged in every way. This view sees technology as having inherent and unlimited capabilities for improving the conditions of people in society. This view holds that technology can solve any problem, in time. This view places great faith in the ability of our institutions to produce technology in such a fashion as to meet the priority demands of people. Those on this side say that technology has immensely helped society to overcome environmental barriers, has increased worker productivity, has helped to feed more people, has reduced the incidence of disease, has increased life expectancy, and in many other ways has led to a better and more secure life for increasing numbers of people.

The opposite view is that technology is an unmitigated curse. It is seen as destroying moral values in favor of materialistic values. It violates privacy and destroys the amenities of life by polluting the atmosphere. It destroys jobs by replacing men with machines. It elevates machines over men and profits over humanity. Worship of the machine challenges traditional religion. Unchecked technology will bring a technocratic society in which men will become automatons subject to rigid controls of some elite group. Technology is seen as having created enormous problems of pollution, social change, weapons of war, moral problems in extending the lives of the seriously ill, and the potential for dictatorship. This group condemns technology for these consequences.

Both extremes are, of course, untenable positions but both have in them truths which are becoming more visible. Generally, the uncritical view of the first group is becoming more challenged than ever before.

The more informed attacks on technology look at its impact in different ways. Commoner, for instance, sees an implacable conflict between pollution control and the drive for productivity. He says that destructive technologies have replaced less destructive products, e.g., detergents have displaced soap, plastics have replaced paper packaging, and synthetic fibers have replaced cotton and wool. He says our present technology course will destroy our society in another twenty to fifty years (1971). Mishan condemns technology for the same reasons expressed by Commoner. He says that nothing short of a sharp and wholesale reversal of present powerful technical, philosophical, and economic trends can prevent disastrous erosion of the quality of life. Specifically, this means a slowing down of growth (1971, 1969). Mumford argues that in today's complex society, based upon the principles and incentives of capitalistic finance, absolute authority has been accorded to machines at the expense of human concerns. The only thing that can save us, says Mumford, is to build a new model for technology which aims not at feeding more human functions to the machine "but to develop further man's incalculable potentialities for self-actualization and self-transcendence, taking back into himself deliberately many of the activities he has too supinely surrendered to the mechanical system" (1970: 395).

Critics of the adverse impact of technology on society are correct in drawing attention to abuses and problems. The answer however, lies not in slowing down the process or reversing it but in redirecting technology. We have already seen dramatic results of new controls. Scarcely a dozen years following the publication of Carson's *Silent Spring* (1962), which first dramatically drew the public's attention to pollution problems, the chemical pollutants she identified have been severely controlled. The basic problem in the past has not been indifference, but a failure of just about everyone, until very recently, to appreciate the exponential growth of pollution problems and to rearrange the incentive system to correct them. With changing incentive systems it is not difficult now to find companies making a profit out of recycling wastes which yesterday were dumped into the atmosphere and waterways. Similarly, adverse impacts of technology on other areas of human interests are more likely to be reduced and eliminated by proper controls than by slowing down the rate of technological development.

Technology is the key element in rising GNP, which in turn is the open door through which millions of underprivileged will move into a much better life, both in the United States and elsewhere. There are a vast range of human demands which must be met by technology to improve the quality of life. To mention just a few, we have not discovered how to eliminate many diseases that kill millions of people prematurely; we need new methods to feed millions of people who will otherwise die of starvation; we can vastly improve many products to the benefit of the nation, such as faster trains, accident-free automobiles and highways; we need new technology to permit us to use our vast coal reserves for producing energy without polluting the environment; and we still have no cure for the common cold. The list of what we need is endless.

The real challenge is not to smash machines, like the Luddites, but to control the development and use of technology. The challenge is to learn how to do this in such a way as to enhance our technological capabilities and at the same time improve the quality of individual lives in our society. In the past the challenge lay in coping with the natural environment. In the future the emphasis will be on controlling our institutional environment, its incentives, tendencies, abuses, and excesses, to produce a technology which is in tune with national goals and priorities. This is likely to be a more difficult goal to reach than yesterday's goal of controlling the natural environment (Wiesner, 1973). In the past the problems of technology were primarily technical and economic. There are added to them today new moral, legal, military, political, and human dimensions.

CAN TECHNOLOGY BE BETTER PLANNED TO MEET SOCIAL NEEDS?

The obvious answer to this question is yes but doing it is very complex. This question should be approached from three angles: first, technological planning in industry; second, planning technology in government; and third, the interrelationships between the two.

Technology Planning in Industry With the rise of comprehensive corporate planning during the past decade there has also been an inevitable increase in long-range technology planning in industry, particularly among the larger companies. Planning R&D is an integral part of overall corporate planning. Emphasis on R&D planning has increased with shortening product life cycles, increasing volume and time devoted to R&D in product development, and the greater dependence of companies on products introduced recently in the product line. With only slight exception the fundamental issues raised in business in the planning process concern technical feasibility, competition, and economic results. That is to say, the basic concern is whether a given expenditure for a particular technology is that which is most likely to have the highest profit return. There are some exceptions, such as the need for a company to meet actual or anticipated pollution regulations; or to gain experience in a technology important in the company's future, irrespective of current profit impact. The criteria for decision-making in the business world which involves technology, however, is fundamentally technical and economic.

Federal Government Technology Planning There are three aspects to better technology planning in the federal government. The first concerns vast defense R&D expenditures which have been carefully planned for many years to maintain the technical capability for the U.S. armed forces. While the planning has been very sophisticated, I am sure that informed analysis will show that improvement is possible. The second area concerns our space program. There is no doubt that the space program of the National Aeronautics and Space Administration (NASA) has been well planned and highly successful in achieving its objectives. Here again, some improvement undoubtedly is possible in NASA long-range planning. The third area is federal planning of technology to meet nondefense needs. Here the record is very spotty. The National Science Foundation was created in 1950 to allocate federal funds to basic research in universities. Other agencies of government, such as the National Institutes of Health, have allocated funds for basic and applied science. These programs, however, were not planned in the full meaning of that word nor were they based on an explicit statement of governmental policy, because there was none. To overcome this policy gap a recent Presidential Task Force recommended that: "The President explicitly enunciate, as a national policy, the need for vigorous, high-quality science and technology, and call for—as one national goal—continuing leadership in science and in the technology relevant to our other national goals and purposes" (Science Policy, 1970). The President followed this recommendation and sent Congress in 1972 the first comprehensive message on technology which was included in his State of the Union message. But it did not lay out "a plan" for the United States.

With the major exception of the National Science Foundation the great bulk of federal expenditures for R&D have been treated as means to achieve other program objectives. For instance, the federal government-supported research on miniturization was not undertaken to get smaller communications equipment but rather to accommodate the goals of getting less weight in space craft, aircraft, and missiles. As long as federal programs which had high priority also were R&D-intensive the total national R&D budget rose. Currently, however, the priority of such programs is declining and so is the R&D budget. ". . . the shift to low R&D-intensity programs," says Weidenbaum, "requires a rethinking of the role of science and technology in national priorities. Perhaps 'R&D' or 'technological innovation' or 'national investment in progress' (or some other proper-sounding term) should be elevated to the status of an end-purpose, at least to a greater extent than at present" (1973: 5). Our needs for increased nondefense R&D are enormous and growing and they cannot all be met by industry. A rational national R&D expenditure plan is urgently needed.

Federal-Industry Interrelationships In a number of different ways the federal government has stimulated industrial technological growth, e.g. tax incentives, agricultural experiment stations, patent protection, but these programs have not been "planned" to meet specific societal goals. It is likely, as will be discussed shortly, that in the future there will be a much closer relationship—and a planned one—between the government and industry in technological development. This will involve government efforts to increase industrial productivity, to meet foreign competition, and to resolve important technical economic and social problems.

Barriers to Better Planning If we decide to do so we can do a much better job of planning our technology. But the gap between deciding to do it and doing an effective job is enormous. Planning technology is not an exercise in itself; it should be done within a comprehensive planning program involving the entire society. This we do not know how to do. A fundamental and significant constraint is the fact that we have not achieved a national consensus about the highest objectives and priorities of this society. We have not developed a consensus about the goals and priorities for technology. Nor have we reached agreement about the responsibility of the federal government in financing R&D to achieve nondefense objectives for technology. We do not know how to inject social values into the present industrial technology decision-making process except in a rather crude way.

One of the great needs in meeting the future in a confident way is to have a better planning system in the public sector. We are doing a little better job today than in the past and it is likely that we shall improve but probably not as rapidly as desirable.

CAN TECHNOLOGY BE BETTER PLANNED TO AVOID UNWANTED IMPACTS?

As noted previously the critics of technology are quick to point out the unwanted impacts of technological developments. At the present time the planning (if it can be called that) to contain such impacts has been the approach of Donneybrook Fair—"hit a head when you see it." Our traditional practice is to wait until crisis strikes and then take action rather than to foresee potential threats and move to meet them.

Technology Assessment On October 13, 1972, President Nixon signed the Technology Assessment Act which created the Office of Technology Assessment (OTA), the first new organization in the legislative branch of government since 1921. Beginning around 1966 there was a growing concern about having available to the Congress information about impacts of technology to permit more informed decision-making.

There is today no consensus about what is meant by technology assessment. The term is generally considered to cover much more territory than the phrase "environmental impact" discussed in Chapter 14. Congressman Daddario's early definition of technology assessment is a useful one because it expresses the objectives sought. He said: "Technology assessment is a form of policy research which provides a balanced appraisal to the policymaker. Ideally, it is a system to ask the right questions, and obtain correct and timely answers. It identifies policy issues, assesses the impact of alternative courses of action and presents findings. It is a method of analysis that systematically appraises the nature, significance, status, and merit of a technological program. . . . [It] is designed to uncover merit of a technological program. . . . [It] is designed to uncover three types of consequences—desirable, undesirable, and uncertain. . . . To assess technology one has to establish cause and effect relationships from the action or project source to the locale of consequences. . . . The function of technology assessment is to identify (all impacts and trends)—both short-term and long-range. . . . The focus of technology assessment will be on those consequences that can be predicted with a useful degree of probability" (U.S. Congress, House Committee on Science and Astronautics, 1967: 12–13). A more academic definition is: "Technology assessment may be defined as the systematic study of the effects on society that may occur when a technology is introduced, extended, or modified, with special emphasis on the impacts that are unintended, indirect, and delayed. . . . Technology assessment emphasizes the secondary or tertiary effects of new technology rather than the primary [intended] effects . . ." (Coates, 1971: 225).

The OTA has a policymaking and controlling board with thirteen members, six from the Senate, six from the House of Representatives, and the director. It has an advisory council of twelve members, ten from the public, to be appointed by the board; the comptroller general of the United States and the director of the Congressional Research Service. The basic function of OTA is "to provide early indications of the probable beneficial and adverse impacts of the applications of technology and to develop other coordinate information which may assist the Congress." In doing this the OTA will identify existing or probable impacts of technology or technological programs; where possible, ascertain cause-and-effect relationships; identify alternative technological methods of implementing specific programs; identify alternative programs for achieving requisite goals; make estimates and comparisons of the impacts of alternative methods and programs; present findings of completed analyses to the appropriate legislative authorities; and identify areas where additional research or data collection is required to provide adequate support for the assessments and estimates. For the fiscal year 1973–1974 the OTA was allocated $5 million for operations.

There is no one way to make a technology assessment nor is there one discipline which can assure the "right answers" (U.S. Senate, Technology Assessment, 1972). To make a technology assessment, using the above definitions, involves many disciplines of knowledge and different approaches. The cost/benefit approach discussed in Chapter 14 can be used. Another approach, used by the National Academy of Engineering (NAE) in making several technology assessment experiments, follows these steps: (1) identify and define the subject to be assessed; (2) delineate the scope of the assessment and develop a data base; (3) identify alternative strategies to solve the selected problems with the technology under assessment; (4) identify parties affected by the selected problems and the technology; (5) identify the impacts on the affected parties; (6) evaluate or measure the impacts; and (7) compare the pros and cons of alternative strategies (NAE, 1969). There are other variations of these steps (Jones, 1972). Other methods include Delphi, panels of experts, and cross-impact matrices such as suggested in Chapter 14.

Senator Humphrey is reported to have observed that "a key factor in the erosion of Congressional power has been the inadequacy of its independent staff, and the OTA will give Congress the capability to make its own independent judgments" [*Business Week*, 1973(A)]. It is easy to develop high hopes for technology assessment in the decision-making process in government because of its potential and the enormity of the problems it is designed to address. But the concept, methodology, and use have many limitations (National Academy of Science, 1969; Hahn, 1973; Green, 1973). One limitation concerns the accuracy of the assessment. Even though the OTA is staffed with skilled experts it will be impossible to forecast the manifold consequences to society of major technological changes over a period of many years. Even though consequences might be foreseen different people will see them with different eyes—some as a curse and some as a joy. But it is possible to forecast the impacts of a wide range of new technological developments on important segments of society. We know that technology will provide much more leisure time for working people, intensify pollution problems, choke traffic in cities, and in many other ways bring increasingly serious social problems. These events are not difficult to see in detail. The secondary impacts, however, are harder to forecast (Bauer, 1969).

A second major limitation concerns the usage of expert data in the decision-making process. Suppose the technology assessment is so creditable that every expert can agree that the recommendations should be implemented. Will they be? The answer may well be no because the political process involves a very different set of decision criteria than the technical assessment methodology. Taking action will affect the lives and pocketbooks of many people and groups, and they may not see the impact in the same way as the expert assessment researchers. Furthermore, there are the problems, discussed above, of adapting our social, political, economic, and other systems and institutions to avoid unwanted impacts. No further elaboration is needed about the matter here, but the point may be made, for example, that financing airport construction to avoid congestion upon the introduction of new jet transports turns out to be an unbelievably complex problem, the solution to which rests not in one, but in a number of different hands.

Despite these, and many other problems, technology assessment is a social invention with great potential. It is a new and relatively untried measuring and decision-making tool and is likely to improve if for no other reason than that it attracts many experts to policy problems which perplex legislators. There is danger that the methodology will be used to inhibit invention (Peltzman, in Steiner, 1974) or to delay action for emotional reasons. However, it gives promise of raising emotional debates (such as the congressional debate over the supersonic transport) to informed technical levels. It is obvious, says Madden, that "technology assessment contributes significantly to changing the content of such notions as productivity, cost, wealth, and price in the direction of down-valuing forms of wealth which are entropy-heightening and up-valuing forms which are entropy-offsetting" (1972: 46).

Technology assessment is not completely new in either government or business. The Food and Drug Administration and the pharmaceutical industry have made technology impact studies for many years. The thrust and scope of the action taken by the Congress in setting up OTA, however, is much different from the past. It is not at all difficult to forecast that in both government and business there will be new programs to make technological assessments. At this writing several universities are building curricula in technology assessment, and a few companies are making studies of the impact of proposed new technology other than those required by government.

Business Responsibility for Anticipating Impacts How much responsibility does the businessman have to anticipate the consequences of his technological endeavors? Austin thinks that responsible business leaders should make some appraisal of the social effects flowing from their strategic policy decisions and technological advances. When an estimate of the social effects of its activities are made, a business must then look at the kind of action which should be taken, and by whom, to meet the problems of social change (Austin, 1965: 51–52). In many instances a company can take positive action, such as training employees who might be displaced by a change, or correcting a noise problem introduced into a community by a new facility. At the other extreme, is the management of a plant making computers responsible for forecasting and making efforts to modify unwanted impacts on employment growing out of the introduction of these machines? In this particular case the answer, I think, is no. If a manufacturer does foresee serious consequences, however, such as from the introduction of the jumbo jet transport or the addition of more automobiles, he has a responsibility to try to get the proper public authorities to act. The aircraft manufacturers have done this with respect to airports, and automobile manufacturers have pushed planning of future highways; but they should not be responsible for making detailed studies of social impact nor for specifying what should be done. In instances where managements have control, such as in the internal affairs of the firm, they do have responsibilities to foresee the consequences of technological change within their area of control. When the impact lies outside the authority of the company and is of broad social consequence, the obligation lies with responsible governments.

HOW FAR SHOULD GOVERNMENT SUPPORT R&D?

From the beginning of this nation, the federal government has supported R&D for and in industry. George Washington, for example, wanted to create a national university with a center of scientific research. The government has done much to promote R&D. It has supported R&D through its own efforts (mapping the frontier), by subsidizing technological developments (grants of land for early railroad growth); by creating and subsidizing organizations to conduct R&D (the Hatch Act of 1887 set up at land grant institutions the experimental stations for agricultural research which were so important in stimulating the productivity revolution in agriculture), and by purchasing R&D products from industry (the National Aeronautics and Space Administration [NASA] Apollo program). It has been only in recent years, however, that the federal government has emphasized so strongly its R&D efforts. Up to then, the government had lagged behind industry and universities in pioneering and supporting R&D efforts. There has also been a shift in emphasis in federal support of R&D. Up to 1940, federal efforts were largely to aid the general development of science and technology. Since then, the bulk of federal funds has been spent to support R&D in specific areas. Programs have been dominated by mission-oriented research, primarily for national defense and space. In 1972, 77 percent of federal R&D expenditures were made by the Department of Defense (DOD), NASA, and the Atomic Energy Commission (AEC). Grants to universities for research were estimated at around $2.3 billion in 1973.

A cluster of issues surrounds federal support of R&D, such as: What is the fundamental justification for government support of R&D? Should the government spend money for other than strictly essential defense projects? Should the government spend R&D funds through industry or in its own laboratories? Can and should R&D funds be better balanced among disciplines? What should the total federal R&D budget be?

How can large R&D expenditures by government be justified? Since most R&D funds are for national defense, the first and most obvious answer is that if such outlays contribute to and are needed for the defense of the nation, there is no alternative. From 1941 to 1973 the United States was involved in an actual fighting war or a "cold" war of impressive dimensions. It is not surprising that this was the very period of rapid buildup in federal R&D expenditures. We live in a hostile world in which our military power must be capable of defending the nation from any potential threat. Since military power rests increasingly on technology, the preparedness posture of this nation obviously hinges significantly on R&D outlays for defense.

What is the justification for NASA expenditures? NASA R&D expenditures are for a number of purposes, but the most important one has been to make the United States superior to the Russians in space technology. Stimulated by the launching of the Russian Sputnik in October 1957, the NASA program has been kept at a high enough level to compete successfully with and better the Russian effort. This has been justified also because of the potential benefit of the space program to military space applications and to nonmilitary uses of the technology developed.

Some types of R&D which are desperately needed cannot be ratably costed to the public. In this class, for example, are R&D expenditures for medical research, costs associated with new city design, and transportation. Programs such as these are justified because they are said to produce gains for the community above the costs incurred. Government also spends money to extend the state of technical knowledge, to exploit the unknown, and to stimulate all scientific and technological activities. While this objective has been given emphasis only recently, it is likely to grow in the future. Many NASA space probes are in this classification. Then there is a variety of miscellaneous reasons for government spending. The supersonic transport, for example, received federal R&D support up to 1972 because, presumably, such a plane would help to maintain the prestige of the United States as a producer of superior aircraft. Pressure is now being put on the federal government to support R&D for new commercial aircraft in order to permit American manufacturers to produce products they otherwise could not finance and, in turn, protect future balance of payments. Pressure is building for the federal government to support other industrial research, such as electronics, to help reverse a decline in our exports of high-technology products which dropped from around $10 billion in 1970 to around $6 billion in 1972.

There is a growing incentive for private firms to undertake R&D with the hope of meeting a consumer demand at a profit, but there is no question about the fact that the total needs of society will not be met by private initiative. One reason is that many requirements —communication satellites, for instance—necessitate engineering or scientific endeavors far beyond the financial capability of private industry to finance. Furthermore, many needed programs, even if financed by private industry, could not be ratably charged to consumers. Technology generally can be stimulated by federal R&D expenditures. For these reasons there is an advantage to society in having the government support R&D.

How far should the government go? The theoretical answer is that expenditures should yield a social benefit greater than their social costs, and a net return equal to if not greater than returns on other types of expenditure programs.

This is a generalization but impossible to implement in practice with any precision. As will be shown shortly, even our measures of the impact of R&D on general economic conditions are not very accurate. Although we have improved cost-benefit analyses greatly, this method cannot help much in determining whether it is best to spend $1 billion for more space probes, for medical research, or for recreation parks. Major federal nondefense R&D programs result from a combination of political pressures, available funds, historical precedent, and judgments of those in the executive branch and in Congress. The final outcome results from the operation of the political process. In a real sense, the level of R&D expenditures for the military and space programs also is the result of this process rather than of conclusive, objective measures. In a political democracy this is the way such decisions should be made; but we are desperately in need of better knowledge about costs and benefits, priorities, timing, and levels of funding to feed to decision-makers to help them make more informed decisions.

Since the bulk of federal R&D expenditures is made through industry, the question naturally arises: Why not spend federal funds in government departments rather than in industry? Prior to World War II the government spent very little for R&D and that which it did spend was mostly in arsenals, which it owned and operated to develop and produce military equipment. The old arsenal concept was abandoned during World War II and never revived. It was simply much more efficient and effective to look to industry rather than to its own departments for research, development, and production of military and space equipment. While it cannot be said that the aerospace industry, for instance, is private like the automobile industry, the aerospace-government industrial complex follows much more closely the private industrial than the governmental model.

Granted that the federal government is justified in spending R&D funds for reasons other than strictly military purposes, how may these expenditures be best balanced? Is the civilian sector getting a fair share relative to the military? What nondefense programs should be supported and with how much money? Would not scientific and technical progress be greater and at lower cost if allocations were better balanced? These are very difficult questions to answer with any conviction. One must begin with a consideration of whether the R&D in question is to support a mission determined by government, such as financing a cure for cancer, or to maximize knowledge about the world around us with the trust that it will eventually contribute to the social welfare. If it is the first, the justification for the basic mission must be set. The major issue of R&D, once the mission is justified, is simply one of agreement among experts on the amount, timing, and direction to achieve the requirements of the basic mission objective. If the objective is to support science per se, the problem is much more complex. In this case, the highest priority ought to be given to those scientific efforts that will have the most significantly stimulating impact on the rest of science. The trouble with this guide is that the impact of one discovery on another may not show up for years and is exceedingly difficult to forecast. It is easy to forecast that reasonable men would come to radically different conclusions about what constitutes the best balance among scientific disciplines. A different question of balance lies in support to be given to various disciplines. Federal support of research in the social sciences, for example, is very small compared to medical and health research and minuscule compared with defense-space research. There are signs, however, that the crust of long-standing resistance to social science research support has been broken and that increases will be made in the future.

TECHNOLOGY AND GNP GROWTH

Joseph Schumpeter (1949) was one of the first economists who recognized the great contribution of technology to economic development. He said industrial growth depended upon technical innovation and the ability to translate technology into profits. Contemporary economists emphasize the fact that research and development leads to new techniques which create demand for capital goods and bring about investment and growth.

The GNP is the result of output per man-hour worked. Rises in output per man-hour are due to a number of forces, such as greater use of capital equipment, more efficient allocation of resources within a business, increased education and skill of labor and management, and technology. From 1889 to 1919 the average annual increase of output per man-hour was 1.6 percent. Between the two world wars it was 2.3 percent, and since then it has been around 3.2 percent. Independent studies concluded that about 90 percent of the increase in output per man-hour in the past half century was due to capital improvements and better skills (Solow, 1957; Fabricant, 1954; and Massel, 1960).

This means, of course, that the bulk of the growth was due to some combination, the precise mix of which is unknown, of technology, better organization, better management, and higher worker skills. This means, also, that in national policy on economic growth major emphasis should be put on technological progress and the factors which support it. Technological change has been responsible for the bulk of growth of some individual companies. For companies like DuPont, Union Carbide, General Electric, Bell and Howell, and many others, the development of new products and sales levels are dependent upon R&D. But even for these companies, the calculation of what R&D has contributed to profits cannot be made with any precision (Steiner, 1969: 683–86). It is unfortunate that we have no precise measures of the impact of technical change on economic growth, but the evidence we do have says it is extremely important.

TECHNOLOGY AND EMPLOYMENT PROFILES

Technology has had an enormous impact on employment, wages, and work skills. A few dimensions of the impacts are presented below.

Is Technological Unemployment to Be Feared? From the Industrial Revolution until today there has been resistance to technological change as a result of the fears of workingmen that their jobs will be lost and they will not find others, and that their share of total income will decline. Because of such fears workers destroyed the spinning frames of Hargreaves, painters are still avoiding the use of spray guns, and dockworkers resist containerization. On the other hand, the United Mine Workers Union under the leadership of John L. Lewis long ago accepted mine machinery, even though it meant a decline in employed miners; those who remained got higher wages and fringe benefits. Nevertheless, fears of unemployment because of the introduction of machinery still are deep among workingmen.

There is no doubt at all about the fact that new glass-blowing machines displaced glass blowers, and new automated refineries displaced workers. But, does such technological development bring about a decline in the aggregate demand for workers and a reduction in the share of the national income paid to workers? The answer is no. Economists for many years have held to the notion that while workers are displaced by the introduction of new machinery, the demands for workers growing out of the new inventions will be greater than the displacement. Indeed, there has been no more rapid introduction of new machinery in our history than during the ten years from 1958 to 1968, and the total unemployment rate actually declined, from 6.8 percent of the labor force in 1958 to 3.6 percent in 1968. Given sufficient aggregate expenditures in the economy, there is no reason to assume that technological developments will bring about a reduction in the total demand for labor. The truth of the matter in the past has been just the reverse (Nelson, Peck, and Kalachek, 1967: 137–39).

In the short run, however, real difficulties can result. The introduction of machinery in the coal mines of the Appalachian area has left a hard-core residue of unemployed. From the end of World War II to today, there has been more than a 50 percent drop in the number of agricultural workers. The bulk of these workers have found jobs in industry, but many are hard-core unemployed in ghettos. Society now recognizes that it has an obligation to assist in the transition of displaced workers to productive jobs, but the programs are still not as effective as needed.

Real Wages, Work Skills, and Hours of Work While technology may have caused displacement of workers, as noted above, the overall net impact on workers has been highly positive. To illustrate, hourly earnings in nonagricultural occupations almost doubled, in real terms, from 1948 to 1972. This impressive improvement in economic well-being in only one generation has been due in large part to advancing technology.

An obvious consequence of rising technology is the need for a more skilled work force. As employees develop their skills they command higher wages and salaries. This is beneficial. On the other hand, as society has become more complex and technically oriented the number of jobs for unskilled workers has declined in absolute terms. This fact is partly responsible for some poverty in the midst of plenty when the heads of households are unskilled and cannot find work. It also makes more urgent public and private programs to educate workers.

As society becomes more technologically advanced the proportion of employees in industry who are technically trained naturally increases. A company having a large number of employees with advanced degrees and technical skills is a much more complex company to manage than one that has employees with routine skills. The problem of managing highly skilled staff and production workers, whose demands for more participation in decision-making and whose value systems are considerably different from manual workers, to make a contrast, is one which only recently has assumed major proportions in business.

Does Technology Alter the Business Structure? Technology affects the structure as well as the management of businesses in many ways. For example, technology is changing the vertical structure of businesses. One outstanding change is the trend toward automating more of the basic work processes, mechanizing much of the activity of middle managers, improving the capabilities of top managers to deal more effectively with more managerial problems, and multiplying staff experts to help line managers. The horizontal structure of businesses is altering under the impact of technological change. For instance, finance, marketing, and research and development are becoming more important relative to production. These trends are reflected not only in the time managers spend on these subjects, but also in the numbers of people employed in these areas.

Present-day technology makes it possible for a company to grow very large and still remain highly efficient. At the same time it permits small companies to compete effectively with large companies. The development of the computer, better techniques for comprehensive corporate planning, and newer quantitative tools such as automatic inventory replacement policy and linear programming are illustrations of technical knowledge that helps large companies grow and become more efficient.

Production technology obviously has an impact on business organizational structures. Joan Woodward (1965) studied 100 companies in England, divided among small-batch and unit-production firms, large-batch production firms, and process-production businesses. She found wide variations among these three types in layers of management authority, span of control, and location of responsibility for production. In a study I made (with Ryan) of project management organization, a significant change in organization structure and authority relationships was found as a new technical innovation moved from the idea and concept formulation stage into development, then into prototype, and finally into production (Steiner and Ryan, 1968). Murphy found that the more complex and dynamic the technological processes in a company the more decentralized it was (1973).

CONCLUDING OBSERVATION
It is in point to comment that technology is becoming ever important in the affairs of society. A special study group of the European Organization for Economic Cooperation and Development said: "The most important conclusion of our Committee is that the new orientation of our societies towards the qualitative aspects of growth and towards broader concepts of welfare will require a much closer integration of science policy with the totality of economic and social policy, especially in relation to the long range human objectives of economic development" (OECD, 1971: 1). This integration should involve not only policy but operations in the form of more technically oriented people in policy-making positions who also have a broad economic, political, and social outlook.

CHAPTER TWENTY

Affluence, Growth, and the Post-Industrial Society

INTRODUCTION

Viewers of our contemporary society see two strikingly different pictures. On the one hand are those who see the most productive society in the history of the world, showering luxuries on a huge population. On the other hand are those who see poverty, environmental pollution, social disorder, and unhappiness. The first see "the affluent society" becoming even more affluent in a very few years. The second group sees a catastrophic collapse of society in a few generations unless drastic changes are made.

Which view is correct is not a question to be settled in this chapter. In many ways, this issue threads its way through much of the discussion in this book. What I hope to accomplish in this chapter is to delineate the core features of the affluent society, to throw light on the validity of the opposing views expressed above, to examine some of the overriding issues concerning the allocation of resources between the private and public sectors, and to look ahead at prospects for this society.

NATURE OF THE AFFLUENT SOCIETY

The phrase "the affluent society" was coined by John Galbraith for his book of the same name in 1958 and has since caught on as the label symbolic of the nature of today's society. In his book Galbraith did not define the word "affluent" except inferentially, as will be explained later. The word "affluence" means abundance and opulence, which are characteristics of today's society. But that society also contains pockets of impoverishment and scarcity. Let us look at these two sides of today's society.

Impressive Productivity An astute British observer of the American economy recently said:

> The main historical fact about America today is not that it presents the all-too-usual spectacle of a major human story being badly mishandled. It is that it is demonstrating the most productive use of resources ever achieved by man—and this at a time when knowledge (which is transmittable between people) has become by far the most important of the economic resources (Macrae, 1969: 20).

Income statistics of the affluent society capture simply and clearly its wealth-producing capability and the way it is distributed. In 1973 the GNP of the United States was $1,285 billion, an aggregate just about twice the size of the next largest nation. The United States, with a population of about 6 percent of the world, produced goods and services in 1973 equal to about half that produced throughout the entire world. Since the end of World War II this nation's GNP has tripled, in constant prices.

Income Distribution Accompanying this growth has been a substantial increase in real income per person and for the average family. Per capita disposable personal income has grown (in 1972 prices) from over $1,900 in 1945 to over $3,800 in 1972. It is important to note that the pyramid of income levels of the average family is becoming inverted. In 1947 (in 1966 prices) 60 percent of the nation's families had incomes under $5,000; only 8 percent had incomes over $10,000. By 1972 (in 1966 prices), 24.9 percent of families had incomes under $5,000 and 48.5 percent had incomes over $10,000. Black families, however, continue to record incomes lower than white families. The median income of white families in 1972 was $11,550 compared with $7,100 for black families. However, the salaries of college-educated blacks and whites are closer to being equal (U.S. Bureau of the Census, 1973).

Poverty While millions of individuals have moved out of poverty, there are today too many poor Americans. What is poor, of course, is a relative question. Fundamentally, poverty is a condition where there is insufficient food, clothing, shelter, and health services to meet minimum standards. The federal government has calculated the income required to meet these standards for persons and families living under different circumstances. For a nonfarm family of four, for example, the poverty income line for 1972 was $4,275. For a farm family of four, the line was $3,643.

On the basis of these estimates, there were in 1972 about 19.6 million people living in households with incomes below the "poverty line." This is much too large a number, but it is noteworthy that the cornucopia of the affluent society had cut this number from the 40 million similarly situated in 1960. In the mid-1930s it was widely accepted that one-third of the nation was ill-fed, ill-clothed, and ill-housed. Today, those living under the poverty line represent about 10.3 percent of the population. The "poverty gap," or the difference between the actual incomes of the poor and the incomes necessary to put them above "the poverty line," has also dropped. This gap fell from $14.1 billion in 1959 to $7.6 billion in 1972 in current dollars (U.S. Bureau of the Census, 1973).

Contrary to popular belief, most of the poor are white. In 1972 67.8 percent of all poor families and 80.6 percent of all poor unrelated individuals were white. The incidence of poverty among non-whites, however, was much greater than among white households, being one in 3.4 compared with one in 14.1 among whites. Furthermore, only in recent years has the reduction of poverty among non-whites matched the decline among whites (U.S. Bureau of the Census, 1973).

To what extent is there wretched, abject poverty in this group? Generally, the great proportion of these people have access to goods of the economic machine through the welfare system. There is, however, a shocking incidence of malnutrition, protein deficiencies, anemia, vitamin deficiencies, and consequent serious health problems. It is embarrassing that in a nation that has exceptionally comprehensive and penetrating statistics on most economic activity, the data about poverty in general are not as complete as they should be, and data about abject poverty are very skimpy and controversial. While there are too many cases of severe poverty, the total undoubtedly is declining impressively as a result of welfare and a spreading affluence.

Between World War II and the mid-1960s, discussions of poverty were few. Poverty was something most people did not think about; and if they did, they dismissed it without much further thought. In recent years, however, much to the credit of the American people, there has been a growing determination to moderate and finally to eliminate poverty. The wisdom of that prominent social moralist Sophie Tucker is one with which many Americans can agree: "I've been rich and I've been poor," she said, "and, believe me, rich is best" (Hinkle, in Bartels, 1963: 63–64).

If past and current trends continue, the incidence of poverty should be negligible in the United States in the next few decades. But achieving this will require the elimination of institutions and practices that stubbornly resist efforts to erase poverty. For instance, housing in low-income areas is much more expensive in relation to quality of service received than in higher income areas; poor citizens have fewer opportunities for improving their own housing than wealthier ones; many subsidies benefit the wealthy more than the poor (housing, urban renewal, and federal sewer and water grants); the lowest quality schools and the least qualified teachers are generally found in low-income poverty areas; welfare systems discourage self-improvement; new jobs are being created away from central city low-income areas; police practices maximize the probability that young men—especially blacks—will develop police records; and on and on (Downs, 1968).

Quality of Life The nature and character of the affluent society should be measured also in terms of the quality of life it provides people, but we have no convincing measures as discussed in Chapter 5 and later in this chapter. It is easy to find a distressing list of disamenities in life. For instance, it is wholly incongruous in this wealthy nation to find school systems completely shut down for months because of insufficient funds. Incredible stresses and strains are put on people by a multiplicity of events and phenomenon—wars and threats of wars, people congestion, inadequate transportation systems, inflation, invasion of privacy, inadequate medical care, electricity brownouts, and demonstrated erosion of morality in high places of government. To top it all are shrill warnings of total disaster if something is not done to reduce the growth of population, industrial output, and pollution.

On the other hand, it must be underscored, relative to only the recent past, tens of millions of people can and do achieve a quality of life in the United States undreamed for them twenty-five years ago, and achieved then only by a few of the wealthy. This has been made possible principally because of rising real income but also because of greater concern for individuals. For contrast, consider that roughly two-thirds of the human beings on this earth have annual incomes of $200 or less and in their constant search for food have no time for amenities.

An Overview On net balance, the affluent society reveals on the one hand a thrilling capability to produce great material wealth for a huge population. On the other hand, there is poverty in the midst of plenty; there is too much human misery that is allowed to go unnoticed; and we display ineptness in dealing with our major social problems. Talk of the affluent and post-industrial society has, I think, tended to make people believe that the United States economy can satisfy all needs instantly. This is not true. The American economy is still one of scarcity. There simply are not enough resources to make everyone affluent today. There are insufficient resources to meet all the urgent social needs of this society. Given time, intelligent direction, and a reasonably stable social setting, however, the American economy will indeed provide affluence and a quality life for all our people. This, of course, is a relative standard, but in terms of living conditions today and yesterday, the future can be one in which no one is poor. This day will not come without careful direction of the politico-socio-economic system. In the meantime there are massive imbalances in the affluent society between its capabilities and its ideals that must be corrected.

MAJOR ISSUES IN THE AFFLUENT SOCIETY

Galbraith's Thesis In his stinging and brilliant analysis of the affluent society, John Kenneth Galbraith in 1958 zeroed in on what to him was its major issue. Simply stated, it was that the affluent society should no longer be preoccupied with production, but with the better distribution of the products of the economic system. Much that is produced is of secondary importance, he said, and could be eliminated without loss. What is needed, in its place, is an increase in the output of public goods and services. We need, he says, a much better "social balance" or an improved relationship between privately and publicly produced goods and services. "Failure to keep public services in minimal relation to private production and use of goods is a cause of social disorder or impairs economic performance. . . . By failing to exploit the opportunity to expand public production we are missing opportunities for enjoyment which otherwise we might have had" (Galbraith: 259). We need, he said, more schools, hospitals, slum-clearance, urban development, sanitation, parks, playgrounds, and other such public goods and services. Among other things to redress the imbalance, he advocated a system of taxation which automatically increases the share of income made available to public authority for public purposes (Galbraith: 311).

Written in his typically shock-producing, eloquent style, the following passage captures the essence of the contrast and need (Galbraith: 253):

> The family which takes its mauve and cerise, air-conditioned, power-steered, and power-braked automobile out for a tour passes through cities that are badly paved, made hideous by litter, blighted buildings, billboards, and posts for wires that should long since have been put underground. They pass on into a countryside that has been rendered largely invisible by commercial art. (The goods which the latter advertise have an absolute priority in our value system. Such aesthetic considerations as a view of the countryside accordingly come second. On such matters we are consistent.) They picnic on exquisitely packaged food from a portable icebox by a polluted stream and go on to spend the night at a park which is a menace to public health and morals. Just before dozing off on an air mattress, beneath a nylon tent, amid the stench of decaying refuse, they may reflect vaguely on the curious unevenness of their blessings. Is this, indeed, the American genius?

Conventional thinking, says Galbraith, is obsessed with the idea of maximizing the production of whatever consumer goods the market brings forth. (He asserts that "production creates the wants it seeks to satisfy" by advertising.) What is needed is a reconsideration of social goals and values. Why should not the central goal of society be "investment in human as distinct from material capital"?

Throughout his book he hammered away at "the myth that production, by its overpowering importance and its ineluctable difficulty, is the central problem of our lives" (Galbraith: 281). This was true when men fought economic insecurity, competitive inequalities, unpredictable economic depressions, and low and unequal incomes. But the affluent society solved the production problem. There are other things, said Galbraith, at least as important as production for the private market, and as desirable a goal as productive efficiency. So long as men hold to the "myth of production," he says, there will be major distortions and contradictions in the distribution of goods and services. Men will view frivolous goods with pride, but consider public services at best to be a necessary evil and at worst "a malign tendency against which an alert community must exercise eternal vigilance." Automobiles will have greater importance than the roads on which they are driven. We will welcome capital expenditures for improving telephone service, but reject capital expenditures to improve the postal service.

One must agree with Galbraith that we do overemphasize production and that in an affluent society attention should turn more to the individuals in it. The fundamental question is, what should be done about it? Galbraith set forth a number of proposals to divert funds from private to public purposes, but he never suggested any particular dollar volume.

Before looking at the changes in public expenditures I want to pause a moment to make a few comments on the Galbraithian thesis. Galbraith is correct in pointing to frivolous private spending, but it should be observed that there is plenty of nonsensical public spending. There is plenty of evidence to suggest that even if public spending is greatly increased, the chances that politicians will further misallocate public funds are very high. Running through Galbraith's book is the thought that the private and public sectors are separate monolithic entities and that somehow they are irrevocably differentiated. This, of course, is not true, as has been amply demonstrated in previous chapters and will be further shown later. Out of this view, which is not really explicitly stated, comes the idea that public output should be emphasized and private production deemphasized. This is wrong. Both should be emphasized, but public output should be emphasized more than it has been in the past. This is a very important distinction to make. Galbraith takes us to the cliff and asks us to jump, which many are willing to do, but does not tell us how to land, which we would like to know. He tells us what kinds of public goods and services should be expanded (education, hospitals, and so on) but does not tell us how decisions should be made or how much to spend on them.

We must agree on the main point, however, that as an affluent society advances, it must pay increasing attention to the solution of social problems, to the dignity and quality of individual life, and to the rapid improvement of life for everybody. The core idea is that an affluent society must reconsider its goals.

The Rise of Public Spending The issues which Galbraith so bitingly set forth are still major ones. Since he wrote, however, total federal expenditures have increased from $92 billion in 1959 to $232 billion in 1972 and to an estimated $269 billion for fiscal year 1974. Military expenditures and interest on debt are a substantial part of the increase. Nevertheless, all other expenditures rose from $28 billion in 1959 to $136 billion in 1972. The bulk of this increase was for health and welfare, education, community and housing development, transportation, and space technology. In the meantime, state and local expenditures have increased from $49 billion in 1959 to an estimated $190 billion for 1974. All of this increase was for public goods and services. These expenditure trends are faster than for population and, therefore, per capita expenditures have increased significantly. The expenditure increases have been much more rapid than price inflation so that real outlays for public purposes have grown impressively. Furthermore, these huge increases in nondefense public goods and services did not come from any massive diversion from private production; rather, it was mostly produced from a growing GNP.

Meeting Future Public Demands It will take a long time for today's urgent social needs to be met fully and, in the meantime, other demands for public spending will rise. Billions of dollars can be spent annually in each of many pressing areas, such as city rebuilding, antipollution campaigns, welfare, prison rebuilding, aid to the mentally and physically incapacitated, law enforcement, education, transportation, and on and on. Tax reduction could cost the government billions in revenues. The point is that the timing of the emergence of the society of abundance will depend in no small degree upon the way in which these demands are balanced, because they all cannot be met at once.

Furthermore, massive shifts from private to public expenditure could perhaps create greater problems than they would solve. For instance, tax increases of sufficient size to erode the profit motive could easily have, as has happened in Great Britain, for example, a depressing impact on managerial drive. This, in turn, could bring about a leveling or decline in productive efficiency and output. We need both an increase in public outlays and a continuous pressure for rising productivity per man-hour and total productive output. Although there have been many premature forecasts over the past thirty years that expansion of the public sector would "kill the goose that lays the golden egg" (meaning business), this obviously has not happened. There must be, however, a suitable evolving balance between the two. Any sharp imbalance caused by a too-rapid expansion of the public sector could bring serious consequences in the private sector.

SHOULD WE SLOW DOWN GROWTH?

Throughout our history it has been observed that industrialization has brought adverse impacts on people—unemployment, poor working conditions, occupational disease, overcrowding in slums, and so on. For the most part those who examined such conditions sought redress of losses to the victims either by government aid for laws to prevent injury or by having business bear certain social costs. There was no thought of slowing down industrialization to reduce social costs but rather the pressure was for reform to prevent injustices. Today, there are those who look at the adverse impacts of an affluent society and predict that if present trends and ways of doing things are continued there will be a major disaster to humanity. They assert that nothing short of a reversal and decline of growth can prevent this grim event. Are they right? Should we slow down growth?

Probably the most comprehensive analysis of impending disaster is that made by a team of computer specialists led by Dennis Meadows and published in *The Limits to Growth* (1972). This group reached the grim conclusion that "if present growth trends of world population, industrialization, pollution, food consumption and resource depletion continue unchanged, the limits to growth on this planet will be reached sometime within the next one hundred years. The most probable result will be a rather sudden and uncontrollable decline in both population and industrial capacity" (1972: 23). They say the only way to avoid catastrophe is to stop growth now.

Rise of Growth-Limiting Philosophies Perhaps the earliest, and certainly the best known, growth-limiting philosophy was that of Thomas Malthus who in 1798 advanced the thesis that population tends to increase faster than the means of subsistence. Time has not been true, so far. When he wrote the world population was about 900 million compared with four times that number today, most of whom are eating better than did most of those who lived in the time of Malthus. Those who today demand the limiting of growth, however, say that Malthus was not wrong. Only his timing was off. They say within a very few decades his thesis will be proved correct. The dominant personalities in this school of thought have been noted elsewhere and need only be mentioned here (Carson, 1962; Commoner, 1967, 1971; Ehrlich, 1968; Mishan, 1969; Meadows, 1972). Viewed from different angles this group says that things are different today and if action, drastic action, is not taken we cannot avoid human disaster.

The Argument for Limiting Growth Because it is the most comprehensive and well-known projection of doom, *The Limits to Growth* analysis will be given here. This study built a computer simulation model which interrelated population, industrial output, raw-material reserves, food production, and pollution. All five basic elements are increasing, but at different rates. Population is growing at exponential rates. It took 300 years, from 1650 to 1950, for the world to grow from 500 million people to over 3.5 billion today. If the current 2 percent growth rate continues the world population will be almost 7.0 billion in 2000 and there will be 50 billion people on the planet in the year 2100. Industrial production has been growing at about 7 percent a year which rate, if continued, would yield an output in 2000 of 7.6 times the present, by 2050 it would be 220 times the present output, and by 2100 it would be an incredible 6,500 times present output. Such growth rates will require more food than will be available, nonrenewable resources will became exhausted, and pollution will be intolerable and beyond environmental capacity to absorb.

Meadows and his fellow researchers made a number of computer simulations with varying assumptions and all ended in collapse. A "standard" World Model was based upon the assumption of no major change in the physical, economic, or social relationships that have historically governed the development of the world system. They concluded that, based on these assumptions, ". . . population and industrial growth will certainly stop within the next century, at the latest" (p. 126). The primary force that stops growth, they say, is pollution.

A second model was run on the assumption that nuclear energy will solve the resource problems of the world. It makes no difference, the same fate is in store for us. The reason is that no restraints brought by energy limitations will permit industrial output to expand and rising pollution will again bring disaster. In a third model it is assumed that there will be both a reduction in resource depletion and a reduction in pollution generation. Population will still be rising as will industrial production but the limiting factor will be arable land for food. In a final model it is assumed that the food yield per acre of land will be doubled. Even with pollution controls a pollution crisis will stop further growth. The net conclusion is that *"the basic behavior mode of the world system is exponential growth of population and capital, followed by collapse"* (p. 142).

The M.I.T. group argues that advancing technology will delay but not prevent the ultimate collapse before 2100. They argue that it is better to try to live within natural limits by restricting growth than to hope that another technological leap forward will allow growth to continue longer. They advocate public policies, as follows: (1) stabilize population by setting the birth rate equal to the death rate; (2) allow industrial capital to increase until 1990, when the investment rate should be set equal to the depreciation rate; (3) reduce resource consumption per unit of industrial output to one-fourth of its 1970 value by recycling and conservation; (4) shift public demand from material commodities to services such as education and health; (5) reduce pollution to one-fourth of its 1970 value; (6) give priority to using capital to produce food; and (7) enhance the durability of industrial capital. Such policies, they assert, will yield twice the food output per person consumed in 1970 and will provide an average income per capita for all people of the world of around $1,800, which is much less than half the present American level.

A Critique It is not surprising, with such an explosive conclusion, that *The Limits* was met with radically different appraisals. Many social critics welcomed the study as a scholarly mathematical proof of what they had been predicting. On the other hand the reactions of the technicians—economists, ecologists, system analysists, social observers—have been critical of both the methods and the results. Criticism of the study is somewhat handicapped by the absence of full disclosure of the technical data and mathematical equations on which the simulation runs were made. (These data are promised in a final report not available at this writing.) It is possible, however, to identify some major shortcomings of both the methodology and the results.

First, much of the doomsday quality of the study arises from the assumption that the historical 2 percent annual growth rate of world population will continue. There is much evidence that growth rates of population in both industrialized and underdeveloped nations are slowing down. There are many reasons for declining growth rates, such as the understanding of both governments and peoples of the problems in assuring economic well-being for an unrestrained population growth, the availability of contraceptive devices, the rising costs of food, and the desire of men and women to reduce the size of their families as their incomes rise. It is not likely, says Maddox, ". . . that societies which have somehow managed to survive for the best part of two million years will at this stage in their history exhaust their capacity for taking prudent steps for their own survival" (1972: 44). Past demographic forecasts have proven less reliable than economic forecasts and are likely to be so for some time in the future.

Second is the assumption of a simple relationship between life expectancy and the availability of food. While it is not clear it seems that the study assumes a simple linear relationship between the two. This is not so. The relationships between nutrition and life expectancy are complex and vary with diet, geography, and life styles.

Third, the rate of technological change and problem-solving capability is much underestimated. It is impossible to forecast technological change except, perhaps, in light of what was said in the past chapter, to say it will be faster than in the past. If this is at all correct there is little doubt that we shall see great new technological developments in the future. For instance, it is quite probable that there will be new fertilizers, pesticides, biological control of insects, new seeds, and new foods which will provide more nutrition at lower costs.

One of the assumptions in the M.I.T. study is that there will be no or little substitution of materials and that when one runs out disaster will result. This flies in the face of a vast technology in the recent past which has provided substitutes for all sorts of scarce resources. For instance, long-range forecasts of world resources in 1941, when the basic patent on polyester fiber was issued, did not anticipate the huge expansion of synthetic materials. Today there are almost 2 billion pounds of polyester materials produced at a price of about 35 cents per pound which compares with $1.75 per pound in 1954.

While we are learning more about forecasting new technological developments this is not something that can be done with confidence, especially with respect to timing. Meadows does not ignore the possibility of new technological developments but he does seem to underestimate very much the probabilities that new technology will help us manage and solve our major problems.

The Economist of London commented that the M.I.T. team had fallen into the "central trap before all ecologists . . . ever since economic growth really began with the industrial revolution two hundred years ago, any scientist has always had to forecast world disaster if he plots exponential economic growth against . . . human technology. Since it is exponential growth in technology that is spurring exponential growth in income, of course your computer tells you that you are heading for breakdown if you tell it to assume continuation of the effect without continuance of the cause" (March 11, 1972: 20).

Fourth, there appears to be a basic assumption that pollution is inherent in growth. Actually, we are free today of serious pollutions of the past, such as blankets of soot (from soft coal furnaces) which used to cover cities in the past, and layers of human and animal excrement which was underfoot in cities. We are also observing today, as noted previously, that given the proper incentive structures business is eliminating its pollutions and often at a profit. Technology, given the proper incentives, may well alter radically past relationships between pollution and growth.

Finally, as intimated above, is the underestimation of market forces to induce changes which may avoid the grim future Meadows sees for us. Higher energy prices are today, for instance, reducing energy consumption which in turn is reducing pollution. Higher prices are spurring the search for oil, gas, copper, lead, and other materials with limited observable reserves. Higher prices for food products in the United States at the present time are bringing about increased acreage for cultivation of crops in short supply. The market economy, influenced and augmented by government regulations, will undoubtedly induce great changes among the basic elements in the M.I.T. model, especially with respect to pollution, resource conservation, and food production.

There are other criticisms that have been levied at *The Limits* (Jacoby, in Steiner, 1974; Maddox, 1972; Passell and Ross, 1973; Clark and Fulmer, 1973; Beckwith, 1972). Those presented, however, I think are the most outstanding to consider.

Concluding Comments One of the important conclusions which I draw from the debate is that we should be indebted to the critics of growth. While the premises of *The Limits* are soft and mushy, the thrust of the study rests on a hard truth that the resources of the earth are finite. *The Limits* and other tracts in this vein do a great service in alerting us to problems which lay ahead. But the conclusions must be taken with great reservation. Such studies do not serve us well when, on the basis of soft data, they tell us we must radically change life styles, forms of government, economic systems, and basic human values, or face doom. They will serve us well if they stimulate the development of sufficient information to build more creditable simulation models, if they make more exciting the search for fresh ideas about how to alter present evaluative and decision-making processes in both the public and private sectors so as to reorient present institutions to avoid impending threats, and if they generate new methods to do all this without denying the people of this country and other countries of the world the benefits of continuing economic progress. We have no pat answer about how to do these things but we shall be well-advanced in meeting the future if we understand the real questions.

ZERO POPULATION GROWTH (ZPG) AND BUSINESS

The M.I.T. study provides a strong case for ending the growth of the human population. Careful studies by TEMPO, the General Electric center for advanced studies, reaffirm this view. TEMPO has concluded that the growth of capital stock is amplified by a slower population growth because resources are freed for investment. This makes output grow faster. "The net result is that GNP is virtually unaffected for the first fifteen years after a fertility decline. Thereafter, for the next fifteen or twenty years, in a typical case, GNP rises slightly faster under lowered fertility. Finally, in about twenty-five to thirty years, GNP under constant fertility catches up and surpasses GNP under lowered fertility . . . with almost the same GNP under constant and lowered fertility but with fewer people, GNP *per capita* must rise much faster with declining fertility" (TEMPO: 36). Slowing population will also reduce disparities in income distribution, says TEMPO.

Slowing population growth in the United States may have adverse impacts on some businesses but not on business generally. Even for those businesses which might be adversely affected, the time scale would permit adjustments to exploiting other opportunities which a stable population would provide. As noted above, GNP will continue to grow. Per capita income will continue to rise and people will have more money to spend.

Different industries will be affected differently. For example, a decline in fertility rates will mean a decline in the birth of new babies. This will, of course, mean a declining market for makers of diapers. But it will be some time before the market is flat and, in the meantime, capacity can be directed to other markets such as bedsheets and bath towels.

ZPG is clearly not the same thing as zero economic growth. Indeed, as noted above, ZPG can accelerate economic growth. It is neither feasible nor desirable to try to bring about zero economic growth for reasons which have been given in this and previous chapters. The social benefits of continued economic growth are clearly much beyond social costs. This nation needs economic growth to eliminate poverty, to end pollution, to modernize its industrial equipment, to rebuild cities, to provide needed housing, and to build an adequate transportation system. The problem is not economic growth, but how we guide and direct our economic system in achieving goals society establishes for itself.

FROM GNP TO NEW

We need a better measure of growth than GNP. GNP, which measures the total output of goods and services, is an economic measure of growth which is unconcerned with amenities of life. Nordhaus and Tobin suggest, not as a substitute but as a supplement, Net Economic Welfare (NEW), which measures consumption satisfactions (1971).

NEW subtracts from conventional calculation of GNP those nonmaterial disamenities that have been accruing costs to the economy whether or not they have been charged to industries causing them. In mind, for example, are effluents that pollute the environment. Also deducted are disamenities such as tedious commuting trips to and from work. Added to the conventional calculation of GNP are items now excluded, such as services of housewives in the home, the value of increased leisure, and so on.

Nordhaus and Tobin calculated NEW for the years 1929 to 1965 and compared their findings with the NNP. [GNP includes an allowance for business capital depreciation and when it is subtracted from GNP the result is Net National Product (NNP).] When NNP is deflated for price increases it measures "real" or "uninflated by price" economic growth. Between 1929 and 1965 real NNP rose by 3 percent annually (1.7 percent on a per capita basis) and the NEW rose at an annual rate of 2.3 percent (or 1.0 percent on a per capita basis). From 1947 to 1965 the NEW index advanced 2.0 percent annually but only 0.4 percent each year on a per capita basis. In the meantime, real NNP rose 3.6 percent per year and 2.0 percent on a per capita basis. This first effort confirmed what many people suspected, that there has been a decline in the rate of growth of the quality of life.

The development of this new measure, along with social indicators discussed in Chapter 6, will be helpful in the future in measuring progress. They will also provide a basis for a better understanding of trade-offs between economic growth and improving the quality of life.

PART FIVE

Business and Government

Government-Business Interrelationships: An Overview

INTRODUCTION

Of all the institutions in society none is more intimately associated with business than is government. The spectrum of relationships varies from Christmas-time generosity to tax-exempt enterprises to virtually complete control over all industry during a major war. For all business, the government is a partner—sometimes silent and sometimes quite vocal. For most businesses, government is one of the greatest influences on activity, and often it is the determining influence on many aspects of the operations of a firm—growth, pricing, production, competition, wages, profits, and investment. No simple treatment of the relationship between business and government can do it justice. A mere listing of government points of impact on a typically large business would fill page after tedious page. Rather than attempt any sort of comprehensive coverage of the subject in this section, I want to survey quickly the broad spectrum of interrelationships between business and government. I hope to show by this presentation the exceedingly wide range of possible and actual actions by government that affect business. A number of aspects of the government-business relationship were examined in previous chapters. Many other issues in this nexus will be discussed in subsequent chapters. In this chapter, however, I seek to pull together in a unified brief statement major features of the entire relationship.

SOURCES OF GOVERNMENT ACTION TOWARD BUSINESS

At the outset it should be recalled that there is no such thing as a monolithic government unilaterally exercising power over business enterprises, not even under conditions of constitutional dictatorship, as in World War II. At any one time, the impact of government on business derives from an accumulation of laws applied by individuals in the executive branches of governments or tested in courts of law. These laws and their implementation are, in turn, based upon legal powers given to governments and the administrators of government programs. The fundamental basis for this tower of regulations is the Constitution of the United States.

In the Constitution, most of the economic powers exercised by the federal government are contained in Art. 1, Sec. 8. This section gives Congress the power to levy and collect taxes, to pay debts and provide for common defense and general welfare; to borrow money; to regulate commerce; to establish bankruptcy laws; to coin money and to regulate its value; to fix standards of weights and measures; to stop counterfeiting; to establish post offices and post roads; to promote science and useful arts by granting patents and exclusive rights over writings and discoveries; to punish piracies; to exercise exclusive legislation over the geographical seat of government, military establishments, and other lands owned by the government; and "to make all laws which shall be necessary and proper for carrying into execution these foregoing powers, and all other powers vested by this Constitution in the government of the United States, or in any department or officer thereof." A reasonable interpretation of such grants of authority permits the national government in today's economy to do just about anything that is likely to pass through congressional law-making machinery.

Enumerated grants of authority are more imposing than the expressed limitations on federal economic power. For instance, ex post facto laws are forbidden, taxes cannot be levied on exports, money can be drawn from the Treasury only following appropriations made by law, no appropriation to support armies can be for longer than two years, and the Bill of Rights contains limitations. The Tenth Amendment reserves to the states, or to the people, powers not delegated to the national government by the Constitution, nor prohibited by it to the states. The exercise of state and local government authority has, of course, deeply affected business in many ways, from promotion to control.

The constitutional machinery ensures that decisions by the federal government are determined popularly rather than autocratically. This machinery is designed to ensure that interests of individuals and groups in society can be focused on government so that governmental policies are determined in the interests of the governed—for example, the procedure for electing representatives, the rights of individuals and groups to petition the legislature, the machinery for legislative action, the organization of courts of law, and provisions for amending the Constitution.

The federal government is one of delegated powers from the states, and state governments retain those powers not explicitly or implicitly granted to the federal government or taken by it. States, therefore, may do whatever they choose so long as they are not prevented from doing so by the Constitution or the federal government. Local governments are created by states and find their powers in charters granted by the states. The more important powers exercised by state and local governments over business enterprises concern powers to incorporate businesses, power to levy and collect taxes, and the police power. The first needs no elaboration. The power to tax has been used not only to raise revenue, but to regulate and promote business. The police powers embrace a variety of activities concerning the health, safety, welfare, and morals of people of the states. Such powers enable states to prevent fraud, ensure adequate service at reasonable rates, protect employees from employer exploitation, maintain competition, restrict competition, fix prices of commodities, establish standards for processing food and drugs, establish standards for safety in mines and factories, and in many other ways to regulate and promote business.

PRESSURES FOR GOVERNMENT ACTION AFFECTING BUSINESS

The actions that governments actually take which affect business derive from extremely complex forces in our society. Fundamentally, however, the legislative process is the focal point of a medley of interests that compete for power over government action and the rewards that go with it. The power that individuals and groups seek over the legislative process is, of course, the power to get government to act in their behalf in conformity with their views. The great bulk of legislation at all levels of government reflects the interplay of these forces.

Once legislation is passed, its administration is based on a number of influences. Private individual and group interests are focused on the administrators of legislative enactments and executive orders. Administration is also affected by legal precedents, court decisions, threats of legal action, personal views of administrators, and the philosophies of top elected officials of government.

Finally, of course, are the courts of law. Here, private individual and group pressures are not nearly so influential as in the above two areas, but the Supreme Court does reflect election returns. Alfange in a prize-winning essay observed that "the court . . . has, with but

few exceptions, adjusted itself in the long run to the dominant currents of public sentiment during successive periods of American
history" (1937: 40).

In Chapter 22 the role of business as a pressure group on government will be explored in the context of the larger process of pressure
politics. The point I want to make here is that what the government
does to business is based upon legal precedent, views of administrators, and private pressures exerted on the legislative and administrative process. This is, of course, a simplistic view of the process in
which business is affected by pressures of other groups exerted on
government and is itself a powerful direct and indirect influence on
government to act in the interests of business.

THE GOVERNMENT-BUSINESS PARTNERSHIP

As a result of forces pressing government to act in business life,
including business itself, there exists today an intimate partnership
relationship between government and business. This did not develop
on the basis of any particular set of ideologies or distributions of
power between the two; rather, it has resulted from a pragmatic
response to problems periodically confronting our society. The partnership has been flexible in developing new patterns to meet new
problems. It has sought to allocate responsibility to business and
government according to the areas where each, respectively, has the
greatest comparative advantage, but it has not failed to grant authority to each to operate in the other's historical province when
circumstances seemed to warrant.

Government and business do display distinct characteristics. For
instance, businesses are still considered to be predominantly profit-
seeking economic institutions whose decisions are made on the basis
of more or less authoritarian administrative rules. Government, on
the other hand, is predominantly a political institution where decisions are forged on the anvil of democratic politics. One remarkable
feature of the partnership is not how much government actually
interferes in and influences business, but how much of business is
free of government intervention. The bulk of activity in the private
sector does, indeed, take place without direct governmental interference.

These are generalizations and are, I think, quite valid. The chief
executive of a large company, however, I am sure feels that his hands
are tied and his actions prescribed to an excessive degree by government (Clee, 1962). If we were to examine the operations of a private
firm, large or small, for even one day, we would see how government
influences affect the enterprise at dozens of points. Conversely, we
cannot look at the daily activities of a major government program,
such as national defense, without seeing the thousand-and-one ways

in which business is affected, negatively and positively, by government.

While the hand of government affects both large and small companies significantly, the larger companies are primarily concerned with policies and actions of the federal government. There are exceptions to this generalization. Large public utilities and insurance companies, for instance, are concerned with state legislation affecting their rates. A large manufacturing company also may be vitally interested in local zoning regulations. But, generally, the governmental impacts of most interest to the large corporations relate to federal activities.

Perhaps the outstanding fact about this partnership is that it seems to have worked rather well. Business is strong and vigorous and improving continuously its extraordinary capability of increasing output per unit of input. As pointed out in previous chapters, however, traditional business doctrine fails to meet many current and urgent social problems and is subject to important shortcomings which need correction. As a result, a new profile of government-business relationships is emerging. A major problem for the future is to ensure that a balance between the two will optimize all the interests of society. This is an issue which will be discussed later.

SOME DIMENSIONS OF GOVERNMENT INFLUENCES ON BUSINESS

Unfortunately, there is no simple method to show just how much business activity is determined by government, and vice versa. It does seem useful to try, however, to get some grasp of the extent to which programs of governments, particularly the federal government, affect business. The following taxonomy is not intended to present a complete profile, but merely to illustrate the breadth and depth of the relationship. My intent here is to help the reader grasp the impact of government on business, not to describe it in detail. In the next chapter the way in which business influences government will be studied in depth.

Government prescribes rules of the game. Government prescribes rules of business behavior governing important business relationships within which individuals are comparatively free to act in conformity with their self-interests. Typical rules of the game are those concerning competitive behavior, labor-management relations, the sale of securities, advertising, business incorporation, and safety regulations concerning automobiles. The regulations vary in the extent to which they restrain an individual businessman, but they serve to establish the "rules for playing the game."

Government is a major purchaser of the output of business. The share of the GNP taken off the market by government has shown a remarkable increase. Out of a prospective GNP in calendar 1974 of $1,385 billion, the federal, state, and local governments are expected to purchase $305 billion. Of this total, $117 billion is expected to be spent by the federal government and $188 billion by all other governments. Government purchases range from paper clips to vehicles and associated equipment to land a man on the moon and return him safely to earth. Many companies, and some very large ones, sell their entire output to government. Few companies do not directly or indirectly benefit from some government procurement.

The government uses its contracting power to get business to do things the government wants. It is a case of "no compliance, no contract." For instance, businesses that want government contracts must comply with the following government regulations: subcontract to minority businesses, pay prevailing minimum wages, comply with safety and sanitary work regulations, refrain from discrimination in hiring, comply with all wage and price controls, and meet government pollution standards. Government contracting agencies by law must prefer domestic to foreign products (Buy American Act), ship all military and at least one-half of foreign aid goods in United States vessels (Cargo Preference Act), purchase all brooms and similar items from nonprofit agencies for the blind (Blind-Made Goods Act), purchase only United States-made buses (1969 Defense Authorization Act), and purchase meat only from suppliers who conform to human standards (Human Slaughter Act). Such rules obviously cost something but presumably they are offset by benefits.

Government is a major promoter and subsidizer of business. In a previous chapter the historical promotion of business by government was discussed. The government is still at it, and engages in a complex and powerful network of programs to aid business. Promotion ranges from tariff protections to loans, guarantees of loans, maintenance of high levels of economic activity, and direct subsidies. It is, of course, in the interest of government to ensure growing and vigorous business activity, but the ways in which government promotes business vary enormously and sometimes are highly controversial. For instance, the oil depletion allowance is controversial, but training military pilots who subsequently are hired by airlines is not. Both are promotional and worth calculable dollars and cents to the businesses concerned. In 1960 the Joint Economic Committee compiled a list of classes of subsidy and subsidy-like programs of the federal government that included over 150 groupings (Joint Economic Committee, 1960).

Promotionalism, of course, is not limited to money, but includes all sorts of favorable legislation and administrative action. For instance, rights given by government to operate a TV station, or to fly an airplane between two heavily populated areas, may be extremely valuable. Since the successful promotion of the interests of one group sets a precedent for others, it can be predicted with confidence that governmental promotion of business activity will expand rather than decrease despite the strong pleading of many business leaders for reduced government expenditures and more limited government.

Government is the owner of vast quantities of productive equipment and wealth.   The government is also an important producer of goods and services, often in direct competition with private business. During the 1930s a major conflict arose over the federal government's construction of electric power generating facilities. Today, about 25 percent of all power is publicly produced. Government is a major producer of goods and services in such fields as rubber, high-octane gasoline, ammunition, guns, ships, atomic energy, postal services, weather-reporting services, and dams. The federal government owns vast stockpiles of raw materials and productive equipment which it often lends to private industry.

Government is an architect of economic growth.   It has assumed responsibility for achieving an acceptable rate of stable economic growth. This policy is of enormous benefit to business because it ensures a much more stable environment than was enjoyed in the past, thereby reducing economic uncertainty and making long-range planning much more feasible.

Government is a financer of business.   There is no limit to the extent to which the federal government can guarantee loans. Nearly a third of all mortgages written since 1949 have been financed or guaranteed by federal credit agencies. The federal government helps to finance airport construction, harbor improvements, and construction of canals. It makes loans to small businesses and provides incentives for larger businesses to expand defense production.

Government is the protector of various interests in society against business exploitation.   An extensive range of programs exists in this area. For instance, there are many laws protecting the interests of investors, customers, employees, and the competitors of a business. The last three areas are examined at length in chapters in this book.

Government directly manages large areas of private business. The word "manage" here means that government dictates a certain amount of decision-making. It does not mean that the government is the manager in the way a chief executive of a company manages. In the sense meant here, the government manages important parts of industries, through regulation, supervisory surveillance, and joint decision-making, such as the following: electric light and power, gas, oil, airlines, railroads, communications, insurance, aerospace, trucks and buses, agriculture, financial institutions, security and commodity exchanges, food processors, and drugs.

Government is the repositor of the social conscience, and redistributes resources to meet social ends.   Government redirects resource use, as noted in a previous chapter, by transfer payments, rising R&D expenditures, tax incentives, and subsidies. These traditional means have expanded in recent years. Also, as noted previously, the government exerts moral pressure on business to act in conformity with generally accepted social goals.

This is but a cursory survey of the many ways in which government affects managerial decision-making in business, which I hope conveys the message of the massive and complex impact of government on business.

The Negative/Positive Impact of Government Actions The government impact on business is not necessarily negative. It very often is munificently positive. It is a delusion, held by many, that government interference in business is control and control is ipso facto bad. A little reflection will show that even where government action is restraining, or compelling, the impact may be negative to one person but positive to another. Indeed, I know of no governmental action in economic life that is wholly negative or wholly positive. Largesse for one group may mean restriction on another, and regulation of one may mean freedom for another. One major function of government is to implement the wishes of the people about the kind of freedom that shall be restrained in order to advance another.

At certain periods in our history the totality of federal actions toward business may have been considered predominantly negative or restraining. This might have been the case in the latter part of the nineteenth century; it was certainly the case during World War II. Today, although there is no way to prove the case statistically, I think that the greater impact on business, all things considered, is promotional rather than inhibitory. This does not mean, however, that there are not some unnecessary negative impacts on business that ought to be removed. I do not want to dwell too much on the positive aspects of governmental impact on business, but it does need emphasis to counterbalance the more prevailing view of governmental negativism. The American Telephone and Telegraph Company is a company which is controlled in thousands of ways by governmental action. On the other hand, government also had a positive impact on its operations, as attested by Frederick Kappel, chairman of the board, as follows:

> The telephone business in its early days, back in the last century, was severely limited technically. People could talk and hear for only a few miles, and they usually had to shout.
> Yet the people who ran the business had big ideas. In particular, Theodore N. Vail, the great leader of the Bell System in its formative years, set forth some fantastic goals. He looked ahead to universal service—to a time when anyone could talk with anyone else, anytime,

anywhere. The very charter of the AT&T Company, issued in 1885, spoke of using cables "and other appropriate means" to interconnect cities and towns all over the world.

This big vision literally drove the business into large-scale research and development effort. The effort got into high gear in the early years of this century, under the leadership of Dr. Frank B. Jewett, the first president of Bell Laboratories. Very importantly, Dr. Jewett realized that the scientific method, applied within the industry, offered the best hope of getting the knowledge on which to build a successful technology of communications.

However, there was one other important circumstance. In the early days of the telephone there were many areas where different telephone companies competed against each other. Resources were wasted and the public suffered. And here comes the decisive fact: In the early 1920s the country and the Congress decided that in the interest of good service, overlapping or dual telephone systems might be unified.

This political decision opened the way to nationwide service over a single system that would interconnect the different companies in all parts of the country.

Now I could ask: "Who did the innovating here? What brought about the progress? How did it all come to pass?"

It might be answered that the scientists and engineers were responsible—after all, it was they who developed the technology. But is this really the answer, all by itself? Remember, it was the foresight and drive of Vail the manager that got the technical effort started, so in a sense it was he who was the principal innovator.

Yet the answer is still incomplete. There was one more essential factor—I mean the public consensus, the political decision. In the last analysis, this is what made it possible for the science of Jewett to implement the goals of Vail (*Business Week*, July 17, 1965: 88).

MAINTAINING THE "RIGHT" BALANCE
BETWEEN GOVERNMENT AND BUSINESS

Both governments and business seek to pursue certain broad goals society sets for them, and each is given powers to achieve these goals. Pursuit of these goals results in conflicting as well as complementary actions. Throughout our history the question has continuously arisen as to the proper relationships between the powers of governments and individuals in economic life. The matter has been settled in each age, and in a very broad and general way, I think a proper relationship has been found in the sense that the objectives society has seemed to set for its social and economic system have been pursued with some success and without either government or business overpowering the other.

Unbalance from whatever source, and in the direction of either government or business, is likely to create more rather than less government influence in economic affairs. Too strong powers in the hands of business, as compared with government, can lead to less concern about the production of social goods and services, less concern about the social costs of progress, and increasing devotion to those selfish interests of business that may be in conflict with general social interests. Eventually, a popular reaction is likely to lead to greater government controls in the public interest. It is possible, too, as happened in Germany and Italy prior to World War II, that business domination of government can lead to an authoritarian government which eventually dominates business. Either way, government power increases relative to business power. There is no reason to believe that either scenario is at all likely in the foreseeable future of this country, but the potential for an imbalance of power on the side of business must be considered.

On the other hand, too great and misguided government control of business can weaken the ability of businessmen to operate effectively in achieving the objectives society sets for business. Too rapid expansion of government regulations, for example, can impair the ability of industry to achieve and maintain high levels of economic activity and to increase output per unit of input. If this happens, new pressures for further government action to remedy the situation can be expected.

I think the prospects are excellent that through this century at least, the power relationships between governments and business in the United States will be reasonably balanced. Neither will so dominate the other as to shatter that partnership arrangement in which both contribute to the achievement of the primary goals society sets, and in which private citizens in their economic pursuits enjoy a high level of economic and political freedom. To ensure this result, however, will require conscious effort. The following are a few suggested principles which may be useful in maintaining a proper balance as new problems are faced in the years ahead.

The Principle of Comparative Performance An effort should always be made to determine whether business or government can best perform an activity that is needed by society. Each has strengths and weaknesses. There clearly are certain activities that government can perform more efficiently than individuals in the private sector. For instance, government is the superior institution to express common social goals, to establish policies over a wide range of activities (foreign affairs and national security), and to tax for social purposes.

On the other hand, government has grave deficiencies as compared with other institutions in performing certain functions. For instance, once government undertakes a function, it generates interest groups and constituents. One result of this is virtual impossibility of abandoning the activity even though it is no longer needed. Another is that it generates pressures for expansion of the activity.

Costs of government management of productive facilities are likely to be higher than in the private sector because of a requirement for "accounting for the last penny," because equal attention must be given to the unimportant and the most important elements of the activity, because in government operations personnel loyalty is often more valued than personnel efficiency, and because any activity assumed by government becomes part of a huge bureaucracy having inherent inefficiencies resulting from its size.

Business can avoid these problems more readily than can governments. Even the largest businesses are smaller than governments and therefore enjoy an advantage in flexibility and adaptability. For these reasons, it would seem sensible to assign to governments and businesses the production of those goods and services which clearly are their responsibility and which each can produce at the lowest cost, using that word broadly. Peter Drucker calls for a "reprivatization" of governmental activities (1969(A): 234). What he has in mind is to make the federal government the central social institution of society, establishing policies for social action and using nongovernmental institutions for actual operations, performance, and execution. Such a clean-cut division is not possible, but an effort to approach it is sensible. The federal government has followed this principle with respect to military equipment. This is now produced principally in the private sector, whereas it used to be produced mostly in government arsenals. In many areas, however, government assumes responsibilities which could be carried out in the nongovernmental sector, such as training the unemployed, medical research, construction, and commodity storage, to name a few.

One classic illustration of a need for implementing the principle set forth here concerns the Post Office. For years those who wanted to improve postal service and have it operate profitably have advocated that it be placed in the hands of a privately run corporation. A Presidential Commission on Postal Organization made the latest recommendation for such action in 1968. As a result of the following debates and pressure from the White House, Congress in August 1970 passed legislation which, while not creating a private corporation, has partially removed the agency from political interference. The Postmaster General is no longer a Cabinet officer but is selected by a nine-man board of directors chosen by the President. Within limits this new agency may increase postal rates, raise money through bond issues, and in other ways operate the function somewhat independently of Congress.

In our increasingly complex society the possibilities of effective action in the public interest through joint business-government operations are increasing in number. In a sense, the aerospace industry represents a joint private-public activity. COMSAT is a more recent example in which government and private industry have joined forces to establish a private corporation to purchase and operate communications satellites.

The Principle of Limiting Individual Economic Freedom Individual economic freedom should be limited only to fill a need that is clearly demonstrated to be in the public interest. What is meant here is that complicated and interdependent social and economic relationships demand some limitations on the exercise of individual economic freedom. Each encroachment on individual economic freedom, however, ought to be roughly measured against the gains to society as a whole sought by the control measure. The principle is that individual freedoms should not be restricted unless there results a correspondingly greater increase in benefits to the community as a whole, desired by the community, and achievable in no other way. This is not an easy test to apply or meet. It is difficult at times to determine when the principle is followed. Broadly, for example, it means that a banker is not free to use resources at his disposal as he sees fit. His economic freedom is restrained to protect his depositors. Probably a central issue in increased taxation is the fact that individual rights over income are restricted with every increase in taxes. Presumably, the restriction is justified because the rights of others as well as the individual taxpayer may be advanced by the expenditures of government. If business profits are reduced by taxes to acquire funds to subsidize the income of farmers, an effort should be made to determine whether the public advantage is great enough to justify the tax.

Economic goods may be divided into two types: individual goods and social goods. The two types differ essentially in terms of demand and, from the point of view of government, in the likelihood of private production in socially sufficient quantities. Individual goods are usually divisible, costs of production can be allocated to the purchaser, and the amount produced can be adjusted to individual demand. In this category are such things as apples, nuts and bolts, tractors, locomotives, pencils, etc. Social goods, on the other hand, are usually not divisible, are not equated with individual demand, and may not be produced at all, or may be produced in very limited quantities, by individual enterprises. Such goods benefit the entire community, and the costs are not and cannot be directly borne by individual consumers on the basis of their consumption. Such goods are education, flood control, conservation of resources, and national security. These goods are subject more to collective than to individual demand. How far should the government go in producing them? The abstract maxim is that the government should increase the production of social goods (assuming a community demand) no further than the point at which the marginal social benefit is the same from all government expenditures, per dollar of the expenditures, and is equal to marginal social cost. At this point, the marginal social benefit from government expenditures is equal to the marginal social benefit from individual expenditures on privately produced goods.

Marginal social benefit is the total net gain in satisfactions to the community over time from the production of an incremental unit of a social good. Thus, the marginal social benefit of an expenditure is equal to the total net benefit to the community of the incremental dollar which government spends on a social good. Marginal social benefit would therefore be, in soil conservation for instance, the net satisfactions accruing to the community from the last dollar spent by the government for this purpose. Total benefits are measured by the benefits to persons getting funds from soil conservation, together with benefits to society in many different directions, such as flood control when it is tied into conservation, reforestation, the curtailment of soil depletion, and so on.

Marginal social cost, on the other hand, is the sacrifice to society incurred by the use of resources for producing the social good. It is the cost to society measured by the alternative use of the resources spent on the last unit of the social good. In this illustration, it would be the cost incurred by society as a result of the reduced production of other goods (and the want satisfactions they would have fulfilled) necessitated by the marginal expenditure for conservation.

Additional expenditures for a social good run into a law of diminishing returns. After a certain point is reached, the benefits to society of additional social goods decline. Similarly, the marginal cost mounts with additional expenditures by government for the social good. At some point, theoretically, the production by government of social goods balances with the social cost of producing those goods. At that point, the community is getting the maximum advantage out of the production. Expenditures beyond that point result in a social cost greater than the social benefit. Below that point there may be a spread between benefit and cost that would make additional expenditures worthwhile in the social interest.

Now, quite obviously, it is not possible to apply this measure with any degree of precision. And even if it were possible to apply it with mathematical accuracy, it might not be desirable to do so. For example, the community calculation of social benefit might lag far behind the realities of the need for substantial expenditures, say, for national security. Government leadership in the face of a threat to national security might push the expenditures for national security beyond the point where there is an equation between marginal social benefit and marginal social cost, as the community at the moment might see it. The community may gradually shift its concept of costs and benefits over time, but government as the protector of the social and economic systems may have to act promptly at any one point in time. The whole principle is extremely rough—so rough, in fact, that it remains a general principle rather than a precise yardstick. But it is a principle that is significant in focusing attention on alternative costs of action. It emphasizes the need for government to weigh social and individual advantage against individual and social disadvantage.

Indirect v. Direct Controls Experience shows clearly that indirect controls over business are generally preferable to direct controls. Indirect controls have the great advantage of permitting individuals and businesses wider freedom in decision-making. Direct controls generally are more difficult to administer, inevitably generate additional direct controls, and create inequities in application. The experience with wage and price controls during the past few years illustrates this point.

Other Guides Without elaboration other guidelines to preserving the "best" balance between business and government are as follows. The profit motive is a powerful driving force and to the extent that government can appeal to it by offering the proper incentives the public interest can be advanced by business. The optimum chance of advancing the public interest exists in an evolutionary change in the basic institutions of society as contrasted with a revolutionary change. Hence, new government controls should avoid drastic changes in the basic institutions of the individual enterprise system unless such action is clearly required as, for instance, in time of war. This is a lesson that history has repeatedly taught. New regulations ought to be clear and not fuzzy. Obsolete regulations ought to be eliminated. It goes without saying that new regulations must be formulated and implemented through democratic processes. The more knowledgeable are public servants of business affairs, and vice versa, the more enlightened are the interrelationships of the two likely to be. We simply must, as emphasized previously, learn how to plan better in the public sector.

Requirements on the Part of Business The business-government power balance is also dependent upon business behavior. As noted previously, it is very important for business, especially the larger companies, to step up to their assumption of social responsibilities. Enough has been said about that and the consequences if the obligation is not discharged appropriately.

Individual businesses, and groups of businessmen, also must act responsibly in lobbying and dealing with regulatory agencies. Lobbies and pressure groups can and do perform many valuable services, but if their selfish interests are pursued at the expense of the public interest, the welfare of the nation is not served. There is no implication in this statement that there is always a conflict between selfish business interests and the public interest. Both can be advanced at the same time. For instance, a tax incentive to industry to buy capital equipment at a time of low economic activity can help individual businesses and advance the general welfare.

Honest men differ, of course, about what is or is not in the public interest and about what a proper trade-off should be between the public and private interests. In many cases, however, the answers seem clear across a broad spectrum of political and economic philosophy. For instance, the basic principle seems to be violated when an industry receives special tax benefits without any corresponding resulting calculable public benefits, or when an industry is able to prevent needed safety or health regulations, or when an industry is able to so influence government as to prevent laws affecting it from being applied.

A few other responsibilities of business follow. Business must continue to be efficient in producing the goods and services that society wants. The level of ethics and morality in business must continue to rise. Practices which cheat the consumer, deceive the public, and evade government laws certainly ought to be eliminated by businessmen. Business must maintain an acceptable balance between preserving traditional tested methods for achieving rising productivity and output and the new requirements of society demanding change in business philosophy, practice, and organization.

CHAPTER TWENTY-TWO

The
Political Role
of Business
in Public Affairs

INTRODUCTION

Business most certainly is not a passive agent accepting the regulations, directions, or favors of government. Business collectively, and businessmen individually, assert influence throughout the political processes of the nation. In this chapter, my objective is to examine the many ways in which business seeks to influence public affairs. Arguments for and against political involvement will be examined at some length. The question of how influential the political activity of business really is will also be considered. Finally, a few views will be presented on the question of whether lobbying is good or evil.

THE POLITICAL PROCESS AND THE POLITICAL ACTIVITIES OF BUSINESS

In recognition of the need for individuals in a political democracy to have access to representatives in government, the Constitution provides that "Congress shall make no law . . . prohibiting the free exercise . . . of the right of the people . . . to petition the Government for a redress of grievances." From the beginning, there has been no hesitancy in using this provision by the people individually and in groups. In a very real measure, this sentence constitutes a "bill of rights" for pressure groups and lobbying activities, and such interests so construe the provision. Given the nature of politics, and the fact of government's importance to business, the inevitability of corporate political activity is clear in governmental affairs as well as in the affairs of other institutions in society which vitally affect business interests. But two issues arise immediately. First, irrespective of the long history of business's political involvement, is it necessary and/or desirable for business enterprises to engage in politics? Second, is this involvement legitimate, that is, is it rightful? On both questions the answers given by businessmen and academic scholars cover the ground from a thumping no to an emphatic yes. Later in the chapter we shall return to these questions, but before dealing with them it is essential to understand the nature and experience of political involvement by business and businessmen.

There are two basic areas of political involvement. The first concerns the electoral process and the second relates to governmental activities. In the first would be included such activities as the selection and support of candidates for public office and of political parties, as well as issues to be decided by the voting public. Governmental activities are concerned with efforts by individuals or groups to influence the formulation of legislation, its implementation, its enforcement, and its adjudication.

Is it a corporation or individuals in it, or both, that become politically involved? The answer is that all do. Furthermore, the corporation and individuals in it are members of and support other groups that seek to exert influence in the corporate as well as their individual interests. Corporations as organizations do have interests which may or may not coincide with the interests of persons in it. As pointed out elsewhere, it is generally the case that the interests of top management and those of the corporation as an entity tend to coincide. Generally, too, the interests of most managers are in harmony with broad company objectives. So close are these interests that it is difficult if not impossible at times to determine whether an executive of a company reflects the company or his private interests when he speaks on public issues.

CURRENT TRENDS IN THE POLITICAL
ACTIVITIES OF BUSINESS

Recent patterns of the political involvement of business in governmental activities have been somewhat different from those of the past. First, there is less emphasis today on the electoral process. As will be demonstrated shortly, business still is involved in the electoral process, but neither as directly nor in the same fashion as in the past. Second, corporate leaders are more willing to speak out on political issues. In the past, business leaders generally followed a policy of silence about their political activities. Crawford Greenewalt, when president of E. I. du Pont de Nemours & Co., set the current trend when he said: "It is . . . the corporation's proper duty to oppose, through proper means, any action which threatens the property or the interests of its stockholders, to fight hard if the well-being of its employees is threatened, or if the successful continuity of its life comes under fire. The normal machinery of government provides the platform" (Greenewalt, 1959(A): 9). Third, there has been a recent trend for corporations, particularly the large ones, to engage in political activities themselves and to rely less on trade associations and other organized groups which speak on behalf of business. The major reason for this is that corporations today have particular interests of their own and sufficient funds to exert pressure in behalf of their own interests.

Fourth, the political activity of business is becoming increasingly bipartisan. Although not all businessmen were members of the Republican party in the past, that party was considered to be the party of business and most businessmen supported it. They were not often disappointed, because the Republicans did speak for the business community. In contrast with the past, more and more corporations have adopted the policy of nonpartisanship. In recent presidential campaigns, for instance, the Democratic party candidate has had substantial business support. There are many explanations of this trend. Aside from the particular candidates, it is probably correct to say that the Democratic party in recent years has sought to build cordial relations with the business community. One result has been the substantial increase in the appointments of businessmen to posts in Democratic administrations. Fifth, there has been an increased intermingling of businessmen and government executives in ways which will be illustrated shortly. Sixth, there has been a substantial increase in intracompany political activities as evidenced by the growth of public affairs departments. This, too, will be discussed later. Seventh, there has been an expansion in both the scope and depth of business activities. Eighth, in recent years more and more companies have established public affairs functional offices, and they are increasing their scope of responsibilities. These functions will be examined in some detail in the following section. Altogether, it is fair to conclude that the agility of the businessman in the political arena to satisfy his self-interest is today more sophisticated than in the past. This is especially true among managers of the larger corporations.

THE PUBLIC AFFAIRS FUNCTION IN BUSINESS

Today, just about every large corporation and many smaller ones have public affairs offices. The great majority have been created within the past dozen years (Bradt, 1969). The public affairs function of a company embraces those activities which it pursues to shape the political, social, and economic environment in which it operates.

This activity is somewhat different from the public relations function, which is concerned with the evaluation of public attitudes and the execution of a program to win public understanding and acceptance of views and activities of the company and its managers. The public affairs function conceptually can include the public relations function because it covers a greater area. In some companies, the public affairs function is placed under the jurisdiction of the public relations unit; in others, the public relations unit is under the public affairs unit; in still others, the two are separated. The well-developed public affairs function will encompass the following major areas (NICB, 1968: 1–2):

> **Government Relations** The government relations area covers a review of proposed legislation of interest to the company and contacts with legislators and governmental officials regarding legislation and administration of regulations of interest to the company.

> **Encouragement of Employee Political Activity** Another public affairs function is to encourage political activity. This covers corporate efforts to encourage employees to take more interest in and participate in the governmental processes as voters, supporters of a political party, or candidates for public office. For the most part, such activities are non-partisan, but in some companies they are partisan and are directed at the election of public servants whose attitudes the company finds congenial to its interests.

> **Political and Economic Education** Included in this area are educational programs to promote better understanding among employees of the American political and economic systems.

> **Community Service** Community service activities embrace company contributions to educational, health and welfare, and civic institutions; and the encouragement of employee support of and participation in community service organizations.

> **Environmental Problem Solution** The public affairs office also is concerned with those activities undertaken by a company on its own initiative or in cooperation with other organizations, public and private, to help solve socioeconomic problems such as air and water pollution, job training, transportation, and urban renewal.

The objectives of public affairs departments vary greatly, but for a reasonably comprehensive program, the following stand out (derived from job descriptions of heads of public affairs departments): to maintain a favorable governmental relations climate for the company; to coordinate the public affairs activities of the company; to coordinate and aid individual managers in accomplishing or furthering company objectives in government circles; to develop and recommend company policy in the areas of governmental and public affairs; to promote the sale of company products to government agencies; to advise top management on major political or legislative developments affecting the company; to review and follow up on major legislation of direct concern to the company; to review and follow up on administrative rules of government agencies which affect the company; to present the company position or arrange for presentations regarding government relations to achieve better corporate-community relations; and to conduct corporate political educational programs.

Sethi surveyed larger companies and found that only 14 percent had formal policies concerning political activities. He also found that the larger the company the greater the probability that a formal policy existed. Despite the absence of formal policies in many companies he said that most companies indicated that they felt corporations should participate in bipartisan activities aimed at promoting good government at local, state, and federal levels and also in civic causes in the communities where their operations were located (1972).

THE PURSUIT OF POLITICAL ACTIVITIES

There are many methods by which business pursues its political activities. Some companies have their own public affairs departments and act independently of other companies. Other companies exert their influence through trade associations, other organized groups, or by hiring men and organizations to promote their interests. In addition, of course, there are methods associated with the individual activities of employees. These can take many forms—all the way from managers seeking elective office to managers trying to influence friends in government. Some of the more common and important techniques are discussed below.

Pressure Groups, Lobbies, and Blocs Before proceeding, it is important to define a few of the terms which will be used frequently in this chapter. Pressure groups are associations of individuals that exert influence on government. They are groups of individuals in the community having a common interest or interests which collectively they seek to secure. Their efforts are directed toward getting legislation that favors their interests on the statute books and toward preventing the passage of legislation contrary to their interests, as they see them. The influence exerted by pressure groups frequently extends throughout the political process to include not only the formulation of legislation, but the process of choosing legislative representatives, selecting and hiring government employees, the process by which legislation is interpreted and executed, and the judicial process in which the legality of legislation is tested. Looked at in this way, of course, pressure groups sit astride the political processes.

A lobby is the point of contact of the pressure group in the legislature or in the administrative agencies of government. At this point, representatives of the pressure group seek to influence legislators and the way in which laws are administered. A single individual is called a lobbyist; a group of individuals with a large pressure group behind it is called a lobby. (The Regulation of Lobbying Act of 1946 has a much more elaborate definition of lobbyist.) To most people, the term "lobbyist" is considered a word of opprobrium. Lobbyists do not like it. A California lobby-investigating committee suggested the euphemism "legislative advocate."

A bloc is something more amorphous than either a pressure group or a lobby. It means a combination of pressure groups, friendly legislators, and lobbyists who in alliance influence legislation. For example, by the "farm bloc" is meant congressmen and senators who are friendly to and frequently share the point of view of agricultural pressure groups; the large farm organizations that represent farmers as a broad occupation group; and those farm organizations that represent particular agricultural interests, such as those of the citrus-fruit growers, nut growers, dairy farmers, and so on. Similarly, of course, from time to time labor blocs and business blocs are formed.

Business Interests Organizations There are thousands of national associations organized to represent group interests. No one knows precisely how many. The major national organizations that represent all business, however, are these four: the National Association of Manufacturers (NAM), the United States Chamber of Commerce (USCC), the Committee for Economic Development (CED), and the Business Council.

The oldest of these is the NAM, founded in 1895. It has always been a focal point for the expression of the "business point of view." It boasts a membership of 14,000 companies, mostly small firms having under 500 employees. It is financed, however, by a handful of large corporations. The NAM is a mutual and cooperative association, whose voluntary membership develops policies, points of view, and directions of influence.

The second nationwide organization, the USCC, was founded in 1912 and is today the largest business outpost in Washington, D.C. It is a federation of business organizations embracing some 2,700 local chambers of commerce, 42 state chambers, and 1,200 trade associations and comparable groups. Whereas the NAM speaks for its corporate members, the Chamber is the spearhead of a galaxy of organizations. Policies are determined at annual meetings and by responses from member organizations on pressing issues. Like the NAM, the Chamber undertakes substantial research projects and public educational campaigns on behalf of business. A widely read magazine, *Nation's Business*, carries the word of the Chamber throughout the nation.

The CED, discussed at length in Chapter 9, is unique among business associations. Its lobbying, if it can be called that, is restricted to the enunciation of policy statements read not only by businessmen, but by legislators, government officials, professors, and the lay public. The CED has often differed sharply with the NAM and the Chamber.

The Business Council was founded in 1933, when President Roosevelt asked to have organized a group of top-echelon businessmen with whom the New Deal administrators could exchange views about key economic issues that were then of crucial importance to government and business. Its prestige has grown through the years, and it now includes the heads of the most important corporations, many of whom have held high government posts. The council has several meetings a year, at which its members receive briefings from top government officials, including cabinet officers, and enjoy the company and the ear of Presidents. Beyond the meetings, the council maintains liaison committees which work with individual government departments concerned with the economy, such as Labor, Treasury, Commerce, the Council of Economic Advisers, and the Bureau of the Budget. These committees give unofficial advice to the departments.

In addition to these organizations are the hundreds of national organizations representing business. Virtually every line of industrial and commercial activity has its own association. Simply to illustrate the variety, there are: the American Beekeeping Federation, the American Insurance Association, the American Paper Institute, the Association of Japanese Textile Importers, Inc., the American Iron and Steel Institute, the National Electrical Manufacturers Association, the Distilled Spirits Institute, the Institute of Pharmaceutical Manufacturers, the American Federation of Retail Kosher Butchers, and the Peanut Butter Manufacturers Association. Then there are regional and local business groups, such as the Western States Meat Packers Association and the Southwestern Peanut Shellers' Association.

Prior to World War II these groups often spoke with a single voice, especially in matters concerning labor unions. Since then, however, there has been an increasing divergence of views, and it is not now unusual to find bitter controversy among some of the trade associations. Continuous skirmishes occur, for example, between truckers and carriers, manufacturers and distributors, bankers and borrowers, and raw material producers and end-product manufacturers. Despite these divergences, however, there is within the business group, as within the labor and farm groups, a broad class unity on fundamental issues of concern to business.

Legislative and Administrative Contacts There is an extensive and increasingly intimate range of communications between business and government officials. Businessmen and their spokesmen, for instance, are constantly appearing before legislative committees considering legislative action or investigating some problem. Appearances before committees may be solicited by the committee members themselves or by those businessmen who are likely to be affected by the proposed legislation. Various pieces of legislation provide for business representatives' appearances before administrative committees. The Federal Administrative Procedure Act of 1946, for instance, gives groups affected by an administrative ruling an opportunity to submit their positions to the agency involved. Many agencies ask those who are to be affected by a rule to appear before the agency decision-makers to comment on the proposed decisions.

Joint Government-Business Decision-making There is an increasing meshing of business and government decision-makers on the formulation and execution of public policies. The first important large-scale cooptation of corporate leaders in the government decision-making process occurred during World War I, when many wartime agencies were manned by businessmen on loan to government for the duration of the emergency. These men, many of whom were paid by their companies, acted as government officials and were involved in the administration of controls over industry, often including their own industries and companies. The reason for this was the fact that there was a great scarcity of personnel in government service who had the experience, knowledge, and leadership ability to mobilize industry in the fashion required. During World War II, and again during the Korean War, the government agencies concerned with control over industry were manned principally by businessmen who were drawn temporarily into federal government service. In addition to businessmen who were full-time employees of government, scores of advisory committees were manned mostly by businessmen.

Since the end of World War II, a number of government agencies —notably the Departments of Commerce, Defense, and the Interior— have continued the use of business advisory committees. There are many committees in the federal government composed wholly or principally of men from business, whose recommendations are frequently followed, although the action is taken in the name of the government. Businessmen also participate in the decision-making processes in state and local governments in similar ways.

There are sound reasons for this sort of joint action. The government has found itself deeply involved with the business community in matters of major importance to the economy which require for rational decision-making knowledge found only in the business world. In addition, the increasing delegation of governmental activities to private corporations—such as the space and defense programs —necessitates joint decision-making. As government-industry relationships come closer together, one can expect that these types of relationships will continue to increase and deepen.

Businessmen in Government Positions Businessmen have always been employed in government offices and have thus been in a position to act upon their own views. This is not meant to imply that when a businessman becomes a public official, he will take a parochial business view in making his decisions. Businessmen, like anyone else, can and do act in conformity with the public interest. During my own experience in the federal government, for example, I have seen many businessmen act in what they thought was the public interest at high expense to business interests in general and their own companies in particular. In recent years, the number of business leaders has increased significantly at the top levels of government, as well as in the legislature. In the states, also, there is a trend toward more businessmen accepting appointments as government officials. The reasons given above for this trend apply here. In addition, some politicians think businessmen know how to do things more efficiently than typical government officials, a view which will be examined later.

The Washington Office More companies are establishing offices to represent them in the nation's capital. Among the 200 largest manufacturing companies, a Washington representative is the rule rather than the exception. A study of over 1,000 companies showed that 17 percent maintained a Washington representative (NICB, 1968: 8). This same study showed that fewer than 6 percent of the companies surveyed maintained branch offices in state capitals.

Companies do not look upon their Washington representatives as "ambassadors plenipotentiary." They view them more as a specialized minister than as a representative with full decision-making powers. They are considered to be special staff. The functions of these representatives generally are essentially commercial—gathering marketing intelligence, soliciting sales, and laying the groundwork for better relationships between the company and a government agency. The representative, typically, is in communication with his trade association, often helps government agencies without compensation, arranges appointments between his company and government officials, and appears before legislative committees, but does not enter into politics directly with a view toward defeating some politician or electing a friend (Cherington and Gillen, 1962; Dexter, 1969).

Washington Public Relations Agents There are in Washington, as well as in the capitals of each of the states, individuals and organizations that represent business firms and associations. Many are lawyers and legal firms, many operate as individuals, and many are public relations firms. They are lobbyists, but prefer to be called by such names as public relations experts, government affairs representatives, or business advocates. These individuals and firms provide different services for the firms they represent, and operate in various ways. The following are among the types of functions performed (Rosenbloom, in Roalman, 1968; and Dexter, 1969):

First, there is fact finding. Every day the federal government spews out an ocean of facts that are of importance to business but that are not readily available or understandable to the typical business which should be concerned. The U.S. Government Printing Office is the largest publisher in the world, and every government agency distributes a flood of bulletins. Yet, only a small fraction of the knowledge of government gets into print, and the bulk of that which is made available does not reach the eyes of the businessman who might be vitally interested in it. A Washington representative can provide valuable services by digging out of the mass of knowledge in Washington that which is of concern to his client and getting the information interpreted and to his client. But the function of the Washington representative does not stop at fact finding. It also involves sniffing out pending policies and actions that might be of concern to clients. His activities may take him to Congress to discover pending legislation; to the executive offices of government to uncover impending or new procedures and administrative decisions; or to the many organizations in Washington that can influence a client, such as world financial institutions.

Most Washington representatives go beyond the fact-gathering function. They may analyze what is going on that is of interest to clients and explain why it is happening. If it is of sufficient importance to a client for him to wish to react, the representative will help him decide the best move to make. Another important function of Washington representatives is to inform government about business. Laws, policies, and administrative actions are not made in a vacuum. They are made by people who want to act in a responsible way toward business, and this requires not only knowledge about business, but about potential impacts of proposed actions. When the Congress was considering legislation concerning automobile safety, for instance, the testimony of the automobile producers was sought on all sorts of technical matters.

Many Washington representatives go beyond these functions and seek to influence government action. They then become advocates. Their techniques range from personal influence exerted on the Burning Tree Country Club golf course during a game between two old friends, one of whom happens to be a congressman and the other a lobbyist, to a massive campaign to stir up popular support throughout the nation for their client's point of view. They may even help congressmen write their speeches on pending issues. Finally, a Washington representative can, like a company's office, act as a sales representative before government agencies.

There is no reasonably accurate tabulation of the numbers of such representatives in the seats of government in the United States.

In Washington, D.C., alone there are some 4,000 lawyers who act in one way or another as representatives of business. In addition, of course, there are thousands of employees in public relations firms.

Intracompany Political Activities An NICB survey of over 1,000 corporations showed that 53 percent offered some form of political education that was based on the dissemination of printed materials. Of the 553 companies that provided political education, 278 offered formal in-plant instruction in the form of "practical politics" courses. Most of these courses were conducted a few times a year, but in 77 companies they were continuous (NICB, 1968: 22). Most of these courses were introduced in recent years. The approach is basically to impart information and is nonpartisan, although a number of programs are slanted toward the "business point of view." Most companies offering such courses open them to all employees, although a few limit attendance to salaried and supervisory personnel.

Corporate contributions or expenditures in connection with federal primary or general elections are prohibited by Section 610 of the United States Criminal Code, and more than half the states have similar legislation banning corporate expenditures in state elections. Corporations can, however, encourage employees to engage in electoral political activity. Almost 80 percent of 1,000 companies surveyed encouraged employees to register and vote; 63 percent encouraged employees to express political views; 41 percent encouraged employee contributions to political parties; 36 percent encouraged their employees to hold appointive public office; and 30 percent encouraged them to run for elective public office (NICB, 1968: 16).

Two basic reasons are given for management encouragement of employee contributions to political parties. One is the rising cost of campaigns and the need to broaden the financial support. The other is that managements believe such contributions make the political processes more real to the giver. Officeholding is encouraged for many reasons: It is a natural outgrowth of active participation in politics; and intangible benefits accrue to the firms of employee officeholders. Some firms discourage their employees from accepting or seeking public office because they feel conflicts of interest may develop (NICB, 1968: 16–19).

The Public Relations Function The public relations function has been a part of corporate activity for many decades. Public relations activities may be said to relate to the communications a corporation has with individuals and groups inside and outside the corporation in order to better relate the corporation to its environment so that its basic objectives may be more readily achieved (Eells, 1959: 15; and 1960: 278). Stated in this way, public relations is part of and can be subsumed under the broader definition of public affairs given early in this chapter.

Public relations activities and institutions have arisen for political rather than economic reasons, they are an attempt to influence beliefs through mass communications. While businessmen have said that their public relations were often stimulated by a feeling of moral responsibility to individuals as human beings, to customers, and to society, Raucher concludes that it was rather a reaction to public sentiment and a desire to be free from regulations that caused them to be public relations-minded (1968).

Public relations today in most companies is not mere publicity, propaganda, or advocacy. It is an effort to stimulate good will in the community through all available communications media. This means, among other things, that a public relations department will listen to communications from the outside as well as send out messages. A large corporation has many "publics" with whom communications must be maintained for political, economic, and sociological pur-poses. Among the publics are members of the national community; citizens, voters, and constituents; customers, shareowners, employ-ees, and suppliers of the company; the press; educators; members of and leaders of religious groups; people in government; members of the financial community; members of labor organizations; members of industry and trade associations; members of service organizations; people in professional life; and people in their roles as members of fraternal, cultural, and ethnic associations (Eells, 1960: 290–91). Viewed in this way, public relations may refer to a campaign by a corporation to make its company slogan a household word. For ex-ample, duPont's "Better things for better living through chemistry"; Westinghouse's "You can be sure if it's Westinghouse"; and Ford's "Ford has a better idea." In an entirely different direction, it can refer to efforts to influence voters to pass a local bond issue or to support one proposition over another of concern to business.

BUSINESS AND THE LOCAL COMMUNITY

During the nineteenth and early twentieth centuries the political and social life of many towns was dominated by one or two companies. With the rise of large national corporations and urban growth, cor-porations withdrew from the social and political life of the com-munities in which they did business. In more recent years, however, large corporations have become more interested in local affairs. This is not due alone to the social problems of local communities in which larger companies have an interest, but also to the realization that their noninvolvement led to increasing control by political machines, labor groups, minority groups, and local small businessmen.

The patterns of today's involvement vary a great deal. There are few towns in which large companies dominate social and political life in a fashion reminiscent of the nineteenth century. One such is Bartlesville, Oklahoma, a small town which is the headquarters of the Phillips Petroleum Company. "The town's economy, cultural affairs, civic projects, social activities, and politics," assert two scholars, "are benevolently guided by Phillips or its employees" (Rogers and Zimet, in Berg, 1968: 48). A few other communities and companies in comparable circumstances are Hershey, Pennsylvania, and the Hershey Chocolate Corporation; Kannapolis, North Carolina, and the Cannon Mills Company; and Middletown, Ohio, and the Armco Steel Corporation. A diffusion of power exists in large cities, so that no major corporation is dominant. In large cities, however, coalitions of business interests are frequently formed to influence some social or political action.

The modern trend is toward businesses helping communities to solve their problems. This is illustrated by the creation in 1967 in the Ford Motor Company of the Urban Affairs Department. Its purpose is "to develop positive programs through which the resources of the company could be marshalled to work effectively with governmental and private organizations in attacking urban problems" (Bradt, 1969: 21).

THE CASE FOR THE POLITICAL INVOLVEMENT OF BUSINESS

In the following discussion of pros and cons of business's political involvement, I have in mind principally the effort to influence the making and executing of public policy. Managers and scholars are found on both sides of the issue, and both present a variety of arguments to support their positions. Among these arguments are the following:

To Maintain an Environment Favorable to Business I suppose that if a poll were taken, more businessmen would subscribe to this reason for involvement than any other. There are a number of aspects of this general rationale for involvement.

Business understands that the legislative process is one of compromise in which pressure groups seek government action in their behalf. If business does not speak up, its voice will not be heard except as its point of view may be held by a legislator or government administrator. The volume of proposals before legislatures is increasing, and business finds in much of the proposed legislation measures which, if passed into law, would make its life difficult. More than 26,000 measures were introduced in the 89th Congress. Among the 50 state legislatures in one recent year, there were 127,000 bills and resolutions, of which over 40,000 were enacted into law (NICB, 1968: 6). A large number of these would have restricted business in its operations had not business exerted a counterpressure. This is not to say, of course, that the result is always in the public interest. The point here is that if business did not exert its power in the legislative process, it might be overwhelmed with restrictive laws. Because of the way the political processes operate, of course, business exerts pressure on legislatures to get benefits. Business initiates legislation in its behalf, such as subsidies, favorable tax laws, exemptions from antitrust laws, help in selling abroad, and so on. Businessmen, as V. O. Key points out (1958: 103), are a small minority and highly vulnerable to political attacks. Furthermore, he says, businessmen lack the moral authority that attaches to a tradition of agrarian work ethics, or the inherent rightness conferred by calloused hands. To protect themselves from unjust restraints, they must use their wits and money to influence public opinion and to exercise a counterbalance in the legislative processes.

There are many businessmen who recognize the need to become involved in the political processes, but who do so reluctantly. This is particularly so in the electoral processes and in the formulation of new legislation. They have a negative view of politicians and would rather not become involved in what they consider to be immoral activities (Powell and Nelson, 1966: 42).

There are yet other motivations for the businessman to influence his environment. For instance, he knows that social disruption is not to his advantage and may be catastrophic to him, to his ideology, or possibly to his business. As a result, he becomes more interested in the political processes associated with social problems. He has community spirit and helps in bond drives and welfare appeals not only with his money, but also with his time. He may be public spirited enough to want to serve as a public servant. Clarence Randall, former chairman of the board of Inland Steel, strongly advocated that business serve government. "I hold the conviction," he said, "that the first job of the American businessman is not his duty to his company but his duty to his country. Businessmen should participate in government" (*Wall Street Journal*, July 28, 1954).

To Inject Rational Thinking into Government Not all businessmen are modest when comparing their managerial capabilities with those of government servants. They often assert that it is important for business skills in thinking rationally and in managing efficiently to be introduced into government; and they are the ones, naturally, to do it. If government decisions are made on the basis of businesslike rationality, it is asserted, the government will become more efficient. Greater efficiency and reduced costs of operation will then be of benefit to everyone.

There is little doubt that the injection of some business methods into government will improve efficiency. On the other hand, the problem of improving the rationality of government decision-making and raising the efficiency of its operations is not one which is solvable by transplanting business management to government operations. To begin with, the words "efficiency" and "rationality" mean different things in the two areas. A rational decision generally can be defined as one that effectively and efficiently assures the achievement of the aims for which the means are selected. Effectiveness refers to the accomplishment of purpose, and efficiency relates to the optimum relationship between input and output. While there are many types of rationality in business operations, generally speaking, that decision is most rational which adds most to profits because the fundamental objective of business is to use resources efficiently and in doing so make profits. This test can be applied in but rare instances in government and only where the activity in question is really a profit-making business.

Government objectives are made in the political process and are based upon political and social values, whereas business objectives are fundamentally based on financial self-interest values. Business measures of success, therefore, often are completely inapplicable to governmental operations. The effectiveness of the State Department has nothing to do with how much money it spends or saves. If effectiveness and efficiency are optimized by a federal budget which comes closest to meeting basic objectives at less cost, the President probably can do a better job of this himself without association with Congress. To do so, however, would violate the basic principles of this political democracy (Fisher, 1962).

Furthermore, I have seen businessmen come to high executive positions in Washington with unsullied reputations for superior managerial efficiency and, after a short time, leave in frustration because the governmental managerial task baffled them. Managing in government is far different from managing in business, aside from the differences in rationality and efficiency. The entire milieu is different. Requirements for managerial success are different. Methods of dealing with people are different. The location of power and its impact are different. The rules of the game are different. This does not mean that most of the fundamental principles and practices for efficient business management are inapplicable in government affairs. What it means is that the ways in which they are used, and the conditions which make them effective or ineffective, are very much different between a private business and a governmental agency.

In sum, no one would deny that there is great need for more efficiency, effectiveness, and rationality in government decision-making and management. Furthermore, it is fortunate that government is coming to see that it can use more of the methods of business to achieve these ends. But this does not mean that a business manager can do any better job of managing government affairs than a public servant who has never been inside a business.

To Counterbalance Union Power A major motivation of some businessmen in pursuing corporate political action is to counterbalance what is perceived by them to be a politically powerful labor union movement. For years the strength of the NAM, for instance, was in the businessman's hatred for government and fear of union power. Many businessmen see in union political activity the capability to elect politicians favoring the labor point of view. They feel that union strength not only will result in legislation which curtails their managerial prerogatives and reduces their profits, but will undermine the very foundations of the traditional business system. In this light, business has supported those associations that help combat union political strength.

Labor unions do have political strength, but today it is grossly exaggerated. The AFL-CIO, for instance, has met with consistent failure in Congress in trying to repeal 14(b), the "right-to-work" section of the Taft-Hartley Act. On the other hand, it has won the passage of legislation over the opposition of some businessmen. Labor unions achieved their peak political strength in the mid-1930s. They still pack political wallop, but it is less than it formerly was.

To Promote Political Interests of Managers Executives of companies have personal political interests to which they are committed, and they may, on occasion, use the power of the companies they head or control to further those interests. There seems no doubt about the fact, for example, that the Ford Motor Company is more deeply involved in public affairs than most large companies because of the strong community interests of Henry Ford II. Corporate political activity directed primarily at pursuing the personal political inclinations of a chief executive or major stockholder is generally more likely to be found in medium-sized or smaller companies than among the largest companies. This is so principally because in the larger companies these days, with rare exceptions, power is dispersed and one man cannot easily indulge his desires if others oppose him.

To Revitalize Political Parties Hoyt Steele, when Manager of Government Relations at the General Electric Company, in discussing his company's activities, observed: "We expect political parties —both political parties, as well as political processes in general—to be strengthened and facilitated by this activity. And we profoundly hope that any tendency of the two major political parties to line up primarily as a labor party or business party will be reversed" (1959). Crawford Greenewalt, when president of E. I. du Pont de Nemours &

Co., also spoke of the need for people to become more deeply involved in political processes to insure the strengthening of democracy. He also pointed out too that it "would be unwise for the business viewpoint to associate itself exclusively with one or the other of our two parties" (1959(A): 10). If the top management of a company does not participate in politics, it is unlikely that junior executives will be powerfully motivated to do so. And, while employees are not likely to be too stimulated or deadened by executive example or company educational programs, they will be influenced in some degree. To the extent that corporate political activities are nonpartisan in nature and stir employees to participate in the political processes, the result is probably all to the good.

THE CASE AGAINST THE POLITICAL ACTIVITY OF BUSINESS

Discussions of opposition to business political activity generally refer to efforts to influence political parties, and this will be the focus in the following analysis.

It Dilutes the Basic Business Function Theodore Levitt strongly opposes business political activity because he feels it diverts managers from what should be a single-minded objective of making profits. He says:

> Involvement in politics can lead only to corporate inefficiency and possible ruin. The corporation that becomes deeply involved in party politics will necessarily dilute its basic profit-making function. The politically active corporation will have to become less seriously profit-minded. When that happens, it will cease to deliver the goods abundantly and efficiently (1960: 50).

Levitt seems to envision a far greater concentration of corporate effort on political matters than currently exists or is likely to take place in the foreseeable future. To begin with, there are legal restraints on corporate political activity—for example, the Federal Corrupt Practices Act mentioned earlier. If this law did not exist and corporations spent funds to help political candidates, they would be restrained by stockholders' suits challenging the use of company money for purposes other than the main business of the firm.

Today, the political activities of virtually all companies are relatively small compared to their total activities. Furthermore, that part of the total political activity of a typical company devoted to party politics is exceedingly small. If a company were to spend much time on political activity, it would indeed, as Levitt says, result in less attention to business affairs and inefficiency. Eventually, a company that so dissipated its managerial talents would lose its competitive position.

For this reason, managers are not likely to spend more time on political activities than is necessary to promote an environment more congenial to achieving their long-range profit objectives.

The Fear of Corporate Power There are those who want business to stay out of politics for fear of the power of business. If such views are based upon the economic power of large corporations they are wrong. There is little correlation between the economic power of a corporation and its political power. In the political arena, the power of a corporation will depend upon a great many variables. The pressure that it can bring to bear on any point in the decision-making process is important; but if the decision-maker is strongly opposed, or if the business interest is out of tune with the times, the decision will not be in favor of business. Such was the case, for instance, when powerful automobile manufacturers opposed the passage of federal safety standards legislation in 1968. Indeed, "the influence of interest groups in the legislative process depends more on the harmony of values between the group and the legislators than it does on the ability of a group to wield its 'power' either through skillful techniques or presumed electoral influence" (Zeigler, 1964: 274).

This is not to deny that business does have impressive political power. When all major business pressure groups are aligned in a solid phalanx, they form a bloc that is not likely to be thwarted. But only rarely does this happen. The more frequent situation is one in which business pressure groups stand in opposition to one another. The truth is, as Epstein points out so well: "Although the political power of business firms and their managers is very real and pervasive, it does not presently constitute a danger to the American pluralistic democracy, which continues to produce legislation, rulings, decisions, and programs that are contrary to the desires of significant corporate interests" (1969: 303). To accept this view, which I think is accurate, is to reject views of writers like C. Wright Mills (1956) and Domhoff (1967), who claim that America is ruled by an elitist group. In the case of Mills, the group is composed of military and corporate heads and to a lesser extent of political leaders. Domhoff says that the ruling class is a business elite.

HOW INFLUENTIAL IS THE POLITICAL ACTIVITY OF BUSINESS?

There is, of course, no final conclusive answer to the question of how influential business political activity is. It will vary depending upon the type of activity under consideration, the stage in the political decision-making process at which influence is directed, and the time period under review. Even when business influence is analysed, it is difficult to tell how effective it is. It is often virtually impossible, for instance, to determine whether a piece of legislation was passed or tabled because of the support or opposition of business. The question of influence, nevertheless, must be addressed. But rather than seek a conclusive answer, in the following discussion I will examine different aspects of the issue.

How Can Business Influence Be Effective? When an interest group does not state its case in Washington, it is signaling that it does not really care how a particular decision turns out. Government expects business to speak up about its interests, and the implication is that when it does, its voice will be heard and be influential. How influential it is depends upon many circumstances.

Pressure group activities in general, including those of business groups, are influential because of the enormous complexity of many public issues and the remoteness of those issues to the daily lives of citizens. This leads to public apathy and lack of popular pressure at the point of decision, which, in turn, leads to efforts by pressure groups to "educate" the public and to gain support for the groups' interests, or to neutralize public opinion. Public silence also permits organized groups to purport to speak to representatives of government as "the voice of the people." Pressure groups generally try to make creditable their assertion that what they really want is "in the public interest."

Of even greater importance to the average legislator than this alleged claim of business groups to represent "the public interest" is the service that the business lobby performs by providing expert opinion on technical matters and articulating constituent interests. Many busy legislators are unsophisticated in their knowledge of the substantive contents of business-related legislative proposals. This is so simply because it is virtually impossible for a congressman to be well versed on the merits of each of the several thousand issues on which he must vote each session. Therefore, the lobby may function as a vital source of information about the meaning of proposed programs. The business lobby, like any other lobby, may also serve to "educate" the congressman by providing him with political intelligence. It does this by conveying the opinion of affected business interests within his district or state and indicating how intense these interests are in their support of or opposition to a given bill. Since key local interests are often business interests, the congressman finds this political advice invaluable; when a lobby provides such advice, its ease of access to the legislator is significantly enhanced. The providing of political intelligence by interest groups is thus an important function, and when this intelligence is highly respected by the congressman, the influence of the lobby grows.

Any effort to unravel the degree of business influence is complicated by the fact that legislators themselves may be sources of business influence. Legislators are not always impartial judges of various pressures. Because of background, training, circumstances of election, and general philosophy, a legislator may on a specific issue have an understandable sympathy with the interests of a particular point of view. Often this is identical with a particular business point of view. In such circumstances a legislator need not be prodded by a business lobby. He can be depended upon to initiate action independently. This proposition holds, of course, for a labor point of view, a welfare point of view, and other points of view.

The Businessman's View of Effectiveness In a series of surveys of business and politics extending over a decade, the conclusion persists that businessmen think they carry some political influence but not as much as they should have. In each survey many of the respondents reported that they felt business influence in political affairs was increasing but in each case it was not enough. In each survey respondents, in retrospect, said past activity was limited and not too effective. In each survey, also, most of the respondents expressed an unwillingness to get mixed up in political activity. On the other hand, they strongly disagreed with the view that company activity in politics will hurt business generally. They concluded that improvement in the political climate toward business must await more political activity on the part of business itself (Fenn, 1959; Greyser, 1964 and 1968).

Is Propaganda Effective? The passage of the Public Utility Holding Company Act of 1935 marked a low point in public attitudes toward public utilities. This act provided for some of the most stringent corrective measures ever applied by government to business. After this shattering experience, the utilities began a campaign to remake their public image. This campaign was effective enough that in recent years propositions supported by the utilities which would have been condemned as self-seeking thirty years ago have been considered highly respectable.

In looking at this experience, V.O. Key concludes that while there is no way to measure the effects of business publicity campaigns on public attitudes, there is plenty of reason to believe that when conducted over time they are markedly effective. "The great political triumph of large-scale enterprise," he says, "has been the manufacture of a public opinion favorably disposed toward, or at least tolerant of, gigantic corporations, in contrast with an earlier dominant sentiment savagely hostile to monopolies and trusts. That fact is of fundamental importance in the workings of the American political system" (1958: 107–8).

Effect the Formulation and Execution of Public Policy Business influence is felt throughout the legislative process—from the inception of an idea, through legislative debate, to the administration of passed laws, and finally in the courts. In commenting on the process of influence, one Washington government relations representative observed: "The first place a bill originates is in a man's mind, and that is the easiest and least expensive place to influence a bill. As the measure progresses, it becomes harder to change; and the longer you wait to take action, the less chance you have to win. If you have to fight a bill on the floor, chances are, you've lost" (Rosenbloom, in Roalman, 1968: 187). It is for this reason, of course, that lobby pressures are first exerted to influence the minds of legislators. One visible result of this principle is the simultaneous appearance, on occasion, of scores of identical bills. This is done as a show of strength for a particular bill.

Business seems to have greater power when it pursues specific narrow interests than when dealing with large policy issues. It is more difficult to be persuasive on broad questions. For instance, opposition to a bill because it "violates the principles of free enterprise" is not nearly as persuasive as "if this tariff is not passed, foreign imports will so reduce sales of American companies as to threaten their very existence."

There is nothing as ineffective as advocacy of an idea that is obsolete. Efforts of the American Medical Association, for instance, to prevent Medicare, and efforts by the automobile manufacturers to stop passage of the National Traffic and Motor Vehicle Safety Act of 1966 are cases in point.

Business seems to have significant influence over legislative details of direct concern to it. To illustrate, in 1967 when the Packaging and Labeling Act was debated, the producers of candy bars successfully opposed a provision which would have created machinery for establishing weight standards for candy bars while permitting the manufacturers to set prices. The industry argued successfully that weight standardization of candy bars would make it difficult for a manufacturer to react to price changes in his raw materials. For all practical purposes, Congress was told, the price of a candy bar is 5 cents or 10 cents, not cents in between. When raw material prices change, manufacturers change the weight of the bars and not the price. To reverse this process would create a hardship. Congress accepted this argument.

A Washington representative stated, "I do not care who writes the laws as long as I can write the regulations." This means, of course, that if he can determine how the laws are administered, he can protect his clients. Once laws are passed, the battle then moves to the regulatory agencies. This may involve agency budgets. If lobbyists cannot persuade Congress to defeat a bill unpalatable to them, one ploy is to pressure legislators to allocate only token funds to administer the law.

Another approach, of course, is to influence the regulators. Relationships between business associations and representatives are often very close and do result in business influence on the way laws are administered. Here again, however, there is no way to determine the degree or extent of such influence. Finally, business uses the legal process to challenge legislation and its administration. By threatening to take legal action, a company may forestall unfavorable legislation or administrative action. By legal action a company may reverse a piece of legislation or the way it is administered.

IS BUSINESS POLITICAL ACTIVITY IN BUSINESS AFFAIRS GOOD OR EVIL?

There is, of course, no final answer as to whether business political activity to influence public decisions is good or evil. When this sort of question is asked, the general response is derogatory to business. The activities of pressure groups and lobbyists, including those representing the business community, are popularly considered to be sinister. More sober reflection, however, points clearly to both good and evil effects.

There is no doubt at all that pressure groups, including business groups, create problems. Business lobbyists thwart needed legislation, as for instance when in 1967 a much-needed revision of the copyright laws was stopped by pressure groups. They create and continue injustices, as for instance in 1973 when pressure groups turned a much-needed tax reform bill into a lobbyists' Donneybrook Fair. They have reversed accepted public policy, as for instance when they pushed through Congress exceptions to the antitrust laws. On the other hand, efforts by business or any other pressure group to influence the political process are not evil per se. It is, as we have said, essential in the proper functioning of a political democracy. Influence may be bad if the ends it seeks are evil. If the evil end is achieved, however, it often is the result of an incomplete or poor functioning of the political machinery, the correction of which can bring redress.

There are many ways in which business influence in the political process can be helpful rather than disruptive. To illustrate succinctly, businessmen and their associations can contribute valuable information by means of which the decision-making processes in government can be improved. The joining together of businessmen into groups serves a useful purpose in representing functional interests, as contrasted with only geographical interests. Through this mechanism, minority functional interests can be heard. From a political point of view, influence groups may provide an effective means for discovering the balance of interests in the community. One must applaud those activities of business that seek to prod the government to come to grips with and resolve important public problems. If in this process, however, business successfully replaces social values with its own values, the result may not be to the good.

CHAPTER TWENTY-THREE

The Convergence of Business and Government Planning

INTRODUCTION

Since World War II there has been a growing convergence of government and business planning throughout the world. Planning has become more comprehensive in scope and has extended over longer time periods. In the United States, government-business planning relationships have converged at more and more points, but there has not been any comprehensive overall government-business planning effort as in some countries in the Western world. A growing number of observers of current and prospective problems in the United States, however, conclude that solutions can be found only in a greater convergence of government-business planning.

This chapter is concerned with types of national governmental plans which exist in the world, and especially in the United States; whether or not a national planning system like that of France should be installed in the United States; what planning improvements should be made in this country; and how all of this is bringing business and governmental planning much closer together.

THE NATURE OF PLANNING

It is important to begin this discussion with some understanding of the meaning of the words "planning" and "plan," because these words can be, and are, defined at different levels of abstraction (Steiner, 1969: chap. I; and Waterson, 1965: chap. II). I will not try to settle the matter of definition here, but the following meanings

393

will be used in this discussion. Very simply, planning is a process of setting objectives, of choosing the best alternatives to reach them, and of making decisions accordingly. A plan is the result of a planning process. The time horizon can be short or long, but no matter how long, the process of planning is undertaken to make current decisions in light of current needs and future prospects. What is a proper long-range horizon for one organization may be short-range for another. For all, however, long-range planning blends into short-range planning because its principal function is to make better current decisions.

It is important in thinking about comprehensive long-range planning to distinguish between two major types. The first is intuitive planning, which is done in the minds of executives and is based upon a blend of past experience, instinctive reaction, and innate intellectual mental processes. A second type is systematic and formal, which is undertaken on the basis of organized procedures, is comprehensive in scope and covers an organization as a system, involves the participation of most managers in the system, and results in written plans. While intuitive planning can and often is done without systematic formal long-range planning, the two should be pursued together because the former should be better as a result of the latter. These conceptual definitions apply to governments as well as to businesses.

EVOLUTION OF LONG-RANGE PLANNING

Prior to World War II, planning by governments in the Western capitalistic nations was principally directed at establishing a framework of rules within which individuals were comparatively free to act as their interests dictated. Business planning, following contemporary economic theory, was principally a reaction to current market conditions. During both World War II and the Korean War there was a major deviation from traditional practice. The United States in World War II was, in a real sense, a constitutional dictatorship in which the government exercised comprehensive and complete controls over the economy in the interests of achieving goals established to win the war. Although controls were neither so comprehensive nor severe during the Korean War, comprehensive controls were used to achieve specific national objectives set by the government. In both instances plans were long- as well as short-range. And in each instance controls and plans were abandoned after the war and the government reverted to prewar traditional practices.

Following World War II one country after another in Western Europe developed comprehensive long-range planning systems. The initial impetus to most of these national plans was the Marshall Plan suggested by the United States to revive European economies shattered by World War II. Before receiving American aid, the participating countries were required to prepare an economic program for the four-year period 1948–1952. This was to show for each country the expected available resources and national expenditures, the progress toward growth and equilibrium, and the logical place for foreign aid.

Long-range development planning is a recent phenomenon among the less developed areas. It is true that early in this century there were a few long-range development plans for colonies (for example, the Belgian government investment plan of 1906 for the Belgian Congo railways and mines), but prior to World War II the only nation on earth that had a continuous development plan was the Soviet Union. Since 1950, however, so widespread has development planning become that "the national plan appears to have joined the national anthem and the national flag as a symbol of sovereignty and modernity" (Waterston, 1965: 28). From about 1950 the World Bank has been a strong force in development planning. In Latin America the Alliance for Progress has been a major stimulant to planning. As Western industrialized nations made loans to the underdeveloped nations of the world the latter prepared long-range plans to meet the requirements of the donors.

Beginning around the mid-1950s large companies in the United States took the lead in developing comprehensive long-range plans for their business activities. Although European nations had developed national plans the large companies located there lagged significantly behind American companies in developing formal planning (Steiner and Cannon, 1966).

The counterpart in the United States government of formal business long-range planning is the program-planning-budgeting system (PPBS). This is a long-range planning program for individual government agencies (Novick, 1965). It is not used as a method to prepare a comprehensive national long-range plan. PPBS was introduced in the Department of Defense in 1960 and later in 1965 President Johnson, by executive order, started its use in all major federal agencies. In 1973 the federal government introduced a system of management by objective. Management by objective (MBO) has superseded PPBS but has not completely replaced it. In some respects MBO is a different name for PPBS. The name and technique of PPBS continue to spread to many other government and nonprofit agencies (Novick, 1973).

The net result has been a rapid spread of comprehensive business planning throughout the industrialized world and long-range comprehensive development planning in the great majority of nations, industrialized as well as underdeveloped. In the so-called free enterprise nations of the world, the relationships between business and government in the preparation and use of these plans have been rather loose. In the less developed nations and in the Communist world, the relationships have been generally close and dictated by government.

TYPES OF GOVERNMENT PLANS

National plans may be classified into some combinations of six types, as follows: First are aggregate plans which seek to interrelate major activities, such as production, capital investment, prices, consumption, employment and balance of payments. Second are cross-sectional plans which may be made for any one of these major activities, such as plans for capital investment, or stabilization of prices. Third are project plans which are concerned with a specific end product such as NASA's plans for landing men on the moon and returning them safely to earth. Fourth are sectional plans covering major areas of activity such as agricultural crops, mining, steel, road construction, electric power, education, health, and so on. Fifth are enterprise plans by or for private, public, or mixed enterprises. Finally are spatial plans embracing regional or geographic activities. Each of these plans can also be classified, of course, into short, medium, or long-range. Plans may be divided into strategic and operational, and compulsory and indicative. Plans are often classified between military and nonmilitary. When speaking about government and government-business planning, therefore, it obviously makes a great deal of difference which types of plan one has in mind (Gross, 1965; Shafer, in Gross, 1967).

Looking only at the aggregate type of planning, one finds great variations throughout the world. In Western Europe plans differ widely in terms of scope and government interference with private enterprise. At one extreme is France, with a five-year plan which does have some governmental authority behind it for execution. At the other extreme is the United Kingdom, where "planning" merely sets some forecasts for different industries. No goals are established, and there is no effort to get industry compliance. (I place planning in quotes because it is a grave mistake to assume that forecasting is planning.) To generalize about the wide variations in plans in the Western nations, it is probably fair to say that most are made for four or five years; are constructed by cooperative efforts among government officials, members of industry, labor unions, and economic experts; cover the entire economy in terms of growth objectives, price stability, balance of payments, and major segments of the economy, such as investment required; and are not compulsory for either government or industry (Sirkin, 1968; Millikan, 1967; Verdoorn, 1965; Morales, in Ozbekhan and Talbert, 1969; and Elliott, in Ozbekhan and Talbert, 1969).

At the other extreme is planning in Soviet Russia, which is centralized in the government and commands implementation by all sectors of society. There has been some decentralization of decision-making in recent years, but not much in terms of Western standards. Yugoslav planning is a hybrid of decentralized decision-making at the level of individual firms and centralized investment controls exercised by government (Adizes, 1971). Japanese plans are essentially long-range forecasts that serve as guidelines for economic policies. Targets in the private sector are not goals to be met but are considered, rather, as expectations. Individual firms have much autonomy in decision-making but there is a close interrelationship and harmony among leaders of large companies, banks, and government officials especially in the Ministry of Finance. Since individual firms are dedicated to the interests of the state they accept substantial tutelage from the government (Ball, 1972; Behrman, 1971: 71–79).

Plans in the less developed countries are frequently based upon a model for the entire economy which shows for the major sectors the targets for contributions of individual sectors needed to achieve a designated level of GNP growth. GNP is then allocated to consumption, investment, and export, and goals are set for each of these areas and as many components of each area as are considered necessary. Among the less developed countries there are great differences in the scope of plans, planning models, commitment by government and industry, and exercise of government authority to achieve objectives (Waterston, 1965).

Corporate planners must, of course, examine with the greatest of care, the plans of countries in which they anticipate doing, or are doing, business. They contain new opportunities and establish constraints and threats which may be ignored only at great peril. They will influence factory location, production, employment, financing, export of profits, prices, and so on. The larger the company and the greater its importance in a country the more attention it must give to national plans, no matter what degree of compulsion is attached to them. For a multinational company, says Phatak, this means that its survival, prosperity, and growth will depend upon its ability to blend its planning with that of every country in which it does business (1971).

FRENCH NATIONAL FIVE-YEAR PLANS

Since planning in France is so frequently held out as being exemplary and the way of the future, it is useful to study its composition and methodology. The first French plan was launched in 1946 by Jean Monnet and was called the Plan of Modernization to indicate that its aim was to repair the ravages caused by the war.

Preparing the Plans The French plan begins with a five-year target rate of GNP growth which is agreed upon by the Commissariat General des Plans and the Treasury. This rate is reviewed and changed if necessary by the Social and Economic Council, which is composed of ministers of state and representatives from major economic and academic groups. Estimates of GNP are then broken down into household consumption, public consumption, housing, gross capital formation, and the net balance of trade. From an input-output analysis are derived levels of production and estimates of investment and employment in major sectors. These estimates are then given to commissions whose members are drawn from industry, labor, and government. There are six so-called horizontal commissions (for example, regional developments, finance, productivity, manpower, social security, and scientific and technical research) and twenty-five vertical commissions (for example, transportation, agriculture, steel, energy, chemical industry, and so on). These commissions are divided into many subcommittees. The horizontal commissions deal with economy-wide matters and are responsible for synthesizing the data furnished by the vertical commissions. This means, among other things, that they ensure that the plans are fundamentally balanced in such areas as production, finance, manpower, and regional development. The vertical commissions are concerned essentially with a unified industrial area. These commissions analyze forecasts of demand, investment and labor requirements, relationships with other sectors, feasibility, and so on. Tentative plans are drawn and then are reviewed by the Planning Commissariat. Reconciliations, of course, are made when discrepancies appear. When a workable synthesis is developed, the plan is presented to the Parliament for debate which is followed by approval of the government.

Details of the French plans have differed, but the basic system and approach have remained the same among the six plans that have been prepared. (The Sixth Plan covers the period 1971–1975.) The plans are comprehensive. They are not, however, compulsory. It has been a major objective of the French system of planning to make plans compatible with a democratic free enterprise system. The method of reconciling requirements of the plan with those of a free market economy has been called "concertation," meaning that those who could put the plan into effect would help prepare it and, in this way, consistency among individual decision-makers in government and industry would bring realization of the plans. Implementation, however, is not left completely to individual decision-makers.

Major Characteristics of the Planning System A few outstanding characteristics of the French system of interest to this discussion are as follows: First, the plan is developed for branches of activity and not for companies or products. The plan states the general objectives for particular segments of the economy and individual firms are free to try or not to try to meet the goal. The government intervenes only when there is danger of some important imbalance either nationally, among regions, or between major sectors of the economy.

Second, as noted above, the plan seeks to use the expertise of all major decision-making centers of the country. For the Fifth Plan there were over 2,000 commission members. Business executives and members of various professional organizations, such as trade and industrial associations, made up 40 percent of commission members for the Fifth Plan. Labor unions contributed 14 percent of the members, while the government contributed 29 percent, and other experts 14 percent. The remaining 3 percent were farmers (Schollhammer, 1967).

Third, the plan is implemented by a mixture of psychological, structural, institutional, legislative, and administrative methods. Pierre Massé, for a long time president of the French Planning Commission, used to say the plan was "less than imperative but more than indicative." The French like to depend first upon persuasion, but if this fails they have a variety of incentives and direct action techniques to ensure desired action. The French have shown a readiness to use incentives, which led one observer to comment that the French approach to implementation uses both sticks and carrots, but with more carrots than sticks (Dreze, 1964: 52). Tax allowances, selective tax treatment, and even direct controls (for example, price) are among the tools used to achieve plans. Most of the implementation of the plans, however, rests on the voluntary actions of businessmen and other decision-makers. The interventions of the government, when made, are generally in line with the philosophy of "indicative" planning, that is, setting a general objective to be achieved by persuasion and incentives without any direct sanctions on individual enterprises for failure to comply with plan objectives.

French businessmen have been influenced in their decision-making by the plans. A survey of these businessmen shows that investment and financial decisions are heavily influenced by the plans. This is not surprising, since public authorities control about half the total investment activity of France, and since the banks are nationalized. Market strategy is not significantly influenced by the plans, and research and development decisions almost not at all. Executives of larger companies, as might be expected, say their plans are greatly influenced by the plans; executives of small firms say the plans have little if any influence on their decision-making (Schollhammer, in Ozbekhan and Talbert, 1969).

Some Impacts of Planning French planning has by no means been acclaimed as an unqualified success (McArthur and Scott, 1969). Overly ambitious growth targets have required high investment outlays which have produced serious price inflation particularly during the 1957–1958 and 1962–1963 periods (Jacoby and Howell, 1967; Cohen, 1969). Plans and French government policies have conflicted. Growth has not been as rapid as projected, although France has been the fastest growing economy in Europe in the past twenty years.

The planning process and plans have had other impacts on French business life. On the positive side of the ledger, the system has produced an increasing amount of consistent and useful information for business to use in making more informed decisions. Methods to develop and publicize more reliable economic forecasts have helped to reduce uncertainties for individual businessmen. In government planning, as in business planning, the result of developing a dialogue among various types of decision-makers, in creating a better system of communication among them, and in having them focus their attention on major opportunities and threats is a value that must not be underestimated. There is great benefit in the process of planning itself whether or not the substantive results of the effort are used. For example, the way the planning process is carried out provides an economic education for decision-makers.

On the other hand, there have been negative impacts on economic life growing out of the planning process and the plans. To begin with, most American commentators see in the commission dialogues an extraordinary opportunity for collusive agreements that can restrain competition. The potential is great for two competitors to agree on sharing a market, or not to struggle to improve their respective shares of a market, or to quote comparable prices, or to make investments accommodating one another. Pierre Massé's response to such fears, however, is that ententes between firms are not new in France, and if firms were interested they would get together even if there were no plan. He has commented that they will get together anyhow, and it is better that they do it in the context of economic growth and within the view of the planning authorities. If firms seek to take advantage of forecasts of increasing markets, as presented in the plans, they may overinvest (as Jacoby and Howell noted) and build up excess capacity. This, in turn, may lead to such keen competition as to damage individual firm profits, if not their very survival.

Since most of the representatives from industry on commissions come from large companies, the ground is laid for a cooperative effort between these companies and the government in implementing plans. The plans lay a basis, therefore, for strengthening the large firms and for changing the competitive balances in the economy. The single most powerful factor in implementing plans, so far as the French manager is concerned, is bank lending policy. Activities of individual firms that fit into the plan are more favored in bank lending than are interests that may not coincide with the plan.

In weighing the positive versus the negative impacts of French planning, Schollhammer concluded that the positive impacts do outweigh the real or imagined negative effects. This, he feels, is the major reason for favorable attitudes toward French planning by French businessmen. French executives may ignore but rarely do they oppose the planning system (in Ozbekhan and Talbert, 1969).

OVERALL NATIONAL PLANNING IN THE UNITED STATES

Except in time of war comprehensive long-range planning covering the entire economy has not been tried in the United States. So distasteful is the thought of any comprehensive government planning for the entire economy, except in wartime, that very little effort has been made by government to look ahead on a national scale. Indeed, the first official effort by government to project total federal expenditures into the future was not made until 1960. At that time the Bureau of the Budget made the forecast as a last gesture of the outgoing Eisenhower Administration to shock the public into questioning the promises of the incoming Kennedy Administration. The Eisenhower Administration also took an important forward step in national long-range planning by creating a Commission on National Goals, which made its report in November 1960. This commission covered a surprisingly wide scope, which included national goals for economic growth, unemployment, individuals, equality, the democratic process, education, technological change, agriculture, health and welfare, foreign aid, defense, disarmament, and so on. No comparable set of goals has since been developed.

SECTORAL PLANNING IN THE UNITED STATES

During the past thirty-five years there has been an expansion of government-business planning at the sectoral level. During the depression of the 1930s, for example, the government, together with agricultural interests, began a joint planning effort that has become increasingly intermeshed. Through price supports, export subsidies, production controls, research programs, and other devices, agricultural output and the prices of many commodities are planned. Planning in the beet-sugar industry is but one of many examples in this area. The United States consumes more sugar than it produces, and if the imports of sugar were not controlled, the price would drop on the domestic market. Domestic beet-sugar farmers would then be forced to use their land for something else. Only a handful of American farmers produce beet and cane, but they are scattered in nineteen states and influence the votes of thirty-eight senators. Preventing the bankruptcy of farmers could be done easily by an import duty, but this might produce a high domestic price for sugar. Rather than establish import duties, the Sugar Act of 1934, and subsequent revisions of it, requires the Secretary of Agriculture to divide the domestic market between foreign and domestic producers. Domestic producers are insulated from fluctuations in market demand and foreign competition, and consumers pay higher prices as a result of a neat and tight cartel created by this joint government-business plan.

An interesting combination of sector and individual enterprise planning occurs in what has been called the military-industrial complex. This military-industrial complex includes major elements in our society—technical, industrial, educational, and political. There is not, however, one government plan embracing it all. There are many plans covering parts of the complex. Sometimes plans are coordinated, but more frequently they are not. One area of significance in this complex, where there is extensive joint government-industry planning, concerns the production of military and space equipment in the aerospace industry. Both with the Department of Defense and NASA there is close collaboration between government and members of the industry in the determination of what to make, the design of equipment, the research needed to produce the prototype, and the production of the equipment. Industry members are on committees of these government agencies and become involved in the design-making process. On the other hand, government officers are located in the plants and exercise a close managerial surveillance over the activities of the companies. Former members of the military services find jobs in the aerospace industry and further link the planning of both. Some people looking at this interrelationship, in which congressmen and union leaders participate, see in it a conspiracy to maintain unnecessary military expenditures and to further the purposes of the government departments and the industry.

In but rare instances is the planning a matter of conspiracy. In two excellent discussions of the military-industrial complex, Adams (1968) and Yarmolinsky (1967) conclude that the complex embraces interrelationships among government and many private interests that are more properly described as coalitions or coincidences of interests. These interrelationships spring from the interests of a project officer in getting a star, a defense contractor in not running out of work, a labor union leader in protecting his constituents, a congressman concerned with the prosperity of his district, an aerospace scientist hoping to provide the newest technology for his country's defense, an engineer lending his expertise to government in its formulation of program requirements, and the armed services in wanting more and better equipment.

Being in the military-industry complex is not without its lumps. Many firms avoid defense work because of the hazards of unexpected contract cancellations, risks associated with contract provisions (Meyers, 1969), and low profits relative to sales (Demaree, 1969). Government-oriented companies are valued at lower price-earnings ratios on the stock market than the typical commercially-oriented company.

OTHER TYPES OF GOVERNMENT PLANNING IN THE UNITED STATES

Without going into detail, the point should be made here that there are many other types of plans in the United States than those just illustrated. To use the above classification of plans, we have many cross-sectoral plans, such as those of the Federal Reserve Board to control prices. There are multiple examples of project plans in government, such as airport plans of the Federal Aviation Agency. At the end of this chapter enterprise-type plans will be touched on. Finally, spatial plans are illustrated by reclamation projects of the Army Corps of Engineers and the Department of Interior. We have no shortage of plans and planning systems.

AN ASSESSMENT OF UNITED STATES GOVERNMENT-BUSINESS PLANNING

The results of the government-business planning system in the United States, at least so far as the performance of our socioeconomic system is concerned, have been presented in a number of previous chapters. However, a few things need to be said here as an introduction to an examination of the case for different planning mechanisms in the future.

Since World War II, to pick an arbitrary date for comparisons, the United States has achieved a remarkable comparatively steady economic growth that contrasts sharply with the unpredictable and major booms and busts of the previous two centuries. Per capita incomes have risen impressively, and the benefits of economic prosperity have been widely diffused. A major problem of pre-World War II capitalism has thus apparently been solved and, with luck, will remain solved. On the other hand, complex problems concerning the impact of technology on social systems, new social problems, inflation and coordination of sociotechnical systems have arisen and have not been readily resolved by older planning systems. Progress has been made in dealing with some of these problems, as previously discussed, but the problems seem to be outdistancing solutions.

The major question now, of course, is this: Will these traditional government-business planning mechanisms be satisfactory for the future? Should the United States have some sort of comprehensive five-year plan? What recommendations may be made for future government-business planning? Before addressing this question, it is very important that we be precise about the sort of planning system we are discussing. The type of system in this discussion is generally the French plan, as described before.

THE CASE FOR COMPREHENSIVE PLANS

Adolph Berle, a respected thinker about corporate-government life, said that the high concentration of economic power among large corporations "suggests the time is ripe for a system of national planning —possibly indicative planning like that now used by France" (1969). His belief was that business decisions about the use of productive capital in the past were generally beneficial to society and therefore uncontrolled by society. Today, however, the ways in which productive facilities are used are of major concern to society, and society should therefore have a good bit to say about their use. Comprehensive planning, he felt, was one way to ensure that resources are used in society's interests.

Others see the need for coordinating complex large-scale programs such as space programs, highway systems, urban renewal, water resources, and so on. The necessary coordination, it is alleged, can be found in a long-range national plan. Schollhammer (in Ozbekhan and Talbert, 1969) points to many advantages to the United States from the adoption of a French type of planning system. For instance, he says, long-range projections of up to twenty years would be helpful in designing a broad spectrum of choices to be used as guides to coherent decision-making. The involvement of those who are most instrumental in implementing plans, as in France, can be helpful in creating a framework for coordinated action. Such planning can also be important in stimulating effective planning systems in enterprises.

Ahlbrandt, when he was chairman of the board of Allegheny Ludlum Industries, Inc., urged centralized economic planning to facilitate private companies in competing in world markets. He said that private firms in the United States were, in many instances, not competing against private foreign firms but with managed economies where government made the decisions (1972).

In an examination of the next thirty years, Eric Trist points to a fundamental problem, the solution to which, for him, lies only in planning. He says that the post-industrial society (as described in a previous chapter) is not in the future. It is here now. It has been developing for some time, and its outline form is in our midst. On the other hand, there is not being created at the pace required corresponding changes in our cultural values, organizational philosophies, and ecological strategies. For instance, he says, individuals cannot meet the demands of evolving complex environments. A pooling of resources is required, and emergent values will emphasize communal rather than individualistic behavior. Ecological strategies must change from today's responsiveness to crisis to anticipation of crisis, from short planning horizons to long planning horizons, from small local government units to enlarged local government units, and from separate services to coordinated services. This structural-cultural mismatch will require a new relationship between planning and the political process. He feels that the most important element of French planning is not in the achievement of targets, but in the social learning process. In the post-industrial society man will spend more of his time in politics and in planning. Continuous dialog will take place. "The task of the new politics," he says, "will be the regulation of ecological systems undergoing rapid but uneven change under conditions of increasing complexity, interdependence and uncertainty." We must find new ways to relate planning to the political processes. While he does not specifically say so, the implication is that the requirement is for a comprehensive long-range planning system with plenty of participants and dialog (Trist, 1968).

THE CASE AGAINST COMPREHENSIVE PLANS

A major barrier to central planning is the current widespread resistance to it in both government and the community. Within the business community, as among the population generally, resistance to any sort of overall governmental planning is strong and undoubtedly will persist for some time to come. Quite obviously, the business community sees in such planning a reduction of its powers of decision-making in areas previously unrestrained by government. Central planning is seen as an avenue of expanding government control over business. It is seen as characteristic of authoritarian governments. In sum, central planning of an overall comprehensive nature like that of France is contrary to the value systems and traditional patterns of thinking of the men in government, business, and large segments of the population.

Aside from the reasons against central planning given above, which are accepted in government circles, there are political and administrative implications of such planning that stiffen the resistance of politicians. Such a planning system, for example, inevitably would strengthen the hand of the executive as compared with the legislative branch of government. This would derive from the necessity for the legislative branch to agree to the expenditure of funds over a longer period of time than is the habit of the Congress. In addition, power would tend to shift to the experts involved in the planning process. The necessity to employ experts would also tend to advance the power of the executive compared with that of the legislative branch. No one who has followed even casually the battle for power that has characterized our congressional-presidential relations over the past half-century would underestimate the resistance in Congress to any erosion of its power. The same thing applies to state and local governments. In addition, a French type of planning program would tend to replace geographic representation by functional representation. Many decisions about economic affairs would be made on the basis of economic group interests that cut across geographic lines. Such a change in our political process would not be easily accepted by elected representatives of the people.

There is also a high probability that such planning would be considered illegal. The antitrust laws are quite explicit about competitors discussing and planning to act cooperatively in their economic relationships. Such planning could be declared unconstitutional on the same grounds that the Supreme Court used to invalidate the National Industrial Recovery Act in 1935. This act permitted the President to approve codes of business action prepared for the government by trade associations and businessmen for their respective industries. The Court held that the act was unconstitutional because the broad grant of authority given by Congress to the President represented a virtual abdication of legislative powers, and also because the field of commerce reserved to the states was illegally invaded—for example, intrastate commerce was controlled by the federal government (Shechter Poultry Corp., 1935).

It seems to me, furthermore, that the sheer size and complexity of the American socioeconomic system prevents its being encompassed in one overall, comprehensive long-range plan. The complexity of many American cross-sectoral and sectoral plans is such now as to stretch the capabilities of men and machines to keep them reasonably coordinated and consistent in their own areas. To envision coordination among them such as is attempted in the French system boggles the mind. While the French planning system has had some success, it is questionable whether the United States, with a GNP many times that of France and a society many times more complex, could manage such a planning system, given the cultural and political acceptances required for its operation.

An important argument against comprehensive long-range plans is the potential of getting locked into a system that cannot be easily altered as problems change. This happened to French planning. The First Plan (1947–1952) established growth objectives for France and identified a sequence of investments which would achieve the goals. Emphasis was placed on eliminating bottlenecks in industry which could inhibit output rather than on finding lowest cost or highest profit solutions to resource allocations problems (McArthur and Scott, 1969: 481–82). At the time of the Fifth Plan (1966–1970) the problems of France had changed. France was plagued with inflation, balance of payments deficits, acquisition of industrial assets by American firms, competition from other countries in the Common Market, and lagging productivity. The problem was not to achieve self-sufficiency and balance among major economic sectors, as in 1947, but to assure a selective employment of resources in specific products and industries where the greatest potential returns on investment could be found. While the planners recognized these problems, the planning machinery did not deal well with them. A major difficulty was that the type of information needed to make these decisions did not grow out of previous planning efforts. The planning system also did not provide a means for resolving conflicts of interest in industrial sectors (McArthur and Scott, 1969: chap. XIII).

The planning system used in a country can easily become so inflexible that neither the discovery of new problems nor their solutions are handled very well by it. Herein lies a paradox. Planning undoubtedly is a major method for society to bridge the gap between galloping technology and slow-changing social systems. But, a national plan becomes a social system and is subject to the sluggishness of change of most social systems.

WHAT SHOULD BE DONE?

If the arguments for and against comprehensive national long-range planning are at all realistic, it is clear that there is a case for such planning but that political, administrative, and economic realities reject such a system for the United States, as least in the next few decades. However, we do need better sectoral planning and we do need some sort of overall national planning. What can be done? I think much can be done. Much can be done to improve the planning that is now taking place. Much can be done to develop new organizations, methods, and principles for more and better planning. We can also try to stimulate a greater planning consciousness among the people.

National Goals One obvious thing to do is to develop, more or less continuously, national long-range goals for which there seems to be a general consensus. A Presidential Commission, or goals staff, can develop such a list. Major groups in society, including business, ought to participate in the effort. Such a set of aims, together with estimates of priorities, could serve as a fundamental foundation for planning at all levels of government and in the private sector. There is no suggestion here that anyone in or out of government is obliged to act in conformity with any specific objective. My point is, however, that the mere existence of such a list would tend to motivate decision-makers both in and out of government to act more in conformity with the presumable consensus of society about what it wants from its social and economic system. There is no implication in this suggestion that goals will always correlate. It is recognized that as goals are described at lower levels of abstraction conflicts will increasingly appear. Miller has repeatedly been making a recommendation similar to this (White House Conference, 1972: 87).

Identification of Future Emergencies We need desperately a permanent staff function at the highest levels of government which identifies and anticipates future emergencies and develops alternative strategies to prevent them or soften their severity. This function can, of course, be performed by a group established to develop goals. It should operate continuously and have access to highly knowledgeable and unbiased experts. We simply must perceive problems which lay ahead and take current action to deal with them. For instance, the current energy crisis was foreseen by experts as much as ten years ago but we did little to avoid it. Indeed, we did many things to hasten it.

This function should concentrate only on the most strategic and critical problems. If it covers too many areas it will lose effectiveness. It should clarify alternative approaches and probably should avoid taking an advocacy role although it probably should be encouraged to identify preferred strategies. It ought to avoid becoming Olympian and detached from reality by being forced to make realistic cost and feasibility studies (Rockefeller, 1973).

Budget Forecasts, Analysis, and Data The Congress should no longer be deprived of an annual long-range projection of federal expenditures and revenues. It needs this to improve its current decisions about the allocation of governmental burdens and resources.

Both the executive branch and Congress should know what future budget commitments are likely to be for selected programs. If realistic future expenditures for a particular program are calculated, it is possible that it may not be started at all. At any rate, if long-range costs and benefits of different programs are prepared reasonably realistically, it is possible for the political processes to weigh one against another to determine whether marginal funds should be allocated to schools, highways, defense, space, or other programs. It is not possible, of course, to make a precise cost-benefit calculation which makes clear that an additional $1 billion would benefit society more in a school than a defense program. But when costs and benefits of programs are calculated, better decision-making should result than if such measures are absent.

To facilitate the preparation of such projections and studies we need much more information and better analytical tools. The United States today has by far the most comprehensive, detailed, and illuminating data about activities in its society of all the nations of the world. Yet this information is not enough to meet the planning requirements of today and tomorrow. For example, a substantial increase in knowledge about the consequences of current programs is needed. We do not know enough about the impact of farm subsidies on agricultural production, of the consequences of continuing present railroad regulations to improved transportation systems, of preferred systems to train and employ the unemployed, of the way labor regulations may impede increased labor productivity, of the potential adverse social impacts of a new developing technology, or of the impact of taxes on incentives.

We need much better forecasting tools about future potential social changes. Just as we have economic indicators of change—such as GNP, capital investment, and prices—we need "social indicators" to tell us whether we are getting healthier, controlling pollution, or creating better jobs for more people. It is possible to develop indexes about such social elements and to make forecasts of them.

We need much better methods to evaluate future alternative courses of action. Current cost-benefit techniques are powerful tools for making choices among alternatives, but much improvement can and should be made in them, especially in the development of better benefit measures (Shick, in Joint Economic Committee, 1969: Part V, 817–34).

My purpose here is not to identify all the types of tools and information that should be developed to improve planning, but merely to illustrate the possibilities. It seems obvious to me that our tools and knowledge are not up to the requirements of our present planning systems, and they are most deficient in supporting the type of planning required in the future.

The Systems View We have currently begun to use the systems approach in dealing with sociotechnical problems. This effort must be advanced significantly. For instance, living conditions in many of our huge metropolitan areas are intolerable and getting worse. These areas are governed by hundreds, and in the case of some cities, thousands, of local authorities with overlapping, duplicating, and disjointed responsibilities. Designed for the horse-and-buggy days, this type of government is completely inadequate for today's society. What is needed is a planning program that integrates physical and fiscal planning on an appropriate regional basis. These areas must be viewed as systems of business, residential, transportation, educational, recreational, and service facilities. Suitable goals must be established for the desired quality of living, and plans must be prepared and implemented to achieve the goals. This is planning of a high order which has not yet been perfected in this or any other country.

Reaching beyond metropolitan areas are other problems which must be tackled through the systems planning approach. Regional, and, where appropriate, national plans must be prepared to cope with certain types of problems such as pollution (air, water, solid waste, and noise), conservation of forests and river systems, air terminal congestion, and air traffic safety. These types of plans obviously must be coordinated with financial plans of the federal, state, and local governments.

Planning Principles and Practices There does not now exist a set of planning principles and practices which will guide the planning systems to fit our needs. They should be developed. During the past twenty years the experience of businessmen with long-range comprehensive planning systems has resulted in the accumulation of lessons of experience which are highly applicable to public and public-private planning systems. In addition, of course, public planning systems will require other policy and procedural guidelines. The type of principle in mind, for instance, is that the planning systems should be as loose and flexible as possible while still providing the basic information needed for decision-making. Another example is this: adequate safeguards must be built into the planning systems to prevent private interest groups from injecting into the planning their own interests at the expense of the public interest. Precisely what such principles and practices mean should be described in some detail.

A Planning Consciousness As we move into the post-industrial society and people have more leisure, it is to be hoped that they will spend more time discussing politics and planning. A greater consciousness among the population about the need for and the practicality of planning is an important step in meeting and dealing properly with the complex problems of this society.

There is always the danger that in the evolution of national planning systems, in which government has such an important part to play, government will increasingly encroach upon the decision-making prerogatives now enjoyed in the private sector. To some, as von Hayek states, any planning begun by government inevitably leads to authoritarian control. Indeed, he equates planning with collectivism (Hayek, 1944: 34–35, 56–57). It does not follow that when a government such as ours begins to plan, the end result is dictatorship or the world of "big brother" (Orwell, 1949). We have amply demonstrated during the past twenty years that it is possible for government to develop major plans, with and without business, and to implement them to the improvement rather than detriment of free economic decision-making in the private sector. There is no reason why the same experience cannot hold in the future. Indeed, planning is the key to mastering our environment while maintaining our freedoms.

An enlightened electorate engaged in planning dialog may be

the link to solving both problems. Trist speaks of the planning process as the basis of a new "culture" of politics. He sees it as involving a continuous dialog, in which there is bargaining among interest groups leading to innovative joint problem-solving as the learning process proceeds. The new politics in the post-industrial society, he says, must regulate environmental systems that are undergoing rapid and uneven rates of change. The problem is further complicated because these environmental systems influence one another. Trist sees this type of planning, which relates to all dimensions and levels of society, as "a young and unmastered art representing the basis of the new form that politics is beginning to take. . . . It is a process of unending imperfect co-ordination and of continuously learning more about how to decide among seriously uncertain alternatives so that some of the better futures are kept open" (1968).

Make Haste Slowly, But Make Haste When discussing the introduction of a comprehensive corporate long-range planning system in a business of any size, I caution management "to make haste slowly." What I mean is that the introduction of a planning system for a business is a major action filled with booby traps. Planning is a part of the entire system of management, and it therefore affects all managers and their relationships with each other. Furthermore, in a business of any size the task of getting the process started is intricate, and if not done carefully can lead at best to ineffective planning and at worst to a failure that will sour management on long-range planning for a long time to come.

Effective planning for major sectors of society, for linking plans of major sectors, or for developing overall comprehensive plans must be approached cautiously and with great wisdom. Our problems, however, are multiplying rapidly and increasing in complexity. We must, therefore, move swiftly to improve planning. I think the great effort must be in improving our present systems and not in attempting to create an over-all comprehensive system. A national plan may be possible in the future, but I do not think it is technically or politically possible now. Even if it were, there are grave dangers in trying to produce it. If other planning is done well, rather loose coordination at the very top will be enough.

THE CHANGING BUSINESS-GOVERNMENT PLANNING RELATIONSHIP

If planning develops as suggested above, the business-government planning relationship will obviously become closer. Public priorities, for instance, will increasingly be established to which private business will be persuaded or forced to comply (Cassell, 1972). This association will very likely become even more intimate as two major trends converge. One is the business thrust into social programs and the other is the increasing use by government of incentives to business to assure its deeper involvement in the resolution of society's problems.

A New Public-Private Interrelationship During the past decade the federal government has encouraged business to perform an increasing number of tasks heretofore reserved exclusively for government. In mind is the training of disadvantaged persons, rebuilding ghettos, running the post office, and helping minority entrepreneurs to get their businesses started. These programs have reflected a growing acceptance in government and among the people of a new philosophy concerning public-private roles. The new relationships are based upon four important propositions, generally accepted (CED, 1971: 51):

> That the goals of American society can be realized only through a massive, cooperative effort of government, industry, labor, and education. Increasingly it is felt that the cooperative participation of the private sector is required not only for national defense and space exploration but also for advances in health care, improvement of education, and elimination of poverty.

> That government's basic role through the political process is to determine the nation's goals, set the priorities, develop the strategies, and create the conditions for carrying out the work most effectively to the satisfaction of the public.

> That business, with its profit-and-loss discipline, has an especially significant role in the actual execution of social programs because it is a proven instrument for getting much of society's work done and because its top executives, with their diverse management capabilities and their involvement in community affairs, are normally well fitted to deal with today's socioeconomic problems.

> That the incentive for profit is the only practicable way of unleashing the power and dynamism of private enterprise on scale that will be effective in generating social progress. Social consciousness and good citizenship, while important prerequisites, cannot realistically be expected by themselves to bring business resources to bear on the country's social problems on the massive scale that is needed. To achieve this, government must create the market conditions that will induce business enterprises to apply their operational capabilities to those public tasks they can carry out more efficiently than other institutions.

Government Incentives and Regulations Government influences business planning importantly both by providing incentives and issuing rules. As pointed out in Chapter 16 the government can attract business problem-solving talents by creating adequate markets for business products and services. Rent supplements, subsidies and low interest rates, for instance, have been used to attract business to low-income housing development. This market-creation technique can be and has been used in other areas, such as transportation, education, and medical services. Government contracts with business to do many things. The contract itself, of course, requires planning for completion, such as a NASA space vehicle. But also, as noted previously, government inserts in its contracts requirements for contractor compliance with social policies the government wishes to pursue. Cash subsidies, loans, credit guarantees, tax benefits, and policy standards are other incentives used by government to get business to undertake social programs.

As amply demonstrated in previous chapters there are many government regulations which have impacts on business planning. For instance, the effort to meet pollution standards stimulates business planning.

New Forms of Public-Private Enterprise In addition to the above ways in which business-government planning intermeshes there are new organizations which establish a basis and precedent for more new structures. There is no question about the need to combine the best talents of people in government, business, universities, think tanks, and the community to resolve our social-economic problems. Some forms of public-private organizations, including corporations, provide models for coordinating such talents in the resolution of specific problems. Comsat (Communications Satellite Corporation) and Amtrak (National Railroad Passenger Corporation) are illustrations. Regional planning corporations, such as TVA (Tennessee Valley Authority), can deal with multiple problems crossing governmental authority boundaries. Ramo for a number of years has been urging what he calls social-industrial complexes, fashioned somewhat after the military-industrial complex, to tackle major social problems (1972). Government has been innovative in the past in designing new organizations to meet urgent problems and certainly can be expected to do so again in the future (Spangler and McMillan, 1970).

SOME CONCLUDING OBSERVATIONS

It seems important to underscore the fact that expanding the capability of government to plan better does not necessarily mean a reduction in the decision-making authority of individuals in the private sector. We have always valued highly a divergence between private and public goals (Chamberlain, 1965: 151). This has been a source of dynamism, flexibility, and vitality. Nor does greater planning in government necessarily imply inevitable movement into an authoritarian society. If the recommendations of this chapter are accepted, the result will not be a planned society but a planning society. In it we must employ our best talents in foreseeing and resolving our most pressing problems before they become acute. There is no other way for us.

CHAPTER TWENTY-FOUR

Economic Concentration and Public Policy

INTRODUCTION

The American people have always had a strong antipathy toward concentrations of economic power in and the monopolistic practices of business, and have had tough laws enacted to promote true competition. Our antitrust laws which embody our distaste for monopolistic practices in business constitute a massive set of regulations governing business practice. This fact is noted here because space does not permit any broad exploration of them. The focus in this chapter is on concentrations of economic power in our larger corporations. We do have great concentrations of economic power but there is no unanimity about what to do about them. There are those who wish to break them up into smaller units. Others say that is inappropriate because we do have vigorous competition with all of its beneficial fruits. During the 1960s a new form of large organization, the conglomerate, rapidly advanced to the ranks of our largest companies. Special questions have arisen about the proper public control policy which should be devoted to them. These are the major issues discussed in this chapter following a description of the basic antitrust laws and how the Supreme Court has interpreted them over a long period of time.

LAWYERS, ECONOMISTS, BUSINESSMEN, AND POLITICAL THEORISTS

It is important in reviewing the literature and debate about the anti-trust laws to understand that lawyers, economists, businessmen, and political theorists look at the issues from different points of view. There are, of course, varying opinions among members of each group, but, generally speaking, it still is true that each group looks at antitrust problems in a way which is fundamentally dissimilar from those of the other groups.

The law deals with the preservation of basic relationships among individuals and groups. It is concerned with equity and justice from the individual as well as from the social point of view. Courts of law are therefore on the horns of a dilemma. On the one hand, the law seeks to provide a certain amount of stability by adherence to the principle of *stare decisis*. On the other hand, the law is a formalized code of relationships society wishes to preserve, and when values change, so will the law. It is this reaching for past precedent that may surprise litigants in a case, to whom the outcome may seem clear on the basis of current views. However, observers are also often surprised by a court's rejection of old decisions in favor of newer doctrine.

The economist is interested in the mechanical operation of the economic system so as to ensure the most efficient utilization of scarce resources at minimum cost. The competitive models worked out in economics over a long period of time tend to achieve this objective much better than monopoly or collusive practices. In looking at the nature of competition and monopoly, economists tend to think in terms of their competitive models and favor market structures in which there are many buyers and sellers who have easy access to markets and who are not unduly restrained in their free exercise of choice. Economists tend to look with disfavor on market structures in which there is a concentration of power in the hands of a comparatively few sellers or buyers, and reject as unsuitable situations in which one buyer or seller has complete control over a market. As will be discussed later, however, there are many economists who are more concerned about the performance of markets than about the market structure. Many economists use price flexibility as a basic criterion to test the degree of competition. If price is uniform among sellers and tends to be "sticky" in its movements, there is presumed to be a monopolistic situation. Some economists see advertising and other sales devices as efforts to enhance the power of the firm by differentiating products in the minds of customers. Some see the preoccupation of businessmen with market share as an effort to exclude others.

Businessmen think of competition in terms of what their competitors are doing to take business away from them and what they must do to keep and increase their business. The approaches they take may seem to others to be contrary to antitrust laws, even though there is no intent to violate the law or economic theory. For instance, a businessman's concentration on market share is not so much an effort to exclude competitors, as it is to increase sales which in turn will reduce cost per unit and enhance profits. The businessman sees what the economists call "pure" competition as a situation that is likely to bring cutthroat competition and bankruptcy. The business-man frequently sees that price flexibility is not always the decisive factor in competition; it may rather be nonprice elements, such as quality, service, prestige of the producer's name, terms of payment, repair parts availability, or advertising. Mergers may be formed to develop a synergy between a technical and a nontechnical company, to substitute skilled headquarters management for poor management in the acquired company, or to take advantage of tax or other finan-cial opportunities. The economist and the lawyer may see the result as an increase in the concentration of economic power.

The political theorist (as well as the jurist and the economist) may be moved to distrust concentration of economic power, even though today it is beneficial, because if allowed to continue, it may upset the balances of the pluralistic society. The essence of political de-mocracy is diffused power; the essence of monopoly is concentrated power. Concentration of power if continued leads to increased gov-ernment controls, which in turn may result in diminution of the democratic processes. An overriding aim of antitrust policy is to keep the economy functioning effectively without injecting into it an excess of government regulation. There is also a subtle connec-tion, in the view of the political theorist, between concentration of economic power and the erosion of economic and political freedom.

All these profiles are, of course, oversimplified, but I think they make the point that the major parties in the antitrust arena look at the subject matter and the results from different points of view. This may often explain the disgust with which one group looks at the conclusions of the other. It may explain, too, the heat of the con-troversy.

THE SHERMAN AND CLAYTON ACTS

The two basic antitrust laws are the Sherman Act (passed in 1890) and the Clayton Act (passed in 1914). There have been few amendments to these fundamental laws, but the legality of various practices today is far different from that of ninety, fifty, or even twenty-five years ago. This is partly attributable to changes in the law, but is mainly because of changes in Supreme Court decisions. An examination of the evolu-tion of antitrust policy is valuable as a basis for understanding present law, but it is also a fascinating history of the many ways in which the relationship between business and government has changed over our history.

Background of the Sherman Act The immediate grounds for the passage of the Sherman Act lay in the rapid development of monopolistic practices following the Civil War. The Standard Oil Trust and its many imitators in the 1880s provoked formidable opposition among small businessmen, farmers, and the general population. This was a period of concentration of economic powers, price fixing, market sharing, and other monopolistic agreements among formerly competing companies. So widespread was the opposition to the monopoly movement that the Sherman Act passed the Senate with but one dissenting vote and passed the House without opposition.

Language of the Sherman Act The two most significant sections of the Sherman Act are 1 and 2. Section 1 reads: *"Every contract, combination* in the form of trust or otherwise, *or conspiracy, in restraint of trade* or commerce among the several States, or with foreign nations, *is hereby declared to be illegal"* (italics added). Section 2 says, *"Every person who shall monopolize,* or attempt to monopolize, or combine or conspire with any other person or persons, to monopolize any part of the *trade* or commerce among the several States, or with foreign nations, *shall be deemed guilty* of a misdemeanor, and, on conviction thereof, shall be punished by fine" (italics added).

Much has been written about the purposes of the Sherman Act, but one of the best statements was given in a Supreme Court opinion:

> The Sherman Act was designed to be a comprehensive charter of economic liberty aimed at preserving free and unfettered competition as the rule of trade. It rests on the premise that the unrestrained interaction of competitive forces will yield the best allocation of our economic resources, the lowest prices, the highest quality, and the greatest material progress, while at the same time providing an environment conducive to the preservation of our democratic political and social institutions. But even were that premise open to question, the policy unequivocally laid down by the Act is competition (*Northern Pacific R.R. Co. v. United States*).

At this point it is useful to note that the act did not outlaw some, but *all* contracts, combinations, and conspiracies in restraint of trade. Furthermore, it sought to nip monopoly in the bud by making illegal any attempts to monopolize. This tough language was, of course, subject to interpretation, and the Supreme Court revealed its intellectual ingenuity in some surprising decisions over the years. This legislation did not provide anything legally new, because monopolistic agreements such as those outlawed were held unenforceable under common law prohibitions of agreements that unreasonably restrain trade. The important new feature was that these conspiracies now were offenses against the federal government.

An Illusory Distinction: Commerce v. Manufacturing The first case brought to the Supreme Court following the passage of the act was the Knight case of 1895. In this case a gigantic manufacturing company controlled 98 percent of sugar refining, but the Court said the company had not violated the act, the reason being that the government's lawyers had failed to prove any *intent* to restrain inter-state commerce and, furthermore, that "Commerce succeeds to manufacture and is not part of it." This meant Congress had no power to control manufacturing under the commerce clause of the Constitution (*United States v. E. C. Knight Co.*). With this decision, the Supreme Court seemed to invite businessmen to combine, which was contrary to the intent of Congress. Corporate immunity from the antitrust law in merging was not eliminated until the Northern Se-curities case in 1904 (*Northern Securities Co. v. United States*). Fol-lowing this case one railroad consolidation after another was de-clared illegal in the 1910s and 1920s.

The Rule of Reason The Court's encouragement to combination in the Knight case was reversed in the Northern Securities case, but reversed again in the Standard Oil Case of 1909 and the American Tobacco case of 1911. Both the Standard Oil Company of New Jersey and the American Tobacco Company enjoyed control of around 95 percent of their respective markets. Both exerted the strongest pressures on competitors, including price cutting, to main-tain and increase their market shares. In both cases the companies were judged to have conspired to monopolize and restrain trade in violation of Sections 1 and 2 of the Sherman Act. In passing judg-ment, however, the Court said that there were reasonable and un-reasonable restraints of trade, and if other trusts were to use their powers reasonably, they would not run afoul of the law. The Court did not define clearly the meaning of these words.

The Clayton and Federal Trade Commission Acts Dissatisfaction with the broad wording of the Sherman Act and the uncertainties to business in proving reasonableness led to the passage of the Clayton Act and the Federal Trade Commission Acts in 1914. The Clayton Act sought to identify those monopolistic practices which were pro-hibited by law. In establishing the FTC, Congress put the antitrust laws under the continuous supervision and administration of an agency in the executive branch. Both these acts are long, and the language is often tortuous and fuzzy. Section 7 of the Clayton Act is the most important one for this analysis, and it reads:

> . . . *no corporation* engaged in commerce *shall acquire,* directly or indirectly, the whole or any part of *the stock* or other share capital of another corporation engaged also in commerce *where the effect of such acquisition may be to substantially lessen competition* between the corporation whose stock is so acquired and the corporation making the acquisition *or to restrain such commerce in any section or community or tend to create a monopoly of any line of commerce* (italics mine).

SUPREME COURT DECISIONS CONCERNING FIRM SIZE AND MERGERS UP TO THE 1960s

I want to return now to the trend of thought stimulated by the Standard Oil and American Tobacco cases. In these two cases the Court was more interested in the way power was used to restrict competition than in the forms and structures by means of which power was acquired in a combination. This thinking was in line with precedents going back to the common law. It did begin, however, a thread of inquiry into the significance of bigness per se as a threat to competition. A series of cases made clear the Court's feeling that bigness was not necessarily badness. Much to the disgust of economists, the Court held that by merging with rivals and acquiring power over the market, a company would not necessarily be in violation of the antitrust laws.

In 1916, for instance, the Court refused to order dissolution of the American Can Company even though it had acquired enough companies to control more than 90 percent of the production of cans in the country and was found by the Court to have been organized to monopolize interstate trade in cans. The Court said that the company "had done nothing of which any competitor or any consumer of cans complains, or anything which strikes a disinterested outsider as unfair or unethical" (*United States v. American Can Co.*). It said those in the trade liked the company, and the Court would not destroy it. In another milestone decision in 1920, the Court said that the U.S. Steel Corporation, which controlled two-thirds or more of the American output of a number of basic metal shapes and forms, showed no evidence of unreasonable restraints of trade. The Court said, ". . . the law does not make mere size an offense or the existence of unexerted power an offense. . . ." Furthermore, said the Court, the public interest might be jeopardized if the corporation were dissolved (*United States v. United States Steel Corp.*). This concept was used many times later to reject the government's contention of monopoly on the basis of size and concentration of economic power. In the International Harvester case in 1927, the Court found

64 percent control of the market to be unobjectionable (*United States v. International Harvester Co.*).

The Rule of Reason and "Loose" Combinations The Court applied a different rule of reason to collusive arrangements made through cooperative action of independent companies. In the Addystone case in 1899, the Court held that price fixing was illegal whether the fixed price was or was not unreasonable (*Addystone Pipe & Steel Co. v. United States*). This view was reaffirmed in the Trenton Potteries case in 1927. Through a trade association, 23 companies manufacturing or distributing some 82 percent of the national production of vitreous pottery fixtures had agreed to fix the prices of their products. In a clarion call for free competition, the Court said that price fixing *per se* was illegal, whether reasonable or unreasonable. "The power to fix prices," said the Court, "whether reasonably exercised or not, involves power to control the market and to fix arbitrary and unreasonable prices. The reasonable price fixed today may through economic and business changes become the unreasonable price of tomorrow" (*United States v. Trenton Potteries Co.*).

The Court Encourages Merger The result of these judicial lines of thought stimulated corporate merger. While the Court held loose agreements of many kinds to be illegal per se, whether reasonable or not, mergers of formerly competing companies were not illegal if the combined company behaved itself in the eyes of the Court. What the Court did not see or refused to see, of course, was that a company which held a major share of a market was in a position to exert anticompetitive controls and that if it had such power, it was likely to use it. By these different lines of reasoning the Court, in effect, encouraged the very thing the Sherman Act was designed to stop. In the Appalachian Coal case in 1933 the Court said as much, reversing its past decisions in these words: "We know of no public policy, and none is suggested by the terms of the Sherman Act, that, in order to comply with the law, those engaged in industry should be driven to unify their properties and businesses, in order to correct abuses which may be corrected by less drastic measures" (*Appalachian Coal, Inc. v. United States*). In this case, however, the Court reversed its previously consistent record of rejecting any and all price fixing by holding that 137 rival companies producing 75 percent of the bituminous coal in the Appalachian area, who had fixed prices in order to end injurious competition so as to promote a "fair market," had not violated the law.

Monopoly Power and Size Beginning with the Alcoa case (*United States v. Aluminum Co. of America*), the Supreme Court condemned size as monopoly power and contrary to law, but it did not pin itself down as to what size was illegal and, on occasion, it seemed to reverse itself. In the case of Alcoa, the company had control of 90 percent of the manufacturing of primary aluminum in the United States; the remaining 10 percent was imported. The company also fabricated products from primary ingot. It was charged with illegal actions in squeezing other fabricators between upping its ingot prices and lowering prices of its own fabricated products. The Court held the company to be a monopoly within Section 2 of the Sherman Act and said that Congress "did not condone 'good trusts' and condemn 'bad' ones; it forbade all." Furthermore, said the Court, the mere existence of the power to fix prices inherent in the monopoly position could not be distinguished from the exercise of such power. Any distinction between the existence and exertion of the power was purely formal. When the monopoly entered the market, "the power and its exercise must needs coalesce." The Court said that 90 percent control was enough to constitute monopoly and came near to saying that size in itself was an offense. At least in this case, for the first time the acquisition of control of a market was a primary test of monopolization, and monopoly power need not be abused to be unlawful.

This doctrine was upheld in a number of subsequent cases. In the American Tobacco case of 1946, the Court held that the three big tobacco companies controlled the market and by their practices, including charging identical prices, they were squeezing out small companies who made cheap cigarettes. The Court held the companies were guilty of unlawful acts and that "Neither proof of the exertion of the power to exclude nor proof of actual exclusion of existing or potential competitors is essential to sustain a charge of monopolization under the Sherman Act" (*American Tobacco Co. et al. v. United States*). In other words, when a few sellers dominate a market they violate the law whether they agree to act in concert or not. In the Paramount case (1948), the Court ordered the major studios to divest themselves of their theaters because of their power to exclude competitors from showing films in the theaters. Said the Court, "the existence of power 'to exclude competition when it is desired to do so' is itself a violation of Paragraph 2 (of the Sherman Act), provided it is coupled with the purpose or intent to exercise that power" (*United States v. Paramount Pictures, Inc.*). Here, the court reneged a bit on the other precedents by bringing in intent.

In the same year, in the Columbia Steel case, the Court seemed to slip back into its more permissive attitude. In this case the government sought to stop U.S. Steel from buying, through its subsidiary Columbia Steel, the largest steel fabricator on the West Coast—the Consolidated Steel Corporation. This acquisition, together with a previous one (the Geneva, Utah, plant), gave U.S. Steel over 51 percent of the rolled-steel or ingot capacity of the Pacific Coast area. In a close decision the Court held that there was no violation of the law. Size is significant, it said, but the steel industry itself is big (*United States v. Columbia Steel Co.*).

Section 7 of the Clayton Act as Amended in 1950 Prior to 1914, mergers had resulted in substantial growth of large corporations, and Congress wanted to slow down the movement. Section 7 of the Clayton Act was designed to do this. Since mergers then were generally created through acquisition of stock, Section 7 prohibited the acquisition of stock of one corporation by another in the same line of business where the effect was to lessen competition between the corporation or to tend to create a monopoly. Purchase of stock for investment was not prohibited.

In 1926, the Court held in the Thatcher and Swift cases that if a corporation bought stock in another company and then approved to itself the sale of the assets of that corporation before the FTC instituted proceedings, there was no violation of the act. There was thus a huge loophole through which merger-minded companies could leap (*Thatcher Manufacturing Co. v. FTC*), (*Swift & Co. v. FTC*). In 1934 in the Arrow-Hart & Hegeman case, the court said the same thing again (*Arrow-Hart & Hegeman Electric Co. v. FTC*).

This defect in the Clayton Act was finally corrected in the Celler-Kefauver Amendments to the Clayton Act of 1950. Section 7 now reads: ". . . no corporation . . . shall acquire, directly or indirectly, the whole or any part of the stock or . . . *any part of the assets* of another corporation . . . where . . . the effect of such acquisition may be substantially to lessen competition, or tend to create a monopoly" (italics mine). Congress made it quite clear in discussions of this law that the intent was to stop a trend to monopolization in its incipient state. Acquisitions of stock or assets have a cumulative effect, and the bill was intended to permit intervention in such a cumulative process. The idea was to stop large firms from merging with small ones when the effect would be to lessen competition or tend toward monopoly.

STRUCTURE VERSUS PERFORMANCE AS A BASIS FOR ANTITRUST POLICY

Armed with the new amendment to the Clayton Act, the Supreme Court in the 1960s proceeded to forge new criteria for determining the legality of mergers. While it did not subscribe to any particular economic theory about antitrust policy, its decisions in this decade showed a disposition toward the structural theory. A good bit of the factual economic as well as theoretical evidence which was available seemed to support this policy. However, during the late

1960s and after there grew a body of evidence which at first challenged the older structural theory and gradually built impressive contradictory evidence.

Structure, Performance, and Behavior Twenty-five years ago Edward S. Mason argued in a landmark article that public policy toward industrial organizations ought to aim at promoting sound market structures as well as effective business performance. The market structure and performance tests, he observed, "must be used to complement rather than exclude each other" (1949: 1280). By performance he meant product and process innovation, reductions in costs by various managerial and technical methods which were passed on to consumers in lower prices, suitable capacity in relationship to output, profits not out of line with other industries, and emphasis on product and service rather than excessive advertising expenditures. Since Mason wrote his article there has been sharp controversy between those who argue for a structural public policy and those who support a policy based on performance.

The conventional economic wisdom up to recent years, and still held by many, was that the structure of the marketplace is a reliable index of monopoly power. More precisely, the theory argues that the more concentrated are the sales and assets of a few firms in an industry the greater is the monopoly power of those firms. Not only is there substantial concentration today of sales and assets in individual industries but there is high concentration of all corporate assets in the largest companies in the United States. Since everyone is opposed to monopoly the proper public policy is one that slows down and reverses this trend. If this is not done we shall in three or four decades be completely dominated by concentrations of economic power in our large corporations.

Excessive concentration of market power, it is argued, gives corporate managers discretionary power to fix market prices, determine which products come to market and in what volume, and make excessive profits. Furthermore, monopoly power has produced price inflation, inefficiencies in production and, of course, a decline in competition.

Structuralists argue that if competitive markets can be created by breaking up concentrations of economic power, or by preventing mergers of large firms, individual companies will behave competitively with economically desirable performance. In this light, large concentrations of economic power should be broken up. Antitrust policy will be clearer and more effective if there is some *per se* rule based on structure.

This market concentration doctrine is rebutted by other views. It is argued that concentrations of economic power in large companies are due to market forces and not to motivations to monopolize. Large size is a necessary concomitant to a large economy. There are certain industries where large companies and concentration are essential because of the heavy capital investment needed to do business. Industries will not become concentrated unless there is a basic economic reason for large-scale operations. Business structure is, therefore, the result of underlying economic forces.

Many observers see competition rising rather than declining. They see there are many forms of nonprice competition which take place. Smaller firms can specialize and take advantage of any excessive pricing of large companies. High profits of large firms may be associated more with efficiency than the exercise of monopoly power. Product innovation is a major source of competition by large firms because they can afford heavy research and development expenditures that small firms cannot.

In sum, it is the performance and behavior of large firms which should be examined and not simply structure. An atomistic market structure would be quite out of tune with the demands of modern society and would, in addition, bring about economic distortions and inefficiencies.

A few other issues between the market structurists and the business performists may be presented in capsule form. The structurists reject performance because they say there are no clear and acceptable standards for measuring performance. Those who emphasize performance do so because they say there are no suitable standards to measure acceptable structure. Structure is favored because when it is suitable, there will be many competitors, the market will regulate economic activity, and government interference in the market mechanism will be unnecessary. Those who hold to performance point out the extraordinary change that would be required to bring about anything approaching pure competition. Furthermore, if advantages of size are prevented, will not the cost to consumers be excessively high? Structurists say it is not performance which is sought, but competition. There is an implicit assumption that if structure is acceptable, there will be better products, improved service, and lower prices. On the other hand, it is said that mergers and company expansions are necessary to ensure efficiency, which benefits society. It is pointed out that structure can be perfect, as in atomistic competiton, and performance terrible because market conditions lead to cutthroat competition. And so the arguments, like a shuttlecock, move back and forth from one position to another. To many observers the argument is not an "either/or" situation. Markham, for instance, argues that structure and conduct criteria are complementary and not competitive (in Sichel, 1970).

(This is a highly simplified and incomplete statement of these differing views. For deeper examination of the views see Weston and Ornstein, 1973; Blair, 1973; Markham and Papanek, 1970; and Weston and Peltzman, 1969).

Judicial and Legislative Implications These arguments, and the supporting data for them, are extremely important because they influence public policy. We shall review shortly how the Supreme Court has more and more taken market concentration into consideration in reaching its decisions in recent years. The market concentration point of view has not yet hardened into firm acceptance by the courts of law but the decisions are in that direction. Policy of the Antitrust Division of the U.S. Department of Justice also has supported the structural theory. On the legislative front there have been many bills presented to the Congress which sought the breakup of large companies. The most significant one in recent years is the Hart bill.

Senator Hart introduced into the Congress in mid-1972 his S.1167 called The Industrial Reorganization Act. This bill calls for the establishment of a commission with the power to break up large firms if any one of three conditions are present in an industry. The bill states that: "There shall be a rebuttable assumption that monopoly power is possessed" if (1) a profit rate on net worth after taxes in excess of 15 percent over a period of 5 consecutive years in the most recent 7 years, or (2) no substantial price competition among two or more corporations in three consecutive years out of the most recent five years, or (3) if any four or fewer corporations account for 50 percent or more of sales in any one year out of the most recent three years. While this bill is not likely to pass, one can safely predict that others like it will be before the Congress in the future.

Factual Support for These Views There is a growing body of data related to these different views. Some of the highlights will be presented shortly. Before doing so it is important to observe that while factual information is becoming better it is far from adequate. Vast areas of corporate activity are not made public and, hence, not available either to the government or to private scholars. Much of the government's data from which conclusions are made public are not released so that independent scholars cannot verify the results. Data are not comparable. For instance, corporations increasingly are including foreign assets in their total-asset calculations, which serves to increase concentration ratios compared with the past. Different studies are made for different time periods which can lead to different conclusions. The interrelationships between variables such as concentration, price, and profits are not always clear and rigorous. Such considerations should be kept in mind in reviewing data and conclusions about concentrations of economic power [Bock, 1972(A, B); Bock and Farkas, 1973].

Macroeconomic Concentration When fears are expressed about trends on corporate economic power the benchmark most frequently used is asset growth of the 200 largest corporations. The most often cited numbers show that total assets of the 200 largest companies in 1954 were 50.8 percent of total industrial corporate assets. In 1968 the 200 largest had 62.3 percent of the total (Bock and Farkas, 1973). This is a 11.5 percent rise in fourteen years (Weston and Ornstein, 1973: 5). Now, of course, if this rate were to continue the 200 largest industrial corporations would account for 100 percent of all manufacturing assets in less than forty to fifty years.

There are other ways to look at the data, however. The 200 largest companies in 1954 had 50.8 percent of total industrial corporate assets. In 1968 the same 200 held 51.2 percent of the total, a statistically insignificant increase. They just about maintained their position. What happened, of course, was that other firms became larger in the interim. It is well to note, too, that this period was extraordinary in the sense that it included the great merger wave with the rise of new huge conglomerate firms.

When the position of the largest companies is measured by value added—a more reliable index—the 200 largest accounted for 42 percent of the total for all manufacturing firms in 1967, not 62.3 percent [Bock, 1972(B)].

Depending upon which numbers are used one can say that aggregate concentration is growing or it is not. Whatever the degree in this country today it is not as high as in Europe and Japan.

Microconcentration in Industries Concentration in individual industries is usually measured by the ratio of sales of the largest companies to total sales in the industry. In 1966 there were 33 industries, or 9 percent of the total, where the four largest firms had over 75 percent of the total sales. In 90 industries, or 24 percent of all industries, the four largest had between 50 and 74 percent of the sales; in 154 industries, or 40 percent of all industries, the top four had between 25 and 49 percent of the sales; and in 105 industries, or 27 percent of the total industries, the top four had less than 25 percent of total industry sales (Weston and Ornstein, 1973).

High industry concentration is found in a limited sector of the U.S. economy. Weston concludes that most of the high concentration in 1968 was in six industries: petroleum refining, motor vehicles, steel, industrial chemicals, nonferrous metals, and aircraft. About one-half of the one hundred largest firms in the manufacturing sector are in these industries (in Steiner, 1972).

What about trends? Studies by the staff of the Cabinet Committee on Price Stability (1969) showed no significant change in concentration between 1947 and 1968. Concentration has changed much in particular industries but in the aggregate it does not appear to have changed significantly over a long period of time.

In sum, there is concentration in the United States but it does not seem to be overwhelming us. To accept this conclusion, however, one must look at other data concerning performance.

Price Inflation and Concentration Concentrated industries are responsible for price inflation, it is alleged, because with their power over markets they can accept higher wage rate increases demanded by unions and pass them on to consumers (Blair, 1973). Recent evidence points to no long-run secular relation between concentration and price change (Demsetz, 1973). The greatest rate of average price change since 1967 has taken place in industries with the lowest concentration. The lowest rate of price increase has come about in the highest concentration quartile (Weston, 1972).

Concentration and Profits On the basis of the work of Bain (1951) and later Blair (1973) it has long been accepted doctrine that there was a positive correlation between concentration and high profits. Bain studied the relationship for the period 1936–1940 in forty-two industries and found that in those industries where the eight largest companies accounted for 70 percent or more of value added the profit rate was 11.8 percent. For other industries in a low concentration group the rate was 7.5 percent. For statistical and other reasons Bain was cautious about his conclusions but, generally, it has been conceded that his work, and other studies, confirmed a somewhat weak yet a positive relationship between concentration and above-average profits.

Recent studies do not confirm this conclusion. Brozen took the original Bain sample, more than doubled the number of industries, and then examined the profits in the same time period as the original Bain study and for later periods. He found the profit rate in industries where eight firms did more than 70 percent of the business to be slightly lower than for industries with less concentration [in Weston, 1973, and Brozen, 1971(B)]. In other studies he found that industries with profit rates above the average grew at a faster rate than the average and their profit rates trended down toward the average. Just the reverse was true for industries with below-average profit rates [1970, 1971(A)]. This suggests that both above and below-average profits may be a temporary disequilibrium phenomenon which is not likely to persist for a long period of time. Ornstein confirmed Brozen's findings that profits were not related significantly to market concentration. They were tied more, he found, to industry and firm growth rates and to the minimum efficient scale of production (1972).

Collusion and Concentration Earlier studies provided a basis for the view that concentration resulted in collusion to restrict output, raise price, and lift profits. This idea was incorporated into antitrust policy. In 1969, for instance, Assistant U.S. Attorney-General Richard W. McLaren said he was going to crack down on conglomerates and set up new guidelines to govern their acquisitions because: "Current merger trends create the probability that a community of interest will develop among the leading actual or potential competitors in many industries" (*Los Angeles Times,* May 28, 1969). Standard economic textbooks have for years accepted this view.

Studies by Demsetz do not support a correlation between concentration and collusion. He says that the concentration/collusion hypothesis implies that smaller firms in the concentrated industries should have higher profits than smaller firms in the nonconcentrated industries. He finds no positive correlation between market concentration and profit rates of smaller firms (1973). There is, however, a positive correlation between profits and concentration. His data "strongly suggest that the relatively large firms in concentrated industries produce at lower cost than their smaller rivals" (1973: 22). He concludes that "the relative competitive superiority of large firms grows more significant as concentration increases" (1973: 25–26).

Price Flexibility, Concentration, and Competition The idea that there was a close relationship between concentration and monopoly power gained strength when Gardiner Means published a milestone monograph which showed that corporations were not responding to changes in market conditions by changing prices but were "administering prices" (1935). While he did not specifically link inflexibility with concentration, the basic allegation was there. Since then others have tackled the problem of statistically proving a connection but, as Demsetz says, "There is as yet no reason to elevate the findings of either side to the status of a scientifically established result" (1973: 7).

If one looks only at the way in which price moves in an atomistically competitive model there is price inflexibility in American industry. But there is also a great deal of nonprice competition in American industry. Indeed, these nonprice characteristics are probably the most significant types of competition which any company, especially the larger ones, face. They are new products that replace old ones, service and warranties, credit terms, international competition, and better general management capabilities in competing firms. Jacoby looks at the state of competition today and sees that it is being invigorated and not weakened by the larger companies (1973).

Policy Implications "The thrust of the accumulating evidence," says Weston, "is that the development of concentrated industries or oligopolies is a result of competition and an expression of competitive processes" (1972: 632). In industries such as agricultural implements, cans, steel, etc., competitive forces have reversed concentration. Concentration has increased in other industries formerly having a large number of firms. He feels that for some industries, especially those requiring high investments, the atomistic model of many small firms is inappropriate. Furthermore, "merger activity may be seen a superior alternative to bankruptcy" (Weston and Ornstein, 1973: 245).

In sum, there simply is no substantial or convincing evidence that market concentration is indicative of monopoly power, collusion, price inflexibility, high prices, and/or excessive profits (Demsetz, 1973: 30; Weston and Ornstein, 1973: 246). Newer data are diametrically opposed to the structural theory. In this light legislative proposals such as the Hart bill, if passed and implemented, are more likely to reduce industrial efficiency than to strengthen it.

CONGLOMERATES AND THE SUPREME COURT

The decade of the 1960s witnessed an exceptional expansion of mergers by so-called conglomerates. This movement was the source of great apprehension and concern. Managers of conglomerates were accused of financial manipulations in their merger activities that made no economic contribution to society and posed new threats to competition. They were accused of adding to general economic concentration and concentration in specific industries with all the bad consequences of growing monopoly power. While the wave of mergers of that decade has not subsided the issues still remain and are, therefore, pertinent to this discussion.

Kinds of Mergers In the past, mergers were either vertical or horizontal. A vertical merger takes place when a company acquires others either back in the production chain toward raw material sources, or forward toward consumers of final products and services. When Reynolds Metals Company, a producer of aluminum foil, acquired Arrow Brands, a converter of aluminum foil for the florist trade, this was a vertical merger. A horizontal merger is one that combines the activities of companies within the same industry. When Ling-Temco Electronics, Inc., merged with Chance Vought Corporation, it was a wedding between two firms making electronics and aerospace industry products. Combinations can, of course, be both horizontal and vertical—as when the Brown Shoe Company, a manufacturer and retail seller of shoes, acquired G. R. Kinney, a manufacturer and retail seller of shoes. In recent years, the word "conglomerate" has been used to describe certain types of mergers. This word was first used in 1941 in hearings before the Temporary National Economic Committee, but was not introduced into Court decisions until the late 1960s. A conglomerate merger is generally defined as one that brings together into one company two or more firms engaged in unrelated lines of business. Many businessmen feel that the term conglomerate has pejorative connotations and they do not like it, but Jacoby feels it is in such widespread use today that it is not likely to be discarded (1969: 41).

Weston (1969: 16–17) draws a distinction between the concentric firm and the conglomerate. In the concentric firm there is a common thread of relationship among its product and service families. The Occidental Petroleum Corporation eschews the word "conglomerate," because it says it is a producer and processor of natural resources and its acquisitions are based upon this fundamental mission. In such cases, argues Weston, there is substantial managerial carryover in the sense that the capabilities of the top management of the company, together with staff expertise at headquarters, have high applicability to the subsidiaries. Thus the label conglomerate is inappropriate, since it suggests lack of relationship, and he prefers concentric as a substitute.

Weston identifies four types of conglomerate firms, namely, managerial conglomerate, financial conglomerate, investment company, and individual portfolio holdings. A major distinguishing characteristic among these four is managerial attention by top management of the central corporation to the affairs of subsidiaries and acquired companies. Line and staff specialists apply their knowledge to acquired operating companies in the management and financial types, but the degree of supervision varies considerably among them, depending upon managerial style and purpose. In both cases, however, subsidiaries typically have considerable autonomy, and the success or failure of managers in the subsidiaries rests principally if not solely upon rigorously defined standards, such as profit return on employed investment. Investment companies by law (Investment Company Act, 1940) have less than 5 percent of the stock of any one company, and while this amount might permit some managerial control, there typically is practically none. Similarly, stock acquisitions for individual portfolio investments rarely result in managerial control.

In this chapter I shall follow Weston's definitions. It ought to be noted, however, that there are other definitions which try to distinguish between "concentric" and "conglomerate." For instance, Bock (1969: 8) distinguishes between "convergent conglomerates" (Weston's concentrics) and "divergent conglomerates" (Weston's conglomerate). The FTC (1969) distinguishes among three types of conglomerates. Product extension mergers involve companies having some degree of functional relationship in either production or distribution. Market extension mergers involve companies in the same general product line that sell in different geographic markets. Other conglomerates consist of essentially unrelated combinations.

Merger Activity from 1960 to 1968 Total acquisitions by companies in 1960 were 1,345 and rose to a peak of 4,003 in 1968 (FTC, 1969: 8). While this number is very small compared with the total business population the result was the rise of new huge corporations. In 1960, acquisitions by conglomerates amounted to 71 percent of total mergers with 60 percent of the dollar value. In 1968 they accounted for 84 percent of total acquisitions and 89 percent of dollar asset value.

There was also increased activity in mergers of large companies. The aggregate assets of all acquired firms having assets of $10 million or more as a percentage of the total assets of manufacturing and mining corporations of $10 million or more in asset size was under 1 percent in 1960. By 1968 the ratio had grown to over 3 percent. In 1968 the 200 largest companies acquired a total of 94 companies with aggregate assets of over $8 billion.

Supreme Court Decisions One of the first cases tried on the basis of the amended Section 7 of the Clayton Act was Brown Shoe. In this case the Court held that protecting small independent competitors by prohibiting the merger of two large companies might result in higher costs and prices to consumers, but preventing such mergers and thereby maintaining competition was worth the price.

The Brown Shoe case was a key decision in a number of respects and set precedents that reverberated in subsequent decisions. It is worthwhile, therefore, to look at the case and the later decisions in some detail (*United States v. Brown Shoe Company*). In 1956 the Brown Shoe Company acquired the G. R. Kinney Company. At that time Brown Shoe was one of the leading manufacturers of men's, women's, and children's shoes, but had only 4 percent of the national output of this line. Kinney operated the largest independent chain of retail family shoe stores in the nation, with over 350 outlets, but its share of the nation's shoe output was 1.5 percent and its share of the total national retail shoe sales was 1.2 percent. Together, the companies had 2.3 percent of total retail shoe outlets. Since the industry had close to 800 shoe manufacturers, no one of which had an important share of the market, it was operating close to the pure competitive model. The Court, however, found a threat to competition in both the manufacturing and retail areas.

It found the merger to be exclusionary, in that it would discourage the entry of competitors. It said, for example, that competitors of Brown would be discouraged from selling to Kinney outlets, and a narrowing of Kinney purchases from independent suppliers could be expected. The Court said that the share of the market foreclosed was not enough to make the merger illegal, but that there was reason to believe, on the basis of Brown's past record, that foreclosure would become more serious. Furthermore, there was a trend in the industry toward vertical integration that ought to be impeded. This view was based upon the fact that the thirteen largest shoe manufacturers operated 21 percent of the shoe stores.

On the horizontal front, the Court thought the merger was illegal. The Court examined individual retail markets having over 10,000 population and found that the combined sales of Brown and Kinney as a share of the total market ranged from 5.1 percent to 24.8 percent for men's shoes, from 5.0 percent to 51.8 percent for children's shoes, and from 5.1 percent to 57.7 percent for women's shoes. In 47 cities the combined share of the three types of shoes was over 5 percent. The Court said that "if a merger achieving 5 percent control were approved, it might be required to approve future merger efforts by competitors seeking similar market shares. Then, said the Court, the oligopoly Congress sought to avoid would be encouraged.

This case set a number of guidelines: First, the Court said that the act applied not only to mergers between actual competitors, but also to vertical and conglomerate mergers. Second, mergers could be stopped in cases where the threats to competition were only *potential*. The law could nip in the bud incipient threats to competition. Third, relevant market areas to test anticompetitive behavior could be anywhere in the country. Fourth, excluding competitors from the market is contrary to the Clayton Act. Finally, the merger of two companies of large size in a concentrated industry makes the combination vulnerable to the provisions of the act.

Advantages to Acquired Companies In a series of cases the court took special note of and frowned upon certain advantages that could accrue to acquired companies by virtue of the resources and power of the acquirer.

In *Reynolds Metal Co. v. FTC* (1962) there was applied the "deep pocket" theory. Arrow Brands produced florist foil by coloring and embossing aluminum foil which it bought from Reynolds Metal. Arrow Brands was the largest company in the florist foil business and had 33 percent of the market. Reynolds acquired Arrow, and the Court declared the merger illegal: "The power of the 'deep pocket' or 'rich parent' for one of the florist foil suppliers in a competitive group where previously no company was very large and all were relatively small opened the possibility and power to sell at prices approximating cost or below and thus to undercut and ravage the less affluent competition."

In the Procter & Gamble case (1967), the Court held that a merger was contrary to the act when it gave the acquired company an advantage in advertising expenditures and store display. This case resulted in a key decision and is worthwhile describing more fully (*FTC v. The Procter & Gamble Co.*). In 1957 Procter & Gamble, one of the country's largest manufacturers of soaps and detergents, acquired the Clorox Company, the nation's largest producer of household liquid bleach. The Court was impressed by the statistics of concentration. At the time of the merger, Clorox had 48.8 percent of the nation's sales, but higher percentages in regional sales—56 percent in New England, 72 percent in the Middle Atlantic States, and 64 percent in the New York metropolitan area. When the sales of Purex, the next largest producer of liquid bleach, were added, the two had 65 percent of the national market. The four largest firms had almost 80 percent of the market. Because of the weight of liquid bleach, the product is not usually shipped more than 300 miles. This fact gave Clorox an advantage in some markets because it alone could distribute nationally. Procter & Gamble at the time of the merger was dominant in producing and selling household products, although it did not carry liquid bleach in its product line. Three companies in this industry, including Procter & Gamble, accounted for 80 percent of the sales. The Court was also impressed with the fact that Procter & Gamble was one of the country's largest advertisers (it spent $80 million a year on advertising and another $47 million on sales promotion). It was therefore in a position to get discounts from media, engage in joint promotion, and cut costs of advertising on individual products below levels for other companies producing liquid bleach. It could also get preferred space in distributor stores.

This merger was not horizontal and not vertical—it was a conglomerate. The Court called it a "product extension" merger, and held against Procter & Gamble on several counts. First, the merger created a barrier to entry because the company was so big it could dissuade new companies from entering the market. The fact that Procter & Gamble could command preferred space on market shelves also would discourage competition. Second, if the merger had not taken place, Procter & Gamble, said the Court, would be the most likely new competition to Clorox and Purex. Therefore, a potential independent competitor was eliminated. Third, price competition was likely to decline. Even before the merger the Court noted that smaller companies tended to follow Clorox's lead in this oligopolistic industry. With an even bigger giant such as Procter & Gamble, the Court felt the small companies would be much less aggressive in price competition. The Court also observed that claims by Procter & Gamble that the merger would bring efficiencies in distribution which would benefit the consumer could not be used as a defense when a lessening of competition could not be reversed without losing these economies.

Reciprocity is another action the Court does not favor. This advantage takes place when firms, overtly or tacitly, make concessions to one another in order to promote their own business interests. Consolidated Foods, a major food wholesaler which owned food processing plants and a network of retail food stores, acquired Gentry, a manufacturer of dehydrated onion and garlic. Gentry was one of the two largest domestic manufacturers in this market, although the total size of the market was small. Consolidated did not deny that it had reciprocity contacts with Gentry, but did deny that it exercised pressure. The Court took pains to observe that not every merger was outlawed where there might be some reciprocal sales practices, but where the acquiring company is dominant in an industry, there is a clear probability of reciprocal buying. The Court dissolved this merger in 1965.

Excluding Competitors from the Market In many cases during the 1960s the Courts held mergers to be illegal partly because competitors were excluded from the market. This clearly was shown in the Procter & Gamble case. Notice also in this case that the Court objected to the merger because without the merger Procter & Gamble was the most likely candidate to enter the chlorine bleach market. Exclusion of competitors was also important in the Brown Shoe case.

Elimination of Potential Competition Following the Brown Shoe case, the Court rejected a number of mergers because of the threat of potential competition. In the El Paso Natural Gas case (*United States v. El Paso Natural Gas Co.*) the Court found that although two companies were operating in different geographic areas, they were potential competitors, and the merger was prohibited.

In the Penn-Olin case (*United States v. Penn-Olin Chemical Co.*) the Court for the first time permitted an acquisition challenged under Section 7 to survive. Actually, the "acquisition" was a joint venture between Pennsalt and Olin Mathieson. They formed Penn-Olin in 1960 to produce sodium chlorate in Kentucky. Olin had not manufactured this product, but Pennsalt had been producing it in Oregon. Pennsalt distributed it in the southeast through Olin Mathieson. The Court allowed the venture on the grounds that there was no probability that both companies would have entered the market independently had they not undertaken the joint venture.

Merger of Large Companies in Concentrated Industries In several cases the Court found that when two comparatively large companies combined in an industry where a large share of the market was dominated by comparatively few companies, the combination was contrary to law. In the Continental Can case (*United States v. Continental Can Co., Inc.*), Continental, a large producer of metal containers, acquired Hazel-Atlas, a large producer of glass containers. In the metal container market, six firms had 70.1 percent of the business. In the glass container field, three firms accounted for 55 percent of the market. Both Continental and Hazel-Atlas were dominant in their industries, and the Court held that the combined market shares of these two companies were too high.

Von's Grocery Company's merger with Shopping Bag Food Stores was struck down in 1966 because of excessive concentration in Los Angeles, plus the progressive reduction of small competitors and the increase of large companies in the area (*United States v. Von's Grocery Co.*). Pabst Brewing Company's merger with the Blatz Brewing Company likewise was stopped in 1966. The Court objected to the restraint of competition which it felt was implicit in the merger of two large companies in an industry where independent competitors were declining in numbers and where shares of market of the two were high in certain cities (*United States v. Pabst Brewing Co.*).

ARE THE SUPREME COURT DECISIONS CONCERNING CONGLOMERATES MOVING IN THE RIGHT DIRECTION?

In light of what was said previously about the theory and data concerning the structural versus the performance points of view there is doubt about the correctness of public antitrust policy embedded in a number of recent Supreme Court decisions. There is, however, doubt about this conclusion (Horvath, 1972). It is important, however, to get a little more specific about this.

Did Conglomerates Accentuate Aggregate Concentration? Bock used a list of 63 conglomerates identified by Weston (1973: 222) and concluded that 34 were among the 200 largest manufacturing corporations in terms of total assets in 1967. Of these, 14 were among the 200 largest in total assets in both 1947 and 1967, while the remaining 20 were not in the 1947 listing. She found that between 1958 and 1967 the conglomerate corporations increased assets at an average annual rate of 24.7 percent compared with 11.0 percent for other companies. In the period 1947–1958 the conglomerates had 9 percent of the total assets compared with 91 percent for other corporations. In the 1958–1967 period the conglomerate share was 69 percent compared with 31 percent for other corporations (1973: 32). This indicates, of course, an impressive increase in the share of total assets held by conglomerates. The result, however, has not been any significant increase in aggregate concentration as noted previously.

What Is Behind the Recent Merger Wave? There are those who accuse conglomerate managers of being primarily interested in financial manipulation for their own gain. Others think the predominant motivation is to acquire economic power. At any rate the motives ascribed to conglomerate managers have not been held in high esteem by some observers. On the other hand, there are those who explain the merger wave as being fundamentally motivated by legitimate economic objectives. Jacoby, for instance, says the recent and the previous two merger waves were based on the conjuncture of two conditions. The first was "an accumulation of perceived and unexploited profit-making opportunities for enlarging the scale of enterprises, arising from basic technological and social changes"; and the second was "a buoyant capital market with strong demand for new securities" (1969: 43). This hypothesis rejects the thesis that the movement was fundamentally a desire to achieve monopoly power in the market. Rather, it asserts that the motivations were predominantly drives by businessmen to profit by exploiting opportunities growing out of new demands and the application of new managerial techniques and business organizations.

More specifically, the underlying purposes of mergers include such objectives as: growth of sales and profits, avoidance of dependence on one product line, stability of sales and earnings over the business cycle, acquisition of needed technology, reduction of costs by using an underemployed distribution system, entry into foreign markets, use of surplus cash, acquisition of basic raw materials, use of excess productive capacity, use of technological capabilities, completing a product line, and taking advantage of tax laws. Undoubtedly there have been mergers with the intent to make life more comfortable by eliminating competitors, but the overwhelming drives have been legitimate economic motivations. On the other side of the coin, most company marriages have not been shotgun weddings: the acquired has sought the merger. An aging owner of a company may wish to retire by selling his firm to another company; a firm may be in financial trouble and need access to cash; or it may be apparent to both companies that joint efforts will more readily achieve mutual economic objectives. As Jacoby points out, these underlying drives have paralleled a growing number of opportunities, as well as threats, in the rapidly changing and prosperous environment. New industries have literally been born overnight, opportunities for profitable production of goods and services have been expanding in number, economic activity has been vigorous and reasonably stable, and capital has been available.

Paralleling these trends has been a revolution in management techniques. Formalized long-range planning has facilitated the identification of new opportunities and threats and has formulated the plans to exploit the opportunities and to avoid the threats. New developments in mathematical techniques to solve complex problems and new information systems have helped management immensely to improve decision-making about large and difficult problems. Advances in the theory and practice of management have provided knowledge to help managers to control larger enterprises more effectively. Developments in the behavioral sciences have helped managers to deal more effectively with people in organizations under conditions of rapid change and uncertainty. These and other advances in the art and science of management have given rise to a new breed of manager far different from and considerably more effective than the typical manager of the past. These developments have facilitated the growth of the conglomerate. The rise in the larger corporation of professional staff to help line managers relate their corporation to its environment and to maintain the degree of internal control necessary to business success has also been important. It is not unusual to find at the top of today's large corporation experts in computers, quantitative decision tools, long-range planning, corporate acquisitions, and technology who join hands with older professionals in law, marketing, finance, and accounting. These staffs are costly yet valuable in helping managers to make better decisions. This motivates managers to spread their costs and skills over a growing corporate family.

This does not deny the fact that many of the rapidly rising conglomerates during the 1960–1968 merger wave were led by entrepreneurs who operated upon the basis of their own intuitions without large staffs. Many were moulded after the industrial buccaneers of the late nineteenth century. Their motivations ranged across a wide spectrum—power, the fun of the game, make money, and so on. One study of the merger movement showed that those companies which acquired others on the basis of careful planning did much better than those that did not plan (Ansoff, et. al., 1970).

In sum, the basic drive of the great majority of conglomerate managers has not been monopolistic. It has resulted from rapid changes in the economic environment in which more and more opportunities exist and in which new threats arise, from a buoyant capital market, from new advances in the art and science of management, and from the rise of expert staffs to aid management.

Are Conglomerates Efficient? Weston compared the performance of sixty conglomerates with a broad sample of manufacturing firms and concluded that the conglomerates registered a superior performance. Over the period 1958 to 1967, conglomerate sales, as might be expected, increased at an annual growth rate of 19.9 percent, compared with 7.3 percent for all manufacturing firms. Net income, however, was at an annual rate of 20.3 percent for conglomerates and 9.6 percent for others. Earnings per share for conglomerates were 15.6 percent and 7.6 percent for companies in the Dow-Jones Industrial Average. The return on net worth in 1967 was 12.3

percent for conglomerates compared with 11.4 percent for all manu-facturing. Weston concludes that, while earnings performance on assets and net worth of conglomerates is not significantly different from that of all manufacturing firms, "given the unfavorable earnings opportunities in the industries from which many conglomerates emerged, earnings performance to date is favorable" (1969: 55). The picture during the five-year period ending in 1972, however, is a little mixed. The average annual return on equity of forty-four conglomerates for the period was 11.5 percent compared with 11.4 percent for all industry. Return on total capital of the conglomerate sales growth was 10.4 percent and 9.1 percent for all industry. The annual earnings growth of the conglomerates was 1.3 percent com-pared with 3.6 percent for all industry (*Forbes*, January 1, 1973).

Do Conglomerates Lessen Competition? It has been alleged by many observers, and supported by the Supreme Court in a number of cases, that conglomerates have an unfair competitive advantage in unrelated industries. On the other hand, there are those who feel that just the reverse is true—that conglomerates increase the vigor of competition in the industries in which they make acquisitions. The controversy centers on a number of specific allegations, among which the following stand out:

1. Cross Subsidization. It is said ("deep pocket" theory) that conglom-erates engage in cutthroat and predatory pricing because they subsi-dize less profitable activities, drive competitors out of business, and then make sizable profits. This is not only illegal, but also rare. Typically, general managers of decentralized operations measure per-formance on the basis of return on investment. It is not in keeping with this managerial philosophy to engineer losses, even though profits might rise when competitors are eliminated. Managers reason correctly that even if temporary losses were accepted in price cutting for higher profits later, the higher later price would bring new com-petitors into the market. Furthermore, if a division is unprofitable, the typical response of management is to improve its performance by better management (meaning new products, better marketing, or cost cutting) or to get rid of it.
2. Unfair Competitive Advantages. In several cases the Supreme Court complained that an acquired company gained unfair advantages be-cause it could avoid financial problems, underprice competitors, or gain access to superior advertising and marketing strength. There is truth to this contention, and such advantages are often sought in mergers. It is pointed out by others, however, that this sort of "un-fair" advantage turns out to be efficiency. If one firm has an advan-tage over another because of access to capital, must all competitors by law be assured the same advantage? Advantages enjoyed by larger companies may rest in superior resources and not in the merging of

companies *per se*, although the joining of two companies may produce a synergistic effect. Is it contrary to public policy for the public to benefit by improved nonprice competition? To take this position is to be opposed in principle to competition.

3. Reciprocity. It is charged that conglomerates make it possible for the sales of acquired companies to be based upon mutual sales arrangements because of affiliation rather than because of price or quality. This effect, it is said, is not necessarily clandestinely arranged, but is spontaneous and inevitable. Since a conglomerate will purchase in volume from many sellers, the sellers will "see the wisdom" of reciprocal purchases from divisions of the conglomerate. Again, this may happen, but it is not inevitable because it flies in the face of efficient managerial practice. Many corporations have a basic policy, for instance, that divisions of the company need not purchase from other divisions if they feel they can do better on the open market. Throughout industry, the modern manager wants to be measured on the basis of his performance, frequently centered in return on investment, and reciprocal buying could mean unfair interference by higher management levels. When everything else is equal—price, quality, schedule—spontaneous reciprocity is quite possible. Seldom, however, is everything else equal. "You scratch my back and I will scratch yours" is indeed practiced in industry, but it is doubtful that reciprocity created by conglomerates is of much actual or potential significance in the totality of competition. The more serious cases are clearly illegal.

4. It is alleged that conglomerates make "toehold" acquisitions of firms with small market positions. Once they get in a market they can use their superior financial resources to expand their positions. This can serve to bring about greater competition than before. On the other hand it can bring about injury to small competitors who are intimidated by the presence of the large conglomerate.

Empirical Tests of Hypotheses The FTC examined activities of nine conglomerates to test some of the above hypotheses (1972). The nine companies chosen for in-depth analysis had acquired 348 companies between 1960 and 1968 with total assets of almost $10 billion. In 1968 they accounted for 26 percent of all assets acquired through large (over $10 million in assets) manufacturing and mining mergers. They were considered to be vigorous companies having a wide variety of merger patterns and product lines.

While no statistical analyses were made concerning deep-pocket, unfair competitive advantages, and reciprocity, the FTC reported little if any empirical evidence to support the charges (pp. 5–7). It examined the toehold theory and concluded that the conglomerates did not acquire substantial market positions in new areas. In 53.6 percent of the acquired product classes the individual market shares were under 1 percent; in 28.4 percent of the cases the share was between 1 and 5 percent (p. 197). Post-acquisition changes in market positions acquired by them were predominantly decreases (p. 123). Most of the sample firms engaged in industries which were not highly concentrated. Moreover, the level of concentration of industries in which the sample participated declined between 1963 and 1969 (p. 197). ". . . It does not appear that conglomerates followed a 'toehold' strategy of making small acquisitions in concentrated industries" (p. 198). ". . . They do not appear to have become significant market forces in large sectors of our economy" (p. 199).

While conglomerates may not have lessened competition, a question arises as to whether they may have invigorated competition. General observation shows that in many instances conglomerate mergers reinvigorated competition by providing technical and managerial capabilities, as well as cash, to otherwise potentially failing companies. But the evidence is mixed. Profitability increased for twenty-three of forty-three acquired companies, which were studied by the FTC, and decreased for 20 (p. 79). Bock and Farkas are more positive. They concluded that the top companies in an industry "are, on the average, more productive than other companies in the same industry" (1969: 25). It makes no difference, they found, whether it is the first four or the first eight under analysis; whether the measure is value of shipments per employee or production worker man-hour, or value added per employee or per production worker man-hour. Presumably this conclusion applies to conglomerates when they are dominant in an industry.

The conglomerate has the capability of identifying opportunities in markets and the power to exploit them if it chooses. Both in theory and in practice, therefore, there is no ground to assert that the conglomerate as a business form brings a decline in competition in an industry in which it makes an acquisition. It can in reality invigorate competition. During the less exuberant economic conditions of 1969–1973, however, conglomerates found that rapid growth by external acquisitions may be more difficult to manage than the slower pace of internal diversification.

WHAT SHOULD PUBLIC POLICY BE TOWARD LARGE COMPANIES?

This question is directed, of course, to economic market power of large companies. There is no question, of course, about the need for continuing surveillance of the competitive scene to ensure that actions which really do substantially lessen competition or lead to monopoly are discovered and stopped. When large companies are found guilty of such practices, they should be penalized. But there are many benefits to consumers and society in the development of large companies and the comparatively few abuses of which they are guilty hardly warrant the deprivation to society of their advantages.

All institutions in this society are growing in size, and the size of business firms needs to grow correlatively. The application of artificial barriers to growth at this time seems to serve no public purpose.

It is probably not in the public interest to permit an industrial firm to acquire a bank because of conflict of interest in marketing securities as well as in extending credit to all who seek it. Major doubts arise about the justification for manufacturing conglomerates to acquire insurance and other finance companies, or communications companies. Conglomerates organized for purely financial purposes without regard to economic efficiency may be frowned upon, but this is hardly the reason to inhibit the organization in the first place. If there are illegal financial transactions, there are laws to prevent them. If the net result of the combination is not an efficiency equal to the requirements of the marketplace, the conglomerate will die an economic death. Probably the most significant conclusion drawn from the FTC study of nine conglomerates referred to above (1972) is the fact that public information is lost when firms merge. Today, divisionalized companies, including conglomerates, need not make public accounting information about individual products and markets. This matter is discussed further in Chapter 26. This loss of data is serious and should be corrected. The way to do it, however, is not to stop merger in the first place for this reason.

There are scholars who feel that the structure of markets is all-important. More, however, believe that more attention must be given to performance. To recognize and measure performance, and to balance it with appropriate standards of structure, is more of an economic than a legal task. In this light, public policy would be served by increased research to determine the actual experience of market behavior and structure so that better standards would be available to both government agencies and the courts of law.

The conglomerate form of organization is of relatively minor significance in the industrial structure of today, but it will grow in importance. Issues raised about the conglomerate have served to stimulate debate about its competitive role, as well as that surrounding other organizations and activities. That is all to the good, for vigorous debate on antitrust issues is an important step in preserving competition.

I should like to conclude with a delightful little poem written by Kenneth Boulding (1958: 285):

> Business is a useful beast,
> We should not hate it in the least;
> Its profits should not be sequestered,
> And yet it should be mildly pestered.
> To pester, rather than to bust,
> Should be the aim of Anti-Trust,

For business best can serve the nation
When pushed by gentle irritation.

THE SCOPE OF THE ANTITRUST LAWS

This chapter has focused on but one area of antitrust, namely, market structure and business performance. Every company is subject to a broad range of antitrust laws covering every conceivable element of competition that may be considered unfair, deceptive, as lessening competition, or as tending toward monopoly. There are long lists of exclusionary and discriminatory practices that are illegal. Laws protect competitors from patent infringement and from theft of copyrights, trade secrets, and trademarks. Pricing systems are of special concern to the antitrust agencies.

A mountain of regulation has been erected to substitute for competition. This is particularly important in the transportation, public utility and communications industries, and in agriculture. Over the past half-century Congress has granted many exemptions from the application of the antitrust laws. The Webb-Pomerene Act of 1918, for instance, exempted business combinations making sales abroad. A number of laws have been passed permitting combination of competing companies in the transportation industry. The Merchant Marine Act of 1920 exempted marine insurance companies from the antitrust laws by permitting them to form consolidations to transact marine insurance business here in the United States and abroad. A number of enactments have been passed giving farmers various exemptions from the antitrust laws. The Capper-Volstead Act of 1922 permitted farmers to employ associations in unison in producing, marketing, and pricing specified foodstuffs. This protection was extended to fishermen in the Fisheries Cooperative Marketing Act of 1934. The Guffey Vinson Act of 1937 authorized price fixing of coal by an administrative board. Perhaps the most important exception was given to manufacturers in the Miller-Tydings Act of 1937, which exempted interstate contracts fixing resale prices from the antitrust laws. The McGuire-Keogh Act of 1952 further strengthened this resale price maintenance law. Okun estimated that this law adds more than 1/4 of 1 percent to the national average of consumer prices (1969). This is an impressive figure, but the rise of discount houses and problems in enforcing resale price contracts have been eroding the strength of this law over a number of years. This is a huge problem, but it is not dealt with here because of space limitations and the necessity to include subject matter that seems to me to be more current and exciting.

CHAPTER TWENTY-FIVE

Business and International Policy

INTRODUCTION

During the past ten years, there has been an impressive growth in both the number and size of multinational companies (MNCs). This trend is destined to continue and these companies will do an increasingly larger part of the world's business. Because a large number of these companies are now and in the future will be American-based companies, there is a new dimension added to the interrelationships between business and society. These companies are the only institutions, says Drucker, that create an economic community transcending national lines and yet are respectful of national sovereignties and local cultures (1969(B): 97). They have enormous opportunities for good in the world, but they are faced with serious conflicts and challenges as they go about their work. This chapter deals with the rise of the international business of American firms; the relationships between them, their host, and their base governments; and the opportunities they have for advancing the welfare of the world.

THE SETTING

Relationships Between Business and Government in International Affairs American foreign policy and business interests have always been intertwined, although the purpose has varied considerably from time to time. The U.S. Navy attacked the Barbary pirates in 1801 to stop interference with Yankee shipping, but it may also have been an excuse to secure the presence of the American Navy in the Mediterranean. Admiral Perry's trip to Japan in 1853 and the American intervention in the Boxer Rebellion in China in 1900 had commercial overtones. The United States government has always been protective of American business interests abroad and on many occasions has not failed to show its military muscle to prevent interference with them. Our flag has followed our trade. Indeed, some writers, such as William Appleman Williams (1969), say that American foreign policy has been designed to establish world economic and political hegemony on behalf of the American businessman. While this is an extreme view, it serves to underscore the fact that United States foreign policy and business interests have been closely linked.

This interrelationship has not always served the selfish interests of business, although that has been rather important in the past. Predominantly, it has served the economic and political interests of the United States, for business can be significant in furthering broad national interests. To illustrate, Henry Fowler when he was Secretary of the Treasury said, ". . . let us all understand that the United States government has consistently sought—and will continue to seek—to expand and extend the role of the multi-national corporation as an essential instrument of strong and healthy economic progress throughout the Free World" (1965). He is saying, of course, that it is a major policy of the United States to foster economic progress throughout the world and that the MNC can be and is a strong means to further this aim. Many businessmen accept the idea that business and government are involved in a "joint venture" in foreign activities. For instance, Blackie, when president of Caterpillar Tractor Co., spoke as follows:

> Those of us engaged in international trade, and particularly in operations involving overseas investment, recognize that in the ordinary course of our business we are, or could be, an arm, an instrument of American foreign policy. . . . We do not have in mind any idea that the one would make decisions for the other or that decision making would be a joint responsibility. Each has its separate and proper functions and objectives, but in the long run these should tend to converge on one point or perspective—a strengthening of the United States. In such circumstances, I believe I speak for American business when I say that we are prepared to recognize our responsibilities as an instrument of national foreign policy (in Behrman, 1971: 138).

Despite such expressions of amity and purpose there has been, at the same time, a growing conflict between United States policy and MNC goals. This has been exceeded only by rising complaints of host governments. There is a type of love-hate relationship between MNCs and governments around the world.

Growth of United States Overseas Business Interests During the past few decades direct foreign investments have increased very rapidly, from $11.8 billion in 1950 to $49.5 billion in 1965 and an even faster jump to $94.0 billion in 1972. Direct foreign investment in developed countries totaled $64.1 billion in 1972, or nearly double the investments in developing countries. A majority of the 500 largest American companies have networks of plants and subsidiaries abroad, and thousands of smaller companies have foreign operations. At least 4,000 American firms have foreign subsidiaries. The 1968 sales of foreign plants of United States companies amounted to $120 billion, making these plants, in effect, at that time, the fourth largest economic power in the world, since only three economies then had GNPs higher than this (*Business Week*, 1969: 51). American MNCs account for about 45 percent of the production of all the world's MNCs. All the world's MNCs together account for 15 percent of the World Product of $3 trillion [NICB, 1973(B)].

Foreign Business Investment in the United States While foreign investment into the United States is growing, its pace is slower than foreign investments of our companies. Foreign business investment in the United States in 1962 was $7.6 billion and by 1972 it had risen to about $15 billion. However, the ratio of foreign investment into the United States to foreign investments of United States companies dropped from around 20 percent in 1962 to 15 percent in 1972 [NICB, 1973(B)].

Why Go Abroad? There are many reasons why a company seeks to do business in foreign countries. A sample of businessmen from seventy-six companies were asked why they made foreign investments and the response is shown in Table 25–1. These responses are interesting in that market factors seem to be the most dominant motivations. More will be said later about motivations for foreign investment.

Sources of Conflict for a Multinational Company MNCs are viewed from two extreme positions. On the one hand are those who see in the MNC the most productive development in the twentieth century for raising world economic well-being and for bringing nations together for peaceful purposes to their mutual advantage (Jacoby, 1973: Eells, 1972; and Donner, 1967). At the other extreme Zambia says the MNC "is an instrument of neo-colonialism; it maintains invisible control . . . [over the less-developed countries] and has sharpened contradictions as never before" (in Stevens, 1971: 49). There are many reasons for such opposite views and much depends upon who is looking. Overarching specific complaints about MNCs

Table 25–1. Importance of Reasons for Foreign Investment

WHY FOREIGN INVESTMENT?	MENTIONED BY NO. OF COMPANIES
1. To maintain or increase market share locally	33
2. Unable to reach market from U.S. because of tariffs, transportation costs, or nationalistic purchasing policies	25
3. To meet competition	20
4. To meet local content requirements and host government pressure	18
5. Faster sales growth than in the United States	15
6. To obtain or use local raw materials or components	13
7. Low wage costs	13
8. Greater profit prospects abroad	11
9. To follow major customers	10
10. Inducements connected with host government investment programs	8

SOURCE: NICB, 1972(B).

are fundamental conflicts between the objectives of the MNC and national governments of countries in which they do business.

There are a different definitions of an MNC (Jacoby, 1973; Eells, 1972; Phatak, 1971; Aharoni, 1971; Behrman, 1969). I have in mind, to oversimplify, a company that does business in two or more countries in such volume that the investment is of some importance to the company and to the host country. The headquarters of such a company would like to make decisions on the basis of global alternatives. This means, theoretically, that the management would like to manufacture in those countries where it finds the greatest competitive advantage; it would like to buy and sell anywhere in the world to take advantage of the most favorable price to the company; it would like to take advantage throughout the world of changes in labor costs, productivity, trade agreements, and currency fluctuations; and it would like to expand or contract on the basis of worldwide comparative advantages. Its objectives are to obtain a high and rising return on invested capital; achieve a rising growth in sales; keep financial risks within reasonable limits in relation to profits; and maintain its technological and other proprietary strengths. I do not mean to assert that MNCs reject social responsibilities. The concept here is that MNCs would like to achieve the highest possible level of economic rationality in their decision-making while assuming a reasonable share of social responsibilities (Dymsza, 1972).

Some of the major goals of most countries around the world conflict with these objectives and decision-making processes. In no particular order of importance the following goals are sought by most countries: economic growth, full employment of people and resources, raising skills of workers, price stability, a favorable balance of payments, more equitable distribution of income, improving technology in and productivity of business firms, national hegemony over the economic system, national security, social stability, and advancing certain elements of the quality of life (Boddewyn, in Kapoor and Grubb, 1972).

MNCs have been and can be of enormous help to governments of the world in their efforts to achieve most of these goals, especially the economic ones. At the same time, however, it is clear that conflicts between the two sets of goals and decision-making processes are inevitable. To many countries of the world the sour sauce of American company presence is sweetened by the injection of technology and capital into their cultural systems (Mason and Miller, 1974; Vernon, 1971).

MNCs conflict with interests other than those of host national governments. Figure 25–1 shows other conflict points, a number of which will be examined in the remainder of this chapter.

HOST COUNTRY ISSUES

Unfortunately, there is no international law to which business can look in its foreign dealings, because there is no supranational authority to enforce it. Also, if a host country feels a MNC is doing something it should not be doing there is no world "authority" to whom it can look for adjudication. The conditions under which a company operates in a foreign country are subject to the laws of that country. National sovereignty covers the actions of business corporations. Treaties have been negotiated to reduce and eliminate frictions, but treaties can be skirted by ingenious officials without actually violating the letter of the agreement. A host country can control a MNC, but if the MNC feels the yoke is too tight it can leave. Differences in the exercise of power between the two are tolerable up to a point but the point varies from country to country and issue to issue. All that can be done here is to illustrate some of the conflicts and what might be done to reduce them.

Employment Policy Potential conflicts in employment policy may arise at numerous points. Foreign countries, for example, are often sensitive to layoffs. Raytheon, an American-based company, invested about $25 million in Raytheon-Elsi SpA in Palermo, Sicily, and owned almost 100 percent of it. The company in 1968 had about 1,000 work-

Figure 25–1. Sources of Conflict in the Multinational Corporate Environment

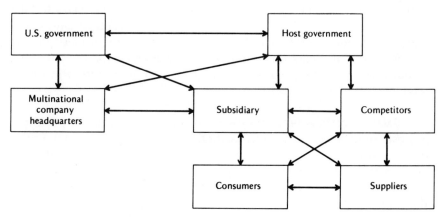

SOURCE: Adapted from Charles F. Stewart, in Ivar Berg, *The Business of America* (New York: Harcourt, 1968), p. 130. Reprinted by permission of the publisher.

ers making cathode ray tubes for television sets and other electronic gear for the North Atlantic Treaty Organization. Faced with sizable losses in 1967 and early 1968, the company tried to reduce operating expenses by laying off 250 workers. This was intolerable to the Italian government, which retaliated by seizing the factory and putting Palermo's mayor in charge. Raytheon reacted by selling out in 1969. Foreign countries are also sensitive to the employment of home talent. Foreign corporations generally are accommodating when unskilled workers are concerned, but are less willing to rely on local technicians when they can move their own skilled workers to the country. Many companies are also unwilling to rely on local managers. Nevertheless, pressures from foreign countries, and the obvious benefits to the company, lead corporations more and more to train and use local managers.

Changing Trade and Production Controls Host countries are anxious to encourage foreign investment that will lead to the home production of items hitherto imported. This has obvious benefits. Corporations have often entered foreign countries to produce an end item requiring imports of components from the company's home base, only to find, after a short period of operations, that a prohibitive tariff has been placed on the importation of the components. In 1947, for example, Sears Roebuck and Company entered Mexico with a plan to import 80 percent of its merchandise for resale in Mexico. By 1954, however, 80 percent of its merchandise was manufactured locally because of the erection of new import walls.

Pressures from Competitors The entry of an American firm into a foreign country may, of course, be viewed with alarm by local competitors, who in turn may put pressure on the host government to take action in their behalf. This was the situation Sears Roebuck and Company encountered in Mexico. Local retailers found themselves unable to compete with Sears for employees as well as customers and tried (though unsuccessfully) to have foreign companies stopped from engaging in retail trade in Mexico.

Balance of Payments Problems Balance of payments problems in host countries often lead to restrictions, many of which may create other problems. Regulation of profit outflows, for example, may deaden the enthusiasm for foreign investment in the host country, which in turn may cause a decline in general economic activity. On the other hand, if a local investment yields high profits which exceed the investment after a few years, the withdrawal of all profits may also have depressing economic consequences. In an effort to control their economies, a natural objective, many countries develop a series of restrictions on imports and exports, currency exchange, and capital outflows that impede the free movement of international goods and cash.

Balance of payments conflicts can arise from other decisions. A country may want the foreign-owned subsidiary to increase its exports so as to improve the balance of payments position. It may be, however, that the costs of the subsidiary are higher than those of another subsidiary in another country. The rational economic decision of the headquarters would be, of course, to export the product from the second subsidiary. The first host country, however, would consider this decision contrary to its best interests.

Foreign Control over Local Activities Most nations of the world want their industries controlled by their nationals. This desire is based on a mixture of nationalism, national security, and fear of arbitrary decision-making in a far-off land. Canada, for instance, for a long time has been concerned that large investments by American companies might result in decisions over which Canada had no control and which would adversely affect Canada. Peruvian business leaders a few years ago asserted that many of their economic problems stemmed from the fact that the extractive industries, most of the manufacturing sector, and the commercial banking sector were largely controlled by non-Peruvian corporations. So, they decided to regain control. Most nations of the world want to control their key industries for national security purposes. This argument, however, is not too sound, because in the event of a national crisis they could expropriate foreign holdings if they felt this was in the interest of national security.

Europeans have been concerned about American control of technology of local firms. Indeed, some Europeans have gone so far as to want to prevent American companies from investing in certain industries. They feel that American control of basic industries like nuclear energy, electronics (especially microcircuits), and computers would block European research in these areas and lead to technological dependence upon America. These are areas in which heavy American investment in Europe has taken place. Dependence on American technology, however, has not taken place. As a matter of fact, American investment in these industries has stimulated technology both in Europe and in the United States.

All nations of the world want to grow economically and welcome foreign inflows of managerial know-how, capital, and technology, but they complain if they think the price is too high. The price to them is not solely economic. It can be resistance to a feeling of dependence. The host country knows that the MNC has a base and it is likely to follow the foreign policy of its home country, a policy the host country may not accept. If one or a few MNCs control most of the capital in a developing country it has great potential influence over the entire society (economic, social, and political) which may, at best, lead to apprehensions and, at worst, to serious conflict with the ways in which the leaders and peoples of the host country want to run their country and see it develop.

Expropriation Expropriation is in a different category from the issues discussed above, but it is naturally in deep conflict with the interests of foreign investors when experienced. Up until recent years expropriation was not a common practice (Root, 1968). It still is not common in light of the world's total business but it seems to be growing. In recent years a wave of expropriations has taken place in Latin America. In 1968, in Peru, a group of military officers ousted the government and seized property of the International Petroleum Corporation valued at $200 million. Bolivia seized installations of the Gulf Oil Company in 1969. Chile, more recently, seized American-owned copper mines and the properties of the International Telephone and Telegraph Company. Currently, the Middle East countries are expropriating American-owned oil company properties.

There is not too much protection against expropriation. The Hickenlooper Amendment to the Foreign Assistance Act of 1961 requires suspension of American foreign aid to any country that expropriates American property without offering prompt, adequate, and effective reimbursement. This act, however, has not been applied in any significant cases. In 1971 the Congress launched the Overseas Private Investment Corporation, and gave it authority to insure high-risk investments of American companies against war and expropriation. In its first two years OPIC has paid seventeen claims amounting to $118 million and had outstanding $2.5 billion in expropriation insurance [*Business Week*, 1973(B)].

Charges of Imperialism Among many of the awakening nations, the American businessman faces what John Fayerweather calls the "lingering curse of exploitation" (1962: 120). The awakening nations look on the foreign businessman with fear and distrust as the follower of an old exploitative colonialism not easily forgotten. It is not difficult for the awakening nations to find current illustrations to support their fears. Since 1962, American investors have taken out of Latin American countries more money than they have invested. This is called economic imperialism by these nations. The refusal of automobile companies to build manufacturing plants in certain Asian and Latin American countries is viewed by them as imperialistic, even though the economics of the situation clearly are against building the facilities. Many less developed nations feel doomed to the role of supplying raw materials and cheap labor because they are denied the technology to develop into an industrialized nation. Their frustrations are leveled at the MNCs exporting their raw materials and cheap labor. In a general way, the sins of the past and allegations of the present cannot easily be erased in the minds of formerly exploited colonies. It is also true that foreign business investors in underdeveloped countries often turn out to be handy scapegoats in political and social crises.

Nontariff Barriers A growing complaint of MNCs is that countries around the world are erecting nontariff barriers which restrain their activities. American distillers may sell bourbon whiskey in Paris, for instance, but cannot advertise it. The Ford Motor Company has complained that because of nontariff barriers its Pinto automobile which costs about $2,700 on the dock in Japan cannot be bought by a Japanese consumer for less than $5,000 (Stigler, 1973). Hundreds of obstacles are placed in the path of American companies doing business abroad. The purpose of these barriers may not necessarily be to thwart American businessmen, although some of them are. They arise in the developed countries from domestic safety, health, and pollution laws. Some of them, however, are aimed at protecting domestic markets and jobs.

What Can be Done to Reduce Conflict? Clearly, one of the first imperatives is for MNCs to act socially responsibly. For the MNC, as for corporations here at home, however, the question is: what precisely are the social responsibilities which we should pursue and how best can they be institutionalized in the decision-making process here and abroad? Answers are slow in coming. It can be said, however, that socially responsible actions would embrace a company's taking measures that avoid offending the national sensibilities of the host country, avoiding actions that raise questions about the self-determination capabilities of the host country, avoiding unnecessary actions that disrupt the social structure, and acting in ways that are in the self-interests of the host country whenever possible while not violating the basic self-interests of the parent company. The importance of greater employment of citizens of a host country is an obvious lesson from past experience. This means, of course, the training and upgrading of local citizens to fill more responsible skilled and managerial jobs. Providing opportunities for an ownership stake in subsidiaries by nationals is important. Some countries insist that nationals own at least 51 percent of the companies in which foreign investment is made. The advantages to the host country of national investment are obvious in terms of control over operations, if that is desired.

MNCs can use local suppliers, bankers, and managers. The possibilities are many and here, as with domestic operations, each company must choose what it wishes to do.

The host country can do many things to ease tensions. It can avoid using the subsidiary as a political weapon to force the parent company's country to take some action desired by the host country. The host country can assure foreign investors that their company need not fear expropriation. The host country can review its tax, production, entry, and other laws to see to what extent they can be altered in both its own and the foreign company's self-interests. It can also assure equal treatment for foreign and local investment.

It is obvious that the development of codes of behavior would facilitate understanding and lessen conflicts. During the past several decades there have been a number of codes, charters, and conventions (Greene, 1971). A recent illustration is "The Pacific Basin Charter on International Investments" (*Fortune*, September 1972). Such agreements will help to solve the conflicts and tensions of MNC activities, but the world becomes more complex, and as the aspirations of the peoples of nations in the world rise, the search for and commitment to accommodation must be intensified.

AMERICAN MNCs AND THE FEDERAL GOVERNMENT

The issues between MNCs and the federal government are many and complex. Cooperation between the two is made difficult, and complexities mount, because there are at least thirty distinct policy areas affecting foreign business activities of American companies plus scores of domestic policies (e.g., wage-price guidelines) having international implications. To complicate the whole setting there are eight major agencies of government having clear authority over major policies of American MNCs and a dozen other agencies asserting some jurisdiction, depending upon the issue (Behrman, 1969). Finally, the Congress is deeply involved in overseas business of American companies.

Balance of Payments During the past two decades the United States balance of payments has been unfavorable. This has resulted in a drain of gold, a series of international monetary crises, and pressure by the federal government on business to repatriate overseas earnings and to restrict new investment in foreign lands. Until 1971 exports of goods and services were greater than imports so the cause of the deficits in international accounts was not a trade imbalance. It was the huge outflow of private investment and government expenditures abroad that were not matched by the trade surplus or by the inflow of foreign capital. The surplus of goods and services reached a high of $8.9 billion in 1964 but declined, until for the first time since 1893 it was in deficit at the end of 1971 and hit a low of $6.9 billion in 1972. The magnitude of the problem is indicated by the fact that the net balance of payments reached a new low deficit of $8.6 billion in 1972. With a weakening of the dollar in international money markets, and an increased world demand for agricultural products the trade balance registered a surplus again in mid-1973. Current prospects are for an increasing trade surplus but a continuing overall net balance of payments deficit.

The federal government in recent years has taken many actions to slow down the outflow of capital. For example, the Interest Equalization Tax of 1964 was designed to narrow the gap between interest rates in the United States and the higher rates abroad, and to reduce the advantage to American investors in buying foreign securities. High interest rates in the United States have narrowed this advantage. In 1965 the federal government sought to get business to slow down its foreign investment on a voluntary basis, and in 1967 more binding controls were enacted. Banks were asked to hold their foreign assets at current levels, direct foreign investors were asked to reduce long-term flows by about 20 percent, and private investors were asked to borrow Eurodollars rather than use American dollars. These efforts did not produce the results desired, so by Executive Order No. 11387, President Johnson on January 1, 1968, severely curtailed direct investments abroad by United States companies. Among other things, this order restricted the transfer of capital from the United States to affiliates in most of continental Europe and, to a lesser degree, prevented other direct foreign investments. These curbs generated heated controversy over the question of whether direct American investment abroad helped or hurt the balance of trade and payments problem.

Businessmen complain bitterly that the net effect of such restraint is injurious to them and to the United States. They maintain that repatriated income from foreign investments is much greater than American investment abroad. To test this hypothesis *Fortune* asked 105 MNCs—which included the bulk of this nation's largest foreign direct investors—to calculate their own balance of payments for the latest fiscal year ending on or before December 31, 1972. The conclusion was that only ten had negative balances, amounting to $446 millions. The total positive balances amounted to $7.7 billions (*Fortune,* 1973). A thorough analysis of MNCs impact on the balance of payments from 1966 to 1970 by the United States Tariff Commission concluded that the MNCs played no role in the deterioration during that period of the United States balance of payments deficit. The contribution to the trade accounts and the huge surpluses on the current accounts more than compensated for the net outflow of long-term and nonliquid short-term capital in these years (U.S. Senate Committee on Finance 1973).

Labor and Industry Problems Accompanying and inherent in balance-of-payments problems were a number of other forces generating discontent in the United States and pleas for government help. For a variety of reasons a number of industries found their international competitive positions deteriorating and imports rapidly increasing over exports. Examples during the past half dozen years are radio and television receiving sets, textile mill products, wearing apparel, and other finished products made from fabrics, shoes, basic shapes and forms, and motor vehicles. Not only was there an adverse impact on the balance of payments but unemployment in these industries also resulted. Loss of jobs in industries adversely affected by foreign competition coincided with a general rise of unemployment in the United States in 1969–1971.

The government responded in many ways. A 10 percent surcharge on imports gave some relief. Pressures on foreign governments to remove nontariff restrictions on United States imports and, in the case of Japan, pressures to reduce exports to the United States of some products, like textiles, also brought relief. Major relief came in 1973 with the substantial devaluation of the dollar in world markets. Before this, however, these relief measures were not enough and major pressures resulted in the introduction into the Congress of the Burke-Hartke bill in 1972.

The specific provisions of this bill are not as important as the forces behind it. While this bill is not likely to pass the Congress, its provisions in one form or another are likely to appear in proposed legislation in the future. In supporting the bill the labor unions altered significantly their hitherto free trade position. They also supported more control over international business than ever before. These views had popular support then and still do. An Opinion Research Corporation survey in 1973 revealed broad-based opposition to the MNCs. The people surveyed were 2 to 1 for federal discouragement of international expansion of business companies. Most people thought such expansion meant fewer jobs here at home and a loss to the United States of tax dollars to foreign governments [*Business Week*, 1973(C)].

Provisions of the Burke-Hartke Bill The Foreign Trade and Investment Act of 1972 (the Burke-Hartke bill) was introduced simultaneously in the Senate (s. 2592) and the House of Representatives (H.R. 10914). Major provisions of the bill would:

> Subject income from foreign subsidiaries of American corporations to United States corporate income taxes in the year the income is earned. Under the present law the income of foreign subsidiaries in general is not taxed until the subsidiary declares a dividend or until the money is repatriated.

> The quantity of imports would be restricted in each important product category to a fixed proportion of the total anticipated domestic market. The proportion would be calculated for each category as the average rate that existed during the period 1965–1969. If an American industry is threatened with serious injury the Foreign Trade and Investment Commission (FTAIC) is empowered to reduce quotas further. The FTAIC, created by the act, is given many powers some of which are now performed by the Tariff Commission.

> International capital transfers are prohibited by United States companies when the transfer would result in a net decrease in employment in the United States. Also, patent holders could not license to foreigners (including foreign subsidiaries of United States corporations) to use the patent when employment in the United States might be adversely affected.

These proposals are the most restrictive measures covering international operations of American companies ever to be considered by the Congress in peacetime. The proponents assert that the net result would benefit labor and the government. Opponents say that the net result would be disastrous to foreign countries and would reduce domestic employment.

Do MNCs Export Jobs? Almost anyone knows that in recent years electronic companies making television sets and semiconductors have gone abroad to use cheap labor in producing components. Americans heretofore making such components no longer are employed to make them. (In 1973 some companies, Zenith, for instance, reduced their dependence on foreign sources for components but the shift has not been great.) Employment in a number of industries, such as shoes, has dropped drastically as imports have risen. Broadly, the unions assert that foreign trade is now reducing domestic employment whereas in the past it increased jobs. In 1971 it was estimated that for the first time more jobs were lost by imports than were created by exports. The difference, or net loss, was 200,000 jobs

(AFL-CIO, 1971). Free trade, now say the unions, is no longer in the interest of American workers (Ruttenberg, 1973).

The facts are quite clear that jobs have been lost in many industries because of foreign competition. What the net loss is, however, from all international activities is far from clear. Serious doubt has been raised about the validity of the AFL-CIO numbers (Jaffee, 1973). Anyway, the employment affects of imports are very small when compared with cyclical changes in employment, employment implications of economic growth, and normal labor turnover (Salant and Vaccara, 1961). Of course, to the person losing his job because of imports these aggregations are not comforting.

How much, if any, domestic unemployment is due to the foreign activities of MNCs is far from clear. Studies that have been made support the view that the MNCs have not in the aggregate exported jobs. Much depends upon assumptions. One thorough study calculated jobs on the following assumptions. In the absence of MNCs foreigners would not have built their own plants but would have imported from the United States. United States firms would hold the share of world exports they enjoyed in 1960–1961. The conclusion was that net employment in manufacturing would gain roughly 500,000 jobs in the United States (U.S. Senate Committee on Finance, 1973: 7). Different assumptions, of course, can produce a net loss of jobs. Other studies show that United States companies which are most vigorous abroad are also the most dynamic at home. MNCs have increased their domestic employment from 1960 to 1970 by 37 percent as compared with the 12 percent increase in all jobs in the United States. (Business International Corporation, 1971). While total United States exports grew by 53 percent during the decade exports of parent MNCs leaped 200 percent (Business International Corporation, 1971; U.S. Chamber of Commerce, 1971; Emergency Committee for American Trade, 1972).

It is true that growing American foreign subsidiary output has replaced exports of the same products. On the other hand, export sales of American components for subsidiary output and industrialization abroad have increased exports of specialized products such as machinery, electrical equipment, electronics, and chemicals. Thus, total American exports have expanded, but the mix has changed. The question then arises as to whether American jobs could have been saved and American exports not eroded for particular products. Generally speaking, I would expect that most managers would rather export their products than produce them abroad so long as they could do so profitably. This decision, however, has often been taken out of their hands, for they have been forced to invest in production facilities in foreign countries. They start manufacturing abroad when trade barriers, foreign government policies, labor costs, and other factors force them to build an overseas plant. Rarely will one find a company that has built a plant abroad while exporting the same product from the United States at a profit and likely to continue to do so in the foreseeable future. The choice they often face is whether to build a plant in a foreign country or not sell their products there at all (Goodyear International Corporation, n.d.).

Restricting imports raises the question of retaliation and the impact of that on jobs. The Department of Commerce estimated that had the Burke-Hartke proposal been in effect in 1971, imports would have been reduced by $10.4 billion from their actual levels, almost 25 percent of the total for that year. Canada would have lost $3.6 billion, or 30 percent of its exports to the United States. Japan would have lost $3.1 billion and Common Market countries would have lost $1.8 billion (Ross, 1973). Such losses would certainly bring retaliation and loss of American jobs.

The Burke-Hartke type of proposals do not seem to be the remedies needed for loss of jobs through international trade. The Trade Expansion Act of 1962 provided for assistance from the federal government to workers and industries adversely affected by imports. This sort of spot therapy has not been used seriously. Some sort of special training assistance to adversely affected industries, or government intervention with foreign governments where "unfair" competitive conditions may seem to prevail, seem more appropriate than the blanket approach of Burke-Hartke.

Free Trade and Tariff Protections Controversy over tariffs has always existed in the United States. Depending upon such forces as economic conditions, manufacturing capacity, the power of influential groups, and Presidential leadership, our tariff barriers have risen and fallen periodically.

The case for free trade is comparatively simple. By virtue of climate, labor conditions, raw materials, capital, management, or other considerations, some nations have an advantage over others in the production of particular goods. For instance, Brazil can produce coffee beans at a much lower price than the United States. Coffee beans could be grown in hothouses in the United States, but not at a price equal to that which Brazil can charge and make a profit. On the other hand, the United States has a distinct advantage over Brazil in producing computers. Resources will be used most efficiently when each produces that for which it enjoys a cost advantage. Gain from specialization and trade is mutually advantageous when the cost ratios of producing two commodities are different in different countries. Furthermore, gain will be maximized when each nation specializes in producing those products for which it has the greatest comparative advantage or the least comparative disadvantage. This is what economists call the law of comparative advantage. It follows that maximum gain on a worldwide basis will be realized if there are no impediments to trade, if there is free competition in pricing, and if capital flows are unrestricted. The greatest profits will result if in each country those goods are produced for which the nation has the greatest comparative advantage. It is not always easy, however, to see just where a nation has a comparative advantage. At the extremes the case is clear, but not at the means. Differences in monetary units, rates of productivity of capital and labor, changes in markets, or elasticities of demand, for instance, obscure the degree of advantage one nation may have over another at one point in time.

Nations use many arguments to convince themselves that erecting tariff barriers is sensible from their point of view. We cannot discuss all the main arguments, but a few issues should be examined, such as the use of tariffs to protect our national security, to protect high American wages, and to equalize costs of production. It is argued that tariffs are needed to maintain skills and productive capability essential to national security. The watchmakers have argued, for instance, that tariffs are needed on imported watches in order to maintain American watchmaking skills because they are necessary to make precision parts of military equipment during national emergencies. There are many problems with this type of argument. For one thing, it is exceedingly difficult to determine precisely what capabilities are needed for national defense. Even if this can be ascertained, it does not follow that tariff protection is the best way to get them. A tariff subsidizes an industry and amounts to a tax on the consumers of the products of that industry. Why should this particular group be taxed in the name of national security? If a capability is really needed for national security, and should be maintained, a much better way to do it would be a direct subsidy by the government to the industry. At least the costs would be clearer.

Another argument is that when imported goods are made with cheap labor and undersell American-made goods, the result will be a drop in American wage rates and/or employment of workers in industries that cannot compete. The argument is that tariffs are needed to protect high American wages and employment. It is pertinent to note that while the American advocates of high tariffs assert the need to protect the American workman from the cheap labor of foreign nations, advocates of high tariffs in foreign nations assert the need because of the more efficient American workman. Those who argue for high tariffs to protect American wage rates are obviously afraid to accept the consequences of the law of comparative advantage. The cheap labor argument for tariffs overlooks the fact that high American wages would not necessarily be jeopardized by a tariff reduction. High wages are due to the productivity of American labor, which is a function of many elements, including applications of capital to labor, the skills of the American workman, motivation, hours of work, and management. There is no doubt but that some workers in, say, the American watch industry probably would have to find new jobs if tariffs were completely removed from imported Swiss watches. This is not inevitable, however, for Americans might invent a new watch that is better and cheaper than those made by the Swiss.

Finally, the argument is made that tariffs are needed to equalize costs of production. On the surface this seems to be fair. If the Japanese can ship steel bars to the United States cheaper than American companies can produce them, why not impose a tariff to equalize costs? Obviously, if this were done throughout the world, all trade would be eliminated because trade is based on cost differentials.

In the past twenty years the United States has substantially reduced tariffs. The tariff question will never be completely settled because there will always be some groups adversely affected by freer trade. The weight of history is on the side of freer trade being in the public interest. So also in the public interest are programs which prevent or ease hardships on industries and workers which are adversely affected by international competition. Special government programs to fit each case are preferable to tariffs.

Antitrust Conflicts Justice Holmes in 1909 said he was surprised to hear that the Sherman Act might be applied outside the jurisdiction of the United States (*American Banana Co. v. United Fruit Co.*). A few years later, however, the Supreme Court held contracts between the American Tobacco Company and the Imperial Tobacco Company of Great Britain to allocate world markets to be illegal (*United States v. American Tobacco Company*). The question of jurisdiction of American law over foreign activities of American corporations raises deep and fundamental issues that can be mentioned only briefly here.

There is no international body that can charter multinational corporations. Nor is there international law (or a legal system) through which their activities can be controlled. They operate in a sort of governmental vacuum. They derive legitimacy from their methods of operation, their strength, their acceptance in different countries of the world, and the prestige of the powerful national governments with which they are most closely associated. This raises major questions about legitimacy and accountability and how multinational companies may be brought within the ambit of public control.

While the actions of these entities do fall under the Sherman Act according to the Supreme Court, the Antitrust Division of the Department of Justice is not at all zealous in enforcing the law (Miller, 1968: 182–83). Even if it were, it would run into serious difficulties abroad. In the past, cartel arrangements that fixed prices and divided markets were made by companies acting alone. Today, governments are involved because they want subsidiaries to act in their interests. This raises the question of how much pressure a foreign government must exert before an American-based company may be relieved of charges of acting in restraint of trade. Also, if foreign governments do not want to cooperate, it is very difficult for the Department of Justice to detect and then to prevent conspiracies in restraint of trade. Then, too, all sorts of complex questions arise as a result of concerted action by the parent and subsidiary, such as fixing intracompany pricing for products one subsidiary buys from another, changing production runs among different plants in different countries, or entering into joint ventures with foreign nationals who might otherwise be competitors. Crude restraints of trade are easy to see, but these interrelationships raise subtleties about which the law is not at all clear (Vernon, 1968). Until such time as there is some sort of legal code, or arrangements for prior consultation and coordination of action among sovereign nations, the legal jungle facing multinational companies will be irritating at best and dangerous at worst (U.S. Senate Committee on Finance, 1973). Any reconciliation of jurisdictional differences among the sovereign nations of the world in the antitrust area does not seem likely in the near future.

Supports to International Companies The list of laws and programs of the government to help American businessmen in their international dealings is almost endless. They range from financing regular transactions to subsidizing high risks, from gathering information about foreign markets to entering into negotiations to help American companies land foreign concessions, from financial to military aid, and from moral support to cash subsidy. To take but one illustration, the Department of Agriculture (which handles the export subsidy program) in 1968 paid subsidies on chickens shipped to Switzerland from American farms. This was in retaliation for European Common Market subsidy policies. It was necessary, said the Secretary of Agriculture, to ensure the fair share of the world market for American producers. The subsidy has since been extended to Greece. In 1962 United States chicken exports totaled 146 million pounds but dropped to 14 million pounds in 1967, largely as a result of subsidized competition in the European market. This raises the question of how much the federal government should help American businessmen in the face of foreign state-supported competition, what we consider to be unfair competitive practices, or arbitrary impediments to normal business activities. There is, of course, no single answer. Each case is a bundle of issues and must be settled individually.

UNITED STATES—HOST GOVERNMENT RELATIONSHIPS

The relationships between the United States government and host country governments are both political and economic and can in many ways affect the operations of multinational companies. For instance, United States aid programs are tied to American exports whenever possible. This means that aid dollars, in degrees specified in legislation and administrative regulations, are spent in the United States as well as in other countries. Depending upon the case, a shift in these allocations can help or injure an American-based company or its foreign-based subsidiary. Friendly political relationships between the United States and another country can obviously help subsidiaries of American companies in the foreign country gain concessions or fight off an unwelcome host country regulation.

ASSESSING THE MNCs: BEAST OR BLESSING

There is no doubt about the fact that a businessman who operates in a foreign country is a "cultural catalyst." American firms can bring to a foreign country needed capital, technology, managerial skills, and other types of expertise. When an American company builds a steel plant in India, a synthetic fiber plant in Nigeria, a refinery in Saudi Arabia, or an automobile assembly plant in Mexico, it is bringing to these economies capital and culture from the United States. In this way the international businessman has an opportunity to advance the well-being of peoples in all the countries in which he does business. There are many illustrations of how a company has furthered American foreign policy and at the same time satisfied the self-interests of both its stockholders and the host country. Firestone Tire & Rubber Company, for instance, has transformed the primarily tribal economy of Liberia into a wage and market economy. This company literally moved Liberia into the twentieth century.

The assessment of whether such influence is good or bad can be made only through the eyes of the company, the host government, and the base country. It cannot be made solely on the basis of economic criteria but must include political, social, military, ethical, and other measures. Each looks at the effect in different ways and uses different criteria. The MNC assesses expected economic gains against perceived risks. Noneconomic activities taken in the name of social responsibilities for the most part will be appraised in terms of the long-range self-interest of the company. The "benefit" which an MNC sees in division of labor among subsidiaries in less developed countries may be considered "costs" to host governments because in the host country view they condemn those countries to low-skilled labor roles. The "benefits" of foreign infusions of capital become "costs" to host countries which must pay interest on capital and dividends on earnings. The base country will look at the outflow of capital also as a "cost" because it upsets its balance of payments. The "benefits" in introducing a less developed country to the twentieth century may be considered as a "cost" to those who wish to maintain old social relationships within their country. And so it goes. Whether beast or blessing depends upon the eye of the perceiver (Johnson, in Kindleberger, 1970).

My assessment is that multinational corporations have been guilty of many abuses in their pursuit of profit but overall they have brought blessings to foreign societies. They have brought capital, technology, and managerial know-how which, in turn, has had three major impacts. First, the per capita income of many countries in which they have operated has risen higher than otherwise. Second, in many cases they have brought skills which people in the host country can use to become more industrialized by their own efforts. Third, and perhaps the most important role of all, they bring change and transition. The result can be beneficial or disadvantageous to host countries, depending upon how they are perceived. But with peace and well-intentioned negotiation, the benefits should be greater than the disadvantages.

The possibilities for continued good are unlimited. In light of this potential one must hope that misunderstandings between MNCs and national governments will be eliminated and that strenuous efforts will be made to reduce conflicts and to regulate the MNCs in the best interests of all parties concerned with peace and prosperity.

CHAPTER TWENTY-SIX

Other Issues in Government Regulation of Business

INTRODUCTION

In most of the preceding chapters, especially the last five, many issues between business and government were mentioned and discussed. In chapters following this one, other important issues will be examined. Despite this coverage, there are additional issues concerning government regulation of business which deserve treatment in this book, and it is the purpose of this chapter to give space to them. They are as follows: the regulatory crisis, the energy problem, government's guarantee of the Lockheed L-1011 loan, corporate disclosure, accounting standards and profit calculations, federal incorporation, and wage/price controls.

THE REGULATORY CRISIS

We face a crisis today in our independent regulatory agencies. Criticisms of policies and management of federal independent regulatory agencies are mounting from all sides of the political and ideological spectrum and their defenders are dwindling. To make matters worse the complaints are more cogent than are the proposed reforms.

The Nature of the Independent Regulatory Agency A large number of federal regulations of business are administered by independent regulatory agencies. There are over fifty of them and they have characteristics and powers not enjoyed by the regular departments of government. They are to a great extent independent from Presidential orders, Congress, the electorate, and the courts. They are established by Congress and are quasi-arms of that body, but are lodged administratively in the executive branch to carry out regulatory responsibilities approved by the legislature. They report to the President, but he can remove commissioners only for good cause, such as malfeasance in office. While they are not completely removed from controls, the authority over them is not direct and unequivocal. They are in fact microgovernments embodying the tripartite powers of government—legislative, judicial, and administrative.

The commissions enjoy legislative powers in the sense that they are delegated responsibilities by Congress to administer laws that give them a good bit of discretion. The Federal Power Commission (FPC), for example, has wide latitude in licensing power-generating plants on navigable rivers, controlling the interstate transmission of electricity, and regulating the price of natural gas entering into interstate commerce. The commissions have administrative powers in the sense that they perform an executive function. They have powers to administer laws by enforcing their rules and regulations. They have subpoena powers. Some of them conduct business operations. The Board of Governors of the Federal Reserve System, for example, participates directly in certain banking functions. They have broad planning functions, such as the ability of the ICC to allocate resource use of transportation systems through regulations, rates, and investigations. The powers and functions of commissions, however, differ a great deal. Commissions also enjoy judicial power. They can determine what the rules will be in the future and enforce them. They act as a judicial tribunal in hearing cases and adjudicating claims within the commission law. The Supreme Court insists that commissions act according to the law, following rules in coming to decisions, and making decisions on the basis of fact. If these principles are not followed, or if there is an issue of constitutional law involved, the Court will review commission decisions. If not, the Court takes the position that the decisions are matters of fact and not of law and will not interfere. In other words, the Court will not review a decision of the commissions to determine whether it is a wise one, even though the Court might come to a different conclusion on the basis of the same facts. The Court intends to review decisions only when they may be contrary to constitutional law. Thus, commission decisions tend to be final.

Economic Criticisms of the Regulatory Commissions The specific attacks on the regulatory commissions are voluminous and what follows is but a sample. The ICC has been attacked because it is said it misallocates resources. Its rate structure, it is said, creates major inequities among systems of transportation, commodities, and communities. Moore concludes that "on the basis of conservative assumptions, it would not be unreasonable to expect that elimination of

(ICC) regulation would result in savings to the economy, in terms of resources, as high as $10 billion a year" (1972: 81). Some economists think that free competition in transportation will be superior to ICC control (Peck, in MacAvoy, 1970). Fellmeth, in a blistering attack on the ICC, recommends abolition of the agency but only to replace it with a new one not encumbered by all the dead timber of the ICC (1970).

The major policies of the Civil Aeronautics Board (CAB) do not coincide with the economist's usual criteria of efficient allocation of resources and market performance (Keeler, 1972; Cave, in MacAvoy, 1970). The control of natural gas rates at low levels by the Federal Power Commission is blamed for some of our current shortages of natural gas. Very low gas rates have encouraged consumption for uses which should have been satisfied with other fuels. At the same time the low rates have inhibited natural gas producers from energetic exploration for new wells. ". . . The regulation of the broadcasting industry by the Federal Communications Commission (FCC)," says one critic, "resembles a professional wrestling match. The grunts and groans resound through the land, but no permanent injury seems to result" (Coase, in MacAvoy, 1970: 96). The FCC also has been accused of intimidating the media to bend more gracefully to the government's rhetoric. The FTC performance was found to be "shockingly poor" by a group of "Nader's Raiders" (Cox, Fellmeth, and Schulz, 1969). A number of economists have contended that the Federal Reserve Board (FRB) has periodically generated too much money which, in turn, has brought inflation. Then, abruptly the FRB has sharply reduced the availability of credit and has thereby created a credit "crunch" with high interest rates to dampen price rises. An economic evaluation of the Federal Aviation Agency concludes that mismanagement of its subsidy program is largely responsible for airport problems such as congestion (Eckert, 1972).

State governments have regulatory commissions which are the targets of the same sorts of criticisms. For example, Posner argues that he sees no general tendency for regulatory agencies to refuse justified rate increases for utilities. But if rate increases are not allowed, he says, the utilities will conceal profits through adroit accounting and/or reduce quality of service (in MacAvoy, 1970). Stigler and Friedland argue that regulatory bodies are incapable of forcing a utility to operate at a specified desirable combination of output, price, and cost (in MacAvoy, 1970).

These criticisms raise a long series of issues, some of which are addressed in other parts of the book. The evidence is mounting that many basic economic policies of certain independent regulatory agencies, such as those mentioned here, are finding less favor among economists as being in the public interest.

Regulations are unjust. Many businessmen feel that federal regulations are unjust. This is, of course, an old complaint. Naturally, what is just or unjust depends upon "whose ox is being gored." Nevertheless, former Attorney-General Robert Kennedy, when he was a senator, agreed with the unjust complaint in saying: "The fact remains . . . that the law administered by these agencies is still not as fair, equitable and expeditious as we have a right to expect" (1967: 71).

Agencies frequently act abruptly and take actions which seem highly inequitable. Very often this is due more to the legislation an agency must administer than to managerial intransigence. Such is the case of the Federal Drug Administration (FDA). Under the Miller Act of 1954, an amendment to the Food, Drug, and Cosmetic Act of 1938, the FDA is required to determine what degree of residue of a pesticide or herbicide is allowable as nontoxic for humans on fruits and vegetables. The Delancy Cancer Amendment of 1958 to the basic legislation allows the FDA no tolerance whatsoever in prohibiting the addition to food of any substance known to produce cancer in any species, in any dosage and under any circumstances. On the basis of the Miller Act the Secretary of HEW ruled that after January 1, 1970, cyclamate-sweetened soft drinks and soft-drink mixes must be removed from the market. This ruling was made upon the basis of research which showed that six of twelve rats that were given the equivalent of fifty times maximum recommended lifetime human daily consumption developed an "unusual" form of bladder cancer. For a person to get as much cyclamate as the rats, he would be obliged to drink several cases of cyclamate-sweetened soft drinks every day for most of his normal human life span! In cases like this many issues arise. Are producers and retailers to be penalized, some rather stiffly, because traces of chemicals not in quantities known to be harmful to humans have been found? Are overweight people to be denied artificial sweeteners which might help them reduce and thus prolong their lives? On the other hand, the increasing use of chemicals must be accompanied by some safeguards to people whose health might otherwise be jeopardized. Where are the safe limits to be established?

This raises another important question: Why does the FDA not have sufficient funds to examine the thousands of products for which it is responsible? It has to date gotten around to testing only a very small fraction of additives and other chemicals directly or indirectly entering into foods. Each one of these issues involves many others. The fundamental issue is how can the public be sure of the scientific integrity of the evaluations, while at the same time being adequately protected from unnecessary scares? Until this question can be answered, there will be inequities in the administration of the law.

Of course, there is literally no way inequities can be eliminated in a system of laws so complex, multitudinous, and far-reaching as exists in this society. The question is further complicated by the fact that the subject matter of legislation is becoming more and more technical. Although we have emphasized injustices, we must not overlook the fact that the great bulk of administrative action is probably acceptably fair to all concerned. In the totality of administrative justice, the glaring inequity is the exception rather than the rule. These exceptions, however, should be eliminated to the extent possible so that businessmen, and the public generally, will be assured of a quasi-judicial mechanism which will secure fair and equitable treatment, the protection of personal and property rights, and expeditious hearings and decisions.

Throughout Galbraith's book on *Economics and The Public Purpose* he complains that public and private organizations react "symbiotically," to use his words (1973). He is complaining about the same thing that many others have referred to as a convergence of the regulator and the regulated.

Those who are regulated understand fully the possibilities of being hurt by the regulators through ignorance, obtuseness, or intransigence. However, a perceptive lawyer, Richard Olney, saw benefits of the ICC which his railroad friends did not see when Congress created it in 1887. He said:

> The Commission, as its functions have now been limited by the courts, is, or can be made, of great use to the railroads. It satisfies the popular clamor for a government supervision of railroads, at the same time that supervision is almost entirely nominal. Further, the older such a Commission gets to be, the more inclined it will be found to take the business and railroad view of things. It thus becomes a sort of barrier between the railroad corporations and the people and a sort of protection against hasty and crude legislation hostile to railroad interests. . . . The part of wisdom is not to destroy the Commission but to utilize it (Josephson, 1938: 526).

This was an astute observation, and the prophecy was fulfilled. A number of commissioners (Durr, 1948) and observers (Hamilton, 1957) of regulatory agencies have commented on the convergence of interests between the regulated and the regulators. The pattern begins with an aroused public that wants correction of some abuse, such as outrageous service or excessive public utility rates. Congress passes a tough law to deal with the matter and creates a regulatory commission to administer the law. The new commission is manned with zealous public servants who exercise the needed controls, and the public goes back to its normal daily life. The regulated companies begin a process of explaining their position and their problems to both the legislative body and the regulatory agency. They are cooperative and friendly. They are reasonable people with real problems, and as they "help in understanding," past battles recede into the distance. When a new problem arises and the regulatory agency takes action, members of Congress cry that their functions are being usurped and begin an investigation which results in delay and administrative restraint. In the meantime, officials of the agency are given jobs in the industry that is regulated and maybe members of the industry accept temporary posts in the agency. To sum it all up briefly in the words of Justice Holmes, the decisions of administrative agencies become "extremely likely to be impregnated by the environing atmosphere."

Commissions take too long to decide. In 1952, for example, the Federal Trade Commission issued a complaint against Pillsbury Mills, Inc. (now the Pillsbury Company), charging the company with violating Section 7 of the Clayton Act by its acquisition of Ballard & Ballard. In mid-1953, after lengthy hearings, the hearing examiner ruled that the FTC had failed to make a case. Late in the year the full commission reversed this decision. It took six years for the case to be tried, and by then the testimony totaled more than 32,000 pages with many more thousands of pages of exhibits. In December 1960 the FTC ruled that Pillsbury's acquisitions had violated the Clayton Act. On January 7, 1966, the Supreme Court held, however, that Pillsbury had been denied a fair hearing. The FTC then had to decide whether to take new evidence, to review the antiquated record, to start all over, or to dismiss the case. It chose the latter, thirteen years after its initial action!

Restore Competition A remedy which is often recommended to eliminate claimed regulatory shortcomings of utilities by agencies such as the ICC, CAB, FCC, and the FPC, as well as state utility agencies, is simply to restore competition. Before commenting further on this remedy it is useful to observe briefly the reasoning upon which government regulation of utilities is based.

The argument is that inevitably cutthroat competition results and one or a few companies survive the wreckage. This concentrated power leads to abuse, such as the extraction of monopoly profits. This is exactly what happened in the railroad industry in the nineteenth century which led to the establishment of the ICC in 1887. There are other characteristics of these industries which also may prevent free and healthy competition. The necessity for huge investments in plant and equipment may be far out of line with current income but justified if a steady volume of traffic can be generated. Under such circumstances new competitors are slow to enter the industry and old ones are slow to leave. A monopoly secured in such an industry can rather easily perpetuate itself. The only alternative is regulation.

There are other reasons given for particular types of regulation. For instance regulation over the airlines is defended for the reasons noted above plus the need to assure airline safety. CAB regulations are also defended because it is necessary to assure adequate service for smaller cities and towns which unregulated airlines presumably would not provide.

Many observers conclude that regulation simply cannot match the benefits brought to the public by competition. Wilcox argues the case this way:

> Taking the place of competition as the method of control, regulation should be expected to yield comparable results. It should not only prevent the regulated industry from charging a monopoly price, impairing the quality of its service, and enjoying a monopoly profit. It should provide an incentive to adopt new methods, to improve quality, to increase efficiency and cut costs, to develop mass markets and expand output by selling at a lower price. It does none of these things.
>
> Regulation, at best, is a pallid substitute for competition. It cannot prescribe quality, force efficiency, or require innovation, because such action would invade the sphere of management. But when it leaves these matters to the discretion of industry, it denies consumers the protection that competition would afford. Regulation cannot set prices below an industry's costs however excessive they may be. Competition does so, and the high-cost company is compelled to discover means whereby its costs can be reduced. Regulation does not enlarge consumption by setting prices at the lowest level consistent with a fair return. Competition has this effect. Regulation fails to encourage performance in the public interest by offering rewards and penalties. Competition offers both.
>
> Regulation is static, backward-looking, preoccupied with the problems of the past. It does nothing to stimulate change, seeking to maintain order on the basis of the old technology. It is slow to adapt to change; new problems appear, but regulatory thinking lags. Competition, by contrast, is dynamic. . . .
>
> Regulation is slower than competition. It must satisfy the requirements of due process: investigate, give notice, hold hearings, study the record, make findings, issue orders, permit appeals. All this takes time and delays action. In some cases, delay may be harmful, as when it permits earnings to rise well above or to fall far below the return required to attract new capital. In other cases, it may be helpful, as when it brakes an inflationary spiral of wages and prices. But here, the merit of regulation lies, not in efficiency, but in its inefficiency (1966: 476–77).

He is not alone. Peck says that a competitive policy is not only possible but desirable in transportation (in MacAvoy, 1970). He admits that there may be problems but "no more vexatious in transportation than in steel or the automobile industries" (p. 92).

Stigler applies this policy to consumer regulations. He says: ". . . public regulation weakens the defenses the consumer has in the market and often imposes new burdens upon him, without conferring corresponding protections" (1971). Peterson says that ". . . free enterprise—the consumer's best servant—is being smothered by interventionistic regulation" (1971: 255). She then recommends phasing out the FDA, FTC, NLRB, ICC, FCC, and CAB.

Charles Phillips argues that Wilcox's position compares alleged shortcomings of regulations with the idealistic benefits of the theoretical competitive model and as a result views regulation too pessimistically, particularly in the nontransport utility area. Actually, utilities have performed well under regulation. Phillips points out that the growth rate of regulated utilities in the postwar period has been much better than that of the nonregulated utilities. The productivity of the regulated utilities has been above any other industrial sector. Utility rates have risen much less than prices generally, and some have actually fallen. Rates of return of utilities have been under those earned by any other industry. Irrespective of the reasons for this performance, Phillips concludes:

> . . . the fact remains that quality has improved, efficiency has increased, and innovation has been introduced under regulation. . . . Many would argue, and the results would seem to substantiate the point, that regulation has been at least as effective as competition, perhaps more so, in encouraging "consumption by setting prices at the lowest level consistent with a fair return." And, while it is true that formal proceedings in the regulatory process are slow, time-consuming, and expensive, even in the past this type of activity has been only a small portion of the commissions' efforts. With renewed emphasis on informal procedures today, even this small portion is declining. Thus, in the author's opinion, regulation has proven to be a more efficient substitute for competition than many claim, although there remains room for improvement (1969: 714).

One obvious middle ground between regulations and competition is to eliminate the generally conceded shortcomings of regulation and strengthen the forces of competition. As argued above, it seems timely to allow more traffic to be allocated in competitive markets. I do not mean to say that injecting more competition into the regulated industries is an easy solution to regulatory problems. Certainly, the airlines would argue today that excessive competition is creating grave financial conditions for them. My thought is that in many instances more competition would be possible and permit abandonment of some parts of the obsolete regulatory apparatus. In the case of the airlines, for instance, as with the railroads, combinations and mergers have the potential of benefiting the carriers and society as a whole. To bring about an increase in competition, a corresponding abandonment of government regulation, and an elimination of major regulatory deficiencies are challenges we have not met very well in the past.

In light of the many imperfections of competition and the ease with which consumers can be induced to buy defective and harmful products, a fact which the National Commission on Product Safety

so clearly revealed, as noted in Chapter 15, it does seem a bit premature to advocate the abolition of agencies such as the FTC and the
FDA, or the new Consumer Product Safety Commission also discussed in Chapter 15. Actually there need be no conflict between
competition and regulation in the consumer area. Regulation is often
needed to preserve, enforce, and vitalize competition and to make
sure it works in the public interest (Cohen in Stigler and Cohen, 1971).

Socialize Industry At the other extreme is Galbraith's prescription to socialize both the weak and the strong industries. One of the
reasons which led him to this conclusion is what he calls "symbiosis"
(1973: 220). He takes the position, contrary to Friedman (1962: 128),
that public monopoly power is preferable to private monopoly power
(pp. 276–277).

It is tempting at this point to digress and examine in detail the
case for and against public ownership of weak and strong industries,
but the analysis is far too complex to be accommodated in the space
which can be devoted to it here. A few things ought to be said, however. To begin with, Galbraith does not spell out in detail precisely
which industries he would socialize, although he does mention, to
illustrate those with great power, housing and transportation. For
years, government-operated arsenals produced all of our military
equipment. They were abandoned in favor of a quasi-private-public
enterprise relationship called the military-industrial complex because
it was thought to be, and proved to be, much more efficient.

It is not true, as some assert, that one finds the incompetent and
inefficient in government and just the opposite in industry. There is
great competence and great incompetence in both (Fisher, 1962). Experience has generally taught, however, that industry is much more
efficient than government in maximizing output per unit of input of
scarce resources. Government is more proficient than business in resolving political conflicts and determining public policy. A great issue
of today is to allocate responsibility to that sector, public or private,
which can operate most efficiently in the public interest. The trend
in the United States today is toward the government's getting rid of
functions which private enterprise can perform more efficiently.

Galbraith's socialization thesis rests on the assumption that government can exercise more control over industries if they are socialized than if they are not. He is after control and not efficiency per se
unless efficiency is used to mean that output is decided by government fiat rather than by a combination of market-government directives. His case for socialization further rests on the assumption that
the only way to control powerful industries is for the government to
own them. While it is true, as noted previously, that government
regulation today needs major overhauling it does not follow that
public ownership will resolve the problems. Every lesson of the past

points to the probability that public ownership would compound the deficiencies found in present regulations. The problem is to control private enterprise in the public interest, which government can now do, while at the same time to clean up the detailed regulatory apparatus, which government has not done well. The way to do this is not public ownership of industry.

Structural versus Strategic Reform In the past thirty-five years we have had five major comprehensive studies of our regulatory commissions. They all were headed by prestigious, responsible and knowledgeable people like former President Herbert Hoover. They all failed to remedy the basic problem of the regulatory agencies largely, says Bernstein, because they focused primarily on structure and not functional strategy (1972). This is not meant to belittle these studies. The latest one (The President's Advisory Council on Executive Organization, 1971), for example, is filled with very useful recommendations but not many, of them have been acted upon. An overarching problem is the cumbersome decision-making processes between the executive and legislative branches of government.

What is most needed is to focus attention on strategies of regulation. Bernstein argues:

> The primary question that we must try to answer as systematically as possible is this: For a given set of objectives, what combination of statutory provisions; regulatory powers, processes, and techniques; incentives and sanctions; political leadership; and administrative resources is likely to achieve results that approximate the goals of a regulatory program? (1972: 26)

This is a more difficult but more fruitful approach than working on organizational structure. Needed, for example, is a thorough reexamination and overhauling of the basic statutory objectives and directives of regulatory agencies. Many of the agencies have broad and ill-defined regulatory powers. The detailed regulations built upon them has erected a patchwork of overlapping jurisdictions, duplications, conflicts, and indefiniteness of policy. The urgency of reexamining the statutory framework is underscored by the strong reservations economists have about the efficiency and appropriateness of a good bit of the regulatory policy. After a careful review of the regulatory crisis a lawyer concluded that there should be an "end of legal dominance of price and entry regulation in favor of economic dominance" (Donahue, 1971: 219).

A number of studies have raised questions about the adequacy of agency leadership and professional capabilities of agency staffs (Man, 1965; Seidman, 1970). I do not like to generalize about this subject but upon the basis of years of working in the executive branch of the federal government, there does seem to me to be plenty of room for improvement in this area.

Reform in these and other areas, however, must be focused on a target different from that of the past. Concludes Bernstein:

> The talent and energy we have devoted to designing regulatory programs to protect the regulated from unfair procedures and to minimize effects adverse to regulated clienteles must now be targeted on the modest problem of designing and improving systems of regulation that have a fighting chance of achieving some useful public result (1972: 26).

The Administrative Conference The Administrative Conference Act of 1964 established the Administrative Conference but it did not begin operations until 1968. Its purpose is to study procedures and make recommendations to individual government agencies and to the President. It has a chairman, a ten-member governing council composed of 50 percent government officials and 50 percent private persons, and an assembly of eighty people. Two-fifths of the assembly are from government and the remainder from private life.

One review of the work of this conference concludes that a great deal of good has been accomplished and there is no reason to expect that many more benefits to improving the regulatory process will not follow (Gardner, in Bernstein, 1972). Such work can be helpful but it is not as likely to accomplish what is required as concentration on strategy, noted above.

Public Interest Advocacy The self-appointed public interest advocate has multiplied rapidly during the past few years. A number of these individuals and groups have assumed the role of monitoring the performance of the regulatory processes. Nader is a good example. He and his group have sought to publicize what regulatory agencies are doing and what he thinks ought to be done to reform them in order to operate more effectively in the public interest. His staff is well represented by lawyers who initiate law suits on behalf of the public. His group exerts pressure on the Congress.

There is no doubt that public interest advocates have brought changes in the regulatory agencies but, at this writing, it appears they have not been as influential in affecting the political process and regulatory agency policies as they wish. It remains to be seen whether they will have a major impact on regulatory agency reform in the future.

Concluding Comment In sum, there is no question about the fact that there is need for major reform and redirection of the independent regulatory agency. Radical reform, such as reverting to "free competition" on the one hand or public ownership on the other, is likely to bring more problems than it seeks to solve. For the next few decades at least, the path which seems to have the greatest chance of advancing the public interest is serious reform of regulatory agency policy and procedures. The focus, however, should be primarily on strategy and not structure.

THE ENERGY CRISIS

We have, at the time of this writing in early 1974, an energy crisis. It has been years in developing and will take years to resolve. An extended discussion of this problem is included here because it demonstrates the intimate interrelationships between business and government.

The Crisis at the Time of Writing In mid-1973 it was generally conceded that in the winter of 1973/74 there would be a 5 percent demand/supply imbalance for gasoline and fuel oil. It was also generally conceded that moderate government action, together with voluntary conservation, could easily bring overall demand into balance with supply but that some hardship would be encountered among certain people and in parts of the country. Then in November 1973 a group of Middle East oil producing countries announced a 25 percent reduction in their oil exports to the world with the intent of forcing the United States government to press Israel to meet Arab demands. The ban was eased considerably soon after for all countries except the Netherlands and the United States. With the oil embargo in effect the United States was faced with an energy deficiency of from 15 to 25 percent of supply.

One of the problems of the energy crisis is that reliable numbers are not available to show the exact deficiencies. Part of this problem arises from "leakage" of oil into the United States and part arises from the sheer complexity of keeping track of energy demand/supply relationships. Nevertheless, it is now clear (January 1974) that the United States faces a number of energy problems. There is indeed a shortage of gasoline and fuel oils for home heating. There are electric power brownouts and threatened rolling blackouts. The nation finds that it must import approximately 30 percent of its daily requirement of about 17 million barrels of oil, much from the Middle East. Imported crude oil prices averaged $3.15 per barrel in early 1973 but in October the price went to $5.12 and jumped to $11.65 in December. Some spot auction prices for limited supplies have brought $25 a barrel. Rising prices will add to the nation's inflation problems, depress the balance of payments, and bring great changes in price relationships. In the Spring of 1974 the embargo was lifted but imported crude oil prices declined only moderately.

While the spot auction price noted above is not likely to be the world price, and while it may be that the $11.65 December 1973 price may not hold, it is altogether likely that the world for some time ahead is faced with much higher oil prices. There are eleven oil exporting countries which have banded together in the Organization of Petroleum Exporting Countries (OPEC). Revenues of these countries in 1973 amounted to about $23 billion. Revenues are expected to rise to $85 billion in 1974, $100 billion in 1975 and $171 billion in 1980, according to the World Bank President Robert S. McNamara (*Los Angeles Herald Examiner,* January 23, 1974). These flows of money will create serious deficiencies in balance of payments of most countries of the world, threaten their economic stability and international trade, and be a source of serious potential financial disruptions in international money markets.

How did we get to this "crisis"?   Rising consumption of energy is a root cause seriously exacerbated by the partial Arab oil embargo. The average American used the energy equivalent of forty-two barrels of oil in 1955. In 1970 it was sixty-one. The prospect for 1985 is ninety-seven. The United States alone uses about one-third of the world's energy output each year.

Our past policies have resulted in a sluggish growth of our gas and oil reserves, a failure of refinery capacity to keep pace with demand, a failure of electric energy output to keep pace with demand, and consequently an increasing reliance on oil imports. As late as 1957 the United States was a net exporter of fuels and lubricants. Since then imports have exceeded exports. In 1960 we depended upon oil imports for 18 percent of our needs and by 1972 foreign countries were supplying 28 percent of our needs at a cost to us of $5 billion a year.

The policy of the Federal Power Commission to clamp a lid on the price of natural gas at the wellhead has provided cheap energy but it also resulted in a lack of incentives to explore for new reserves. At the same time electric utilities have increased their demand for gas because it became progressively relatively cheaper than other fuels and is free of the polluting qualities of other fuels. Before the President increased gas prices in May 1973 the cost of gas at the wellhead was 25 cents per million BTUs compared with 60 cents for crude oil, 80 cents for heating oil, and 35 cents for coal (*Business Week,* April 21, 1973). Gas and oil exploratory wells dropped from 58,000 in 1956 to 27,000 in 1971.

In the face of a rising demand for gasoline of about 7 percent per year our volume of crude oil processed by refiners has risen only 3 percent per year. We are thus short of refinery capacity. There are a number of reasons for this. Environmental restrictions have placed obstacles in the way of finding suitable sites for refineries and have delayed construction. Our oil import quota system has been operated on a year-to-year basis and has created uncertainties for refinery operators about their getting sufficient supplies to operate profitably.

Tax and other economic benefits have been more attractive in other countries of the world for the location of refineries (Simon, 1973).

In 1972, 230 power plants of 300 Mw or larger were scheduled to come on line between 1971 and 1977. For various reasons fifty-three of these, or 23 percent, were delayed. Regulatory and environmental problems were responsible for delays of 27 of them. Hence, a conflict between environmental policy and energy requirements is also partly responsible for our energy shortage (NICB, 1972: 14). In addition, facilities that do exist cannot produce at capacity because of shortages of gas. Also, without special permission, they cannot burn higher sulfur content oil and coal because of antipollution regulations.

The oil companies have been the target of blame. The companies have been accused by the FTC of having behaved "as would a classic monopolist: They have attempted to increase profits by restricting output" (U.S. Senate, Permanent Subcommittee on Investigations of the Committee on Government Operations, 1973). They have been accused of inhibiting competition, of using their power to control and misuse common carrier pipelines, and of investing in refinery capacity abroad when they should have been building capacity here at home (Aspin in Lawrence and Wengert, 1973).

There are really two fundamental energy problems. One is the current crisis and the other are longer range problems which would evolve were we to continue on the courses of energy action and policy pursued during the past ten years. The remedies for each differ significantly.

Meeting the Current "Crisis" Before the Arab oil embargo it became obvious that we were not producing enough energy nor were we exploring for it as diligently as future demands required. As a result the Federal Power Commission increased substantially the wellhead price of gas. In November 1973 the President sent a special message to the Congress on "the energy emergency" which asked for many things most of which the Congress granted. Included was national daylight saving time, a reduction of automobile speeds, permission to build the Alaskan Pipe Line, use of the Elk Hills naval petroleum reserves for civilian purposes, and temporary relaxation of some environmental regulations. The message did not ask for rationing powers because the President had such powers under other legislation. The President, in December 1973, also established the Federal Energy Office and named an "energy czar" to coordinate and centralize federal control over energy problems. This later became the Federal Energy Administration.

A major issue at this writing concerns the use of the price mechanism to deal with the emergency. There are some who feel that gasoline prices should be allowed to reach their natural level. This, it is asserted, would result in a sharp price increase which would reduce consumption and induce exploration, refinery construction in the United States, and greater oil imports. Others feel that instead of letting prices rise on the open market the government should levy a tax of from twenty to forty cents a gallon. This would avoid "windfall" profits to the oil companies and yield billions of dollars for government use in solving the oil shortage. Others assert that the only solution is coupon rationing. Still others, including government officials, think that the use of both price increases and rationing, coupled with more stringent conservation measures is the way to go.

There are powerful arguments against allowing gasoline prices to rise as market conditions permit. Prices would skyrocket for a time, depending on the size of the shortage, but would eventually come down. In the meantime, this type of gyration would be very disruptive. Perhaps more seriously the price increase could well spark another price-wage spiral and add to inflation problems. Also, we simply do not know how much a ten-, twenty-, or thirty-cent increase could reduce consumption. One study by reputable economists concluded that a thirty-cent increase could reduce consumption by 10.7 to 14.8 percent and a forty-cent increase would reduce it from 13 to 19.9 percent (Lawrence, 1973), but no one knows for sure. It is obvious also that a sharp price increase would not bring new refineries or power plants into operation any quicker. It takes years to build such plants.

These issues disappeared in the Spring of 1974 as the oil embargo leaked oil to the United States and was finally lifted. The demand/supply squeeze, however, can easily be applied by OPEC as long as this country does not satisfy most of its consumption by domestic production. There is urgency, therefore, for government-industry cooperation in meeting future energy requirements.

The Problem Through to 1985 If present trends in energy supply and usage continue without change, and assuming there is no Arab oil embargo, we shall be in trouble for a long time. The numbers are staggering. In considering the following projections two points are important. First, they are based upon a continuation of present trends. Second, forecasts in this area have not always been very accurate and, while there seems to be some general agreement with these numbers that does not mean they are correct. I do believe, however, that their magnitudes are reasonable.

The total demand for energy in the United States is expected to just about double from approximately 65 quadrillion BTU's (British Thermal Units) in 1970 to 120 quadrillion in 1985 (Committee on Interior and Insular Affairs, 1972).

To meet such requirements will demand an enormous rise in supplies of fuels, especially gas, oil, coal, and nuclear. Of outstanding significance is the supply of oil. Total demand for oil in the United States is expected to be about 30 million barrels/day in 1985 of which half must be imported and the remainder will be satisfied from domestic sources. This compares with consumption of 17 million barrels/day in the fall of 1973 of which one third was imported. The 1985 projected import of oil is equivalent to the entire Middle East production at the present time. At current oil prices our total payments for imported oil in 1985 could be around $50 billion per year, most to the Middle East oil exporting countries. Such a level of expenditure by the United States would create enormous problems in its balance of payment because there is no way these funds could be used by these countries to import United States produced products and services in any appreciable amount. Furthermore, the United States would be competing with other industrialized nations of the world whose demands for oil will also be rising. The net result will be intensive competition, higher prices, and huge cash reserves in the hands of the Middle East oil producers. The major oil producers in the Arabian peninsula had an estimated income of $5 billion in 1972. If current trends were to continue the Middle East oil producer could have enormous cash holdings in their treasuries by the end of this decade. Such cash flows and reserves could be seriously disruptive to world monetary markets.

Meeting energy demands from domestic sources involves huge expenditures and problems. For instance, to meet nuclear energy requirements involving perhaps 17 percent of our total demand in 1985 would necessitate building 280 nuclear energy plants of 1,000 megawatts each. To raise domestic energy production to projected levels will require capital outlays between now and 1985 of $375 billion (NICB, 1972(A): 34).

Reserves There is no doubt about the fact that the United States has sufficient reserves to meet its future energy requirements. There are problems in making them available, however, and before they are resolved there will be an "energy squeeze." Estimates of our oil reserve range from several hundred million to 590 billion barrels. With present technology perhaps 100 billion is recoverable (Rocks and Runyon, 1972: 15). There are reserves of oil in shale rock estimated at 600 billion barrels but only about 80 billion are now accessible (Nixon, 1973A). There are huge reserves of oil in tar sands in Canada, which presumably would be readily accessible to the United States. The United States Geological survey estimates that we have 2,100 trillion cubic feet of natural gas as yet "undiscovered" [NICB,

1972(A): 25]. We have perhaps 20 percent of the world's coal reserves and they are estimated to be sufficient to meet our needs for 300 or 400 years. Beyond these sources are nuclear energy (breeder and fusion). We have sufficient uranium to satisfy all of our nuclear energy needs for hundreds of years. There are also other possibilities such as solar and geothermal energy (Smil, 1972).

Using these resources is not without problems. Much of our oil reserves are on the continental shelf and present cost and pollution problems. The Alaskan Prudhoe Bay oil field can be exploited only with pollution hazards. At the present time it is uneconomic to produce oil from shale rock and we do not know how to get it without irreparable damage to the landscape. Most of it is found in the mountains of the west and the rock is covered by only a few feet of earth. We have many problems in using our huge coal reserves. Our present technology is not efficient in transforming coal into gas and oil for energy. We have major problems in avoiding destruction of the earth.

What Can Be Done? President Nixon in his special message to the nation on the energy emergency, November 7, 1973, called for a major new endeavor to make the United States self-sufficient in energy. He called it Project Independence and set 1980 as the target date for achievement. This is a tough schedule but, as the President said, with the spirit exhibited in the Apollo project and the determination of the Manhattan Project the goal might be met. Many things will have to be done.

First, a fundamental requirement is the development of coordinated, comprehensive, and realistic national goals, priorities, and policies concerning every important aspect of the energy problem. The Congress, of course, must become deeply involved in the preparation of these guidelines. The petroleum, electric power, and other industries must also become involved in their formulation. Policies then must be administered in a coordinated and efficient manner.

Second, there must be a series of specific actions taken to increase production of needed energy resources. To illustrate, it is essential that research and development be accelerated in a major way. Technological developments really can, in time, solve our energy problems but the costs will be heavy. Federal R&D expenditures for energy amounted to $357 million in fiscal 1969 and rose to $623 million for fiscal 1973. In contrast to this number it was proposed by four U.S. senators in March 1973 that the United States create a new federal agency to oversee research concerned with energy by government-industry research corporations and allocate $20 billion to the effort. Both numbers may be unrealistic. Nevertheless, neither the importance of technology nor the cost should be underestimated. We need, for example, massive research to make efficient the conversion of our enormous coal reserves to gas and oil. Much still has to be done to improve the efficiency of getting oil from shale rock. Much needs to be done to speed up research of breeder and fusion nuclear energy. Looking further ahead much needs to be done to make solar and geothermal energy available at reasonable prices.

There must be incentives to motivate the development of new sources of supply and the means of production of end use fuels. This means permitting gas prices to rise sufficiently to encourage exploration of needed new reserves. It means assuring that there is an appropriate profit incentive for oil companies to explore for new reserves. Naturally, means must be found to avoid excessive profits in the oil and gas industry. Prices should be continuously surveyed by government. There are other things that can be done. Income tax subsidies for the oil and gas industries should be changed to require that funds provided by depletion allowances and other tax preferences be sunk into capital investments in the United States or North America. Past federal policies encouraged investment abroad rather than at home and this was partly the cause of our growing dependence on foreign oil and inadequate refinery capacity. This sort of thing should be stopped.

Nonprice impediments to the development of energy must be reduced and/or eliminated. Problems in locating power plants must be resolved. In the case of the Southern California Edison Company, to illustrate, it is necessary to get clearances for siting from at least thirty different governmental agencies. Some of this problem arises from environmentalists but not all. Speeding up the leasing of federally owned oil and gas lands by cutting bureaucratic tangles is needed. President Nixon estimated that one half of our oil reserves are in these lands (including offshore shelf) and by accelerating leasing we can increase annual energy production by 1.5 billion barrels of oil and 5 trillion feet of gas by 1985. This is 16 percent of our projected requirements for oil, and 20 percent of our gas needs, in that year.

It will be necessary to review very carefully our environmental standards to be sure that they do not create greater problems—albeit different ones—than they were designed to solve. For example, getting more coal out of the ground to provide electricity cannot be done without ecological impairment. How much impairment will be permitted? Very difficult questions will arise and demand answers about a more gradual approach to ecological desires and standards so as to achieve a quicker and lower cost contribution to energy demands. We must learn to make such decisions much better than in the past.

A third program involves the reduction of waste. As a nation we do waste much energy. A careful study of possible conservation was made by the Office of Emergency Preparedness and the conclusion was reached that the United States could save 7.3 million barrels of oil per day by 1980, or two-thirds of projected imports in that year.

The balance of payments saving would be $10.7 billion (in 1972 prices). The proposed conservation measures include such actions as improvement in products (such as more efficient engines), more efficiency in economic activity (e.g., new freight handling systems), new conservation measures (e.g., recycling waste materials), and pricing (such as to increase prices by a fuel tax). The measures proposed do not entail necessarily a slowing down or reversal of economic growth.

Over the long term there must be some price rise for energy to allow the market mechanism to increase supply, as noted above, and to reduce the demand for energy. If a price rise is desired to reduce consumption without expanding the profits of industry the obvious way is to use the excise tax. This, however, is not without its problems. For instance, rising energy costs will discriminate against the poor.

Fourth, the energy problem must be tackled in conjunction with other countries of the world. Energy consumption grows with affluence and as more countries become richer the demand for energy will rise. Increasing requirements of Europe and Japan, for instance, will bring intense competition for available supplies. Secretary of State Kissinger recently called for a cooperative effort on the part of western industrialized nations to come to grips with the energy problem. In another direction, political stability in the Middle East is essential since such a large portion of the world's oil supplies comes from that region and since those nations have chosen to use oil as a weapon in international diplomacy. Reconciling demands for oil and the political aspirations of oil-producing countries will require great skills of diplomacy.

Fifth, there will be required new and more intimate relationships between the federal government and industries involved in and subject to the consequences of the energy problem. Precisely what this relationship should and will be is difficult to say. But clearly the old ways of doing things need change. There is a great lesson in the energy crisis. Our current energy problems have arisen not because of a lack of resources in and available to the United States but because we did not foresee problems ahead and take action in time to meet them. Bluntly stated, we did a thoroughly impoverished planning job. We can resolve our energy problems only by skilled long-range planning and appropriate current program implementation by both government and industry based on plans. If we can meet this challenge it will show that we can master such complex problems. If we do not, the portent for our future survival will be a more important result than the energy problems which will arise.

Finally, energy goals must be more realistic. President Nixon's original aim of Project Independence was virtually complete reliance for energy on our own resources. It is now clear that the costs of meeting this goal are prohibitive. Project Independence now means no greater reliance in 1985 on foreign energy sources than in 1974.

This is an attainable goal, at reasonable costs, which would prevent foreign oil producers from exerting excessive pressure on our foreign policy.

SHOULD THE GOVERNMENT HAVE GUARANTEED LOCKHEED'S LOAN?

In 1971 the government guaranteed a $250 million loan to the Lockheed Aircraft Corporation, presumably saving it from bankruptcy. This case naturally involved a great many issues which will not be examined fully here (Hearings Before the Committee on Banking, Housing and Urban Affairs, 1971). There is a core issue, however, which I do want to present.

Opponents of the measure argued that the guarantee was contrary to the fundamental purposes and operations of our free competitive economic system. They said that the basic objective of free competition was to assure that resources were used efficiently in producing the goods and services that people want. If a firm failed it showed that it had not used the resources at its disposal efficiently. In that case, society is better off to allow the firm to fail so that someone else can use the resources efficiently in producing what society wants. Bankruptcy of an unprofitable firm serves the public interest.

On the other hand, it was argued that to allow Lockheed to go bankrupt would result in the loss of thousands of jobs, bankruptcy for suppliers who were efficient, and perhaps trigger a series of financial disasters which might throw the entire economic system into a downturn. If these fears are at all realistic, they said, the public interest clearly would be served by preventing the company from going into receivership.

These arguments raise a question as to whether public policy will be made on the basis of the older classical principles of the operation of our economic system or some newer cost/benefit philosophy. While in theory it may be true that resources of a company that has failed will be converted and used more efficiently by someone else this result is not certain. The resources can be lost to society. It seems to me that it is wiser to try to find out whether the net advantage to society would be greater than the costs of preventing failure. Hence, for a case such as the Lockheed loan I favor the cost/benefit approach. The great danger in issues such as this are not, it seems to me, in using the cost/benefit approach rather than the older competitive model, but in allowing the guarantee action to establish a precedent for government's continuously preventing companies, large and small, from going bankrupt. I am sure there were many who opposed the loan to avoid this danger. If, however, the government acts affirmatively in such cases only reluctantly, very infrequently, and after thorough analysis of costs and benefits then this option should be kept open in the public interest.

CORPORATE DATA DISCLOSURE

American corporations make available to the public far more information than companies in any other country of the world. Under the Securities Exchange Act of 1934, the SEC has power to force corporations to disclose information needed by investors to appraise the value of corporate securities, and to prescribe and police corporate accounting methods in this regard. Since the passage of this legislation corporations have been asked to make public more and more information and the pressures are continuing. Recently, the movement has assumed more intensity both with respect to current and historical data and to projected earnings.

Historical and Current Information There are many today who would agree with President Roosevelt's observation in 1901 that: "Great corporations exist only because they are created and safeguarded by our institutions; and it is therefore our right and our duty to see that they work in harmony with these institutions. . . . The first requisite [of corporate accountability] is knowledge, full and complete; knowledge which may be made public to the world." Demands for more information about our corporations rest on this philosophical ground as well as on the idea that the type of political-economy system we have functions best when there is a maximum of information available about products and business behavior. Consumers who have more knowledge about products can purchase in a more rational manner. The more knowledge the public has about corporate behavior the less likely there will be abuses, injustices, and illegalities.

As anyone who looks at the typical annual reports and prospectuses of a corporation will see there is available to the public a great deal of information about each public company. What more is wanted? For one thing there are demands for more information about product lines. The SEC now requires reporting of sales of product lines when the contribution to sales or net income is over 10 percent. This cutoff is too high, say some observers. Furthermore, it is argued that the definition of product line is so loose that very large companies do not report by product line on the grounds that all products are related to one technology and therefore can be lumped together. So, demands are being made to clarify SEC regulations to assure deeper reporting of product lines.

The demands for information go far beyond this, however. They cover highly detailed information about individual products, finance, employment, political activity, procurement of supplies and components, product research and development, environmental impacts, and tax information. Recommendations are to make public the income tax returns of corporations, certain social costs, intercorporate financial ties, publicly owned facilities operated or leased by private corporations, and details of corporate foreign operations. (Nader, Mueller, and Adams, in Hearings before the Subcommittee on Monopoly, 1971: Part 2).

Corporations generally resist such demands although studies show that more corporations voluntarily are publishing more information. For one thing there may be heavy costs involved in getting some of this information—costs in terms of executive as well as clerical time. Companies also fear that if too much information is to be made public they may be forced to disclose proprietary data.

Companies generally do not want to reveal product division data, but would rather hide financial problems of particular divisions behind aggregate numbers for the entire corporation. To do so, for instance, gives a company time to solve a divisional financial problem before adverse publicity has a chance to affect the entire company. Anyway, say managers, their companies should be evaluated as a whole, like chop suey. Beyond these considerations, corporations point out that there is no universally accepted formula for allocating overhead costs—administration, interest, and other expenses—to lines of business. These are joint costs and are handled differently by corporations. Top managements of companies, divisional general managers, and the SEC may find it difficult to agree on what is an equitable method to allocate overhead costs among lines of businesses.

On the other hand, the more information an investor has, the greater is his chance of making rational decisions. Analysts claim that in large diversified companies they are unable to come to rational conclusions without knowledge of divisional operations. They also claim they are confused by figures in annual reports. For example, on the same page or at least in the same report it is not at all unusual to find three or four different figures purporting to measure the same thing, such as per-share earnings. There are a number of cases now before the courts claiming stockholder losses because of insufficient and deceptive financial reporting that might have been avoided with fuller corporate disclosure.

Here, as in so many other issues between government and business, there are trade-offs between beneficial and disadvantageous results. Where the balance lies depends a great deal upon who is doing the weighing. However, it is difficult to argue with the proposition that, without strong evidence to the contrary, the public interest is best served by more information being made public about what our corporations are doing.

Making Forecasts Public Following much thought and study the SEC on February 2, 1973, announced a tradition-shattering decision: companies will be allowed to include sales and earnings forecasts in registration and proxy statements, prospectuses, and annual reports filed with the commission. Prior to this time the SEC had taken a strong position against making such forecasts public. This SEC ruling does not make reporting mandatory. The decision to make a forecast public rests entirely with each company. However, the SEC is considering a proposal to require filing of forecasts when such data are given to financial analysts outside the corporation and to the news media. This is entirely logical and follows an argument long made by former SEC Chairman Casey that ". . . when a management confirms an analyst's private projection in a private meeting, it seems to me that an obligation to make that projection public is created" (1972: 52).

Casey also had other reasons for approving the ruling. He felt that there were too many instances where forecasts of things to come were made public at various meetings and that investors who were not at these meetings were being deprived of information that others had. He also reasoned that when a management knew that earnings projections substantially in excess, or below, their own expectations were being given to the investing public it was in their self-interest as well as their obligation to the investing public to make known the company's forecasts or at least issue some sort of public demurrer.

Whether or not to make a forecast public is not a simple decision. Most companies make forecasts, especially of sales and profits, but there are many different types of forecasts, for different periods of time, and with varying degrees of reliability. A survey made by the Financial Executives Institute showed that 334 out of 338 companies said they made forecasts of earnings (*Fortune*, 1973). While most of these companies would consider such forecasts to be confidential another survey showed that 70 percent of the reporting companies gave some kind of help to analysts who were trying to estimate their company's future sales and earnings (*Fortune*, 1973).

A financial forecast can be a simple broad statement, unsupported by research, such as this: "Your corporation expects to increase both earnings and profits over the next five years." It can also be a detailed pro forma profit and loss statement and balance sheet covering each of five future years and produced from a thorough corporate long-range planning system. In between, a financial forecast can be a simple sales and profit projection based upon little more than an extrapolation of past trends modified by a "feel" for future environmental changes. Or, it can be a sincere effort to prepare the best cash flow projection that available time and expenditure will permit.

Forecasts may be in terms of expected earnings per share. They may be in terms of percentage growth expectations or in absolute dollars. They may be expressed as return on investment. The time span varies from company to company. Typically, the formal long-range plans of companies are for five years. There are many companies, however, that plan ahead only one year. There are others who make long-range plans of ten to twenty years ahead.

Most larger companies have some type of formal planning system which includes many projections other than sales and profits. Included are product developments, research, acquisitions, divestment, managerial changes, capital financing, marketing channels, and so on. Once a financial forecast is made public the precedent is set to disclose these other projections. At what point is disclosure contrary to the interests of the company and its investors?

The degree of reliability of forecasts will vary. Every forecast is obsolete the moment it is made because the forecast is made upon the basis of a set of assumptions which are constantly changing. Even the best managed companies have erred badly in forecasting the future.

A few arguments often given against disclosure of forecasts follow. There are those who fear that the naive and unsophisticated investor will really believe the forecasts and invest accordingly. Others feel that managers will be overly conservative in making forecasts so as not to be embarrassed when the results come in. Others may paint a rosy picture of the future to divert attention from current problems. If managers see that they have overestimated future earnings they may cut necessary current expenditures so as to improve profits and thereby meet their projections. This may, however, be at the expense of future profits.

Following are some arguments for publicizing forecasts. It is asserted that companies in the United Kingdom have made public certified forecasts by chartered accountants for twenty-five years and the experience has been generally good (Carmichael, 1973). Making forecasts public will obviously eliminate advantages that insiders now have. Relations between investors and companies should be improved. Making forecasts public will force managers to do a better job of long-range planning (Brown, 1972: Kell, 1973).

Some people are concerned about the possibility of corporate managers being held liable for forecasts that turn out to be wrong. The case of *Dolgow v. Anderson* throws light on this issue. In this case stockholders of Monsanto Company brought suit because they said the company's forecasts turned out to be incorrect and they lost money as a result. The suit was dismissed by the judge of the U.S. District Court who said that the forecasts were well prepared, extensively reviewed, honest, reasonable, and the best estimates qualified people could make. If this case is used as a precedent it can be concluded that if forecasts are carefully and honestly prepared the managers of companies will not be liable if unforeseeable circumstances cause different results.

The SEC ruling on forecasts will bring many important issues to the forefront in the future. Undoubtedly there will be abuses of the right to publicize forecasts. This will raise the issue of whether or not certified public accountants should attest to their reliability. Also, the SEC will be forced to step up to the question of reporting standards including format, the assumptions on which the forecast is based, rules with respect to updating the forecast, and rules of liability (Kell, 1973).

ACCOUNTING STANDARDS AND PROFIT CALCULATIONS

Closely associated with the questions of disclosure noted above are needed reforms in the application of accounting rules. Current rules for corporate accounting permit a businessman to vary reported profits within wide limits. This is not to say that there are no accounting rules. There are. But they can be used in legal ways to produce great variations in the bottom line of a profit and loss statement. Sometimes an opportunistic manager may use the rules to try to influence the price-earnings ratio of his stock so as to acquire greater leverage in acquisitions. There are many accepted rules which can be used to change profits, such as those concerning research and maintenance expense, depletion of inventories held at low cost, introduction of new depreciation schedules, stopping of research temporarily, cutting of advertising temporarily, and selling assets for a "one shot" capital gain. These possibilities suggest also that it is often impossible to compare performance of companies in the same industry.

The American accounting profession is the primary agency for establishing accounting standards. But the government, especially the SEC, also makes rules in this area. The accounting profession over time has made it more difficult for an unscrupulous manager to use legitimate rules to distort earnings but there are still too many alternatives which permit the preparation of misleading statements. It is likely that tighter rules will be recommended by a newly formed Financial Accounting Standards Board of the American Institute of Accountants.

FEDERAL INCORPORATION

Throughout our history corporations have acquired their charters from state governments. Proposals for the federal government to issue charters of incorporation for all businesses have been made throughout this century. Presidents Franklin Roosevelt, Taft, and Wilson, for example, are among prominent persons recommending that the Congress pass a federal incorporation statute. Most of the committees of the Congress investigating antitrust problems have made similar recommendations. Today, activists such as Nader are following the same line. The idea is one which appears logical, compelling, and full of promise. State laws granting corporate charters are loose and permit corporations to do just about anything they wish. More uniformity and a better means of control than present ad hoc legislation and regulatory agency ruling seems desirable.

Why has the Congress never passed federal incorporation laws? Probably the best answer is that such action would certainly restrict the potential area of activity of many companies and would seriously affect the interests of others. For all it would make federal intervention in their affairs much easier and business would fear possible new controls. As a result, business can muster virtual unanimity of opinion and face Congress with a united front and such opposition is very persuasive to the Congress.

The power of incorporation could be used by the federal government as a major instrument of policy and control. Whatever was written into the charter would be binding. It could include controls over acquisitions of other companies, specification of reports to be made public, and disclosure of all sorts of information from managerial stock holdings to campaign contributions. As matters now stand such requirements flow from the usual legislative and regulatory processes.

The only major argument against federal incorporation, in my judgment, is that if the initial statute were written so rigidly as to lock the nation into a particular structure and business operating system the flexibility of the corporation to change with events might be seriously reduced. This could be disastrous. But I do not think that would happen. On the other hand, we are in need of uniform control over many details of corporate reporting and performance which can be accomplished efficiently by federal incorporation.

PRICE INFLATION AND GOVERNMENT CONTROLS

One of the most persistent, dangerous, and complex problems of the United States during recent years has been price inflation. To control inflation the government has applied various types of economic controls over the economy, wages and prices particularly, which affect business in many direct and indirect ways. The issues for business in this area are many and highly intricate and cannot be treated at any length here. But a few comments are in order. First will be noted the basis for governmental policy in controlling prices. Then recent control experience will be presented briefly. Finally, the question is addressed: What needs to be done to control price inflation in the future?

Full Employment Policy of the Federal Government The basic policy for government's anti-inflation policies rests in the Employment

Act of 1946. This was a very important piece of legislation. Section 2 of the act states the declaration of national policy to be as follows:

> The Congress hereby declares that it is the continuing policy and responsibility of the Federal Government to use all practicable means consistent with its needs and obligations and other essential considerations of national policy, with the assistance and cooperation of industry, agriculture, labor, and State and local governments, to coordinate and utilize all its plans, functions, and resources for the purpose of creating and maintaining, in a manner calculated to foster and promote free competitive enterprise and the general welfare, conditions under which there will be afforded useful employment opportunities, including selfemployment, for those able, willing, and seeking to work, and to promote maximum employment, production, and purchasing power.

The act did not state that the government was obliged to ensure employment for all those seeking it, but only to foster conditions that will promote maximum employment. (President Truman sought the stronger language.) It is noteworthy, also, that this objective is to be achieved with means consistent with other national policies and with the free enterprise system. This has been interpreted to mean that action is to be taken to maintain a stable price level, to protect the rights of the states, to preserve the economic freedoms of people, and to promote the private sector rather than to enlarge the government's sphere of operations.

Objectives of the Employment Act of 1946 The looseness of the act's language opens the door for differences of opinion about goals and means to achieve them. Over time, however, there has developed a consensus that the fundamental objectives of the act are to ensure full employment while at the same time securing price stability. So accepted are these goals that Gordon rightly says that if the act were recast today, it would be called "The Full Employment Act" (1967: 1). Full employment generally means that qualified people can find jobs at prevailing wage rates in productive activity without excessive delay. A widely used national target for full employment is that unemployment should not exceed 4 percent of the work force. (It is recognized that frictional and structural unemployment cannot be erased and unemployment reduced to zero.) It also means that housewives and students are not under pressure to take jobs they do not want.

Price-level stability means the absence of any sharp trend or movement in the general price level. A price rise of between 1.5 and 2 percent a year would be considered to be within the goal of price stability. Price indexes are not really precise. The general consumer price index, for instance, is a bundle of market-basket items and services of many kinds. The index does not measure changes in quality of products, and measuring prices such as medical care and recreation raises special problems.

Achieving these goals is of profound significance to society and business. Business is freed from the threat of bankruptcy because of external and sudden unexpected changes in the economic environment. It can plan ahead with reasonable assurance. This, in turn, induces enterprisers to be bolder in undertaking research and development projects having a long-time span for fruition. In turn, new job opportunities are opened and employment is sustained. Masses of workers need not fear sudden denial of jobs for reasons having nothing to do with either their productivity or managerial efficiency. Price instability on the down side can wreak havoc with production plans and business income, which in turn can result in unemployment. On the inflationary side, it can rob people of their incomes and can generate serious conflicts among groups whose purchasing power is eroding. If anyone does not fully appreciate the extraordinary significance of achieving the goals of full employment policy, he should reread very carefully the accounts of the economic and political catastrophes throughout the world brought about by the economic depression of the 1930s.

The Record of GNP, Employment, and Prices Compared with previous experience, there is no question at all that the record of performance of the economy as measured by GNP, employment, and prices has, with the exception of prices during the past half dozen years, been exceptionally good. GNP, as noted in Chapter 4, has moved upward without the huge booms and busts so characteristic of previous economic history. Unemployment has hovered above and below the 5 percent range and, in many years, the objectives of the act have not been met. Prices jumped substantially in the years immediately following passage of the act but were comparatively stable during the 1950s and up to 1966. From that time to this price inflation has been a major problem.

Causes of Inflation After 1965 The present inflation began after President Johnson in 1965 committed a half million troops in the Vietnam War and failed to take the necessary measures on the economic front to counteract the inflationary impact of additional military costs. Annual military spending was lifted by $25 billion, which increased in succeeding years, and this expenditure was not offset by an increase in federal tax revenues even though the economy was then fully employed. In 1967 the President did ask the Congress for an increase in taxes but the Congress refused unless the President agreed to cut rising nondefense expenditures. He declined to do this and the federal deficit rose to over $25 billion in fiscal year 1968. The Congress did not pass tax legislation until 1968. By then it was too late because inflationary pressures could not be contained. Expansion of aggregate demand in an already overheated economy lifted prices which in turn brought rising wage settlements. This pushed costs up. What at first was a demand-pull inflation became a cost/push inflation. Consumer prices rose about 3 percent in 1966 and 1967, 4.7 percent in 1968, 6.1 percent in 1969, 5.5 percent in 1970, and were rising at the rate of 4.8 percent in mid-1971 when comprehensive direct controls were placed on the economy.

In the meantime average hourly compensation and fringe benefits had gone up 13.1 percent in the year before controls. The traditional surplus in the United States balance of trade with the world degenerated into a huge deficit. This deficit, coupled with increased investments abroad by American companies, accelerated downward total balance of payments deficits. Foreign confidence in the dollar eroded and there was a rush to convert dollars into other currencies. Unemployment rates leaped to 6 percent and the prime commercial paper rate was at an unprecedented 8.65 percent in July 1971.

The New Economic Policy President Nixon in August 1971 took action under the provisions of the Economic Stabilization Act of 1970 to combat these adverse forces. The dollar no longer could be converted into gold at a fixed price, an import tax of 10 percent was imposed, and a ninety-day freeze on all wages and prices was announced. This was called Phase I. Phase II began on November 14, 1971. Price ceilings were established with a price commission in charge of the controls. A 5.5 percent guideline on wage increases was imposed with a pay board to oversee the controls. Phase III started in January 11, 1973. Mandatory overall controls on prices were removed but special regulations were kept on food, health services, and construction. It was expected that the voluntary controls of Phase III would blend into decontrol. That did not happen and Phase IV was started in mid-August 1973. Prices were permitted to rise only to cover increases in basic costs. Price rises of major companies, however, were subject to rejection or postponement by the government. Wage rates were held to 5.5 percent but a cost of living council could grant higher levels.

Phase I was rather successful in keeping the annual rate of price rise to about 2.0 percent. Under Phase II the annual rate of increase was 3.6 percent. In Phase III it was 8.3 percent and for 1973 it was over 9 percent. In 1973, also, wholesale prices leaped 18.2 percent, the largest one-year increase since 1946. This foreshadowed sizable price rises in 1974. Wage rates and fringe benefits dropped from 13.1 percent in Phase I to 8.5 percent in Phase II, and to 7.6 percent in Phase III and IV. This rate of Phases III and IV, however, was almost double productivity rates. Price-wage controls were relaxed and then abandoned in 1973–74 and the nation experienced double-digit consumer price inflation.

The Case for and against Direct Wage/Price Controls It has long been standard wisdom that comprehensive direct wage and price controls in a peacetime economy would at best be a failure and at worst a disaster in disrupting complex economic interrelationships. Why then can the President's action in August 1971 in instituting such controls be justified? The fundamental answer is that things were getting out of hand at the time. Rising expectations of greater inflation were likely to be self-fulfilling prophecies. Some shock treatment was necessary to dampen expectations and inflation. There is good evidence that this premise was accurate. There is also good evidence that the Phase I program was successful in dampening expectations and in reducing the rate of price inflation and compensation per man hour.

During Phase I there was little evidence to support the view that controls generally brought productive inefficiency in industry. But as time moved on the number of specific disruptions grew. A good illustration was the sharp rise in food prices in late 1973 because of previous price controls on food supplies.

The lesson from the experience is that comprehensive direct economic controls can be successful for a short period of time. The longer the controls exist in a peacetime economy the greater are the distortions, disruptions, and inequities which result and the less effective are the controls in achieving the objectives originally designed for them. A number of other industrial countries of the world have had the same experience in recent years (Ulman and Flanagan, 1973).

The view of the typical businessman about such economic controls has generally followed this experience. He was in favor of Phase I but as one phase followed another he became disenchanted and progressively opposed controls.

Why Worry about Inflation? It is generally conceded that price inflation rates beyond, say, 3 percent a year are unacceptable. It is well known that inflation is the pickpocket of the poor, the robber of those on fixed incomes, and the distorter of price interrelationships throughout the economy. It encourages speculation and inflates expectations of further inflation which in turn creates an upward wage/price spiral. Despite sticky prices in many parts of the economy the price mechanism does serve to allocate resources in conformance with society's priorities. It does bring a certain order in the intricate interplay of people, organizations, and transactions in society. Not only does it inject a rationality into economic life but it provides a predictability to economic activity. Persistent inflation makes the whole process less rational and predictable. Unchecked serious inflation can and likely will bring financial, economic, and perhaps social and political collapse. It is a serious matter and must be avoided (Friedman, 1973).

Is Inflation Inevitable? Inflation in the United States has been a recurring problem for over thirty years. This experience leads many observers to conclude that we as a people are conditioned to expect price inflation, which is one factor in making it inevitable. It is buttressed by other forces. For political reasons the government reacts more readily to prevent depression and high unemployment than to institute controls at times of inflation which may bring unemployment and a squeeze on profits. Also, it is said, the demands upon the federal budget in the future will be too strong to deny. Revenues will lag behind expenditures, and we shall have chronic deficits which are, of course, inflationary. It is also argued that at full employment levels, wage-rate increases will generate inflation. For such reasons as these, many people believe inflation is inevitable.

Past experience, however, does not lead one to the conclusion that inflation is inevitable. The price inflations visited on this country during the life of the Employment Act of 1946 have been preceded by wars. During the interwar periods the average annual price increases have been around 1.5 percent. But the fact of wars is not the sole cause of inflation. Wars bring out the worst features of an economy. In addressing the question of the root causes of inflation in Western societies Gardner Ackley said the contributing factors were: mistakes in using fiscal and monetary tools to secure full employment; the ability of unions to get wage rate increases above productivity improvements; the ability of semi-monopolistic manufacturers to pass higher prices on to consumers; various monopolistic practices legalized by governments; downward rigidities in many individual prices; "the increasing aspirations of every group in our societies for rapidly rising real incomes, and the tendency everywhere for the fulfillment of people's aspirations—in all areas of economic, political, and social life—to be pressed ever more aggressively and insistently"; various psychological, sociological, and institutional factors which foster inflation; and the importation of inflation into a country from others (1971).

These deficiencies point, of course, to requirements for avoiding inflation in the future. We are not as skillful as we should be in using monetary and fiscal policy, partly for political reasons but also because we do not know as much as we should about their use. The Congress is too slow in altering fiscal policy and the President ought to be given the right to raise or lower personal and corporate income tax payments by up to 10 or 15 percent. Full employment policy should be reinforced by a vigorous attack on structural defects in the economic system that reduce competition, stifle business incentives, or prevent economic flexibility. I have in mind moderate—not major—reforms in laws and practices to remove barriers to international trade, house construction, agricultural price flexibility, and competition. Neil Jacoby suggests that there be established in the

Office of the President an Office of Competition to coordinate and stimulate government activities to improve the state of competition in the United States (Jacoby, 1974). This is a good idea because it would coordinate federal programs to assure greater competition in business and would continuously draw attention to the significance of having stronger competition in industry. Finally, we need to develop more appropriate direct control mechanisms. Fiscal, monetary, and free market processes are apparently not enough in this complex world. From time to time more direct measures will be required. Comprehensive direct wage and price controls can have a powerful impact (except in wartime) for only a very limited period of time. There are many other possibilities, such as persuasion by the President, guidelines established by government within which price and wage adjustments can be made voluntarily, review boards of various types with differing powers, application of controls to only major corporations and labor unions, and some reorganization of government to deal more directly with inflationary problems (Pohlman, 1972). In the latter category would be federal coordinating agencies, such as the Federal Energy Office to pay more attention to supplies of scarce commodities. Inflation is likely to be a persistent problem in the years ahead and we must be better prepared to deal with it.

PART SIX

Business and Its Employees

CHAPTER TWENTY-SEVEN

The Changing Role
of People
in Organizations

INTRODUCTION

This is an age when the individual is becoming more and more the center of attention. In the past, except at the very top, people in organizations accommodated themselves to the organization. Today, organizations are more and more changing to accommodate those working in them. After defining work, and noting how concepts towards it have changed in the past, the complaints and desires of people in the work place are examined. Then, the many ways in which organizations are changing to favor individuals are presented. The chapter closes with a discussion of the interrelationships between business and leisure and business and the family. There is no question about the fact that the roles of individuals in organizations are changing significantly, a trend which will continue into the future. This chapter seeks to capture the highlights of this powerful force in society.

BUSINESS AND THE CHANGING MEANING OF WORK

Work Defined Work is often considered to be "paid employment." This definition is weak, however, because it neglects activity such as housework. For this reason the "pay" part of the definition is eliminated by some observers and work is defined as "an activity that produces something of value for other people" (HEW, 1973: 3). This definition, however, misses several points of importance. First, it implies that if you paint a picture as a leisurely diversion, and someone thinks it has value and buys it, your "play" then becomes "work." Also, I think there is the element of continuous activity associated with work that ought to be included in the definition (Dubin, 1958). Hence, my definition would read: "work is a continuous activity that is designed to produce something of value for other people."

Changing Attitudes Toward Work Work has undergone major changes in the history of man. First, it has lost its pre-Christian association with degradation and slavery, a view held in the Greek and Roman cultures. Second, it has lost much of the religious significance attached to it by medieval philosophers and Calvinists (see Chapter 2). Third, it has lost the utopian significance attached to it by Karl Marx, who thought that work, when freed from capitalist exploitation, would become a joy (Tilgher, 1964).

Great changes have taken place in the meaning of work in the United States. Work was a grim necessity for survival in the pre-industrial colonial period, but overtones of religious obligation softened the long and hard labor. In the pre-Civil War period economic opportunities opened up (except, of course, for those in slavery), and farmers found craft and self-employment work in cities. During this period an industrial work force grew, and the ordinary man was able to become rich through work. The opportunities to work and to accumulate wealth were important incentives for the immigrants flowing into the United States. During the latter part of the nineteenth century, large companies tied men pitilessly to machines for long hours at low wages and Horatio Alger possibilities of wealth for the ordinary man disappeared in factory tedium and grime. In the early twentieth century, under the influence of Frederick Taylor, managers sought to increase worker productivity by careful measurements of work activities and machine-man relationships. Mass production industries brought highly specialized but routine tasks, satirized in Chaplin's classic movie, *Modern Times*. Work underwent important changes in the mid 1930s as the nation sought to reemploy millions of jobless in order to buttress their self-esteem. The human factor in the work place began to be considered by more businessmen and government. Then, during World War II, the driving motive of work became patriotism. Today, the key focus of attention is on the quality of working life (QOWL) and how to improve it.

TROUBLES IN THE WORK PLACE

In a monumental study the Department of Health, Education and Welfare concluded that a significant number of American workers were dissatisfied with the quality of their working lives and this was a source of great national concern (HEW, 1973). There are two paradoxes in this conclusion. First, alienation of workers with work is taking place at a time when physical working conditions and monetary rewards for work have never been better. Second, when workers are asked: "Is your work satisfying?" positive responses are made by 80 to 90 percent of those polled. Yet the HEW studies find great dissatisfactions. One is reminded of a passage in Arthur Miller's one-act play "A Memory of Two Mondays":

> The workplace must seem dirty and unmanageably chaotic. . . . It is a little world, a home to which, unbelievably perhaps, these people like to come every Monday morning, despite what they say.

These paradoxes are hard to explain but if there is one it is that the root cause of worker dissatisfaction with work is not so much because of working conditions and pay but because of changing worker needs, aspirations, and values.

Personal Needs and the Meaning of Work The meaning of work to an individual varies with his needs and the extent to which they are satisfied in a work situation. Maslow (1943) has captured these changes in his hierarchy of needs classification, as follows:

1. Physiological needs of hunger, thirst, sleep, and sex.
2. Safety needs for protection against danger, threat, and deprivation.
3. Love needs for satisfactory associations with others, for belonging to groups, and for giving and receiving friendship and affection.
4. Esteem needs for self-respect and the esteem of others, often referred to as ego or status needs.
5. Self-realization, self-fulfillment, or self-actualization needs to achieve the potential within an individual for self-development, creativity, and self-expression.

These needs may be satisfied in different ways. Fundamentally, some can be met away from the job, such as when a man's pay is used to join a group of friends at the local tavern. Other needs can be satisfied from a work environment around a job. Finally, some needs can be met in actually doing a job. In our society a man's job is generally, although not always, his most important means of meeting the basic needs expressed above.

It is probably true that most individuals will seek a higher-order need when lower-order needs are satisfied. Motivation, however, does not always move in this neat progression. Many individuals will seek all or many needs at the same time. Generally, however, once lower-level needs are met, workers will become increasingly interested in having business meet their higher-level needs. This is a fact of great significance for business.

It is obvious that the intensity of need, the way it is best satisfied, and the extent to which one is motivated to satisfy a need in a job, will vary much depending upon the individual. Furthermore, the mix is likely to change over a man's career.

Job Satisfaction versus Job Dissatisfaction Herzberg suggests an explanation of the second paradox noted above which embodies significant insights. Factors producing job satisfaction and motivation, he says, are separate and distinct from those producing job dissatisfaction. Job satisfaction and dissatisfaction are not opposites of each other. "The opposite of job satisfaction is not job dissatisfaction but, rather, *no* job satisfaction, and, similarly, the opposite of job dissatisfaction is not job satisfaction, but *no* job dissatisfaction" (1968: 56). Dissatisfaction may arise from such factors as low pay, poor supervision, or dirty working conditions. Their removal, however, will not necessarily lead to job satisfaction. Satisfaction depends upon such factors as sense of accomplishment, responsibility, and recognition. This is more a function or work content whereas dissatisfaction is more a result of environment of work.

A survey of 1,533 workers at all occupational levels asked how important some twenty-five aspects of work were to them. The highest ranked in order of importance, were interesting work, enough help and equipment to get the job done, enough information to get the job done, enough authority to get the job done, good pay, opportunity to develop special abilities, job security, and seeing the results of one's work (Survey Research Center, 1970). This clearly lends credence to the view of Herzberg that job content is more important than working conditions to the removal of job dissatisfaction.

Other Factors in Job Dissatisfaction As pointed out in earlier chapters this is an age of discontent, a malaise which is reflected in the work place. It is an age of rising expectations, a fact also reflected in the work place. The number of self-employed workers is declining. In the middle of the nineteenth century less than half of all employed were wage and salary workers. Today the proportion is 90 percent (HEW, 1973: 21). A higher proportion of workers are in large companies in large cities. Workers are better educated and want to use their brain power. Discrimination of minorities in the work place is more visible and less tolerable today. There are many other sources of discontent which are briefly presented in *Work in America* (HEW, 1973; Chapter II).

Rather than examine the sources of discontent in further detail turn to the question of what can and should business do about it? The basic questions here, of course, are: What do workers want that they are not getting or think they are not getting? Can and should business respond in an acceptable way? These questions have answers which differ for various classifications of workers.

What Do Blue-Collar Workers Want? *Work in America* observed that more than a hundred studies in the past twenty years have shown that workers want "to become masters of their immediate environments and to feel that their work and they themselves are important—the twin ingredients of self-esteem" (HEW, 1973: 13). Workers realize that some of the distasteful jobs can only be made less intolerable. What they object to is the avoidable oppressive features of work such as constant supervision and coercion, monotony, meaningless tasks, and coercion. But they want more than an end to that. They want jobs that have some prestige and give them some ego gratification. They rate self-determination highest among the elements that define an ideal job. Content of work generally is more important to workers than getting promoted. Most workers are happier when employed as a member of a group than in isolation. They prefer interaction with other workers. They want pay that will support an adequate standard of living. Generally, they do not think their pay is high enough but if pay is adequate getting more is not high on their needs list. They want opportunities to get promoted and to develop their special talents. Job security for older workers is, naturally, of importance to them. Finally, workers do not want bad physical working conditions (HEW, 1973: 94–96; Survey Research Center, 1970).

The White-Collar Workers' Needs Traditionally there was a higher status associated with white-collar jobs (secretaries, clerks, office machine operators, etc.) than with blue-collar jobs. Today, however, there is little to distinguish a computer operator from an assembly line worker and the positions often differ little in prestige. *The Survey of Working Conditions* (Survey Research Center 1970) found the needs of white-collar workers similar to but not the same as factory workers. White-collar workers feel more strongly than blue-collar workers that their talents are not being used, that the problems they deal with are not hard enough, and that they do not have an ample opportunity to develop their own special abilities.

Managerial Needs A recent study of 2,821 American managers showed that 70 percent are less than minimally satisfied with their present careers and expect to be searching for ways to make career changes in the near future [Tarnowieski, 1973(A)]. The level of satisfaction, as one might expect, rises with status. Only 27 percent of the top executives said they were dissatisfied with their career advancement and sense of personal fulfillment as compared with 40 percent of the middle managers and 52 percent of lower managers. On the other hand, when asked whether or not they believe the organization for which they work will provide them adequate opportunities to realize overall goals and aspirations a surprising 62 percent said yes. The older the person and the higher his status the greater the chance of a yes response.

When asked what considerations most likely would influence them to change jobs (but not occupational fields) the managers responded, in descending order of importance, as follows: enhanced occupational status and authority, salary considerations, opportunity to spend more time with family, opportunity to reduce tension and health hazards, opportunity to make a meaningful contribution to civic and/or charitable endeavors, opportunity to spend more time on hobbies and personal interests, enhanced status in peer group, and better benefit programs. These considerations differ for age and status but fundamentally, for both, they were in this order of importance. The definition of success of the managers were in terms of (in order of importance) achievement of goals (means a general reaching of all major aims); self-actualization; harmony among personal, professional, family, and social objectives; making a contribution to a greater good; happiness or peace of mind; greater job satisfaction; self-respect and the respect of others; enjoyment in doing or in being; and job and financial security.

The Case of the Middle Managers The real meaning of the above considerations varies, of course, from individual to individual. For middle managers, for example, need and reality can lead to high frustration. A study of the American Management Association of middle managers in more than 500 business organizations showed a "widespread disenchantment with the prevailing state of corporate affairs." Some of the causes are desires for changing life styles, pressures for making profits under difficult economic conditions, external pressures for business and organizational reform, waning managerial opportunities. More and more of the managers, for instance, perceive or imagine themselves as caught in a situation where a single error— sometimes serious, sometimes not—in their dealings with either superiors or subordinates may cost them their job, their security, and perhaps even their career (Tarnowieski, 1973(B): 49–50).

The Case of the MBA In a study of MBA students the following were considered, in the order given, to be "very important": advancement determined by ability, challenge of the job, sense of meaning and accomplishment on job, personal growth, job allow for self-expression, opportunity to make a meaningful contribution, variety in work. Not one of these desires was expected to be met by the MBAs (Greenberg, et. al. 1969). The factors considered most unlikely to be found in the first entrance into business life by these students were authority to make decisions at the outset, fewer working hours, ability to influence change, democratic organization, maximum use of personal resources, jobs that allow for individuality, jobs that allow for self-expression, and advancement to top executive positions.

Young Workers and the Changing Work Ethic Since about one-quarter of the work force is under the age of thirty the views of youth are important in looking at sources of discontent in the work place. As pointed out in Chapter 8 the values of our young people are changing and will have an impact on the work place and their sense of satisfaction. Generally, they have accepted the basic values of this society but there are some important differences. *Life* commissioned Louis Harris and Associates to interview a national cross section of some 26 million Americans between the ages of fifteen and twenty-one. When asked what were the most important factors in choosing a job they responded: enjoyable work, pride in the job, pleasant working conditions, creative satisfactions. The least important factors were: short hours, recognition by society, and achieving status. When asked whether they would be willing to work in a factory production line 56 percent said no (*Life*, January 8, 1971).

Yankelovich made several surveys of young people some of whom were in college and some were not. Among those in college were those who were "practical-minded" and others who were designated as "forerunners" or those whose views were believed to foreshadow more prevailing views in the future. Asked whether they accepted more power and authority of the "boss" in a work situation they responded as follows: no college, 74 percent; practical college, 60 percent; and forerunners, 52 percent. They all agreed that more emphasis should be given to work being meaningful in its own right (in the order noted above, 85, 78, 88 percent). Asked whether they could accept having little decision-making power in the first few years on a job they responded in the above order: 48 percent, 38 percent, and 23 percent. Could they accept laws they did not agree with? The response was, in order again: 43 percent, 35 percent, and 21 percent. On the whole they thought that business would not allow self-development of the individual, self-expression, or individuality. Today's young have, apparently, a lower attachment to work on the same job than their elders. They have a lower commitment to work. They want quicker self-satisfactions (*Fortune*, 1969).

Minority Workers Minority workers have, for the above classifications, similar needs, aspirations and frustrations. But there are also others unique to this group. For example, as pointed out in Chapter 20 there is an important difference in money incomes between the national average and minorities. They probably are more worried about security and survival than other workers. They certainly are concerned about racial and ethnic discrimination.

Women Workers A major social force today is the movement for equality in women's rights. While there may be differences of view about the meaning of the women's liberation movement, there is no disagreement that women have been grossly discriminated against in the work place. Central demands are for equal pay and equal opportunity. But they, too, want the types of things in the work place discussed above.

It was not until 1848 that the suffragette movement was born and not until 1919 that it resulted in the nineteenth amendment to the Constitution which gave women the right to vote. The turning point in the economic field came in World War I when one-fifth of American women were in the labor force, but after the war they returned to their homes. In World War II they once again moved into the labor force, but this time they stayed there. In 1947 there were 16.7 million in the work force, or about 24 percent of the total. By 1972 they numbered over 33 million and were over 37 percent of the total. By 1980 it is expected they will number 46 percent of the labor force (NICB, 1973(C): 22).

Two reinforcing sets of forces have given the women's movement for equality of pay and opportunity a strong thrust. On the one side a series of congressional enactments, executive orders, and court decisions, have solidly established the legal foundation. These pieces of legislation and decisions were presented in Chapter 16. To that list should be mentioned an order of the OFCC of December 4, 1971, which required affirmative action goals by government contractors to increase representation of women in job categories in which they were underrepresented. A second stream of force has come from interests of women themselves in getting into the labor force. Rising levels of education have made many women dissatisfied with their traditional boundaries, and rising demand in industry, particularly the service industries, for their efforts gave them opportunities for work outside the home. Declining family size, the growing permissiveness in society, new expectations, and labor-saving devices in the home, are a few of the factors giving the movement its drive (General Electric, 1972).

There is no doubt that there has been discrimination of women in the work place. Women have been confined to certain occupations such as secretaries, schoolteachers, waitresses, nurses, and clerks in service industries. Comparatively few enter managerial, professional or technical jobs. As a result, in 1971, 45 percent of the working males made over $10,000 per year while only 8 percent of the women made that much. In that year 71 percent of the women made less than $5,000 whereas only 27 percent of the men were in this pay bracket (NICB, 1973: 30).

Pay for the same work is less for women than men. In 1970 women took home only 59 percent as much pay as men for similar employment. Education and work experience may account for some of this differential. But, after adjusting for such factors, there still remains a differential of around 20 percent between the earnings of men and women (Council of Economic Advisers, 1973: 106). Most of this, if not all, is due to discrimination. Generally, however, women are discriminated against more often in the form of job segregation than in unequal pay. They are being penalized more by being underutilized than underpaid (HEW, 1973: 61–62; Fretz and Hayman, 1973).

Quality of Working Life (QOWL) From all this it is now possible to develop a concept and definition of QOWL. Altogether, there appears to be no significant shift away from workers valuing work per se but there is a declining willingness to take on meaningless work in authoritarian settings. Some people wrongly have concluded that the work ethic has declined. They see that there has been an erosion of the Puritan Ethic since people, generally, no longer work for the glory of God. But the drive of people for work is stronger than ever. The moral and doctrinal elements of the work ethic have been replaced by a strong economic and psychological need. The new demand today is for a meeting of old demands associated with improved working conditions, such as better pay and fringe benefits, safe and healthy working conditions, shorter hours, and elimination of incompetent supervision. Added to this, and having far greater priority among workers, is their demand for greater control over their immediate work environment. In business, as one moves up the hierarchical chain the meaning of this aspect of the work ethic changes in content and emphasis. For most employees it means meaningful work; the use of available skills; the chance to grow and achieve; the opportunity to find interesting and challenging work, facilities to do the assigned job correctly and well; and an end to monotonous, meaningless tasks performed in isolation; and satisfactions (Walton, 1973). To the extent that business can meet this challenge it will be improving the QOWL.

MEETING THE DEMANDS FOR A BETTER QOWL

While there is controversy about how much employees of business firms are satisfied or dissatisfied with their work life, there is no question but that their needs and desires are changing and are outpacing what they find on the job. More and more people in organizations are expecting more self-actualization, to use Maslow's words.

Business is cognizant of this and is doing something about it. The following is addressed to some of the issues which are present when business tries to meet employee expectations, some of the methods employed, and some speculations about the future role of people in organizations.

CONFLICTS BETWEEN INDIVIDUAL AND BUSINESS AIMS

Everyone knows that for many workers there often are serious conflicts between their interests and those of the enterprise in which they work. The degree of conflict in organizations between personal and business aims varies from none to a great deal. An owner-manager of a small enterprise may find a complete congruence between his personal and his company's objectives. Such enterprises have more the characteristics of individuals than of institutions. Heads of very large companies also may find a perfect matching of their aims in life with the aims of their companies. Not surprisingly, Porter (1964) concluded after studying 2,000 managers that higher-level managers fulfill their needs for recognition, autonomy, and self-realization more than do those in lower levels. He also found that line managers better met their higher-level needs than did staff men.

Granted that there are conflicts as well as correlations between business objectives and aims of people working in enterprises, what can and should management do? McGregor observed (1967) that a person's motivations, potential for development, capacity for assuming responsibility, and readiness to direct behavior toward organization goals are all present. As a consequence, an appropriate managerial strategy is to create conditions that enable the individual to achieve his own goals (including those of self-actualization) by directing his efforts toward organizational goals. Effective managers and behavioral scientists are convinced that this observation is true, given certain circumstances. One primary circumstance is the acceptance of the importance of the aims of the enterprise. Each member of the enterprise must feel that its aims are genuinely important to him and that he is making a useful contribution toward achieving them.

Likert advanced a principle of supportive relationships reflecting these conditions. He says:

> The leadership and other processes of the organization must be such as to ensure a maximum probability that in all interactions and all relationships with the organization each member will, in the light of his background, values, and expectations, view the experience as supportive and one which builds and maintains his sense of personal worth and importance (Likert, 1961: 103, italics omitted).

Likert feels this is a fundamental formula that can be used to tap every basic motive and harness it in each employee to organizational ends. To do so, however, involves a new way of managing, in which each person in an organization is a member of one or more work groups, each of which has a high degree of group loyalty, effective skills of interaction, and high performance goals (Likert, 1961: 104).

These are, of course, worthwhile objectives for managers, but precisely how they are to accomplish such results is not clear. Each situation will vary. Furthermore, there are limitations on the extent to which an organization can satisfy all the wants of the individuals in it and still accomplish the basic aims society expects it to achieve. In mass production industries, for instance, work has given men increasing economic freedom through higher wages, but at the same time has restrained their freedom on the job. While organizations are means to fill some human needs, they also obligate men to subordinate certain of their wants to the interests of organizational ends. All organizations demand that individuals direct their behavior toward accomplishing the purposes of the organization.

A business enterprise must have firm economic and social ends, and it must have discipline in meeting them. These ends, today at least, are predominantly economic and not social. As individuals in an enterprise satisfy their economic needs, the social and self-fulfillment needs are felt more keenly. To expect business organizations to satisfy all such needs is neither possible nor desirable. One serious question is whether an organization reaching for predominantly economic ends can or should be a means for total satisfaction of individual aims. Managerial efforts to satisfy all the needs of an individual should be viewed with alarm, for this is impossible. It should be recognized that some of the objectives of individuals, perhaps most, must be met outside a business. The management of each enterprise, however, is challenged to find that balance which will properly optimize personal with organizational ends. Having said this, I think it also must be observed that business managers have a responsibility to reconcile employee and company objectives to the fullest extent possible while preserving the fundamental capability of the firm to prosper in its environment.

CONFORMITY VERSUS INDIVIDUALISM IN BUSINESS LIFE

The American, like the Faustian, is accused of making a bargain with the devil technology: for the material wealth of the machine, he accepts a life of dull, grinding, and routine work, completely dominated by the demands of the machine. The employee's ability to be creative is thus completely eroded by pressures for conformity. This trend, to some writers, is increasing and will eventually engulf us all in a massive, impersonal, and dehumanized system where order, routine, and conformity deprive men of those qualities needed for fulfilled lives (Huxley, 1932; Orwell, 1949). But there are those who assert that this is a completely distorted view. The modern business is one in which individuals have and will increasingly get opportunities for self-expression.

As one looks at these extreme positions, many questions arise. Of central importance, of course, are: What is meant by conformity and individualism? What is the situation in business today that tends to force conformity? What are the trends leading to increased creativity?

Meaning of Conformity and Individualism   William Whyte's book, *The Organization Man* (1956), has become a classic exposition of the nature of and pressures for conformity in business. Whyte said that today's organization man was in search of a rationale for his conformist role and that he has found it in "the Social Ethic" (the successor of the Protestant Ethic) which makes morally legitimate the pressures of society against the individual. In essence, he says, the individual is isolated, meaningless; only as he collaborates with others does he become worthwhile. By sublimating himself in the group, he helps produce a whole which is greater than the sum of its parts. The Social Ethic rationalizes the organizational demand for fealty and gives those who accept it a sense of dedication in doing so. Unorthodox action is dangerous to the organization man. He is loyal to his company; wants to be of service to it; is indoctrinated in and thinks as one with its ethos; and believes that ideas come from the the group, not the individual.

Individualism in organizations is the reverse of the coin. Individualism treats people as ends, not means; it fosters their desire for independence and self-expression; it stimulates their imagination, creativity, and innovation; and it permits freedom of thought and action, up to a point, even though it conflicts with the firm's values and aims.

Whyte's concept of the organization man is overdrawn, but its popularity attests to the fact that it hit a sensitive target. At the other extreme, no business firm can accept the pure concept of individualism for everyone.

The issue is not conformity or individualism. There are deeper questions. If conformity is enforced in a company, does it so reduce innovation as to raise doubts about the survival of the company? What is the trade-off between conformity and individualism? Where is the balance? To what extent should a man dedicate himself to his company and to what extent should he devote his energies to his private life? These are difficult but vital questions for business enterprises, the people who work in them, and their families.

One among many difficulties in considering such issues as these is that there is not one but may types of conformity, and there is not one but many types of individualism. For example, one can speak of conformity to the standard values of a group in which an individual finds himself. There can be conformity to the procedures, values, and objectives of organizations; conformity to social standards, for example, middle-class standards; conformity to professional standards; and conformity to the values and objectives of superiors. Individualism, too, is multifaceted. It may, for example, be associated with freedom of thought, with flexibility in accepting job assignments, with having superiors accept and support a man's dignity, or with the ability of a plant manager to run his activity in relative freedom from central headquarters' authority. Put this way, there is no method to measure the degree of conformity or individualism in American industry. It is possible, however, to examine major trends in business today which seem to foster conformity, on the one hand, and individualism, on the other.

Trends Toward Conformity in Business As a business grows larger, it takes on characteristics of a bureaucracy. Some of the major characteristics of bureaucracy are a division of labor into detailed functional specializations, fixed job descriptions, well-defined hierarchies of authority, a complete and detailed system of rules and procedures governing the conduct of individuals, and impersonal relationships among individuals. An organization following this model literally would surely force conformity and stifle individualism.

General criticisms of bureaucracies are as follows: They are unresponsive and inflexible because of elaborate and detailed rules and stifling of initiative. They generate low levels of morale. They foster dull environments. They stimulate self-centered managers who avoid responsibility but have a quest for power, often in petty ways. They generate conformity and "group think" consensus. They lack an adequate juridical process. Their communications system (and flow of creative ideas) is thwarted, blocked, and distorted by standard procedures. The full capabilities of individuals are neither appreciated, used, nor wanted. Mistrust and fear are the norm.

There is no doubt that in both large and small corporations there is a tendency to develop rigid rules of behavior, to avoid making decisions, to block self-expression, and, metaphorically, to develop arteriosclerosis in vital arteries. On the other hand, it is perfectly obvious that many major American corporations have not only grown rapidly, but maintained great vitality and vigor. They clearly do not evidence the stereotype of a bureaucracy described above.

How Business Fosters Individualism There is a wide variety of organizational structures and administrative techniques which business managers today use to stimulate entrepreneurship, innovation, creativity, general self-expression, and individual self-development. A number of the more important ones are described below.

Developing top-flight managers who have a firm understanding of the functions of managers, and how people can best be motivated, is a major method to stimulate individual initiative and productivity. This is, in a sense, an overriding requirement for the factors which follow, because poor management can negate any one of them. More democratic management, or participative management, can stimulate and motivate people more than autocratic or traditional authoritarian management (Milutinovich, 1971). On the other hand, evidence exists to show that organizations do not flourish with excessively democratic supervision, especially when it is done at the expense of appropriate controls (Sayles, 1963: 192–93). An effective comprehensive corporate planning system seeks to develop creative ideas in all managers. It is designed to bring change in a company and, by participating in the exercise, managers accept and adapt to change. Management by objective, or the practice of developing a hierarchy of objectives which individuals seek to achieve, is a powerful motivating force. The more individuals participate in setting their own objectives, the more motivated they are. The more flexibility they have in achieving their objectives, the more creative they are (Thompson, 1969).

Certain types of organization can stimulate individual initiative. Project management organization, for instance, is best performed when individuals have considerable freedom in the initial design stages (Steiner and Ryan, 1968). This has been a powerful motivator of creative people. Decentralization, especially when comparatively free of home office controls, permits managers to operate as if they were running their own businesses. Indeed, one important reason for decentralization in businesses is to encourage experimentation, fresh thinking, and innovation. Functional staffs in large organizations develop loyalties to their group and emphasize their functional point of view in corporate decision-making. If this effort is not thwarted by top management, it will stimulate creativity. Business corporations are hiring increasing numbers of professional employees—scientists, lawyers, economists, accountants, behavioral scientists, mathematicians, engineers, and so on. These specialists generally are self-motivated and will not stay in an organization where they cannot express themselves. As management becomes more professional and welcomes the professionalism of experts, the doors of managerial life are opened wider to the winds of individualism.

The computer is likely to improve rather than downgrade individualism in managerial ranks. It should free management from routine jobs and thus permit it to engage more deeply in the development of strategies and the solution of interesting and important unstructured problems. Finally, there is a great range of methods for stimulating individual initiative in the area of merit awards, fringe benefits, job training, job design, and job enrichment. The practice of sending managers and craftsmen to schools and professional meetings is a step toward individualism and away from conformity.

Pressures for or against conformity or individualism are not related to business size. As large organizations evolve, they tend to develop rigidities that stifle individual initiative, but this is not an inevitable pattern. Employees in many large organizations, especially at managerial levels, have far greater freedom than in many small companies. And just the reverse is also true. What is the balance? There is little question about the fact that the organization man is not a myth. There are important forces shoving employees toward conformity. There is a paradox in organizational life spotted by Strauss (1964), when he noted that managers want individuals to coordinate their efforts, and with enthusiasm and imagination. The trouble is that enthusiasm and imagination may well conflict with coordination, and individualism may conflict with the conformity needed for coordination. If management permits too much individualism, there may be too much lack of coordination as subgroups look to their own interests. If coordination forces too much conformity, there may be too little initiative from individuals. It is no wonder, therefore, that we find conflicting trends in industry.

At the managerial level, I think the trend in business, on net balance, is towards more individual self-expression and away from conformity. More large organizations understand the dangers of conformity to their very survival, and for this and other reasons are opening new avenues for self-expression. In most corporations a free-wheeling individualist is out of place, but there are occasions when a creative manager can by his aggressiveness benefit himself and his company. On many other occasions his best interests, and those of his company, are served by a certain amount of conformity. It has been my observation of business life that the successful manager knows when to conform and when to be aggressively creative.

How about nonmanagerial employees? There are many things that management can do to ease the pain of necessary conformity and to further the drive for creativity. Managers can stimulate employees to invent new ways of doing things, by awards, job enrichment, and other benefits. Management can be more imaginative about organizing group projects. It may be, however, that the major effort here must be to speed up automation, reduce the number of hours and increase pay, and to help employees enrich their lives by better use of their expanding free time. It cannot be forgotten that the total number of workers in mass production industries is declining relative to the total, and the number performing repetitive jobs is also declining. In many other areas—services, for instance—opportunities for worker initiative and creativity are great and increasing.

JOB ENRICHMENT: A CASE STUDY

It was noted above that job enrichment was an important method to permit individuals in organizations to be more creative and to meet their psychological needs. In the past few years there have been many experiments in job enrichment which have been successful and which probably in the future will be much more widely used (Taylor, et. al., 1973; HEW, 1973; Davis, 1972; Marrow, 1972; Paul, et. al., 1969; Herzberg, 1969). Following is a brief analysis of a successful experiment at the Pet Food Plant of General Foods in Topeka, Kansas.

This plant was plagued with low employee morale, frequent shutdowns, and evidence of severe worker alienation. For instance, there were serious instances of sabotage and violence. Changes were introduced, as follows:

Work teams of from eight to ten employees were formed and given responsibility for large pieces of the production process. The teams decided who would perform what tasks. In the performance of these tasks the team members taught one another their jobs.

Support functions, such as maintenance, quality control, engineering, and personnel, which heretofore were performed separately, were now part of the operating team responsibility.

In establishing tasks to be performed an effort was made to include functions which would challenge team members by requiring higher abilities and more responsibilities. Efforts were made to eliminate routine and dull jobs, but members who had to continue to perform such jobs were also given other more demanding tasks.

Team members were rewarded for mastering new tasks performed by the team as well as in the rest of the plant. Since all team members could qualify for higher pay if they mastered a job they were encouraged to teach each other.

Instead of a "supervisor," a "team leader" was appointed to facilitate team development and decision making. Information was given to the teams to permit them to make decisions at the operating level which before had been made at higher levels of management.

Top management decided not to lay down in advance plant rules but rather to let them evolve out of experience.

Status symbols were eliminated, such as preferred parking space and special office decor. Physical arrangements were designed to encourage rather than discourage team meetings.

The results were impressive. The company thought that 110 workers would be required for operations but the manning level was less than 70 once the teams got into operation. More importantly, major economic benefits came from minimization of waste and smooth uninterrupted operations. Perhaps of even more importance has been the improvement in attitudes of workers. Greater democracy in the plant has led to more civic activities of the worker (HEW, 1973: 96–99).

Not everyone agrees that job enrichment by management is the proper solution to job discontent. The unions take the position that "just as job dissatisfaction in the workplace yielded to trade union solutions in the past, such dissatisfaction can be decreased to the extent that trade union solutions are applied today. . . . If you want to enrich the job," says Winpisinger, a vice-president of the Machinists, "enrich the pay check. The better the wage, the greater the job satisfaction. There is no better cure for the 'blue-collar blues' " (1973: 9). Union opposition has been overcome, however, in some companies (Myers, 1971).

There are also criticisms of job enrichment in the academic world as well as in management, a summary of which Sirota recently presented (1973). There seems to be some agreement on the basic principles of job enrichment. However, if it is not done right the results may not be those desired (Morse, 1973). Also, too much should not be expected from job enrichment because there are many worker complaints that it will not satisfy (e.g. job insecurity) (Sirota, 1973; Sirota and Wolfson, 1972).

THE JOINING-UP PROCESS

The preferred desires of college graduates in the work place, especially new MBAs, was noted previously. Because their expectations have not always been met they have been frustrated and job turnover has been rapid. At the same time, the companies they join have been denied the fruits of their skills.

One possibility for reducing the expectation-reality gap is for business to manage better the joining-up process. Business has certain expectations from new employees which are not often explained. For instance, business expects an ability to learn the various aspects of a position while on the job, to discover new methods of performing tasks, to solve novel problems, to present a point of view effectively and convincingly, to work productively with groups of people, to supervise and direct the work of others, to make responsible decisions without assistance from others, to plan and organize work efforts for oneself or others, to use time and energy for the advantage of the company, to accept company demands that conflict with personal prerogatives, to conform to the folkways and customs of the company, to maintain a good public image of the company, to take on company values and goals as one's own, and to initiate appropriate activity when something needs to be done (Kotter, 1973: 93).

When there is an exchange of expectations at the time an employee joins a company the results have been excellent for the company and the new employee. Costs to the company have been reduced and the level of productivity, commitment, and innovativeness of the new people employed by the company are enhanced.

WORKER SAFETY

Improving safety conditions on the job is in a different category than the above but of high importance in the QOWL. There are many pieces of legislation covering worker safety but still the work place is dangerous. Justification for passing the Occupational Safety and Health Act (OSHA) of 1970 was based upon the assertion that there are 14,000 deaths and 2,200,000 disabling accidents per year in the work place.

OSHA is one of the most far-reaching pieces of safety legislation ever passed. It covers some 57 million workers in over 4 million business establishments and sets some 22,000 standards in such areas as unguarded machinery, excessive noise, hazardous materials, and worker safety devices. The law has teeth in it since standards are enforced by fines up to $10,000 per violation and prison terms for corporate managers responsible for violations.

There is no question but that OSHA will improve safety in the work place. Since the act became effective in mid-1971 companies not only have tightened their policies and procedures but have increased expenditures for safety devices (Petersen, 1973). It is entirely likely that industry will be rewarded as well as the employees. Records show that accident prevention, which is the basic aim of OSHA, is generally accompanied by cost savings greater than the safety expenditure (Simonds, 1973).

FUTURE BUSINESS ORGANIZATIONAL AND LEADERSHIP PATTERNS

Forces driving toward organizational and leadership patterns that will increase job satisfactions appear to be considerably stronger than those which bring conformity and job tedium. But both sets of forces will exist for a long time.

Is Democracy Inevitable? Bennis and Slater assert that democracy in industry is inevitable, not because people think it would be nice and want it, but because under certain conditions it is more efficient and more capable than other patterns of ensuring the survival of the firm in a world of rapid change and chilling threats. By democracy in business they do not mean permissiveness or laissez-faire leadership. Democracy to them is a system of values in a company which includes free and full communications at all levels and among levels without restraint, decision-making by consensus, influence by virtue of knowledge rather than rank or personal whims, stimulus to emotional expression and task-oriented acts, and acceptance of conflicts between individuals and the organization with convergence through rational deliberation (1968: 4).

Democratic organizations are more in tune with current and projected business problems. As already mentioned, the pace of business environmental change today is greater than ever before and will accelerate in the future. Old style, thoroughy bureaucratic companies are notoriously slow to react to environmental developments, and will either reorganize or disappear when confronted with major change. Many large and growing companies have found it much more efficient to divide themselves into many subcompanies, each of which needs different combinations of talents and has a good bit of autonomy. In a world of increasing threats to company survival, but expanding opportunities for profitable growth, the need for imaginative and complex collaboration among managers and staff experts has been recognized by a rapidly growing number of companies in their introduction of formal comprehensive planning. There is little question about the fact that professional managers, working effectively with professional experts, will spark new ideas and vitality which must yield competitive advantages. For these and other reasons discussed in this chapter, it does indeed appear that survival for most businesses will depend upon the extent to which old bureaucratic restrictions are lifted and democratic forms of organization replace them (Mee, 1973).

Temporary Systems Bennis (1966) and Bennis and Slater (1968) predict that business organizations in the future will be predominantly temporary. By this they mean that groups of managers and experts will be organized in task forces to solve problems, and once the problems are solved the task forces will break up and will reform in different groups to tackle other problems. There is nothing new in this approach because it is widely practiced today (Steiner and Ryan, 1968). But Bennis and Slater give the impression that in those industries faced with rapid change, the predominant characteristic, the norm and not the exception, of organizational life will be these adaptive and constantly changing temporary systems. "This is the organization form," they say, "that will gradually replace bureaucracy as we know it" (Bennis and Slater, 1968: 74).

There are, of course, many implications of such a change. Managers will become "linking pins" or coordinators of the talents in and activities of these task groups. Men in organizations must be more adaptive; quick to change activities, loyalties, and personal relationships; and able to overcome the psychological consequences of such a life. Bennis and Slater think such a life might not be a "happy" one because of social strains and psychological tensions. Paradoxically, a world of such temporary systems which provides great opportunities for personal fulfillment will also force conformity. Whyte's organization man will reappear in different form. There will be need in this type of organization for people to interchange easily. This collaborative climate requires that men interrelate easily and accommodate to values of peers. As with Whyte's and Riesman's (1950) organization men, they must be "other-directed." This type of world, assert Bennis and Slater, will lead to "a totally new concept of leadership." The fundamental element in this concept is that a leader's substantive knowledge about a subject will be of much less importance than his understanding of people and complex systems.

No Single Universal Pattern Bennis and Slater do not specify a particular period of time when the business world will be one massive temporary system, so it is difficult to quarrel with them. To the turn of the century, however, I think the likelihood is high that there will be a mix of systems embodying some features of present bureaucratic organization and leadership patterns and some of those Bennis and Slater foresee.

There can be little doubt that present trends in business organizations to provide more challenging jobs and enable individuals to achieve their full capabilities, especially at managerial levels, will accelerate. There can be little doubt that the drift is toward increasingly temporary group task-oriented systems and the new patterns of leadership most successful in managing this type of organization. On the other hand, there will still be demands for authoritarian types of enterprises, since they will be the most efficient for certain kinds of jobs that have to be done. Furthermore, even when an adaptive type of organization may be most effective, there will be many people who cannot perform in such an environment. In crises, the only alternative in a company may be tough-minded, one-man control.

The fact of the matter is that in the foreseeable future there is no single type of organization or leadership pattern that will be universally appropriate. At one extreme will be the assembly line, much as it is today. At the other extreme will be basic research laboratories with their virtually complete permissiveness and autonomy. In between will be combinations of today's patterns. The trend will be, however, increasingly in favor of the individual compared with the organization.

BUSINESS AND LEISURE

There are three basic relationships between business and leisure. First, the technological developments so greatly advanced by business have made possible an expanding amount of time for leisure. Second, consumption associated with activities outside the work week has created a large and growing market for goods and services produced by business. Finally, the way in which men spend their free time will have an important impact on society, which in turn will affect business. These interrelationships are extremely complex, and a substantial literature is being developed to analyze them; space limitations permit only the sketchiest account here.

Definition of Leisure Leisure, as defined by *The Random House Dictionary*, refers to "freedom from the demands of work or duty," "free or unoccupied time," "unhurried ease," and "unrestricted time." This is not, however, the classical Greek and Roman meaning of leisure. To them, the life of leisure was the only one to live; leisure was supreme among human activities. The Greeks wanted to be wise, and to be wise one had to have leisure. This type of leisure was a state of being in which activities were undertaken for their own sake, not as means to an end. To lead the good life, the quality life, meant to cultivate the mind and to seek self-improvement.

The latter is not the antithesis of work, nor is it the same thing as free time or vacant time. De Grazia points to a number of differences between the two (1962: 347–50). To measure leisure by time is totally irrelevant. Furthermore, to many people time has become an obsession as they seek to use free time. Leisure activity refers principally to activity of the mind, but spending free time generally connotes physical or other types of activities. Fun is thought to be the essence of spending free time, but fun does not dominate leisure. Free time is opposed to work, but a man engaged in leisure may be working his head off in the view of another person. At the end of this analysis I will comment on why it is important to distinguish between vacant time and leisure.

Development of Leisure As noted above, the only life fit for the Greek was a life of leisure. The Romans adopted the Greek idea. Then leisure disappeared for centuries under the yoke of work. In our early colonial period many of the Founding Fathers were men of leisure, but most people literally worked from sunup to sundown. One hundred years ago a steelworker was on a twelve-hour shift, seven days a week (de Grazia, 1962: 87). Today, the average work week is under forty hours and provides plenty of opportunity for a life of leisure for a large number of people. In the future, more leisure will be possible for more people. By the turn of the century, it may be possible to produce the necessary goods and services with a work week under thirty hours, many more and longer vacations, and earlier retirement. There will, however, be unevenness among occupations. Managers, professors, and artists are likely not to find their formal hours of work so reduced, but to many of them the edge of work and leisure blend.

What people will do when faced with the possibility of reduced hours is not at all certain. People seem to want to work to meet certain needs. The great majority of people respond affirmatively to this question: "If by some chance you inherited enough money to live comfortably without working, do you think that you would work anyway?"

If leisure is defined in the future as most people define it today, for example, looking at TV, outdoor recreation, attending spectator sports, gardening, and racehorse betting, they will want to work if for no other reason than to increase their incomes to buy the equipment associated with their free-time activities. Costs of equipment for many free-time activities can escalate to substantial levels with each step-up in standards—for instance, boating.

Implications for Business One important implication for business, of course, is that present concepts of leisure will provide large and growing markets. The greater consequence to business will be the way in which people think about leisure and the changes leisure will bring to values in this society.

It is not clear what future attitudes will be toward leisure. If people decide they want much more free time, this will, of course, lead to pressures on business to reduce hours and to maintain and increase wage rates. If the concept of leisure moves toward the classical view, there will be a more thoughtful work force with different demands in their work situations. As free time increases, it is quite likely that pressures will be exerted on business to make leisure time more meaningful by improving advertising, TV, and other entertainment programs. Business in the past has responded to such demands, but only when the masses clamor for more substance is there a quick response. Improvement is likely to be slow.

The Value of Leisure De Grazia asks: Why preserve the ideal classical definition of leisure? His answer is that there are great benefits to society (1962: 413). Creativity, the search for truth, and the expansion of freedom are stimulated. Since philosophy and politics are two principal forms of leisure, the political system may be much more easily directed to solving pressing problems while maintaining the fundamental values society wishes to preserve. More leisure in the classical sense should create a more tranquil society, a more rational society, and a more enlightened society. In such a society business would flourish, although it would lose influence in relation to intellectual pursuits. The importance of leisure to society and to business will become greater, for what happens to society and business will reflect what people do in their leisure time.

BUSINESS AND THE FAMILY

That business has had a profound impact on family life has long been understood by sociologists and anthropologists. The relationship between business and family life is exceedingly complex and in many areas a matter of sharp controversy. In this section I want to do no more than open up the subject and make a few brief comments about changes in family life brought about by business. Business influences family life mostly through employment, employment practices, income distribution, and advertising. The impact of these forces is felt principally on family authority relationships, roles of members of the family, child-rearing, and values transmitted to children.

Over the past hundred years there have been major changes in the authority structure of the typical family. The dominant role of the father has declined as families have been separated in work, as members of families became independent through work, and as other institutions arose to meet a variety of needs (for example, schools, nurseries, and welfare agencies) formerly met in family circles. An important cause of changed authority in family life has been the growth of married women in the work force. Today, 37 percent of all workers are women, and some three-fifths of this group are married women. Traditionally, the male of the family has assumed the occupational-earner role and the woman the child-rearing role. These roles are now mixed and in some cases are reversed.

Automation has created special employment problems for teenagers since they do not have the skills required for available jobs. One result is to postpone the assumption of the wage-earner role by the male. Nevertheless, the teenage group represents a rapidly rising and large market for business because of the affluence of the typical family. Much advertising today is geared to this market. The question has arisen as to whether business has fostered a youth culture or merely reflected it. The question has also arisen as to whether business has contributed to the so-called generation gap by catering to youth.

The changing family paradigm also reacts on business. Obviously, for instance, the new authority relationships between father and son weaken the drive for the son to follow in his father's occupational footsteps. In many other ways, the views of the younger generation about business and their careers are influenced by changing family organization and style of living (Rodman and Safilios-Rothschild, in Berg, 1968: 313–25).

OTHER ISSUES

It will be recalled that in Chapter 16 business activities in hiring the hard-core unemployed and assuring equality of treatment of minorities in hiring and promotion were discussed. A major issue now before the nation concerns pension programs. This question was not examined in this chapter because of space limitations and also because what is done to correct present problems will be dictated by government. While many companies have built up rather generous pension systems over a long period of time there have been many cases of abuses and many workers who thought they had pensions were for a variety of reasons denied them (Nader and Blackwell, 1973). A much less significant issue concerns whether or not removing causes of worker dissatisfaction results in increased productivity. Many issues revolve around labor union influence over managerial processes. This will be treated in the next chapter.

CHAPTER TWENTY-EIGHT

Labor
Unions
and
Managerial
Authority

INTRODUCTION

The relationships between business and labor have been and are unique, complex, and volatile. The way in which business and labor interact is not something they alone can decide. It is dependent upon government policy, legal decisions, and prevailing attitudes in society, as well as the power of labor and business.

In this chapter, rather than attempting a survey of the many interrelationships between business and labor, I shall concentrate on one overriding issue. It is, in effect: "Who is in charge here?" On the one hand, managers prefer to have no interference in their exercise of managerial authority. On the other hand, organized labor when it is able to exert its power does in fact restrict managerial authority.

COLLECTIVE BARGAINING, MEDIATION, AND ARBITRATION

The main thrust of labor's efforts in recent years has been toward organization, higher wages, job security, and better working conditions. Organization has been the most important, because with it labor has power to bargain collectively with employers. The collective bargaining and arbitration processes are immensely significant for many reasons, but probably none is more important than that they have produced a sort of "constitutionalism" for labor. Together they have evolved a formal system to adjudicate grievances at the work place and a body of rules and regulations that are tantamount to a "common law" governing labor-management relations.

Collective bargaining, simply, is the process in which employers and employees join in conference from time to time, and agree upon the terms of employment for workers. While the words "collective bargaining" were not used until this century, the process itself extends far back in time (Chamberlain and Kuhn, 1965: 1–50). Current collective bargaining has a number of important characteristics. It is not a discrete event or a one-time bargain, but rather is a continuing, legal relationship. It consists of a series of negotiations conducted between representatives of the unions and employers. Once a union is certified by the National Labor Relations Board as being the representative of employees, the management of a company has no alternative but to deal with the union. Collective bargaining ends in mutual agreement or a strike, usually the former. Since both sides generally have different points of view, the process is one of persuasion. The ultimate consent is derivative from many sources—economic, legal, social, and political. In other words, negotiation reflects not only economic circumstance, but past procedures, previously bargained-for rights, legal principles forged in arbitration, and other values relevant to the negotiations. Federal laws do not determine the outcome of collective bargaining. Rather, governmental regulations over collective bargaining only set the framework within which negotiation takes place. The national policy is that within this framework labor and management should bargain in good faith and come to their own agreement. On occasion, however, Congress has stepped in to impose compulsory arbitration on the railroad unions.

A major result of collective bargaining is a written contract. Prior to the 1930s, contracts were general statements setting forth broad principles and purposes. Today, they are detailed documents covering minute agreements about every conceivable situation, each of which has a long historical legislative and judicial background as to rights and language. Naturally, such lengthy and legalistic documents raise many questions of interpretation. These issues may be settled in two basic ways. One is by mediation, in which someone looks at each side of an issue and makes recommendations which the parties are free to accept or reject. Under the terms of the Taft-Hartley Act, labor and management are required to notify one another of a desire to modify a collective agreement sixty days before it expires, and to notify the Federal Mediation and Conciliation Service within thirty days after that if an agreement is not reached in the meantime. The service becomes involved by law in national strikes that threaten the public health and safety, but can be used by any employer and union.

Arbitration is the second and most favored method to settle disputes. About 95 percent of all contracts contain binding clauses prohibiting strikes and lockouts during the life of the agreement. The ultimate recourse of both unions and employers, therefore, is the arbitrator. Arbitrators enjoy considerable legal authority. The Supreme Court has taken the position (comparable to that of the independent regulatory commission) that it will not second-guess the arbitrator concerning his line of reasoning or his conclusions. It will only review the question of whether the arbitrator, under the terms of the contract, has the right to deal with the grievance at issue, and even with this question the Court proceeds with restraint. The result is that arbitrators have established a sort of case law governing labor-management relationships. It is, according to Justice Douglas, a "common law of the shop" and is binding on the parties.

This judicial approach to arbitration first began during World War II and picked up impetus afterward. The arbitrator cannot deal with any and all issues at dispute between employers and employees, but rules only on alleged violations of the contract.

UNION CHALLENGE TO MANAGEMENT AUTHORITY

Union power challenges business in two important areas—the legislative process, and the managerial process. In the first area, the prize is legislation favoring the working man in his dealings with employers as well as in his social and political life. In the second area, union representatives sit face to face with employers in a collective bargaining process. While both challenge the power of businessmen, it is in the latter area that unions threaten to encroach more upon the traditional prerogatives of managers in running their businesses as they see fit.

Management Attitudes About Decision-making Authority There are still many managers who cling to the view that ownership of property carries with it the right of control. Even when managers own only a small fraction of a company's stock, they assert that the stockholders really own the property and they manage it for them. Collective bargaining may be accepted, but that does not mean it should deny the owners their rightful authority over their property. Managers look at the encroachments of union authority on traditional managerial prerogatives and complain that their ability to meet the demands of the competitive market is being hobbled as a result. They fear that reductions in their authority will lead to losses in productivity, which will erode the fundamental strength of this society.

Managers fear that unions have too much power and will use it to usurp managerial prerogatives whenever they can. Roger Blough, chairman of the U.S. Steel Corporation, put the matter this way:

> The power of labor unions and their dominance over a most essential part of the productive process of the many companies in entire industries, together with the effective collaboration among the unions, adds

up to a force which no one company or even any one industry could begin to equal—a force which well surpasses the strength of any group of private organizations this country has ever known (1959: 62–63).

Although most businessmen today would like to run their companies without any interference from labor unions, as they did fifty years ago, they also understand and respect the right of workers to organize and bargain collectively. As the CED has said, "To return to the situation which existed before 1932, or before 1947, or before 1959, would be highly undesirable." The particular task force writing these words also said that ". . . the national labor legislation adopted in the past generation, taken as a whole, has been constructive" (1964: 12). Even though managers may understand the need for labor unions, they watch the continued erosion of their power over their businesses by the unions and they do not like it. They do not want to share their managerial authority, and most of them would prefer to regain authority they have already lost. They are more frustrated than bitter, and more promanagement than antilabor. Managers are concerned about the present level of union influence in their decision-making, and they are apprehensive about the future because they see no end to the encroachment on their authority and to the increase in their labor costs.

Labor's Attitudes Toward Managerial Rights Labor interests, unions have consistently insisted, are to improve wages and working conditions and not to run businesses. Unions have always supported the capitalistic system and have seen no inconsistency in using their power to force employers to do things on behalf of workers. Indeed, unions have sought to better their position within the general growth of the economic system. They have accepted the wage system and have applied business values in their collective bargaining. Chamberlain goes further in saying that the alleged radicalism of labor is really its conservatism. He means by this that labor has become involved in managerial decision-making to further its ends, but this is evidence that labor wanted to join with management in keeping the struggle between the two and out of the political arena (in Mason, 1960: 125).

Unions say that it is not the managerial prerogative they wish to challenge, but rather the free hand of management in dealing with workers. If managers were completely free in disciplining, promoting, laying off, and recalling, the worker would be protected only by the competitive market, and he has found that to be not enough. Workers have today accumulated important rights and benefits in their jobs, and they insist that they be protected. Without protection, workers with seniority, pensions, and various fringe benefits would be too vulnerable to arbitrary management decisions. Labor unions do not view their challenge to management decision-making as being a fundamental denial of managerial authority, but rather as the pursuit of concessions needed to maintain the skills and motivation of the worker. Without the benefits workers have received, and their protection, productivity and industrial peace would deteriorate. Furthermore, say unions, if workers voluntarily give up their freedom to strike in a collective bargaining contract, why should not the manager also give up some of his freedom in order to protect worker rights?

The Right to Manage and Worker Rights This latter point deserves further comment. The old view that any union activity should not interfere with managerial rights over property—such as price, output, and transfer—on the surface seems quite acceptable. Yet, managerial control over property does not carry with it an obligation on the part of working people to be managed. Cooperation of workers in the use of company property cannot be commanded, but is won by consent. There is no legal compulsion for workers to cooperate, and there is nothing in the law that says that workers cannot extract as a price for their cooperation a voice in matters which management heretofore considered to be its sole responsibility. Managers therefore find it essential to share authority in order to ensure the cooperation of workers. Henry Nunn, a large shoe manufacturer, accepted this principle in 1915 and said to his workers: "Everything in the future will be mutually agreed upon. . . . Everything management does in the future and every act will be subject to review and question. The only authority that will be used is the authority that you have accepted" (Nunn, 1962: 79–80).

Many employers today accept the view, albeit reluctantly, that collective bargaining is based on an ethical principle "that those who are integral to the conduct of an enterprise should have a voice in decisions of concern to them" (Chamberlain and Kuhn, 1965: 134). These authors call this the "principle of mutuality," which recognizes that ownership of property is a basis for authority over it, but that authority over men requires their consent. There are some, including the Supreme Court, who accept the idea that ". . . a kind of property right inheres in the existing beneficial conditions of employment" (Kuhn, in Berg, 1968: 303). In this view, when a job or good working conditions are arbitrarily taken away from a worker, he has lost something of value. It is as if he lost a piece of property. These values therefore constitute one important basis for collective bargaining.

The Widening Scope of Collective Bargaining Demands of workers still focus on wages in the collective bargaining process, but there is growing interest in a wide range of benefits conveniently encompassed in the concept of quality of working life, discussed in the previous chapter.

Collective bargaining today extends beyond wages to pensions, guaranteed hours, unemployment benefits, retirement age, vacations, medical care, recreation facilities, work environment, and so on. Collective bargaining moves beyond even these bounds, which are of primary interest to employers and employees, to cover areas of national scope, such as training of the unemployed and their place in the company work force, price inflation, automation, foreign competition, national productivity, balance of payments, ecology, and economic stability. As the issues of collective bargaining broaden, the limitations of the process become more significant, and the potential for clashes between employers and employees grows.

Limitations on Managerial Authority The previous discussion of the impact of union power on managerial authority has been rather general; now it is time to become specific. The traditional authority of managers covers such matters as determining wage rates, where to locate a plant, what to produce in it, how to make a product, the price to be charged, the purchase of new machinery, the size of the work force, work assignments, promotion of employees, numbers of shifts, and overtime. In every one of these areas, and in many others, collective bargaining agreements and arbitration decisions have reduced managerial authority. The collective bargaining process itself, of course, results in restrictions on managerial authority to the extent that unions can get concessions in their behalf. Over a long period of time, collective bargaining contracts have, of course, built-in protections for workers concerning wages, hours, working conditions, fringe benefits, and assorted rights which restrict the area of management decision-making. Space does not permit illustration of all cases, but a few comments about wage rates and fringe benefit costs may serve as examples of the issue.

Employers have lost the power to set wage rates and fringe benefits unilaterally. If a union and an employer can hold wage and fringe benefit increases to increases in worker productivity, the implications for the employer are not serious. If these costs rise much above productivity increases, however, managerial alternatives are seriously affected. An employer is then faced with the necessity of increasing prices to maintain his profit position, cutting costs elsewhere, or watching his profits decline. Choosing any one of these possibilities can lead to other problems. A price increase, for instance, may lose him his market. Reduced profits may alienate his investors. To cut costs he may be forced to take distasteful actions, such as firing workers. Collective bargaining has tended to create a downward rigidity in wages, which in turn makes prices more stable in a business downturn than would be expected if wage rates were more flexible. On the other hand, collective bargaining has produced upward flexibility in wage and fringe benefit costs in booming economic conditions. In either case, managerial decision-making has been somewhat restricted. In today's dynamic economy, it is not at all a foregone conclusion that a manager who accepts a wage settlement greater than his workers' productivity will be able to maintain his profits with a price increase. Changing volume, product mix, consumer demand, competition, and other factors make a direct relationship between wage-rate increases and price rises very unstable.

As pointed out previously, there is a rapidly expanding body of law, growing out of arbitration of disputes concerning contractual provisions, that impinges on managerial authority. The drift of this law is toward increasing restrictions on managerial authority. Management takes the position that what is not spelled out in the contract with a union is reserved for management. This is the "theory of management reserved rights." More specifically, "management's authority is supreme in all matters except those it has expressly conceded in the collective agreement and in all areas except those where its authority is restricted by law" (Prasow and Peters, 1970: 31). These authors point out that this theory is a necessary frame of reference for contract interpretation in arbitration, but that it is subject to considerable qualification. The unions, for example, take the position that matters affecting their interests should be discussed with them before action is taken, whether or not the contract so stipulates. This is a position the arbitrators and the Supreme Court accept. A prevailing doctrine in this connection is that once an employer and a union agree to arbitration, the only matters excluded from arbitration are those specifically excluded in the labor agreement. Therefore, if a matter of concern to employees arises after the contract has been set and is not a part of that contract, it may become the subject of arbitration procedure. In one milestone case (*United Steel Workers v. Warrior and Gulf Navigation Company*), the Supreme Court held that an issue was arbitrable even though the contract contained a clause saying, "Issues . . . which are strictly a function of management shall not be subject to arbitration," and even though the unions had been unsuccessful in including the subject in collective bargaining. In this case the Court ruled that "strictly a function of management" refers only to that which in the contract specifies management control and unfettered discretion.

At issue in this particular case was a practice of contracting out which the company had followed for twenty years and which the employees unsuccessfully sought to reject in the collective bargaining agreement. In the arbitration of the case, however, an "outsider" settled the issue in favor of the union, and the decision was binding on the company. Some writers believe that because of rulings such as this, arbitration clauses in contracts may deprive "an employer of a very substantial portion of the management rights he has always believed he possessed" (Bangks and Fraser, 1963: 51). However, simply because a particular issue may be arbitrable, whether included in the contract or not, does not necessarily mean that a decision will

go against an employer. But employers find that the collective bargaining contract itself and the arbitration decisions arising from conflicts in contract interpretation have increasingly reduced their authority. The following cases illustrate the point.

Employer responsibilities to employees have been broadened,
for instance, in plant relocation. In 1957 the Stetson Hat Company
decided to move its finishing shop from Danbury, Connecticut, to its
Philadelphia plant. It had shortly before signed a three-year contract
with the union which happened to be the same union as the one in
the Philadelphia plant. When the Philadelphia plant heard about the
matter, it threatened a sympathy strike unless the company kept the
Danbury plant open. The company had offered jobs to those who
wanted to move to Philadelphia and severance pay for those who did
not choose to relocate. The arbitrator laid down a principle, upheld
in subsequent court cases, that the company had a right to move its
business in the expectation of becoming more efficient, but it also
had an obligation to discuss such an important matter with the union
and to be generous with older workers who might be permanently
unemployed as a result of the move (*John B. Stetson Company v.
United Hatters, Cap and Millinery Workers International Union*). In a
later case (*NLRB v. Rapid Bindery*) a U.S. Court of Appeals held that
the company had a right to move its plant, but because it did not
discuss the move with the union, it was in violation of the National
Labor Relations Act. The court ordered the company to give workers
"immediate and full reinstatement to their former or substantially
equivalent position privileges." In general, the legal view is that companies have the right to relocate, but they must discuss the matter
with unions and they cannot abrogate employee rights acquired
through long service to the company. So, managerial prerogatives are
indeed restricted in the area of plant location.

Managers strive to use their resources as efficiently as they can,
but their decision-making, if left unchecked, may be contrary to the
interests of workers in protecting their jobs, pay, and benefits. Court
decisions have, as a consequence, prevented managers from taking
action which presumably they felt would improve efficiency. For
instance, a company was prevented from subcontracting janitorial
service even though it was in financial difficulties (*Stockholders Publishing Company v. American Newspaper Guild*). The arbitrator, however, ruled against the company not on substantive grounds, but because the union with which it had a contract was not consulted. On
the other hand, an arbitrator said that a company could introduce a
new machine to improve efficiency and reorganize the work without
prior negotiation with the union (*General Baking Company v. Bakery
& Confectionery Workers International Union of America*). Arbitrators view with disfavor efforts by management to take advantage of
situations that deprive workers of pay, work, vacations, and so on due

them in conformity with the terms of an agreement (Ginzberg and Berg, 1963: 81).

The "doctrine of implied obligations" asserts that an employer has the right to alter or abolish an employee benefit when the contract is open for renegotiation, but once it has been signed, he can no longer withdraw existing benefits. Managers are stopped from withdrawing benefits during the course of the contract because the union is precluded from striking to preserve that benefit. The application of this principle depends upon each case, and different arbitrators may apply it in various ways. In one case, for instance, an employer installed new equipment which employees could tend without dirtying their hands. Their previous equipment was dirty, and the company gave employees the last ten minutes of their shift to wash up. When the new equipment was installed, management revoked the wash-up time. The arbitrator ruled for the employer, but some arbitrators might well have decided that the company had an implied obligation to continue the wash-up time until the contract expired (Prasow and Peters, 1970: 39). Does this imply that a manager has no control over work assignments upon the introduction of a new machine? Arbitrators generally have ruled that, in the absence of "an express provision guaranteeing the continuation of a job, a contract does not ordinarily bar the employer from laying off employees for various reasons, including increased efficiency attained by new equipment or new methods of utilizing old equipment" (Prasow and Peters, 1970: 41–42). Employees, however, may enter claims for certain lost benefits, but whether they receive redress will depend upon contractual terms and the specifics of the case.

In concluding this section, it should be mentioned that unions often accede to managerial interests and facilitate decisions managers wish to make. For example, unions have been known to restrain wage demands and accept wage reductions when a company is in financial difficulties. Unions have often provided employers with important information about worker morale and have offered employers expert knowledge gathered by union staffs.

Limitations on Union Power No one doubts, least of all the manager, the great strength of many labor unions. There are, however, a number of serious limitations on the power of unions that must not be overlooked.

Generally, the more competition exists in an industry, the less is the power of unions. Under perfect competitive conditions, there would be no advantage in collective worker activity as compared with individual bargaining. The economic system would compel workers and businessmen to conform to its requirements or suffer reduced profits, unemployment, or both. When markets are not fully competitive, there is room for discretion in bargaining between employers and unions. It is not magnanimity that leads unions to support monopolistic practices among local businessmen, such as construction contractors, truckers, barbers, and so on. Were these businessmen competing freely, the discretion permitted at the bargaining table would be minimal. It is to the advantage of unions to prevent cutthroat price-cutting because it inevitably leads to a reduction in wages. The more a market shows monopolistic manifestations—such as oligopoly, product differentiation, and price leadership—the greater is the discretion permitted at the bargaining table, other things being equal. In such instances, wage-rate increases are more easily passed on to the consumer in higher product prices.

But even in monopolistic markets the power of unions is limited. The degree of elasticity of demand for products, for example, can exert a limitation on union bargaining power. If a product evidences a high elasticity of demand, it reflects the availability of substitute products. In such a case manufacturers will find their market declining if they try to pass on wage increases by raising product price over that of competitors. Even in cases of high elasticity, however, managers may accept higher wage rates on the assumption that they can maintain profit levels without increasing prices by raising worker productivity, or by increasing volume. When products show high inelasticity, there is room for passing on wage-rate increases in the form of higher prices without the loss of demand. There is a limit, of course, to protection from a price rise, for in the highly dynamic American market, any excessive price increases in areas of product inelasticity quickly attract competitors, and product demand then loses its inelasticity. The threat of a strike to achieve union demands, which is, of course, the ultimate weapon of organized labor, is not likely to be effective in an industry or company that is not operating at full capacity. In such instances, managers might view a temporary work stoppage with some relief.

Automation has weakened labor's position and strengthened the hand of management. As unions press harder for higher wages, managers find it increasingly attractive to buy machinery to replace men. The greater the automation, the easier it is to continue operations with fewer workers. In such cases, and they are growing in numbers, supervisors and higher-level managers are able to keep the plant in operation while workers are on strike. This potential sometimes makes a strike threat a hollow gesture.

Foreign competition also restrains union demands in those industries threatened by foreign imports. As noted in Chapter 25, the invasion of the American market by foreign producers has been increasing and has cost American jobs in some industries.

How Influential Are Unions In Raising Wage Rates? This turns out to be a very difficult question to answer with certainty. In periods of high and rising aggregate demand and price inflation, organized labor finds its strength at a maximum in extracting favorable collective bargaining agreements. At other times, as noted above, its strength is less. There have been few if any conclusive studies, however, about precisely how influential unions are in getting higher wage rates. Generally, studies which have tried to assess union power in the market place have been of two types. The first has measured the extent to which unions have increased their wages in relation to nonunion workers. The second has measured the increase in total share of national income going to unions. All such studies have been inconclusive primarily because so many factors which are not measurable bear heavily on the results (Pohlman, 1972).

Wages do tend to be higher in unionized industries, but wages were higher in these industries before unions became strong, so the probability exists that wages in these industries would be higher today even if unions were not strong. Since World War II, wages in unionized industries increased a little faster than in nonunionized industries, but some of the largest increases occurred in nonunion areas such as domestic workers. Such comparisons are not too useful, however, because union strength in bargaining for higher wages has resulted in raising all wages. Employers of nonunionized workers must pay them more or watch them move to unionized companies. In a sweeping way, the demand for and supply of labor has a governing influence over wage rates and fringe benefits, but within the broad restraints of economic conditions, unions have exerted and will continue to exert enough strength to get more generous settlements than managers would be willing to pay were there no unions. What the difference is quantitatively, however, no one really knows.

Assessing the Erosion of Managerial Authority   Everyone agrees that managerial authority has been reduced by collective bargaining and arbitration. There are widely differing views, however, about the importance of the erosion, its trend, and the significance to management.

There are ways to look at the erosion of managerial authority other than in terms of specific decisions affected by labor power and arbitration decisions. I think it is fair to say that the heartland of managerial authority has not been seriously invaded. In major operational decisions, the impact of union power has not been great. Nor have many of labor's gains cost business much money. Whatever the costs have been, there has also been an offsetting advantage in the avoidance of widespread industrial strife. Furthermore, labor's gains have not been absolute. If management felt the need to make a change in collective bargaining agreements, it could do so, at a price.

What has really happened is not that management powers have been stripped, but that the perimeters within which management functions have been changed. Management cannot manage as it did in the old days. The closer its decisions come to affecting working conditions, job security, pay, and other worker interests, the more it must act with reference to employees. It must consult with workers before certain moves are made, and it must defer sometimes to employee interests even though the result may not be precisely what management would do if it were unhindered. Employees have acquired rights which must now be respected, and they have benefits to offer management in return for the protection of those rights.

Clark Kerr and a special study group sponsored by the CED found a more global beneficent relationship between union power and managerial authority. The group concluded that today's collective bargaining strengthens management in the long run because "the United States has been uniquely fortunate among developed and free-enterprise economies in having an industrial work force and labor movement that accepts . . . [our] basic political and economic framework and seeks to advance its interests within that framework" (CED, 1961: 33).

In sum, there is no doubt about the conclusion that managerial prerogatives in traditional terms have eroded with collective bargaining and court decisions which extend the areas of dispute for arbitration. On the other hand, the collective bargaining and arbitration processes have developed a stability in industrial relations which probably could not otherwise have been accomplished short of massive government intervention. In this light, net managerial capabilities for free action may have been advanced.

THE CURRENT STATE OF COLLECTIVE BARGAINING

Collective bargaining has come of age, it has matured. One mark of maturity is the small number of strikes and the absence of violence. Even in "the year of strikes," 1946, total man-days lost was only 1.4 percent of total man-days worked. In no year since then has the total been over 1/2 of 1 percent, and in most years it has been much less than that. This record is all the more remarkable in light of the fact that very few of the over 150,000 collective bargaining agreements are nationwide. There is no satisfactory measure of violence, but the level today is far below that of a few decades ago. Indeed, today's strikes sometimes verge on being ritualistic.

The reasons for peaceful negotiations are many. So far as management is concerned, there is a widespread acceptance today of the labor union. Acceptance of the union removes the survival issue for unions, an issue which can always be relied upon to engender violence. Of great importance also is the fact that both employers and employees approach the bargaining table in a sophisticated fashion. Each has learned the importance of having information about the issues and each does his homework. Experts are employed on both sides to analyze data. This stands in sharp contrast to past take-it-or-leave-it positions that were formed with limited facts and analysis. Only rarely are there strikes over grievances that arise during the term of contracts. Both employers and employees have learned how to use arbitrators to settle disputes. Other marks of the maturing process are the increasing number of bargaining relationships that take place long before the termination of existing contracts. There is growing awareness of the public interest in negotiations. Negotiations are more problem-oriented and are not based upon polarized abstract principles. There is a growing mutual trust between the parties involved.

This is a far different situation than that which existed twenty or thirty years ago, but it still is some distance from solving all the problems between employers and employees. Despite all the machinery and experience of peaceful settlements, there have been instances recently where settlement has come only after long, bitter, and costly strikes. Furthermore, many settlements have not taken place despite the use of the strike. The seriousness of some of these strikes to public health and safety must not be underestimated. A strike of subway workers, garbage collectors, transportation workers, or milk delivery-men can have widespread implications throughout society.

There are methods by means of which officials at all levels of government may intervene in different types of strikes that affect the public health, safety, and welfare. They include mediation, voluntary arbitration, appointment of fact-finding boards, injunctions, and persuasion by high political figures. The Taft-Hartley Act lays down a lengthy procedure for settling work stoppages that imperil national health or safety, but the procedure does not necessarily lead to a settlement.

Collective bargaining today works reasonably well when the subject concerns wages and working conditions between an employer and a group of employees. The process is strained when the issues go beyond this, such as in cases where settlements are associated with national anti-inflationary policy. Collective bargaining does not work well in the case of a declining industry that needs relief, for example, railroads. As prosperous industries automate, the issue of jobs comes front and center. Management cannot be expected to employ people no longer needed, and unions will find it difficult to concede that their members are superfluous. Where an industry tries to get unions to bargain their members out of a job and their union out of existence, it is easy to predict trouble. The collective bargaining process also has its costs. The very success of the process in bettering working conditions makes it difficult to change these conditions as might be required to improve productivity. The impact of strikes on third parties, such as travelers on a shut-down airline, can be inconvenient and expensive. All things considered, however, collective bargaining today works reasonably well and, except in periods of severe turbulence, is likely to mature even more if the principles of the Experimental Negotiating Proposal, to be discussed next, are more widely accepted in the future as I think they will be.

THE EXPERIMENTAL NEGOTIATING PROPOSAL

One of the most important developments in collective bargaining in forty years was an agreement between the United Steelworkers of America and ten steel companies, employing about 350,000 union members, which assured labor peace for a three-year period from mid-1974 to mid-1977. The agreement was reached in March 1973 to apply to the negotiations undertaken in the summer of 1974. It was called the Experimental Negotiating Proposal.

Every year, almost like clockwork, the nation has been faced with the threat of a steel strike at the time annual negotiations between the union and the company managements were to begin. Just as rhythmically, users of basic steel shapes and forms built up their inventories to protect themselves from the possible strike. The result was that even if there was no strike employment and production in the steel industry fluctuated in boom and bust cycles. Both the unions and managements deplored such swings. Not only were such gyrations extremely costly to the companies in lost production and revenues, and to workers in lost wages, but they also were responsible in part for attracting large volumes of foreign steel imports which continued after negotiations and strikes were ended. This, in turn, not only had a continuing adverse impact on the industry and its employees but on the United States balance of payments. As one union leader expressed it, "Nobody can win a strike anymore."

The new agreement commits the union not to strike for a period of three years. In the meantime all issues will be resolved by binding arbitration. Under the new procedure the right to strike is permitted only at a particular operation over a local issue unique to that operation. The steel companies agree to increase wage rates a minimum of 3 percent each year and to give workers a one-time bonus payment of $150.

It is to be hoped that this plan will work to the satisfaction of both parties because if it does it is likely to be extended to many other industries and to the public sector. One significant phenomenon in the labor movement during recent years has been the rapid growth of unionism in the not-for-profit sector, a trend likely to continue in the 1970s. Accompanying it in recent years has been a growing number of strikes and threatened strikes, all of which raise serious questions about the right of public employees to strike. Each time there is a strike in the public sector cries are heard to outlaw the strike and install compulsory arbitration. Most leaders of public employee unions oppose compulsory arbitration but do favor voluntary arbitration of contract issues that cannot be resolved through the collective bargaining process (Stieber, 1973).

THE POLITICAL POWER OF UNIONS

The power of organized labor confronts that of business not only at the conference table, but also in the political arena. Hutchinson (1962) observes three major changes in the recent past in labor's political activities. First, the legislative objectives of labor have widened. Prior to the 1930s labor interests centered principally on the bargaining table. The depression of the 1930s, however, politically activated the rising and aggressive CIO and stirred organized labor to pressure Congress for measures to revive the faltering economy, to support collective bargaining, and in many other ways to improve the workingman's position. From that day to this there have been few issues before Congress on which labor is nonpartisan.

A second change has occurred in the political methods employed. The Smith-Connally Act of 1943 and other attempts to control strike and union activities prompted the creation of the CIO's Political Action Committee, the first modern effort by labor to establish nationwide organization to influence electoral votes. The Taft-Hartley Act of 1947 stimulated the AFL to establish a comparable arm. When the two merged in 1955, the AFL-CIO's Committee on Political Education (COPE) was formed as a means to influence electoral as well as legislative activities.

The third major political change has been the decline in theory and practice of nonpartisanship in politics. The old AFL was nonpartisan and the early CIO assumed a nonpartisan stance, but over time the relationship of organized labor to the Democratic party has become ever closer. This relationship is not solely associated with national elections, but is deep in state and local governmental politics. Hutchinson says, "It would be wrong to infer that labor either dominates or is dominated by the Democratic Party; or that the relationship is effectively exclusive, always smooth or wholly welcome on either side. But the alliance is national, enduring, and close, a major political fact, more important than the ceremonies which might appear to deny it" (1962: 140).

Granted the deepening interests of organized labor in politics, the widening scope of its interests, and its close relationships to one party, how powerful is it in politics? This is not a question to which there is a simple categorical answer, but a review of different aspects of it may be enlightening. To begin with, it is noteworthy that there is no "labor" party in the United States. This is partly due to the fact that in the past when labor did have grievances which merited attention, the issue was accepted and advanced by one of the two major political parties. Of more importance, however, is the fact that labor could not have created an effective political party even though it might have wanted to. Bernstein points to a number of impediments to a labor party in the United States, as follows: The political climate is hostile to a class-based party. Union members are a small proportion of the voting population and are distributed in a lopsided fashion from the standpoint of political effectiveness. They are highly concentrated in the industrial states and sparse in the rural and agricultural areas. Anyway, there is no certainty that union members would vote for a labor party, if there were such a party (1962: 10).

How powerful is labor in electing public officials and in influencing legislation? Labor generally has not been able to deliver the vote in a bloc sense. Organized labor does have many common aims, such as wages, hours of work, and working conditions; but workers do not identify themselves as a class, and their identification with the working group is not very close. This means that when a worker's basic aims are reasonably well satisfied, as they are in prosperous conditions, his vote will be influenced more by other issues—religion, the appearance of candidates, attitudes of friends, prejudice, or views of candidates on issues irrelevant to the workers' economic interests. When the workers' economic interests are in jeopardy, however, he is more likely to vote as his union officials suggest. The influence of unions over the vote of their members is in inverse relationship to general economic conditions. Furthermore, it is important to keep in mind that most workers are not members of unions.

On the legislative front, organized labor's influence has been more impressive. Methods of lobbying employed by organized labor are the same as those used by other powerful interest groups. Organized labor has successfully fought for important pieces of legislation, such as the Employment Act of 1946, the Social Security Act of 1935, and many recent enactments concerning consumer interests. On the other hand, organized labor has been violently opposed to the Taft-Hartley Act, but has not been able to amend or rescind it. In the future, organized labor will concentrate more on legislative processes. As the scope of collective bargaining moves further and further from issues of immediate concern to employer-employee relationships and matters they can resolve, the focus of attention will shift to the national scene. This process will be accelerated the higher the objective of quality of life becomes for workers. Issues of job security in the face of rapid automation, full employment with price stability, foreign competition, medical care, welfare, unemployment compensation, or protection of consumers cannot always or easily be dealt with in the collective bargaining process and will therefore be the focus of political attention at all levels of government.

FORECASTS FOR 1984–1985

In 1968 the NICB asked a number of business executives to describe what labor relations and collective bargaining would be like, in their view, in 1984. The spectrum of the responses is captured in the following profiles:

> If the present trends continue, with increasing governmental regulation of industry and commerce, management will have lost its right to manage, and we will no longer have a free society. The present socialistic trends will bring about an impossible situation that will in turn lead to the establishment of authoritative government either of the right or the left, and those who are responsible for operating production units will be doing so as instruments of the state.
>
> Very possibly by 1984 the disputes between management and labor will be fought out on political rather than economic battlegrounds. That is, unions will have largely given up their right to strike, and business will have given up its right to set prices. The great economic disputes will be resolved by government-appointed arbitrators, while what strikes we do have will probably be political in nature, as in Europe, to influence legislators and government administrators. . . .
>
> In most respects the labor relations and collective bargaining of 1984 will probably not be dramatically different from today's. This conclusion is based on two premises: (1) both unionism and collective bargaining are relatively mature institutions which are not likely to undergo any self-generated changes, and (2) the collective bargaining system is working well enough that major changes will not be imposed from without. This second premise seems somewhat more questionable than the first . . . by 1984 we will see a more mature and practical relationship between labor and management, one that has been developing over the past 20 years and will continue to develop. This relationship will be improved over the years ahead through the development of greater confidence on the part of labor and management in each other. I also think that both parties will play a more active role in facing up to their responsibilities for contributing to a stable and healthy economy. By this I mean that labor leaders will recognize the importance of the relationship of productivity improvements to wage and benefit improvements, and a more responsible attitude on the part of management in sharing a fair portion of the productivity improvement with the labor force* (Curtin and Brown, 1968: 54–55).

Which of these is the most plausible? I side with the last.

Gordon and LeBleu used twenty-two expert panelists in an application of the Delphi technique to forecast changes in employee benefits. They examined some fifty-five benefits—divided into general, income security, family protection, employee services, time off

* The publisher of the *Conference Board Record* is the National Industrial Conference Board, New York. Quotes above are from respondents to a National Industrial Conference Board survey and are not the views of the Conference Board.

with pay, medical costs, and retirement—and concluded that in terms of strength and direction, none of today's trends will decrease, although a few will remain constant. Many are expected to increase greatly in strength and direction, such as medical coverage, pension programs, and time off with pay. The panelists agreed that "employees will come to regard benefits as rights even more so than at present" (1970: 96). Except for a thrust of unions for longer vacations, the main push will be to protect the living standards of workers against inflation before and after retirement.

The panelists also agreed that a number of new benefits would be demanded and granted by 1985, among which are the following (Gordon and LeBleu, 1970: 99–101):

> Cooperative benefit programs among companies on a nationwide basis
> Company assumption of all benefit costs
> Retraining conducted by employers as part of severance benefits
> Annual wage guaranteed by employers
> Minimum government-guaranteed annual income
> Guaranteed employment for most employees under contract to employers, and a job guarantee by the government as the employer of last resort
> Medical coverage to extend to such service as new prosthetics (e.g., artificial hearts) and new exotic medical practices (e.g., aging control)
> Optional retirement at age 55 with no loss of benefits
> Pension plans extended to include education, medical services, legal services, etc.
> Employers to pay most insurance for a wide variety of protections
> Credit assistance to employees through employer credit cards or cosigning notes
> Subsidized employee housing
> Free concert, theater, and other entertainment
> Company in-house advanced degree programs
> Shortening of workday by employer counting travel time to and from work
> Educational leave for employees

The net impact by 1985, conclude Gordon and LeBleu, is to "guarantee all employees reasonable wages, more education and leisure, safer and more pleasant working places, and the avoidance of most of the fiscal hazards associated with accidents, ill health, and old age" (1970: 102).

PART SEVEN The Future

CHAPTER TWENTY-NINE

Future Forces and Patterns in the Business-Society Relationship

INTRODUCTION

In *A Tale of Two Cities* Charles Dickens wrote that the setting was in the best of times, the worst of times, the age of wisdom, the age of foolishness, the epoch of belief, the epoch of incredulity, the season of light, the season of darkness, the spring of hope, and the winter of despair. This could be said about the present because it catches the extremes and the paradoxes of our times. Will we be able to say the same thing in 1985 or 2000? No one knows, but one can agree with John Gardner that "the prospects never looked brighter and the problems never looked tougher." He goes on to say that anyone who is not stirred by this statement is too tired to be of much use to us in the days ahead (1968: 168).

This chapter presents those major foreseen trends and events which most likely will shape the future of the business-society relationship to the end of the century. Upon this basis, the outstanding characteristics of what I consider to be the most probable emerging society will be presented. A number of fundamental considerations in the shaping of the future will then be examined. It is not at all certain that the future will be anything at all like that which is here considered to be the most probable. As a consequence, it is useful to examine alternative scenarios even though the probabilities for them are thought by most observers to be below those of the emerging society discussed in the chapter. (The word scenario is used in this chapter to mean a hypothetical description of the main characteristics of a possible society in the future.)

ON SOCIAL PREDICTIONS

Irving Kristol has asserted, "The beginning of wisdom, for any social analyst or critic, is to know that the future is unknowable" (1969). The history of forecasting societal phenomenon is strewn with so many glaring failures that anyone approaching the subject should do so with humility. Yet despite the hazards, it is very useful to look ahead at what may take place because it provokes thought about the future.

Anyone trying to foresee future business-society interrelationships must be aware of four major analytical problems. First, the future will be a reflection of the present and the past. Which forces of the present and past will be reflected in the future, however, is not clear. Also, the further ahead in time the less will current forces be influential. Second, there are major discontinuities which will also affect the relationship. Peter Drucker says, for example, that human history is and will become more than in the past a discontinuous process [1969(A)]. He says that four major discontinuities are now convulsing our society and our lives. They are new technologies which are radically changing our world, the move from an international economy to a world economy, the changing responsibilities of and interrelationships among our major institutions (for which we have no adequate political or social theory to deal with this reality), and, finally, the creation of a "knowledge society" which we do not know how to manage. Third, most of the information available to use as a basis for projections is speculative, qualitative, and imprecise. Finally, there is great uncertainty about the way in which forces will ebb and flow and mix at any particular point of time.

The assumption made here is that in the absence of some catastrophe the society of the next twenty-five years in the United States will be determined largely by the momentum of present forces adjusted by significant decisions made by managers of our basic institutions. These forces will generate different patterns over time depending upon the strength and thrust of each and the combinations which evolve. Since this exercise in projection cannot be made by a neutral scientific methodology the projections are influenced by personal biases.

THE WORLDWIDE SETTING

No view of future business-societal relationships in the United States can ignore significant worldwide forces. What happens here is affected by what is occurring outside our boundaries.

Among all the foreseeable forces operating in the world the most significant to the United States is its involvement in wars. Wars bring major changes in societies. To the extent, therefore, that the United States becomes embroiled in military engagements in the future, deep and powerful forces will be stirred up—forces whose impact on business-societal relationships will depend upon their level of violence, the popular consensus about them, and their timing.

Worldwide population growth is and will continue to generate a broad range of forces. The projected rate of growth is explosive. Between now and the year 2000 the population of the world will grow from about 3.5 billion today to about 7 billion, assuming present rates of growth. The rate of growth is slowing down in the more developed nations but it still is rapid in the less developed countries. As countries become more developed there is prospect of a decline in the birthrate, but in the less developed countries the rate of growth is not likely to drop significantly over the next few decades provided that mortality conditions do not deteriorate and no major disasters with great loss of life are encountered.

Unchecked population growth can be the greatest threat to the future well-being of man on this globe. Slowing the rate of population growth is essential in solving many of the world's great problems, such as widespread hunger, rising levels of unemployment, and a deteriorating physical environment. If this is not done it is predicted by some observers as noted in Chapter 20, that the result in the twenty-first century will be worldwide disaster (Meadows, 1972). Despite rising gross national products in the underdeveloped countries, population growth can slow down per capita GNP growth and may, in some countries, bring about a reduction in standards of well-being.

There are encouraging counterforces. The idea of population control is spreading rapidly. Rising productivity of farming, new high-yield foods, and commercially prepared synethetic protein foods will increasingly relieve food shortages. Spreading technology around the world will advance industrialization. The population of the world is becoming better educated. Transportation and communications systems are rapidly improving. Global economic activity is becoming better coordinated thanks much, but not entirely, to the spread of multinational corporations (Brown, 1972).

Political changes with potential impacts on the United States will also take place. Kahn and Weiner in their book *The Year 2000* (1967) set forth different possible political changes the world may see in the next twenty-five years. If there are major shifts in governance among important nations, they will be reflected in the United States.

There will be, of course, other significant forces operating in the world which will influence United States business-society interrelationships, such as technology, international monetary systems, economic blackmail (e.g., the oil embargo), ideologies, and business practices. No one can now foretell precisely what the impacts will be, but there is no question that they will be important.

In sum, there are deep underlying forces operating in the world which increase complexity, tension, and instability. There are also counterforces.

THE EMERGING AMERICAN SOCIETY

Over the next several decades the current affluent society will move toward a much different kind of society. Daniel Bell calls it the "post-industrial" society, a name which seems to be widely accepted. This is a deceptive phrase, however, because society in the stretch to the year 2000 still will be highly industrialized. Some call it a "learning" society because of the heightened role of knowledge and education. Lyndon Johnson called it the "Great Society." Whatever the name given it, however, it will differ much from today's society. (For other names see Marien, 1973.)

Basic Premises of Projections The following concepts are based on the assumption that worldwide forces will create major problems for the United States but that they will not cause disastrous disruptions. It is assumed that there will be no global wars but that the United States may become engaged in limited wars. It is assumed that there will be no internal political, economic, or social catastrophes which would importantly change the course of events. It is assumed that the major trends which underlay the development of Western society for many centuries will continue, although there may be some significant discontinuities. Each of the trends shown in Exhibit 29–1 has its own set of premises but space does not permit their description.

Exhibit 29–1. One Hundred Probable Domestic Major Trends and Events to 1985 and Beyond of Importance to the Business-Society Relationship*

A. *National Economics*
1. GNP is expected to grow, in real terms, at an average rate of 4 percent per year. This will lift GNP (in 1973 prices) from $1,285 billions in 1973 to $2,056 billions in 1985, and to $3,700 billions in the year 2000. GNP per capita will rise from $6,119 in 1973 to $8,290 in 1985 and $13,214 in the year 2000 (in 1973 prices). (See #16 for population estimates.)
2. Economic activities will become even more service-oriented, rather than production-oriented, than today.

      3. The work week will decline through the century.

      4. Price inflation is likely to continue between the range of annual increases of 3.5 to 6 percent in the consumers price index.

B. *The Government Sector*

      5. Federal government outlays are expected to rise only slightly as a percentage of GNP. From estimated outlays in FY 1974 of $269 billions it is expected that the total, in 1973 prices, will rise to $432 billions in 1985 and to $777 billions, or 21 percent of GNP, in the year 2000.

      6. Considerably more output of goods and services will be directed toward the public sector in relation to the private sector of the society.

      7. There will be a growing interdependence among major institutions in society, especially the federal government, state governments, local governments, educational institutions, and larger businesses.

      8. The rate of growth (past ten years) of total R&D expenditures will slow down. Federal government expenditures for nondefense R&D, both in government and outside it, will expand enormously, both absolutely and relative to defense and space R&D.

      9. Government programs will shift slowly from operations and management to goal-setting, funding, catalyzing, measuring, and setting standards for performance.

      10. By 1985 there will be a set of national goals which will be revised periodically.

      11. Government regulations over business activities will continue to grow.

      12. The efficiency of government, measured on any reasonable standard, is not likely to improve as fast as more complex societal problems appear.

      13. There will be increased government influence on business, especially in dealing with social problems.

      14. Toward the end of the century the Congress will legislate that all corporations doing interstate business must be chartered by the federal government.

      15. The convergence between business and government planning will accelerate.

C. *Population*

      16. The population is projected to grow from 210 million in 1973 to 248 million in 1985 and to 280 million in the year 2000.** (For the year 2000 the following fertility rates will produce the following population: 2.11 = 271 million; 2.45 = 288; 2.78 = 305; and 3.10 = 322.)

17. Major shifts will take place in age mix. The greatest leap will be a 75 percent increase in the 35–49 age group from now to the year 2000. Those over 65 will grow by 38 percent, and those between 50–64 will grow by 27 percent. Young adults from 20 to 34 will grow by 21 percent, and teenagers will increase by 5 percent.

18. Concentration in urban centers is expected to continue from 73.5 percent of the population today to 77 percent in 2000.

19. In 1985 more married women will be working outside the home than are engaged solely in the home.

D. *Social Values*

20. While it is likely there will be a continuing commitment to basic American values very much along present-day lines, important changes will have taken place in social values. Increased emphasis will be placed on such values as social justice, esthetics, humanitarianism, social consciousness, personal comfort and security, leisure, and internationalism. Less emphasis will be placed on piety, patriotism and national pride, civic pride, the work ethic, materialism, conformity, centralization, and authority.

21. While there may appear to be an erosion from time to time of the basic optimism of people in the future of this society, optimism will continue to be a strong fundamental value held by most people.

22. While there will be only minor erosion of the work ethic, there will be significant new demands of workers at all levels for control over and satisfactions from the work place.

23. As population ages, social values will change more slowly and become slightly more conservative.

24. There will gradually be developed a set of social indicators measuring elements in the "quality of life" that eventually will match Gross National Product measurement in social importance.

25. The strong current trends will continue for a wider distribution of power in society. At the same time per capita power will continue to increase.

26. Increasing emphasis will be given to improving the quality of life of the population. All institutions, including business, will be obliged to participate in the process.

E. *Technological*

27. STOL and VSTOL giant passenger transports will be produced by the year 2000.

28. Reliable and long-range weather forecasting will be possible.

29. The United States will not be self-sufficient in energy by 1985 because of the heavy costs needed to be so. However, dependence on foreign energy sources in 1985 will be relatively no greater than today and perhaps a little less. This will result from new discoveries of oil and gas reserves; the use of nuclear power, including breeder reactors; gasification and liquefication of coal; shale oil recovery; automated underground coal mining; and perhaps new discoveries of energy sources.
30. Controls will be possible over hereditary and congenital defects.
31. Widespread automation in industry will exist.
32. Oceans will be farmed for foods and minerals.
33. Cheap, reliable, and no-side-effect birth-control methods will be available.
34. Real-time automated credit and bank charge account systems will be in operation.
35. Efficient, fast, and cheap underground tunneling machines will be in use.
36. Efficient automobile smog control devices and/or new nonsmog-producing automobile engines will be in use.
37. There will be worldwide TV broadcasting.
38. Two-way television will be widespread.
39. There will be better control of the aging process and increased longevity.
40. Small, powerful batteries with long life will be available.
41. Miniaturization of integrated circuits will continue and expand usage to all sort of products from toys to complicated machinery.
42. Sea water will be cheaply desalinized.
43. Enzyme technology will become a major new industry by 1985.
44. There will be widespread use of computers to interpret medical symptoms.
45. Implanted plastic organs will be commonplace.
46. New strong and light metals will be in use.
47. Modular house construction will be widespread.
48. Many foods will be produced synthetically.
49. Many chemical pesticides will be phased out and insect hormones will be widely used as pesticides.
50. There will be more emphasis on technology in more companies. Increasingly new technologies will arise in areas other than those to which they are related (e.g., the computer did not arise in the office equipment industry). Technological change will continue to be rapid.

51. Drugs to control human moods and mental problems will be widespread and effective.

F. *Education*

52. 1985 and beyond will be much more of a learning society.
53. Education in 1980 and beyond will represent an enormous market for business.
54. Managers of the future will take periodic retraining courses as do scientists and engineers today.
55. New information technologies will transform libraries into facilities which will disseminate information quickly and cheaply.
56. Programmed learning will be widespread in and out of the classroom.
57. Industry will experience a relative decline as the prime motivating force in society as government and educational institutions become more innovative in economic and social life.

G. *Business Management*

58. Criticisms of business will ebb and flow over the remainder of the century but will continue to be severe and may well become more widespread as the population becomes better educated and society becomes more complex.
59. In the business world, the emphasis will shift importantly from concentration on production to strategy in relating the business to its environment.
60. Boards of directors of the larger corporations will be composed more and more of outside members and boards will exercise more direction over the affairs of firms than today.
61. Classical profit maximization ideology increasingly will yield to the doctrine of social responsibility. Yet, in the year 2000, the business firm will be conceived as fundamentally an economic institution having social responsibilities.
62. Forecasting changing social values will become of increasing importance in business appraisal of environment.
63. More and more companies will attempt to forecast the societal impact of the technologies they introduce.
64. The computer will greatly change middle-management work, but certainly not eliminate it. In some industries middle managers will disappear, but in all industries their numbers will increase. Their job content will change substantially.
65. Expectations of individuals will increase for self-expression and self-fulfillment in their work. The

role of people in organizations will be dominant rather than subservient.

66. Business firms will be increasingly managed in permissive and democratic ways to meet new market-place challenges as well as demands of employees.

67. Employees will be more mobile, less loyal to an individual employer or company.

68. Some companies will have vice-presidents for education. Some large businesses and universities will give joint courses and degrees.

69. There will be a system of accounting for the human assets in most companies.

70. Business will become much more deeply involved in solving social problems because of (a) identifying major profit-making opportunities, (b) the financial support of government, and (c) assumption of social responsibilities not directly related to profits.

71. By 1985 most large companies will prepare a comprehensive annual audit of their social performance.

72. Rapid changes in communications systems—computers, video tapes, closed circuit television systems—will bring great changes in information systems, advertising, and decision-making methods.

73. There will be a growing use of manager-specialist combinations in the decision-making process.

74. Rapid expansion in the use of computers will continue.

75. The tools for managerial decision-making will be expanded and sharpened, but the complexities of the managerial task will, on net balance, increase.

76. Tomorrow's managers will be more flexible and adaptable to change than today's. More managerial decisions will be unstructured than today.

77. There will be major problems at all levels of management because of difficulties in adjustment to rapid change.

78. By 1985 the proportion of women in management ranks will have grown impressively.

79. The relative influence of unions will decline. Nevertheless, union influence will still be very important in economic and political life.

80. Unions will seek and get many new benefits in collective bargaining agreements and these will be considered more of a right than at present.

81. Strikes will decline as a union weapon and voluntary arbitration will spread broadly.

82. Average age of retirement in the last decade of this century will be sixty or less.

83. Corporations will continue to grow in size but concentration of sales and assets in the largest firms will show no appreciable rise.
84. Antitrust cases will be decided less in terms of market structure and more in terms of performance.
85. There will be greater decentralization of operations and dispersion of managerial functions, and business organizations will be more flexible.

H. *Major Social Problems*
86. By 1985, environment pollution problems will continue to be vigorously attacked but not completely solved.
87. By 1985, there will be major city rebuilding, and new cities constructed, but the task will by no means be completed to society's satisfaction.
88. By 1985, major strides will have been made in improving the lives of minority groups.
89. By 1980, there will be an effective floor for income below which no one will fall, and it will be above a liberally derived "poverty level."
90. Racial tensions will diminish with rising affluence and equality of opportunity.
91. While the ratio between technological changes and social organizations and instruments to cope with them will narrow, the gap in 1985 will still be wide and leave the United States, therefore, with major problems. Problems in adjusting to rapid change will create all sorts of tensions for people in all walks of life.

I. *International Economics*
92. American-based multinational companies will continue to grow in sales, profits and number of countries in which each does business.
93. American manufacturers face increasing competition in foreign markets as other industrialized countries improve their productivity relative to the United States.
94. More American-based companies will do business in foreign countries and the total investment will expand.
95. Multinational companies will be increasingly challenged and restricted by host governments and find themselves in conflict with nationalistic goals. Foreign capital investment in American companies will continue to expand. With the growth of affluence in the United States and other developed nations of the world the demands for limited resources will grow. One result will be inflated prices for them. Another will be continuing shortages of raw materials.

This will disrupt economic activity but also provide opportunities for substitutes at lower prices.

96. Higher prices for oil will upset international balance of payments among all nations of the world and cause serious financial strains until the 1980s.

97. Multinational computer systems will grow and enhance the power of multinational corporations over the nation-state. At the same time, however, the systems will bring growing uniformity of business practices around the world.

J. *Military*

98. The United States will likely become involved in limited wars but in no major world-wide conflagration of a classical type, such as World War II or a nuclear war.

99. Aside from aberrations brought by limited wars the military budget will grow absolutely but register a declining proportion of GNP. Manpower costs (including pensions) will consume a growing proportion of the military budget.

100. Military equipment expenditures will continue to be concentrated in a few strategic programs.

---

* These projections were partly accumulated from many sources some of which follow: Gordon and Helmer, 1964; Kahn and Wiener, 1967; General Electric Company, 1969; Drucker, 1969B; Wilson, 1970; Nanus, 1971; Smil, 1972; Bell, 1973.

** The fertility rate reached a high in recent years of 3.8 and has been declining since. The average number of children per woman today is 2.3. Past population projections for the United States have not been very accurate, and this record may be duplicated in the future. These projections can accommodate the relatively modest immigration of current years.

Major Characteristics Outstanding characteristics of our emerging society included in, or derivable from, the list of events and trends in Exhibit 29–1 are as follows:

1. It will be an enormously productive society and provide the means for everyone to have a high level of material goods and services. Poverty will be virtually eliminated by a guaranteed floor income for everyone.

2. More and more national activity will take place outside business and the traditional market economy. The production of public goods and services will increase relative to private production and will be determined by government through its expenditures. More and more activities will be service rather than production oriented. Employment in manufacturing will decline as a share of total employment.

3. Knowledge, education, and learning will be of central importance.

Organizations in which theoretical knowledge is preserved and expanded will become more important innovators in society. A much higher percentage of the population will be getting advanced degrees, and more and more adults will continue their education. It will be a learning society.

4. Public authorities will face more deep and complex problems than ever before in our history. This is so, Daniel Bell observes, because:

> Social issues are more and more intricately related to one another because the impact of any major change is felt quickly throughout the national and even the international system. Individuals and groups, more conscious of these problems as problems, demand action instead of quietly accepting their fate. Because more and more decisions will be made in the political arena than in the market, there will be more open community conflict. The political arena is an open cockpit where decision points are more visible than they are in the impersonal market; different groups will clash more directly as they contend for advantage or seek to resist change in society (Bell, 1967b: 645–46).

5. Business and government will be more closely related and in a much less antagonistic fashion than today. Indeed, the two will cooperate more in the achievement of the public interest.

6. Change will speed up in technology, ideas, and values. It will be more and more but not completely controlled by better public and private planning.

7. It will be an extremely complex society in which great opportunities for and threats to the business institution, and its relationships with society, will increase. As this society and others become more affluent shortages of raw materials will increase around the world. Rising complexities will result in disruptions at vital points which may be very difficult to foresee and correct. On the other hand, a society of affluence and dynamism creates opportunities in new industries, ideas, and ways of doing things.

8. The organization and management of individual business firms, especially large companies, will be considerably different than today. Increasing emphasis will be placed upon individuals in and out of a firm and positive response to societal expectations of business. The concept of accountability reporting to constituencies for all major institutions will grow.

9. Today's major social problems will continuously come under firmer control and resolution.

10. It will be a society which seeks and embodies the characteristics of the "Great Society" dreamed of by President Johnson in his imaginative speech to the graduating class of the University of Michigan, May 22, 1964. "The purpose of protecting the life of our nation and preserving the liberty of our citizens," he said, "is to pursue the happiness of our people." The extent to which we can do this is the measure of the success of our nation. We have in the half century just passed created the most affluent society the world has ever known. He continued, "The challenge . . . is whether we have the wisdom to use that wealth to enrich and elevate our national life—and to advance the quality of American civilization."

The Great Society, he said, "demands an end to poverty and racial injustice," and is "a place where every child can find knowledge to enrich his mind and enlarge his talents." It is also a place of beauty and one which inspires for its inhabitants a desire and hunger for renewed contacts with nature. In this society people will work for the joy of creating something for its own sake. It is a place where all people can lead satisfying and enriching lives, he concluded. In essence, he said that we now have the capability of shaping our lives, and we must do it in such a way as to build for each citizen a richer life of mind and spirit. We have learned to be materially wealthy. Now, we must use the exploits of man's genius to enrich his life.

CONSIDERATIONS ON THE ROAD TO THE NEW SOCIETY

To reach this new society will require the resolution of many thorny problems. On the way there will be great changes in and among our major institutions of which the business corporation is of special interest here. Some observations about the road to the new society follow.

Possible Disasters The above potentialities are rather optimistic. There is no certainty that the American society toward the end of this century will be superaffluent—or even exist. There are distressing possibilities which must not be overlooked. It is so trite, yet so important, to say that man's nuclear weapons can destroy him, although at the moment the prospect of nuclear war seems remote. As other nations of the world acquire nuclear and delivery capability, however, and as potential worldwide political instabilities intensify, the probability of nuclear war may increase. Limited wars will likely occur and may create conditions that alter the politico-socioeconomic patterns of society in such a way as to delay—or even cancel—the arrival of the great prizes of the supersociety. International political and economic forces may put a brake on American movement toward the superculture. Continuing disparity between the rich and poor nations of the world will raise tensions among nations. A collapse of the international monetary system would have a shattering impact on the American economy. The turning of the people of the United States away from foreign political and military involvement could lead to a sort of neo-isolationism that might at first stimulate the economy, but eventually would be harmful.

All these possibilities have varying degrees of probability that will change in ways which cannot now be predicted. The possibilities for disaster must be matters for deep concern and constant vigilance for they, and they alone, can block the creation of the great society of the future.

Institutional Lags A key source of conflict and frustration will continue to be the lag between growing social problems and the ability of our institutions to resolve them. A galloping environmental pace of change is paralleled by a lagging ability of our institutions to adjust to it, and the result is less than suitable resolution of social problems. This force is likely to be very serious unless there is a stepped-up rate of institutional change and increased planning.

Our political institutions were created for a small society which was comparatively simple, and they were designed to check the exercise of central power. In many cities, for example, the distribution of power is scattered among hundreds and even thousands of jurisdictions to avoid power concentration. Now and into the future, of course, complicated problems are demanding solutions which these old institutional arrangements cannot meet satisfactorily. The result is not only exacerbation of the problems, but frustrations which in turn bring new social problems. The answer is not to tear down these institutions and start building anew, as some advocate. History has amply demonstrated that a society which tries this solution winds up either with a dictator or institutions no better and probably worse than those torn down. The answer lies in greater adaptability to change, self-renewal, and planning.

As pointed out previously, there has been imaginative adaptability of old institutions and creation of new ones during the past ten years to meet new demands. But the rate of change has not been fast enough and must be accelerated in the future. For instance, a few regional bodies have been created to handle issues that cut across local political lines. But, technical and economic problems lie in areas that transcend political boundaries. The easy answer is to set up a special authority, but such authorities often take on a semi-autonomous and self-perpetuating status with only indirect, if any, connection with the electorate. This then creates other problems. A river pollution problem, for instance, raises puzzling questions about who is to pay and who is to benefit. An upstream community whose water is clear may be unwilling to join a regional authority to clean up the river, whereas the city at the mouth of the river may be looking for help. The first community is reluctant because it will receive no direct benefits and may have to pay, while the second group will look forward to receiving benefits well over its costs. There is no simple answer to this issue of equating costs and benefits.

John Gardner has repeatedly called for institutions that are self-renewing. He is not advocating abolition of present-day institutions, but their redesign to meet today's problems. Our institutions are subject to instant antiquity, he says, as they confront problems which they cannot easily solve. He complains, and rightly, that we have exceptional skills to accomplish scientific and technical objectives, but that we have learned very little about the art of changing human institutions to serve in a dynamic world. To meet this need will require a renaissance of ingenuity such as that which brought innovations like the Bill of Rights, the land grant colleges, the Federal Reserve System, and the Urban Coalition. One way to stimulate this development, of course, is to bring about a shift in priorities to elevate the importance of achieving institutional redesign. Although this can be done through opinion leaders' eloquence, a massive increase in nontechnical research and development expenditures would also be helpful.

Self-renewing organizations require more than redesign to create new ways of doing things. Behind innovative capability are fundamental values and other skills. For example, there must be capacity to learn from experience and to retain relevant knowledge; an ability to understand how to redesign an organization and when to time the introduction of innovation; and a skill in planning which involves not only past knowledge, sharpened methodology, and adaptiveness, but foresight in perceiving future needs and making proper changes today to meet them.

A force of extraordinary power for good will be comprehensive integrated systems planning. Whereas in the past our strategy was to respond to crises, increasingly it will be necessary that we anticipate them. Planning time horizons in the past were short and must become longer in the future. Over time there has been a tendency for problem-solving to move from local governments to state governments and then to the federal government. This trend will accelerate despite efforts to reverse it. The only reversal, of a sort, will be more enlarged local governmental problem-solving units. Comprehensive long-range planning which integrates the operation of multiple governing units and problems, if perfected, will be a coordinating and directing power of the highest social importance. Developing such a system may be a test of our ability to govern ourselves.

The Great Social and Economic Problems Our great social problems, such as racial discrimination, ghettos, pollution, transportation, energy, inflation, and poverty will not be solved for a long time to come. If our institutions are revitalized, however, and if we plan better, it is to be hoped that they will be managed and gradually decline in severity. But these problems will persist over time and will be significant forces impacting on the whole of society. Coming to grips with them will raise deep, profound, and controversial issues the solutions to which will affect powerfully the interrelationships between business and society. For instance, rising expectations for instant well-being for everyone cannot be reached. Trade-offs are inevitable in developing priorities among social programs, within

social programs themselves, and between social and defense programs. Difficult decisions will be required concerning the extent to
which current costs should be incurred to provide a better quality
of life for the children of the future. Our society is honeycombed
with intricate balances that must be maintained in harmony for the
whole to operate in the greatest public good. Our society, paradoxically, is extremely strong and resilient to shock and strain and
yet it is sensitive to and can disintegrate from internal divisions and
conflict. How these issues will be settled, and the outcome on social
progress or decay, will depend much upon changing social values
and will, in turn, influence social values.

Changing Social Values The impact of shifting social values on
the business-society interrelationship has been a theme running
throughout this book. It is, of course, possible that changing social
values in the next twenty-five years could dramatically influence both
business and society. One cannot look at the list of probable trends
and events in Exhibit 29–1 without sensing bases for strong shifts in
values. In contemplating evolving events, however, one must not
overlook the powerful forces for stability in society. There seems to
exist a consensus about many traditional values upon which this
society has been and is based. Even when the nation was engaged
in a very unpopular war, opinion polls showed that the great majority
of our youth, whose views were thought to be radical, embraced the
fundamental values held generally by society and were optimistic
about the future.

Since then, as noted previously, opinion polls show a strong
stability of basic values. This is likely to be reinforced as the population ages in the future. Forces unleashed by changing social values
will be powerful, but it seems that enough stability exists in society
to channel these pressures into reform rather than revolution. One
problem of the future, of course, will be to ensure that this is really
the actuality.

Economic Strength The extraordinary strength of the American
economic system has been described throughout this book and
needs no further comment here. It is pertinent to note that there is
not now nor does there seem likely to be in the future any counter-
force that will significantly alter for long the forward thrust of this
system. There are, of course, tough problems ahead in combating
inflation, in diverting resources from the private to the public sector,
in absorbing a rising population into meaningful occupations, in
solving the energy problem, and so on. But in the absence of a
shattering blow from outside the country, such as involvement in

a major war, there is every prospect that this system will continue its productivity and bring ever higher per capita material well-being.

There are those who decry this affluence, but it is only as a result of it that we have come to understand that affluence is not enough. As the material well-being of increasing millions of people is provided by this system, the expectation is induced generally that everybody can achieve a satisfying economic life. And the system generates expectations that affluence can bring new values of joy, personal growth, and other characteristics of a quality life to increasing millions.

The American capitalistic system continues to display an inner vigor, adaptiveness, and creativity. Competition is more rigorous than in many past periods. A distinctive and almost unique feature of the system is its remarkable ability to increase wealth on the basis of free and decentralized decisions reached on the open market. While government does set the ground rules for much of the operation of this system and does itself make decisions which directly affect the market mechanism, the great bulk of decision-making is done by individuals undirected except for their own view of their interests. If we manage our affairs properly and are lucky, this system is capable of becoming even more productive and thereby providing a firmer underpinning for resolving outstanding problems in an orderly way in an evolving, stable society. Of all the industrial nations of the world, this one of private capitalism has become closest to the socialist goal of abundance for all classes of people.

Technological Change Economic activity gives rise, of course, to technological change, a matter discussed at length throughout this book. We need not add to this discussion here except to underline the fact that here is a central force affecting all levels of society. Controlling technology to achieve as much of our social goals as possible will raise many puzzling issues in the future.

The Public v. The Private Sector A current trend which I think will continue is the shift in government from operational programming to a role of goal-setting, policy-making, funding, stimulating, and measuring performance. As demands increase in government's policy-setting role and difficulties mount in its effective operation of activities, the shift will gain speed. This movement obviously has many significant implications for business.

Along with this force is another of equal importance, namely, government's influence in increasing the production of goods and services for the public sector as contrasted with the production of goods and services for the private sector. The trend toward diverting production to the public sector will continue. Maintaining a proper balance between the two is a high challenge for the years ahead.

Controlled Growth One theme running through this book is that economic growth per se is no longer a sufficient over-all end sought by this society. Unrestrained economic growth has certain side effects which society wants reduced or eliminated. Furthermore, it is becoming clear to more people that a certain amount of control over growth, coupled with advance planning, not only is required to prevent catastrophic disasters but is essential to achieving in a minimum of time the major goals of society concerned with the quality of life. This spells increasing government intervention in the market economy.

Education and Knowledge Increased knowledge, together with rising affluence, undoubtedly will influence men's attitudes toward work and leisure. The knowledge industry, as mentioned before, is a growing market for business products and services. One result may be an even more accelerating technology. The point needs no further elaboration that the pursuit of education and the accumulation of knowledge are forces of untold potential impact on business and society.

Assumption of Social Responsibilities by Business The shift from narrow short-range to enlightened long-range self-interest in business decision-making will continue and will reflect more social consciousness. More businessmen will find that the assumption of social responsibilities can be profitable in both the short and long run. Many forces pushing in this direction have been identified in this book, and they are likely to become more powerful motivators in the future.

The assumption of social responsibilities by business can have profound implications for business-society relationships. For one thing, business action may lessen the motivation for government to act to the disadvantage of business. Attacks on business by groups in society might lessen. Business can make a huge contribution to the resolution of social problems which in turn can strengthen and stabilize society. There is no end to the good that business assumption of social responsibilities can bring, so long as there is no erosion of the profit motive.

It is not likely that in the next decade or two the profit motive will be eroded, and businesses will continue to be fundamentally economic institutions having some political and social characteristics. If so, business can be a powerful force economically as well as socially, and the two forces can strengthen one another.

Dispersal of Power There is a current groundswell of demand by more and more people and groups to participate in the decision-making processes that govern events affecting them. The result will be a relative decline in the power of business in decision-making processes in those areas where business has traditionally concentrated its influence. There are vast areas of activity in society where business has not been particularly involved in the past and where, if it exerts itself in the future, it will increase its opportunity to participate in the development of society. The area about which I speak is more in the social than in the economic domain, such as concern for human values within and without business. But even in the economic realm, business may contribute significantly to the development of society with an enlightened, as compared with an austere selfish, explanation to society of how business operates and why it is of such central importance to the kind of society most of us want.

The Moon and Earth The thrilling Apollo 11 flight that took the first man to the surface of the moon threw into sharp contrast America's amazing technological capability and its stubborn, massive socioeconomic-political problems. After that first step on the moon, the question has been repeatedly asked: If we can land a man on the moon and return him to earth, why is it that we cannot solve our pressing problems here on earth?

This is a difficult question to answer, but any answer must recognize the differences between the two types of problems. Getting to the moon—despite the cost of $25 billion, spread over ten years, and the involvement of thousands of men, businesses, and government agencies—was a relatively simple matter compared with solving major social problems. The goal was clear-cut, and when achieved had no immediate and direct impact on the lives of individuals in terms of their status quo, relationships with others, power, and so on. Getting to the moon directly involved a comparatively few brave men and the application of more or less immutable laws of physics, chemistry, and astronomy. The atoms and electrons which were manipulated were quiet, docile, and did what they were told. There were no atoms that said one thing and did another, that had one social point of view which differed from others, or that had one color as compared with others. In contrast, the major problems of society are much more complex because people are involved. To achieve social goals, peoples' lives are changed in direct and uncertain ways. These changes are difficult to accomplish because, as Bengelsdorf (1969) says, "from birth, people . . . come overlaid with traditional prejudices, encrusted with hoary cultures, and swaddled in ancient customs. And these are hard to change."

Will the Challenge Be Met? There is little doubt in my mind that the evolving society will be one in which the difficulties standing in the way of social problem-solving will be of a radically different dimension than those of the past. It will be a more fragile society, more susceptive to hostile polarizations of major and minor groups, more complex, and with a wider gulf between technical capability and social expectations. Solutions will not be ready-made. But this should not lead to despair. The Apollo 11 flight demonstrated dramatically what can be done when clear-cut goals are established and there is determination to achieve them. Its technical solutions may have limited applicability to socioeconomic problems, but its managerial techniques and spirit should have high transferability. The project demonstrated how vast resources, many people, and many different public and private organizations can work harmoniously to accomplish complex tasks (Alexander, 1969).

I agree, however, that although the lessons of Apollo 11 in teaching us how to manage great undertakings are important, organizational solutions to social problems demand much more. Fortunately, we have powerful mechanisms to deal with these problems. At the top of the list is the fantastic productivity of our economic machine, whose strength in helping to solve social problems should never be underestimated. The solution to socioeconomic-political problems is always easier under circumstances of increasing per capita wealth. Although John Gardner's warnings about the adaptability of our institutions must be taken seriously, it must also be recalled that in the past our institutions have adapted to changing demands and continue to do so today. In the past, our society, has shown timely imagination, skill, and flexibility in changing its institutions and creating new ones to meet new needs. Public corporations, regional compacts and authorities, nonprofit organizations, public-private coalitions, and large intergovernmental cooperative programs are cases in point. Furthermore, the federal government has demonstrated remarkable skill in planning when there was a consensus about goals and priorities. Unfortunately, this has not happened often enough.

In the past, generally, reforms and solutions have come only after a problem has become quite serious. We have not won high marks in adapting old and creating new institutions to meet anticipated problems. In appraising the future, we must not mistake caution and delay for paralysis. In the future, as contrasted with the past, however, we cannot afford to let major problems fester without treatment. An urgent task for the future is to define our highest objectives, to settle upon the priorities for them, and to make the necessary commitments to achieve them. We know a great deal about how to do this, but we need to know more. We also know much about the planning processes required to achieve desired results, but we need to know more. And this knowledge must be matched with new innovations in the means for achieving our goals.

All things considered, I cast my lot with those who are cautiously optimistic that we shall deal with the tough problems in our socioeconomic-political systems in a way which will facilitate transition into the new advanced society and which will produce an equitable distribution of its benefits. There will be, of course, agonizing delays in changing our ways as entrenched groups jockey for position and problems defy known solutions. In the end, however, and in the absence of wars having high levels of violence, the present expectations of the evolving society should become actualities. Only the timing is in doubt.

ALTERNATIVE FUTURES

The future which has just been discussed seems to me to be the most probable among all those which can be conceived for the next twenty to thirty years. A few others which are possible during this period and beyond are briefly discussed here. What is presented here is but a thumbnail sketch of some basic characteristics of what one might envision in the identified futures. There is no consensus among "futurists" about their nature, timing, or probability of happening. (For details see Kahn and Bruce-Briggs, 1972; Madden, 1972; Meadows, 1972; Linstone, 1972; Kahn and Weiner, 1967.)

Status Quo One possibility is that we will struggle along as we are today, doing the same things in the same old ways. In this scenario government will more often follow than lead and generally will be inept in foreseeing problems as well as in managing them. Our basic institutions, aside from government, will operate as of now with only grudging incremental changes made under great pressure. Dissident elements will be alternately accommodated and restrained. Underlying racial tensions in society will continue. The disparity between individual incomes will continue if not expand. Business will resist undertaking new social obligations except as token measures to appease pressure groups. Major social problems will be relieved slowly. Massive societal efforts to correct problems will be taken only when major crises strike. In an unstable world environment military expenditures will be high relative to welfare expenditures. Proponents of slowing down growth may succeed in reducing the rate of economic growth.

The Corporate State Rising internal disorders might lead powerful groups in society to band together for their own protection and the preservation of a society they wish. In different ways this is what happened in Nazi Germany under Adolph Hitler and in Italy under Benito Mussolini during the 1930s. The result was a fascist state in which, at first, powerful business groups, labor unions, and other power centers cooperated in controlling the state. In each case the political arm eventually tightly controlled the economy.

There are many different possible types of corporate states. The type of monolithic business-government structure which Galbraith says exists now in the United States would be one type (1967). Madden thinks that the current Japanese order is an adaptation of the corporate state (1972: 105). In Japan there is a type of coordination among top business, government, and financial leaders that links their efforts in forging basic economic policy for the nation. Problems of United States companies in competing in international trade with companies closely associated with and supported by government conceivably could lead to some sort of consortium among powerful business, labor, and other groups, with government to counteract conceived international competitive disadvantages.

Bucolic Nirvana At the other extreme is a possibility that Reich (1970) could be right and that someday a radically different mood in this country could lead to a rejection of current institutions and create a world in which each individual could thrive and be free to do what he chose to fulfill his desires. Linstone (1972) describes the scenario as follows. There is a belief that the "system" and its institutions are unworkable and should be reconstructed. There is a drive to eliminate obsolete institutions and rewrite the Constitution. There is emphasis on experimentation involving new social arrangements and groupings and an encouragement of diversity. Decision-making is decentralized and increased autonomy is given to regional and local bodies. There is a massive decline in funding of federal programs such as national security and retaliatory space systems. Financial control shifts from federal to regional and local organizations. The influence of business and the military declines sharply.

Authoritarianism Both the corporate state and the state of bucolic nirvana could lead to authoritarianism. As Madden so nicely puts it: "The danger of cooperative planning is that conventional wisdom would lead the march to the sea, but the march would proceed in orderly, disciplined ranks. The romantic revolution threatens a decline in the machinery of the economy out of sheer indifference which, to follow the metaphor, is no less a march to the sea, but one that proceeds in permissive and meandering ways" (1972: 106). Authoritarian rule can come also, of course, out of disasters such as wars, internal upheavals, revolutions, or the rise of powerful leaders.

Major failures in existing societies generally lead to authoritarianism. Both Napoleon and Hitler, in two different worlds, were responses to deeply serious internal problems. Madden describes two different scenarios (1972: 106–107).

Authoritarianism of the "right" is as follows:

reactionary, inflexible regime based on military and populist, fundamental support;

intolerance toward, and suppression of, minorities;

use of communist or other threats to motivate and unite the population;

aggressive foreign policy;

harsh policy of law and order;

control of mass media and universities; and

rigidly authoritarian planning to capture the economy.

Authoritarianism from the "left" is an old story of how disciplined revolutionaries have captured control of romantic revolutionary movements. Madden describes it as follows:

seizure of coalition government of the "left" by disciplined revolutionaries;

temporary adaptation of the regime to liberalizing elements;

with consolidation of power, a gradual liquidation of liberalizing elements;

takeover by the state of ownership and/or control of industry, banking, communications, and universities;

interpretation of political criticism as "reaction" punishable by imprisonment; and

alliance with communist regimes.

Socialism Another possibility is that society will accept Galbraith's advice to nationalize industry and public welfare institutions. He asserts that there is a socialist imperative that powerful monopolistic businesses be nationalized to prevent their exploitation of the public. Also, there are certain industries that cannot function effectively in the market system, such as those that provide shelter, health services and local transportation of people. These, too, should be nationalized, he says. He says that weapons makers also should be nationalized. Galbraith's basic presumption is that strong companies are uncontrolled and that this leads to unequal development since they grow rapidly. Other industries, which he equates with the needs of the public, grow more slowly than desired. Also, he says, public bureaucracy while less responsive than private monopoly power is not exploitative and thus not malign (1973). Galbraith's facts are incorrect, and the drift today is in the opposite direction from his prescription, but socialism in the sense of nationalized industry cannot be ruled out as a possibility in the distant future.

Doomsday As noted in Chapter 20 there are those who predict that we are headed directly into a situation where the world will collapse under the pressures of overpopulation and overpollution. As noted in that chapter the probabilities of this happening are not high, but exist in sufficient degree to warrant the inclusion of this scenario here.

Concluding Comment These scenarios are not as probable, in my judgment, as the continuation of present forces modified by reform, new ideas, new institutions and ways of doing things. The further out in time one looks, however, the greater is the uncertainty. Civilizations have risen and fallen as Toynbee so painstakingly has told us (1947). For the next twenty-five years, however, it is difficult to see a massive civilization change in the United States.

CONCLUDING OBSERVATIONS

It seems fitting to conclude with a general comment on the current and evolving world in light of the diametrically opposed views which exist about whether it is going to heaven or hell. Thomas Macaulay more than a century ago presented a view that has applicability to today's world. He said, "Those who compare the age in which their lot has fallen with a golden age which exists only in imagination, may talk of degeneracy and decay; but no man who is correctly informed as to the past will be disposed to take a morose or desponding view of the present." There are many who seek instant solutions to current problems and speak of the sickness of society when they are not found. A different perspective says that in recent years this society has corrected grave problems, has healed festering sores, and has massively alleviated widespread economic hardship. The same mechanisms that achieved these results, stimulated by new incentives, freshened with new institutional interrelationships, and operated on the basis of imaginative planning, can continue the social healing processes needed in the future.

In contemplating our present problems and future course a perspective on the human scale of progress may be comforting. The apes, after 2.5 million generations, lived much like their earliest ancestors. Then came man. In contrast, man accumulated his learning in 3 percent as many generations as the apes since modern man was born some 80 thousand generations ago. But almost all that we know today was discovered in the most recent ½ percent of these generations. Agriculture was invented 500 generations ago. Recorded history began 200 generations ago. The Golden Age of Greece existed 100 generations ago. Our entire scientific era is only 20 generations

old. Our Declaration of Independence was forged but six generations ago. The era of nuclear power is but one generation old. The
rise of our great socioeconomic problems came literally in the past
handful of years. The awareness of the possibility of universal abundance is only a few years old (Gorney, 1972: 569). We should be im-
patient with inept solutions of our problems but, at the same time,
this time perspective should give confidence in a better world ahead.

The contents of this book reveal current powerful forces which
will continue into the future. Some of these forces are disruptive,
some generate almost insoluble problems, and some are barriers to
rational decision-making. There are others which improve man's
ability to govern himself and to correct, or at least manage, his problems. There are some that make for evolutionary rather than revolutionary social change, and there are some that produce an improved
quality of life for growing numbers of people. While it is not now
clear whether the positive underlying forces will produce a society
that will really lead to a condition which satisfies in fuller measure
the human desires of all of our people, they can do so. My vote is
that they will, but the timing will not be as rapid as society demands
nor as quick as more rational thinking could make possible. But
when has man been consistently rational?

In the future, as in the past, the relationships between business
and society will continue to be strategic determinants of what happens in each area. Like a kaleidoscope, the patterns will be ever-
changing. They can be favorable for all mankind.

Bibliography

Aaker, David A., and George S. Day. "Corporate Responses to Consumerism Pressures," *Harvard Business Review*, November–December 1972.

Abramovitz, Moses. "Resources and Output Trends in the U.S. Since 1870," *American Economic Review*, May 1956.

Abrams, Charles. *The City is the Frontier.* New York: Harper & Row, 1965.

Abt, Clark. "Managing to Save Money While Doing Good," *Innovation*, January 1972(A).

———. "Social Audits—The State of the Art." Presented at Conference on Corporate Social Responsibility. New York. October 1972(B).

Ackerman, Robert W. "How Companies Respond to Social Demands," *Harvard Business Review*, July–August 1973.

Ackley, Gardner. *Stemming World Inflation.* Paris: The Atlantic Institute, 1971.

Adams, Walter. "The Military-Industrial Complex and the New Industrial State," *American Economic Review*, March 1968.

———, and Horace Gray. *Monopoly in America: The Government as Promotor.* New York: Macmillan, 1955.

Addeystone Pipe and Steel Co., United States v., 85 Fed. 271 (1899).

Adizes, Ichak. *Industrial Democracy: Yugoslav Style.* New York: Free Press, 1971.

———, and J. Fred Weston. "Comparative Models of Social Responsibility," *Academy of Management Journal,* January 1973.

AFL-CIO. *Needed: A Constructive Foreign Trade Policy.* Washington, D.C.: Industrial Union Department, AFL-CIO, October 1971.

Aharoni, Yair. "On the Definition of a Multinational Corporation," *Quarterly Review of Economics and Business,* Autumn 1971.

Ahlbrandt, Roger S. "For Whom the Steel Bell Tolls." Speech before the

Steel Industry Economics Seminar, Wayne State University. Detroit, Michigan, April 12, 1972.

Alexander, Tom. "The Unexpected Payoff of Project Apollo," *Fortune*, July 1969.

Alfange, Dean. *The Supreme Court and the National Will*. New York: Doubleday, 1937.

Aluminum Co. of America, United States v., 148 Fed. 2d 416 (1945).

American Banana Co. v. United Fruit Co., 213 U.S. 347, 355 (1909).

American Can Co., United States v., 230 Fed. 859 (1916).

American Institute of Certified Public Accountants. *Social Measurement*. New York: American Institute of Certified Public Accountants, Inc., 1972.

American Tobacco Co., United States v., 211 U.S. 106 (1911).

American Tobacco Co., et al., United States v., 328 U.S. 781 (1946).

Anderson, Rolph E., and Marvin A. Jolson. "Consumer Expectations and the Communications Gap," *Business Horizons*, April 1973.

Andrews, Kenneth R. *The Concept of Corporate Strategy*. Homewood, Illinois: Dow Jones-Irwin, Inc., 1971.

Anshen, Melvin. "Changing the Social Contract: A Role for Business," *Columbia Journal of World Business*, November–December, 1970.

Ansoff, H. Igor, et al. "Does Planning Pay? The Effect of Planning on Success of Acquisitions in American Firms," *Long-Range Planning*, December 1970.

Appalachian Coals, Inc., United States v., 288 U.S. 344 (1933).

A. P. Smith Manufacturing Company v. Barlow, et al., 26 N.J. Super. 106 (1953), 98 Atl. (2d) 581, 346 U.S. 861 (1953).

Arrow-Hart & Hegeman Electric Co. v. FTC, 291 U.S. 587.

Arts Management. "Company Hires Culture Head, Nation's First," November–December 1972.

Austin, Robert W. "Responsibility for Social Change," *Harvard Business Review*, July–August 1965.

Baier, Kurt, and Nicholas Rescher (eds.). *Values and the Future*. New York: Free Press, 1969.

Bailey, Stephen Kemp. *Congress Makes a Law*. New York: Columbia University Press, 1950.

Bain, J. S. "Relation of Profit Rate to Industry Concentration: American Manufacturing," *Quarterly Journal of Economics*, August 1951.

Ball, George W. "Japan and the World Trading System," *The Conference Board Record*, January 1972.

Banfield, Edward C. *The Unheavenly City: The Nature and Future of Our Urban Crisis*. Boston: Little, Brown & Co., 1970.

Bangs, John R., and Frank A. Fraser. "The Impact of the Courts on Arbitration and the Right to Manage," *California Management Review*, Summer 1963.

BankAmerica Corporation, "Bank of America's Standards for Top Executives," undated.

Barber, Richard. *The American Corporation: The Power, Its Money, Its Politics*. New York: Dutton, 1970.

Barkley, Paul W., and David W. Seckler. *Economic Growth and the Environmental Decay.* New York: Harcourt, 1972.

Barnard, Chester I. "Elementary Conditions of Business Morals," *California Management Review,* Fall 1958.

Bartels, Robert (ed.), *Ethics in Business.* Columbus: Bureau of Business Research, College of Commerce and Administration, Ohio State University, 1963.

Bartimole, Roldo. "Keeping the Lid on: Corporate Responsibility in Cleveland," *Business and Society Review/Innovation,* Spring 1973.

Bauer, Raymond A. *Second-order Consequences: A Methodological Essay on the Impact of Technology.* Cambridge, Mass.: M.I.T. Press, 1969.

────── and Dan H. Fenn, Jr. *The Corporate Social Audit.* New York: Social Science Frontiers Series, Russell Sage Foundation, 1972.

────── and Stephen A. Greyser. *Advertising in America: The Consumer View.* Boston: Division of Research, Graduate School of Business, Harvard University, 1968.

Baumhart, Raymond. *Ethics in Business.* New York: Holt, Rinehart and Winston, 1968.

──────. "How Ethical Are Businessmen?" *Harvard Business Review,* July–August, 1961.

Baumol, William J., Rensis Likert, Henry C. Wallich, and John J. McGowan. *A New Rationale for Corporate Social Policy.* New York: Committee for Economic Development, 1970.

────── and William G. Bowen. *Performing Arts—The Economic Dilemma.* New York: Twentieth Century Fund, 1965.

Beard, Miriam. *A History of Business,* 2 vols. Ann Arbor: Ann Arbor Paperbacks, University of Michigan Press, 1962; first printing, 1938.

Beckwith, Burnham P. "The Predicament of Man: A Reply," *The Futurist,* April 1972.

Behrman, Jack N. *Some Patterns in the Rise of the Multinational Enterprise.* Chapel Hill, N.C.: Graduate School of Business, University of North Carolina, 1969.

──────. *U.S. International Business and Governments.* New York: McGraw-Hill, 1971.

Bell, Daniel. "The Corporation and Society in the 1970's," *The Public Interest,* Summer 1971.

──────. "Notes on the Post-industrial Society," *The Public Interest,* Winter and Spring, 1967.

──────. "The Year 2000—The Trajectory of an Idea," *Daedalus,* Summer 1967.

Bell, J. Fred. *A History of Economic Thought.* New York: Ronald Press, 1967.

Bell Report. *Toward a Social Report.* U.S. Department of Health, Education, and Welfare. Washington, D.C.: U.S. Government Printing Office, 1969.

Bengelsdorf, Irving S. "After Apollo, Why Can't We Solve the Other Problems?" *Los Angeles Times,* July 24, 1969.

Benham, Thomas W. "Trends in Public Attitudes Toward Business and the Free Enterprise System." Presented at the White House Conference on the Industrial World Ahead. Washington, D.C., March 1972.

Bennis, Warren G. *Changing Organizations.* New York: McGraw-Hill, 1966.

————, and Philip E. Slater. *The Temporary Society.* New York: Harper & Row, 1968.

Berg, Ivar. *The Business of America.* New York: Harcourt, 1968.

Berle, Adolf A., Jr. *The American Economic Republic.* New York: Harcourt, 1963.

————. *Power Without Property.* New York: Harcourt, 1959.

————. "Second Edition/Corporate Power," *The Center Magazine,* January 1969.

————. *The 20th Century Capitalist Revolution.* New York: Harcourt, 1954.

————, and Gardiner C. Means. *The Modern Corporation and Private Property.* New York: Macmillan, 1932.

Bernstein, Irving. "The Growth of American Unions, 1945–1960," *Labor History,* Spring 1961.

————. "Labor's Power in American Society," *California Management Review,* Spring 1962.

Bernstein, Marver H. *The Job of the Federal Executive.* Washington, D.C.: Brookings Institution, 1958.

————, (ed.). *The Government as Regulator. The Annals of the American Academy of Political and Social Science.* March 1972.

Berry, Leonard L. "Marketing Challenges in the Age of People," *MSU Business Topics,* Winter 1972.

Blair, John M. *Economic Concentration: Structure, Behavior and Public Policy.* New York: Harcourt, 1973.

Bleichen, Gerhard D. "The Social Equation in Corporate Responsibility," Speech made at the Boston University Law School Centennial, 1972.

Blodgett, Timothy B. "Showdown on 'Business Bluffing,' " *Harvard Business Review,* May–June 1968.

Blough, Roger. *Free Man and the Corporation.* New York: McGraw-Hill, 1959.

Blum, Fred H. "Social Audit of the Enterprise," *Harvard Business Review,* March–April, 1958.

Blum, Milton L., John B. Stewart, and Edward W. Wheatley, "The New Corporate Approach to Consumer Affairs." Paper presented at the Program for the Study of Consumer Affairs, University of Miami, 1972.

Bock, Betty. *Antitrust Issues in Conglomerate Acquisitions.* Studies in Business Economics, No. 110. New York: National Industrial Conference Board, 1969.

————. *Concentration, Oligopoly, and Profit: Concepts vs. Data.* New York: National Industrial Conference Board, 1972(A).

————. *Mergers and Markets.* Studies in Business Economics, No. 93. New York: National Industrial Conference Board, 1966.

————. *Statistical Games and the '200' Largest Industrials: 1954 and 1968.* New York: National Industrial Conference Board, Inc., 1970.

————. "The Conglomerate and the Hippogriff," *The Conference Board Record.* February 1972(B).

————, and Jack Farkas. *Concentration and Productivity.* Studies in Business Economics, No. 103. New York: National Industrial Conference Board, 1969.

————, and Jack Farkas. *Relative Growth of the "Largest" Manufacturing*

Corporations, 1947–1971. New York: National Industrial Conference Board, 1973.

Boulding, Kenneth E. *Principles of Economic Policy.* Englewood Cliffs, N.J.: Prentice-Hall, 1958.

Bowen, Howard R. *Social Responsibilities of the Businessman.* New York: Harper & Brothers, 1953.

Bowen, William. "Auto Safety Needs a New Road Map," *Fortune,* April 1972.

Bower, Joseph L. "Planning Within the Firm," *The American Economic Review,* May 1970.

Bradt, William R. *Current Trends in Public Affairs.* New York: National Industrial Conference Board, 1972.

————. *Organizing for Effective Public Affairs.* New York: National Industrial Conference Board, 1969.

Branch, Melville C. "Delusions and Diffusions of City Planning in the United States," *Management Science,* August 1970.

Brandeis, Louis. *Other People's Money.* Princeton, N.J.: 1932.

Brayman, Harold. *Corporate Management in a World of Politics.* New York: McGraw-Hill, 1967.

Bridges, Hal. "The Robber Baron Concept in American History," *The Business History Review,* Spring 1958.

Brown, James K., and Seymour Lusterman. *Business and the Development of Ghetto Enterprise.* New York: National Industrial Conference Board, 1971.

Brown, Lester R. "An Overview of World Trends," *The Futurist,* December 1972.

Brown, R. Gene. "Ethical and Other Problems in Publishing Financial Forecasts," *Financial Analysts Journal,* March–April 1972.

Brown Shoe Co., United States v., (US S Ct. 1962) 1962 Trade Cases, Par. 70,366.

Browne, M. Neil, and Paul F. Haas. "Social Responsibility and Market Performance," *MSU Business Topics,* Autumn 1971.

Brozen, Yale. "The Antitrust Task Force Deconcentration Recommendation," *The Journal of Law and Economics,* October 1970.

————. "Bain's Concentration and Rates of Return Revisited," *The Journal of Law and Economics,* October 1971(A).

————. "Concentration and Structural and Market Disequilibrium," *Antitrust Bulletin,* Summer 1971(B).

Brunk, Max E. "Consumerism and You," *Foundation For American Agriculture,* 1971.

Burack, Elmer H., F. James Staszak, and Gopal C. Pati. "An Organizational Analysis of Manpower Issues in Employing the Disadvantaged," *Academy of Management Journal,* September 1972.

Burck, Charles G. "Let's Take a New Look at Automobile Pollution," *Fortune,* June 1973.

Burck, Gilbert. "DuPont 'Gave Away' Billions—and Prospered," *Fortune,* January 1973.

Bureau of the Census. *Minority-Owned Businesses: 1969.* Washington, D.C.: U.S. Government Printing Office, 1971.

Burnham, James. *The Managerial Revolution.* New York: John Day Co., 1941.

Business and Society Review/Innovation. "A Who's Who of Corporate Responsibility Action Groups," Winter 1972–73.

Business International Corporation. *International Investment and Trade Study.* New York: Business International Corporation, 1971.

Business Week. "Congress Gears up to Assess Technology." January 13, 1973(A).

———. "Crash Program That is Changing Detroit." February 27, 1971(A).

———. "Dow Cleans Up Pollution at No Net Cost." January 1, 1972.

———. "Meet Ralph Nader's Most Outspoken Critic." July 24, 1971(B).

———. "Multinationals: Congress Has Second Thoughts on OPIC." March 24, 1973(B).

———. "Multinationals: The Public Gives Them Low Marks." June 9, 1973(C).

———. "What You Will Pay For Safer Cars of Future." March 8, 1971(C).

Butcher, Bernard. "The Program Management Approach to the Corporate Social Audit." Paper presented at conference on "Corporate Social Policy in a Dynamic Society," University of California, Berkeley. November 9–11, 1972.

Butler, William F., Chairman. *Annual Report of the Council of Economic Advisers,* New York, 1972.

Cabinet Committee on Price Stability, *Studies by the Staff of the Cabinet Committee on Price Stability.* Washington, D.C.: U.S. Government Printing Office, 1969.

Carmichael, D. R. "Reporting on Forecasts: A. U.K. Perspective," *The Journal of Accountancy,* January 1973.

Carr, Albert Z. "Is Business Bluffing Ethical," *Harvard Business Review,* January–February 1968.

Carruth, Eleanore. "The 'Legal Explosion' Has Left Business Shell-Shocked," *Fortune,* April 1973.

Carson, Rachel. *Silent Spring.* Greenwich, Conn.: Fawcett, 1967 (paperback); first published by Houghton Mifflin, 1962.

Case, Frederick E. "Housing the Underhoused in the Inner City," *The Journal of Finance,* May 1971.

———. *Inner-City Housing and Private Enterprise.* New York: Praeger, 1972.

Casey, William J. "Responsibilities and Liabilities in Corporate Life," *The Conference Board Record,* February 1972.

Cassell, Frank H. "The Politics of Public-Private Management," *MSU Business Topics,* Summer 1972.

Center for Law and Social Policy. *A Proposal on Corporate Responsibility.* Washington, D.C., 1969.

Chagy, Gideon, (ed.). *Business in the Arts '70.* New York: Erikson, 1970.

———, (ed.). *The State of Arts and Corporate Support.* New York: Erikson, 1971.

Chamberlain, Neil W. *Enterprise and Environment.* New York: McGraw-Hill, 1968.

———. *Private and Public Planning.* New York: McGraw-Hill, 1965.

———, and James W. Kuhn. *Collective Bargaining.* New York: McGraw-Hill, 1965.

Chamber of Commerce of the United States, Council on Trends and Perspective. *The Corporation in Transition*. Washington, D.C.: Chamber of Commerce of the United States, 1973.

Chase Manhattan Bank. *Business in Brief*. April 1972.

Chase Manhattan Corporation. *Annual Meeting of Stockholders*, New York, 1971.

Cheit, Earl F. (ed.). *The Business Establishment*. New York: John Wiley & Sons, 1964.

Cherington, Paul W., and Ralph L. Gillen. *The Business Representative in Washington*. Washington, D.C.: Brookings Institute, 1962.

Cheyney, Edward P. *An Introduction to the Industrial and Social History of England*. New York: Macmillan, 1912.

Christoffel, et al. *Up Against the American Myth*. New York: Holt, Rinehart and Winston, 1970.

Churchman, C. West. *Challenge to Reason*. New York: McGraw-Hill, 1968.

Clapp, Norton. "Corporate Responsibility to the Community," *University of Washington Business Review*, Spring 1968.

Clark, J. M. *Social Control of Business*. New York: McGraw-Hill, 1934.

Clark, John W. *Religion and the Moral Standards of American Businessmen*. Cincinnati: South-Western, 1966.

Clark, Thomas B., and Robert M. Fulmer. "The Limits to the Limits of Growth," *Business Horizons*, June 1973.

Clasen, Earl A. "Marketing Ethics and the Consumer," *Harvard Business Review*, January–February 1967, 79–86.

Clee, Gilbert H. "The Appointment Book of J. Edward Ellis," *Harvard Business Review*, November–December 1962.

Coates, Joseph F. "Technology Assessment: The Benefits . . . the Costs . . . the Consequences," *The Futurist*, December 1971.

Cochran, Thomas C. *Basic History of American Business*. New York: D. Van Nostrand, 1959.

Cohen, Stephen. *Modern Capitalist Planning: The French Model*. Cambridge, Mass.: Harvard University Press, 1969.

Cohn, Jules. "Is Business Meeting the Challenge of Urban Affairs?" *Harvard Business Review*, March–April 1970.

———. *The Conscience of the Corporations*. Baltimore: The Johns Hopkins Press, 1971.

Collins, John W. "Formulating Corporate Social Policy: Consideration of the Effect of Managerial Attitudes." Paper presented at the Thirty-Third Annual Meeting of the Academy of Management, Boston, August 1973.

Columbia Steel Co., United States v., 335 U.S. 495 (1948).

Committee for Economic Development. *An American Program of European Economic Cooperation*. New York: CED, 1948.

———. *Anti-Recession Policy for 1958*. New York: CED, 1958.

———. *Economic Development Assistance, A Long-term Policy for Assisting Economic Growth and Encouraging Independence in the Underdeveloped Nations of the Free World*. New York: CED, 1957.

———. *Economic Policy for American Agriculture*. New York: CED, 1956.

———. *Educating Tomorrow's Managers—The Business Schools and the Business Community*. New York: CED, 1964.

———. *Education in the Ghetto*. New York: CED, 1968.

———. *The Education of Businessmen*. New York: CED, 1960.

————. *The European Common Market and the Balance of Payments Problem.* New York: CED, 1959.

————. *Financing the Nation's Housing Needs.* New York: CED, 1973.

————. *Fiscal and Monetary Policies for Steady Economic Growth.* New York: CED, 1969.

————. *Innovation in Education: New Directions for the American School.* New York: CED, 1968.

————. *Managing a Full Employment Economy.* New York: CED, 1966.

————. *The Public Interest in National Labor Policy.* New York: CED, 1961.

————. *Raising Low Incomes Through Improved Education.* New York: CED, 1965.

————. *Social Responsibilities of Business Corporations,* New York: CED, 1971.

————. *Taxes and the Budget.* New York: CED, 1947.

————. *Toward a Realistic Farm Program.* New York: CED, 1957.

————. *Toward More Production, More Jobs, and More Freedom.* New York: CED, 1946.

————. *Trade Negotiations for a Better Free World Economy.* New York: CED, 1964.

————. *Union Powers and Union Functions: Toward a Better Balance.* New York: CED, 1964.

Committee on Interior and Insular Affairs. *Energy 'Demand' Studies: An Analysis and Appraisal.* U.S. House of Representatives, Ninety-Second Congress. Washington, D.C.: U.S. Government Printing Office, 1972.

Committee on Science and Astronautics, U.S. House of Representatives. *Science & Technology and The Cities.* Washington, D.C.: U.S. Government Printing Office, 1969.

Commoner, Barry. *The Closing Circle.* New York: Alfred Knopf, 1971.

————. *Science and Survival.* New York: Viking Press, 1967.

Continental Can Co., Inc. (Hazel-Atlas Glass Co.), United States v. (DC NY 1964), 1964 Trade Cases, Par. 71,264.

Cook, Paul W., Jr., and George A. von Peterffy. *Problems of Corporate Power.* Homewood, Ill.: Richard D. Irwin, Inc., 1966.

Coppock, R., M. Dierkes, H. Snowball, J. Thomas. "Social Pressure and Business Actions," Paper presented at the Seminar on Corporate Social Accounts. Battelle Seattle Research Center, November 10–11, 1972.

Cordiner, Ralph J. *New Frontiers for Professional Managers.* New York: McGraw-Hill, 1956.

Corson, John J. *Business in the Humane Society.* New York: McGraw-Hill, 1971.

————, and George A. Steiner. *Measuring Business Social Performance: The Corporate Social Audit.* New York: Committee for Economic Development, 1974.

Council for Financial Aid to Education. *Corporate Support of Higher Education.* New York: 1972.

Council of Economic Advisers. *Economic Report of the President.* Washington, D.C.: U.S. Government Printing Office, 1973.

Council on Economic Priorities. *Economic Priorities Report, Environmental Steel,* 1973.

Council on Environmental Quality. *Environmental Quality*. Washington, D.C.: U.S. Government Printing Office, 1970.

————. *Environmental Quality*. Washington, D.C.: U.S. Government Printing Office, 1972.

Cox, Edward F., Robert C. Fellmeth, and John E. Schulz. *The Nader Report On the Federal Trade Commission*. New York: Richard W. Baron, 1969.

Cross, Theodore L. *Black Capitalism*. New York: Atheneum, 1969.

Curtin, Edward R., and James K. Brown. "Labor Relations Today and Tomorrow," *The Conference Board Record*, August 1968.

Daedalus. *Perspectives on Business*. Winter 1969.

————. *Toward the Year 2000: Work in Progress*. Summer 1967.

Dahl, Robert. *Who Governs?* New Haven, Conn.: Yale University Press, 1962.

Dalkey, Norman C., with Daniel L. Rourke, Ralph Lewis, and David Snyder. *Studies in the Quality of Life*. Lexington, Mass.: D. C. Heath, 1972.

————, and O. Helmer. "An Experimental Application of the Delphi Method to the Use of Experts," *Management Science*, April 1963.

Davidson, Mark. "The New History: Can It Free Us From the Past?" *The UCLA Monthly*, November 1971.

Davis, John P. *Corporations*. New York: Capricorn Books, 1961; first printed circa 1897.

Davis, Keith. "Can Business Afford To Ignore Social Responsibilities?" *California Management Review*, Spring 1960.

————, and Robert L. Blomstrom. *Business and Its Environment*. New York: McGraw-Hill, 1966.

Davis, Louis E., and James C. Taylor. *Design of Jobs*. England: Penguin Books, Ltd., 1972.

Day, V. B. "The Social Relevance of Business." Paper presented at the Annual College-Business Symposium, Providence, Rhode Island, December 3, 1969.

de Grazia, Sebastian. *Of Time, Work, and Leisure*. New York: Twentieth Century Fund, 1962.

Demaree, Allan T. "Defense Profits: The Hidden Issues," *Fortune*, August 1969.

Demsetz, Harold. *The Market Concentration Doctrine*. Washington, D.C.: American Enterprise Institute for Public Policy Research, 1973.

De Nevers, Noel. "Enforcing the Clean Air Act of 1970," *Scientific American*, June 1973.

Denison, Edward F. *The Sources of Economic Growth in the United States*. New York: Committee for Economic Development, 1962.

Dennis, Lloyd V. *Community Performance: An Action Report of California Bankers*. San Francisco: California Bankers Association, 1973.

Department of Health, Education and Welfare. *Work in America*. Cambridge, Mass.: M.I.T. Press, 1972.

Destler, Charles McArthur. "Entrepreneurial Leadership Among the 'Robber Barons': A Trial Balance," *Journal of Economic History*, Supplement, 1946.

Dewhurst, J. Frederic, et al. *America's Needs and Resources*. New York: Twentieth Century Fund, 1950.

Dexter, Lewis Anthony. *How Organizations Are Represented in Washington.* Indianapolis and New York: Bobbs-Merrill, 1969.

Demhoff, G. William. *Who Rules America?* Englewood Cliffs, N.J.: Prentice-Hall, 1967.

Donahue, Charles, Jr. "Lawyers, Economists, and the Regulated Industries: Thoughts on Professional Roles Inspired by Some Recent Economic Literature," *Michigan Law Review,* November 1971.

Donner, Frederic G. *The World-Wide Industrial Empire.* New York: McGraw-Hill, 1967.

Douglas Commission. *Urban Housing Needs Through the 1980's: An Analysis and Projection.* National Commission on Urban Problems. Washington, D.C.: U.S. Government Printing Office, 1968.

Downs, Anthony, "Up and Down with Ecology," *The Public Interest,* Summer 1972.

Dreze, Jacques H. "Some Postwar Contributions of French Economists to Theory and Public Policy," *American Economic Review,* June 1964.

Drucker, Peter F. *The Age of Discontinuity: Guidelines to Our Changing Society.* New York: Harper & Row, 1969(A).

———— (ed.). *Preparing Tomorrow's Business Leaders Today.* Englewood Cliffs, N.J.: Prentice-Hall, 1969(B).

Dubin, Robert. *Human Relations in Administration.* Englewood Cliffs, N.J.: Prentice-Hall, 1961.

————. *The World of Work: Industrial Society and Human Relations.* Englewood Cliffs, N.J.: Prentice-Hall, 1958.

Durant, Will and Ariel. *The Lessons of History.* New York: Simon & Schuster, 1968.

Durr, Clifford J. "The Voice of Democracy." Address at the Convention of National Lawyers Guild, Sheraton Hotel, Chicago. February 21, 1948.

Dymsza, William A. *Multinational Business Strategy.* New York: McGraw-Hill, 1972.

E. C. Knight Co., United States v., 156 U.S. 1 (1895).

East, Robert A. "The Business Entrepreneur in Colonial Economy," *The Tasks of Economic History,* Supplement VI. Papers presented at the annual meeting of the Economic History Association. New York: New York University Press, 1946.

Eckert, Ross D. *Airports and Congestion.* Washington, D.C.: American Enterprise Institute for Public Policy Research, 1972.

Economic Priorities Report. *Minding the Corporate Conscience,* January–March 1973.

Edmunds, Stahrl, and John Letey. *Environmental Administration.* New York: McGraw-Hill, 1973.

Edwards, Edgar O. (ed.). *The Nation's Economic Objectives.* Chicago: University of Chicago Press, 1964.

Eells, Richard. "Business for Sale: The Case for Corporate Support of the Arts," in Ivar Berg, (ed.), *The Business of America.* New York: Harcourt, 1968.

————. *Corporate Giving in a Free Society.* New York: Harper & Brothers, 1956.

————. "The Corporate Image in Public Relations," *California Management Review*, Summer 1959, 15–23.

————. *The Corporation and the Arts*. New York: Macmillan, 1967.

————. "Executive Suite and Artist's Garret," *Columbia Journal of World Business*, Fall, 1965.

————. *Global Corporations: The Emerging System of World Economic Power*. New York: Interbook, Incorporated, 1972.

————. *The Government of Corporations*. New York: Free Press, 1962.

————. *The Meaning of Modern Business*. New York: Columbia University Press, 1960.

Ehrlich, Paul R. *The Population Bomb*. New York: Ballantine Books, 1968.

————, and Anne H. Ehrlich. *Population, Resources, Environment*. Freeman, 1970.

Elbing, Alvar O., Jr. and Carol J. *The Value Issue of Business*. New York: McGraw-Hill, 1967.

Elliott-Jones, M. F. "Matrix Methods in Corporate Social Accounting: Some Extensions of Input-Output Economics." Presented at Seminar on Corporate Social Accounts, Battelle Seattle Research Center, November 10–11, 1972.

El Paso Natural Gas Co., United States v., (DC Utah 1965), 1965 Trade Cases, Par. 71,453.

Emergency Committee for American Trade. *The Role of the Multinational Corporation in the United States and World Economies*. New York: Emergency Committee for American Trade, 1972.

Environmental Protection Agency. *The Quality of Life Concept*. Washington, D.C.: Office of Research and Monitoring, Environmental Studies Division, 1973.

Epstein, Edwin M. *The Corporation in American Politics*. Englewood Cliffs, N.J.: Prentice-Hall, 1969.

Erpf, Armand G. "Interface: Business and Society." *Columbia Journal of World Business*, May–June 1967.

Ewing, David. "Who Wants Corporate Democracy?" *Harvard Business Review*, September–October 1971.

Fabricant, S. *Economic Progress and Economic Change*. New York: National Bureau of Economic Research, 1954.

Farmer, Richard N. "The Pros of Black Capitalism," *Business Horizons*, February 1970.

————, and W. Dickerson Hougue. *Corporate Social Responsibility*. Chicago: Science Research Associates, Inc., 1973.

Fayerweather, John. *Facts and Fallacies of International Business*. New York: Holt, Rinehart & Winston, 1962.

Federal Trade Commission. *Conglomerate Merger Performance: An Empirical Analysis of Nine Corporations*. Washington, D.C. National Technical Information Service, U.S. Department of Commerce, November 1972.

————. *Current Trends in Merger Activity, 1968*. Washington, D.C.: FTC, March 1969.

————. *Report to Congress Pursuant to the Federal Cigarette Labeling and Advertising Act*. Washington, D.C.: FTC. June 30, 1968 (mimeographed).

————. *Trade Regulation Rule for the Prevention of Unfair or Deceptive Advertising and Labeling of Cigarettes in Relation to the Health Hazards of Smoking.* Washington, D.C.: FTC, June 22, 1964.

Fellmeth, et al. *The Interstate Commerce Omission.* New York: Grossman Publishers, 1970.

Fenn, Dan H., Jr. "Business and Politics," *Harvard Business Review,* May–June 1959.

Finley, Grace J. *Business and Education: A Fragile Partnership.* New York: National Industrial Conference Board, 1973.

————. *Mayors Evaluate Business Action on Urban Problems.* New York: National Industrial Conference Board, 1968.

Finn, David. *The Corporate Oligarchy.* New York: Simon & Schuster, 1969.

Fisher, John E. "Efficiency in Business and Government," *Quarterly Review of Economics and Business,* August 1962.

Flamholtz, Eric. "Human Resource Accounting: A Review of Theory and Research," *Proceedings of the 32nd Annual Meeting of the Academy of Management,* 1972.

Folsom, Marion B. *Executive Decision Making.* New York: McGraw-Hill, 1962.

Ford Foundation. *Letter,* February 1, 1973.

Ford, Henry, II. *First Quarter Report to Stockholders,* Spring 1972.

Fortune. "A Big Boost for the B. O. P." August 1973.

————. "How Big Does the FTC Want to Be." February, 1972.

————. "What They Believe," A *Fortune*/Yankelovich Survey, January 1969.

————. "Who Needs Earnings Forecasts?" January 1973.

Fowler, Henry H. Remarks Before the U.S. Council of the International Chamber of Commerce, Hotel Pierre, New York. December 8, 1965.

Freeman, A. Myrick, III, and Robert H. Haveman. "Clean Rhetoric and Dirty Water," *The Public Interest,* Summer 1972.

Fretz, C. F., and Joanne Hayman. "Progress for Women—Men Are Still More Equal," *Harvard Business Review,* September–October 1973.

Friedman, Irving S. *Inflation: A World-Wide Disaster.* New York: Houghton Mifflin, 1973.

Friedman, Milton. *Capitalism and Freedom.* Chicago: University of Chicago Press, 1962.

————. "Does Business Have a Social Responsibility?" *Bank Administration,* April 1971.

————. "The Social Responsibility of Business is to Increase Its Profits," *The New York Times Magazine,* September 13, 1970.

Fuchs, Victor R. *The Service Economy.* New York: National Bureau of Economic Research, 1968.

Fullerton, Kemper. "Calvinism and Capitalism," *The Harvard Theological Review,* 1928.

Gaddis, Paul O. *Corporate Accountability.* New York: Harper & Row, 1964.

Gaedeke, Ralph M. "The Movement for Consumer Protection: A Century of Mixed Accomplishments," *University of Washington Business Review,* Spring 1970.

Galbraith, John Kenneth. *The Affluent Society.* Boston: Houghton Mifflin, 1958.

——. *American Capitalism: The Concept of Countervailing Power.* Boston: Houghton Mifflin, 1952.

——. *Economics and the Public Purpose.* Boston: Houghton Mifflin, 1973.

——. "Economics and the Quality of Life," *Science,* July 10, 1964.

——. *The New Industrial State.* Boston: Houghton Mifflin, 1967.

Gallup Poll. *Los Angeles Times,* April 17, 1960.

Gardner, John W. "How 20th Century Man Let His Institutions Go to Pieces: A View from the 23rd Century," *The Futurist,* December 1969.

——. *No Easy Victories.* New York: Harper & Row, 1968.

Garrett, Thomas M. *Business Ethics.* New York: Appleton-Century-Crofts, 1966.

——. Raymond C. Baumhart, Theodore V. Purcell, and Perry Roets. *Cases in Business Ethics.* New York: Appleton-Century-Crofts, 1968.

General Baking Company v. Bakery & Confectionary Workers International Union of America, Local 50 (AFL) 14 LA 83 (1950).

General Electric. *General Electric Investor.* New York: General Electric, Summer 1973.

——. *General Electric's Commitment to Progress In Equal Opportunity and Minority Relations.* New York: General Electric, 1970.

——. *Our Future Business Environment: A Reevaluation.* A Business Environment Working Paper. New York: General Electric, 1969.

——. *Women and Business: Agenda for the Seventies.* New York: General Electric, March 1972.

General Motors Corporation. *Report on Progress In Areas of Public Concern.* Warren, Michigan: GM Technical Center, 1972.

Gerstenberg, Richard C. Remarks at the Institutional Investors Conference, General Motors Technical Center, Warren, Michigan. February 8, 1973.

Gilmore, Frank F. "Strategic Planning's Threat to Small Business." *California Management Review,* Winter 1966.

Ginzberg, Eli (ed.). *Business Leadership and the Negro Crisis.* New York: McGraw-Hill, 1968.

——, and Ivar E. Berg. *Democratic Values and the Rights of Management.* New York: Columbia University Press, 1963.

——, and Alfred E. Eichner. *The Troublesome Presence.* New York: The Free Press and Mentor Books, 1964.

——, Dale L. Hiestand, and Beatrice G. Reubens. *The Pluralistic Economy.* New York: McGraw-Hill, 1965.

Goldman, Marshall I. *The Spoils of Progress: Environmental Pollution in the Soviet Union.* Cambridge, Mass.: The M.I.T. Press, 1972.

Goldston, Eli. *The Quantification of Concern: Some Aspects of Social Accounting.* Pittsburgh: Carnegie-Mellon University, 1971.

Golembiewski, Robert T. *Men, Management, and Morality.* New York: McGraw-Hill, 1965.

Goodyear International Corporation. *Information on the Multinationals.* Akron, Ohio: Goodyear International Corporation, ca. 1972.

Gordon, T. J., and Olaf Helmer. *Report on Long-range Forecasting Study,* P-2982. Santa Monica, Calif.: RAND Corporation, September 1964 (multilithed).

——, and R. E. LeBleu. "Employee Benefits, 1970–1985," *Harvard Business Review,* January–February 1970.

Gorney, Roderic. *The Human Agenda.* New York: Simon and Schuster, 1972.

Graham, Frank, Jr. *Since Silent Spring:* Boston: Houghton Mifflin, 1970.

Graubard, Stephen R., (ed.). "Perspectives on Business," *Daedalus,* Winter 1959.

Green, Harold P. "Technology Assessment and Democracy: Uneasy Bedfellows," *Business and Society,* Spring 1973.

Green, Mark J., Beverly C. Moore, Jr., and Bruce Wasserstein. *The Closed Enterprise System: On Anti-trust Enforcement.* New York: Grossman, 1972.

Green, Robert W. (ed.). *Protestantism and Capitalism: The Weber Thesis and Its Critics.* Boston: D. C. Heath, 1959.

Greenberg, Philip, Steve M. Panzer, and Gary Silverman. "The Expectations of Today's MBAs and the Potential Impact on Business Management," *Special Report,* Graduate School of Business Administration, UCLA, 1969.

Greenewalt, Crawford H. "A Political Role for Business," *California Management Review,* Fall 1959(A).

———. *The Uncommon Man.* New York: McGraw-Hill, 1959(B).

Greenman v. Yuba Power Products, Inc., 377 P. Cal. 2d 897 (1963).

Greenough, William C. "The Power of Institutions: They Can Influence Corporate Role in Society," *New York Times, Business Section,* May 2, 1971.

Greyser, Stephen A. "Business and Politics, 1964," *Harvard Business Review,* September–October 1964.

———. "Business and Politics, 1968," *Harvard Business Review,* November–December 1968.

Griggs v. Duke Power Co., 401 U.S. 424 (1971).

Gross, Bertram M. (ed.). *Action Under Planning: The Guidance of Economic Development.* New York: McGraw-Hill, 1967.

———. "The Great Vista: National Planning Research," *Social Science Information,* June 1965.

Hacker, Louis M. *The Triumph of American Capitalism.* New York: Columbia University Press, 1947.

———. *The World of Andrew Carnegie.* Philadelphia: J. B. Lippincott, 1968.

Hahn, Walter. "Technology Assessment & Corporate Planning," *Planning Review,* June 1973.

Hamilton, Alexander. *Report on Manufactures.* Submitted to the U.S. Congress, 1791. New York: Harper & Row, 1964.

Hamilton, Walton. *The Politics of Industry.* New York: Alfred Knopf, 1957.

Harris, Louis. "The Public Creditability of American Business," *The Conference Board Record,* March 1973.

Hayek, Friedrich A. *The Road to Serfdom.* Chicago: University of Chicago Press, 1944.

Heald, Morrel. *The Social Responsibilities of Business: Company and Community, 1900–1960.* Cleveland: The Press of Case Western Reserve University, 1970.

Hearings Before the Committee on Banking, Housing and Urban Affairs. *Emergency Loan Guarantee Legislation.* United States Senate, Ninety-second Congress, First Session. Washington, D.C.: U.S. Government Printing Office, 1971.

Hearings before the Subcommittee on Monopoly of the Select Committee on Small Business. *Role of Giant Corporations*. Ninety-second Congress, First Session. Parts 1, 2, 3. Washington, D.C.: U.S. Government Printing Office, 1971.

Heermance, Edgar L. *Codes of Ethics: A Handbook*. Burlington, Vt.: Free Press Printing, 1924.

Heilbroner, Robert L., et al. *In the Name of Profit*. New York: Doubleday, 1972.

Henderson, Hazel. "Should Business Tackle Society's Problems?" *Harvard Business Review*, July–August 1968.

Henningsen v. Bloomfield Motors, Inc., 32 N.J. 358, 161 A 2d 69 (1960).

Henry, Harold W. "Environmental Protection Impacts in Major Corporations," College of Business Administration, University of Tennessee, December 1972.

Herzberg, Frederick. "One More Time: How Do You Motivate People?" *Harvard Business Review*, January–February 1968.

Hess, John. "Public Policy as a Function of Perception of Business Ethics," *The Economic and Business Bulletin*, Spring 1968.

Hetherington, J. A. C. "Fact and Legal Theory: Shareholders, Managers, and Corporate Social Responsibility," *Stanford Law Review*, January 1969.

Heyne, Paul T. "The Free-Market System is the Best Guide for Corporate Decisions," *Financial Analysts Journal*, September–October 1971.

———. *Private Keepers of the Public Interest*. New York: McGraw-Hill, 1968.

Hobson, J. A. *Free-thought in the Social Sciences*. London: George Allen & Unwin, 1926.

Hoffenberg, Marvin. "Comments on 'Measuring Progress on Social Goals: Some Possibilities at National and Local Levels'," *Management Science*, August 1970.

Hofstadter, Richard. *Social Darwinism in American Thought*. Boston: Beacon Press, 1955.

Horvath, Janos. "Measuring Conglomerate Concentration: A Proposal." *The Antitrust Bulletin*, Fall 1972.

Houser, Theodore V. *Big Business and Human Values*. New York: McGraw-Hill, 1957.

Humble, John. *Social Responsibility Audit: A Management Tool for Survival*. London: Foundation for Business Responsibilities, 1973.

Hunter, Floyd. *Community Power Structure*. New York: Doubleday, 1963.

Hutchinson, John. *The Imperfect Union*. New York: Dutton, 1970.

———. "Labor and Politics in America," *The Political Quarterly* (London), April–June 1962.

Huxley, Aldous. *Brave New World*. New York: Harper & Row, 1932.

International Harvester Co., United States v., 247 U.S. 643 (1927).

Jacoby, Neil H. *Can Prosperity Be Sustained?* New York: Henry Holt, 1956.

———. "The Conglomerate Corporation," *The Center Magazine*, July 1969.

———. *Corporate Power and Social Responsibility*. New York: Macmillan, 1973.

———. "Impacts of Scientific Change upon Business Management," *California Management Review*, Summer 1962.

————. Speech Before Antitrust Conference, National Industrial Conference Board. March 7, 1974.

————. "What is a Social Problem?" *The Center Magazine*, August 1971.

————, and James E. Howell. *European Economics, East and West*. Cleveland: World Publishing, 1967.

Jaffe, Eugene D. "In Defense of MNC's: Implications of Burke-Hartke," *MSU Business Topics*, Summer 1973.

Janger, Allen R. *Employing the Disadvantaged: A Company Perspective*. New York: National Industrial Conference Board, 1972.

————. "What's Been Learned About Managing the Disadvantaged," *The Conference Board Record*, December 1969.

————, and Ruth G. Shaeffer. *Managing Programs to Employ the Disadvantaged*. Studies in Personnel Policy, No. 219. New York: National Industrial Conference Board, 1970.

Johnson, E. A. J., and Herman E. Krooss. *The Origins and Development of the American Economy*. New York: Prentice-Hall, 1953.

Johnson, Harold L. *Business in Contemporary Society: Framework and Issues*. Belmont, Cal.: Wadsworth Publishing Company, Inc., 1971.

Johnson, Lawrence A. *Employing the Hard-core Unemployed*. New York: American Management Association, 1969.

Joint Economic Committee. *Subsidy and Subsidylike Programs of the U.S. Government*. Eighty-sixth Congress, Second Session. Washington, D.C.: U.S. Government Printing Office, 1960.

Jones, Martin V. "The Methodology of Technology Assessment," *The Futurist*, February 1972.

Josephson, Matthew. *The Politicos, 1865–1896*. New York: Harcourt, 1938.

————. *The Robber Barons*. San Francisco: Harcourt, 1934.

Kahn, Herman, and Anthony J. Wiener. *The Year 2000*. New York: Macmillan, 1967.

————, and B. Bruce-Briggs. *Things to Come*. New York: Macmillan, 1972.

Kapoor, A., and Phillip D. Grubb, (eds.). *The Multinational Enterprise in Transition*. Princeton, N.J.: The Darwin Press, 1972.

Kapp, K. William. *The Social Costs of Private Enterprise*. Cambridge, Mass.: Harvard University, 1950.

Kappel, Frederick R. *Vitality in a Business Enterprise*. New York: McGraw-Hill, 1960.

Keeler, Theodore E. "Airline Regulation and Market Performance," *The Bell Journal of Economics and Management Science*, Autumn 1972.

Kell, Walter G. "The SEC's New Disclosure Rule on Forecasts," *Michigan Business Review*, May 1973.

Kennedy, Robert. "Robert Kennedy on: Government Injustice to Business," *Nation's Business*, June 1967.

Key, V. O. *Politics, Parties and Pressure Groups*. New York: Thomas Y. Crowell, 1958.

Kindleberger, Charles, (ed.). *The International Corporation*. Cambridge, Mass.: The M.I.T. Press, 1970.

Kolko, Gabriel. *Wealth and Power in America*. New York: Praeger, 1962.

Kotter, John Paul. "The Psychological Contract Managing the Joining-Up Process," *California Management Review*, Spring 1973.

Krishnan, Rama. "Business Philosophy and Executive Responsibility," *Academy of Management Journal,* December 1973.

Kristol, Irving. "The New Era of Innovation," *Fortune,* February 1969.

Krooss, Herman E. *American Economic Development.* Englewood Cliffs, N.J.: Prentice-Hall, 1966.

Langer, Susanne K. *Philosophical Sketches: A Study of the Human Mind in Relation to Feeling, Explored Through Art, Language and Symbol.* New York: Mentor Books, 1964.

Larson v. General Motors Corporation, 391F. 2nd 495 (8th Cir. (1968)).

Lave, Lester B., and Eugene P. Seskin. "Air Pollution and Human Health," *Science,* August 21, 1970.

Lawrence, John F. "Tax Could Cut Gas Thirst 15%, Study Finds," *Los Angeles Times,* December 21, 1973.

Lawrence, Robert M., and Norman I. Wengert, (eds.). *The Energy Crisis: Reality or Myth. The Annals,* November 1973.

Learned, Edmund, Arch Dooley, and Robert Katz. "Personal Values and Business Decisions," *Harvard Business Review,* March–April 1959.

Lecht, Leonard A. *Goals, Priorities, and Dollars.* New York: Free Press, 1966.

Leff, Arthur Allen. "The Closed Enterprise System," Quoted in a book review, *New York Times Book Review,* April 30, 1972.

Lerman, Louis. *Michelangelo. A Renaissance Profile.* New York: Alfred A. Knopf, 1942.

Letwin, William. "The Past and Future of the American Businessman," *Daedalus,* Winter 1969.

Levitt, Theodore. "Business Should Stay Out of Politics," *Business Horizons,* Summer 1960.

———. "The Dangers of Social Responsibility," *Harvard Business Review,* September–October 1958.

———. "The Morality (?) of Advertising." *Harvard Business Review,* July–August 1970.

Leys, John Albert. *Ethics for Policy Decisions.* Englewood Cliffs, N.J.: Prentice-Hall, 1952.

Leys, Wayne A. R. "Ethics in American Business and Government: The Confused Issues," *The Annals,* July 1968.

Life, "Change, Yes—Upheaval, No." January 8, 1971.

Likert, Rensis. *New Patterns of Management.* New York: McGraw-Hill, 1961.

Linowes, David F. "Measuring Social Programs in Business," *Social Audit Seminar—Selected Proceedings,* Washington, D.C.: Public Affairs Council, July 1972.

Linstone, Harold A. "Four American Futures: Reflections on the Role of Planning," *Technological Forecasting and Social Change,* 1972.

List, Friedrich. *The National System of Political Economy, 1841.* London, New York: Longmans, Green & Co., 1922.

Longstretch, Bevis and H. David Rosenbloom. *Corporate Social Responsibility and the Institutional Investor.* New York: Praeger, 1973.

Louis, Arthur M. "The View from the Pinnacle: What Business Thinks," *Fortune,* September 1969.

Lovell, Michael, and Edward Prescott. "Money, Multiplier-Accelerator Interaction and the Business Cycle," *Southern Journal of Economics,* July 1968.

Lund, Leonard. "Pollution Abatement Proceeds—Unabated," *The Conference Board Record,* May 1973.

Lundberg, Craig C. "The Golden Rule and Business Management: Quo Vadis?" *Economics and Business Bulletin,* January 1968.

Lundberg, Ferdinand. *The Rich and the Super-Rich.* New York: Bantam, 1968.

MacAvoy, Paul W. (ed.). *The Crisis of the Regulatory Commissions.* New York: W. W. Norton, 1970.

MacEachen, Allan J. *Profiles of Involvement,* Vol. I–III. Philadelphia: Human Resources Corporation, 1972.

MacPherson v. Buick Motor Company, 217 N.Y. 382, 111 N.E. 1050 (1916).

Macrae, Norman. "The Neurotic Trillionaire," *The Economist,* Reproduced in Atlas, 1970.

Madden, Carl H. *Clash of Culture: Management in an Age of Changing Values.* Washington, D.C.: National Planning Association, 1972.

Maddox, John. *The Doomsday Syndrome.* New York: McGraw-Hill, 1972.

Malkiel, Burton G., and Richard E. Quandt. "Moral Issues in Investment Policy," *Harvard Business Review,* March–April 1971.

Malthus, Thomas Robert. *An Essay on the Principle of Population as It Affects the Future Improvement of Society.* London, 1798.

Mann, Dean, and Jameson W. Doig. *The Assistant Secretaries.* Washington, D.C.: Brookings Institution, 1965.

Manne, Henry G. "Shareholder Social Proposals Viewed by an Opponent," *Stanford Law Review,* February 1972.

————. "Who's Responsible? What the Anti-Corporate Zealots are Pushing is Coercion," *Barron's,* May 17, 1971.

Mansfield, Edwin. *The Economics of Technological Change.* New York: W. W. Norton, 1968.

———— (ed.). *Monopoly, Power, and Economic Performance.* New York: W. W. Norton, 1964.

McAdam, Terry. "How to Put Corporate Responsibility Into Practice," *Business and Society Review/Innovation,* Summer 1973.

McArthur, John H., and Bruce R. Scott. *Industrial Planning in France.* Boston: Graduate School of Business Administration, Harvard University, 1969.

McConnell, Grant. *Private Power and American Democracy.* New York: Alfred A. Knopf, 1966.

McCoy, C. B. "How Should Business Respond to its Critics?" Remarks before The Business Council, Hot Springs, Virginia. May 7, 1971.

McGregor, Douglas. *The Human Side of Enterprise.* New York: McGraw-Hill, 1960.

————, Warren G. Bennis, and Caroline McGregor (eds.), *The Professional Manager.* New York: McGraw-Hill, 1967.

McGuire, E. Patrick. "Consumer Product Safety," *The Conference Board Record,* September 1973.

McGuire, Joseph W., and John B. Parrish. "Status Report on A Profound Revolution," *California Management Review,* Summer 1971.

McQuade, Walter. "Mortgages for the Slums," *Fortune,* January 1968.

Marien, Michael. "Herman Kahn's 'Things to Come,' " *The Futurist,* February 1973.

———. "Who Coined 'Post-Industrial Society'?" *The Futurist,* December 1973.

Markhan, J. W. and G. F. Papanek (eds.). *Industrial Organization and Economic Development.* Boston: Houghton Mifflin, 1970.

Marrow, Alfred J. *The Failure of Success.* New York: AMACOM, American Management Association, 1972.

Maslow, A. H. "A Theory of Human Motivation," *The Psychological Review,* July 1943.

Mason, Edward S. (ed.). *The Corporation in Modern Society,* Cambridge, Mass.: Harvard University Press, 1960.

———. "The Current Status of the Monopoly Problems in the United States," *Harvard Law Review,* June 1949.

Mason, Robert Hal, Dale D. Weigel, and Robert R. Miller. *The Economics of International Business.* New York: John Wiley & Sons, 1974.

Massell, B. F. "Capital Formation and Technological Change in United States Manufacturing," *The Review of Economics and Statistics,* May 1960.

Meadows, Dennis, et al. *The Limits to Growth.* New York: Universe Books, 1972.

Means, Gardiner C. *Industrial Prices and Their Relative Inflexibility,* Senate Document 13, Seventy-fourth Congress, First Session, Washington, D.C.: U.S. Government Printing Office, 1935.

Mee, John F. "The Manager of the Future," *Business Horizons,* June 1973.

Melman, Seymour. *Pentagon Capitalism: The Political Economy of War.* New York: McGraw-Hill, 1970.

Mermelstein, David. "Large Industrial Corporations and Asset Shares," *American Economic Review,* September 1969.

Merton, Robert K., Leonard Broom, and Leonard S. Cottrell, Jr. (eds.). *Sociology Today: Problems and Prospects.* New York: Basic Books, 1959.

Mesthene, Emmanuel G. "How Technology Will Shape the Future," Reprint No. 5, *Program on Technology and Society.* Harvard University, 1968.

———. *Technological Change.* Cambridge, Mass.: Harvard University Press, 1970.

Meyers, Harold B. "For Lockheed, Everything's Coming Up Unk-Unks," *Fortune,* August 1969.

Michelman, Irving S. *Business at Bay.* New York: Augustus M. Kelley, 1969.

Miliband, Ralph. *The State in Capitalist Society.* New York: Basic, 1969.

Mill, John Stuart. *Principles of Political Economy.* New York: D. Appleton & Co., 1870.

Miller, Arjay. "New Roles for the Campus and the Corporation," *Michigan Business Review,* November 1966.

Miller, Arthur Selwyn. *The Supreme Court and American Capitalism.* New York: Free Press, 1968.

Millikan, Max F. (ed.). *National Economic Planning: A Conference of the Universities—National Bureau for Economic Research,* New York: Columbia University Press, 1956.

Milutinovich, Jogoslav S. "Comparative Study of Job Satisfaction Under Different Leadership Styles Among Blue-Collar and White-Collar Workers," in M. William Frey (ed.). *New Developments in Management and Organization Theory*. Proceedings of the Eighth Annual Conference, Eastern Academy of Management, May 1971.

Mintz, Morton, and Jerry S. Cohen. *America Inc*. New York: Dial, 1971.

Mintzberg, Henry. *The Nature of Managerial Work*. New York: Harper & Row, 1973.

Mishan, Ezra J. "On Making the Future Safe for Mankind," *The Public Interest*, Summer 1971.

————. *Technology & Growth: The Price We Pay*. New York: Praeger, 1970.

Mitchell, Arnold. "Changing Values," *International Associations*, April 1971.

Mitford, Jessica. *The American Way of Death*. New York: Simon and Schuster, 1963.

Monsen, R. Joseph, Jr. *Modern American Capitalism: Ideologies and Issues*. Boston: Houghton Mifflin, 1963.

————, and Mark W. Cannon. *The Makers of Public Policy*. New York: McGraw-Hill, 1965.

Moore, Thomas Gale. *Freight Transportation Regulation*. Washington, D.C.: American Enterprise Institute for Public Policy Research, 1972.

Moore, Wilbert E. *The Conduct of the Corporation*. New York: Random House, 1962.

Morse, John J. "A Contingency Look at Job Design," *California Management Review*, Fall 1973.

Moss, Frank E. *Initiative in Corporate Responsibility*. Consumer Subcommittee, Committee on Commerce, U.S. Senate, Ninety-second Congress, Second Session. Washington, D.C.: U.S. Government Printing Office, 1972.

Muller, Herbert J. *The Uses of the Past: Profiles of Former Societies*. New York: Oxford University Press, 1957.

Mumford, Lewis. *The Myth of the Machine: The Pentagon of Power*. New York: Harcourt 1970.

Murphy, David Charles. "Decentralization: The Effects of Technology," *Proceedings of the Thirty-Second Annual Meeting of the Academy of Management*. Minneapolis, Minnesota, 1972. (Published 1973.)

Myers, M. Scott. "Overcoming Union Opposition to Job Enrichment," *Harvard Business Review*, May–June 1971.

Nader, Ralph (ed.). *The Consumer and Corporate Accountability*. New York: Harcourt, 1973.

————, and Mark J. Green (eds.), *Corporate Power in America*. New York: Grossman, 1973.

————. *Unsafe at Any Speed*. New York: Pocket Books, 1966.

————, and Kate Blackwell. *You and Your Pension*. New York: Grossman, 1973.

Nanus, Burt. "The World of Work: 1980," *The Futurist*, December 1971.

National Academy of Engineering. *A Study of Technology Assessment*. Report to the Committee on Science and Astronautics, U.S. House of Representatives. Washington, D.C.: U.S. Government Printing Office, 1969.

National Academy of Sciences. *Technology: Processes of Assessment and Choice*. Report of the National Academy of Sciences to Committee on

Science and Astronautics, U.S. House of Representatives. Washington, D.C.: U.S. Government Printing Office, 1969.

National Commission on Product Safety. *Final Report Presented to the President and Congress.* Washington, D.C.: U.S. Government Printing Office, June 1970.

National Goals Research Staff. *Toward Balanced Growth: Quantity and Quality.* Washington, D.C.: U.S. Government Printing Office, 1970.

National Industrial Conference Board. *Antitrust Problems and National Priorities.* New York: NICB, 1972.

————. *Challenge to Leadership: Managing in a Changing World,* New York: Free Press, 1973(A).

————. *Economic Almanac, 1967–68.* New York: Macmillan, 1968(A).

————. *Energy and Public Policy in 1972.* New York: NICB, 1972(A).

————. "Foreign Direct Investment in the United States," *World Perspectives,* NICB, No. 10, August 1973(B).

————. *The Role of Business in Public Affairs.* Studies in Public Affairs, No. 2. New York: NICB, 1968(B).

————. "U.S. Direct Foreign Investments: The Views of Businessmen," *World Perspectives,* NICB, No. 10, August 1972(B).

————. *Women.* New York: NICB, 1973(C).

National Labor Relations Board v. Rapid Bindery. 293 F 2nd 170 (1961).

National Science Board. *Environmental Science: Challenge for the Seventies.* Washington, D.C.: U.S. Superintendent of Documents, 1971.

National Science Foundation. *National Patterns of R&D Resources.* Washington, D.C.: U.S. Government Printing Office, September 1969.

Nation's Business. "Why Cars Are Getting Safer," May 1966.

Nelson, Richard R., Merton J. Peck, and Edward D. Kalachek. *Technology, Economic Growth and Public Policy.* A RAND Corporation and Brookings Institution Study. Washington, D.C.: Brookings Institution, 1967.

Nickels, William G., and Noel B. Zabriskie. "Corporate Responsiveness and the Marketing Correspondence Function," *MSU Business Topics,* Summer 1973.

Nixon, Richard M. *Manpower Report of the President.* Washington, D.C.: U.S. Government Printing Office, 1969.

————. "Special Message to the Congress Concerned With Pollution." February 10, 1970.

————. "Special Message to the Congress on Energy." April 18, 1973(A).

————. *State of the Union Message.* Washington, D.C.: U.S. Government Printing Office, March 1973(B).

————. "The Energy Emergency." An Address to the Nation, November 7, 1973(C).

Nordhaus, William, and James Tobin. "Is Growth Obsolete?" Cowles Foundation Discussion Paper No. 319. New Haven: Yale University, October 7, 1971.

Northern Pacific R. R. Co., United States v., 356 U.S. 1 (1958).

Northern Securities Co., United States v., 193 U.S. 197 (1904).

Nossiter, Bernard. *The Mythmakers.* Boston: Beacon Press, 1964.

Novick, David, (ed.). *Current Practice in Program Budgeting (PPBS).* New York: Crane, Russak, 1973.

————, (ed.). *Program Budgeting.* Cambridge, Mass.: Harvard University Press, 1965.

Nowlan, Stephen E., and Diana Russell Shayon. *Profiles of Involvement.* Philadelphia: Human Resources Corporation, 1972.

Nunn, Henry L. *Partners in Production.* Englewood Cliffs, N.J.: Prentice-Hall, 1962.

O'Connell, J., and Arthur Myers. *Safety Last.* New York: Random House, 1966.

Office of Emergency Preparedness. *The Potential for Energy Conservation.* Washington, D.C.: U.S. Government Printing Office, October 1972.

Office of Minority Business Enterprise. *Progress Report: The Minority Business Enterprise Program, 1972.* Washington, D.C.: U.S. Department of Commerce, October 1972.

————. *Special Catalog of Federal Programs Assisting Minority Enterprise.* Washington, D.C.: U.S. Department of Commerce, Summer 1971.

Ohmann, O. A. "Skyhooks," *Harvard Business Review,* May–June 1955.

Okun, Arthur M. "Policies for Sustaining Prosperity." Speech Before the 1969 Stanford Business Conference, San Francisco, California. February 19, 1969.

Olafson, Frederick A. *Society, Law, and Morality.* Englewood Cliffs, N.J.: Prentice-Hall, 1961.

Organization for Economic Cooperation and Development. *Science Growth and Society: A New Perspective.* Paris: OECD, 1971.

————. Social Indicator Development Programe. *List of Social Concerns Common to Most OECD Countries.* Paris: OECD, Manpower and Social Affairs Directorate, 1973.

Ornstein, Stanley I. "Concentration and Profits," *Journal of Business,* October 1972.

Orwell, George. *1984.* New York: Harcourt, 1949.

Ozbekhan, Hasan, and Gene E. Talbert (eds.). *Business and Government Long-range Planning Impacts, Problems, Opportunities.* Proceedings of of the Eleventh Annual Symposium on Planning, The TIMS College on Planning. Providence, R.I.: Institute of Management Science, 1969.

Pabst Brewing Co., United States v., U.S. S Ct (1966), 1966 Trade Cases, Par. 71,790.

Packard, Vance. *The Hidden Persuaders.* New York: McKay, 1957.

————. *The Waste Makers.* New York: McKay, 1960.

Paramount Pictures, Inc., United States v., 334 U.S. 131 (1948). .

Passell, Peter, and Leonard Ross. *The Retreat from Riches: Affluence and Its Enemies.* New York: Viking Press, 1973.

Patrick, Kenneth G., and Richard Eells. *Education and the Business Dollar.* New York: Macmillan, 1969.

Patterson, James M. "Corporate Behavior and Balance of Power," *Business Horizons,* June 1969.

Penn-Olin Chemical Co., United States v., U.S. S Ct (1967) 1967 Trade Cases, Par. 71,571.

Petersen, Donald J. "The Impact of OSHA on Management—A First Look," *The Conference Board Record,* October 1973.

Peterson, Mary Bennett. *The Regulated Consumer.* Los Angeles: Nash Publishing, 1971.

Petit, Thomas A. *The Moral Crisis in Management.* New York: McGraw-Hill, 1967.

Phatak, Arvind V. *Evolution of World Enterprises.* New York: American Management Association, 1971.

Phelan, James, and Robert Pozen. *The Company State: On DuPont in Delaware.* New York: Grossman, 1972.

Phillips, Charles F., Jr. *The Economics of Regulation.* Homewood, Ill.: Richard D. Irwin, 1969.

Pitofsky, Robert. "The Changing Focus in the Regulation of Advertising," *Concerned Business Students' Report,* May 1973.

Pohlman, Jerry E. *Economics of Wage and Price Controls.* Columbus, Ohio: Grid, Inc., 1972.

Porter, Lyman W. *Organizational Patterns of Managerial Job Attitudes.* New York: American Foundation for Management Research, 1964.

Powell, Reed M., and Dalmas H. Nelson. "Business Executives View the Politician," *Business Horizons,* October 1960.

Prasow, Paul, and Edward Peters. *Arbitration and Collective Bargaining: Conflict Resolution in Labor Relations.* New York: McGraw-Hill, 1970.

Presidential Task Force on Antitrust (Neal Report). *White House Task Force Report on Antitrust Policy.* Reprinted in BNA *Antitrust & Trade Regulation Report,* May 27, 1969.

Presidential Task Force on Appliance Warranties. *Presidential Report of the Task Force on Appliance Warranties and Service.* Washington, D.C.: January 8, 1969 (mimeo).

Presidential Task Force on Productivity (Stigler Report). *Task Force Report on Productivity and Competition.* Reprinted in BNA *Antitrust & Trade Regulation Report,* June 10, 1969.

Presidential Task Force on Science Policy. *Science and Technology: Tools for Progress.* Washington, D.C.: U.S. Government Printing Office, 1970.

President's Advisory Council on Executive Organization. *A New Regulatory Framework: Report on Selected Independent Regulatory Agencies.* Washington, D.C.: U.S. Government Printing Office, January 1971.

President's Commission on National Goals. *Report of the President's Commission on National Goals.* Washington, D.C.: U.S. Government Printing Office, 1960.

Procter & Gamble Co. (The), FTC v. (U.S. S Ct 1967) 1967 *Trade Cases,* Par. 72,061; (FTC opinion and final order 1963) 1963 *Trade Cases,* transfer binder, Par. 16,673.

Purcell, Theodore, S. J. "Work Psychology and Business Values: A Triad Theory of Work Motivation," *Personnel Psychology,* Autumn 1967.

Ramo, Simon. "Economic Policy, National Goals, and Antitrust," *Antitrust Problems and National Priorities.* New York: National Industrial Conference Board, 1972.

———. "Toward a Social-Industrial Complex," *The Wall Street Journal,* February 11, 1972.

Randy Knitwear v. American Cyananid Company, 181 N.E. 2d 402, N.Y. (1962).

Raucher, Alan R. *Public Relations and Business, 1900–1929.* Baltimore, Md.: Johns Hopkins Press, 1968.

Reich, Charles A. *The Greening of America.* New York: Random House, 1970(A).

———. Quoted in *The New York Times,* October 21, 1970(B).

Reiss, Alvin H. *Culture & Company.* New York: Twayne, 1972.

Reynolds Metal Co., FTC v., (U.S. S Ct 1962) 1962 Trade Cases, Par. 70,741.

Richman, Barry M. "The Corporation and the Quality of Life: Part I: Typologies," *Management International,* Vol. 13, 1973.

Riesman, David. *The Lonely Crowd.* New Haven: Yale University Press, 1950.

Roalman, A. R. *Profitable Public Relations.* Homewood, Ill.: Dow Jones-Irwin, 1968.

Roche, James M. "Understanding: The Key to Business-Government Cooperation," *Michigan Business Review,* March 1969.

Roche, John P. "Paper Tiger," *Herald-Examiner,* Los Angeles, July 29, 1969.

Rockefeller, David. Address to the Advertising Council. Reported in *Los Angeles Times,* January 3, 1971.

———. *Creative Management in Banking.* New York: McGraw-Hill, 1964.

Rockefeller, John D., 3rd. *The Second American Revolution.* New York: Harper & Row, 1973.

Rocks, Lawrence and Richard P. Runyon. *The Energy Crisis.* New York: Crown, 1972.

Roosevelt, Theodore. *First Annual Message to the Congress.* December, 1901.

Root, Franklin R. "The Expropriation Experience of American Companies," *Business Horizons,* April 1968.

Rose, Arnold. *The Power Structure.* New York: Oxford University Press, 1967.

Rose, Sanford. "Bigness Is a Numbers Game," *Fortune,* November 1969.

Ross, Irwin. "Labor's Big Push For Protectionism," *Fortune,* March 1973.

Ruckelshaus, William D. "It's Time for Environmental Truth or Consequences," *Public Relations Journal,* May 1973.

Rust, Edward B. "Ralph Nader—Friend of U.S. Capitalism," Speech before a National Insurance Men's Meeting in Chicago. Excerpted in *Los Angeles Times,* September 26, 1973.

Ruttenberg, Stanley H. "Updating the World of Trade," *The American Federationist,* February 1973.

Salant, Walter S., and Beatrice N. Vaccara. *Import Liberalization and Employment.* Washington, D.C.: Brookings Institution, 1961.

Sayles, Leonard R. *Individualism and Big Business.* New York: McGraw-Hill, 1963.

Schechter Poultry Corp., United States v. 295 U.S. 495 (1935).

Schmookler, Jacob. *Invention and Economic Growth.* Cambridge, Mass.: Harvard University Press, 1966.

Schöllhammer, Hans. *French Economic Planning and Its Impact on Business Decisions.* Doctoral Dissertation. Graduate School of Business, Indiana University, 1967 (mimeo).

Schriftgiesser, Carl. *Business Comes of Age,* New York: Harper & Brothers, 1960.

Schultz, Charles L. *Setting National Priorities: The 1971 Budget.* Washington, D.C.: Brookings Institution, 1970.

Schumpeter, Joseph A. *The Theory of Economic Development.* Cambridge, Mass.: Harvard University Press, 1949.

Schwartz, George. "Marketing: The Societal Concept," *University of Washington Business Review,* Autumn 1971.

Scott, Bruce R. "The Industrial State: Old Myths and New Realities." *Harvard Business Review,* March–April 1973.

Segal, Ronald. *The Americans: A Conflict of Creed and Reality.* New York: Viking Press, 1969.

Seidman, Harold. *Politics, Position, and Power: The Dynamics of Federal Organization.* New York: Oxford University Press, 1970.

Selekman, Sylvia Kopald, and Benjamin M. Selekman. *Power and Morality in a Business Society.* New York: McGraw-Hill, 1956.

Sethi, S. Prakash. "Political Action: A Business and Society Survey of Corporate Practices," *Business and Society Review,* Summer 1972.

Shaeffer, Ruth G. *Nondiscrimination in Employment: Changing Perspectives, 1963–1972.* New York: National Industrial Conference Board, 1973.

Shapiro, Harvey D. "Social Responsibility Funds Get Off to a Bad Start," *Business and Society Review/Innovation,* Spring 1973.

Sheldon, Oliver. *The Philosophy of Management.* London: Sir Isaac Pitman & Sons, 1923.

Sichel, Werner (ed.). *Antitrust Policy and Economic Welfare.* Ann Arbor, Michigan: Bureau of Business Research, Graduate School of Business Administration, The University of Michigan, 1970.

Silk, Leonard S. *The Research Revolution.* New York: McGraw-Hill, 1960.

Simon, William E. Testimony Before the House Committee on Interstate and Foreign Commerce. July 10, 1973.

Simonds, Rollin H. "OSHA Compliance: 'Safety is Good Business,' " *Personnel,* July–August 1973.

Sirkin, Gerald. *The Visible Hand: The Fundamentals of Economic Planning.* New York: McGraw-Hill, 1968.

Sirota, David. "Job Enrichment—Another Management Fad?" *The Conference Board Record,* April 1973.

————, and Alan D. Wolfson. "Job Enrichment: Surmounting the Obstacles," *Personnel,* July–August 1972.

Smil, Vaclav. "Energy and the Environment—A Delphi Forecast," *The Futurist,* December 1972.

Smith, Adam. *An Inquiry into the Nature and Causes of the Wealth of Nations,* 1776. New York: Modern Library, 1937.

Smith, George Albert, Jr., and John Bowers Matthews, Jr. *Business, Society, and the Individual.* Homewood, Ill.: Richard D. Irwin, Inc., 1967.

Solow, Robert. "Technical Change and the Aggregate Production Function," *The Review of Economics and Statistics,* August 1957.

Spangler, Miller B., and Sterling McMillan. *Case Studies of Government Cooperation in Funding New Industries: With Implications for Marine Resource Developments.* Washington, D.C.: National Planning Association, 1970.

Sparks, C. Paul. "Changing Perspectives on Nondiscrimination," *The Conference Board Record,* August 1973.

Spencer, Herbert. *Social Statics*. London: Williams and Norgate, 1868.

Sporn, Philip, Leon E. Hickman, and Luther H. Hodges. *The Ethics of Business: Corporate Behavior in the Market Place*. New York: Columbia Graduate School of Business, Columbia University, 1963.

Standard Oil Co., United States v., 221 U.S. 1 (1911).

Stanton, Frank. "Art and Business: The Creative Alliance," *The MBA*, October 1967.

Steele, Hoyt P. "The Corporation's Role in Politics." Address before the Public Relations Institute, Madison, Wisconsin. July 12, 1959.

Steiger, Paul E. "Nontariff Barriers—Keeping Lid on World Markets," *Los Angeles Times*, February 14, 1973.

Steiner, George A. *Cases in Business and Society*. New York: Random House, 1975.

———— (ed.). *The Changing Business Role in Modern Society*. Los Angeles: Graduate School of Management. UCLA, 1974(A).

———— (ed.). *Contemporary Challenges in the Business-Society Relationship*. Los Angeles: Graduate School of Management. UCLA, 1972(A).

————. *Government's Role in Economic Life*. New York: McGraw-Hill, 1953.

———— (ed.), *Major Issues in the Business-Society Relationship*. Los Angeles: Graduate School of Management. UCLA, 1974(B).

————. "The Redefinition of Capitalism and Its Impact on Management Practice and Theory." *Proceedings of the Thirty-Second Annual Meeting of the Academy of Management*. Minneapolis, Minnesota, 1972(B).

———— (ed.). *Selected Major Issues in Business' Role in Modern Society*. Los Angeles: Graduate School of Management. UCLA, 1973(A).

————. "Social Policies for Business," *California Management Review*, Winter 1972(C).

————. *Summary Results of Survey of Development Efforts to Measure the Social Performance of Business*. New York: Committee for Economic Development. 1973(B).

————. *Top Management Planning*. New York: Macmillan, 1969.

————, and Warren Cannon. *Multinational Corporation Planning*. New York: Macmillan, 1968(A).

————, and William G. Ryan. *Industrial Project Management*. New York: Macmillan 1968(B).

Stetson, John B., Company v. United Hatters, Cap and Millinery Workers International Union. BNA 28 LA 514 (1957).

Stevens, Robert Warren. "Scanning the Multinational Firm," *Business Horizons*, June 1971.

Stieber, Jack. *Public Employee Unionism: Structure, Growth, Policy*. Washington, D.C.: Brookings Institution, 1973.

Stigler, George J., and Manuel F. Cohen. *Can Regulatory Agencies Protect the Consumer?* Washington, D.C.: American Enterprise Institute, 1971.

Stockholders Publishing Company, Inc. v. American Newspaper Guild (CIO). 16 LA 644 (1951).

Strauss, George. "Organization Man—Prospect for the Future," *California Management Review*, Spring 1964.

Survey Research Centers. *Survey of Working Conditions*. Ann Arbor, Michigan: University of Michigan, 1970.

Sutton, Francis X., Seymour E. Harris, Carl Kaysen, and James Tobin. *The*

American Business Creed. Cambridge, Mass.: Harvard University Press, 1956.

Swift & Co. v. FET. 272 U.S. 554 (1926).

Sypher, A. H. "Why Safety Laws Aren't Safe," *Nation's Business*, March 1968.

Tarnowieski, Dale. *The Changing Success Ethic*. New York: AMACOM, American Management Association, 1973(A).

————. "Middle Managers' New Values," *Personnel*, January–February 1973 (B).

Taylor, James C., Judith Landy, Mark Levine, and Divakar R. Kamath. *The Quality of Working Life: An Annotated Bibliography*. Los Angeles: Center for Organizational Studies, Graduate School of Management, UCLA, 1973.

TEMPO. *The Economics of Slowing Population Growth*. Santa Barbara, 1972.

Terleckyj, Nestor E. "Measuring Progress Toward Social Goals: Some Possibilities at National and Local Levels," *Management Science*, August 1970.

Thatcher Manufacturing Co. v. FTC, 272 U.S. 554 (1926).

Thompson, Stewart. *Management Creeds and Philosophies*. New York: American Management Association, 1958.

Thompson, Victor A. *Bureaucracy and Innovation*. Birmingham: University of Alabama Press, 1969.

Tilgher, Adriano. *Homo Faber: Work Through the Ages*. Chicago: Henry Regnery, 1964.

Time. "Black Capitalism: Mostly an Empty Promise," July 9, 1973.

————. "The Great Breeder Dispute," November 1, 1971.

Toffler, Alvin. *Future Shock*. New York: Random House, 1970.

Towle, Joseph W. (ed.). *Ethics and Standards in American Business*. New York: Houghton Mifflin, 1964.

Toynbee, Arnold. *The Industrial Revolution*. Boston: Beacon Press, 1956; (First edition, 1884).

————. *A Study of History*. Abridgement of volumes I–VI by D. C. Somervell. New York: Oxford University Press, 1947.

Trenton Potteries Co., United States v., 273 U.S. 392 (1927).

Trist, Eric. "Urban North America: The Challenge of the Next Thirty Years, a Social Psychological Viewpoint." Paper presented at the Annual Meeting and Conference of the Town Planning Institute of Canada, Minaki, Ontario. June 26–28, 1968.

Trivoli, George W. "Has The Consumer Really Lost His Sovereignty?" *Akron Business and Economic Review*, Winter 1970.

Turner, James S. *The Chemical Feast*. New York: Grossman, 1970.

Ulmann, Lloyd, and Robert J. Flanagan. *Wage Restraint: A Study of Incomes Policies in Western Europe*. Berkeley: University of California Press, 1973.

United Church of Christ. *Investing Church Funds for Maximum Social Impact*. New York City, 1970.

U.S. Bureau of the Census. *The Social and Economic Status of the Black Population in the United States, 1972*. Washington, D.C.: U.S. Government Printing Office, 1973.

U.S. Chamber of Commerce. *Multinational Enterprise Survey.* Washington, D.C.: U.S. Chamber of Commerce, 1971.

U.S. Congress, House Committee on Science and Astronautics. *Inquiries, Legislation, Policy Studies Re: Science and Technology: Review and Forecast.* Second Progress Report to Subcommittee on Science, Research and Development, Eighty-ninth Congress, Second Session. Washington, D.C.: U.S. Government Printing Office, 1966.

U.S. Congress, House Committee on Science and Astronautics. *Technology Assessment, State of Subcommittee on Science, Research and Development,* Ninetieth Congress, First Session. Washington, D.C.: U.S. Government Printing Office, 1967.

U.S. Congress, Select Committee on Small Business. *Investigation of 'Preselected Winners' Sweepstakes Promotions.* Hearings Before the Subcommittee on Activities of Regulatory Agencies Relating to Small Business. House of Representatives, Ninety-first Congress, First Session. Washington, D.C.: U.S. Government Printing Office, 1970.

U.S. Congress and Senate. *Establish a Department of Consumer Affairs.* Hearings on S. 860 and S. 2045 before the Subcommittee on Executive Reorganization of the Committee on Government Operations, Ninety-first Congress, First Session, March, April, July, 1969.

U.S. Congress and Senate. *To Establish a Consumer Protection Agency.* Hearings on S. 1177 and H.R. 10835 before the Subcommittee on Executive Reorganization and Government Research of the Committee on Government Operations, Ninety-second Congress, First Session. Washington, D.C.: U.S. Government Printing Office, November 1971.

U.S. Department of Health, Education and Welfare (Bell Report). *Toward a Social Report.* Washington, D.C.: U.S. Government Printing Office, 1969.

U.S. Public Health Service. *Smoking and Health—Report of the Advisory Committee to the Surgeon General of the Public Health Service.* Public Health Service Publication, No. 1103. Washington, D.C.: U.S. Department of Health, Education, and Welfare, January 11, 1964.

U.S. Riot Commission (Kerner Commission). *Report of the National Advisory Commission on Civil Disorders.* New York: Dutton, cloth edition; Bantam Books, paperback, 1968.

U.S. Senate, Committee on Finance. *Implications of the Multinational Firms for World Trade and Investment and for U.S. Trade and Labor.* Report to the Committee on Finance of the United States Senate and Its Subcommittee on International Trade on Investigation No. 332-69, Under Section 332 of The Tariff Act of 1930. Washington, D.C.: U.S. Government Printing Office, February 1973.

U.S. Senate. Permanent Subcommittee on Investigations of the Committee on Government Operations. *Investigation of the Petroleum Industry.* Washington, D.C.: U.S. Government Printing Office, July 1973.

U.S. Senate. *Technology Assessment for the Congress,* Staff Study of the Subcommittee on Computer Services of the Committee on Rules and Administration, Ninety-second Congress, Second Session. Washington, D.C.: U.S. Government Printing Office, 1972.

United States Steel Corp., United States v., 251 U.S. 417 (1960).

United Steelworkers of America v. Warrior and Gulf Navigation Co. 363 U.S. 574 (1960).

Verdoorn, P. J. "Government-Industry Planning Interrelationships," *California Management Review,* Winter 1965.

Vernon, Raymond. "Antitrust and International Business," *Harvard Business Review,* September–October 1968.

———. *Sovereignty at Bay: The Multinational Spread of U.S. Enterprises.* New York: Basic Books, 1971.

Viner, Jacob. "Adam Smith and Laissez Faire," *Journal of Political Economy,* April 1927.

Vogel, David. "The Books That Shaped The Public's View of Business," *Business and Society Review/Innovation,* Summer 1973.

Von's Grocery Co., United States v., U.S. S Ct. (1966) 1966 Trade Cases, Par. 71,780.

Votaw, Dow. "Genius Becomes Rare: A Comment on the Doctrine of Social Responsibility," *California Management Review,* Winter 1972.

———. "The Nature of Social Responsibility: 'You Can't Get There From Here,' " *Contemporary Business,* Winter 1973.

———. "What Do We Believe About Power?" *California Management Review,* Summer 1966.

Walker, Charles R. *Technology, Industry, and Man: The Age of Acceleration.* New York: McGraw-Hill, 1968.

Walton, Clarence C. (ed.). *Business and Social Progress.* New York: Praeger, 1970.

———. *Corporate Social Responsibilities.* Belmont, Calif.: Wadsworth, 1967.

———. "Critics of Business: Stonethrowers and Gravediggers," *Columbia Journal of World Business,* Fall 1966.

———. *Ethos and the Executive.* Englewood Cliffs, N.J.: Prentice-Hall, 1969.

Walton, Richard E. "Quality of Working Life: What Is It?" *Sloan Management Review,* Fall 1973.

Walton, Scott D. *American Business and Its Environment.* New York: Macmillan, 1966.

Waterston, Albert. *Development Planning: Lessons of Experience.* Baltimore: Johns Hopkins Press, 1965.

Watson, John H., III. *Industry Aid to Education.* New York: National Industrial Conference Board, 1965.

Watson, Thomas, Jr. *A Business and Its Beliefs.* New York: McGraw-Hill, 1963.

Weber, Max. *The Protestant Ethic and the Spirit of Capitalism.* New York: Charles Scribner's Sons, 1952 edition.

Webster, Frederick E., Jr. "Does Business Misunderstand Consumerism?" *Harvard Business Review,* September–October 1973.

Weidenbaum, Murray L. "Government Spending and Innovation: An Exploratory Analysis of the Use of Government Expenditure Mechanisms to Foster R & D." Report prepared for the Office of National R & D Assessment. The National Science Foundation, July 1973.

Weinstein, James. *The Corporate Ideal and the Liberal State.* Boston: Beacon Press, 1968.

Weiss, E. G. "The Corporate Deaf Ear," *Business Horizons,* December 1968.

Wells, William D. "It's A Wyeth, Not a Warhol, World," *Harvard Business Review,* January–February 1970.

Weston, J. Fred. *Corporate Firms and Business Diversification*. Los Angeles: UCLA Printing and Production Office, 1969.

―――. "Implications of Recent Research for The Structural Approach to Oligopoly," *Antitrust Law Journal*, August 1972.

―――, and Stanley I. Ornstein. *The Impact of Large Firms on the U.S. Economy*. Lexington, Mass.: D. C. Heath, 1973.

―――, and Sam Peltzman (eds.). *Public Policy Toward Mergers*. Pacific Palisades, Calif.: Goodyear Publishing, 1969.

White House Conference. *A Look At Business in 1990*. Washington, D.C.: U.S. Government Printing Office, November 1972.

White, Lynn. "Technology and Invention in the Middle Ages," *Speculum*, 1940.

Whitehead, Alfred North. *The Dialogues of Alfred North Whitehead as Recorded by Lucien Price*. New York: Mentor Books, 1956.

Whyte, William H., Jr. *The Organization Man*. New York: Simon & Schuster, 1956.

Wierzynski, Gregory H. "Our Most Wrenching Problem Is Finding a Place for Ourselves in Society," *Fortune*, January 1969.

Wiesner, Jerome B. "Technology is For Mankind," *Technology Review*, May 1973.

Wilcox, Clair. *Public Policies Toward Business*. Homewood, Ill.: Richard D. Irwin, 1966.

Williams, Robin. "Individual and Group Values," *Annals of the American Academy of Political and Social Science*, May 1967.

Williams, William Appleman. *The Roots of the Modern Empire*. New York: Random House, 1969.

Wilson, Ian H. "How Our Values Are Changing," *The Futurist*, February 1970.

―――. "The New Reformation: Changing Values and Institutional Goals," *The Futurist*, June 1971.

Winpisinger, William W. "Job Satisfaction: A Union Response," *AFL-CIO American Federationist*, February 1973.

Winter, Ralph K., Jr. *The Consumer Advocate Versus The Consumer*. Washington, D.C.: American Enterprise Institute for Public Policy Research, 1972.

Woodward, Joan. *Industrial Organization: Theory and Practice*. London: Oxford University Press, 1965.

Wright, Myron A. *The Business of Business*. New York: McGraw-Hill, 1967.

Yankelovich, Daniel. "The Real Meaning of the Student Revolution," *The Conference Board Record*, March 1972.

Yarmolinsky, Adam. *The Military Establishment: Its Impacts On American Society*. New York: Harper & Row, 1971.

Yarrington, B. Y. "Corporate Social Responsibility: Ritual or Reality?" Remarks delivered to the International Assembly of Better Business Bureaus. May 23, 1972.

Zeigler, L. Hormon. *Interest Groups In American Society*. Englewood Cliffs, N.J.: Prentice-Hall, 1964.

Index

Aaker, David A., 260
Abrams, Charles, 297
Abt, Clark, 197, 203–204
Accounting standards, profits and, 488
Ackerman, Robert W., 188
Ackley, Gardner, 494
Acton, Lord, 107
Adams, Walter, 485
Addystone Pipe & Steel Co. v. U.S., 421
Adizes, Ichak, 154, 397
Administrative Conference Act, 474
Advertising, cigarette, 266–269
Aerojet General Corp.: Watts Mfg. Co.
  and, 291
Affirmative Action, 286–289
AFL-CIO, 457, 537
Affluent Society: Chapter Twenty; in-
  come distribution, 339; major issues
  of, 342–345; nature of, 338–342; pov-
  erty in, 339–340; productivity of, 339;
  public spending in, 344
Agricultural revolution, 26–27
Aharoni, Yair, 447
Ahlbrandt, Roger S., 404
Air Pollution Control Act, 248

Alaskan Pipe Line, 477
Alexander, Tom, 562
Alfange, Dean, 357–358
Allegheny Conference on Community
  Development, 299–300
Alliance For Progress, 395
American Banana Co. v. United Fruit
  Co., 460
American Beekeeping Federation, 376
American Federation of Retail Kosher
  Butchers, 376
American Institute of Certified Public
  Accountants, 205, 488
American Insurance Association, 376
American Iron and Steel Institute, 376
American Medical Assn., 390
American Paper Institute, 376
American Revolution, 32–33
American Telephone and Telegraph Co.:
  government and, 362–363; size of,
  111
American Tobacco Co. et. al. v. U.S.,
  422
Anderson, Rolph E., 258
Andrews, Kenneth R., 155, 165

Anshen, Melvin, 164–165
Ansoff, Igor, 438
Antitrust (see Economic concentration)
Apollo program, 331, 561, 562
Appalachian Coal, Inc. v. U.S., 421
Aquinas, St. Thomas, 21
Arrow-Hart & Hegeman Electric Co. v. FTC., 423
Art Institute of Akron, 317
Arts, business and: Chapter Eighteen; common goals, 318–319; defined, 315–316; support of, 316–318
Association of Japanese Textile Importers, Inc., 376
Aswan Dam, 244–245
Austin, Robert W., 330
Automobile: emission and pollution, 240–241; product safety case, 272–278

Baier, Kurt, 122, 127–129, 132, 133
Balance of payments, 450, 454–455, 481–482
Ball, George W., 397
Banfield, Edward C., 305
Bank of America: executive promotion policy, 102–103; social programs, 191
Banks, John R., 529
Barkley, Paul W., 159
Barnard, Chester, 224–225
Barry Corporation, human asset reports, 197
Bartels, Robert, 211, 212, 340
Bartimole, Roldo, 300
Bauer, Raymond A., 201, 329
Baumhart, Raymond, 159, 214–216, 217, 226
Baumol, William J., 166, 316
Beard, Miriam, 17, 18
Beckwith, Burnham, 349
Behrman, Jack N., 397, 445, 447, 453
Bell, Daniel, 135, 159, 553, 554
Bell, J. Fred, 171
Bell Report, 88
Bengelsdorf, Irving S., 561–562
Benham, Thomas W., 70
Bennis, Warren G., 516–517, 518
Berg, Ivar, 139, 382, 521, 527, 531
Berle, Adolph A., Sr., 80, 105, 108, 110, 111, 114, 117, 166, 171, 404
Bernstein, Irving, 538
Bernstein, Marver, 474, 475
Berry, Leonard L., 280
Bill of Rights, 356
Black Death, 22
Blair, John M., 426, 428
Bleichen, Gerhard, 163
Blough, Roger, 109–110, 144, 146, 147, 148, 525–526

Blum, Fred H., 204
Blum, Milton L., 259
Bock, Betty, 427, 431, 436
Boulding, Kenneth, 442
Bowen, Howard, 155, 178
Bowen, William, 272, 275
Bowen, William G., 316
Boxer Rebellion, 445
Bradt, William R., 190, 382
Branch, Melville C., 300
Bronfenbrenner, Martin, 71, 171
Brown, James K., 293, 294, 296, 539
Brown, Lester R., 487
Browne, M. Neil, 160
Brozen, Yale, 428, 429
Bruce-Briggs, B., 563
Brunk, Max E., 258, 259
Burack, Elmer H., 293
Burck, Gilbert, 259
Burnham, James, 111
Bubble Act, 28
Burke-Hartke Bill, 455–458
Business: ancient times, 17–18; constituents of, 78; criticisms of, 69–72; defined, 5–6; demands on, 94–98; dominant role of, 46–48; economic concentration in, 110–111; economic environment of, 74–75; employment of disadvantaged, 289–293; ethics in today, 214–216; government environment of, 77–78; ideologies of, Chapter Nine; impact on environments, 81; internal environment of, 77–78; legal environment of, 75–76; legitimacy, 115–117; managerial philosophies of, 101–103; Maslow's needs and, 83; in medieval world, 20–24; mercantilism, 24–25; minority enterprises and, 293–296; national priorities and, 82; pluralism and, 79–80; population growth and, 349–350; power of, 81, 109–110; public affairs function of, 372–374; quality of life and, 87–94; rising expectations and, 83–84; role in economic growth, 52–53; in Roman world, 18–20; social environment of, 73–74; social expectations of, 98–101; social goals and, 85–87; social problems and, 176–177; Supreme Court and, 63–64; wars and, 64
Business Council, 376
Business Ethics Advisory Council, 222
Business and the family, 521
Business and Government (see Government; Business)
Business and leisure, 518–520
Businessmen: antitrust views of, 416–417; conflict with individual aims, 508–509; defined, 5–6; dominant role of, 46–48; ethical problems of, 212–

Businessmen (cont.)
214; importance of, 142–143; powers of, 114–115; role in organization, 61–62; source of ethos, 217–220
Business-society relationships: alternative futures, 563–567; areas of, 7; characteristics of analysis, 9–14; fundamental interrelationships, 8–9; importance of, 3–5; institutional lags, 556–557; major trends to 1985 and beyond, 546–555; nature of issues, 5–6; operation of, 9, 38–39; paradoxes in, 69–70; possible disasters to, 555–556; social and economic problems of, 557–558; spectrum of, 7–8
Butcher, Bernard, 197
Butler, William, 243

Cabinet Committee on Price Stability, 428
Caesar, Julius, 19
Calvin, 23
Campaign, G. M., 174
Cannon, Warren, 143, 149, 395
Capitalism: antecedents of, Chapter Two; assumptions of, 39–45; criticisms of, 70; individual freedom and, 41–42; institutions of, 27–29; market mechanism and, 38–39, 42; profit motive and, 40–41; property and, 40–41; redefinition of, 81–82; rise of, 25–26; role of government in, 37, 42–43; strength of, 558–559; theory of, Chapter Three
Capper-Volstead Act, 443
Carmichael, D. R., 487
Carr, Albert Z., 224–225
Carruth, Eleanore, 76
Carson, Rachael, 234, 253, 257, 324, 346
Case, Frederick E., 285, 297, 300
Casey, William S., 44, 486
Cassell, Frank H., 411
Caves, Richard E., 466
Center for Law and Social Policy, 174
Chagy, Gideon, 316
Chamberlain, Neil W., 9, 413, 524, 526, 527
Cheit, Earl F., 151
Cherrington, Paul W., 378
Cheyney, Edward P., 24
Child Protection and Toy Safety Act, 262
Church Project on U. S. investments in Southern Africa, 174
Churchman, C. West, 13–14
CIO, 537
Civil Aeronautics Board, 466, 469, 471
Civil Rights Act, 286
Clapp, Norton, 163
Clark, J. M. 171

Clark, John W., 226
Clark, Thomas B., 349
Clasen, Earl A., 213
Class action suits, 76–77
Clayton Act: 261, 417–420, 469; Celler-Kefauver amendments to, 423
Clausen, A. W., 103
Clean Air Act, 237–238, 248
Clean Water Restoration Act, 248
Clee, Gilbert H., 358
Coase, Ronald H., 466
Coates, Joseph F., 328
Cochran, Thomas C., 50
Cohen, Manuel F., 472
Cohen, Stephen, 112, 400
Cohn, Jules, 181, 285, 300
Collective bargaining, 523–524, 527–528, 534–537
Collins, John W., 188
Commission on National Goals, 401
Committee for Economic Development; 144, 145, 146, 148, 150, 151, 163–164, 190, 199, 207, 208, 209, 297, 375–376, 412, 526, 534; listing of social programs, 155–158
Committee on Political Education, 537
Commoner, Barry, 323, 346
Companies Act, 28–29
Competition: 38–39, 141; conglomerates and, 439–441; deregualte for, 469–473; economic concentration and, 429–430; need to improve, 495; structure v. performance, 423–430
COMSAT, 55–56, 365
Conglomerates: economic concentration and, 430–442; and efficiency, 438–441
Constitution of the United States, 63, 356, 370–371
Consumer Advocate, 257, 258–259
Consumer Protection Credit Act, 262
Consumerism: (see Consumers); 253–254; business response to, 259–260, 279–280; defined, 253–254; journalistic exposés, 257; perspectives on, 278–279; sources of, 255–258
Consumers: (see Consumerism); 141–142; advertising and, 264–266; advocates for, 257, 258–259, 474; deceptive promotion, 255–256; discontent, 255; guarantees, 256; freedom of choice and, 266–269; legislation for, 260–263; manufacturer liability, 270–272; poor service to, 257; product obsolescence, 269–270; product safety: case of automobiles, 272–278; rising expectations of, 257–258; sovereign or captive?, 42, 263–264; unsafe products, 255
Cook, Paul W., 108, 278
Coppock, R., 172

Cordimer, Ralph S., 144, 145, 146, 147
Corporation: (see International Policy and Business); accountability, 199–201; constituent demands, 202–204; data disclosure, 484–488; early, 28–29; growth of, 61–62; incorporation laws, 49–50, 488–489; making public forecasts, 485–488; need for big firms, 146–147; legality of philanthropy, 178–180; powers of, Chapter Seven (see Power); realities of decision-making in, 186–188; rise of, 48–50; value systems of, 152
Corson, John S., 87, 190, 197, 199, 207, 208, 285
Cost-benefit analysis: Lockheed loan and, 483; nature of, 132–133; pollution and, 242–244
Council of Economic Advisors, 507
Council on Economic Priorities, 204, 205
Council on Environmental Quality: 232, 235, 238, 249, 250, 251; pollution cost calculation, 242–244
Cox, Edward F., 278, 466
Cremin, Lawrence, 309
Cross, Theodore L., 294
Crusades, 21, 22
Curtice, Harlow, 309
Curtin, Edward R., 539
Cyclamates, 467

Daddorio, Congressman, 327–328
Dahl, Robert, 111
Dalkey, Norman C., 87–88, 93–94, 132
Dartmouth College case, 49–50
Data disclosure, 484–488
Davidson, Mark, 13
Davis, John P., 28
Davis, Keith, 155, 182
Davis, Louis E., 514
Day, George S., 260
Day, V. B., 166–167
DDT, 234, 246, 249, 266
Declaration of Independence, 31
De Grazia, 519, 520
Delphi, 132, 133–134
Demaree, Allan T., 403
Demonstration Cities and Metropolitan Development Act, 298
Demsetz, Harold, 428, 429, 430
Denenberg, 254
De Nevers, Noel, 245
Denison, Edward F., 52
Dennis, Lloyd V., 285
Depression of 1930s, 54–55
Depressions, impact on business, 63
Destler, Charles A., 48
Dewhurst, S. Frederic, 51
Dexter, Lewis A., 379

Dickens, Charles, 58, 543
Dingell, Congressman, 256
Disadvantaged minorities: business employment of, 289–293; business and enterprises of, 293–296; business and equal opportunities of, 286–289; business role and, 283–286; training and employment of, 289–293
Dodge v. Ford Motor Co., 178
Dolgow v. Anderson, 487
Demhoff, G. William, 112, 387
Donner, Frederic G., 144, 446
Donohue, Charles, 473
Dooley, Arch, 217
Douglas Commission, 298–299
Douglas, William, 525
Downs, Anthony, 237
Drew, Don, 212
Dreyfus Third Century Fund, 175
Dreze, Jacques H., 399
Drucker, Peter F., 77, 87, 307, 365, 444, 544, 553
Dubin, Robert, 500
Durant, Will and Ariel, 34, 181
Durr, Clifford S., 468
Dymsza, William A., 447

Eckert, Ross, 466
Economic concentration: Chapter Twenty-four; collusion and, 429; competition and, 429–430; conglomerates and, 430–442; court decision about size, 420–423; court encourages merger, 421; deep pocket theory, 439; good and bad trusts, 422; monopoly power and size, 421–423; price flexibility and, 429–430; price inflation and, 428; profits and, 428; public policy for, 441–442; reciprocity and, 440; rule of reason, 419, 421; statistics of, 110–111, 427; structure v. performance, 423–430; "toehold" acquisitions, 440; types of mergers, 430–432
Economic growth: should we slow it down?, 345–349
Economic Priorities Report, 174
Economic Stabilization Act, 492
Economists, antitrust views of, 416
Edmunds, Stahrl, 245, 250
Education, business and: Chapter Seventeen; business programs of, 310–313; education in future, 550; historical relations, 307–308; market of, 313; rationale for business support, 308–310
Edwards, Edgar O., 85
Eells, Richard, 108, 159, 308, 309, 310, 316, 317, 319, 380, 381, 446, 447
Ehrlich, Paul R., 83, 236, 346

Eisenhower, Dwight D., 401
Elbing, Alvar O., 135
Elliott-Jones, M. F., 204
Emergency Committee for American Trade, 457
Employment Act, 62, 146, 489–491, 494, 538
Energy Crisis: conservation savings, 481–482; dimensions of, 475–476, 478–479; origins of, 476–477; pollution and, 239–240, 241; Project Independence, 480; reserves, 479–480; what can be done?, 480–482
Environmental Impact Studies, 250
Environmental Protection Agency, 94, 232, 233, 237–238, 250
Epstein, Edwin M., 70, 112, 387
Equal Employment Opportunity Commission, 286
Equal Opportunity and Affirmative Action, 286–289
Equal Pay Act, 286
Erpf, Armond, 318
Estes, Robert, 72, 97, 98, 99
Ethics of business (see Social responsibilities of business; Social audit; Business ideologies): Chapter Thirteen; in business today, 214–216; critical questions, 222; defined, 211–212; forces upon, 225–226; game ethics, 223–224; improving company behavior, 226–227; legal system and, 219; philosophical systems, 218–219; popular guides to, 220–224; principle of proportionality, 221; problem in business, 212–214; professional codes, 219–220; source of, 217–220; structural change in organization and, 223; types of moralities, 224–225; why be ethical?, 216–217
European Common Market, 461
Ewing, David, 113, 131, 172–173
Expectations: identifying, 202; recording, 203; v. reality, 98–101
Experimental Negotiating Proposal, 536–537

Fabricant, S., 334
Fair Packaging and Labeling Act, 262
Farkas, Jack, 427
Farmer, Richard N., 159, 296
Fayerweather, John, 452
Federal Administrative Procedure Act, 377
Federal Aviation Agency, 403, 466
Federal Cigarette Labeling and Advertising Act, 267
Federal Committee on Pest Control, 249
Federal Communications Commission, 466, 469, 471

Federal Energy Administration, 477
Federal Energy Office, 477, 495
Federal incorporation, 488–489
Federal Manpower Programs, 289–293
Federal Pest Control Review Board, 249
Federal Power Commission, 465, 466, 469, 476, 477
Federal Reserve Board, 403, 465
Federal Trade Commission, 261, 264, 265, 267, 431, 432, 440–441, 466, 469, 471, 472, 477
Federal Trade Commission Acts, 419–420
Federal Water Pollution Control Act, 249
Fellmeth, Robert C., 466
Fenn, Dan H., Jr., 201, 389
Fight, 173
Financial Executives Institute, 486
Finley, Grace S., 302, 312
Finn, David, 112, 179
First Water Pollution Control Act, 248
Fisher, John E., 384, 472
Flammable Fabrics Act, 261
Flanagan, Robert S., 493
Folsom, Marion B., 144, 146
Food and Drug Administration, 260, 261, 262, 279, 330, 467, 471, 472
Food, Drug, and Cosmetic Act, 261, 279, 467
Ford, Henry II, 167, 290, 385
Foreign Assistance Act, 451
Foreign investments, 446
Fowler, Henry, 445
Franklin, Benjamin, 23
Fraser, Frank A., 529
Free market mechanism: (see Capitalism), 38–39
Freeman, A. Myrick, III, 249
French National Plans, 397–401
French Planning Commission, 399
Fretz, C. F., 507
Friedland, Claire, 466
Friedman, Milton, 160–161, 162, 267, 472, 494
Fugger, Jacob, 25
Full employment policy of government, 489–490
Fullerton, Kemper, 23
Fulmer, Robert M., 349

Gaddis, Paul D., 115
Gaideke, Ralph M., 263
Galbraith, John K., 112, 113, 114, 135, 257, 262, 263, 278, 279, 338, 342–344, 468, 564, 565
Gallup poll, 130
Gardner, John, 543, 557, 562
Garrett, Thomas M., 221, 226

General Banking Company v. Bakery & Confectionery Workers International Union of America, 530

General Electric Co.: constituent demands of, 95–98; equal opportunity policy, 287–288; pollution policy, 251; profit policy, 166–167

General Foods Corp.: Pet Food plant, job enrichment, 514–515

General Motors: Corporate Public Policy Committee, 189; size of, 111

Generations, as scale of human progress, 566–567

Gillen, Ralph L., 378

Ginzberg, Eli, 531

Golden Rule, The, 220

Goldman, Marshall I., 236

Goldsmith, Oliver, 231

Goldston, Eli, 173, 180

Gordon, T. S., 132, 539–540, 553

Gorney, Roderic, 266–267

Government: controls of, 54–56; economic powers of, 356; efficiency in, 385; environment, 77; future trends, 547; marginal social benefit of outlays, 366–368; role of, 37, 140–141, 145–146; support of R & D, 322, 331–334

Government-business planning: Chapter Twenty-three; assessment of, 403; case against comprehensive planning, 405–407; case for comprehensive planning, 404–405; changing relationships, 411–414; French National Plans, 397–401, nature of, 393–394; PPBS, 395; sectoral planning, 401–403; types of government plans, 396–397; what should be done?, 407–411

Government-business relationships: businessmen in, 378; federal incorporation, 488–489; fundamental, 9; future scenarios for, Chapter Twenty-nine; government influences on, 359–363; historical, 53–56; joint action in, 377–378; Lockheed L-1011 loan, 483; maintaining "right" balance, 363–369; MNC's v. Federal government, 453–461; overview, Chapter Twenty-one; partnership of, 358–359; political role of business in, Chapter Twenty-two; pressure for government action, 357–358; regulation of business, Chapter Twenty-six; regulatory crisis, 464–475; socialize industry, 472–473; source of action, 356–357; structural v. strategic reform, 473–474

Graham, Frank Jr., 234

Granger Laws, 47, 54

Graubard, Stephen R., 113

Great Society, 555

Green, Harold P., 329

Green, Mark S., 112

Green, Robert W., 24

Greenberg, Philip, 504

Greenewalt, Crawford H., 144, 147, 371–372, 385–386

Greenman v. Yuba Power Products, 271

Greenough, William C., 175

Greyser, Stephen A., 389

Griggs v. Duke Power Co., 287

Gross, Bertram M., 396

Growth, control of, 560

Grubb, Phillip D., 448

Guffey Vinson Act, 443

Haas, Paul E., 160

Hacker, Louis M., 111

Hahn, Walter, 329

Hamilton, Alexander, 44

Hamilton, Walton, 108, 468

Hammurabi, code of, 18

Harris, Louis, 100, 101, 138, 505

Hart, Senator, 279, 426

Hatch Act, 331

Haveman, Robert H., 249

Hayek, Friedrich A., 162, 410

Hayman, Joanne, 507

Heald, Morrel, 171, 283–284

Heermance, Edgar L., 219

Heilbroner, Robert L., 112, 114, 151, 257

Helmer, Olaf, 132, 553

Henderson, Hazel, 161

Henningsen v. Bloomfield Motors, 271

Henry, Harold, 251

Herzberg, Frederick, 502, 514

Hess, John, 214

Hetherington, J. A. C., 165

Heyne, Paul T., 161

Hickman, Leon E., 222

Highway Safety Act, 275

Hill, John W., 163

History, lessons of, 12–13

Hobson, J. A., 37

Hodges, Luther H., 222

Hoffenberg, Marvin, 94

Hofstadter, Richard, 59

Hogue, W. Dickerson, 159

Holmes, Oliver W., 12, 59, 460

Hoover, Herbert, 473

Horvath, Janos, 436

Houser, Theodore, V., 114, 147

Housing, substandard, 297–301

Housing Act, The, 298

Housing and Urban Development Act, 297

Howell, James E., 400

Human values (see Values; Quality of life)

Humphrey, Hubert, 329

Hunter, Floyd, 112
Hutchinson, John, 537
Huxley, Aldous, 509

Ideologies of business: Chapter Nine; changing, 139–140; classical, 140–144; defined, 137–139; gaps in, 148–149; inconsistencies in, 149; interest theory, 138; major themes of, 151–152; managerial philosophies, 101–103; in modern business, 144–148; of small business, 143–144; strain theory, 138; whither the business ideology?, 150–152
Income distribution, 339–340
Independent regulatory agency, 464–469
Individual freedom, 36–37, 41–42
Individualism: 30–31, 57–58; v. conformity, 509–514
Industrial Reorganization Act, 426
Industrial Revolution, 26–27
Inflation (see Price inflation)
Institute of Pharmaceutical Manufacturers, 376
Institutional lags, 556–557
International Policy and Business: Chapter Twenty-five; antitrust conflicts, 460–461; balance of payment problems, 450, 454–455; export of jobs by MNC's, 455–458; expropriation, 451–452; host country issues, 448–453; MNC's: beast or blessing?, 462–463; MNC's v. The Federal Government, 453–461; sources of conflict, 446–449; the setting, 444–448; trade and tariff protection, 458–460; U.S. v. host countries, 461–462
Interstate Commerce Commission, 260–261, 465, 466, 468, 469, 471
Investment Company Act, 431
Iron Law of Wages, 51–52

Jacoby, Neil H., 83, 112, 114, 129, 349, 400, 429, 431, 437, 446, 447, 495
Jaffee, Eugene D., 457
Janger, Allen R., 290, 291, 292, 293
Job opportunities in the business sector, 290
Johnson, E. A. J., 28
Johnson, Harold, 163, 167, 171
Johnson, Lyndon B., 262, 290, 317, 395, 454, 491, 555
Joint Economic Committee, 409
Joint stock companies, 28–29
Jolson, Marvin A., 258
Jones, Martin V., 129
Josephson, Matthew, 112, 468

Kahn, Herman, 545, 553, 563
Kalachek, Edward D., 335
Kapoor, A., 448
Kapp, R. William, 177
Kappel, Frederick, 144, 147, 362–363
Katz, Robert, 217
Keeler, Theodore, E., 466
Kell, Walter G., 487, 488
Kennedy, John F., 254, 258
Kennedy, Robert, 467
Kerr, Clark, 534
Key, V. O., 383, 389
Kindleberger, Charles, 462–463
King, Martin Luther, 173
Kissinger, Henry, 482
Kolko, Gabriel, 112
Kotter, John P., 515
Krishman, Rama, 173
Kristal, Irving, 544
Kroos, Herman E., 28, 144
Kuhn, James W., 524, 527

Labor unions and business: Chapter Twenty-eight; arbitration, 524–525; in business ideology, 142; challenge to management, 525–534; collective bargaining, 523–524, 527, 528, 534–537; do MNC's export jobs?, 457–458; experimental negotiating proposal, 536–537; forecasts for 1984–1985, 539–540; influence in raising wage rates, 532–534; limitations on management authority, 528–531; limitations of power, 531–534; mediation, 524; political power of, 537–538
Laissez-faire, 31–32, 43–44, 53–54, 57–58
Langer, Susanne K., 315
Larson v. General Motor Corp., 271
Lave, Lester B., 243
Lawrence, Robert M., 477, 478
Lawyers, antitrust views, 416
Learned, Edmund, 217
LeBleu, R. E., 539–540
Lecht, Leonard A., 85
Leff, Arthur A., 259
Legitimacy, 115–117
Leisure and business, 518–520
Letey, John, 245, 250
Levitt, Theodore, 161–162, 266, 280, 386
Lewis, John L., 335
Leys, John A., 214, 219, 222, 226
Likert, Rensis, 508–509
Linestone, Harold A., 563, 564
Linowes, David F., 197, 204
List, Friedrich, 44
Locke, John, 29
Lockheed Aircraft Corp. loan guarantee, 464, 483
Longstretch, Bevis, 175

Louis, Arthur M., 308
Lowell, James Russell, 162
Lund, Leonard, 251
Lundberg, Craig C., 220
Lundberg, Ferdinand, 112
Lusterman, Seymour, 293, 294, 296
Luther, Martin, 22–23

McAdam, Terry, 158
McArthur, John H., 399, 406, 407
MacAvoy, Paul W., 466, 470
McConnell, Grant, 112
McCullock v. Maryland, 49
MacEachen, Allan J., 285, 295
McGregor, Douglas, 508
McGuire, Joseph W., 272, 285
McGuire-Keogh Act, 443
Machlup, Fritz, 307
McKinsey lectures, 144–148
McLoren, Richard W., 429
McMillan, Sterling, 413
MacPherson v. Buick Motor Co., 271
McQuade, Walter, 300
Madden, Carl H., 330, 563, 564–565
Maddox, John, 347, 349
Malkiel, Burtom G., 175
Malthus, Thomas R., 345
Management (see Business; Corporations): accountability of, 116; by objectives, 191, 395; changing practices, 103–104; fostering individualism, 511–514; future leadership patterns for, 516–518; future trends, 550–553; modern ideology of, 144–148; needs of, 503–504; philosophies of, 101–103; union challenge to, Chapter Twenty-eight; view of social responsibilities, 171–173
Manne, Henry G., 162, 175
Mansfield, Edwin, 162, 321
Manufacturer liability, 270–272
Markham, J. W., 425, 426
Marrow, Alfred J., 514
Marx, Karl, 500
Maslow, A. H., 83, 501, 507
Mason, Edward S., 108, 144, 424, 526
Mason, Robert Hal, 448
Massé, Pierre, 399
Materialism, 58
Mathews, John B., 226
Means, Gardiner, 111, 429
Meadows, Dennis, 84, 236, 345–349, 545, 563
Meat Inspection Act, 261
Medieval World, 20–24
Mee, John, 517
Melman, Seymour, 112
Mercantilism, 24–25
Merchant Marine Act, 443
Mergers, 430–442

Mesthene, Emmanuel, 129
Meyers, Harold B., 403
Michelangelo, 11
Mickelman, Irving S., 69
Miliband, Ralph, 112
Military-industrial complex, 402
Mill, John Stuart, 44–45
Miller Act, 467
Miller, Arjay, 164
Miller, Arthur S., 460, 501
Miller, Robert R., 448
Miller-Tydings Act, 443
Millikan, Max F., 396
Mills, C. Wright, 112, 130, 387
Milutinovich, Jososlav S., 512
Minorities (see Disadvantaged minorities; Women)
Minority enterprise small business investment companies, 295, 296
Mintz, Morton, 112
Mintzberg, Henry, 113
Mishan, Ezra J., 236, 323, 346
Mitchell, Arnold, 130, 131, 134
Mitford, Jessica, 257
MNC's (see International policy)
Monnet, Jean, 397
Monopoly: (see Economic concentration), antipathy to, 58, 59
Monson, R. Joseph, 138, 143, 149
Moore, Wilbert E., 108, 112
Morality (see Ethics)
Moss, Frank E., 172
Motor Vehicle Safety Standards Act, 275
Muller, Herbert J., 321
Mumford, Lewis, 323
Myers, Arthur M., 273

Nader, Ralph, 112, 173, 254, 257, 259, 262, 273, 278, 485, 492
Nanus, Burt, 553
National Academy of Engineering, 328
National Academy of Science, 255–256, 329
National Aeronautics and Space Administration, 325, 331, 332, 396, 402, 413
National Alliance of Business, 290–291, 292–293
National Association of Manufacturers, 375
National Business Council for Consumer Affairs, 262
National Bureau of Standards, 261
National Canners Association, 260
National Commission on Product Safety, 255, 262
National Council on Arts, 317
National Electrical Manufacturers Association, 376
National Environmental Policy Act, 249, 250

National Foundation on the Arts and Humanities, 317
National goals, 407–408
National Highway Traffic Safety Administration, 275
National Housing Act, 297
National Industrial Conference Board, 104, 300, 301, 373, 378, 380, 382, 479, 506, 507, 539
National Industrial Recovery Act, 406
National Labor Relations Board, 471, 524
NLRB v. Rapid Bindery, 530
National Minority Purchasing Council, 295
National priorities, 82
National Railroad Passenger Corporation, 413
National Science Board, 239
National Science Foundation, 325, 326
National Traffic and Motor Vehicle Safety Act, 390
Natural laws, 29–30
Nelson, Dalmas H., 383
Nelson, Richard R., 335
Net Economic Welfare, 350–351
Newton, Sir Isaac, 29
Nickels, William G., 280
Nixon, Richard M., 232, 233, 234, 235, 253–254, 262, 291, 298, 327, 479, 480, 481, 482
Noise Control Act, 248
Nordhaus, William, 350–351
North Atlantic Treaty Organization, 449
North Carolina Highway Safety Research, Center, 278
Northern Pacific Railroad Company v. U.S., 418
Northern Securities Co., v. U.S., 419
Nossiter, Bernard, 112
Novick, David, 395
Nowlan, Stephen E., 173
Nunn, Henry, 527

Occupational Safety and Health Act, 516
O'Connell J., 273
Office of Competition, 495
Office of Consumer Affairs, 262, 279
Office of Emergency Preparedness, 247, 481–482
Office of Federal Contract Compliance, 286
Office of Industry Assessment, 327, 328, 329, 330
Office of Minority Business Enterprise, 294–295
Ohman, O. A., 217
Okun, Arthur M., 443
Olafson, Frederick A., 219
Olney, Richard, 468
Opinion Research Corporation, 455

Oppenheimer, J. Robert, 11
Optimism, 58
Organization for Economic Cooperation and Development, 88, 337
Organization of Petroleum Exporting Countries, 476, 478, 482
Ornstein, Stanley I., 426, 427, 428, 430
Orwell, George, 410, 509
Overseas Private Investment Corporation, 451
Ozbekhan, Hasan, 396, 399, 401, 404

Packaging and Labeling Act, 390
Packard, Vance, 257
Papanek, G. F., 426
Parrish, John, 285
Passell, Peter, 349
Pati, Gopal C., 293
Patrick, Kenneth G., 308, 309, 310
Patterson, James M., 223
Peanut Butter Manufacturers Association, 376
Peck, Merton S., 335, 466, 470
Peltzman, Sam, 279, 329, 426
People in organizations: Chapter Twenty-seven; conflict between individual and business aims, 508–509; conformity v. individualism, 509–514; future pattern of, 516–518; is democracy inevitable?, 516–517; meaning of work, 499–500; job enrichment, 514–515; job satisfaction and dissatisfaction, 502–503; joining-up process, 515–516; problems of, 500–507; what people want, 500–508; work safety, 516
Perloff, Harvey, 283
Peters, Edward, 529, 531
Petersen, Donald J., 516
Peterson, Mary B., 263, 278, 470–471
Phatak, Arvind V., 397, 447
Phelan, James, 112
Phillips, Charles, 471
Pitofsky, Robert, 265, 266
Planning: authoritarianism and, 410–411; evolution of, 394–396; nature of, 393–394, planning programing budgeting system, 395; in post-industrial society, 405, 411, 557
Plato, 18
Pluralism, 62, 78–80
Pohlman, Jerry E., 533
Political Action Committee, 537
Political role of business: Chapter Twenty-two; case against, 386–387; case for, 382–386; current trends of, 371–372; good or evil?, 391–392; how influential, 387–391; types of activities, 374–381
Political theorists: antitrust views of, 417

Pollution: Chapter Fourteen; air, 232; auto emissions, 240–241; business response, 251–252; city life style and, 240; conflicts with other systems, 239–243; cost/benefit analysis, 242–243; energy crisis and, 239–240, 241; environmental impact studies, 250; growth and, 345–349; issue-attention cycle, 237; noise, 233; pesticides, 234; population and, 235; price mechanism and, 247–248; schools of management about, 236–237; solid wastes, 233; system analysis of, 244–245; trade-off analysis for, 244; water, 233; what is an acceptable environment?, 237–239; who is to blame?, 234–236; who should pay?, 245–248; why be concerned?, 232

Population: 51, 235, 282, 545, 547–548; growth and, 345–349; zero growth and, 349–350

Poverty, 339–340

Powell, Reed M., 383

Power: Chapter Seven; of business, 81, 109–110; of the chief executive, 187; concepts of, 107–108; do large firms have monolithic power?, 112–114; dispersal of, 561; economic concentration of, 110–111; of labor unions, 528–534, 537–538; of large firms, 112–114; literature of, 111–112; monopoly power and size, 421–423; spheres of business, 108; used responsibly?, 114; will it be controlled?, 114–115

Pragmatism, 59–60

Prasow, Paul, 529, 531

President's Advisory Council on Executive Organization, 473

President's Advisory Council on the Arts, 317

Presidential Commission on Postal Organizations, 365

Presidential Task Force on Appliance Warranties, 256

Presidential Task Force on Science Policy, 325–326

Price inflation: causes of, 491–492; concentration and, 428; controls over, 489–495; is it inevitable?, 494–495; why worry?, 493–494

Principle of proportionality, 221

Product obsolescence, 269–270

Product safety: case of the automobile, 272–278

Productivity, 339

Profile Bread, 265

Profits: accounting standards and, 488; constituent interests and, 153–154; General Electric view, 166–167; in ideology, 141; maximization of, 153–154; medieval world, 21; motive, 40–

41, 47; opinions, of, 72; policy for, 193–194; profits and economic concentration, 428; social responsibility and, 153–154, 158–159, 166–168

Project on Corporate Responsibility, 173–174

Project Independence, 480

Property: 40–41; passive receptive, 116; possessary, 116

Protestant ethic, 23–24, 34, 57, 510

Public Utility Holding Company Act, 389

Punic Wars, 18

Purcell, Theodore, 159, 226

Pure Food & Drug Law, 261

Puritan ethic, 143, 507

Puritans, 23

Quality of life: 87–94, 341; net economic welfare, 350–351

Quality of working life, 500, 507–508

Quandt, Richard E., 175

Ramo, Simon, 303

Randall, Clarence, 383

Randy Knitwear v. American Cyanamid, 271

Raucher, Alan R., 380

Refuse Act, 248

Regulation of Lobbying Act, The, 375

Reich, Charles, 71, 84, 112, 113, 114, 130, 564

Reiss, Alvin H., 316

Religion and business: 57–58, 217–218; Catholic Church and, 20–21; medieval world, 22–23; protestant ethics, 23–24; in Rome, 19–20

Rescher, Nicholas, 122, 127–129, 132, 133

Research and development (see Technology): outlays of government for, 321–322; 331–334; 480–481

Revenue Act of 1935, 179

Reynolds Metal Co. v. FTC, 433

Richman, Barry M., 154

Riesman, David, 518

Roalman, A. R., 379, 390

Roche, James, 146, 281

Roche, John, 130

Rochester Business Opportunities Corp., 295

Rockefeller, David, 70, 144, 167

Rockefeller, John D. III, 81, 159, 170, 408

Rocks, Lawrence, 479

Roets, Perry, 226

Roman World, 19–20

Roosevelt, Franklin D., 55, 261, 376

Roosevelt, Theodore, 484

Root, Franklin R., 451

Rose, Sanford, 112

Ross, Franklin R., 458
Ross, Leonard, 349
Ruff, Larry, 247
Runyon, Richard P., 479
Rust, Edward, 259
Ruttenberg, Stanley H., 456–457
Ryan, William, 337, 512, 517

Salant, Walter S., 457
Santa Clara case, 50
Sayles, Leonard R., 512
Schollhammer, Hans, 399, 401, 404
Schriftgiesser, Carl, 144
Schulz, John E., 466
Schumpeter, Joseph, 334
Schwartz, George, 194
Scott, Bruce C., 399, 406, 407
Sea Food Act, 261
Seckler, David W., 159
Securities and Exchange Commission, 261, 485, 486, 487, 488
Securities Markets Review Act, 262
Security Pacific Bank, social program, 191
Segal, Ronald, 84
Seidman, Harold, 473
Selekman, Sylvia and Benjamin, 108
Seskin, Eugene, 243
Sethi, S. Prakash, 374
Shaeffer, Ruth G., 287, 293
Shapiro, Harvey D., 175
Shareholder proposals, 173–176
Sharon, Diana R., 173
Shaw, George Bernard, 220
Shecter Poultry Corp., 406
Sheldon, Oliver, 216
Sherman Act, 417–419, 460
Shultz, George, 286
Sichel, Werner, 425
Sierra Club, 238
Silk, Leonard S., 113
Simonds, Rollin H., 516
Sinclair, Upton, 261
Sirkin, Gerald, 396
Sirota, David, 515
Slater, Philip E., 516–517, 518
Small Business Administration, 295
Smil, Vaclav, 480, 553
Smith, Adam, 29, 32, Chapter Three
Smith, A. P., Manufacturing Co. v. Barlow, et al, 178–179
Smith-Connally Act, 537
Smith, George Albert, Jr., 226
Social audit: Chapter Twelve; accountability audit, 201; corporate accountability and, 199–201; make mandatory?, 206–208; measurement problem of, 204–206; nature of, 196–198; obstacles to, 207; why make?, 198–199
Social contract, 8

Social Darwinism, 59
Social ethics, 510
Social goals, 85–87
Social indicators, 88–92
Social policies for a company, 192–195
Social predictions, 544
Social problems, can we manage them?, 561–563
Social responsibilities of business (see Ethics; Social audit): Chapter Ten; assessment of argument, 166–168; boards of directors and, 189; business in South Africa, 170, 175; case against, 160–162; case for, 162–165; criteria for determining, 180–184; defined, 154–159; in decision-making process, 185–186; in future, 560–561; institutionalizing social action, 185–186; investment managers and, 175–176; major programs of business, 200; making operational, Chapter Eleven; management by objective and, 191; measurement problem, 204–206; perceived by managers, 171–173; performance measurement, 191–192; profits and, 153–154, 158–159; shareholder proposals and, 173–176; social costs and, 176–178; social policies for, 192–195; voluntary programs, 169–171
Social Security Act, 538
Society, defined, 6
Solid Waste Disposal Act, 249
Solow, Robert, 334
Southern California Edison Co., social programs, 191
Southwestern Peanut Shellers' Assn., 376
Spangler, Miller B., 413
Spencer, Herbert, 59
Sporn, Philip, 222
Standard Oil of New Jersey, size of, 111
Stanton, Frank, 318
Staszak, James, 293
Steele, Hoyt, 385
Steiner, George A., 69, 70, 71, 72, 75, 82, 97, 98, 99, 103–104, 112, 168, 171, 190, 192–194, 197, 199, 207, 208, 219, 226, 279, 285, 329, 334, 337, 349, 393, 395, 427, 512, 517
Stetson, John B. Company v. United Hatters, Cap and Millinery Workers International Union, 530
Stevens, Robert W., 446
Stewart, John B., 259
Stieber, Jack, 536–537
Stigler, George, 466, 470, 472
Stockholders Publishing Company v. American Newspaper Guild, 530
Strauss, George, 513
Sugar Act, 402
Supreme Court, 49–50, 63–64, Chapter Twenty-four, 465

Survey Research Center, 502, 503
Sutton, Francis X., 138, 143, 148
Swift & Co. v. FTC, 423
Sypher, A. H., 277
Systems analysis, 244–245, 409–410
Systems approach, 13–14

Taft-Hartley Act, 385, 524, 535, 538
Talbert, Gene E., 396, 401, 404
Tarnowieski, Dale, 503, 504
Tax incentives, pollution and, 246–247
Taylor, Frederick, 500
Taylor, James C., 514
Technology, business and: Chapter Nineteen; assessment of, 327–330; business structure and, 336–337; defined, 321; destroyer or savior?, 322–324; future trends of, 548–550; government expenditures for, 480–481; government support of, 331–334; growth and, 334; unemployment and, 335–336
TEMPO, 349–350
Temporary National Economic Committee, 431
Tennessee Valley Authority, 413
Terleckyj, Nestor E., 94
Thatcher Manufacturing Co., v. FTC, 423
Thompson, Stewart, 219
Thompson, Victor A., 512
Tilgher, Adriano, 500
Tobin, James, 138, 350–351
Tocqueville, Alexis de, 58, 83
Toffler, Alvin, 81, 322
Towle, Joseph W., 219
Toynbee, Arnold, 566
Trade and tariff protection, 458–460
Trade-off analysis, 244
Trist, Eric, 404, 405, 411
Trivoli, George W., 264
Truth-In-Lending Act, 258
Turner, James S., 278
Twain, Mark, 264

Ulman, Lloyd, 493
United Church of Christ, 170, 175
United Mine Workers Union, 335
United States Atomic Energy Commission, 331
United States Department of Agriculture, 261, 461
United States Department of Commerce, 377
United States Department of Community Development, 298
United States Department of Consumer Affairs, 262
United States Department of Defense, 331, 377, 395, 402

United States Department of Housing, Education and Welfare, 467, 499, 501, 503, 507, 514, 515
United States Department of Interior, 377, 403
United States Department of Justice, 460
United Steelworkers of America, 536
U.S. Chamber of Commerce, 170, 375, 457
U.S. Geological Survey, 250
U.S. Steel Corporation, size of, 111
U.S. Tariff Commission, 455
U.S. v. Aluminum Co. of America, 421–422
U.S. v. American Can Co., 420
U.S. v. American Tobacco Co., 460
U.S. v. Brown Shoe Co., 432
U.S. v. Columbia Steel Co., 422–423
U.S. v. Continental Can Co., Inc., 435
U.S. v. El Paso Natural Gas Co., 435
U.S. v. E. C. Knight Co., 419
U.S. v. Pabst Brewing Co., 436
U.S. v. Paramount Pictures, Inc., 422
U.S. v. Penn-Olin Chemical Co., 435
U.S. v. Trenton Potteries Co., 421
U.S. v. United States Steel Corp., 420
U.S. v. Von's Grocery Co., 436
United Steel Workers v. Warrior & Gulf Navigation Co., 529
Urban affairs: business guidelines for, 303–304; government guidelines for, 304–305
Urban Coalition, 300

Vaccara, Beatrice N., 457
Values: antipathy to monopoly, 58–59; attitudes toward government, 60; business and human, 147; in business ideology, 143; causal origins of, 128–130; changing in society, 57, 72–73, 558; Chapter Eight; clusters of, 122, 123–125; conceptual types, 127–128; cost/benefit analysis of, 132–133; defined, 122; future changes in, 131–135, 548; forecasting methods of, 131–133; issues for business, 135–136; materialism, 58; model of change, 126–127; optimism, 58; pragmatism, 59–60; register of, 123–125; social ethic, 510; work needs and, 500–506
Verdoorn, P. J., 396
Vernon, Raymond, 468
Viner, Jacob, 37
Vogel, David, 257
Votaw, Dow, 82, 107, 159

Walton, Clarence, 69, 213, 270
Walton, Richard, 507
Washington, George, 331

Washington representatives of business, 378–380
Watergate, 226
Water Quality Act, 248
Water Quality Improvement Act, 248
Waterson, Albert, 393, 395, 397
Watson, John H., 309, 311
Watson, Thomas, 144, 147, 152
Webb-Pomerene Act, 443
Weber, Max, 24
Webster, Frederick E., 259, 260
Weidenbaum, Murray L., 326
Weiner, Anthony J., 545, 553, 563
Weinstein, James, 112
Wengert, Norman I., 477
Wesley, John, 23
Western States Meat Packers Assn., 376
Weston, J. Fred, 154, 426, 427, 428, 430, 431, 436, 438–439
Wheatley, Edward W., 259
White, Lynn T., 13, 22
Whitehead, Alfred North, 319
White House Special Assistant for Community Affairs, 262
Whyte, William, 510, 518
Wierzynski, Gregory H., 310
Wiesner, Jerome B., 324

Wilcox, Clair, 470
Williams, Robin, 122
Williams, William A., 445
Wilson, Ian, 134, 553
Winpisinger, William W., 515
Winter, Ralph K., 259, 279
Wish, John, 171
Wolfson, Alan D., 515
Woodward, Joan, 337
Women, work needs, 506–507
Wool Labeling Act, 261
Work: changing attitudes toward, 500; changing ethics of, 505; defined, 499–500; job enrichment of, 514–515; job satisfaction and dissatisfaction, 502–503; safety of, 516; troubles in work place, 500–507; women and, 506–507
Wright, Myron A., 144

Yankelovich, Daniel, 259, 505
Yarmolinsky, Adam, 402
Yarrington, B. Y., 164

Zabriskie, Noel B., 280
Zeigler, L. Hormon, 387